Interpretations of
American History

Interpretations of American History

Patterns and Perspectives

THIRD EDITION

**Gerald N. Grob &
George Athan Billias**

Volume II
since 1865

THE FREE PRESS
A Division of Macmillan Publishing Co., Inc.
NEW YORK

Collier Macmillan Publishers
LONDON

E
178.6
G68
Vol. 2

79150

The Free Press
A Division of Macmillan Publishing Co., Inc.
866 Third Avenue, New York, N.Y. 10022

Collier Macmillan Canada, Ltd.

Library of Congress Catalog Card Number: 77–087574

Printed in the United States of America

printing number

2 3 4 5 6 7 8 9 10

Library of Congress Cataloging in Publication Data
Grob, Gerald N.   ed.
    Interpretations of American history.

    Includes index.
    CONTENTS:
v.2.   Since 1865.
    1.   United States--History--Addresses, essays,
lectures.   2.   United States--History--Philosophy--
Addresses, essays, lectures.   I.   Billias,
George Athan   joint ed.   II.   Title.
E178.6.G68   1978   973'.08   77-87574
ISBN 0-02-912720-3

for
GLORIA ORESKY

CONTENTS

PREFACE TO THE THIRD EDITION

This two-volume book of essays and readings continues to be based upon our philosophy of teaching American history to college students. Simply stated, this philosophy holds to four premises: (1) that the approach to history should be analytical, not factual; (2) that students should be exposed to the newest viewpoints as well as to traditional interpretations; (3) that beginning students should be provided with a brief historiographical background in order to appreciate more fully the selections assigned for outside readings; and (4) that reading assignments should be a joy rather than a chore.

The first purpose of this work, then, is to bring together selections which approach American history from an analytical point of view. In most instances these readings represent interpretive pieces which illuminate different problems and periods in America's past. Students will be struck, however, by one thread that runs through both volumes and ties together the diverse readings. The selections reproduced here underscore a single major theme: that the view of American history has been a constantly changing one.

Generally speaking, new interpretations in American history have arisen for two reasons. First, the perspective of American historians of a given generation has been shaped in large measure by the sweep of events in the external world in which they have lived. Scholars, in short, have tended to reflect either consciously or unconsciously in their works the problems and predilections of the age in which they have written. Each succeeding generation, therefore, seems to have rewritten American history to suit the felt needs of its time. Some selections in this work are indicative of this generational change. We have sometimes sought to show how the age in which the historian was writing often influenced starting assumptions, collection of evidence, and the interpretation of events. In recent years, for example, the consciousness of historians has been influenced by distinctive social changes reflecting the forces of racism, sexism, war, violence, and economic and urban problems that have profoundly affected the lives of most Americans.

The second reason for the constantly changing picture of our nation's past is the result of internal intellectual changes within the historical profession itself. History, like most other academic disciplines, seems to have a built-in tendency toward self-generating change. When scholars sense that they have reached the outer limits in applying the tenets of what has become an accepted interpretation, they do one of two things: introduce major revisions to correct the prevailing point of view, or strike off in a new direction. Some articles in this work, therefore, represent the writings of scholars who seek to revise some of the more traditional interpretations; other selections reflect the work of a current generation of historians who apply concepts borrowed from the social and behavioral sciences and employ quantitative techniques. The decades of the 1960's and 1970's have been notable for efforts to create a "new" social history, a "new" political history, and a "new" economic history. These efforts have focused primarily, though not exclusively, on the study of group behavior, with the group being defined by a set of variables which lend themselves to quantification. Other efforts of a non-quantitative nature are either cross-disciplinary in purpose or resort to new methodological approaches.

To meet the needs of our third premise, we have written chapter-length introductions to each group of selections. These introductions will enable students to approach the readings with greater ease and understanding by providing a historiographical context for the topic under discussion.

Finally, we have searched the literature for selections which have a lively literary style. It is our firm conviction that the readings represent spirited writing as well as sound scholarship. Much of the exciting work in American history has been done by scholars who possess a real flair for literary expression. Students will discover the rewards and pleasures of history when they read in these pages the articles by (among others) Daniel J. Boorstin, Perry Miller, Bernard Bailyn, Gordon Wood, David H. Fischer, Stanley Elkins, Eugene D. Genovese, Gabriel Kolko, Herbert Gutman, Arthur M. Schlesinger, Jr., John Kenneth Galbraith, and Marvin Meyers.

In preparing this work, we have drawn upon the help of several friends. In particular, we should like to thank two of them, Ronald Petrin and Bruce Zellers, for their aid in bringing this work to completion.

G.N.G.
G.A.B.

1

Introduction

"Every true history is contemporary history." Thus wrote Benedetto Croce, the great Italian philosopher and historian, over a half century ago. By his remark Croce meant that history—as distinguished from mere chronicle—was meaningful only to the degree it struck a responsive chord in the minds of contemporaries who saw mirrored in the past the problems and issues of the present.

Croce's remark has special relevance to the writing of American history. Every generation of American scholars has reinterpreted the past in terms of its own age. Why is this so? One compelling reason, no doubt, has been the constant tendency of scholars to re-examine the past in light of the prevailing ideas, assumptions, and problems of their own day. Every age has developed its own climate of opinion—or particular view of the world—which, in turn, has partially conditioned the way it looks upon its own past and present. Thus, each succeeding generation of Americans has rewritten the history of the country in such a way as to suit its own self-image. Although there were other reasons for this continual reinterpretation of American history, the changing climate of opinion more than any other single factor caused historians to recast periodically their view of the past.

Changing interpretations arose also from the changing nature of American historians and their approach to the discipline. The writing of history in America, broadly speaking, has gone through three distinct stages. In the first stage—the era of Puritan historians during the seventeenth century—historical writing was dominated by ministers and political leaders of the Puritan colonies who sought to express the religious justification for their New World settlements. The second stage— the period of the patrician historians—saw the best history being written by members of the patrician class from the early eighteenth century to the late nineteenth century. Patrician historians—often gentlemen of leisure with private incomes—normally had little or no connection with the church or other formal institutions, as had the Puritan historians. They were stirred to write history by a strong sense of social responsibility that characterized the class from which they sprang, and by a personal conviction that each individual had a moral obligation to employ his best talents for the betterment of mankind. Their works, as a general rule, reflected the ideology and preconceptions of their class. Although they were amateur scholars for the most part, many patrician writers succeeded in reaching a high level of literary distinction and accuracy. The third stage—the period of the professional scholars—began during the 1870's and may properly be called "the age of the professional historians." These scholars qualified as professionals on several counts: they were specifically trained for their craft; they supported themselves by full-time careers of teaching, writing, and research at colleges and universities; and they looked to their professional group to set the standards of achievement by which historical studies were evaluated. Their work has been characterized by constant revisionism: they attempted to correct one another, to challenge traditional interpretations, and to approach old historical problems from new points of view.[1]

During each of these three stages of historical writing, the intellectual milieu in America was distinctly different. In the seventeenth century, the best histories were written by Puritan ministers and magistrates who saw history as the working out of God's will. Theirs was a Christian interpretation of history—one in which events were seen as the unfolding of God's intention and design. Borrowing the concept of a Chosen People from the ancient Hebrews, they viewed the colonization of America in Biblical terms. They cast the Puritans in the same role as the Jews in the Old Testament—as a regenerate people who were destined to fulfill God's purpose. New England became for them New Canaan— the place God had set apart for man to achieve a better way of Christian living. Massachusetts, therefore, was more than simply another colony. In the words of John Winthrop, it was to be a "city upon a hill"—a model Utopia to demonstrate to the rest of the world that the City of God could be established on earth along the lines set forth in the New Testament.

The major theme of most Puritan historians, whether they were ministers or lay leaders, was the same—to demonstrate God's special concern for His Chosen People in their efforts to build a New Canaan. New England's history served their purposes best because it was here that God's mercy could be seen more clearly than in any other part of the globe. To the Puritans, New England's history was one long record of the revelation of God's providence toward His people. Their disasters as well as their triumphs were seen only in relation to God, and the setbacks they suffered were viewed as evidence of God's wrath and displeasure.

Of all the Puritan histories, William Bradford's *Of Plimouth Plantation* was, perhaps, the preeminent work of art. Written in the 1630's and 1640's while Bradford was governor of the colony, this book recounted the tale of the tiny band of Pilgrims who fled first to Holland and then to the New World. No other narrative captured so perfectly the deep feeling of religious faith of New England's early settlers. None illustrated

---

[1]John Higham *et al.*, *History* (Englewood Cliffs, N.J., 1965), pp. 3–5.

better the Puritan ideal of a plain and simple literary style, or mastered so well the rhythms of Biblical prose. Yet, like most Puritan literature, it was written during the few spare moments that Bradford could find from his more important activities as a governor of a new community in the wilderness.

The patrician historians of the eighteenth century replaced the Puritan historians when the church ceased to be the intellectual center of American life. The Christian theory of history with its emphasis on supernatural causes increasingly gave way to a more secular interpretation based upon the concepts of human progress, reason, and material well-being. Influenced by European Enlightenment thinkers, American historians came to believe that man, by use of his reason, could control his destiny and determine his own material and intellectual progress in the world.

The patrician historians were profoundly influenced also by ideas derived from the writings of Sir Isaac Newton. This seventeenth-century English scientist, by applying a rational, mathematical method, had arrived at certain truths, or "natural laws," concerning the physical universe. Newton's systematization of scientific thought led many men to conclude that the same mathematical-scientific method could be employed to formulate similar natural laws in other fields. In order to develop a theory of history in keeping with Newtonian thought, writers began to postulate certain natural laws in the field of history. Thus, patrician historians abandoned the Christian theory in which God determined the events for a view of the universe in which natural laws were the motivating forces in history.

This shift from a Christian interpretation of history to a more secular approach was reflected in the change of leaders among American historians. Minister-historians were increasingly replaced by members of the patrician class—political leaders, planter-aristocrats, merchants, lawyers, and doctors.[2] In the eighteenth century, for example, America's outstanding historians included Thomas Hutchinson, member of the Massachusetts merchant aristocracy and royal governor of that colony; William Smith of New York, doctor, landowner, and lieutenant-governor of that colony; and Robert Beverley and William Byrd of Virginia, who were planter-aristocrats, large landowners, and officeholders. Most of these men possessed a classical education, a fine private library, and the leisure time in which to write. With the growth of private wealth and the opening up of new economic opportunities, more members of the upper classes were in a position to take up the writing of history as an avocation.[3]

The reaction against the Christian interpretation of history was par-

---

[2]Harvey Wish, *The American History* (New York, 1960), p. 25.
[3]Higham, *History*, p. 3.

ticularly evident in the writings of Thomas Jefferson. In his *Notes on the State of Virginia*, first published in 1785, Jefferson stressed reason and natural law instead of divine providence as the basis for historical causation. Jefferson believed also that men were motivated by self-interest, and he employed this concept as one means of analyzing the course of historical events. As he wrote in his history of Virginia, "Mankind soon learn to make interested uses of every right and power which they possess, or may assume."

Jefferson's history showed the impact of yet another major influence—nationalism—which affected historical writing after 1776. As author of the Declaration of Independence, Jefferson felt a fierce, patriotic pride in the free institutions that emerged from the Revolution. He was convinced that America as a democratic nation was destined to pave the way for a new era in world history. A whole new generation of patrician historians sprang up after the Revolution, writing in a similar nationalistic vein—David Ramsay, Mercy Otis Warren, Jeremy Belknap, and Jared Sparks. They likewise contrasted America's free institutions with what they considered to be Europe's corrupt and decadent institutions.

During the first three quarters of the nineteenth century, the writing of history continued to be dominated by patrician historians. The influence of the romantic movement in the arts with its heightened appreciation of the past, emphasis upon pictorial descriptions, and stress upon the role of great men, caused history to be viewed increasingly as a branch of literature. Many outstanding literary figures—Washington Irving, Francis Parkman, Richard Hildreth, William H. Prescott, and John Lothrop Motley—wrote narrative histories about America, other lands, and other times, in a romantic style calculated to appeal to a wide reading public. Such authors were often part of a trans-Atlantic literary culture, for many English historians were writing in the same vein.

America's patrician historians, however, were not always content to provide only a colorful narrative. Writing within a developmental framework, they sought to reveal some of the underlying principles which they believed lay behind the rational evolution of historical events. For the most part, their writings reflected certain assumptions that were common to many historians on both sides of the Atlantic in the first half of the nineteenth century—the idea that history was essentially the story of liberty; that man's record revealed a progressive advance toward greater human rights down through the ages; and that peoples of Anglo-Saxon origin had a special destiny to bring democracy to the rest of the world.

Many of these American historians, influenced by the pronounced nationalism of the period, used such broad assumptions within a chauvinistic framework. They felt a responsibility to help establish the national identity of the new United States. Thus, they employed history as a didactic tool to instruct their countrymen along patriotic lines and presented America's story in the best light possible. Running through their writings were three basic themes: the idea of progress—that the story of America was one of continuous progress onward and upward toward greatness; the idea of liberty—that American history, in essence, symbolized the trend toward greater liberty in world history; and the idea of mission—that the United States had a special destiny to serve as a model of a free people to the rest of mankind in leading the way to a more perfect life. The last theme, in effect, was nothing more than a restatement of the idea of mission first set forth by the Puritan historians.

George Bancroft, the most distinguished historian of the mid-nineteenth century, organized his history of the United States around these three themes. After studying in Germany in the 1820's, Bancroft returned to America determined to apply Teutonic ideas of history to the story of his own country. Bancroft believed in the progressive unfolding of all human history toward a future golden age in which all men would eventually achieve complete freedom and liberty. This march of all mankind toward a greater freedom was in accordance with a preordained plan conceived by God. One phase of God's master plan could be seen in the way that a superior Anglo-Saxon people developed a distinctive set of democratic institutions. The United States, according to Bancroft, represented the finest flowering of such democratic institutions. American democracy, then, was the fruition of God's plan, and the American people had a unique mission in history to spread democracy throughout the rest of the world. Such was the central theme of Bancroft's famous twelve-volume work, *History of the United States from the Discovery of the American Continent*, written between 1834 and 1882.

Francis Parkman, a patrician historian from New England, held many views similar to those of Bancroft. Writing about the intercolonial wars in his work, *France and England in North America*, Parkman portrayed the American colonists as democratic Anglo-Saxons of Protestant persuasion whose superior qualities enabled them to conquer authoritarian-minded French Catholics in Canada. But in many other ways the two writers were quite different. Parkman was more representative of the gentlemen-historians of the nineteenth century who, being drawn from the upper classes, usually reflected an aristocratic bias in their writings, advocated a conservative Whig philosophy, and were distrustful of the American masses. Bancroft, on the other hand, eulogized the common man and was a Jacksonian in politics; his history was distinctly democratic in outlook.

By the 1870's two profound changes began to influence the writing of American history. The first was the change in leadership from amateur patricians to professional historians. Until the last quarter of the nineteenth century, American history had been written almost exclusively by men who had received no special training as historians—except, of course, for a few individuals like Bancroft. From this point on, however, the writing of history was dominated by professionally trained scholars educated in the universities of America and Europe. Professionalization in the field was made possible by developments in higher education as graduate schools appeared in increasing numbers in America to train college history teachers. In the last three decades of the century, this trend proceeded at a rapid rate: the Johns Hopkins University, the first institution devoted to graduate study and research, began its activities in 1876; the American Historical Association was founded in 1884; and the *American Historical Review* made its appearance in 1895.

The advent of professional historians brought about a marked transformation in the field. No longer was historical writing to be vested mainly in the hands of amateurs—though it should be emphasized that many patrician historians had been superb stylists, creative scholars, and researchers who made judicious use of original sources. Nor would historians be drawn almost exclusively from the patrician class in the Northeast, particularly from New England. Professional scholars came from all walks of life, represented a much broader range of social interests than the patricians, and hailed from different geographic regions. Finally, instead of being free-lance writers, as many patricians had been, professionals made their living as teachers in colleges and universities.

The second major development affecting the writing of American history was the emergence of a new intellectual milieu that reflected the growing dominance of novel scientific ideas and concepts. Influenced by Darwinian biology and its findings in the natural sciences, historians began to think of history as a science rather than as a branch of literature. Why couldn't the historian deal with the facts of history in much the same way that the scientist did with elements in the laboratory? If there were certain laws of organic development in the scientific field, might there not be certain laws of historical development? What historian, wrote Henry Adams, with "an idea of scientific method can have helped dreaming of the immortality that would be achieved by the man who should successfully apply Darwin's method to the facts of human history"?[4]

The first generation of professional historians—who held sway from about 1870–1910—was best exemplified by two outstanding scholars, Henry Adams and Frederick Jackson Turner. Henry Adams, a descendant of the famous Adams family that contributed American presidents, statesmen, and diplomats, turned to history and literature as his avoca-

---

[4]Henry Adams, "The Tendency of History," *Annual Report of the American Historical Association for the Year 1894* (Washington, D.C., 1895), p. 19.

tion after his hopes for high political office were dashed. In 1870 he was invited to Harvard and became the first teacher to introduce a history seminar at that institution. Adams pioneered in training his students in the meticulous critical methods of German scholarship, and searched for a time for a scientific philosophy of history based on the findings in the field of physics. His nine-volume history of the United States during the administrations of Jefferson and Madison was destined to become one of the classics of American historical literature. Although he left Harvard after a few years, his career symbolized the transformation from patrician to professional historian and the changing intellectual climate from romanticism to a more scientific approach in the writing of American history.

While Henry Adams was attempting to assimilate history and physics, Frederick Jackson Turner—perhaps the most famous and influential representative of the scientific school of historians in the first generation of professional historians—was applying evolutionary modes of thought to explain American history. Born and reared in a frontier community in Wisconsin, Turner attended the University of Wisconsin, received his Ph.D. from the Johns Hopkins University, and then went on to a teaching career first at Wisconsin and later at Harvard. Like Adams, Turner believed that it was possible to make a science out of history; he attempted, therefore, to apply the ideas of Darwinian evolution to the writing of history. Turner emphasized the concept of evolutionary stages of development as successive frontier environments in American wrought changes in the character of the people and their institutions. As one frontier in America succeeded another, each more remote from Europe than its predecessor, a social evolutionary process was at work creating a democratic American individualist. The unique characteristics of the American people—their rugged individualism, egalitarianism, practicality, and materialistic outlook on life—all resulted from the evolutionary process of adapting to successive frontier environments. Turner's famous essay "The Significance of the Frontier in American History," written in 1893, remains a superb statement of one approach that was employed by the scientific school of historians.

Between 1910 and 1945, a second generation of professional scholars—the Progressive historians—came to maturity and helped to transform the discipline by introducing new ideas and methodologies. Many of them were influenced by the Progressive movement of the early 1900's—a period when the future of American democracy appeared to be threatened by new economic and social forces arising from the rapid industrialization of American society. Rejecting the views of the older and more conservative patrician historians, the Progressive scholars viewed history as an ideological weapon that might explain the present and perhaps help to control the future. In sympathy with the aims and objectives of the Progressive movement between 1900 and 1920, these

scholars continued to write history from a Progressive point of view
even after the decline of the Progressive movement following the First
World War.

Unlike the New England patrician historians of the nineteenth century, the Progressive scholars tended to hail more than the Midwest and
South. These Progressives complained that in the past American history
had been presented mainly as an extension of the history of New England. American civilization, they argued, was more than a transplanted
English and European civilization that had spread out from New England; it had unique characteristics and a mission all its own. But while
the Progressive historians were as nationalistic as the patrician school,
their nationalism was different in nature. The patricians had conceived
of nationalism as a stabilizing force, preserving order and thus assuring
the continued ascendancy of the aristocratic element in American life.
The Progressives, on the other hand, considered nationalism a dynamic
force. To them the fulfillment of democracy meant a continued and
protracted struggle against those individuals, classes, and groups who
had barred the way to the achievements of a more democratic society in
the past.

In changing the direction of American historical writing, Progressive
scholars drew upon the reform tradition that had grown out of the effort
to adjust American society to the new demands of an urban-centered
and industrialized age. This tradition had originated in the 1890's and
reached maturity in the early part of the twentieth century with the
Progressive movement. Drawing upon various sources, the adherents of
the Progressive movement rejected the idea of a closed system of classical economic thought which assumed that certain natural laws governed
human society. Society, these reformers maintained, was open-ended
and dynamic; its development was determined not by immutable laws,
but by economic and social forces that grew out of the interaction between the individual and his environment.

Reacting against the older emphasis upon logic, abstraction, and
deduction, these reformers sought a meaningful explanation of human
society that could account for its peculiar development. Instead of focusing upon immutable laws, they began viewing society and individuals as
products of an evolutionary developmental process. This process could
be understood only by reference to the past. The function of the historian, then, was to explain how the present had come to be, and then to
try and set guidelines for future developments. As a result of this approach, history and the other social sciences drew together, seeking to
explain the realities of social life by emphasizing the interplay of economic, technological, social, psychological, and political forces.

History, according to its Progressive practitioners, was not an
abstract discipline whose truths could only be contemplated. On the
contrary, historians had important activist roles to play in the construc-

tion of a better world. By explaining the historical roots of contemporary problems, historians could provide the knowledge and understanding necessary to make changes which would bring further progress. Like the Enlightenment *philosophes*, historians could reveal prior mistakes and errors, and thus liberate men from the chains of tyranny and oppression of the past. When fused with the social sciences, history could become a powerful tool for reform. "The present has hitherto been the willing victim of the past," wrote James Harvey Robinson, one of the greatest exponents of Progressive history; but "the time has now come when it should turn on the past and exploit it in the interests of advance."[5]

Clearly, the sympathy of this school lay with change and not with the preservation of the *status quo*. Committed to the idea of progress, they saw themselves as contributing to the better and more humane world of the future. Consequently, they rejected the apparent moral neutrality and supposed objectivity of the scientific school in favor of a liberal philosophy of reform. In so doing, they rewrote much of American history, greatly widening its scope and changing its emphasis. Instead of focusing on narrow institutional studies of traditional political, diplomatic, and military history, they sought to delineate those determinant forces that underlay human institutions. In their hands American history became a picture of conflict—conflict between polarities of American life: aristocracy versus democracy; economic "haves" versus "have-nots"; politically overprivileged groups versus those underprivileged; and between geographical sections, as the East versus West. In short, the divisions were between those dedicated to democratic and egalitarian ideals and those committed to a static conservatism.

Believers in inevitable progress, the Progressive historians assumed that America was continually moving on an upward path toward an ideal social order. Not only was American society growing in affluence, but in freedom, opportunity, and happiness as well. The primary determinant of progress was the unending conflict between the forces of liberalism and those of conservatism. Thus all periods in American history could be divided into two clear and distinct phases: periods of active reform and periods of conservative reaction. As Arthur M. Schlesinger, Sr., wrote in 1939: "A period of concern for the rights of the few has been followed by one of concern for the wrongs of the many."[6]

Just as Henry Adams spoke for the scientific school of history, so did Frederick Jackson Turner, Charles A. Beard, and Vernon L. Parrington speak for the Progressives, each in his own way. After his epochal essay on the frontier in 1893—an essay that emphasized unity rather than

---

[5]James Harvey Robinson, "The New History," in *The New History: Essays Illustrating the Modern Historical Outlook* (New York, 1912), p. 24.

[6]Arthur M. Schlesinger, Sr., "Tides of American Politics," *Yale Review*, XXIX (December, 1939), p. 220.

conflict—Turner's interest turned elsewhere, particularly to the idea of sectional conflict. From the late 1890's until his death in 1932, he elaborated and refined his sectional conflict hypothesis. Turner and his students attempted to understand not only how a section came into being, but also the dynamics of conflict that pitted the East against West, North against South, labor against capital, and the many against the few. Under Turner's guiding hand, American scholars wrote a series of brilliant monographs as well as broad interpretive studies that emphasized the class and sectional divisions in American society. Although a few favored the conservative side, the overwhelming majority of historians made clear their preference for democratic liberalism and progress.

While Turner was developing and elaborating his sectional approach, Charles A. Beard was applying the hypothesis of an overt class conflict to the study of American institutions. His book *An Economic Interpretation of the Constitution,* written in 1913, was perhaps the most influential historical work of the twentieth century. Beard attempted to demonstrate that the Constitution, far from representing a judicious combination of wisdom and idealism, was actually the product of a small group of propertied individuals who were intent upon establishing a strong central government capable of protecting their interests against the encroachments of the American masses. In a series of books, climaxed by *The Rise of American Civilization* in 1927, Beard argued that American history demonstrated the validity of the class conflict hypothesis between "haves" and "have-nots." Time and again, he showed the paramount roles that economic factors played in determining human behavior. Fusing his ardent faith in progress with a qualified economic determinism, Beard made clear that his sympathies lay with the forces of democracy as opposed to those of reaction and privilege.

The culmination of the Progressive interpretation came with the publication of Vernon L. Parrington's *Main Currents in American Thought.* Using literature as his vehicle, Parrington portrayed American history in clear and unmistakable terms. The two central protagonists of Parrington's work were Jefferson and Hamilton. Jefferson stood for a decentralized agrarian democracy that drew its support from the great mass of people. Hamilton, on the other hand, represented a privileged and aristocratic minority seeking to maintain its dominant position. American history, according to Parrington, had witnessed a continual struggle between the liberal Jeffersonian tradition and the conservative Hamiltonian one. Underlying Parrington's approach was one major assumption that had also governed the thought of Turner and Beard, namely, that ideology was determined by the materialistic forces in history. Like Turner and Beard, Parrington clearly preferred the forces of reform and democracy, but there were times when he was much less certain of their eventual triumph than his two intellectual companions.

The Progressive point of view generally dominated the field of

American historical scholarship down to the end of World War II. Class and sectional conflict, Progressive historians implied, was a guarantor of progress. Even during those eras in American history when the forces of reaction triumphed—as in the post-Civil War period—their victory was only temporary; ultimately the forces of progress and good regrouped and thereby gained the initiative once again. Such an approach, of course, led to broad and sweeping interpretive syntheses of American history, for the basic framework or structure was clear and simple, and the faith of historians in the ultimate triumph of good over evil remained unquestioned.

Beginning in the 1930's, however, some American scholars began to question the idea of progress that was implicit in this view. The rise of Nazism in the 1930's and 1940's, and the menace of Communism in the 1950's and 1960's, led to a questioning of older assumptions and generalities. How, some asked, could one subscribe to the optimistic tenets of liberalism after the horrors of Auschwitz, Buchenwald, Hiroshima, Nagasaki, and the threat of modern totalitarianism? Indeed, had not American historians, through their own optimistic view of history and their faith in progress, failed to prepare the American people for the challenges and trials that they would face during the middle of the twentieth century? Parrington himself had recognized as early as 1929 that the Progressive faith was under attack by those who did not subscribe to its basic tenets. "Liberals whose hair is growing thin and the lines of whose figures are no longer what they were," he wrote, "are likely to find themselves today in the unhappy predicament of being treated as mourners at their own funerals. When they pluck up heart to assert that they are not yet authentic corpses, but living men with brains in their heads, they are pretty certain to be gently chided and led back to the comfortable armchair that befits senility. Their counsel is smiled at as the chatter of a belated post-Victorian generation that knew not Freud, and if they must go abroad they are bidden take the air in the garden where other old-fashioned plants—mostly of the family *Democratici*—are still preserved."[7]

Following the end of the World War II, a third generation of professional historians appeared on the scene to challenge the Progressive point of view. They were sometimes called "neo-conservatives" because they seemed to hark back to the conservative historical position that had prevailed prior to Turner and Beard. Their rise was partly a result of pressures—both external and internal—upon the historical profession in the postwar era.

---

[7]Vernon L. Parrington, *Main Currents in American Thought* (3 vols.: New York, 1927–1930), III, p. 401.

External pressures resulting from changing political conditions in the world at large brought about a major change in the mood of many Americans. Some neo-conservative historians reflected, either consciously or unconsciously, an outlook that pervaded the United States as the nation assumed the sober responsibility of defending the world against the threat of Communism. During the Cold War era, when the country felt its security endangered from abroad, these scholars wanted, perhaps, to present an image to the rest of the world of an America that had been strong and united throughout most of its history. Hence, the neo-conservative scholars pictured American history in terms of consensus rather than conflict.

Internal pressures within the profession itself likewise brought changes. Particular points of view expressed in any academic discipline seem to have an inner dynamism of their own. After subscribing to a given interpretation for a time, scholars often sense that they have pushed an idea to its outermost limits and can go no farther without risking major distortion. A reaction inevitably sets in, and revisionists begin working in a different direction. Such was the case of the Progressive interpretation of history. Having written about American history from the standpoint of conflict and discontinuity, scholars now began to approach the same subject from an opposite point of view—that of consensus and continuity.

One way this new group of scholars differed from the Progressives was in their inherent conservatism. Progressive historians had had a deep belief in the idea of progress. Neo-conservative historians, on the other hand, often rejected progress as an article of faith. Skeptical of the alleged beneficial results of rapid social change, they stressed instead the thesis of historical continuity.

Given their emphasis on continuity, the neo-conservatives were less prone to a periodized view of American history. Progressive scholars had seen American history in terms of class or sectional conflicts marked by clearly defined turning points—the Revolution, the Constitution, the Jeffersonian era, the Jacksonian period, the Civil War, and so forth. These periods represented breaks, or discontinuities, from what had gone on before. For the Progressive, American history was divided into two distinct phases that followed one another in a cyclical pattern—periods of reform or revolution when the popular and democratic forces in society gained the upper hand and forced social changes, and periods of reaction and counterrevolution, when vested interests resisted such changes. For the neo-conservative scholars, however, the enduring and unifying themes in history were much more significant. To them the continuity of common principles in American culture, the stability and longevity of institutions, and the persistence of certain traits and traditions in the American national character, represented the most powerful forces in history.

Consensus, as well as continuity, was a characteristic theme of the neo-conservative historians. Unlike the Progressives, who wrote about the past in terms of polarities—class conflicts between rich and poor, sectional divisions between North and South or East and West, and ideological differences between liberals and conservatives—the neo-conservatives abandoned the conflict interpretation of history and favored instead one that viewed American society as stable and homogeneous. The cement that bound American society together throughout most of its history was a widespread acceptance of certain principles and beliefs. Americans, despite their differences, had always agreed on the following propositions: the right of all persons in society to own private property; the theory that the power of government should always be limited; the concept that men possessed certain natural rights that could not be taken from them by government; and the idea of some form of natural law.

One of the foremost neo-conservative historians writing in the 1950's was Louis Hartz. In his book, *The Liberal Tradition in America*, Hartz took issue with those Progressive historians who had viewed the American Revolution as a radical movement that fundamentally transformed American society. America had come into being after the age of feudalism, Hartz claimed, and this condition had profoundly shaped its development. Lacking a feudal past, the country did not have to contend with the established feudal structure that characterized the *ancien regime* in Europe—a titled aristocracy, national church, national army, and the like. Hence, America was "born free" and did not require a radical social revolution to become a liberal society—it was one already. What emerged in America, according to Hartz, was a unique society characterized by a consensus upon a single tradition of thought—the liberal tradition. The absence of a feudal heritage enabled the liberal-bourgeois ideas embodied in the political principles derived from England's John Locke to flourish in America almost unchallenged. "The ironic flaw in American liberalism," wrote Hartz, "lies in the fact that we have never had a conservative tradition."[8]

What, then, of the "conservatives" in American history about whom the Progressive scholars had written? When viewed within the context of comparative history, Hartz said, American conservatives had much more in common with their fellow American liberals than with their European counterparts. Many of the presumed differences between so-called American "conservatives" and "liberals" was in the nature of shadow-boxing rather than actual fighting, he concluded, because both groups agreed on a common body of liberal political principles. The Federalists, for example, were not aristocrats but whiggish liberals who misunderstood their society; they misread the Jeffersonian Democrats as

[8]Louis Hartz, *The Liberal Tradition in America* (New York, 1955), p. 57.

being "radicals" rather than recognizing them as fellow liberals. What was true of the Federalists and Jeffersonians held for the other political confrontations in American history; if measured in terms of a spectrum of thought that included European ideologies, the American conflicts took place within the confines of a Lockean consensus.

Daniel J. Boorstin, another major neo-conservative historian, also offered a grand theory which pictured American history in terms of continuity and consensus. Boorstin, like Hartz, stressed the uniqueness of American society, but he attributed this development to other causes. A neo-Turnerian, Boorstin postulated an environmental explanation of the American national character. To him the frontier experience was the source of America's conservatism.

In two books written in the 1950's—*The Genius of American Politics* and *The Americans: The Colonial Experience*—Boorstin denied the significance of European influences and ideas upon American life. Boorstin's premise was that the Americans were not an "idea-centered" people. From the very beginning Americans had abandoned European political theories, European blueprints for utopian societies, and European concepts of class distinctions. Americans concerned themselves instead with concrete situations and the practical problems experienced by their frontier communities. Thus, they developed little knack for theorizing or any deep interest in theories as such. The "genius of American politics" lay in its emphasis on pragmatic matters—its very distrust of theories that had led to radical political changes and deep divisions within European societies.[9]

The American way of life which evolved during the colonial period, wrote Boorstin, set the pattern for the nation's later development. That pattern placed a premium on solutions to practical problems, adaptations to changing circumstances, and improvisations based upon pragmatic considerations. Lacking a learned class or professional traditions, the colonists were forced to create their own ways of doing things in the areas of education, law, medicine, science, diplomacy, and warfare. During this process the "doer" dominated over the "thinker" and the generalist over the specialist. Over the course of time, this nontheoretical approach developed into a distinctive American life style—one characterized by a naive practicality that enabled Americans to unite in a stable way of life and to become a homogeneous society made up of undifferentiated men sharing the same values.

The "cult of the 'American Consensus'," as one scholar called it, made the nation's past appear tame and placid; it was no longer a his-

---

[9]Daniel J. Boorstin, *The Genius of American Politics* (Chicago, 1953), and *The Americans: The Colonial Experience* (New York, 1958). Boorstin further elaborated on his views in two more volumes: *The Americans: The National Experience* (New York, 1965), and *The Americans: The Democratic Experience* (New York, 1973).

tory marked by extreme group conflicts or rigid class distinctions.[10] The heroes in America's past—Jefferson, Lincoln, Wilson, and Franklin D. Roosevelt—became less heroic because there occurred no head-on clash between individuals on the basis of ideology since all Americans shared the same middle-class Lockean values. Conversely, the old villains—Hamilton, Rockefeller, and Carnegie—became less evil and were portrayed as constructive figures who contributed much to their country. The achievements of the business community in particular were glorified. Without the material achievements of American entrepreneurs, according to some scholars, the United States could not have withstood the challenges to democracy during World War I and World War II. The underdogs in American history—the reformers, radicals, and working class—were presented as being less idealistic and more egocentric as neo-conservative scholars sought to demonstrate that the ideology of these elements in society were no less narrow and self-centered than that of other elements. The "cult" of the neo-conservatives continued into the 1960's—though "cult" was perhaps too strong a term, and implied a unanimity rarely found in the historical profession.

Besides Boorstin and Hartz, other neo-conservative scholars published specialized studies which revised the Progressive point of view in virtually every period of American history. The neo-conservative trend, marked by a new respect for tradition and a de-emphasis on class conflict, brought many changes in American historiography: the revival of the filiopietist approach to the Puritans; the treatment of the American Revolution as a conservative movement of less significance; the conclusion that the Constitution was a document faithfully reflecting a middle-class consensus; the favorable, if not uncritical, attitude toward the founding fathers of the new republic; the diminution of the traditional ideological differences between Hamiltonianism and Jeffersonianism; the consensus interpretation of the Jacksonian era; the enchanced reputation of America's business tycoons; a renewed appreciation of such controversial political leaders as Theodore Roosevelt; the inclination to play down the more radical aspects of the Progressive and New Deal periods; the predisposition to support the correctness of America's recent foreign policy; and the tendency to view American society as being satisfied, unified, and stable throughout most of the nation's history. Implicit in the neo-conservative approach was a fear of extremism, a yearning to prove that national unity had almost always existed, and a longing for the security and way of life America presumably had enjoyed before becoming a super-power and leader of the free world.

---

[10]John Higham, "The Cult of the 'American Consensus': Homogenizing Our History," *Commentary*, XXVII (February, 1959), pp. 93–100.

During the decades of the 1960's and 1970's, the assumptions and conclusions of the neo-conservative historians were rudely overturned by two major developments. First, the mood of the American people shifted markedly as the seemingly placid decade of the 1950's was succeeded by tumultuous events in America's foreign and domestic affairs. Second, within the historical profession itself a reaction to the neo-conservative point of view led to the rise of many revisionist interpretations. The result was a pronounced fragmentation in the field of American historiography.

The prevailing mood among the American people shifted dramatically in the 1960's and 1970's because of a series of shattering events on the domestic scene. Gone were the complacency, national self-confidence, optimism, and moral composure that seemed to have characterized the 1950's. Many historians were stirred by the great social upheavals that undermined previously held assumptions. A marked trend toward racial divisions within American society appeared with the new-found militancy among blacks during the civil rights movement. The resulting hostility to integration among many whites showed that American society was hardly as homogeneous as had been previously believed. At the same time, an increased tendency toward violence during the urban riots in the 1960's indicated that Americans were not always committed to the idea of peaceful compromise. President Kennedy's assassination in 1963 followed by that of Martin Luther King and Robert Kennedy revealed that the United States was as vulnerable to political terrorism as other societies. There was also a renewed awareness of poverty with the economic downturn in the 1970's, and some scholars began voicing doubts about the supposed social mobility within American society, the virtues of technological change, and the benefits of economic growth.

The appearance of numerous social protest movements during those two decades also made many American historians more conscious of the importance of minority groups in the nation's past. Having witnessed protest movements by the blacks, the poor, and the women's liberation movement, some scholars took a greater interest in black history, women's history, and to protest groups like the Populists and I.W.W. Generally speaking, historians became more sympathetic to the role of the underdog in American history.

Changes in America's foreign affairs during these decades similarly had a profound effect on the writing of history. The Vietnam war, above all, divided the American people. Students participated in large-scale antiwar demonstrations, and college campuses were transformed into centers of political protest and activism. Many intellectuals grew disenchanted with the government's military policy and became increasingly suspicious of the political establishment in general. The Vietnam war also exposed the dangers of what one historian termed the imperial presidency. President Nixon and the Watergate scandal revealed further the threat posed to constitutional government by this concept of the presidency. As some historians grew more critical of America's foreign policy, they began to question the credibility of the government both in the present and in the past.

During the course of the 1960's and 1970's, scholars were affected also by sweeping intellectual changes within the historical profession itself. Some began by challenging the traditional approach to history—one that assumed the discipline was separate and self-contained. Acting on the premise that the other social sciences—psychology, sociology, anthropology, and political science—could contribute to the study of history, they turned more to an interdisciplinary approach. In doing so, these historians applied concepts, laws, and models from other social sciences in order to understand the conduct of individuals and social groups in the past. This interdisciplinary approach could hardly be called "new" for it had been employed during the first half of the twentieth century. Still, there was a stronger tendency among scholars to apply social science techniques during these two decades.

A second major development was the use of new methodological approaches to the study of history. Some historians began relying more on quantitative techniques in their efforts to derive scientifically measurable historical data to document their studies. Other scholars turned to a comparative history approach—comparing entire societies or segments of societies—to illuminate the American past. Quantitative and comparative history were but two of a number of methodological approaches which were employed with greater frequency in the 1960's and 1970's.

It was within this general context that there arose a significant challenge to the neo-conservative historians in the 1960's from a group of younger radical scholars known as the "New Left." Like the older Progressives whom they considered their predecessors, these historians sought to fuse historical scholarship with political activism. Unlike the neo-conservatives who emphasized consensus, continuity, and stability, the New Left saw social and economic conflict as the major theme in American history. Of all historians, the individuals identified with the New Left were the most disenchanted with the course of events in recent American history. As a result they presented a radical critique of American society and took a more jaundiced view of the American past.

These scholars reinterpreted American history along more radical lines and insisted that their colleagues pay far greater attention to the lower classes and minority groups of all kinds. Members of the New Left were exceedingly critical, in particular, of those neo-conservative scholars who tended to celebrate the virtues and achievements of the American people. Because the neo-conservatives had excluded conflict in their interpretation, the New Left argued, the American people were unprepared to cope with the social upheavals that occurred in the

1960's. These younger historians declared that the resort to violence by social groups to achieve their goals was a theme that had deep roots in the American past. The New Left historians sought to create a "usable past"—a history that would account for the country's social problems such as racism, militarism, economic exploitation, and imperialism, and would serve as the basis for reforming American society. American history had too often been written from "the top down"—that is, from the point of view of elites and the articulate like Washington, Lincoln, and Franklin D. Roosevelt. History, they argued, should be written "from the bottom up," a perspective which would reflect the concerns of the common people, the inarticulate masses, and non-elites. Viewing history in this way, scholars would discover the radicalism inherent in the American past.

In their treatment of America's foreign policy, for example, the New Left developed a much more critical interpretation than previous historians. America from its very beginnings, they argued, had been an aggressive, expansionist, and imperalist nation. It expanded first at the expense of the Indians, and then later at the expense of its weaker neighbors like Mexico. The United States turned subsequently to an overseas imperialist foreign policy based on its need for foreign markets, raw materials, and investment opportunities. This expansionist foreign policy had global ramifications, the New Left claimed. America had played a major role in precipitating two world wars and was primarily responsible for bringing about the Cold War. The Vietnam war, according to the New Left, was simply a logical extension of America's aggressive and expansionist foreign policy.

The New Left view of American history never attained the importance of cohesion of either the Progressive or the neo-conservative interpretation. One reason was that few Americans were prepared to accept either the analysis or the solutions proposed by these radical historians. Another was that the American withdrawal from Vietnam and the economic downturn of the 1970's brought a halt to most radical protest movements. Although New Left scholarship failed to develop the potential many had expected of it, some of its insights and concerns were absorbed by nonradical historians seeking to break out of the mold and limitations of the neo-conservative approach of the 1950's.

A much more significant challenge to both the neo-conservatives and to some Progressive scholars was the "new" social history of the 1960's and 1970's. This group of scholars, in general, were concerned with defining the nature of America's social structure and its changes over time. They were called the "new social historians" to distinguish them from the "old" social historians who had been occupied primarily with descriptive and narrative history which dealt with the manners and mores of the common people.

The "new social historians" criticized both the neo-conservatives and

Progressives for their choice of subject matter and use of evidence. These historians claimed that older scholars had focused too narrowly upon political, diplomatic, and institutional matters. Older scholars, moreover, were interested in describing isolated historical events. The "new social historians" hoped to widen the scope of history by showing that the relationship between social, economic, and political events inevitably involved changes in the social structure.

These scholars claimed also that earlier historians had sometimes made generalizations based on vague and limited evidence. Historical evidence, according to the "new social historians," should be more precise and approached in a more scientific manner. If at all possible, evidence should be expressed in quantifiable terms so that it might be measured to provide a greater degree of precision. It should be subjected also to systematic analysis in order to test broad conceptual hypotheses about human behavior advanced by the other social sciences. Their hope for history was likewise more ambitious than their predecessors. They aimed to create a "new social history" that would illuminate America's social structure and explain social change throughout all of American history.

The growing interest of American historians in the "new" social history was the result of several influences. First, French scholars since the 1930's had been moving away from narrow political and institutional studies and raising new questions which employed novel methodologies. The most significant outlet for the work of these European scholars was the *Annales*, a French publication. The aim of this distinguished journal was to break down the traditional disciplinary barriers and to create a new and unified approach to the understanding of the totality of human activity within a given society or geographical region. Under the editorship of two French scholars, Lucien Febvre and Marc Bloch, the *Annales* became the acknowledged leader in creating the new field of social history or historical sociology. Continuing its innovative beginnings after World War II, the *Annales* increasingly served scholars employing quantitative and demographic techniques, or resorting to multidisciplinary approaches. Slowly but surely, the influence of this French scholarship made itself felt in the United States.

A second influence shaping the "new" social history was the proliferation of work in the social and behavioral sciences after World War II on contemporary problems that vitally affected the lives of many Americans. Among these were included the issue of race relations, family problems, patterns of social and geographical mobility, crime, and educational as well as economic opportunities. Inevitably American historians began to examine the historical roots and antecedents of these social problems.

The final influence was the increased use of the computer and new quantitative techniques which permitted these newer scholars to analyze historical evidence from heretofore unusable sources. Before the advent of the computer, scholars found it difficult, if not impossible, to collect and analyze massive amounts of data. Historians, for instance, were now able to make use of the manuscript census schedules which formed the basis for the published federal and state censuses. These census schedules, which provided much information about individuals and households in the past, had remained unused for the most part because of problems encountered in reducing such a mass of discrete bits of information to usable form. Computer technology made it possible to gather and manipulate these data, while new quantitative techniques enabled researchers to analyze the information in more meaningful ways.

Although the "new social historians" were more or less unified in their desire to examine social structure and social change, their approaches to these problems led them in many different directions. The fragmentation characteristic of American history in general during this period was especially true among these scholars. It manifested itself in the appearance of a number of separate groups of historians who focused upon specific problems all of which came under the general heading of the "new" social history.

The so-called "new economic historians" were among the first to employ quantitative techniques and computer technology. Their outstanding characteristic was the use of historical data to test hypotheses derived from economic theories. One of their main interests was to describe and explain the patterns of America's economic growth. They hoped also to identify in a more precise manner the forces that had shaped the complex pattern of the economy, the role of entrepreneurs, and the development of different kinds of labor groups and systems.

The "new political historians" represented another fragment group. These scholars were especially influenced by the behavioral approach of the political scientists. Unlike older scholars, these newer historians were less concerned with describing presidential elections and political developments in traditional terms. These scholars were interested instead in quantitative analyses of voting behavior, roll-call analyses of legislatures, and shifts in public opinion on political issues. In studying political behavior, they introduced new techniques for the collection and measurement of data, and developed and refined concepts for analyzing the political process. In doing so, they moved political history closer to social history by seeking to portray the social bases of political behavior.

Yet a third group consisted of the "new urban historians" who studied many processes that occurred within a city setting. These scholars examined such diverse topics as the process of urbanization, growth of suburbs, development of neighborhoods, educational systems, and the rise of political bosses and machines. In approaching these topics, these scholars also made use of computer technology and quantitative techniques to analyze new sources such as manuscript census schedules, city directories, and municipal records. At the same time, many of them resorted to multidisciplinary approaches which drew heavily from concepts of the social and behavioral sciences.

These three groups represent only a few of the new departures undertaken by the "new social historians." In their attempts to understand the American social structure and social change over time, still other scholars in this tradition turned to demography—the study of population in terms of statistical analyses of rates of births, deaths, and marriages. Many of these demographic studies focused upon the family and the community as units of analysis, and led to the establishment of two subfields within the "new" social history—family history and community studies. Others examined the experiences of ethnic and racial groups, giving rise to what was sometimes called an "ethno-cultural approach" to American history. Still others turned to a study of the social, economic, and geographical patterns of mobility in order to identify the conditions that led to success or failure within American society.

Concern with social structure and social change led also to a greater interest in previously neglected social groups. In researching the history of welfare and dependency, scholars studied the ways American society had responded to these groups. The means to care for the poor, the unemployed, the sick and infirm, the insane, and the aged were subjected to close scrutiny. This interest was accompanied by a corresponding concern for the history of crime and delinquency as historians sought to deal with the experiences of the less fortunate and less successful in American society.

The fragmentation of American history so obvious in the many manifestations of the "new" social history was even more marked with the emergence of four other approaches to the discipline which continued along more traditional lines. First of all, the old Progressive tradition was continued after World War II by a group of historians who might be called "neo-Progressives." These scholars approached the study of American history in ways similar to the older tradition, but they modified the Progressive interpretation in many significant ways.

Another development along similar lines was the extension of the work of Perry Miller and other older intellectual historians into the post-World War II era by the so-called "new intellectual historians." Like Miller and others, these more recent scholars placed more emphasis on analyzing rather than describing ideas. Many of these historians reflected a different orientation from the Progressives because they stressed the primacy of ideas as determinants in history.

The two other developments—comparative history and the organizational school of scholars—likewise represented a continuation of the more traditional approaches to history. The comparative historians usually studied the histories of two or more countries in search of similarities or dissimilarities in national experiences. At other times they compared ideas and concepts like "democracy," "nationalism," or "imperialism" to discover to what extent these concepts were the same or different within diverse historical settings. The organizational school of scholars, on the other hand, developed a new synthesis to explain American history since the advent of industrialism. They regarded the rise of bureaucratic structures in society and the acceleration in professionalization as the most significant influences shaping American life since the closing of the frontier in the 1890's. These scholars emphasized the history of organizations and bureaucratic systems, claiming that the behavior of individuals might be better understood when seen within an organizational context.

The fragmentation within the discipline during the 1960's and 1970's prevented the rise of any new major synthesis of American history comparable to the neo-conservative or older Progressive interpretations. As one of the most perceptive scholars on American historiography, John Higham, concluded at the end of the 1960's, "we have today no unifying theme which assigns a direction to American history and commands any wide acceptance among those who write it."[11]

Diversity and disagreement, then, were the hallmark of American historians as the decade of the 1970's moved toward a close. Scholars could only agree that America's past was infinitely more varied and complex than earlier generations of historians had imagined. It may well be that the writing of American history in the future—given the diverse social backgrounds and varied interests of its practitioners—may never again attain the degree of unity that was sometimes achieved in the past.

This introduction postulates two major assumptions regarding the writing of American history: that "every true history is contemporary history" because external pressures of contemporary events have tended to color the view of scholars writing about the past; and that scholars have been affected also by internal pressures within the historical profession to re-evaluate or revise their points of view. If these premises were valid in the past, we can be certain that our view of American history is bound to undergo changes in the future.

---

[11]John Higham, "American Historiography in the 1960's," *Writing American History* (Bloomington, Indiana, 1972), p. 173.

2

The Reconstruction Era

Constructive
or Destructive?

To students of American history, the Civil War years stand in sharp contrast to those of the Reconstruction era. The war years represented a period of heroism and idealism; out of the travail of conflict there emerged a new American nationality that replaced the older sectional and state loyalties. Although the cost in lives and money was frightful, the divisions that had plagued Americans for over half a century were eliminated in the ordeal of fire. Henceforth, America would stand as a united country, destined to take its rightful place as one of the leading nations in the world.

The Reconstruction era, on the other hand, conjures up a quite different picture. Just as the war years were dominated by heroism, the postwar period was characterized as being dominated by evil, power-seeking scoundrels intent upon pursuing their narrow self-interest regardless of the cost to either the South or the nation. The result was a tragedy for all Americans—Northerners, Southerners, whites and blacks alike. Nothing short of a revolution, it seemed, could displace the forces of evil from power and restore the South and the nation to its rightful rulers.

Between 1890 and 1930 few historians would have disagreed with this contrast of the two periods. If anything, most scholars during these years characterized Reconstruction in even harsher terms. Led by Professor William A. Dunning of Columbia University—who literally founded the school of Reconstruction historiography that still bears his name—the historical profession set out to prove that the years following the Civil War were marked by tragedy and pathos because men of good will were momentarily thrust out of power by the forces of evil. This period, in the words of one historian, "were years of revolutionary turmoil.... The prevailing note was one of tragedy.... Never have American public men in responsible positions, directing the destiny of the Nation, been so brutal, hypocritical, and corrupt. . . . The Southern people literally were put to the torture."[1]

Underlying the interpretation of the Dunning school were two important assumptions. The first was that the South should have been restored to the Union quickly and without being exposed to Northern vengeance. Most Southerners, it was argued, had accepted their military defeat gracefully and were prepared to pledge their good faith and loyalty to the Union. Secondly, responsibility for the freedmen should have been entrusted to white Southerners. Blacks, these historians believed, could never be integrated into American society on an equal plane with whites because of their former slave status and inferior racial characteristics.

Working within the framework of these two assumptions, historians in the Dunning school tradition proceeded to study Reconstruction in terms of a struggle between elements of good and evil. On one side stood the forces of good—Northern and Southern Democrats and Republicans of the Andrew Johnson variety. These men, recognizing the necessity for compassion and leniency, were willing to forget the agonies of war and to forgive the South. On the opposing side were the forces of evil—scalawags, carpetbaggers, and above all, a group of radical and vindictive Republicans intent upon punishing the South by depriving the native aristocracy of their power and status, thereby ensuring the dominance of the Republican party in that section. Caught in the middle of this struggle were the helpless, impotent, and ignorant blacks, whose votes were sought for sinister purposes by Radical Republicans who had little or no real concern for the welfare of the freedman once he had left the ballot box.

The result of such a political alignment in the South, according to the Dunning school, was disastrous. The Radical carpetbag state governments that came into power proved to be totally incompetent—in part because they included illiterate blacks who were unprepared for the responsibilities of self government. Still worse, these governments were extraordinarily expensive because they were corrupt. Most of them, indeed, left nothing but a legacy of huge debts. "Saddled with an irresponsible officialdom," one Dunning school historian concluded, "the South was now plunged into debauchery, corruption, and private plundering unbelievable—suggesting that government had been transformed into an engine of destruction."[2]

The decent whites in the South, the Dunning argument continued, united out of sheer desperation to force the carpetbaggers, scalawags,

[1]Claude G. Bowers, *The Tragic Era: The Revolution After Lincoln* (Cambridge, 1929), pp. v–vi.

[2]E. Merton Coulter, *The South During Reconstruction 1865–1877* (Baton Rouge, 1947), p. 148.

and blacks from power. In one state after another Radical rule was eventually overthrown and good government restored. By the time of the presidential campaign of 1876 only three states remained under Radical control. When the dispute over the contested election was resolved, Hayes withdrew the remaining federal troops from the South, and the three last Radical regimes fell from power. Thus the tragic era of Reconstruction came to an end.

For nearly three decades after the turn of the century the Dunning point of view was dominant among most Americans historians. Many monographs on the history of individual Southern states were published, but most of them simply filled in pertinent details and left the larger picture virtually unchanged. All of these studies, despite their individual differences, agreed that the Reconstruction period had been an abject and dismal failure. Not only had Reconstruction destroyed the two-party system in the South; it had left behind an enduring legacy of bitterness and hatred between the races.

The first selection by Albert B. Moore is a good example of a historian writing about Reconstruction within the Dunning tradition. The events between 1865 and 1877, Moore argues, had the effect of converting the South into a colonial appendage of the North. To put it another way, the Reconstruction period was simply one phase of the process whereby the North attempted to remake the South in its own image; it was an attempt by a victor to punish the vanquished. Rejecting completely the assertion that the North was lenient, Moore emphasizes property confiscations, mental torture, and vindictive military rule. The political enfranchisement of blacks, which laid the basis for Carpetbag government, is to Moore perhaps the most incredible event of an incredible era. The result was the continued exacerbation of Southern economic, political, and social problems. The South, he concludes, was still paying for the dark legacy of Reconstruction in the twentieth century.

In the late 1920's, however, historians began to look at the events between 1865 and 1877 from a new and different perspective. These revisionists—a term that distinguishes them from followers of the Dunning school—were much less certain that Reconstruction was as bad as had been commonly supposed. Influenced by the Progressive school of American historiography—which emphasized underlying economic factors in historical development—the revisionists began to restudy the entire Reconstruction period. As a result, they posed a sharp challenge to the Dunning school by changing the interpretive framework of the Reconstruction era.

Generally speaking, the revisionists accepted most, if not all, of the findings of the Dunning school. The disagreement between the two groups, therefore, arose from their different starting assumptions and the consequent interpretation of data rather than over disputed empirical data as such. Unlike the Dunningites, the revisionists could not view events between 1865 and 1877 in terms of a morality play that depicted Reconstruction as a struggle between good and evil, white and black, and Democrats and Radical Republicans. Nor were the revisionists willing to accept the view that responsibility for the freedmen should have been entrusted to native white Southerners. Given these differences, it was understandable that the revisionist interpretation should differ sharply from that of the Dunning school.

In 1939 Francis B. Simkins, a distinguished Southern historian who published with Robert Woody in 1932 one of the first revisionist studies, summed up some of the findings of the revisionist school. Pointing out that the overwhelming majority of Southerners lived quietly and peacefully during these years, he emphasized many of the constructive achievements of this era. Simkins, as a matter of fact, denied that the Radical program was radical within the accepted meaning of the word; indeed, the Radicals failed because they did not provide freedmen with a secure economic base. Past historians, he concluded, had given a distorted picture of Reconstruction because they had assumed that blacks were racially inferior. The result was a provincial approach to Reconstruction that was based on ignorance and priggishness. Only by abandoning their biases could historians contribute to a more accurate understanding of the past, thereby making possible rational discussion of one of the nation's most critical dilemmas.[3]

While the revisionists often disagreed as much among themselves as they did with the Dunning school, there were common areas of agreement that gave their writings a certain unity. Most revisionists viewed the problems of American society during these years in a broader context and concluded that they were national rather than sectional in scope. Corruption, to cite but one example, was not confined to the South. It was a national phenomenon in the postwar era and involved all sections, classes, and political parties alike. To single out the South in this regard was patently unfair and ahistorical.

Revisionist historians attempted also to refute many of the familiar assertions of the Dunning school. In the first place, they denied that the Radical governments in the South were always dishonest, incompetent, and inefficient. On the contrary, they claimed, such governments accomplished much of enduring value. The new constitutions written during Reconstruction represented a vast improvement over the older ones and often survived the overthrow of the men who had written them. Radical governments brought about many long-needed social reforms, including state-supported school systems for both blacks and whites, a revision of the judicial system, and improvements in local administration. Above all, these governments operated—at least in

---

[3]Francis B. Simkins, "New Viewpoints of Southern Reconstruction," *Journal of Southern History*, V (February, 1939), pp. 49–61.

theory—on the premise that all men, white and black alike, were entitled to equal political and civil liberties.

Second, the revisionists drew a sharply different portrait of blacks
during Reconstruction. They denied that developments in the post-war
South resulted from black participation in government or that the
freedmen were illiterate, naîve, and inexperienced. In no Southern
state, they pointed out, did blacks control both houses of the legislature.
Moreover, there were no black governors and only one black state supreme court justice. Only two blacks were elected to the United States
Senate and fifteen to the House of Representatives. Such statistics
hardly supported the charge that the supposed excesses of Reconstruction were due to political activities of black Americans.

Indeed, the revisionists maintained that blacks, as a group, were
quite capable of understanding where their own interests lay without
disregarding the legitimate interests of others. The freedmen were able
to participate at least as intelligently as other groups in the American
political process. As Vernon L. Wharton concluded in his pioneering
revisionist study of the Negro in Mississippi after the Civil War, there
was "little difference . . . in the administration of . . . counties [having
blacks on boards of supervisors] and that of counties under Democratic
control. . . . Altogether, as governments go, that supplied by the Negro
and white Republicans in Mississippi between 1870 and 1876 was not a
bad government. . . . With their white Republican colleagues, they gave
to the state a government of greatly expanded functions at a cost that
was low in comparison with that of almost any other state."[4]

If black Americans were not the dominant group in most Radical
governments, where did these governments get their support? In attempting to answer this question, revisionists again endeavored to refute the Dunning school contention that these governments were controlled by evil, power-hungry, profit-seeking carpetbaggers and renegade
scalawags who used black votes to maintain themselves in power. The
stereotype of the carpetbagger and scalawag, according to revisionists,
was highly inaccurate and far too simplistic. Carpetbaggers, to take one
group, migrated to the South for a variety of reasons—including the lure
of wider and legitimate economic opportunities as well as a desire to
serve the former slaves in some humanitarian capacity. The scalawags
were an equally diverse group. Within their ranks one could find former
Southern unionists and Whigs, lower class whites who sought to use the
Republican party as the vehicle for confiscating the property of the
planter aristocrats, and businessmen attracted by the promise of industrialization. The Radical governments, then, had a wide base of indigenous support in most Southern states.

---

[4]Vernon L. Wharton, *The Negro in Mississippi 1865–1890* (Chapel Hill, 1947), pp. 172,
179–180.

Finally, the revisionists rejected the charge that the Radical governments were extraordinarily expensive and corrupt, or that they had saddled the South with a large public debt. It was true that state expenditures went up sharply after the war. This situation was due, however, to understandable circumstances and not to inefficiency or theft. As in most postwar periods, the partial destruction of certain cities and areas required an infusion of public funds. Deferring regular appropriations during the war years also meant that a backlog of legitimate projects had accumulated. Most important of all, the South for the first time had to provide certain public facilities and social services for its black citizens. Southern states and communities had to build schools, and provide other facilities and services for blacks which did not exist before the 1860's and for which public funds had never been expended prior to this time. It is little wonder, then, that there was a rise in spending in the Reconstruction era.

In examining the financial structure of Southern governments between 1865 and 1877, the revisionists also found that the rise in state debts, in some instances, was more apparent than real. Grants to railroad promoters, which in certain states accounted for a large proportion of the increase in the debt, were secured by a mortgage on the railroad property. Thus, the rise in the debt was backed by sound collateral. The amount of the debt chargeable to theft, the revisionists maintained, was negligible. Indeed, the restoration governments, which were dominated by supposedly honest Southerners, proved to be far more corrupt than those governments controlled by the Radicals.

Although revisionists agreed that the Dunning interpretation of Reconstruction was inadequate—if not misleading—they had considerable difficulty themselves in synthesizing their own findings. If there was one idea on which the revisionists were united, it was their conviction that economic forces, which were related to the growth of an urban and industrialized nation, somehow played a major role during this period. Beneath the political and racial antagonisms of this era, some revisionists argued, lay opposing economic rivalries. Anxious to gain an advantage over their competitors, many business interests used politics as the vehicle to further their economic ambitions—especially since the South, like the North and West, was ardently courting businessmen. The result was that economic rivalries were translated into political struggles.

Revisionists also emphasized the crucial issue of race. During Reconstruction many former Whigs joined the Republican party because of its pro-business economic policies. These well-to-do conservatives, at first, were willing to promise blacks civil and political rights in return for their support at the polls. Within the Democratic party, however, lower class whites, fearful of possible encroachments by blacks upon their social status and economic position, raised the banner of race. Conservatives found their affiliation with the Republican party increasingly uncomfortable and they slowly began to drift back into the Democratic party. The fact that both parties were under the control of conservatives made it easier for former Republicans to shift their political allegiance. One result of the political alignment was that it left Southern blacks politically isolated and without allies among the whites. When the move to eliminate blacks from political life in the South got started, they could find little support among Southern whites. This political move came at a time when Northerners were disillusioned by the failure of the Radicals to achieve many of their idealistic aims for the freedmen. Tired of conflict and turmoil, Northerners became reconciled to the idea of letting the South work out its own destiny—even if it meant sacrificing the black people. Northern businessmen likewise became convinced that only Southern conservatives could restore order and stability and thus create a favorable environment for investment.

The result was both a polarization of Southern politics along racial rather than economic lines and the emergence of the Democratic party as the white man's party. For whites of lower class background, the primary goal was to maintain the South as a white man's country. Upper class whites were also contented with the existing one-party political structure because they were permitted the dominant role in determining the future economic development of their section.

The end of Reconstruction, according to the revisionists, was closely related to the triumph of business values and industrial capitalism. When the contested presidential election of 1876 resulted in an apparent deadlock between Rutherford B. Hayes, the Republican candidate, and Samuel J. Tilden, his Democratic opponent, some prominent Republicans saw an opportunity to rebuild their party in the South upon a new basis. Instead of basing their party upon propertyless, former slaves, they hoped to attract well-to-do former Whigs who had been forced into the Democratic party as a result of events during the Reconstruction. To accomplish this goal, a group of powerful Republican leaders began to work secretly to bring about a political realignment. If Southern Democratic congressmen would not stand in the way of Hayes' election and also provide enough votes to permit the Republicans to organize the House of Representatives, these leaders were willing to promise the South federal subsidies—primarily for railroads—and also to name a Southerner as Postmaster General.

The "Compromise of 1877," as this political deal was called, was not fully carried out, but its larger implications survived unscathed. As C. Vann Woodward, the revisionist historian who propounded the thesis of such a political bargain, concluded, the Compromise "did not restore the old order in the South, nor did it restore the South to parity with other sections. It did assure the dominant whites political autonomy and nonintervention in matters of race policy and promised them a share in the blessings of the new economic order. In return the South became, in effect, a satellite of the dominant region. So long as the Conservative Redeemers held control they scotched any tendency of the South to combine forces with the internal enemies of the new economy—laborites, Western agrarians, reformers. Under the regime of the Redeemers the South became a bulwark instead of a menace to the new order."[5]

Since the early 1950's, a new school of Reconstruction historiography called the neo-revisionists has emerged. These historians emphasized the moral rather than the economic basis of Reconstruction. The differences between the revisionists and neo-revisionists were often minimal since the latter frequently relied upon the findings of the former to reach their conclusions and it is difficult, if not impossible, to categorize certain historians as belonging to one group or another. Generally speaking, while the neo-revisionists accepted many findings of the revisionists, they rejected the idea of interpreting Reconstruction in strictly economic terms. The Republican party, the neo-revisionists maintained, was not united on a pro-business economic program; it included individuals and groups holding quite different social and economic views.

In interpreting Reconstruction, the neo-revisionists stressed the critical factor of race as a moral issue. One of the unresolved dilemmas after the Civil War, they claimed, was the exact role that blacks were to play in American society. Within the Republican party, a number of factions each offered their own solution to this question. Andrew Johnson, who had been nominated as Lincoln's running mate in 1864 on a Union party ticket despite his Democratic party affiliations, spoke for one segment of the party. To Johnson blacks were incapable of self-government. Consequently, he favored the state governments in the South that came back into the Union shortly after the end of the war under his own plan of reconstruction and went along with the Black Codes that denied black Americans many of their civil rights.

Although Johnson was President as well as titular head of the Republican party, there was a great deal of opposition to his policies by a group known as the "Radicals." Who were the Radical Republicans and what did they stand for? To the Dunning school the Radicals were a group of vindictive politicians who were utterly amoral in their quest after power; they were merely interested in the black man for his vote. To revisionists the Radicals represented, at least in part, the interests of the industrial Northeast—men who wanted to use black votes to prevent the forma-

[5]C. Vann Woodward, *Reunion and Reaction: The Compromise of 1877 and the End of Reconstruction* (Boston, 1951), p. 246.

tion of a coalition of Western and Southern agrarian interests against the industrial capitalism of the Northeast.[6]

To the neo-revisionists, on the other hand, the Radicals were a much more complex group. Many of the Radicals, they claimed, joined the Republican party in the 1850's for moral and idealistic reasons—their antislavery zeal—rather than for economic motives. These men, seeking to eradicate all vestiges of slavery, were consistent in their demands before and after the war that blacks be given the same rights as white Americans. Their beliefs, of course, brought them to a face-to-face confrontation with President Johnson in the postwar period. In the ensuing struggle, the President, because of his political ineptness, soon found himself isolated. Taking advantage of the situation, the Radicals first won the support of conservative Republicans and then set out to remake Southern society by transferring political power from the planter class to the freedmen. The program of the Radicals, therefore, was motivated in large measure by idealism and a sincere humanitarian concern.

In 1965 Kenneth M. Stampp published an important synthesis that emphasized the moral dimension of the Reconstruction years. Stampp rejected the traditional stereotype of the average Radical as a figure motivated by vindictive considerations. He argued that the issues of the 1860's were not artificial ones as the Dunning school had claimed. The central question of the postwar period was the place of the freedmen in American society. President Johnson and his followers believed in the innate racial inferiority of blacks; therefore they rejected any program based upon egalitarian assumptions. The Radicals, on the other hand, took seriously the ideals of equality, natural rights, and democracy. Indeed, most of these men had been closely associated with the antebellum abolitionist crusade. Stampp did not deny that the Radicals had other motives as well, for he admitted that they saw black Americans as valuable additions to the Republican party. But most politicians, he insisted, identify the welfare of the nation with the welfare of their party. To argue that the Radicals had invidious and selfish motives, Stampp concluded, does them a severe injustice and results in a distorted picture of the Reconstruction era.

The Radicals, according to the neo-revisionists, ultimately failed in their objectives. Most Americans, harboring conscious and unconscious racial antipathies, were not willing to accept blacks as equals. By the 1870's the North was prepared to abandon blacks to the white South for three reasons: a wish to return to the amicable prewar relations between the sections; a desire to promote industrial investment in the South; and

---

[6]This point of view was best expressed by Howard K. Beale, one of the fathers of the revisionist school, in *The Critical Year: A Study of Andrew Johnson and Reconstruction* (New York, 1930).

a growing conviction that the cause of black Americans was no longer worth further strife. The tragedy of Reconstruction, the neo-revisionists maintained, was not that it occurred, but that it had ended short of achieving the major goal sought by the Radicals.

The struggle over Reconstruction, nevertheless, had not been in vain. In addition to the many achievements of the Radical governments, the Radicals had succeeded in securing the adoption of the Fourteenth and Fifteenth amendments. These amendments, in Stampp's words, "which could have been adopted only under the conditions of radical reconstruction, make the blunders of that era, tragic though they were, dwindle into insignificance. For if it was worth four years of civil war to save the Union, it was worth a few years of radical reconstruction to give the American Negro the ultimate promise of equal civil and political rights."[7]

In the second selection in this chapter Allen W. Trelease sums up the neo-revisionist interpretation of Reconstruction. Given a commitment to racism that by 1865 was deeply embedded in the minds of a majority of white Americans, Trelease argues that Southerners could hardly be expected to abandon their antipathies toward blacks after emancipation. Although blacks were simply seeking the same rights enjoyed by whites, the latter were unable to accept the former as equals. Seeing the race question as crucial, Trelease insists that Radical Reconstruction failed because the seed of biracial democracy was planted on barren ground in the South. Moreover, the federal government failed to nurture the seeds of democracy. Despite significant achievements in the years following the end of slavery, most Radical state governments were quickly overthrown by a society committed to inequality.

The heroic (though tragic) interpretation of Reconstruction offered by Stampp and, to a lesser extent, by Trelease did not remain unchallenged. Given the internal strife engendered by the continued existence of economic, political, and legal inequality, and the seeming resurgence of a radical critique of American institutions and society in the 1960's, it was not surprising that historians associated with the "New Left" would slowly begin to re-evaluate the events of the postwar years in a way that took sharp issue with scholars such as Stampp. Staughton Lynd, for example, argued that it was pointless to debate endlessly the issue whether Northern policy was too hard or too soft following the end of the Civil War. Historians should focus instead on a discussion of the strategies of planned social change that might have succeeded in avoiding the tragedies that followed. Conceding that Reconstruction failed and that American society during the succeeding century would reflect this failure, Lynd concluded "that the fundamental error in Reconstruction policy was that it did not give the freedman land of his own.

---

[7]Kenneth M. Stampp, *The Era of Reconstruction* (New York, 1965), p. 215.

Whether by confiscation of the property of leading rebels, by a vigorous Southern homestead policy, or by some combination of the two, Congress should have given the ex-slaves the economic independence to resist political intimidation."[8]

Nor were the "New Left" scholars alone in rejecting the revisionist or neo-revisionist view of Reconstruction. Although not sufficiently in agreement to constitute a specific school, some individual historians began to place specific events during Reconstruction within a different structural setting. In his study of the presidential election of 1876, for example, Keith I. Polakoff came to conclusions that were at variance with those expressed by C. Vann Woodward nearly twenty-five years earlier. Woodward assumed that national political parties were centralized organizations under the control of their leaders. Polakoff, on the other hand, was influenced by the work of more recent social and political historians. Where Woodward saw decentralized authority, Polakoff saw structural weakness; he insisted that American political parties at this time were decentralized:

> Not only was factionalism practically the central characteristic of both parties, but the precise balance existing between the various factions remained remarkably stable; and no wonder: each faction had its own little constituency on which it could always depend. The diffuseness of power in the Republican and Democratic parties was merely a reflection of the remarkable diversity of the American electorate. If there was one thing nineteenth-century parties did well, it was to represent their constituents. In the process rational programs of government action were trampled underfoot.... The resulting irrelevance of much of the political process was actually one of its principal sources of strength. Because the stakes involved were more symbolic than substantial, much like the outcome of the Army-Navy football game a century later, politicking served as a way of transcending the dull routine of everyday life, a means of identifying with the distinctive democratic greatness of the United States while socializing with like-minded men.[9]

Whether Polakoff's approach would lead to a more generalized reinterpretation of national politics between 1865 and 1877 is as yet unclear; suffice it to say that if his emphasis on structural weakness is correct, then historians may very well have to re-examine the political dimensions of Reconstruction.

The differences between the various schools of Reconstruction historiography were partly a result of the particular milieu in which each

---

[8]Staughton Lynd, ed., *Reconstruction* (New York, 1967), p. 8. See also Lynd's article, "Rethinking Slavery and Reconstruction," *Journal of Negro History*, L (July, 1965), pp. 198–209.

[9]Keith I. Polakoff, *The Politics of Intertia: The Election of 1876 and the End of Reconstruction* (Baton Rouge, 1973), pp. 321–322. See also Allan Peskin, "Was There a Compromise of 1877?" *Journal of American History*, LX (June, 1973), pp. 63–75, and C. Van Woodward, "Yes, There was a Compromise of 1877," *ibid.*, pp. 215–223.

had grown to maturity. The Dunning point of view, for example, originated in the late nineteenth century and flowered in the early part of the twentieth. During these years the vast majority of white Americans assumed that blacks constituted an inferior race, one that was incapable of being fully assimilated into their society. Most Southerners had come to this conclusion well before the Civil War many Northerners had come to the same conclusion after the debacle of Reconstruction seemingly vindicated this belief. Racism in America was buttressed further by the findings of the biological and social sciences in the late nineteenth century. Influenced by evolutionary concepts of Darwinism, some scientists argued that blacks had followed a unique evolutionary course which resulted in the creation of an inferior race. The racial prejudices of many Americans thus received what they believed to be scientific justification.

Given these beliefs, it is not difficult to understand why the Dunning school interpretation gained rapid acceptance. The attempt by the Radicals to give equal rights to a supposedly inferior race did not appear to be sensible; state governments that included black officials and held power in part through black votes were bound to be inefficient, incompetent, and corrupt. Moreover, the Southern claim that responsibility for black people had to be entrusted to whites seemed entirely justifiable. The findings of the Dunning school that Reconstruction was a tragic blunder doomed to failure from its very beginning came as no surprise to early twentieth-century Americans, most of whom were prepared to believe the worst about black Americans.

The revisionist school, on the other hand, originated in a somewhat different climate of opinion. By the 1920's American historiography had come under the influence of the Progressive or "New History" school. This school, growing out of the dissatisfaction with the older scientific school of historians that emphasized the collection of impartial empirical data and eschewed "subjective" interpretations, borrowed heavily from the new social sciences. The New History sought to explain historical change by isolating underlying economic and social forces that transformed institutions and social structures. In place of tradition and stability it emphasized change and conflict. Progressive and democratic in their orientation, Progressive historians attempted to explain the present in terms of the dynamic and impersonal forces that had transformed American society.

The revisionists, then, rejected the moralistic tone of the Dunning school. They sought instead to identify the historical forces responsible for many of the developments following the Civil War. Economic and social factors, they maintained, were basic to this era. The real conflict was not between North and South, white and black; it was between industrial capitalism and agrarianism, with the former ultimately emerging victorious. Thus, the question of the status of black people in American society was simply a facade for the more basic conflicts that lay hidden beneath the surface. Reconstruction, they concluded, was the first phase in the emergence of the United States as a leading industrial and capitalist nation.

The neo-revisionist school, although owing much to the revisionists, was influenced by the egalitarian emphasis of the 1940's and the period following the Second World War. Indicative of changing attitudes toward blacks was the publication in 1944 of the monumental study by Gunnar Myrdal and his associates, *An American Dilemma: The Negro Problem and Modern Democracy*. Myrdal, a distinguished Swedish sociologist, was commissioned by the Carnegie Foundation in the late 1930's to undertake a comprehensive study of black people in the United States. Although emphasizing that a variety of complex factors were responsible for the depressed condition of American blacks, Myrdal argued that the problem was basically a moral one. Americans, he wrote, held a political creed that stressed the equality of all men. This ideal, however, was constantly confronted with the inescapable reality that in the United States white citizens refused to accept blacks as their equals. Thus many Americans were caught in a dilemma between theory and practice, causing them to suffer an internal moral conflict. Myrdal's work anticipated, in part, the thinking behind the civil rights movement of the 1950's.

In evaluating events between 1865 and 1877, neo-revisionist historians began to shift the focus of previous schools. The issue of equal rights for blacks, neo-revisionists maintained, was not a false one even though it was complicated by economic and other factors. In a real sense, the fundamental problem of Reconstruction was whether or not white Americans were prepared to accept the freedmen as equal partners. Even though the Radicals ultimately failed in achieving their egalitarian goals, they left an enduring legacy in the form of the Fourteenth and Fifteenth amendments. These amendments gave black people citizenship, promised them equal protection under the laws, and gave them the right to vote. That America did not honor these promises in the decades after Reconstruction in no way detracted from the idealism of those responsible for these amendments. Indeed, the importance of these amendments took on a new meaning as they gave legal sanction to civil rights after the Second World War.

Historians of the "New Left," on the other hand, saw Reconstruction as a failure because Americans had not faced up to the problems arising out of the end of slavery. Reflecting their own disillusionment and dissatisfaction with contemporary America, they condemned the post-Civil War generation for its failure to restructure society and thereby give blacks (and other poor groups as well) an equitable share of America's wealth. Reconstruction, they argued, represented but another unhappy chapter of American history; the past as well as the present merely revealed the widespread hypocrisy and corruption of ruling groups in the United States.

Although it is possible to demonstrate that particular interpretations grew out of and reflected their own milieu, historians must still face the larger and more important problem of determining the accuracy or inaccuracy of each interpretation.[10] Was Reconstruction, as the Dunning school argues, a tragedy for all Americans? Were the revisionists correct in stressing the achievements as well as the partial failures of this period, and emphasizing the fundamental economic factors? Were the neorevisionists justified in insisting that the major issue during Reconstruction was indeed a moral one? Or were "New Left" historians correct in their assessment of the general failure of Reconstruction and American society? Did the particular structural form of state and national politics preclude effective governmental action in dealing with the problems growing out of emancipation?

To answer these questions, historians must deal also with a number of subsidiary issues. Should the North have forgotten that it had taken four years of bloody and expensive conflict to keep America united and welcomed the South back into the Union in 1865 with open arms? Or was it proper for Northern Republicans to lay down certain conditions to ensure that slavery, legal or implied, would never again exist within the United States? What should have been the proper policy for both the federal and state governments to follow with regard to black Americans, and how were the voices of blacks to be heard during policy formation and implementation? Were Southerners justified in their belief that blacks were incapable of caring for themselves and that their future should be left in the hands of white men? Or were the Radicals correct in insisting that blacks had to be given the same legal and political rights that all Americans enjoyed?

The answers to some of these questions will, in large measure, determine the broader interpretive framework of the Reconstruction era. Although that period is nearly a century away from our own, some of the basic conflicts common to both remain unresolved and as pressing as ever. Time and circumstance may have changed; new leaders may have emerged; yet the fundamental dilemma of what role black people should play in American civilization remains a controversial and vital one.

---

[10]For a discussion of most schools of Reconstruction historiography see Gerald N. Grob, "Reconstruction: An American Morality Play," in *American History: Retrospect and Prospect*, edited by George A. Billias and Gerald N. Grob (New York, 1971), pp. 191–231.

Albert B. Moore

ALBERT B. MOORE (1887–1967), taught at the University of Alabama from 1923 to 1958, where he also served as Dean of the Graduate School and Chairman of the Department of History. He was the author of several books on the history of the South. The selection reprinted above was his presidential address before the Southern Historical Association in 1942.

The South has long been, and to some extent still is, in the throes of being reconstructed by forces operating from outside the region. Ramifications of this reconstruction process account in large degree for certain conditions in the South today and for its place in the nation. They explain how the South has acquired a colonial status, not only in the economic system but also in the psychology, sentiment, culture, and politics of the nation.

While this address is concerned primarily with the reconstruction of the South after the Civil War, it takes cognizance of the fact that the reconstruction of the South by the North has been going on more than one hundred years. Prior to the Civil War it took the form of a savage attack upon slavery and southern society, though it had other connotations. The Northeast with its western extensions, possessed of what one writer has called "egocentric sectionalism"—that is, the conviction that it was not a section but the whole United States and that, therefore, its pattern of life must prevail throughout the country—undertook after 1830 to reconstruct the South into conformity and into a subordinate position. With furious denunciations and menacing gestures and actions it drove the South into secession and war, destroyed its power, and reconstructed it with a vengeance and violence remarkable in the history of human conflict. This is not to give the South a clear bill of health; but whatever the rights and wrongs of the controversy, the Civil War, broadly speaking, was the tragic drama of a movement to reconstruct the South.

We have formed the habit of examining the phenomena of the reconstruction of the South after the Civil War—that is, the period 1865–1877—in a very objective, almost casual, way and with little regard to their essence and their significance in southern and national history.

"One Hundred Years of Reconstruction of the South," *Journal of Southern History*, IX (May, 1943), pp. 153–65. Copyright 1943 by the Southern Historical Association. Reprinted without footnotes by permission of the Managing Editor.

While avoiding the emotional approach one should not forget that it was, after all, a settlement imposed by the victors in war, and should be studied in all its effects, immediate and far reaching, on its victims. An investigation of the effects on the victors themselves would also be an interesting adventure. It is a chapter in the history of the punishment of the defeated in war. The observations of a competent historian from another country, coming upon the subject for the first time, taking nothing for granted and making a critical analysis of its severity compared with the punishment of losers in wars in general, would make interesting reading.

The war set the stage for a complete reconstruction of the South. Furious hatred, politics, economic considerations, and a curious conviction that God had joined a righteous North to use it as an instrument for the purging of the wicked South gave a keen edge to the old reconstruction urge. The victories of bullets and bayonets were followed by the equally victorious attack of tongues and pens. Ministers mounted their pulpits on Easter Sunday, the day following President Lincoln's tragic death, and assured their sad auditors that God's will had been done, that the President had been removed because his heart was too merciful to punish the South as God required. An eminent New York divine assured his audience that the vice-regent of Christ, the new president, Andrew Johnson, was mandated from on high "to hew the rebels in pieces before the Lord." "So let us say," with becoming piety and sweet submissiveness he enjoined, "God's will be done." Whether the ministers thought, after they discovered that Johnson was opposed to a reign of terror, that the Lord had made a mistake is not a matter of record. As Professor Paul H. Buck has said, "It was in the churches that one found the utmost intolerance, bitterness, and unforgiveness during the sad months that followed Appomattox." Henry Ward Beecher, one of the more moderate northern preachers, thought the South was "rotten." "No timber," said he, "grown in its cursed soil is fit for the ribs of our ship of state or for our household homes." The newspapers spread abroad the preachers' gospel of righteous vindictiveness and expounded further the idea that drastic punishment of the South was essential for the security of the Union.

Many unfriendly writers invaded the South, found what they wanted, and wrote books, articles, and editorials that strengthened the conviction that the South must be torn to pieces and made anew. Books, journals, and newspapers stimulated the impulse to be vigilant and stern, to repress and purge. A juggernaut of propaganda, stemming from the various sources of public instruction, prepared the way for the crucifixion of the South. The South of slavery and treason, of continuous outrages against the Negroes and Northerners, of haughty spirit and stubborn conviction, and of superiority complex, must be humbled and made respectable or be annihilated, so that it could never become again a strong factor in national politics.

The South did little or nothing to neutralize Radical northern propaganda. To be sure, a few journalists, like A. T. Bledsoe, complained about "the cunningly devised fables, and the vile calumnies, with which a partisan press and a Puritanical pulpit have flooded the North," but their vituperative responses to vituperative attacks did more harm than good. There was, in the very nature of things, little that the South could do to disabuse the Radical northern mind that was disposed to believe evil of it. There was simply no escape for Southerners from an awful scourge. Even more courage and fortitude than they had displayed on the battlefield would be required to endure what was in store for them.

As much as Reconstruction has been studied in this country it should not at this late hour be necessary to point out its severity, its permanent effects upon the South, and its influence upon various aspects of our national history. Yet few have examined critically the harshness of it and its persistent and manifold effects. While crucifying the South, the dominant Radical group of the North, thanks to the blindness of hatred, believed it was being lenient. Because no lives were taken—but there are some things more agonizing than death—for the "crimes of treason and rebellion," the North has prided itself on its magnanimity; and its historians have been strangely oblivious of property confiscations and mental tortures. It seemed to the late James Ford Rhodes "the mildest punishment ever inflicted after an unsuccessful Civil War." But this was no ordinary civil war, if, indeed, it should be classed as a civil war. The thesis of leniency has oddly persisted. When the Germans protested to high heaven against the severity of the Versailles Treaty they had sympathizers in this country who compared the generosity of the North in its treatment of the South with the harshness of the Versailles Treaty. But the late Professor Carl Russell Fish of the University of Wisconsin, in his article on "The German Indemnity and the South," discredited the theory of generosity on the part of the North. He showed that the South was punished more than Germany, though he touched upon only a few phases of the South's burdens.

Professor Buck in his delightful and highly informative book, *The Road to Reunion*, recognized Reconstruction as "disorder worse than war and oppression unequalled in American annals," but made a serious error when he stated that "virtually no property" was confiscated. He overlooked the confiscation of large quantities of cotton—estimated in the minority report of the Ku Klux Klan Committee at two million bales—then selling for a very high price and most of which belonged to private citizens. The abolition of slavery wiped out about two billion dollars of capital and reduced the value of real estate by at least that amount. This was confiscation of property and the repudiation of Confederate currency, the Confederate bonded debt, and the war debts of the states, all amounting to no less than three billion dollars, was confiscation of property rights. As inevitable as much of this was, it represented a frightful confiscation of property.

The freeing of the slaves not only cost the South two billion dollars but it also forced upon that section an economic and social revolution. It subverted a mode of life almost as old as the South itself. The repudiation of its debts impoverished the South and destroyed its financial relationships. While the South lost its debts, it had to pay its full share of the northern debts which amounted to about four-fifths of the total northern war expenses. The money for this debt was spent in the North for its upbuilding. It paid also its share of the $20,000,000 returned by the Federal treasury to the northern states for direct taxes collected from them during the war, and of extravagant pensions to Union soldiers. Professor James Sellers estimates that the South paid in these ways an indemnity of at least a billion dollars to the North.

The South accepted the results of the war—the doom of slavery and the doctrine of secession—as inevitable and its leaders sought to restore their respective states as speedily as possible to their normal position in the Union. But despite its acceptance in good faith of the declared aims of the North, the South was forced through the gauntlet of two plans of Reconstruction. The people conformed in good faith to the requirements of President Johnson's plan, but Congress repudiated this plan and forced the South to begin *de novo* the process of Reconstruction. Pending its restoration, it was put under the heel of military authority, though there was no problem that exceeded the power of civil authority to handle. Objectively viewed, it is a singular fact that it took three years to restore the South to the Union. It is little short of amazing that for a dozen years after the war Federal troops were stationed in the South among an orderly people who had played a leading role in the building and guidance of the nation since colonial times, and who now sought nothing so much as peace and surcease from strife. For much of the period government was a hodgepodge of activities by the civil authorities, the army, and the Freedmen's Bureau, with the President of the United States working through any or all of these agencies. Most of the serious problems of government were precipitated by outside influences and conspiracies.

The political enfranchisement of four million Negroes, from whose necks the yoke of slavery had just been lifted, is the most startling fact about Reconstruction, and a fact of tremendous impact in southern history. There is nothing in the history of democracy comparable to it. To give the Negroes the ballot and office—ranging from constable to governor—and the right to sit in state legislatures and in Congress, while depriving their former masters of their political rights and the South of its trained leadership, is one of the most astounding facts in the history of reconstruction after war. It was a stroke of fanatical vengeance and design. The basic purpose of this sort of political reconstruction was to vouchsafe for the North—while chastising the South—the future control of the nation through the Republican party. The South was never again to be allowed to regain the economic and political position which it had occupied in the nation prior to 1860.

Negro voting laid the basis for the Carpetbag regime. For eight years Radical northern leaders, backed by the Washington authorities and the army and aided by some native whites, pillaged and plundered and finished wrecking the South. Northern teachers who invaded the South to reconstruct its educational and social system, and northern preachers who came down to restore the unity of the churches by a reconstruction formula that required Southerners to bend the knee and confess their sins helped the politicians, the Freedmen's Bureau, and the Loyal League to undermine the Negroes' confidence in their white neighbors. The reconstruction policy of the churches did its part in stirring up both racial and sectional enmities. The *Nation* remarked, in 1879, the "Churches are doing their full share in causing permanent division." Reconstruction affected the religious life of the country for fifty years and more after the Radicals were overthrown. The character of the Carpetbag-Scalawag-Negro governments was well stated by the New York *Herald* which said the South is "to be governed by blacks spurred on by worse than blacks. . . . This is the most abominable phase barbarism has assumed since the dawn of civilization. . . . It is not right to make slaves of white men even though they have been former masters of blacks. This is but a change in a system of bondage that is rendered the more odious and intolerable because it has been inaugurated in an enlightened instead of a dark and uncivilized age."

It would be safe to say that the people of the North never understood how the South suffered during the Radical regime. The Radicals who controlled most of the organs of public opinion were in no attitude of mind to listen to southern complaints, and most people were too busy with the pursuit of alluring business opportunities that unfolded before them to think much of what was going on down South. In some respects conditions in the South at the end of the Radical regime remind one of the plight of the Germans at the end of the Thirty Years' War.

The South staggered out of the Reconstruction, which ended *officially* in 1877, embittered, impoverished, encumbered with debt, and discredited by Radical propaganda. It had won after many frightful years the right to govern itself again, but there were still white men who could not vote and for many years there was danger of the federal regulation of elections and a resurgence of Negro power in politics.

The tax load had been devastating. The lands of thousands upon thousands had been sold for taxes. Huge state and local debts, much of which was fraudulent, had been piled up. So many bonds, legal and illegal, had been sold that public credit was destroyed. The people stood, like the servant of Holy Writ, ten thousand talents in debt with not one farthing to pay. They had to solve the paradoxical problem of scaling down public debts—a bewildering compound of legal and illegal and far too large to be borne—while restoring public credit. Northern hands had imposed the debts and northern hands held the repudiated bonds. Repudiation became another source of misunderstanding between the sections and another basis for charges of "Southern outrages."

Reconstruction profoundly and permanently affected the political life of the South. It gave the South the one party system. The white people rallied around the Democratic party standards to overthrow the Radical regime, and their continued co-operation was necessary to prevent the Negroes from acquiring again the balance of power in politics. The terrible record of the Republican party during the Radical regime was an insuperable obstacle to its future success in the South. Hostility toward this party promoted devotion to the Democratic party. The complete domination of the latter party not only invested southern politics with the disadvantages of the one party system, but proved to be costly to the South in national politics. The Democratic party has been out of power most of the time in national politics and the Republican party naturally has not felt under obligation to do much for the South when it has had control of the national government. Even when the Democratic party has been in power the South has not had its share of patronage and appropriations, or of consideration in the formulation of national policies. The inequitable distribution of federal relief funds between the states since 1930 is an illustration in point. Political expediency has been the controlling consideration and not gratitude for party loyalty, which calls to mind an old Virginian's definition of political gratitude. Political gratitude, he said, is a lively appreciation of favors yet to be received.

Radical Reconstruction corrupted southern politics, and the prejudice aroused against Negro participation in politics led ultimately to the disfranchisement of most of the Negroes. Political habits formed in counteracting Carpetbag machinations and the presence of Negro voters continued to influence politics. Fraudulent methods were employed to control the Negro votes and when factions appeared among the whites they employed against each other the chicanery and frauds which they had used against the Radicals.

Reconstruction contributed to the proscription of the South in national politics and to provincialism in southern politics. Southerners so feared a recrudescence of Reconstruction in some form or other that for a generation they generally shrank from active participation in national affairs. Their attitude, generally speaking, was that if the North would leave them alone it could direct national affairs. This begat provincialism and made the continued proscription of the South easier. Such a situation was not good for either the South or the North.

Race friction and prejudice were engendered by Reconstruction, which was an unfortunate thing for both races and especially for the Negroes. It caused greater discriminations against the Negroes in politics and education, and in other ways. The Negroes had been so pampered and led as to arouse false notions and hopes among them and to make them for many years lame factors in the rebuilding of the South. The Negro after Reconstruction, and in large degree because of it, continued and continues to be a source of division between the North and South. The North either could not or would not understand the necessity of race segregation, and the idea that the Negro must have a definite place in the scheme of life was obnoxious. Disfranchisement of the Negro, occasional race riots, and the sporadic mobbing of Negroes accused of heinous crimes gave rise to continued charges of "Southern outrages." Criticisms from the North, generally based upon a lack of understanding of the problem, seemed more a matter of censure than of true interest in the Negro. Thus, those who expected to see sectional strife over the status of the Negro disappear with the emancipation of the slaves were disillusioned.

The Negro has been the cause of more misunderstanding and conflict between the sections than all things else. The North freed the Negro from slavery but by repressing and exploiting the South it has contributed much to conditions that have deprived him of some of the opportunities that a free man should have. If southern whites have suffered the pangs and restraints of poverty, the lot of the Negro has inevitably been worse. The shackles upon the Negro's economic and cultural advancement have been formidable and deadening in their effects. Their inescapable lack of educational opportunities has been epitomized by the saying that the South has had the impossible task of educating two races out of the poverty of one.

In some respects the South has not pursued an enlightened policy toward the Negro. In ways it has exploited him. In the struggle for existence the Negro too often has been overlooked. Prejudice, too, resulting to a large extent from Reconstruction experiences, has done its part. Southerners, determined that the political control of Negroes back in the old Reconstruction days shall not be repeated, and probably too apprehensive about the breaking down of social barriers between the two races, have been conservative and slow to see adjustments that need to be made and can be made for the good of both races. Northerners with little information, but sure of their superior understanding, have scolded and denounced after the fashion of the old abolitionists. They have protested and cast sweeping aspersions without making constructive suggestions or troubling themselves to procure information upon which such suggestions could be based. Occasional violence against Negroes by ignorant mobs and discriminations against the Negroes in the enforcement of laws have evoked brutal and indiscriminating attacks from the northern press that remind one of journalism in the old Reconstruction days. Needless to say, such criticisms have contributed nothing to the southern Negro's welfare or to national unity.

The growing political power of the Negro in the North is adding to the Negro problem in the South. Many northern politicians to gain the political support of the northern Negroes—and, eventually, those of the South—are now supporting radical Negro leaders in their demand for a sweeping change in the status of the Negro in the South. But efforts to subvert the social system of the South will lead to more friction between the North and South and to bitter racial antagonisms.

The impoverishment of the people by Reconstruction and the heavy debt load imposed by it were most serious impediments to progress. They hindered economic advancement and educational achievement. Vast hordes of children grew to maturity unable even to read and write. It is impossible to measure the cost to the South of illiteracy alone resulting from the War and Reconstruction. Conditions brought about by Reconstruction also caused a tremendous loss of manpower. They caused a large exodus of the white people of the South to diverse parts, and made the Negroes unfit to apply their productive powers. The loss of whites is well illustrated by Professor Walter L. Fleming's statement that Alabama lost more manpower in Reconstruction than it lost in the War.

The poverty attending Reconstruction laid the basis for the crop lien system and promoted sharecropping, and these more than all things else have hindered rural progress. Hundreds of thousands of both the landless and the landed had nothing with which to start life over and the only source of credit was cotton. Merchants, with the assistance of eastern creditors, advanced supplies to farmers upon condition that they would produce cotton in sufficient quantity to cover the advances made to them. The merchant charged whatever prices he chose to and protected himself by taking a lien upon the cotton produced. Under the system the great mass of farmers became essentially serfs. To throw off the shackles required more resources than most of them possessed.

Even at present a majority of southern tenant farmers depend for credit on their landlords, or on the "furnish merchants" for their supplies. The landlord, moreover, who stakes all on cotton or tobacco, is a bad credit risk. For this reason he pays interest rates as high as twenty percent, and naturally his tenants pay more. It has been estimated that those who depend on the merchant for supplies pay as much as thirty percent interest even on food and feed supplies. Credit unions and the Farm Security and Farm Credit Administrations have helped many of the farmers, but farm credit facilities are still sadly lacking in the South.

Louis XIV's remark that "Credit supports agriculture, as the rope supports the hanged" has been abundantly verified in the South.

Thus, Reconstruction made a large contribution to the development of a slum-folk class in the rural South. The sharecropper-crop-lien farm economy of the South has produced a human erosion system more costly than soil erosion. In fact the two have gone hand in hand. These things always come to mind when in this day of national championships the South is referred to as the nation's "Economic Problem No. 1."

Reconstruction and its aftermath prevented the flow of population and money into the South. The 37,000,000 increase in population between 1870 and 1900 was largely in the North. The South's increase, except in Florida and Texas, was principally native and, as has been observed, it lost part of this increment. Northerners who moved and the millions of Europeans who came in either flocked to the industrial centers of the North or settled down on expansive fertile lands between Ohio and Kansas, made available by the Homestead Act. Most of the nation's capital and credit resources were put into railroad building and industrial and business pursuits north of the Mason and Dixon line. By 1890 the railroad pattern was laid and most of the roads had been built to feed the North. In every phase of economic activity the South was a bad risk compared with the North. Not the least of the things that kept men and money out of the South were its debt load and the stigma of debt repudiation. Northern newspapers and journals lambasted the South for the sin of repudiation and warned investors and emigrants to shun the South. In addition to other risks, they would find, the *Nation* said, that in the South the "Sense of good faith is benumbed, if not dead," and if they had anything to do with the South they would make themselves a part "of a community of swindlers." Even Henry Clews, who had conspired with the Carpetbag racketeers to sell shoddy Reconstruction bonds to gullible buyers in the North and Europe, railed out against the spectacle of "Southern robbery." The notion of southern depravity was long-lived.

Between 1865 and 1900 a new republic of tremendous wealth and productive power was forged and concurrently there was a great educational development and a general advance in culture throughout the North. The South was a mere appendage to the new nation advancing through these epochal transformations; Reconstruction had assigned it a colonial status in all its relations with the North. J. M. Cross of New York City, for example, wrote to John Letcher of Virginia on March 8, 1867, that "Northern civilization must go all the way over the South, which is only a question of time." Some of those who had wanted to make the northern way of life the national way lived to see their wish a *fait accompli*. The patterns of national life were forming and henceforth were to be formed in the North and national unity was to be achieved by the conformity of the South to these patterns. Northerners have made little or no distinction between the North and the nation. The idea has become deeply imbedded throughout the country. For example, Professor Buck unconsciously expresses this attitude when he says, "The small farm worked in countless ways to bring Southern life into closer harmony with the leaven of graceful living. But to the older generation it seemed idea is carried in one of the chapter titles—"Nationalization of the South"—in Professor William B. Hesseltine's recent *History of the South*. When the South has failed to conform it has been stigmatized as backward, provincial, and sectional.

By 1900 the Old South was largely a thing of memory. Yearning for some of the good things of life, impulsive young men rejected antebellum traditions as inadequate to the needs of the new South which must be built. They sneered at "mummies," "mossbacks," and "Bourbons" who cherished the Old South. Others, just as avid about the future of business and industry, hoped to bring over into the New South of their dreams the best of the old and thus merge "two distinct civilizations" into a compound that some good day would surpass anything the North could show. They would leaven the lump of crass materialism with the leaven of graceful living. But to the older generation it seemed that those who were breaking loose from old moorings were bending "the knee to expediency" with little or no regard for principle.

Allen W. Trelease

ALLEN W. TRELEASE (1928–   ) is Professor of History at the University of North Carolina, Greensboro. He is the author of several books, including *Indian Affairs in Colonial New York: The Seventeenth Century* (1960), *Reconstruction:The Great Experiment* (1971), and *White Terror: The Ku Klux Klan Conspiracy and Southern Reconstruction* (1971).

After promoting for a generation and more the idea of innate Negro inferiority in order to justify slavery, Southerners could hardly be expected suddenly to abandon it with the coming of emancipation, especially in the wake of military defeat. The newly freed slave, regarded as occupying an intermediate stage between humanity and the lower orders of animal life, fell into a niche already prepared for him—that of the ante-bellum free Negro. As such, he was not a citizen and had no civil or political rights except those which the white community deemed proper to confer. "He still served, we still ruled," as Cable pointed out a few years later; "all need of holding him in private bondage was disproved. . . . Emancipation had destroyed private, but it had not disturbed public, subjugation. The exslave was not a free man; he was only a free Negro." In effect Negroes were now the slaves of every white man. As subordination and discipline had been enforced by the lash before, it continued to be so now, but without the restraining influence of the slaveholder's self-interest. "The pecuniary value which the individual negro formerly represented having disappeared," Carl Schurz reported in 1865, "the maiming and killing of colored men seems to be looked upon by many as one of those venial offenses which must be forgiven to the outraged feelings of a wronged and robbed people." Most whites, he said, appeared to believe that Negroes existed for the special purpose of providing for their needs. If Schurz exaggerated, the history of the Ku Klux Klan will show that he did not do so very much. Certainly whipping and corporal punishment were regarded as the white man's right and duty, emancipation or no emancipation; organized regulators or vigilantes took up this task with the advent of emancipation, and the Klan further institutionalized the practice.

Negroes often suffered by their liberation.

> As a slave [a Mississippi official pointed out in 1871], the negro was pro-
> tected on account of his value; humanity went hand in hand with the interest
> of the owner to secure his protection, to prevent his being overworked,
> underfed, insufficiently clothed, or abused, or neglected when sick. But as a
> free man, he was deprived of all the protection which had been given to him
> by his value as property; he was reduced to something like the condition of a
> stray dog.

For all the talk of white suffering during the Reconstruction era, it was
the black man who experienced the greatest deprivation and mistreatment, first and last. But it was a rare freedman who regretted emancipation; stories to the contrary could almost invariably be traced to white
men's rationalizations of slavery.

Negroes wanted the same freedom that white men enjoyed, with
equal prerogatives and opportunities. The educated black minority emphasized civil and political rights more than the masses, who called most
of all for land and schools. In an agrarian society, the only kind most of
them knew, landownership was associated with freedom, respectability,
and the good life. It was almost universally desired by Southern blacks,
as it was by landless peasants the world over. Give us our land and we
can take care of ourselves, said a group of South Carolina Negroes to a
Northern journalist in 1865; without land the old masters can hire us or
starve us as they please. A major failure of Reconstruction was that,
except for a favored few, they never got it. Not only did they lack money
or credit, but the government made no substantial effort to help them
obtain it. Whites in many areas refused to sell, or even rent land to
Negroes when they did not have the means to buy, and often actively
conspired to keep them from acquiring it. Negro landownership would
have enhanced the economic and social well-being of the entire section,
but it smacked too much of equality and independence. Some Negroes
who did acquire farms of their own were driven off by mobs or the Ku
Klux Klan. A Negro state senator in Florida believed that there was a
general understanding among whites to deprive blacks of a great part of
the income and property they had rightfully acquired. In many places
this was correct.

The desire for education was reflected in the avidity with which
blacks of all ages took advantage of the limited schooling made available
to them immediately after the war. Knowledge and literacy too were
associated with freedom. Some of this enthusiasm was transitory, particularly among the elders, but parents continued to send their children
to schools, where they existed, and to cry for their establishment where
they did not.

Although a minority of Negroes moved to town—occasionally driven there by white terrorism—the overwhelming majority stayed on the land as wage laborers and sharecroppers. There was little motivation to work harder than they had under slavery. Many whites repeated the stock attitudes regarding Negro character: they were lazy, irresponsible, wasteful, and careless of property; they procrastinated, lacked forethought or perseverance, and derived no satisfaction from a job well done; they engaged in petty thievery and had no sense whatever of right and wrong or truth and falsehood. These characterizations were valid in varying measure—the natural defense mechanisms generated by a life of slavery. One well-disposed Northerner trying to cope with a Georgia cotton plantation reiterated nearly all of these traits from experience with his own laborers, but pointed out that the one thing which seemed to overcome Negro heedlessness was the desire to own their own land. Native Southerners admitted, however, that Negroes were performing far better than they had had any reason to expect at emancipation. A few proclaimed Negro labor the best in the world. The truth seems to be that, after a brief exultation with the idea of freedom, Negroes realized that their position was hardly changed; they continued to live and work much as they had before.

But white men generally agreed on the Negroes' good behavior after the war, and it was for many a matter of pleasant surprise; they had assumed that slavery alone could keep the blacks in good order. Most freedmen were as submissive and deferential to white men as before the war. The great majority were totally dependent upon white favor for a livelihood, and self-interest dictated subservience as a matter of second nature. If some aggressive souls—usually a minority of younger Negroes and other free spirits—talked back or refused to give up the sidewalk, this "insolence" was rare. Seldom were Negroes willing to stand up to a white man and resist or defy him to his face; those who did automatically incurred the wrath of the white community, and risked their lives. Concerted resistance was almost never successful and was apt to prove fatal. Whites were more numerous in most areas, and better armed. More important, they were used to commanding and the blacks to obeying. Next to poverty and economic dependence, this was the freedman's greatest handicap in asserting real freedom during the Reconstruction era.

When Negroes did strike back or defy the master race it was more often the product of impetuosity and extreme aggravation than forethought and planning. Whites commonly ascribed Negro violence, whether directed against them or (more often) among the blacks themselves, as the product of a congenitally passionate nature. The blacks were like children, it was said, who flared up without thought of consequences and then almost as quickly subsided. Negroes seemingly committed fewer murders than whites in proportion to their number, and most of these were crimes of passion in which other Negroes were the victims. Certainly black men were more often the victims than the perpetrators of interracial violence.

A partial exception to the rule of Negro passivity was the crime of arson. The fires almost invariably occurred at night, with barns, gin houses, and other outbuildings the chief targets, and the culprits were seldom discovered. This was, in fact, one of the few relatively safe ways Negroes had of evening the score with white terrorism, although the fire victims were not always those guilty of the terror. Whites frequently imagined incendiary plots when there were none, just as they had long imagined servile insurrections.

But the chief crime complained of was petty thievery. Most thefts occurred after dark, with no witnesses, and it was almost impossible to discover the culprits. Cotton and corn were stolen from the fields, hams were abducted from smokehouses, tools and equipment disappeared from sheds and barns. Occasionally cows, sheep, and hogs were stolen and slaughtered. Some planters who had raised their own meat supplies before the war now gave up trying to keep livestock. Negro larceny, too, was a legacy of slavery: a poverty-stricken people, systematically denied the fruits of their labor and having no property of their own to consider sacred, appropriated what they needed to make life more livable. . . .

Whites of every class united in opposition to what they called social equality—a completely integrated society—as leading inevitably to inter-marriage and degeneration of the white race. In that event, a South Carolinian declared, "we shall become a race of mulattoes . . . another Mexico; we shall be ruled out from the family of white nations. . . . It is a matter of life and death with the Southern people to keep their blood pure." A Republican of Georgia pointed out, "If you talk about equality, they at once conclude that you must take the negro into your parlor or into your bed—everywhere that you would take your wife. They seem to be diseased upon that subject. They do not seem to consider that he is merely to be equal before the law, but take it, I suppose designedly, to mean equality in the broadest sense; and hence they stir themselves up and lash themselves into a fury about it."

Emancipation increased the Southern white rape complex because freedom presumably stimulated the Negro's innate passion for white women and removed external restraints. This was the supreme taboo, which evoked white supremacy in its most virulent form. Whether or not Negro rape of white women actually increased during Reconstruction, it certainly was not widespread; more important was the fact that whites *thought* it was on the increase. The only penalty sufficient to deter the tendency was violent and speedy death—lynching without the delay and dignity of formal trial. The Fayetteville (Tennessee) *Observer* echoed widespread opinion when it condoned the lynching of an alleged Negro rapist in 1868: "The community said amen to the act—it was just and right. We know not who did it, whether Ku Klux or the immediate neighbors, but we feel that they were only the instruments of Divine vengeance in carrying out His holy and immutable decrees." Here too the Ku Klux Klan helped to institutionalize a practice which preceded and long outlived it.

The physical and psychological necessities of keeping Negroes in subordination led to the wildest inconsistencies of attitude and expression. On the one hand the black man was best fitted by nature and temperament for a life of servility and happiest in his carefree dependence on white protectors. On the other hand he was only a degree removed from the wild beasts of the jungle, and the most constant surveillance was needed to keep him from bursting the bonds of discipline and turning upon his friends and protectors in a bloody insurrection. The first theory was necessary to rationalize slavery and the ensuing peonage, but as it never fully squared with the facts, the second argument served to justify necessary repressive measures. Both reinforced Negro subordinance. . . .

Northern Reconstruction policy evolved against this background of myths and realities. Again, the race question was crucial. The North began fighting the Civil War to defeat secession and ended by abolishing slavery as well. Emancipation brought the unavoidable problem of defining the freedmen's status. Northern Democrats generally shared the racial views of the white South and sanctioned the most minimal adjustments required by the ending of legal servitude. This was also the tendency of Abraham Lincoln and of Andrew Johnson afterward. Most Republicans fell between this conservatism and the Radicals' advocacy of full legal and political equality at war's end, but they were gradually driven toward egalitarianism by the course of events between 1865 and 1867. And as theirs was the majority party in the North, that drift determined federal government policy.

Lincoln had assumed the right to reorganize the South and guide her back into the Union, largely on his own authority as commander in chief. During the war, therefore, he sponsored new Loyal or Unionist state governments in Virginia, Tennessee, Louisiana, and Arkansas. Following Appomattox and Lincoln's death, Andrew Johnson took advantage of a Congressional recess to organize the remaining seven states of the late Confederacy. Seemingly all that remained was for Congress to seat the senators and Representatives chosen under these governments. But Congress delayed and ultimately refused to do so.

While the Lincoln and Johnson regimes were dominated in the South by men who had taken a back seat in the secession movement, or opposed it altogether, and who accepted the end of slavery as a price of military defeat, they subscribed as a matter of course to the view that white men must continue to rule in the South. To this end they enacted a series of Black Codes in 1865 and 1866 which clearly and deliberately relegated the Negro to a second-class citizenship. No state extended the right to vote to black men, even to the few who might be educated or well-to-do. Nor was any hope extended for equality someday in the future.

When new horizons did open up for the Negro, as they soon did, it was because of the Republican majority in Congress. Just as the war closed, Congress created a Bureau of Refugees, Freedmen, and Abandoned Lands, attached to the Army, primarily to care for the newly freed black population. The Freedmen's Bureau, as it was called, always suffered from inadequate funds and personnel to perform the tasks assigned it, but the services it did provide were indispensable. Under the direction of General O. O. Howard it distributed food and clothing to those of both races who needed them, protected Negroes against the most blatant forms of exploitation and mistreatment, arranged labor contracts with employers, and attempted with some success to enforce these contracts against infractions on either side. It established hospitals, schools, and colleges for its black charges with the cooperation of Northern charitable agencies.

The Bureau represented an unprecedented extension of federal authority, regulating the economic, social, and legal affairs of individual persons within the respective states. Intended as an emergency device to cope with wartime and immediate postwar conditions, it was due to expire a year after the war ended. But the needs it was created to meet showed no sign of disappearing. Negroes were continually subjected to exploitation, discrimination, and outright violence, which they were powerless to combat alone. The new state governments not only failed to protect them or to assume the educational and other responsibilities of the Freedmen's Bureau, but their Black Codes actually perpetuated many of the hallmarks of slavery. So far as the Northern war effort had become a crusade to free the slaves, the victory seemed in danger of becoming undone. Thus the Republicans pushed through Congress in July 1866, over President Johnson's veto, a law continuing the Bureau for two years more.

In the same spirit were the Civil Rights Act and its sequel, the Fourteenth Amendment, which the Republican majority enacted over the President's objections in April and June of 1866. The former measure defined United States citizenship to include Negroes and extended to them the basic civil rights to sue and to testify in the courts, to hold and convey property, and most importantly, to enjoy equal benefit of the laws with white people. The Fourteenth Amendment, which was ratified and went into effect in 1868, incorporated the provisions of the Civil Rights Act into the Constitution; it also set forth a program for Southern Reconstruction which represented a compromise between the quick restoration favored by the white South and President Johnson and the stricter requirements (such as Negro suffrage) advocated by Radical Republicans. . . .

A basic assumption behind the Reconstruction Acts was that the Negro freedmen would support Congressional Reconstruction and would vote for the party which had freed them and granted them civil rights and the ballot. The assumption proved sound, for Negroes backed the Republican party overwhelmingly as long as they had the chance to do so. In fact they provided the bulk of the Republican electorate; in most states white supporters were more important for their leadership than for their numbers. No matter how dependent the freedmen were upon their former masters, or how much they continued to trust and confide in them as individuals, only a tiny minority of Uncle Toms willingly cast their ballots for the party of white supremacy.

Negroes were elected to office in every state, leading Conservatives in moments of bitter abandon to characterize the whole policy as one of "Negro rule," an accusation made partly for political effect but also arising from the common conviction that racial sovereignty was indivisible. If whites did not rule blacks, it must therefore be the other way around. The charge of Negro rule was absurd, for blacks never held office in proportion to their total number and they rarely held the most prominent posts. This situation resulted in part from the race prejudice which white Republicans shared, or which they sought to appease in nominating attractive party slates. But equally important was the plain fact that slavery was a poor training ground for the responsibilities of publice office. The quality of those Negro officeholders high and low who did pass the barrier was not notably better or worse than that of white men who held comparable posts at that time, before, or later. Some, especially in the lower levels, were illiterate, but so were some of their white counterparts of both parties. Incompetent and illiterate officials did not begin or end with Reconstruction, nor were they typical of that period.

The so-called carpetbaggers—Northerners who settled in the South during and after the war and affiliated with the Republican party—were only a tiny minority numerically. They had great influence, however, particularly in the deep South where the Negro population was heavy and there was no significant native white Republican element to provide leadership. The term "carpetbagger" was another canard. These men supposedly descended on the South like a swarm of locusts, bringing no more than they could carry in a carpetbag; their purpose was to prey on the defenseless region through political manipulation of the gullible freedmen. Actually most of these persons moved South by 1866, well before Radical Reconstruction was conceived or the Republican party was even organized in most of the South. Some were stationed there by the Army or Freedmen's Bureau, but most moved South for the same reasons of economic betterment that led greater numbers to go West.

When the Republican party was organized and new governments were in process of formation these men filled a need for educated and occasionally experienced leadership. In fact, they usually raised the caliber of Radical government rather than lowering it. Of course, their motives, abilities, and accomplishments ran the usual human scale; along with the incompetent or corrupt there were honest and highly able men whom posterity would have celebrated under other circumstances. Active Republicans required a tough skin and often great physical courage to withstand the social ostracism, economic boycott, verbal abuse, character assassination, and physical violence to which they were commonly subjected by Southern whites. In a few cases at least, this courage was inspired by a high degree of dedication. "That I should have taken a political office seems almost inexplicable," wrote General Adelbert Ames a quarter-century after he had been forced out of the governorship of Mississippi:

> My explanation may seem ludicrous now, but then, it seemed to me that I had a Mission with a large M. Because of my [earlier] course as Military Governor, the colored men of the State had confidence in me and I was convinced that I could help to guide them successfully, keep men of doubtful integrity from control, and the more certainly accomplish what was every patriots' [sic] wish, the enfranchisement of the colored men and the pacification of the country.

Men of Northern origin were to be found in local and subordinate offices here and there, and they served conspicuously in Congress, as governors, and in other high offices.

The native white Republicans—scalawags to their enemies—were drawn from every walk of Southern life. Some had been Democrats and others were Whigs before the war. A few had served the Confederacy in conspicuous fashion, but most were wartime Unionists; the more uncompromising their Unionism had been, the more apt they were to embrace the Republican party afterward. Although they could be found, at least as isolated examples, throughout the South, most white Republican voters were concentrated in the hilly and mountainous regions where slavery had gained little foothold. The Appalachian highlands from western Virginia to northern Alabama and the Ozark Mountains of Arkansas were the major strongholds of white Republicanism during Reconstruction and for generations afterward. The term "scalawag" was of course another form of political abuse; the personal character of Southern Republicans did not suffer by comparison with their accusers. Many joined the Republican party because it was the Unionist party and it opposed the planter interest as they themselves had done for years. Most of them shared in some measure the racial views common to the white South, and this helped make the Republican coalition unstable, but for the most part they lived in regions where the Negro was hardly more of a factor locally than in the North. In such places they commonly filled all of the political offices and supplied nearly all of the Republican votes. At the state level, particularly in the upper South, they filled many of the higher offices as well. A few members of the ante-bellum ruling class, usually ex-Whigs who had not been enthusiastic secessionists, also joined the Republican party, hoping to hold it to a moderate course and exercise a paternalistic rein on the Negroes while profiting by their strength at the polls. Such men carried great prestige and, were given some of the highest offices in an effort to make the party more appealing to the white population generally, but the number of these converts was small. Governor James L. Alcorn of Mississippi belonged to this class, as did former Governors Lewis E. Parsons of Alabama and James L. Orr of South Carolina.

In terms of ideology, Republicans were clearly the democratic party of the Reconstruction South. Unquestionably there was an element of political expediency involved in the raising of Negroes to civil equality with white men, but a great many believed in it as a matter of principle. The Charleston *Daily Republican*, a voice of moderation and a critic of corruption and ineptitude within the party in South Carolina, attacked Democratic predictions that white men must at some near day control the state again.

> Such talk is as wickedly idle as for colored men to say that their race shall have complete control. It is not to be a matter of race at all. It is to be a matter of citizenship, in which colored and white are to have their rights and their due share of power; not because they are white, not because they are colored, but because they are American citizens. By-and-by we shall stop talking of the color of a man in relation to citizenship and power, and shall look at his wealth of mind and soul.

Radicalism was also aimed less spectacularly at raising the status of poorer whites. Within limits the Republican party was a poor man's party which sought to obliterate racial lines as much as popular prejudice made it politically safe to do. Democrats defeated the effort, as they later did when the Populists tried it, by crying "nigger"; most Southern whites placed white supremacy above all other issues.

Many public offices which had been appointive were now made elective, sometimes at the cost of efficiency. In some states, but not all, more home rule was extended, making local government more responsive to local wishes and less subject to central control. Property qualifications for officeholding, where they still existed in 1867, were removed. Legislatures were reapportioned to provide more equal representation, although Negro counties in some states were slighted. By far the most important democratic extension was the granting of Negro suffrage. This had been required by the Reconstruction Acts, and it was incorporated in all the new constitutions.

The only exception to universal manhood suffrage lay in the partial and temporary disfranchisement of ex-Confederates. This provision had been written into the Reconstruction Acts to help ensure further that the new state governments would be organized by Unionists, but state law governed the matter thereafter. Where disfranchisement survived as a significant factor—in Tennessee and Arkansas—Republicans felt themselves outnumbered and regarded it as a continuing necessity to keep the former rebels and the Democratic party from taking control. However dubious this policy may have been in those states, a free and unfettered majority rule permitted Republican victories in most states, and disfranchisement was abandoned either at once or very soon. Much the same was true of eligibility for public office, which was more nearly determined by federal law. By 1872 Congress had removed the disqualifications of all but a relative handful of ex-Confederate leaders. The Radical governments made no effort to outlaw the Conservative opposition or create a dictatorship. On the contrary, they were too lenient in enforcing law and order against those who used force to overthrow them.

There was corruption, electoral as well as financial, in nearly every state during the period of Republican control. Conservatives at the time succeeded in pinning on the Radical regimes a blanket charge of dishonesty which has never worn off, but the actual picture was not so simple. Corruption was rampant throughout the country after the war, and Democrats North and South were about as guilty as Republicans. The Tweed Ring in New York City supposedly stole more than all Southern politicans combined, if only because New York had more to steal. Within the South corruption varied widely from state to state. It flourished most in South Carolina, where it had been comparatively unknown, and in Louisiana, where it was endemic. In South Carolina the Republicans at least partially cleaned their own house under Governor Chamberlain after 1874. In Louisiana both parties were corrupt and remained so for generations. In Mississippi an honest Republican administration gave way to less honest Democratic regimes after 1875. During the period of Republican control, moreover, minority Democratic officials were sometimes as venal as their Republican counterparts, and Democratic businessmen sometimes offered the bribes that Republicans accepted. In the matter of electoral, as opposed to fiscal, corruption generalization is easier. Republicans were occasionally guilty of manipulating election returns, but these practices paled in comparison with the massive campaigns of fraud and intimidation, symbolized by the Ku Klux Klan, with which Democrats sought to return to power in nearly every state. It was largely owing to these methods that they did assume power in one state after another during the 1870's....

Radical egalitarianism for the Negro was primarily political and legal, but it also extended to economic and social matters. Republican governments repealed nearly all of the earlier laws requiring racial discrimination, and in some states it was specifically forbidden. A few states enacted laws to prevent racial segregation in railroad cars, theaters, restaurants, and hotels, but compliance was never complete and actual practice varied widely. It is mistaken to say that segregation did not begin until well after Reconstruction, although positive laws requiring it certainly were hostile to Republican policy. Both constitutional and legal enactments guaranteed racial equality before the law.

The greatest and most enduring achievement of the Radical governments was the establishment of a functioning public school system for the first time in Southern history. As in politics, the greatest change lay in the fact that Negroes were included in the new dispensation. Building on the work of the Freedmen's Bureau and various charitable agencies before 1868, they created school systems which could not compare with most of those in the North, but which represented a great accomplishment in the light of Southern traditions and resources. Straitened finances and the difficulty of securing qualified teachers plagued the new school systems in every state. Economy was hampered further by the fact that almost everywhere separate schools were established for the two races—Negroes seldom demanded integrated facilities, which were opposed even by most white Republicans. Often churches or other buildings were converted to school purposes, and many schools were erected by groups of individuals on their own initiative, sometimes, in the case of Negro schools, with financial aid from interested whites. Local whites served as teachers of both white and Negro schools; literate Negroes also taught in Negro schools, as did white men and women from the North. Most who taught in Negro schools did so at the price of social ostracism and sometimes physical danger; they required a high degree of dedication and a high resistance to poverty, given the pay scales. The new state governments provided support for higher education for both races. In some cases this meant the creation of Negro colleges and universities, and in others it entailed efforts, largely unsuccessful, to desegregate existing institutions.

New hospitals, orphanages, insane asylums, poorhouses, and other institutions were created, and older facilities enlarged. Jails and penitentiaries were built on a larger scale than before. Negro emancipation had rendered all of this necessary, for as slaves they had been under the wardship of their masters and rarely used public facilities. Moreover, the Radicals were somewhat readier than their predecessors to assume public responsibility for the welfare of citizens of both races, in many respects adopting attitudes and precedents which had been gaining headway in the North for a generation or more but which had lagged in the South.

The Radical regimes generally shared the old Whig-Republican willingness to use government power to stimulate business activity and economic growth, especially in the field of transportation. As elsewhere in the country, the major beneficiaries of public aid were railroads, although a good deal of money was spent on roads, bridges, levees, and other public works. These projects were expensive, taken collectively, and some states assumed greater debts than the returns justified. Everywhere, North and South, politics and personal profiteering motivated some of these expenditures. For the most part, however, they were relatively sound, and in the South they decidedly enhanced the region's economic growth and prosperity. Some of the projects were essential to repair wartime deterioration and destruction.

Radical governments did comparatively little to alter the conditions of labor or raise the incomes of citizens of either race; no governments did in nineteenth-century America. The Freedmen's Bureau continued most of its operations through 1868 and then gradually closed down because of Congressional nonsupport, suspending altogether in 1872. This was a misfortune, especially for the Negroes, as the state governments lacked the funds, personnel, and legal power to advise and protect them as effectively in relations with the white community. Even in Republican-controlled localities, the scales of justice were weighted against the impoverished freedmen. A number of states did enact laws, however, to protect persons against foreclosures of all their property for debt. These homestead exemptions were designed to appeal to both races, and some Democrats found them to be embarrassingly popular with poorer whites.

One of the most cogent criticisms of Radical Reconstruction is that it failed to distribute land to the freedmen while it was giving them the ballot. Continuing economic dependence on the whites endangered every other right the Negro received. Some halting steps were taken by the federal government and the state of South Carolina to provide land to Negroes on easy terms, but they came to almost nothing, requiring as they did a social concern and an expenditure of tax money which most people in that generation did not have or were unwilling to make. At the same time, Southern whites were suspicious of Negro landownership and continued to discourage it, sometimes by outright violence. This was another service rendered by the Ku Klux Klan.

The Radical governments spent more money and levied higher taxes than Southerners had been used to, as it was. But public needs were also unprecedented. Even the Johnson governments had raised taxes and expenditures to repair war damage, but left much yet to be done. The necessary new social services and especially the schools were extremely costly by previous governmental standards. When the aid extended to railroads is also added in, it is no wonder that both taxes and public debt rose unprecedentedly at every level of government. States, counties, and municipalities all raised what money they could and then mortgaged the future to meet immediate needs and finance improvements which required time to repay themselves. If debts occasionally climbed beyond a prudent level this was by no means universal; Democrats sometimes raised them further when they returned to power in the 1870's.

Even with these increases the Southern tax level remained considerably below that which prevailed in the North. The average tax rate in the eleven ex-Confederate states in 1870, including all state, county, town, and city taxes, was 1.57 per cent of assessed valuation; the comparable figure in all the remaining states was 2.03 per cent. The Southern states were much poorer than the Northern, and less able to afford improvements and services; but this poverty was usually reflected in lower assessed valuations and hence a lower tax return at the same rate. Taxes levied by the Radical governments were extravagant only by comparison with the section's previous parsimonious standards.

Equally controversial as the level of taxes and debts was the matter of who paid the taxes and who derived the benefits. Landowners, who had previously governed the South in their own interest, now found themselves bearing the major tax burden while the benefits went in large measure to businessmen and Negroes. Republican fiscal policies thus further infuriated the old ruling class and convinced them that civilization had given way to barbarism.

Republicans were often accused of partiality in law enforcement, winking at black criminality. Law enforcement was always difficult in the sparsely settled South, and lawlessness increased with the unsettled conditions that prevailed during and after the war. Negro criminality, chiefly petty theft, may well have grown temporarily, but it was always comparatively easy to convict Negro criminals when they were known. Republican officials (including Negroes) usually leaned over backward to demonstrate their impartiality in this respect. Republican governors were also accused of pardoning Negro criminals indiscriminately. This charge too was exaggerated if not wholly false. Whatever substance it may have had probably derived from the fact that some pardons were granted (after proper investigation) to redress the manifest injustices of many Southern courts against Negroes in interracial cases. White Conservatives often recommended such pardons in individual cases, but collectively it was easy to accuse the Radicals of yet another outrage against white civilization.

Actually it was white men who committed most of the violence, and much of it was racially and politically inspired. When these overtones were not present, it was punished about as effectively, or ineffectively, in areas of Republican control as Democratic, and as was true in earlier and later periods of Southern history. A great deal of violence was deliberate and organized, however, committed by mobs and by armed bands in and out of disguise. A disproportionate share was directed at Negroes and white Unionists, partly to avenge real or imaginary injuries arising from the war, partly to keep the Negro "in his place" economically and socially, and partly to overthrow the Republican party by intimidating, exiling, or assassinating its members. The Ku Klux Klan examplified this kind of violence in the most spectacular way, but it extended far beyond the Klan. The greatest short-run deficiency of the Republican regimes—it would soon prove fatal—was their physical weakness. In the face of implacable white resistance they proved unable to preserve law and order, or their own existence, against attempts at violent overthrow. In certain parts of the South the authorities were almost paralyzed by organized lawlessness.

When conspiracies to obstruct justice assumed this dimension the only solution was armed force. Republican officials repeatedly called on the Army for help in suppressing combinations which they could not handle by the usual means, but the results were usually discouraging. In the first place, too many troops were mustered out of service too quickly amid the euphoric celebration of victory in 1865. Only 20,000 troops remained on duty in the South by the fall of 1867, and this number gradually fell to 6,000 by the fall of 1876; moreover, one-quarter to half of these were stationed in Texas, chiefly on frontier duty. A much larger occupation force would have had trouble in maintaining order through-out the South. Furthermore, the traditional constitutional and legal safeguards against military power now sharply restricted the Army's peacekeeping potential. Its political and legal jurisdiction disappeared as soon as the new state governments were recognized by Congress. The military were limited thereafter to intervention only on application from, and in subordination to, the civil authorities. Where the latter did not act effectively, through incapacity, fear, or sympathy with the outlaws, the soldiers had little more than symbolic value.

For this reason most of the states organized militias, the traditional standby in times of emergency. But this weapon too was of doubtful value under the peculiar circumstances of Reconstruction. A militia composed in large part of the very white men who were engaged in lawlessness, or were sympathetic with it, seemed worse than useless. The only safe recruits were white Unionists and Negroes, but mobilizing these was equivalent to arming one political party against the other. The arming of Negroes in particular inflamed Conservatives and added fuel to the fire it was intended to quench. It summoned up the old fear of Negro insurrection and portended a race war which no Southern official was prepared to be responsible for. In the deep South, where white Republicans were few and far between, militia were seldom mobilized and they played a negligible peacekeeping role. Governors in the upper South organized white Unionist recruits, for the most part, to stamp out Democratic terrorism, a tactic that was relatively effective but highly dangerous politically, for it fed Conservative charges of military des-potism.

In the last analysis, Radical Reconstruction failed because the seed of biracial democracy which it planted fell on barren ground in the South, and the artificial nurture it received from the federal government was soon discontinued. Democracy has always required a high degree of popular homogeneity and consensus, a precondition which was altogether lacking in the South. Conservative opposition to Reconstruction was about as deeply felt as political opposition ever gets. As South Carolina whites expressed it in a protest to Congress in 1868:

> Intelligence, virtue, and patriotism are to give place, in all elections, to ignorance, stupidity and vice. The superior race is to be made subservient to the inferior.... They who own no property are to levy taxes and make all appropriations.... The consequences will be, in effect, confiscation. The appropriations to support free schools for the education of the negro children, for the support of old negroes in the poor-houses, and the vicious in jails and penitentiary, together with a standing army of negro soldiers [the militia], will be crushing and utterly ruinous to the State. Every man's property will have to be sold to pay his taxes.... The white people of our State will never quietly submit to negro rule.... By moral agencies, by political organization, by every peaceful means left us, we will keep up this contest until we have regained the heritage of political control handed down to us by honored ancestry. That is a duty we owe to the land that is ours, to the graves that it contains, and to the race of which you and we are alike members—the proud Caucasian race, whose sovereignty on earth God has ordained....

Such views contrasted sharply with the vision of a biracial democracy quoted already from the Charleston *Daily Republican*.

Conservatives mercilessly pilloried the Negroes, carpetbaggers, and scalawags who staffed and supported the Republican regimes. The Democratic newspaper press—which far outstripped the Southern Republican press in numbers and circulation—played a vital role in stimulating and disseminating hatred of all things Radical. The wildest allegations and *ad hominem* arguments were at least half believed and unblushingly broadcast because they fit preconceived notions. Moreover, character assassination and slander were resorted to even when editors did not believe them, because they "served a good end" in discrediting the enemy. The Little Rock *Daily Arkansas Gazette,* for example, characterized the state constitutional convention of 1868 as "the most graceless and unconscionable gathering of abandoned, disreputable characters that has ever assembled in this state, outside of the penitentiary walls ... a foul gathering whose putridity stinks in the nostrils of all decency." Altogether the whole tone of Southern government had been debased, Conservatives felt, and they proceeded to debase the tone of political discourse correspondingly. "So far as our State governments is [sic] concerned, we are in the hands of camp-followers, horse-holders, cooks, bottle-washers, and thieves," declared General James H. Clanton of Alabama. "We have passed out from the hands of the brave soldiers who overcame us, and are turned over to the tender mercies of squaws for torture. . . ." Negroes were characterized as unfit to vote, much less hold office, and Democrats excoriated the federal and state enactments which had brought these things to pass. Few Southern Democrats in public life had any constructive proposal to make in behalf of the freedman. The whole thrust of their policy was to "put him back in his place" economically, socially, and politically. Some Conservatives disapproved in principle of universal manhood suffrage, even among whites, regarding it as a denial of character and intelligence in government and a threat to property; Negro suffrage was simply the ultimate outrage. An increasing number of so-called New Departure Democrats, like Benjamin H. Hill of Georgia, reluctantly accepted Negro suffrage as a *fait accompli* and hoped to control the black vote as they controlled black labor, but a majority rejected the idea out of hand and pledged themselves to repeal or nullify it at the earliest opportunity.

To Conservatives, Republican affiliation was itself a sign of moral turpitude which only the flimsiest additional evidence sufficed to confirm. The laws of libel had no practical existence in that day, and such evidence was commonly embroidered or manufactured to suit the occasion. Those Republicans who mingled socially with Negroes were morally depraved; those who refused to do so were hypocrites who betrayed their own political teachings. Those who came from the North were outlanders having no ties of knowledge or sympathy with the land and people they despoiled; those who were native to the South were traitors to their race and section and therefore equally unworthy of trust or confidence. Those who had owned slaves were now discovered to have treated them cruelly; those who had not owned them were the dregs of society who would never have risen to the surface in decent times. The greatest opprobrium was always heaped on those who associated most with the freedmen or who had substantial Negro followings. Eric Hoffer has remarked that hatred requires a vivid and tangible devil. Conservative Southern whites conjured them up by the hundreds.

But although Radical policies were condemned as a matter of course, Democrats in fact supported some of them unobtrusively. This was true of the exemption of homesteads from foreclosure, and also a great proportion of the railway expenditures. Opinion was divided on the subject of public schooling, especially for Negroes, but most Democrats accepted the policy and continued it when they later assumed power. Opposition was strongest in Mississippi, as noted earlier, but schools were unpopular with many rural people everywhere. The major complaints arose from the unprecedented cost of establishing and maintaining them and from the fact that Republicans sponsored the policy. Many persons objected less to Negro schools per se than to the Negro and Yankee teachers who staffed them. Most of these were advocates of racial equality, and some were quite militant about it. Hence Southerners resented them as they did the political carpetbaggers—outside agitators whose main purpose and effect was to alienate Negroes from the white population and make them less docile. H. C. Luce, a Northerner living in western North Carolina who had never engaged in politics at all, wrote of threats he received after establishing a school for local Negro children: "It is one of the perils of a Northern man residing in such a community that, however unexceptionable his conduct may be, if he is kind to the negroes and tries to help them, a report will very soon be put in circulation that he is inciting the negroes to revenge, and the chances are against him if he does not promptly and publicly convince his neighbors of their mistake in believing the report." Like countless teachers or sponsors of Negro schools across the South, Luce became a target of the Ku Klux Klan.

In general, Conservatives advocated retrenchment and economy at the expense of many social services favored by the Radicals. Apart from white supremacy, their most popular and effective cry was for economy in government and lower taxes—a cry that often came from the heart as they compared present and past tax bills. The position of most Democrats on most issues was plainly reactionary. They appealed largely to a rural, agrarian, racist past which had become increasingly hostile to new ideas, and except for the most minimal accommodations required by the war's outcome they proposed to return to it. Later, after the Radicals had been swept aside, they were to become more enamored of the vision of an industrialized New South.

The bitterest opposition was always reserved for those Radical policies that portended racial equality. This was the supreme Radical sin. Laws enacted for that purpose "have no binding force or moral sanction," the New Orleans *Times* declared in July 1868, "and will be disregarded and declared null and void as soon as the inalienable rights of the people are again recognized.... No privilege can be secured to the negro to which his white neighbors do not consent, and if he attempts to enforce privileges on the strength of carpetbag authority he will simply destroy his claims of future peace, and heap up wrath against the day of wrath." Political and legal equality for the Negro was rendered all the more noxious by the common assumption that it would lead inevitably to social mixing. "[If] I sit side by side in the Senate House, or on the judicial bench, with a coloured man," one gentleman inquired indignantly, "how can I refuse to sit with him at the table?... If we have social equality we shall have intermarriage, and if we have intermarriage we shall degenerate; we shall become a race of mulattoes; ... we shall be ruled out from the family of white nations."

The Radical revolution, as some contemporaries on both sides regarded it, was only a halfway revolution. Within the South, Radical Reconstruction was clearly revolutionary in its overthrow of the old ruling class and above all in its establishment of political and legal equality for Negroes; hence the bitterness of the Conservative reaction. But economically and socially there was far less change, and most blacks remained a landless peasantry subject to manifold discrimination. In the larger national context, Radical Reconstruction reflected a revival of the old nationalistic constitutional doctrine of Hamilton and Marshall submerged by the state rights creed of Jefferson, Jackson, and their successors before 1860. The Radicals were not revolutionary by traditional American standards; if they appeared to be so it was chiefly because of the archaic social and political structure of the South. Nor did most of them regard themselves as revolutionaries. Southern Republicans, in trying to broaden their base of support at home, denied the charge and sought repeatedly to identify themselves with established political traditions. They claimed to stand for state rights within the higher national context and for the liberation doctrines expressed in the Declaration of Independence. The Fourteenth and Fifteenth Amendments, the Reconstruction Acts, the civil rights legislation, and other related laws attempted to guarantee Negro rights and a loyal South within the accepted federal framework set forth in the Constitution. National authority and military rule were applied only partially and temporarily after 1865, and often reluctantly at that. The chief reliance in day-to-day government rested on the existing civil authorities. When the new state governments were formed after 1867, national and military control were withdrawn and the new regimes had to rely for their survival on customary legal institutions.

The experiment failed, and these regimes were overthrown in a few years because the ideas underlying them had become alien to the South during a generation or more of defending slavery, and because the Radicals' adherence to traditional forms weakened their resistance to attack. Radical regard for the civil liberties of ex-Confederates enabled the latter to sabotage the Reconstruction program almost from the start. Democrats had full access to the polls almost everywhere after 1868 and controlled hundreds of county and local governments throughout the period; they exercised the right to express themselves freely on every occasion, and they controlled the great majority of the section's newspapers. When they were charged with illegal activity and violence they had full access to the courts—in fact often dominated them. In such cases it was often impossible to get grand juries to indict, prosecutors to prosecute, or petit juries to convict, even if sheriffs were willing to arrest or judges to try them. This was even true in Republican-controlled localities. All of the safeguards for the accused in the Anglo-Saxon system of justice were mobilized to enforce the higher law of white supremacy. The Republicans themselves insisted upon certain limits to federal authority, and this was another source of weakness. Conservative violence against Negroes and Radicals involved crimes which had always fallen within state rather than federal jurisdiction, and as a result the federal government refused to intervene soon enough or strongly enough to check the error effectively. Thus the Radicals were defeated within a few years by their very conservatism and unwillingness to employ more than halfway measures.

3

The American
Businessman

Industrial Statesman or Robber Baron?

For many students of American history, the problems of war and peace appear to be the dominant ones in the years from 1850 to 1877. Yet during this same period the country was undergoing an industrial and urban transformation that inevitably resulted in profound changes in the structure of American society. Few individuals or institutions remained unaffected by the forces at work and the nation as a whole was destined to experience fundamental changes which enabled it to emerge as a leading world power by the close of the nineteenth century. "The old nations of the earth," Andrew Carnegie observed in 1886 with considerable pride, "creep on at a snail's pace; the Republic thunders past with the rush of the express. The United States, [in] the growth of a single century, has already reached the foremost rank among nations, and is destined soon to outdistance all others in the race. In population, in wealth, in annual savings, and in public credit; in freedom from debt, in agriculture, and in manufactures, America already leads the civilized world."[1] Industrial growth and the accumulation of wealth, Carnegie suggested, would lay the cornerstone of a better America: ultimately, material progress would lead to spiritual and intellectual progress.

Although this new burst of industrialism gave the United States one of the highest standards of living in the world, it was not always greeted with unrestrained enthusiasm. To some the new industrialism was destroying the very traits that had given America immunity from class strife, internal divisions, and rivalries that had long plagued Europe. Others feared the greed and ugliness that accompanied the industrial transformation. Walt Whitman, in *Democratic Vistas*, summed up the

---

[1]Andrew Carnegie, *Triumphant Democracy* (New York, 1886), p. 1.

opposition. "The depravity of the business classes of our country is not less than has been supposed but infinitely greater. The official services of America, national, state, and municipal, in all their branches and departments, except the judiciary, are saturated in corruption, bribery, falsehood, mal-administration; and the judiciary is tainted. The great cities reek with respectable as much as non-respectable robbery and scoundrelism. . . . In business, (this all-devouring modern word, business,) the one sole object is, by any means, pecuniary gain. . . . [M]oney-making is our sole magician's serpent, remaining to-day sole master of the field. . . . I say that our New World democracy, however great a success in uplifting the masses out of their sloughs, in materialistic development, products, and in a certain highly deceptive superficial popular intellectuality, is, so far, an almost complete failure in its social aspects, and in really grand religious, moral, literary, and esthetic results."[2] In short, America was adversely affected by the material forces at work.

The differences between the views of Carnegie and Whitman were by no means atypical; Americans have always been ambivalent in their attitudes toward material affluence. While emphasizing the virtues of acquisitiveness, individualism, and competition, they have been unable to throw off the influence of their religious heritage and the sense that the nation as a whole has a mission. At times this dual heritage has created an internal conflict because attempts to harmonize American materialism and idealism have not always succeeded. Some Americans have dealt with this conflict by proclaiming that material well-being is a prerequisite of spiritual and intellectual achievement; others have criticized a system that emphasizes material values at the expense of other values; still others have insisted that America's abundance was proof of its superior moral character.

This ambivalent attitude toward our heritage has exercised a profound impact on the writing of American history. Historians, on the whole, have also displayed divided attitudes when studying the rise of industry and its implications for American society. Nowhere can this dichotomy of thought be better seen than in the changing image of such great entrepreneurs as Rockefeller and Carnegie. To many historians, these captains of industry represented more than the rise of industrialism; they symbolized some of the basic characteristics of modern American culture.

The first attempts to evaluate the achievements of these industrial giants occurred at the beginning of the twentieth century. Many of the early studies took their cue from the writings of Henry Demarest Lloyd. A journalist and a scholar, Lloyd until his death in 1903 played a signifi-

---

[2]Walt Whitman, "Democratic Vistas," in *Prose Works 1892*, Floyd Stovall, ed. (2 vols.: New York, 1963–1964, II, p. 370.

cant part in reform movements that developed out of the social and economic unrest of that era. Critical of laissez faire and corporate monopoly, he insisted that the American people were confronted with a choice between reform or revolution. Public ownership of monopolies and an increased role for government were absolutely necessary, according to Lloyd, if the American people were to avoid the fratricidal class struggles that had wracked other nations in the Western world.

In 1894 Lloyd spelled out his case in *Wealth Against Commonwealth*, a book that anticipated the writings of later muckrakers and Progressive journalists and also set the stage for much of the controversy among historians over the captains of industry. The book ostensibly was a study of the Standard Oil Company and the techniques used by John D. Rockefeller to gain a virtual monopoly over the petroleum industry. Actually *Wealth Against Commonwealth* was an indictment of the entire capitalistic system as it then existed. Businessmen, wrote Lloyd, paid lip service to the ideal of competition, but their true purpose was to achieve monopoly. If the captains of industry continued to have their way, the result would probably be a violent and bloody class struggle. There was little time to act, declared Lloyd, for the nation was already faced with "misery, plagues, hatreds, national enervation."[3]

While Lloyd's principal purpose was to issue a call for national regeneration, he had drawn an unfavorable yet influential portrait of the typical industrial tycoon to make his point. His stereotype of the American businessman was in many respects similar to the one held by other American reformers, including the Populists as well as many Progressives. Much of the debate over reform in the years from 1900 to 1917, indeed, centered about the unbridled power and selfishness of the captains of industry—a group, many claimed, who were motivated only by a desire to amass great wealth regardless of the cost to the American people. The specific political issues of the Progressive era—monopolies, trusts, federal regulation—were all based upon the proposition that Americans could no longer afford to permit these autocratic barons to shape the nation's destiny.

Many of the studies dealing with the American businessman written prior to the First World War were done not only by historians, but by social scientists and, to a lesser extent, socialists seeking to prove that the system of capitalism was identified with social and individual selfishness and egoism. Among the social scientists were economists and sociologists like Thorstein Veblen and E. A. Ross, who implicitly denounced the predatory, profit-seeking, amoral businessman for refusing to recognize the pressing needs of society. In the latter category were Gustavus Myers and Algie Simons, who portrayed businessmen as malefactors of wealth and looked forward to their eventual extinction as

---

[3]Henry Demarest Lloyd, *Wealth Against Commonwealth* (New York, 1894), p. 517.

the historical process reached its inevitable destiny in the emergence of a socialist utopia.

While the interpretation of the businessman as robber baron was being etched in the public's imagination, historians, under the influence of the "New History," were themselves beginning to inquire into the economic realities of capitalism in order to buttress their own predilection for democracy and reform. But not until the 1920's—a decade that was notable for the debunking activities of a small group of intellectuals—did historians turn their full attention to the study of the rise of American industry. With the publication in 1927 of Charles and Mary Beard's *Rise of American Civilization* and the first volume of Vernon L. Parrington's monumental *Main Currents in American Thought*, the scene was set for a radical reevaluation of the role of the businessman in American history.

Although the Beards refrained from any direct or outward condemnation of the industrial tycoon in their panoramic study of American civilization, their description suggested the analogy of a medieval baron—an individual who was despotic and autocratic within his own sphere. The story of American industry, they wrote, is "the story of aggressive men, akin in spirit to military captains of the past, working their way up from the ranks, exploiting natural resources without restraint, waging economic war on one another, entering into combinations, making immense fortunes, and then, like successful feudal chieftains or medieval merchants, branching out as patrons of learning, divinity, and charity. Here is a chronicle of highly irregular and sometimes lawless methods, ruthless competition, menacing intrigues, and pitiless destruction of rivals."[4]

Parrington, on the other hand, was much clearer and far less ambiguous in his description of postwar industrial developments. Writing within a Jeffersonian agrarian framework which stressed individualistic values, he sought to defend his particular vision of liberalism. In Parrington's eyes the predatory and materialistic tycoon of industry represented the greatest threat to those humane and democratic values that had made America great. Businessmen had created the America of the present, with "its standardized life, its machine culture, its mass-psychology—an America to which Jefferson and Jackson and Lincoln would be strangers." These giants of industry, Parrington wrote in colorful and emotion-laden terms, "were primitive souls, ruthless, predatory, capable; singleminded men; rogues and rascals often, but never feeble, never hindered by petty scruple, never given to puling or whining—the raw materials of a race of capitalistic buccaneers."[5]

---

[4]Charles and Mary Beard, *The Rise of American Civilization* (2 vols.: New York, 1927), II, p. 177.

[5]Vernon L. Parrington, *Main Currents in American Thought* (3 vols.: New York, 1927–1930), III, pp. 12, 26.

The debunking atmosphere of the 1920's and depression years of the 1930's provided a favorable climate of opinion for the growing idea of the businessman as a robber baron. For decades the business community had taken great pains to convince the American people that the nation's greatness rested on the achievements of ambitious and energetic entrepreneurs. A. C. Bedford, a tycoon in the oil industry, made this point very clear in 1925. In his eyes, work was even of more importance than love, learning, religion, or patriotism. "I have come to the conclusion," he wrote, "that industry is the fundamental basis of civilization. The high office of civilization is to train men to productive effort."[6] Other business leaders during the 1920's echoed Bedford's observations; if anything, they were even more ecstatic in extolling the contributions of business to American civilization. With the exception of a dissenting minority of reformers, many Americans agreed with President Coolidge's dictum that "The business of America is business."

Having taken credit for the apparent prosperity of the 1920's, the business community, ironically enough, was forced to accept responsibility for the catastrophic depression of the 1930's. The capitalist free enterprise system, which supposedly accounted for the greatness of America, seemingly failed in 1929. Millions who sought work were unable to find jobs; bankruptcies increased at an astounding rate; and many Americans even faced a real threat of starvation. Indeed, the United States appeared to be on the threshold of disaster. For once the business community found that the time-honored cliché that wealth was the product of ambition, talent, and drive, no longer held true. Capitalism and free enterprise perhaps had come to the end of the road, many argued, and new approaches were required if the needs of a modern complex industrial society in America were to be satisfied.

Given these conditions, it was not surprising that much of the historical scholarship of the 1930's took an anti-business turn. Beard and Parrington had anticipated this development; their writings during the late 1920's echoed some of the critical literature of this era. Sinclair Lewis' unforgettable portrait of Babbitt, while not wholly intended to debunk businessmen, contributed to a stereotype already widely held. The massive attack on the image of the American businessman, however, came in the great depression. During the 1930's, the robber baron idea came to full bloom.

In presenting a highly unfavorable portrait of the industrial tycoon, most writers in this tradition were implicitly attacking an economic system that they thought had failed to live up to its promises and expectations. Oddly enough, many—though not all—of the critical studies during the 1930's were written by non-academic figures who were critical of capitalism rather than by academic historians. Thus Lewis Corey, a so-

---

[6]Quoted in James W. Prothro, *The Dollar Decade: Business Ideas in the 1920's* (Baton Rouge, 1954), p. 67.

cialist, in his book *The House of Morgan* (1930), detailed the techniques whereby a major banking and investment concern exercised near dictatorial control over corporations having assets well in excess of twenty billion dollars. His lesson was not lost upon his readers. It was Corey's purpose to marshal as much evidence as possible to demonstrate the evil, selfish, and corrupting nature of industrial and finance capitalism. Other historical and literary writers, attracted by Marxian ideas, lent support to the growing body of critical studies of the American economic system.

The book that did the most to fix in American historical scholarship the enduring stereotype of the late nineteenth century industrialist, however, was Matthew Josephson's brilliantly written *The Robber Barons: The Great American Capitalists 1861–1901*, which appeared in 1934. Fittingly enough, Josephson dedicated his book to Charles and Mary Beard, who themselves had interpreted American history in terms of a struggle between haves and have-nots, debtors and creditors, agrarians and industrialists, workers and capitalists. Josephson set the tone of his work in his introduction. "This book," he began, "attempts the history of a small class of men who arose at the time of our Civil War and suddenly swept into power.... these men more or less knowingly played the leading roles in an age of industrial revolution.... Under their hands the renovation of our economic life proceeded relentlessly: large-scale production replaced the scattered, decentralized mode of production; industrial enterprises became more concentrated, more 'efficient' technically, and essentially 'cooperative,' where they had been purely individualistic and lamentably wasteful. But all this revolutionizing effort is branded with the motive of private gain on the part of the new captains of industry. To organize and exploit the resources of a nation upon a gigantic scale, to regiment its farmers and workers into harmonious corps of producers, and to do this only in the name of an uncontrolled appetite for private profit—here surely is the great inherent contradiction whence so much disaster, outrage and misery has flowed." Josephson conceded that the robber barons had many imposing achievements to their credit. On the other hand, the debits far outweighed the credits. Ultimately, he concluded, the "extremes of management and stupidity would make themselves felt.... The alternations of prosperity and poverty would be more violent and mercurial, speculation and breakdown each more excessive; while the inherent contradictions within the society pressed with increasing intolerable force against the bonds of the old order."[7] The implications of Josephson's ideas were obvious.

At the same time that the robber baron concept was reaching matur-

---

[7]Matthew Josephson, *The Robber Barons: The Great American Capitalists 1861–1901* (New York, 1934), pp. vii–viii, 453.

ity, another school of thought was emerging. Although it is difficult to give this school a particular name, the designation "business history" is not wholly inaccurate. The foundation of business history had already been laid by the 1930's. As a result of the work of Norman S. B. Gras and others at the Harvard Graduate School of Business Administration as well as the publication of a number of sympathetic biographies of individual business leaders, some historians and economists began to depart from the unfavorable stereotype of the American industrialist. Business history, however, was not merely a reevaluation of the contributions of industrialists; it represented a radically new approach to the study of American economic history, Indeed, business historians by the 1950's—because of their differences with other academic historians—had created their own professional organization, developed a new vocabulary and research techniques, published their own journal, and in some cases had even founded new departments within the university separate from regular history departments.

Generally speaking, business historians insisted that the careers of industrial leaders were far more complex than earlier scholars had realized. Business leaders were not predatory money seekers. Indeed, in many cases they were talented individuals whose creative contributions to the economy—and to American society as a whole—were very great. Allan Nevins, who published a major revisionist biography of John D. Rockefeller in 1940, argued that much of the blame heaped on this man was unwarranted. It was true, Nevins conceded, that Rockefeller used methods that were of dubious moral character. On the other hand, the kind of monopoly control attained by Standard Oil was a natural response to the anarchical cutthroat competition of the period and reflected the trend in all industrial nations toward consolidation. To Nevins, Rockefeller was not a robber baron; he was a great innovator who imposed upon American industry "a more rational and efficient pattern." Rockefeller's objective was not merely the accumulation of wealth; he and others like him were motivated by "competitive achievement, self-expression, and the imposition of their wills on a given environment."[8]

Thirteen years later Nevins pushed this thesis even further when he published a second biography of Rockefeller. He was, Nevins forcefully argued, an "innovator, thinker, planner, bold entrepreneur." Taking a confused and disorganized industry, Rockefeller organized it with completeness, efficiency, and constructive talent; in his philanthropy he set a model for all to follow. Had it not been for men like him—men who helped to create within a brief span of time great and powerful industrial units in steel, oil, textiles, chemicals, electricity, and automotive

---

[8]Allan Nevins, *John D. Rockefeller: The Heroic Age of American Enterprise* (2 vols.: New York, 1940), II, pp. 707–714.

vehicles—"the free world might have lost the First World War and most certainly would have lost the Second."[9]

The points that Nevins made about Rockefeller were not fundamentally different from those made by other students of business history. The great nineteenth century entrepreneurs, business historians emphasized, actually played a vital role in making the United States the greatest industrial power in the world and giving its people the highest standard of living. Far from being immoral, unethical, or evil individuals—although sometimes their methods involved questionable tactics—these industrial statesmen stepped into a disorganized, unstructured, anarchic economy, restored order and rationality, created giant organizations that were in a position to exploit fully the great natural resources of the nation, and took full advantage of the potentialities of the American economy.

Like students in the robber baron tradition of American historiography, business historians began with certain underlying assumptions that undoubtedly influenced the way in which they approached their subject. It is quite clear that they rejected the hostile critique of Progressive historians who believed that the social and economic costs of late nineteenth century industrialization could have been far lower and less painful and degrading to the great mass of Americans, and that the result need not have been a dangerous centralization of economic power that ostensibly threatened freedom and democracy. On the contrary, business historians tended to eulogize rather than to disparage the American economic system. Did not the growth and development of the large corporation, they maintained, give the American people the highest standard of living in the world and make possible the victory against totalitarianism? Was not America's industrial capacity responsible for the strength of a large part of the free world in the struggle with Communism? To put it another way, these historians concluded that the large corporation, despite its monopolistic and oligopolistic position, was far more of an asset than a liability. Unlike Progressive historians who defined the problem in terms of a tension between democracy and the menace of the concentration of economic power in the hands of a few, business historians minimized the threat of such dangers and opposed efforts to employ historical analysis as an ideological anti-corporation weapon.

Perhaps the most sophisticated example of recent developments in business history is the work of Alfred D. Chandler, Jr. Unlike even Nevins, Chandler was notably disinterested in the biographical ap-

---

[9]Allan Nevins, *Study in Power: John D. Rockefeller, Industrialist and Philanthropist* (2 vols.: New York, 1953), I, pp. viii–ix, II, p. 436. For a direct confrontation of views see the enlightening article "Should American History be Rewritten? A Debate Between Allan Nevins and Matthew Josephson," *Saturday Review,* XXXVII (February 6, 1954), pp. 7–10, 44–49.

proach that sought to vindicate the career of an individual against his detractors. He was more concerned in the process whereby new forms, methods, and structures came into being in the late-nineteenth and twentieth century. In a major work published in 1962 Chandler identified four stages in the development of large industrial enterprise. First came a period of expansion and the accumulation of resources. During the second period these resources were "rationalized." In the third phase the organization expanded its operations to include new products in order to ensure the most efficient use of existing resources. In the fourth and final phase new structures were created to promote effective use of resources in order to meet immediate and long-range demands. Borrowing heavily from work in the social sciences, Chandler saw large corporations as complex economic, political, and social systems with common administrative problems. He insisted, moreover, that most large firms went through similar stages of development. "Strategic growth," he noted, "resulted from an awareness of the opportunities and needs—created by changing population, income, and technology— to employ existing or expanding resources more profitably. A new strategy required a new or at least refashioned structure if the enlarged enterprise was to be operated efficiently."[10] The result was the large, decentralized, multidivisional corporation. Less concerned with the moral dimensions of industrial entrepreneurship, Chandler attempted to analyze the forces that led businessmen to develop new products, new markets, and new sources of raw materials. By 1900, he pointed out, these industrial leaders had created the modern corporation, which integrated the functions of purchasing, manufacturing, marketing, and finance. Each of the major processes was managed by a separate department, and all were coordinated and controlled by a central office. Such a complex organization was a response to the emergence of the urban market that followed the creation of a national transportation system. Minimizing the role of technological innovation, Chandler concluded that entrepreneurs like Rockefeller and others were successful because they accurately analyzed the economic situation and responded in a creative manner. Their contributions, he suggested, played an important role in the dramatic growth of the economy and the creation of an affluent society.[11]

Business historians tended to see the large corporation as essentially an economic organization. Other scholars, however, were less concerned with understanding the corporation in structural and functional terms; they were more concerned with the political aspects of business

---

[10]Alfred D. Chandler, Jr., *Strategy and Structure: Chapters in the History of the Industrial Enterprise* (Cambridge, 1962), p. 15.

[11]Alfred D. Chandler, Jr., "The Beginnings of 'Big Business' in American Industry," *Business History Review*, XXXIII (Spring, 1959), 1-31.

and the threat to democratic institutions posed by such huge conglom-
erations. This concern took two different forms in the 1950's and 1960's.
The first was a sophisticated body of scholarship that examined business
in a critical vein, though not with a view that sought the end of
capitalism and the establishment of a socialist society. Typical of this
approach was the work of Carl Kaysen, an economist who also served
for a time as the Director of the Institute for Advanced Study in Princeton, New Jersey. Kaysen noted the overwhelmingly disproportionate
importance of large corporations in the economy. Because of their size,
these large units were less influenced by changes in economic activity
and exercised considerable power over their smaller suppliers and customers. Their investment decisions and research activities, moreover,
had important implications for society. The bigger market power which
absolute and relative size gave to the large corporation also resulted in
political and social as well as economic power. Kaysen noted that
American society possessed three alternate ways of controlling business
power: the promotion of competitive markets; control by agencies external to business; and institutionalization within the firm of responsibility
for the exercise of power. Traditionally the United States relied on the
first in the form of antitrust activities, although far more could have been
done along this line. Kaysen's conclusions were equivocal, for he felt
that effective control of business power remained an unfinished task.[12]

Scholars like Kaysen were essentially in a reform tradition; they
sought to eliminate imperfections in American society rather than overthrow it. By the early 1960's, however, a small but growing number of
scholars in a variety of disciplines were coming to the conclusion that
American society was fundamentally immoral and that a radical change
in its structure was required. This point of view was best expressed by
historians associated with the "New Left." War, poverty, racism, they
argued, were direct outgrowths of American capitalism. If this were so,
then only the abolition of capitalism could make possible the establishment of a just and peaceful society. This belief, of course, led to a
rejection of those scholars who had defended business as well as those
who were critical of it but did not seek its destruction.

One of the first monographs embodying a "New Left" approach was
Gabriel Kolko's *The Triumph of Conservatism: A Reinterpretation of American History, 1900–1916*, which appeared in 1963. Kolko argued that the
distinctive feature of American society—what he designated as political
capitalism—dated only from the first two decades of the twentieth century. Rejecting the belief that large-scale business enterprise was inevitable, Kolko maintained that competition was actually increasing at the
turn of the century. Even the merger movement and the capitalization of

---

[12]Carl Kaysen, "The Corporation: How Much Power? What Scope?," in *The Corporation
in Modern Society*, ed. by Edward S. Mason (Cambridge, 1959), Chapter 5.

new combinations on an unprecedented scale failed to stem the tide of competitive growth. Corporate leaders, therefore, turned to government to control competition and to prevent the possibility of a formal political democracy that might lead to a redistribution of wealth. The result was a synthesis of business and government, with the former emerging as the dominant element. In contrast to Chandler, Kolko believed that large-scale units turned to government regulation precisely because of their inefficiency. The lack of a viable alternative to political capitalism at that time made its victory a certainty, for neither the Populists nor the Socialists (who themselves accepted the necessity of centralization) understood that the Progressive movement—far from being anti-business—was actually a movement that defined the general welfare in terms of the well-being of business.[13] An excerpt from Kolko's book is the first selection in this chapter.

Kolko's controversial thesis did not persuade other scholars, many of whom rejected his radical ideological assumptions and questioned his conclusions. Shortly after Kolko published his study of railroad regulation in 1965, Edward A. Purcell, Jr., criticized his thesis that businessmen favored government regulation because they feared competition and desired to forge a government-business coalition in which they would be the dominant partner. In an examination of the attitudes of businessmen during the passage of the Interstate Commerce Act of 1887, Purcell came to a quite different conclusion. Rejecting the idea that the actions of businessmen grew out of a particular ideology, he insisted that entrepreneurs and managers were more interested in solving particular problems than they were in adhering to any coherent body of thought. Hence some favored regulation while others opposed it. In general, Purcell concluded, diverse economic groups who felt threatened by the new national economy and rate discrimination turned to the federal government in the hope of protecting their interests. Political control of the economy was not their ultimate goal; they simply wanted to protect their own interests. Purcell's article is included as the second selection in this chapter.

In assessing businessmen and corporations since the late-nineteenth century, it is important to understand that differing interpretations often reflect diverging viewpoints regarding the very nature of economic development. Ironically enough, adherents of the robber baron and "New Left" school implicitly (and sometimes explicitly) extol the virtues of a competitive economy when they criticize the monopolistic objectives of most entrepreneurial and financial leaders. Business historians, on the other hand, tend to argue that the movement toward consolidation

---

[13]In addition to *The Triumph of Conservatism: A Reinterpretation of American History, 1900–1916* (New York, 1963), see Kolko's *Railroads and Regulation 1877–1916* (Princeton, 1965) for an illustrative case study of his interpretation.

arose out of a cutthroat and disorganized economy whose productive potential could never have been realized without the large, decentralized, multidivisional corporation. Still others see the problem within a far more complex framework; decisions made by individuals often gave rise to results that were not anticipated.

Which of these viewpoints is correct? Was consolidation a necessary prerequisite for the emergence of a complex industrial economy? Is bigness synonymous with efficiency? On both these issues opposing schools of thought give very different answers. The upholders of the robber baron and "New Left" approach insist that the monopolistic control that often accompanies large productive units frequently reflects the inability of those units to meet the challenges of smaller competitors who do not have high overhead and fixed costs. Thus, consolidation actually reflects inefficiency rather than efficiency. Some of these historians, moreover, argue that the movement toward consolidation was the result of bureaucratic business reorganizations rather than an effort to increase efficiency. Most business historians, on the other hand, reject this interpretation. They tend to correlate consolidation with order and efficiency; thus the great entrepreneurs are viewed as creative individuals interested not in profit alone but in productive efficiency as well.

In the final analysis, any interpretation of the careers and accomplishments of American industrialists and the role of the large corporation will depend in large measure on the starting assumptions and values of the individual making the particular judgment. Despite claims of objectivity, it is difficult, if not impossible, for historians to divest themselves of beliefs and standards that influence their analysis of this problem. In some ways an evaluation of business and businessmen is even more controversial than other problems in American history. For underlying such an evaluation is the larger problem of the quality and meaning of the American experience. To some historians the significance of America is directly related to its productive capacity. America, they maintain, has demonstrated to the world that an affluent society is possible to achieve within a democratic capitalist framework. Thus the American economy—a creation of industrial pioneers and bold entrepreneurs—has far more to its credit than many have admitted. Other historians, however, argue in a much different vein. The social costs of industrialism, they maintain, could have been far lower had it not been for the greed and quest after power that marked this process. By placing a premium on acquisitive and amoral values, by creating a system of great inequality of wealth, they conclude, these entrepreneurs and large corporations contributed to the narrowness and materialism of American life. Political capitalism, moreover, was responsible for continued war, racism, and poverty in the twentieth century. Any judgment on this historical problem, then, often becomes a judgment on the nature and quality of American civilization itself.

Gabriel Kolko

GABRIEL KOLKO (1932–   ) is Professor of History at York University. He has
written a number of books on the history of domestic and foreign policy,
including *Railroads and Regulation 1887–1916* (1965) and *The Politics of War: The
World and United States Foreign Policy, 1943–1945* (1968).

Not merely present-day historians but also contemporary observers of
the growth of big business were virtually unanimous in believing that
the concentration of economic power and the growth of "monopoly"
and the "trust" was an inevitable result of the modern capitalist *and*
industrial process. This unanimity was shared not only by the conventional celebrators of the status quo—the businessmen, conservative
journalists, and intellectuals—but also by the critics of capitalism. Indeed, at the turn of the twentieth century a belief in the necessity, if not
the desirability, of big business was one of the nearly universal tenets of
American thought.

It is to be expected, of course, that the large majority of the important
businessmen who contemplated and wrote about the growth of big
business were ideologically receptive to a rationale of it. The similarity of
economic values held by both small and big businessmen was sufficiently great to undermine the serious possibility of the sort of social
analysis capable of challenging the big businessman's belief in the
necessity and desirability of the economic world as he saw it evolving.
This agreement on fundamentals, needless to say, has never meant
there could not be very substantial disagreement among businessmen
on particular issues of specific importance to one type of industry, or to a
business of a certain size. But the signal fact of American business history
is the consensus among businessmen, of varying degrees of importance
and in different industries, that the capitalist system is worth maintaining in one form or another; this has resulted in a general attitude that has
not necessarily been opposed to decisive innovation in the economic
sphere, but which has opposed radical economic programs that might,
in the process of altering the concentration of economic power, also
undermine the stability, if not the very existence, of the status quo. If the
small businessman has at times joined anti-monopoly crusades, the least

that can be said is that he has never pursued his beliefs to the point where his own stake in the existing economic order has been endangered.

But, even granting the belief of so many historians in the existence of small businessmen who have challenged the supremacy of the great business enterprises, the evidence indicates that the vast majority accepted the inevitability of the monopoly movement in the economy even if they believed it undesirable. The prevalent nonacademic analysis at the turn of the century was that the cold, hard facts of industrial life and technology favored the growth of big business, and that little could be done to change the limitations these facts placed on political programs for economic change. Such assumptions, based on a few years' experience with the merger movement, were as much wish-fulfilment as descriptions of reality. By 1907 many big businessmen were aware that their world was more complicated, and their utterances were increasingly to become celebrations of a situation they hoped to attain rather than the world they actually lived in.

The Inevitable Monopoly

Important businessmen and their lawyers in the first years of this century were convinced that big business was necessary, inevitable, and desirable as a prerequisite to rationally organizing economic life. And the destructiveness of competition and the alleged technical superiority of consolidated firms were the catalytic agents of change which made industrial cooperation and concentration a part of the "march of civilization," as S. C. T. Dodd, Standard Oil's lawyer, phrased it. Although there was a formal commitment to varieties of laissez faire economic theory in most of the academic world, big businessmen developed their own functional doctrine very much opposed to competition as either a desirable mechanism or as a goal. " . . . the 'trust,'" wrote James J. Hill in 1901, "came into being as the result of an effort to obviate ruinous competition." "Competition is industrial war," wrote James Logan, manager of the U.S. Envelope Company in the same year. "Ignorant, unrestricted competition, carried to its logical conclusion, means death to some of the combatants and injury for all. Even the victor does not soon recover from the wounds received in the conflict." The instinct of survival made combination inevitable, for combination was "caused primarily by the desire to obviate the effects of competition"—or at least this was the dominant contemporary view of the matter.

At the same time, combinations were the logical outcome of technological considerations, according to big business opinion. The larger the output the smaller the cost of production, suggested Charles M. Schwab of United States Steel, and this meant lower supervision costs, better goods, and lower prices.

The validity of the notion that corporate consolidation leads to industrial efficiency will be examined later. But a belief in this proposition was shared by virtually all of the important businessmen who wrote or commented on the matter in the pre-World War I period, and it is this belief which became the operational basis of their actions. Buttressed by this conviction, men such as Schwab, Elbert H. Gary, John D. Rockefeller and John D. Archbold were certain that their economic behavior was "inevitably" preordained. This synthesis of the doctrines of the efficiency of consolidations and the destructiveness of competition is echoed again and again in the latter part of this period. Even when the big business community developed an involved and often shifting set of political goals it never ceased to view itself as making the technologically efficient and inevitable response to the evils of unrestricted competition. "Unrestricted competition had been tried out to a conclusion," an American Tobacco Company executive wrote in 1912, "with the result that the industrial fabric of the nation was confronted with an almost tragic condition of impending bankruptcy. Unrestricted competition had proven a deceptive mirage, and its victims were struggling on every hand to find some means of escape from the perils of their environment. In this trying situation, it was perfectly natural that the idea of rational co-operation in lieu of cut-throat competition should suggest itself."

At least a decade before his younger brothers embarked on that grey, pessimistic intellectual discourse which now has a classic place in American intellectual history, Charles Francis Adams, Jr., president of the Union Pacific Railroad from 1884–1890, was announcing that "the principle of consolidation . . . is a necessity—a natural law of growth. You may not like it: you will have to reconcile yourselves to it." "The modern world does its work through vast aggregations of men and capital. . . . This is a sort of latter-day manifest destiny." Periods of intense competition were perpetually followed by combinations and monopolies, according to Adams. "The law is invariable. It knows no exceptions." But, ignoring the fact that the essence of Brooks and Henry Adams' generalizations on the role of the corporation in modern life can be found expressed with great clarity in the earlier writings of their older brother, what is significant is that the widespread belief among important businessmen in the inevitability, if not the desirability, of the concentration of economic power was shared by most contemporary intellectuals and journalists. And although many intellectuals and journalists were critical of the functions or even the nature of the massive corporation, most, like Charles Francis Adams, Jr., resigned themselves to their necessity and shared the consensus on the character and future of the American economy.

Academic economists of the historical school were less concerned about the classical preoccupation with the nature and conditions of competition than they were with fostering a positive attitude toward minimal government regulation of the economy. It was this tacit acceptance of a theory directed toward redressing the existing balance of social and economic power via political means that meant that, on an analytical basis at least, the probably most sophisticated group of American economic thinkers accepted the same fundamental premises on the nature of the industrial structure as most major businessmen. The variations on the businessman's essential theme are as diverse as academic minds are subtle, but a clear pattern can be distinguished. Richard T. Ely, for example, maintained that large-scale business was inevitable, but that, save for certain types of services, monopolies in the pure sense were not preordained; the burden of his writings was concerned with the desirability of government regulation of "artificial" monopolies that had sprung up rather than with regulation as a means for restoring purely competitive conditions. Henry C. Adams, one of the founders of the American Economic Association, saw in monopoly, which was "natural" only in railroads, the possibility of "cheapness and efficiency," and was attracted by its advantages—provided it was controlled by minimal government regulations. By and large historical economists such as E. Benjamin Andrews, Arthur T. Hadley, Edwin R. A. Seligman, and Simon N. Patten were ready to "accept," with little empirical analysis, the existence of a trend toward monopoly as a starting point on which to provide proof of their theories on the desirable relation of economics to government. And virtually all assumed that, whether monopolistic or not, combined capital avoided the waste of small-scale production.

It is to be expected, of course, that the movement toward corporate concentration had less sophisticated supporters in the academic world as well. S. A. Martin, president of Wilson College, told the Civic Federation of Chicago's Trust Conference in September, 1899, ". . . trusts are here and here to stay as the result of the inevitable laws of industrial development." Less detached defenses of the alleged monopoly movement were as common as big business' interest in cultivating a rationale for its existence. George Gunton, popular economist who spent a number of his years as editor of *Gunton's Magazine* while on an annual retainer of $15,000 from Standard Oil of New Jersey, defended the necessity and desirability of big business. John Moody, whose data-gathering service probably gave him more factual insights into the workings of business than any of his contemporaries, was convinced that "The modern Trust is the natural outcome or evolution of societary conditions and ethical standards which are recognized and established among men to-day as being necessary elements in the development of civilization."

But even among the critics of business there was a general acceptance of the inevitability, and often the ultimate desirability of the "trust." Ray Stannard Baker and John B. Walker, for example, thought monopoly to be progressive. Hardboiled Lincoln Steffens, who maintained that business was the source of political corruption, was nevertheless convinced that business concentration was inevitable. Only a small minority of the muckrakers were concerned with the causes rather than the consequences of the alleged business debauching of politics, and most of them assumed that there were always certain constraints in American society, among which were "the trusts."

It is ironic that the greatest celebrators of the alleged trend toward corporate monopolies could be found among that element in American politics with attitudes sufficiently critical of the status quo to suggest programmatic alternatives to the growth of monopoly—the socialists. After the demise of the Populist movement, only the socialists were in a position to explicitly reject a policy of economic change limited, as in the case of the advocates of laissez faire, by a conservative fear of undermining the fundamental institution of private control of the economy in the process of attempting to restore competition. But American socialists were Marxists, and Frederick Engels, with characteristic sharpness, had made it clear that "the progressive evolution of production and exchange nevertheless brings us with necessity to the present capitalist mode of production, to the monopolisation of the means of production and the means of subsistence in the hands of the one, numerically small, class. . . ." Thus armed, American socialists shared the general belief in the inevitability of corporate concentration and monopoly, even after key business leaders began realizing it no longer fitted the facts.

". . . one cannot but acknowledge the natural development of the successive steps of this [Standard Oil] monopoly," the Social Democratic Party's *Campaign Book of 1900* declared. "No better way could be invented by which the natural resources may be made available for the world's need. The lesson of the trust, how to secure the greatest satisfaction for the least expenditure of human energy, is too good to be lost." W. J. Ghent, a socialist writer, saw "an irresistible movement—now almost at its culmination—toward great combinations in specific trades. . . ," and these combinations would dictate the terms of existence for the small business permitted to survive. Even Henry Demarest Lloyd, who was not a Marxist but eventually joined the Socialist Party, gave up his vagueness on the possible alternatives to monopoly expressed in *Wealth against Commonwealth* and concluded "centralisation [was]. . . one of the tendencies of the age."

But the resignation of the socialists to inevitable monopoly was not merely a passive commitment to an article of faith. It stimulated many of them to a personal admiration of big businessmen unequalled by most paid eulogists. Indeed, big businessmen were the vehicles of progress and the guarantors of socialism, and worth defending from personal attacks for the parts they played in an impersonal industrial process. For the socialists "are not making the Revolution," *The Worker* declared in April, 1901. "It would be nearer the truth to say that Morgan and Rockefeller are making it." When Ida Tarbell's *History of Standard Oil* appeared, Gaylord Wilshire, publisher of the mass circulation socialist *Wilshire's Magazine*, criticized her for not being more sympathetic to Rockefeller as an individual. The system was predestined and "Mr. Rockefeller was forced by unavoidable circumstances to pursue his path of consolidation. . . . The fault exists not in the individual but in the system." When J. P. Morgan died in 1914, the Socialist *Call* wrote "if Morgan is remembered at all, it will be for the part he played in making it [socialism] possible and assisting, though unconsciously, in its realization."

Although crucial aspects of the intellectual consensus on the role of big business in the American economy were challenged now and again, and a Louis Brandeis might question the necessary relationship between size and efficiency or an Edward Dana Durand could suggest that monopoly was not inevitable and competition was somehow attainable, the significant fact is the pervasiveness of the proposition that economic concentration, if not monopoly, is inevitable and is the price to be paid for maximum industrial efficiency.

Mergers and Promoters

At the turn of the century the vast majority of the businessmen who defended monopoly and corporate concentration believed in it as a goal, and often strove to attain it, but their beliefs were based on a very limited experience which they thought would extend into the future. Monopoly, however, was the exceptional and not the routine characteristic of most industries, and the use of the term "monopoly" or "trust" by defenders of the status quo was based more on wish-fulfillment than on economic reality. (By "trust" I mean effective control of an industry by one firm or a working alliance of firms. Contemporary usage of the term usually equated it with mere large size or concentration, without any specific reference to the extent of market control but with the implicit assumption that large size could be equated with control.)

Many big businessmen, such as Elbert H. Gary, knew that monopoly and the total concentration of economic power did not exist even as they defended it as inevitable. What they were defending was concentration and their monopolistic aspirations, aspirations that never materialized despite their enthusiastic efforts. These key businessmen believed concentration and combination led to efficiency and lower costs, and therefore worked for them energetically. And although we might find this inconsistency natural among the militantly unreflective, it can be suggested that what these men were defending was the status quo, their past actions and consolidation, their future actions and, hopefully, industrial domination.

Certainly it can be said that there was a revolution in the American business structure from about 1897 on—a revolution caused by the sudden rise of a merger movement and the capitalization of new combinations on an unprecedented scale. But the revolution was abortive, whereas the intellectual conclusions based upon it were projected into the future and survived long after the revolution's death. Indeed, the preoccupation with monopoly, which seemed imminent at the turn of the century, led to general intellectual confusion as to the important distinction between monopoly and concentration, and this confusion has seriously interfered with subsequent efforts for a proper understanding of the nature of the American economy and politics in the Progressive Era.

In 1895 only 43 firms disappeared as a result of mergers, and merger capitalizations were $41 million. In 1898, 303 firms disappeared, and merger capitalization was $651 million; and in 1899 the peak was reached when 1,208 firms disappeared as a result of mergers, and merger capitalizations soared to $2,263 million. In 1900 the movement declined precipitously to 340 firm disappearances, and a capitalization of $442 million, and in 1901 the last great merger movement, largely centered about the formation of United States Steel, occurred when 423 firms disappeared, and capitalization amounted to $2,053 million. But the merger movement declined sharply after 1901, despite the permanent impact it had on the modern American intellectual tradition. During 1895–1904 there was an annual average firm disappearance of 301 companies and a total annual average capitalization of $691 million. During 1905–1914 an average of only 100 firms disappeared each year, and average capitalization was $211 million. More important, from 1895 to 1920 only eight industries accounted for 77 percent of the merger capitalizations and 68 percent of the net firm disappearances. In effect, the merger movement was largely restricted to a minority of the dominant American industries, and that for only a few years.

The merger movement was caused primarily by the growth of a capital market for industrial stocks after the return of economic prosperity in late 1897. The railroad industry, which was the main preoccupation of European investors who had plunged $3.0 billion into the United States by 1890, was overexpanded and unprofitable. Capital invested in manufacturing increased 121 percent from 1880 to 1890, and despite the depression of 1893–1897 increased 51 percent over the next decade. In this context of shifting economic interests, the history of the 1890's is one of sharpening and extending the existing institutional structures for raising capital, and thereby creating movements for mergers, concentration, and, hopefully, monopoly in the American industrial structure.

The stock exchanges of the major financial centers had specialized in railroads until the 1890's, although the Boston Stock Exchange had a copper mine section in the early 1850's which helped establish that city's domination over the American copper industry until the end of the century. Boston, in addition to textiles, was also to dominate the capital market for the electrical and telephone industries until the turn of the century. In 1890 no more than ten industrial stock issues were quoted regularly in the financial journals. By 1893 the number increased to about thirty, and by 1897 to over two hundred.

Industrial capital until the late 1890's came mainly from short-term loans and self-financing out of profits, aiding instability and bankruptcies during the periods of economic decline or depressions. By the 1890's industrial shares became widely available as a result of the creation of new issues from mergers and the reconversion of many trusts, in the literal sense, into unified corporations. And many industrial leaders, ready to retire or diversify their fortunes—Andrew Carnegie is the most notable example—were anxious to develop outlets for their shares. Each new wave of mergers created new sources of capital in a sort of multiplier fashion, and, quite ironically, the very creation of mergers and new industrial combinations led to the availability of funds in the hands of capitalists which often ended, as we shall see, in the creation of competing firms.

The director and coordinator of this industrial metamorphosis was the promoter. To the extent that the dominant stimulus for the promoter was watered stock and his charge for the transaction, the economic concentration which took place at the turn of the century was based on factors other than technological elements inherent in any advanced industrial society. But even if not interested in the transaction fees per se, the promoter was invariably motivated by concern for his own profit position and financial standing, and merely regarded promotion as the means of maintaining or re-establishing it.

Promoters included in their ranks both members of firms being merged and outsiders seeking to stimulate consolidations in order to obtain a share of the profits of the merger. In a number of spectacular instances the insiders of a group of firms sought to interest outside promoters capable of financing or organizing the merger. Quantifications of the nature and source of all or a significant number of promotions do not exist, but some of the more important variations can be illustrated.

William H. Moore and his brother, James H. Moore, were among the three or four most significant promoters. It would be difficult to regard them as anything more than brilliant gamblers. In 1898 William H. Moore organized, at the request of a committee of manufacturers, the American Tin Plate Company out of a group of thirty-five to forty plants. He took options on the component companies and obtained loans to pay for them and provide working expenses. After choosing all officers and directors, he sold $18 million in preferred and $28 million in common stock to bankers and capitalists. Out of this sum he awarded himself $10 million. The Moore brothers were not always so fortunate, however. In 1899 they gave Andrew Carnegie $1 million for an option to try to raise $350 million from bankers to float the sale of Carnegie Steel. They failed, and Carnegie pocketed the money. Similar failures in 1896 forced the Moore brothers into insolvency.

Not infrequently a single manufacturer would turn promoter in order to try to eliminate competition or instability. John W. Gates successfully proved in a law suit that he earned less than $400,000 through underwriting profits and the exchange of shares in the promotion of American Steel and Wire Company in 1899. His only substantial profits were on his component properties that he turned over to the new firm. In the case of the Amalgamated Copper Company, formed in 1899 to gain effective control over the copper industry, outsiders and insiders united. Thomas Lawson, Henry H. Rogers, and William Rockefeller, none of whom had any special competence in the copper industry, cooperated with Anaconda Copper. J. P. Morgan, the largest single industrial promoter and the dominating figure in railroad mergers, resorted to nearly every variation of insider and outsider promotions. Morgan, the Moore brothers, John R. Dos Passos, Moore and Schley, and Charles R. Flint collectively probably accounted for a minority of the total mergers and less than half of the value of all mergers; in addition, there were innumerable single individuals and investment bankers involved in the merger movement.

If the merger movement as organized by promoters was the result of "inevitable" impulses within the capitalist economy, as well as technological imperatives to maximum efficiency, we should determine whether the organization of these new corporations was arranged in such a manner as to: (1) make the competitive entry of new firms increasingly difficult, and (2) avoid the accusation of being organized primarily to create the profits of promotion. It is understood that unless the merger of firms within an industry obtained control of a crucial raw material, patents, or trade advantage, it would have to maintain a reasonable price and profit level or else run the risk of attracting new competitors or allowing existing ones to grow, the risk being scaled to the capital requirements of successful entry. Overcapitalization of the stock of a merged firm, therefore, is an indication of the extent to which a merger was executed to obtain maximum industrial efficiency, control over the competitive annoyances of the industry, or the profits of promotion and speculation. Watered stock meant higher prices in order to pay dividends, and higher prices opened possibilities of new competitive entries.

It is significant, of course, that the heyday of the merger movement was restricted to a few years, and ended almost as abruptly as it began. There are now few academic defenders of the thesis that the merger movement was primarily the outcome of industrial rationality or a desire for control of economic conditions. Charles R. Flint, one of the more important promoters and organizer of twenty-four consolidations, naturally claimed that mergers were intended mainly to attack the evils of competition, and that the profits of promoters were greatly exaggerated by critics. Capitalization, he maintained, was not overinflated, and Flint published data showing that the average return on the *market value* of the stock of forty-seven merged firms was 13.6 percent.

The evidence is overwhelming, however, to indicate that the watering and overcapitalization of the securities of merged companies was the general rule. This fact was widely acknowledged at the time by economists, by most promoters, and by many businessmen. It was simply not generalized upon or related to contemporary theories on the necessity and inevitability of the trust. Indeed, the incompatibility between the obvious ulterior motives behind the merger movement and social theory was ignored even by those attacking the evils of watered stock. J. P. Morgan's lawyer, Francis Lynde Stetson, frankly admitted that he opposed any scheme for limiting overcapitalization that risked "taking away from men of enterprise their paramount motive for corporate organization. . ."

A government study in 1900 of 183 industrial combinations shows that stocks and bonds valued at $3,085,000,000 were issued for plants with a total capital worth of $1,459,000,000. The Department of Labor, in the same year, claimed that a substantial group of combinations they studied issued stocks valued at twice the cost of reproducing active plants. Arthur S. Dewing, in a study of fourteen mergers, found that the average overcapitalization was well in excess of 50 percent of the assets. The large majority of mergers clearly capitalized their firms on the basis of preferred stock representing the cost of the real property or assets and common stock representing the costs of promotion, the expenses of amalgamation, and the expectations of future earnings as a result of the merger. John W. Gates, Henry O. Havermeyer, and John R. Dos Passos freely admitted that common stock represented the promoter's estimate of the potential earning power of consolidations. The profits of underwriters, in many instances, came exclusively from the sale of securities, not anticipated dividends, and this fact alone placed a premium on overcapitalization.

Seven of the combined forms that later entered the United States Steel merger paid out $63 million in stock as commissions to promoters, excluding bonuses and other forms of commission. The tangible assets and property of United States Steel on April 1, 1901, were worth $676 million, and the average market value of the shares it acquired was $793 million in 1899–1901. The total capitalization of the firm was $1,403 million, and the cost of promotion and underwriting consumed over $150 million of this amount. United States Rubber, in much the same way, based its capitalization on 50 percent watered stock, the common shares representing "the increased earning capacity by reason of the consolidation. . . ."

Promotion, with its premium on speculation to maximize its profits, soon extended its heady gambling mentality to the general stock market. Brokers emphasized the more profitable speculative stock orders rather than investment buying, and they directed their customers to the speculative issues. The commission rates on speculative orders made investment orders less profitable, and by no later than 1904–1907 the volume of transactions on the stock market far exceeded investment demand. This trend alarmed a number of more conservative capitalists primarily concerned with the means, not the ends, of the merger movement, and led to dire predictions, most of which were realized by 1932. Russell Sage wrote in 1901 that watered stock "has also . . . produced a feeling of unrest and disquiet, industrial and political, that threatens, sooner or later, to bring serious results." Henry Clews, the banker, was less restrained.

> Many of these [combinations] have been organized in disregard and defiance of legitimate finance, and have exposed the stock market and all the monetary interests depending upon them to risks and disastrous disturbances inseparable from organizations whose foundations rest largely on wind and water. . . .

J. P. Morgan persistently overcapitalized his promotion schemes whenever he was able to do so. His greatest triumph was United States Steel, but when the merger initiative came from insiders, as in the case of International Harvester, Morgan restricted himself to more limited, yet amply lucrative profits. In every case, however, Morgan sought to obtain substantial, if not total, managerial control or board representation.

Morgan's efforts were generally marked by success, and had he avoided managerial responsibilities his fortunes might have been larger and his reputation would certainly have been better. In the case of the formation of the International Mercantile Marine Company, Morgan became deeply involved in a grossly overextended venture. His firm initially received $5.5 million in preferred and common stock at par, and a share of the $22 million paid to bond underwriters. An additional $6 million went to shipper-promoters, and the new firm was burdened with a total of $34 million in merger fees on a preferred and common stock issuance of $120 million and $50 million in cash. But the company was poorly conceived and poorly managed: in the end the Morgan firm lost about $2 million, and International Mercantile Marine went out of business after World War I. In the case of American Telephone and Telegraph, Morgan fought for effective control of the board, which he managed to obtain in 1907. As part of an over-all effort to replace New England management and financial connections, a Morgan-led syndicate obtained a $100 million bond flotation, but was able to dispose of only $10 million before giving up the effort in 1908. Although Morgan's philosophy of trying to obtain managerial control along with the profits of promotion was, on the whole, profitable, it is questionable whether he increased managerial or industrial efficiency. The primary goal of promotions was, as Francis Lynde Stetson admitted, profits. Insofar as Morgan's profits were not immediate or short-range, but tied to the managerial and profit performance of the new company, Morgan tended to do relatively poorly. And in several spectacular instances Morgan either lost money or, as in the railroad industry, bankrupted companies.

To the extent that promotions and mergers were organized among competing firms, the dominant causal factor behind the merger and consolidation movement can be said to have been the existence of internecine competition. A market for industrial securities did not exist in any significant form before 1897, but it most certainly continued after the decline of the merger movement in 1901, and the history of the movement must be explained by more than a market for securities. In the period 1897–1901 the merger movement was the unique result of the rise of a market for securities and an impetus to eliminate competition, and the success of outside promoters was dependent on both factors. But the decline of mergers was due to the collapse of the promises of stability, profits, and industrial cooperation. Save for the outside promoter who took his profit immediately and then broke his ties with the consolidation, the larger part of the mergers brought neither greater profits nor less competition. Quite the opposite occurred. There was *more* competition, and profits, if anything, declined. Most contemporary economists and many smaller businessmen failed to appreciate this fact, and historians have probably failed to recognize it altogether. This phenomenon, I maintain, is a vital key to understanding the political history of the period of reform preceding World War I.

Most important businessmen did not comprehend the general demise of the merger and consolidation movement save in their own industry, and were unable to understand the larger economic context in which they operated. Businessmen, as a group, are not prone to reflection, much less theoretical generalization, but they did act to ameliorate their own illnesses. Now and again, however, a business journal commented on the failure of the merger movement and on the real trends, as opposed to commonly accepted mythology, in the American economy as a whole. In late 1900 *The Iron Age* lamented:

> Experience has shown that very few of the promises of the promoters of consolidations have materialized. That some of them are satisfactorily profitable is undoubtedly true.... Others are less so; some are conspicuously unprofitable; some have dissolved, and more will have to dissolve within the next two or three years. Before another wave of the consolidation movement overtakes us, if it ever does, the experiment will have proved itself by the test of time.

The first decades of this century were years of intense and growing competition. They were also years of economic expansion and, in a number of industries, greater internal concentration of capital and output. But neither of these phenomena was incompatible with increased competition. From 1899 to 1904 the number of manufacturing firms in the United States increased 4.2 percent, and from 1904 to 1909 they increased 24.2 percent—a growth of 29.4 percent for the entire decade. Of the nine manufacturing industries with a product value of $500 million and up in 1909, only one, the iron and steel industry, had less than 1,000 establishments, and the exception had 446. In the thirty-nine industries with products valued at $100–500 million, only three had less than one hundred establishments. The numbers of business failures from 1890 on followed the classic pattern of being high in depressions and low in periods of prosperity, and there is no evidence whatsoever that failures due to competition were any more numerous in 1900 than in 1925.

The new mergers, with their size, efficiency, and capitalization, were unable to stem the tide of competitive growth. Quite the contrary! They were more likely than not unable to compete successfully or hold on to their share of the market, and this fact became one of utmost political importance. The very motives behind the merger movement, and the concern with promotion of enterprises irrespective of the health of the component firms or the advantages of combination, led to an immediate apprehension among well-informed businessmen. "One question of great interest in relation to our new industrial combinations is whether a proper readjustment of their hugely inflated capital and excessive charges will place them permanently in a condition of efficiency, productiveness, solvency, and prosperity, or whether they will ultimately drift, one by one, into the hands of receivers..." said Henry Clews at the opening of the century.

This skepticism was more than justified by subsequent events, since the promises of the promoters were, by all criteria, mirages. Forty-eight pre-World War I manufacturing mergers studied by the National Industrial Conference Board had a nominal return on their net worth in 1903–1910 averaging 5.8 percent—no greater than the average to other firms.

Arthur S. Dewing, studying thirty-five mergers of five or more firms in existence at least ten years before 1914, discovered that the steep fixed interest charges and contingent preferred stock dividends imposed by promoters led to a radical deflation of promoters' promises. The earnings of the pre-merger firms were about one-fifth greater than the ten-year average profits of the new consolidation. Promoter estimates of expected ten-year earnings turned out to be about twice the actual performance. Another study by Dewing reveals that heavy fixed charges on the basis of expected earnings, administrative difficulties, and continued competition caused ten mergers to earn an average of 65 percent of their pre-consolidation profits. Shaw Livermore, in a study seeking to defend the success of 328 mergers formed during 1888–1905, nevertheless was forced to conclude that only 49 percent were "successes" in the sense that their rate of earnings compared favorably after 1918 to other companies in their field. Forty percent failed altogether, and 11 percent limped along at lower than average profit levels. He judged the main causes of failures to be poor judgment by promoters, dishonesty, and the decline of the industries.

The inescapable conclusion is that mergers were not particularly formidable and successful, and surely were incapable of exerting control over competitors within their own industries. "Mere bulk, whether of capital or of production, is not, *per se,* an element of strength," *The Iron Age* commented in 1900. "Some of the new plants are better equipped, carry less dead weight of unproductive assets and can produce more cheaply per unit of output than the consolidations can. So far as can be judged, the great industrial aggregations, instead of discouraging competition, have rather encouraged it." Most of the new mergers started out with less than monopoly control, and virtually all lost their initial share of the market. This failure, discussed in detail later in the chapter, was due to the rise of important new competitors and the significant economies of size attainable at lower production levels. Thirteen consolidations studied by Dewing controlled an average of only 54 percent of the output of their industries upon organization, and the U.S. Industrial Commission studied a sample with an average market share of 71 percent. Of seventy-two mergers listed by Ralph L. Nelson, twenty-one controlled 42.5 to 62.5 percent of their markets upon formation, twenty-five controlled 62.5 to 82.5 percent, sixteen controlled over 82.5 percent, and ten controlled "large" portions.

There is also data to suggest that very large corporations as a whole did poorly—and many of these were recent mergers. Alfred L. Bernheim studied the 109 corporations with a capitalization of $10 million and up in 1903. Sixteen of these failed before 1914 and were dropped from the list, leaving ninety-three. Only twenty-two of the remainder paid common stock dividends of over 5 percent during 1900–1914, and twenty-four paid nothing. Their average dividend on common stock over the period was 4.3 percent. The market value of the common stock of forty-eight of the companies declined over 1900–1914, and rose in only forty-five instances.

In the light of such mediocre profit records it should not surprise one to discover that the mobility of giant firms out of the ranks of the largest hundred industrial corporations was high. Of the fifty largest companies in 1909, seven could not be found in the ranks of the top hundred in 1919, and twenty could not be found there in 1929; for the top hundred corporations in 1909 the figures are forty-seven drop-outs by 1919 and sixty-one by 1929. By comparison, of the top one hundred industrials in 1937, only twenty-eight could not be found in that category in 1957. Bernheim studied the fate of the ninety-nine largest industrials of 1909 by 1924, and found that forty-seven of them could not be found among the largest two hundred corporations of every type. Of this forty-seven, seven had dissolved, three had written down their capital to realistic proportions and were disqualified, nine had become unable even to pay their preferred dividends in full, two had paid no common dividends, ten had merged or reorganized without loss, and sixteen had failed to grow fast enough after 1909.

Many large corporations soon found their overcentralization unprofitable, and tried to reduce plant sizes and distribute plants more widely throughout the nation. In the case of United States Steel, as we shall see, the organizational structure was centralized only at the very highest policy level, and autonomous operating units and specialized staffs have been a general trend in the large corporate structure since the turn of the century. To the extent that Joseph A. Schumpeter was correct in holding that each significant new innovation was embodied in a new firm and the leadership of new men in a still dynamic capitalism—and that firms that do not innovate die—it can also be said that important competitive trends were inherent in the economic structure. The growth in the number of individual patents issued until the peak year of 1916 indicates that innovation was very much a part of the American economy and technology until World War I. Even if organized corporate and government research and development now dominates the field, and many private patents are purchased just to be suppressed, or are infringed merely because most private inventors are economically helpless, enough individuals were able to break into established fields, or to create entirely new ones, to make a significant economic difference. For all of these reasons *The New York Financier*, in opposition to the vast majority of contemporary writers and modern historians, was correct when it observed in June, 1900, that "The most serious problem that confronts trust combinations today is competition from independent sources. . . . In iron and steel, in paper and in constructive processes of large magnitude the sources of production are being multiplied, with a resultant decrease in profits. . . . When the papers speak of a cessation of operation in certain trust industries, they fail to mention the awakening of new life in independent plants . . . ."

This "awakening of new life" in the economy is the subject of the case studies that follow. The examples are significant not only because of their economic role, but also because of their political roles. Moreover, although these typologies reflect a trend, they also involve industries which most historians have been inclined to think proved the conventionally accepted thesis that the tendency in industrial life at the beginning of the century was toward economic concentration and monopoly. They are the "classic" examples of the "trust"—steel, oil, telephones, meat, and a number of others. And in all of these cases we find a fluidity of economic circumstances and radical changes generally slighted by the historian. The shifting markets and resources, the loss of relative power by the dominant companies, the specific failure of the merger movement in attaining either stability or economic control—these are the significant features that emerge from our case studies. . . .

Theory and the American Reality

The American experience justifies different theoretical conclusions than those reached by Marx, Weber, or Veblen. Any reasonable generalization on the phenomenon of progressivism must necessarily take into account the economic realities and problems of the period, and the responses that were set in motion. Yet the crucial factor in the American experience was the nature of economic power which required political tools to rationalize the economic process, and that resulted in a synthesis of politics and economics. This integration is the dominant fact of American society in the twentieth century, although once political capitalism is created a dissection of causes and effects becomes extraordinarily difficult. The economy had its own problems, dictated by technological innovation, underconsumption, crises, and competition. But these difficulties were increasingly controlled by political means to the extent that the consideration of economic problems outside their political context is meaningless. The "laws of capitalist development" were not self-contained imperatives in the technological, economic, or political sphere, but an inseparable unification of all three elements.

The object of such a combination was not merely capital accumulation, although it was that as well, but a desire to defend and exercise power through new media more appropriate to the structural conditions of the new century: the destructive potential of growing competition and the dangerous possibilities of a formal political democracy that might lead to a radical alteration of the distribution of wealth or even its total expropriation. Politics and the state become the means of attaining order in the economic sphere and security in the political arena. And they were accessible tools because the major political parties and leaders of the period were also conservative in the sense that they believed in the basic value of capitalist social relations—of some variation of the status quo. The resilience of capitalism, under these circumstances, becomes something that cannot be evaluated in isolated economic terms. Behind the economy, resting on new foundations in which effective collusion and price stability is now the rule, stands the organized power of the national government. The stability and future of the economy is grounded, in the last analysis, on the power of the state to act to preserve it. Such support does not end crises, nor does it eliminate antagonisms inherent in the very nature of the economy, but it does assure the ability of the existing social order to overcome, or survive, the consequences of its own deficiencies. The theory of the national government as a neutral intermediary in its intervention into the economic process is a convenient ideological myth, but such a contention will not survive a serious inquiry into the origins and consequences of such intervention. The rhetoric of reform is invariably different than its structural results. Such mythology is based on the assumption that those who control the state will not use if for their own welfare.

It is important to stress that under conditions of political capitalism the form of the industrialization process, and of the political machinery of society, take on those characteristics necessary to fulfill the peculiar values, attributes, and goals of the ascendant class of that society. The rationalized, dominated, and essentially totalitarian decision-making process is not a consequence of forces inherent in industrialism, but in political capitalism in all its components. The organization of industry is based on the decisions of men whose motives have nothing whatsoever to do with inexorable destiny. Mergers, the scale of effective production, the nature of the production itself, and the direction given to the fruits of technology—all these were decisions made by men whose motives, interests, and weaknesses were peculiar to the basic capitalist assumptions upon which they operated. Their errors were many, as were the possibilities for their failure; but the national government stood behind them so that the consequences of their mistakes would not be calamitous. Perhaps industrialization would not have permitted democratic control and direct participation in the work process under any circumstances. All one can do is point to the large extent to which the concentration of industry in this period had nothing to do with considerations of efficient technology, and suggest that no effort whatsoever was ever made to democratize the work situation and industrial control, much less consider the desirability of reducing technological efficiency, if necessary, in such a way as to make decentralization or workers' control possible.

Nor is there any evidence to suggest that the bureaucratization of the political machinery of society, to the extent it took place, was as inevitable as the concentration of industry. It was perfectly logical for men who had spent years solving their economic problems or making their fortunes through political means to also welcome the intervention of a centralized state power to meet problems they could not solve themselves. Social forces, dynamic institutional factors, were the cause of bureaucratic developments in the form of new political agencies and the strengthening of many of the older ones. American capitalism was not merely interested in having law that operated like a piece of machinery, as Weber suggested, but in utilizing the state on terms and conditions which made bureaucratic functions class functions. Bureaucracy, in itself, needed a power base in order to operate in a roughly continuous, systematic fashion. Since it had no economic power itself, it had to support, and hence be supported by, powerful economic groups. This was especially true in a situation where the conditions of political activity were defined by political parties which in turn reflected economic interests, or where the idea of the bureaucracy originated with those operating in the very area in which the bureaucracy was to function.

The skeptical reader may ask whether political capitalism changed after 1916, or perhaps whether capitalism was made more socially responsible by virtue of the stability and rationalization it attained through political means. The question is a moot one, and would take at least one more volume to answer properly. All one can do is point to the continuity in the nature of the political parties and their key leaders, but, more important, to the perpetuation of the same distribution of wealth and the same social relations over the larger part of this century. The solution of economic problems has continued to take place in the political sphere, and the strength of the status quo is based ultimately on the synthesis of politics and economics. Crises have been overcome, or frozen, as much by the power of the state as by internal economic resources applied by business in isolation.

The question remains: Could the American political experience, and the nature of our economic institutions, have been radically different than they are today? It is possible to answer affirmatively, although only in a hypothetical, unreal manner, for there was nothing inevitable or predetermined in the peculiar character given to industrialism in America. And, abstractly regarding all of the extraneous and artificial measures that provided shape and direction to American political and economic life, and their ultimate class function, it would be possible to make a case for a positive reply to the question. Yet ultimately the answer must be a reluctant "No."

There can be no alternatives so long as none are seriously proposed, and to propose a relevant measure of fundamental opposition one must understand what is going on in society, and the relationship of present actions to desired goals. To have been successful, a movement of fundamental change would have had to develop a specific diagnosis of existing social dynamics and, in particular, the variable nature and consequences of political intervention in the economy. It would have, in short, required a set of operating premises radically different than any that were formulated in the Progressive Era or later. Populism rejected, on the whole, the values of business even as it was unable to articulate a viable alternative. Intellectually it left a vacuum, and, more important, the movement was dead by 1900. The Socialist Party suffered from the fetishistic belief in the necessity of centralization that has characterized all socialist groups that interpreted Marx too literally, and it had a totally inaccurate estimate of the nature of progressivism, eventually losing most of its followers to the Democrats. The two major political parties, as always, differed on politically unimportant and frequently contrived details, but both were firmly wedded to the status quo, and the workers were generally their captives or accomplices. No socially or politically significant group tried to articulate an alternative means of organizing industrial technology in a fashion that permitted democratic control over centralized power, or participation in routine, much less crucial, decisions in the industrial process. No party tried to develop a program that suggested democracy could be created only by continuous mass involvement in the decisions that affected their lives, if the concentration of actual power in the hands of an elite was to be avoided. In brief, the Progressive Era was characterized by a paucity of alternatives to the status quo, a vacuum that permitted political capitalism to direct the growth of industrialism in America, to shape its politics, to determine the ground rules for American civilization in the twentieth century, and to set the stage for what was to follow.

Edward A. Purcell, Jr.

EDWARD A. PURCELL, JR. (1941–   ) is Associate Professor of History at the University of Missouri, Columbia. His book, *The Crisis of Democratic Theory: Scientific Naturalism and the Problem of Value* (1973), received the Frederick Jackson Turner Prize of the Organization of American Historians.

Historians have generally seen the Interstate Commerce Act of 1887 as the first major step on the road to federal regulation of business. While much of the rhetoric of American politics painted the issue in terms of "the people" or "the farmers" against "business," scholars have long been aware of the inadequacy of that view. Rather than opposing all government regulation, businessmen were often involved in sponsoring and supporting such legislation. Within the last two decades historians have published several important studies concerning the origin and purpose of the Interstate Commerce Act of 1887. Lee Benson, studying the New York State movement toward regulation of the roads, was able to delineate the impact of railroad development on various economic interest groups in the state and explain the conflict generated among them. He focused mainly on merchants, especially those in New York City, and their fight for more favorable freight rates. "New York merchants," he concluded "constituted the single most important group behind the passage of the Interstate Commerce Act."

More recently, Gabriel Kolko finished an examination of federal regulation from 1877 to 1916, which concentrated on the machinations and motives of railroad leaders. The railroads were ruining themselves by cutthroat competition, Kolko argued; and hence they actually sought government regulation to stabilize their industry and to make it more profitable. He amply demonstrated that many railroad men both accepted the premise of federal regulation and strongly supported certain proposed laws. Although railroad managers were obviously not alone in urging federal action and often disagreed among themselves, Kolko maintained that "the railroads, not the farmers and shippers, were the most important single advocates of federal regulation from 1877 to 1916."

Edward A. Purcell, Jr., "Ideas and Interests: Businessmen and the Interstate Commerce Act," *Journal of American History*, LIV (December, 1967), pp. 561–578. Reprinted by permission of the Organization of American Historians.

It was "businessmen" and not "the people" or "farmers" who were the most important advocates of federal regulation, Benson and Kolko agreed; but, of course, they disagreed over which businessmen were most important. Other historians, examining the role of businessmen in the nineteenth century, have generally concurred that economic changes caused by the growth of rail transportation forced various groups to support federal regulation. A study of the relationship between the competitive economy of the late-nineteenth century and the ideas of American businessmen would clarify the attitude of various groups toward government regulation as well as suggest more accurately the meaning and importance of the Interstate Commerce Act. Obviously, nonbusiness groups endorsed and influenced legislation for their own motives; but the purpose here is to examine only the reaction of American businessmen to the railroad problem and to relate their responses to the complexity of the economic system in which they were caught.

During the last quarter of the nineteenth century, American businessmen operated in an impersonal economic structure. In order to meet their competition, individuals whose businesses depended on shipping goods had to control as much as possible their major transportation connections. The rapid and far-reaching railroad system, which had developed after the Civil War, altered older economic relationships and placed many businessmen at a competitive disadvantage. The railroads, for example, diverted much trade from the water routes that followed the Great Lakes and the Erie Canal, and deprived merchants along the waterway of much of the business they had previously enjoyed. In addition to disrupting trade channels, the roads offered cheap, long-haul transportation that enabled distant merchants to compete with smaller businessmen who had earlier been able to control their local markets. Flour millers in St. Louis and Chicago, for instance, took advantage of low through-rates in order to compete for southern markets. Millers in Nashville, a local center, lost much of their market, including Atlanta, a traditional customer, and suffered greatly as a result. Moreover, the complicated rate structures worked new hardships on many individuals and areas. The grain merchants of Pittsburgh lost much of their trade when the railroads began charging ten cents per hundred pounds more for grain from Chicago to Pittsburgh than they did on the much longer haul from Chicago to New York. Later, both the Pittsburgh Chamber of Commerce and the Grain and Flour Exchange heartily endorsed the Interstate Commerce Act, including the controversial long-and-short-haul clause.

Businessmen recognized the importance of the railroads, and those who were not in a position to influence railroad policy but who depended on railroad service, feared and resented the rate discriminations and the power that characterized the transportation system. Even Poor's

Manual, a staunch advocate of both railroad practices and interests, admitted that the charge of discrimination was the major complaint made in all quarters against the roads. When the developing railroad system added the threat of potentially ruinous rate differentials to the already highly competitive and dynamic economy, those businessmen who were unable to take advantage of such differentials began to consider the desirability of government regulation. That truth was further substantiated when the biggest shippers, who could command rebates and profit from the differentials, were almost alone in opposing government regulation.

The widespread support for federal legislation did not mean, however, that most businessmen agreed on the specific type of law that was needed. Frank J. Firth, president of the Erie and Western Transportation Company, implicitly recognized the diversity and conflict among businessmen when he testified before Senator Shelby M. Cullom's committee investigating interstate commerce in 1885. Firth attempted to defend the roads and at the same time place them in a position superior to their many antagonists. "The transporter or merchant appearing before you," he politely told the senators, "speaks from the narrow field of observation within which this modern science of division of labor has confined him." Since each businessman saw only the one aspect that influenced his own business, Firth argued, then such a man could not give a comprehensive analysis. Firth's obvious conclusion was that the Cullom committee should not listen to complaining merchants but should rely instead on railroad men—those who understood the whole situation and knew all of the facts necessary to formulate an interstate commerce law.

Spokesmen for those businessmen who feared rate discrimination disagreed wholeheartedly with Firth and espoused their own brand of federal railroad regulation. Not all of them were enthusiastic about government interference, but their experience told them it was necessary. William H. Beebe, a member of a Chicago merchant firm, represented those diverse shipping groups when he addressed the Cullom committee. "While I do not lean very much toward paternal legislation on the part of the Government," he explained, "still I am decidedly of the opinion that when the railroads begin to touch the point of discrimination, regulation by a commission or by some other governmental agency would be beneficial."

The question of discrimination was puzzling and complex. Railroad men and shippers engaged in and suffered from various planned and purposeful discriminations. The whole transportation system also almost unavoidably resulted in widespread inequalities, which were themselves unintentional and accidental. Geographical location, size of shipments, competition from other transportation systems, and varying railroad overhead all combined to make uniform rates an impossible goal. The new railroad network pulled local merchants inextricably into a complex web of trade patterns, forcing them to compete with distant rivals. Trade areas overlapped more and more until a dozen cities could serve one section of the country that had previously relied on one local center. Individuals throughout the nation whose business depended on the shipment of goods had to have favorable transportation costs, not just for growth and profits, but for survival.

The foundation of the transportation system lay in the five great trunk lines that tied the East to the West and Midwest and dominated the transportation of goods in intersectional and international trade. Each directly connected the trans-Appalachian region with one or more of the major eastern seaports: Boston, New York, Philadelphia, and Baltimore. The merchants in these cities engaged in a constant struggle with one another to protect and increase their share of the western trade, just as the trunk lines fought with one another over the available freight. Thus, in 1881, the New York Central cut its rates in an attempt to increase its freight and to win more trade for New York. The other trunk lines responded with similar cuts, and soon rate wars followed. Businessmen in the four cities entered the fight immediately because they feared that their competitors would secure more favorable differentials. Both the railroads and the ports tried to work out agreements on differentials in the interest of peace and steady profits, but their failure led to constant dissatisfaction and rate-cutting. Conflicts even divided the interests of the trunk lines from those of their original terminals. The various roads found it profitable to carry goods to rival cities, and the merchants of the terminal cities took advantage of cheaper rates from other lines.

Edward Kemble, a Boston merchant, was typical of the businessmen who needed low rail rates. When the rates were temporarily disadvantageous he called for government regulation to improve his competitive position. "Massachusetts and a good portion of New England are, in my judgment, to-day laboring under an outrageous railroad discrimination," he claimed. The railroads were favoring New York with relatively cheap rates, Kemble argued, and they were thus robbing Boston of her share of the trade. Earlier, when the differentials weighed against New York, the city's Chamber of Commerce had petitioned Congress for relief from the unjust discriminations that were injuring "the producing, commercial, and other interests of the state, and particularly those of the City of New York." Railroad executives, too, disliked the open competition and despaired at the continual and debilitating rate wars. Even Albert Fink, the staunch supporter of private pooling, came to believe that only federal legislation could establish a viable pooling system.

Competition among producers and shippers in the Midwest and the South was as sharp and unrelenting as it was in the East. Chicago and St. Louis, the major centers in the Midwest, had a long history of com-

mercial rivalry that the advent of railroad transportation only intensified. They were challenged, however, by an increasing number of
regional competitors which were anxious about their own share of the
growing commerce. Kansas City, Louisville, Cincinnati, New Orleans,
Peoria, and many other cities struggled for prominent places in the
burgeoning commerce of the Midwest. Under the influence of shippers
in Minneapolis and St. Paul, for example, the Chicago, Burlington &
Northern lowered rates to improve the competitive position of the Twin
Cities against Chicago and St. Louis. After 1876, merchants in Milwaukee, enjoying a rate differential over competitors in Chicago, cut
into their business until the latter were able to command equal rates.

One of the most spectacular examples of the expansion of competition created by railway growth centered on the lucrative trade which St.
Louis enjoyed in Latin American products—especially sugar, molasses,
crockery, and coffee—that were shipped through New Orleans and up
the Mississippi, the shortest trade route from the South. Chicago businessmen challenged the merchants of New Orleans and St. Louis by
allying with importers in Baltimore and winning the support of the
trunk lines seeking additional westbound freight. Utilizing freight reductions from Baltimore of up to ninety percent, Chicago merchants
were able to offer lower delivery prices on goods from Latin America
and to divert the trade from New Orleans and the Mississippi route,
thus profiting themselves, the trunk lines, and the Baltimore importers.

Businessmen in smaller cities and interior distribution points refused
to accept, without putting up a strong fight, the loss of trade and influence that the expansion of competition caused. They supported both
state and federal regulation as a means of preserving their economic
positions. The businessmen in Dubuque, Iowa, and other river towns
led the fight for state regulation to protect themselves from roads offering low through-rates to Chicago. They received support in the interior,
not so much from the Grangers but from the small businessmen in the
prairie towns who also suffered from rate discriminations. Together they
were able to pass the famous Iowa Granger law, bringing the roads
under state control. In 1877, when the railroads imposed a temporary
embargo on the city's grain, the Kansas City *Times* vigorously attacked
the move as "a vital stab at the business interests of the city." Earlier the
Journal of Commerce, a local business publication, had urged a federal
antipooling law to protect local interests. Merchants in Montgomery,
Selma, and Mobile joined forces in 1881 to establish Alabama's first
railroad commission, which they hoped would protect their endangered
commercial positions from the consolidation of local roads under the
control of the Louisville and Nashville. Braxton Bragg Comer, who later
led the movement for further state regulation in Alabama, was himself a
victim of the expansion of competition. Rivals in St. Louis and other

northern centers had ruined his Birmingham milling trade and forced him out of business.

Discriminatory railroad practices existed not only between competing businessmen in different regions but also between merchants in the same city or area. In New York the Chamber of Commerce opposed two key provisions of the proposed Interstate Commerce Act, while the members of the Board of Trade and Transportation supported them both. The result of the situation, declared the president of the New York Produce Exchange, had been to aid certain favored merchants, who were often large stockholders in the roads, to the detriment of their local competitors. Such practices caused great damage to the helpless merchants, he believed, and were wholly unjust. Perhaps there is no stronger motivation than the combination of a feeling of injustice with the fear of unprofitability. A Chicago businessman stated it clearly: "It is simply in effect letting one man steal another man's business."

Rate policies often divided local businessmen in different lines of commerce. In Boston, for example, where most merchants who dealt in goods shipped by rail were angry about differentials made in favor of New York and other cities, the exporting merchants stood strongly in favor of the existing rates. William H. Lincoln, manager of a Boston steamship line, explained that his export trade had grown immensely after the railroads began shipping large quantities of goods from the West. Since the roads had cut the rate from Chicago to Boston on goods intended for export, Boston had gained an advantage over New York in the export trade. Kemble, acknowledging that exporters benefitted from existing rates, declared that the majority of Boston businessmen were not helped by the rates. "It is of no benefit to her merchants," he broadly declared, "it is of no benefit to her banks, it is of no benefit to her insurance companies, it is of no benefit to her real-estate interests."

Again, at other times, rate differentials divided the interests of those in the same business. From the standpoint of the origin of the Interstate Commerce Act, one of the most important local conflicts existed in western Pennsylvania between the Rockefeller forces and the competing independent oil producers. Through the ability to command exorbitant rebates from the railroads, Rockefeller was slowly forcing his rivals out of business. In self-defense the independents joined to bring pressure on their congressman for government regulation of the railroads, especially for an antirebate law. Their campaign led directly to the introduction of John H. Reagan's bill into the House of Representatives in 1878. While that bill eventually became the basic House bill and was in large part made law in 1887, it came too late for the independent oil producers who had surrendered to Rockefeller by 1880.

Other business groups throughout the country joined the attack on discriminatory railroad practices. Merchants handling dairy goods in the north-central states complained because they were charged much higher rates on butter and cheese than the merchants shipping meats or lard had to pay. There seemed to be no defense against such injustices, they argued, and they called for federal action to end them. Steamboat operators also objected to the railroad practice of cutting rates to the bare minimum when competing with water lines. The railroads could make up their losses on noncompetitive lines; the steamships could not. By such methods, explained J. B. Wood, an agent of the St. Louis and New Orleans Anchor Line, railroads tried to ruin the steamship lines. Even those men engaged in the jewelry trade were critical of the railroads and wanted some type of regulation. The roads generally did not want to bother with the small but valuable jewelry trunks and made it very difficult for the jewelers to transport their goods. That was unfair, the jewelers argued; they were willing to assume the risk for their goods, if they could only get the reasonable transportation services that the roads had previously refused them.

The new system of railroad transportation not only established a wider sphere of competition and made advantageous freight rates a major factor in commercial success but also fragmented the interests of American businessmen. Gradually, businessmen made alliances on the basis of their attitude toward government regulation of the railroads, each operating from his own motives and for his own interests. The struggle over the role government should play in the railroad system divided businessmen into four main groups. The largest of them, composed of the men who suffered from unfavorable differentials, strongly urged government action to protect their interests or, as they phrased it, to insure the public welfare. "In our judgment the time has arrived," read a statement of the Toledo Produce Exchange, "when Congress should assume its undoubted right and duty to the whole of the country, to supervise the whole system of transportation in this country." The Peoria Board of Trade was even more specific: "The best method of preventing extortion and discrimination," it declared, "is by means of stringent laws passed by Congress."

Often businessmen who favored strong legislation to control interstate commerce revealed marked antipathy to the railroads. Eastern merchants shared much the same attitude traditionally associated with midwestern farmers. The railroads "have come to the conclusion apparently that they are masters of the situation," charged James H. Seymour, representing the New York Mercantile Exchange, "and they treat it as if it was a business of their own, a private business, not a public business, and do not seem to regard themselves as doing business for the public." James Spear, a Philadelphia manufacturer, took another tack, striking at an obvious failing of the roads. "My complaint," he stated, "would be simply a general complaint of bad management of all the railroads in the United States. . . ."

The great majority of the businessmen who favored government regulation gave wholehearted support to the idea of a watchdog commission that would be empowered to prohibit unfair railroad practices. In large part, general confidence in the commission system stemmed from relatively successful experiences, especially in Massachusetts, during the previous decade. "It seems reasonable," remarked J. D. Seeberger, a wholesale hardware dealer in Des Moines, Iowa, referring to the commission plan, "that, according to the working of the commission in this State, it might operate successfully in an enlarged sphere." Businessmen wanted effective regulation, not some untried experiment. They felt that the commission system had proved itself, and they were willing to support it.

Many businessmen disagreed about the exact amount of control that the commission should exercise; yet they wanted it to have enough authority to be effective. Many suggested that either the commission be given judicial powers to decide law suits brought against the roads or have its findings made *prima facie* evidence in any court of law in the nation. Few would have gone along with M. A. Fulton, a Wisconsin merchant, who urged that Congress should pass an "absolute law" which would establish rates throughout the country. Such a plan was much too rigid.

A second, smaller group of businessmen took a more cautious approach. Their economic positions demanded some type of government regulation, but they were unsure as to both the type of legislation needed and all the ramifications of such action. "My opinion is that Congress should go pretty slow upon the subject of regulating, or attempting to regulate, freight rates," declared E. O. Stanard, a St. Louis mill owner, "especially at this time, when everything is so depressed." Charles Ridgely, president of the Springfield Iron Company, expressed the same concern that government action might harm business activity in general. "Less damage to business is likely to occur from doing too little in the way of regulation of interstate commerce than from doing too much," he told the Cullom committee. Still, under the circumstances, both men acknowledged the need for federal regulation.

In spite of their fear that regulation might cause further economic hardships and an inbred suspicion of government interference, many businessmen allowed economic necessity to overcome most of their doubts. *Bradstreet's* best represented many of the businessmen in that group; and although the magazine did not support the Cullom bill, it did concede that "With this demand for the passage of a national law, there exists a general acquiescence even on the part of railroad men themselves in the principles of a national railroad commission."

A third group, much smaller than the first two, formed around those men—predominantly railroad men and investors in weaker railroad bonds—who advocated government regulation not for the protection of the public but for the welfare of the struggling roads. James D. Furber, the manager of the Boston and Maine Railroad, asked Congress for a law prohibiting rebates. "They are very annoying in your accounts and annoying to the railroads," he explained; "there is nothing fair about it to the public or to the railway. . . ." W. G. Raoul, president of the Central Railroad and Banking Company of Georgia, went even further by suggesting that Congress should pass laws to insure fairer profits for the railroads and a just return on capital investments. Furber and Raoul drew support from such railroad presidents as John King of the Erie, J. C. Clarke of the Illinois Central, Frank S. Bond of the Reading, and George B. Roberts of the Pennsylvania, all of whom favored federal regulation that would aid the lines suffering from overexpansion and rate wars.

The major railroad journals gave voice to the same demands and the same goals. They defended the roads as essential to the well-being of the American economy and argued that they deserved to be protected from harmful legislation. The *Railway World* declared that the roads had "rendered an immense amount of service to the American people, and done more than any other single agency to generate national prosperity." Not content with such self-praise, the *Railway Age* insisted that: "The vast interests represented in and connected with the operation of railways are entitled not only to protection from injustice but to friendly fostering by the government." The other journals took similar stands, admitting both the right and need for federal action, but contended that the legislation should help rather than hinder the railroads.

Although Chauncey M. Depew of the New York Central had declared that "all the leading railroad men, I think, admit the principle of government supervision and are anxious for it," railroad men clearly disagreed with the type of legislation that most other businessmen had in mind. The economic structure of late nineteenth-century America forced railroad men, as it had forced other businessmen, to seek the protection of the federal government.

A fourth distinct group of businessmen rejected the idea of federal regulation of the railroads and were driven by two entirely different motives. One such group of men opposed railroad regulation because they thought that any such legislation would only aid the railroads to the detriment of everyone else. Regulation in their minds was actually a crutch for the roads. Francis B. Thurber, a New York wholesale grocer who had long been interested in the problems of transportation, spoke for this group when he told the Cullom committee that the railroads were the chief supporters of federal regulation: "The trouble is, with many railroad men who have failed in the tasks required of them, to pay dividends on the capitalization, that they want now to appeal to the Government to help them out." He advised them to stay with the doctrine of competition, even though it might work temporary hardship on some people. A similar view was expressed by J. H. Walker, a Massachusetts manufacturer, who stated that "great injury... would be done to the country by any effort to protect the owners of the railroads." Although they overestimated by far the number of railroad men who favored the final Interstate Commerce Act, Thurber and Walker were well aware of the attempt made by railroad men to secure the passage of a favorable regulatory law.

The other group that opposed government regulation argued from both practical and theoretical bases; they combined the plea that the complexities of railroad management were beyond the competence of legislation with their adherence to principles of laissez faire and free enterprise. Although the members of that group may have believed firmly in their laissez-faire principles, they were also usually individuals who prospered under the status quo—either spokesmen for companies that enjoyed profitable rate differentials or owners of high-dividend railroad stocks. Charles A. Pillsbury, one of the major and most successful shippers in the nation as well as one who commanded lucrative rebates, was a perfect example. "We have no complaints to make," he truthfully informed the committee.

Charles E. Perkins, president of the Chicago, Burlington, and Quincy Railroad, was the most outspoken member of that small but determined group. Not only did he refuse to admit the existence of any but the rarest case of railroad abuse but also he attacked just about every proposal of regulation that had been suggested. He denounced the plan of publicized railroad rates, denied the possible efficacy of any scheme of rate-fixing, attacked uniform accounting laws, justified pools and price discriminations, and rejected the idea of annual railroad reports to the government.

"The wisdom of any legislation which may look to changing the conditions which have produced results on the whole so beneficial," he confidently stated, "may well be doubted." The real evil, he suggested, was that an erroneous public opinion might force the passage of laws that would seriously harm the whole economic structure of the nation and very likely lead to complete government ownership of the railroads. "Among the evils of Government ownership and control," he predicted, "would undoubtedly be higher charges and increased taxation." Perkins' resentment against the Interstate Commerce Act died hard. Two years after its passage, in a pamphlet published by the C. B. & Q., he called the law unwise, impractical, and one of the greatest burdens under which the roads had to operate.

Perkins had one prominent counterpart. The *Commercial and Financial Chronicle* led a determined opposition against government regulation and defended a strict version of laissez faire. In 1874, commenting on the business recession, it had noted:

> trade is suffering from those general sources of commercial disturbance which have been often demonstrated to be as far beyond the reach of human

legislation as are the meterological [sic] forces that bring about a late spring or a wet summer, or a copious harvest. As the world grows wiser men are getting to recognize more and more the marvellous wisdom of the great doctrine of the French economists, *"laissez-faire et laissez-passer."*

Following its guiding principle, the *Chronicle* continually attacked the idea of government regulation of the railroads. "Hardly anything can be more dangerous just now than any further extension of Congressional power," it declared in 1879; and two years later, it noted that federal regulation "can be anything but a failure we have but the slightest expectation." When Congress was preparing the final version of the Interstate Commerce Act in 1886, the *Chronicle* angrily insisted that "The measure as proposed is so full of crudities and so totally at variance with all economic and we might almost say moral laws that it passes comprehension how an intelligent body of men can countenance or recommend certain of its provisions."

In spite of the air of certainty and authority that marked its pages, the *Chronicle* represented only a small minority of the businessmen concerned with interstate transportation. Few American businessmen shared the journal's belief in the benevolent workings of laissez-faire economics, at least in regard to the problem of the railroads. They were much more interested in operating their businesses more efficiently and profitably. Most business groups saw government regulation as a necessary means to that end.

Businessmen showed little interest in philosophical distinctions. The great majority of them rejected laissez-faire economics and cared little for the theory of the survival of the fittest, often considered the basis of business philosophy. Hardly anyone who testified before the Cullom committee even mentioned the concept. Businessmen were much more concerned with the evils of rate discrimination, the effects of pooling, and the value of long-and-short-haul legislation than they were with the laws of nature, the benevolence of competition, or the loss of an abstract liberty. The very few men who even made reference to the concept clearly rejected it. John H. Devereux, the president of the Cleveland, Columbus, Cincinnati, & Indianapolis Railroad, who claimed that "absolutely the railroad interests of this country are going to destruction," believed that regulation was necessary for the good of the roads. The chaos in the railway industry was "not to be remedied by waiting upon 'the survival of the fittest.'" That "misapplied phrase" had nothing to do with the condition of the railroads, Devereux explained, and was of no help in attempting to improve the situation. "The law of 'survival' may apply to animals," he emphasized, "but not to railroads...." George W. Parker, vice president and general manager of the St. Louis, Alton, & Terre Haute Railroad, expressed the same pragmatic attitude when he said simply that "the theory of the 'survival of the fittest' does not apply to railroads. . . ." Parker, like Devereux, accepted the necessity of regulation and urged pooling as the solution to railroad conflict. Even Poor's *Manual*, which complained of the difficulties that afflicted the roads in 1885, declared firmly that the theory of survival did not work in the railroad business. "Railroads," the editors argued, "unfortunately, seem to reverse the rule of 'the survival of the fittest,' to 'the survival of the unfittest.'"

Businessmen were thus more interested in solving particular problems than they were in adhering to any "business philosophy." Perhaps on a different issue they might have appealed to the theory of survival of the fittest or to the principles of free competition, but when it was clearly contrary to their interests they readily abandoned both of them. There could be no question that the vast majority of them viewed some type of government action as a necessity for their economic welfare.

When Congress was seriously debating the interstate commerce bill in 1885 and 1886, businessmen throughout the nation supported the idea of regulation in overwhelming numbers. During the first session of the Forty-ninth Congress petitions from business groups were almost unanimous in favoring federal action. Criticism grew only after the Senate-House conference had worked out a final proposal. Then, businessmen who would have been harmed by the specific type of regulation Congress had accepted protested against the offending provisions in the bill, especially against the antipooling and long-and-short-haul clauses. Since those merchants located close to markets favored the long-and-short-haul clause, most opposition to that provision came from shippers in western cities such as Chicago and Springfield. These opponents of the interstate commerce bill did not attack the idea of regulation; they complained only that certain parts of the bill would be harmful to their economic positions. Regulation would be fine, they argued, so long as it was "helpful" regulation.

The opposing reactions of millers in St. Louis and Minneapolis, rivals in the flour trade, were typical of the reactions among competing businessmen across the nation. Since Minneapolis had a great advantage over St. Louis before 1887, due to the availability of cheap water transportation and the ability of her millers to force large rebates from the competing roads, Minneapolis flour merchants were unanimous in attacking the conference bill—saving special condemnation for the long-and-short-haul clauses. St. Louis merchants, however, hoping that the new provisions would enable them to compete more favorably with the northern center, favored the bill and expected it to accomplish "a great deal of good." The *Weekly Northwestern Miller*, a journal of the Minneapolis milling interests, frankly summarized the opposing reactions by observing that the interests of the two cities seemed "diametrically opposed." The editors were not surprised that most St. Louis businessmen supported the bill.

Although many railroad men had supported legislation favorable to the roads, most of them agreed that the interstate commerce bill was not the law they had wanted. Although Kolko's assertion that railroad men agreed to the principle of federal regulation is undoubtedly true, his conclusion that the roads favored the final bill and for the most part "welcomed the signing of the new railroad law" is quite doubtful. Kolko himself admits that John Murray Forbes and William Bliss, two leading railroad men, were hostile to the new act. They were not alone. The presidents of most roads were dissatisfied with the House-Senate compromise bill and worked against its passage. They focused their opposition on Congress, bringing special pressure to bear on their senators and representatives. The presidents of all five of the Vanderbilt lines opposed the bill throughout 1887 and into 1888. Jay Gould and Leland Stanford denounced it. Samuel Sloan, president of the Delaware, Lackawanna, and Western, claimed that "The bill is impracticable and ought not to pass," while Clement A. Griscom, a director of the Pennsylvania, thought that there had already been too much legislation. "The Inter-State Commerce Bill...," wrote Frederick J. Kimball, president of the Norfolk and Western, "will, I think, break up the entire through transportation business of the country and will work great harm to all business interests."

Moreover, the actual positions of the major railroad journals ranged from general dissatisfaction to bitter hostility. The *Railroad Gazette*, the least antagonistic of the major industry journals, tended to accept the new law but still did not like it and declared that "it hampers business as badly as a much severer law" and could do "a great deal of harm." Although that journal claimed that the new law could be the basis for something better, its whole argument was that only if the roads obeyed the law could they show both the legislators and the public how bad it actually was, and hence bring about "something better."

The *Railway Review*, which showed much less restraint in its attack on the new law, stated that it was passed "by the votes of men who do not believe in it," because "their votes were forced from them by popular clamor." Referring to charges made during debate on the bill, the *Review* agreed that members of Congress "did not like the law" and that the bill was one "that nobody understood, that nobody wanted." It also charged that "The bill, as it now stands, places too great, too autocratic power in the hands of five men, and subjects them to too severe temptations." It was "unwise and unjust." The *Review* went far beyond the attacks of the other industry journals. "In fact, if the act had been devised by the enemies of the government and of the people of the United States," it declared on January 22, 1887, "the most merciless malice and the most careful deliberation could hardly have hit upon a measure more deadly and far-reaching in its effects."

The other leading industry journals also expressed grave doubts and deep fears over the proposed measure. The Reagan-Cullom bill "will seriously jeopardize the efficiency of numerous links of the existing through railways systems," declared the *Railway World.* "That any important movement in such a direction will be a serious error can scarcely be doubted." The mainspring for much of the regulatory legislation, the *World* asserted, "seems to be furnished by a supposition that plans can be devised whereby the nation can be enriched by impoverishing the railways." "This is sorry work for an American congress," the *World* concluded. "The injurious effects of the interstate commerce law ought to cause serious reflection on the part of the makers and supporters of this law," declared the *Railway Age,* which continued to oppose the act into 1888 and 1889. "The law has put a premium on reckless competition and incited all kinds of sharp practices" in the competitive railroad industry. "The utter heartlessness of the law" marked it off from all other regulatory attempts. "In some of its features the interstate commerce law defies the natural principle of justice and equity, and hence it cannot endure without reform." Even the commission which was supposed to interpret the law "conservatively" drew the scorn of that journal. The members "seem to have moved with the current of popular opinion into the feeling that the interstate commerce law was intended solely for the repression and punishment of the railway interest," the *Railway Age* complained bitterly, "and not to any degree for its protection."

Thus there was widespread and vocal opposition to the Interstate Commerce Act on the part of many railroad executives. That they generally welcomed the bill appears doubtful. Granted, some railroad managers—for various reasons—did either support or accept the act. The point is that there was strong and determined opposition and much division of opinion. Railroad men were neither satisfied with the bill generally nor were they its strongest supporters. Very likely the great division of opinion among the roads gave other interests a greater weight than they might otherwise have had against a united railroad lobby.

Just as the railroads were not the major advocates behind the Interstate Commerce Act, neither were the New York merchants nor any other single group. Support for government regulation was, in fact, widespread among businessmen; and that near unanimity was more important in forcing federal action than was the endorsement by any one group. The primary dynamism behind the drive for regulation was the threatening pattern of economic changes that forced most businessmen in all lines of commerce to seek federal intervention as a means of protecting their own individual interests. The desire for economic protection was the one and only unifying force among those who supported regulation; and it cut across all commercial and geographic boundaries and swept up the great majority of American businessmen into an effective movement for the assertion of their interests through the federal government.

It was neither "the people" nor "the farmers"—nor even "the businessmen"—who were responsible for the government regulation of railroads. Rather, it was many diverse economic groups in combination throughout the nation which felt threatened by the new national economy and sought to protect their interests through the federal government. Often they were unsure of the exact means to be used, but they were clear about the end they hoped to accomplish. The railroads were necessary for the prosperity of most businessmen, and they intended to force the roads to serve their purposes. The so-called "business philosophy" of the late-nineteenth century meant little to most businessmen, at least when it conflicted with their practical commercial needs. "We are not aware that there is the slightest principle involved in the question," observed the *Banker's Magazine* in discussing the issue of railroad regulation; "it is one purely of self-interest." Such a broad statement might perhaps be harsh, yet it surely described the attitude of American businessmen toward the Interstate Commerce Act.

4

The Advent of Industrial Society

Conflict or Acquiescence?

American society during the second half of the nineteenth century underwent a series of profound changes. In addition to rapid physical growth, the nature and quality of life, personal and social relationships, political and economic structures, and work habits and goals all underwent a fundamental transformation. Consequently, the American people were faced with a series of major problems that seemed to threaten many traditional institutions and values that had given them a sense of stability, order, and purpose.

Although historians were aware that the United States was undergoing a basic transformation, they were by no means agreed about either its nature or its desirability. Some—particularly those in the Progressive tradition of American historiography—were ambivalent toward change. Conceding that industrialization had certain beneficent consequences, they nevertheless insisted that it could have been achieved in a more humane manner and in ways that would have diminished social and economic inequalities. These scholars emphasized the themes of conflict and discontinuity; they interpreted social change as a product of a creative tension between the mass of people and a much smaller hegemony-seeking business class. Other historians—especially those in the neo-conservative tradition—were less critical of the process of industrialization, which they believed had given to the American people an unprecedented level of material prosperity and a more just social order. Still other scholars who were associated with the newer organizational school and who supported the use of social science concepts and methodologies were somewhat less concerned with offering moral judgments; they were primarily interested in describing and analyzing the process of industrialization and the ways in which it shaped the lives of millions of people from different walks of life.

Until 1950 most scholars writing about the emergence of industrial society were affiliated with the Progressive school of American historiography. Committed to an ideology based upon the twin pillars of democracy and progress, they remained ambivalent in their approach. On the one hand, they conceded that economic growth and technological change provided the American people with a steadily rising standard of living. On the other hand, they disliked the excesses and evils accompanying industrialization, particularly the efforts of special interest business groups to dominate the economy and control politics. Hence they interpreted American history in terms of a perpetual conflict between the people and their would-be oppressors.

Such a conceptualization helped to create a unique kind of periodization in which liberal reform and conservative consolidation followed each other with almost monotonous regularity. The character of each period was most accurately reflected in its politics. Political struggles mirrored the clash of the people versus special interests; key presidential elections represented dramatic turning points. Implicit in the work of Progressive historians were three vital assumptions: first, that most political actions were motivated by economic self-interest; second, that voting behavior reflected with a high degree of certainty the self-interest of the electorate; and third, the national party platforms were synchronized with the views of the voting public.

Typical of the political emphasis of Progressive historians was Horace S. Merrill's study of midwestern politics from 1865 to 1896. The most conspicuous and dynamic class in America after the Civil War, Merrill insisted, was the "industrialist and financier clan." With a singular purpose and unprecedented speed these entrepreneurs turned the nation's resources and people "into instruments of unprecedented gain." Over a period of time, however, opposition forces made up of discontented farmers and unhappy wage-earners slowly entered politics in an effort to redress the imbalance. Initially their efforts failed, largely because the Democratic party remained under the control of a "cabal of industrialist-financier entrepreneurs operating within the Democratic party.... [Their] task was to occupy the only really vulnerable outpost in the political-economic empire of big business, the discontented agrarian Middle West." The nomination of Bryan in 1896 signaled a defeat for these conservative Democrats. Although Bryan lost his bid for the presidency, later liberal leaders from Wilson's New Freedom to Franklin Delano Roosevelt's New Deal "utilized the experience of 1896 as an invaluable guide.... The people were learning."[1]

Given the emphasis on the primacy of politics and the division of American society into two distinct groupings, it was not surprising that Progressive historians avoided detailed studies of specific groups. Al-

---

[1]Horace S. Merrill, *Bourbon Democracy of the Middle West 1865–1896* (Baton Rouge, 1953), pp. 1–2, 272–274. See also Matthew Josephson's *The Robber Barons: The Great American Capitalists 1861–1901* (New York, 1934) and *The Politicos, 1865–1896* (New York, 1938).

though writing about farmers and workers, they ignored the persistence of ethnic, racial, religious, and social groups. Committed to an assimilationist and democratic model of society, these historians never imagined that the loyalty of individuals was not necessarily unitary in nature, nor was it defined solely in economic terms. Instead they assumed the existence of a mass of undifferentiated Americans held together by "common cosmic forces of morality and reason." Similarly, their opponents included "limited cultural and economic groups which sought special power and privilege."[2]

After the Second World War the Progressive synthesis slowly came under attack by neo-conservative historians who approached the American experience with quite different assumptions. These scholars were less inclined to emphasize conflict and discontinuity; they saw consensus and continuity as the major themes of American history. Nor were neo-conservatives inclined to denigrate their nation; compared with regimes elsewhere in the world the shortcomings of the United States paled into relative insignificance.

Nowhere were the differences between Progressive and neo-conservative historians better revealed than in Daniel J. Boorstin's trilogy *The Americans*. In the second and third volumes, dealing with the nineteenth and twentieth centuries, Boorstin all but ignored the earlier political periodization of American history. In its place he substituted a set of enduring traits shared by most Americans, including a pragmatism and an ingenuity that permitted individuals to develop their nation in novel ways.

The decades after the Civil War, Boorstin noted in the opening pages of his third volume, were the halcyon days of the "Go-Getters" who went in search of what others had never imagined. "The Go-Getters made something out of nothing, they brought meat out of the desert, found oil in the rocks, and brought light to millions. They discovered new resources, and where there seemed none to be discovered, they invented new ways of profiting from others who were trying to invent and to discover." At the same time innumerable communities of consumers came into existence, without which the entrepreneurial and inventive drive of individuals would have been frustrated. These consumption communities, Boorstin noted, were quick, nonideological, democratic, public, vague, and rapidly shifting. "Consumption communities produced more consumption communities. . . . Never before had so many men been united by so many things." Even after nearly four centuries Americans continued to live between the wild and the frontier; their world had never become "settled."[3] Throughout his tril-

---

[2] Samuel P. Hays, "The Social Analysis of American Political History, 1880–1920," *Political Science Quarterly*, LXXX (September, 1965), p. 375.

[3] Daniel J. Boorstin, *The Americans: The Democratic Experience* (New York, 1973), pp. 3, 90, 600.

ogy Boorstin's tone remained celebratory; he interpreted the American experience largely in terms of an underlying and basic unity.

Neo-conservative historians, however, never attained the dominant position once enjoyed by their Progressive predecessors. Indeed, by the 1950's a number of historians had already begun to create a new synthesis that described and explained the rise of modern American industrial society. Based upon insights drawn from the social and behavioral sciences, these historians developed an approach best subsumed under the title the "organizational school." Their assumption was that the most important characteristic of modern America was the existence of large-scale, national, and formal organizations that were bureaucratically structured. These organizations cut across political, economic, occupational, and social boundaries, and gave order and coherence to American society.[4]

Concern with the role of organizations in defining the character of modern society, of course, was not new. By the early part of the twentieth century Max Weber, the seminal German social theorist, had already emphasized the importance of hierarchical and bureaucratic authority in modern society. Weber distinguished between charisma and bureaucracy. The former was characterized by decision-making by individuals who were bound by no rules. In a bureaucratic setting, by way of contrast, power was allocated according to abstract rules, which defined responsibility and authority. Decision-making thus became impersonal; "experts" filled positions, which survived intact even when personnel changed. To Weber the triumph of the organizational model was due to its emphasis on efficiency. "Experience," he noted, "tends universally to show that the purely bureaucratic type of administration . . . is, from a purely technical point of view, capable of attaining the highest degree of efficiency and is in this sense formally the most rational known means of carrying out imperative control over human beings."[5]

After the Second World War interest in the implications of organizational growth intensified. Despite the enduring popularity of the ideology of the self-made man, it was evident that large and complex organizations had sharply transformed the nature of American society. Bureaucracies in one form or another dominated the economy, played a central role in the exercise of public authority, and shaped all aspects of life. To most individuals in modern America the choices they faced were largely determined by the activities of private and public organizations.

One manifestation of this heightened concern with the role of organization was the publication during the 1950's and after of a number

---

[4]For an analysis of the organizational school see Louis Galambos, "The Emerging Organizational Synthesis in Modern American History," *Business History Review*, XLIV (Autumn, 1970), pp. 279–290.

[5]Quoted in Louis Galambos, *The Public Image of Big Business in America, 1880–1940: A Quantitative Study in Social Change* (Baltimore, 1975), p. 4.

of scholarly works that explored the full ramifications of this phenomenon. Many of these studies were read by a large audience, and their influence extended beyond the disciplines of their authors. In 1950 David Riesman published his study of the changing American character. He traced the transition from the "inner-directed" person of the nineteenth century to the "other-directed" person of the twentieth. The latter, Riesman maintained, was a response to the fact that most individuals functioned in a bureaucratic and organizational setting where success was a function of the approval of others. Two years later John Kenneth Galbraith's analysis of American capitalism appeared; he noted that the growth of certain kinds of organizations immediately stimulated the growth of other organizations to act as a countervailing force. In 1953 Kenneth Boulding's *The Organizational Revolution* appeared; it was among the earliest works to delineate explicitly the impact of organizational change upon the lives of people. In 1956 William H. Whyte's *The Organization Man* popularized a theme that had its fictional counterpart in Sloan Wilson's *The Man in the Gray Flannel Suit*. During this same decade C. Wright Mills, a sociologist whose writings played an important role in the radicalism of the 1960's, also published a number of studies that analyzed specific occupational groups within an organizational setting. While all of these authors stressed the crucial importance of organizational growth, they did not necessarily agree on its desirability or morality. Some were neutral; some were favorable, and some were hostile because of the negative effect of bureaucracy on individual personality and the degree to which private organizations exercised public power.[6]

A heightened sensitivity toward a contemporary issue invariably influences the direction of historical research. It was not surprising, therefore, that some historians would begin to borrow concepts and data from the social and behavioral sciences in order to develop an organizational and bureaucratic framework capable of illuminating the structure of modern American society. The emerging organizational school began with the proposition that the single most important change in American history was the shift from small, local, and informal structures to large, bureaucratic, and regional or national organizations. In this new society, they emphasized, the means of production and distribution were mechanized; social relations became impersonal; and the advent of mass communications created more uniform attitudes. Moreover, industrial

---

[6]David Riesman, *The Lonely Crowd: A Study of the Changing American Character* (New Haven, 1950); John Kenneth Galbraith, *American Capitalism: The Concept of Countervailing Power* (Boston, 1952); Kenneth Boulding, *The Organizational Revolution: A Study in the Ethics of Economic Organization* (New York, 1953); Sloan Wilson, *The Man in the Gray Flannel Suit* (New York, 1955); William H. Whyte, *The Organization Man* (New York, 1956); C. Wright Mills, *White Collar: The American Middle Classes* (New York, 1951), and *The Power Elite* (New York, 1956).

discipline and regularized work patterns replaced older and more informal work habits, and efficiency and faith in science and technology became dominant social values in American society.

This shift in perspective had important consequences for the writing of American history. It implied, for example, that the study of particular individuals or small groups, no matter how prominent, was not as significant as the study of larger aggregate groups or those impersonal forces that determined relationships between groups. Whereas earlier scholars identified and studied key leaders, organizational historians were more concerned with groups, especially their values, roles, and the manner in which they related to each other. In place of the simple dualisms that posited an undifferentiated people struggling against special interests, newer historians emphasized a pluralistic approach. They identified groups by using a variety of characteristics, including class, race, culture, religion, ethnicity, and occupation, to cite only a few. Even conflict was no longer defined exclusively in economic terms; organizationally minded historians noted that many inter-group conflicts revolved around cultural, religious, and moral issues. Indeed, by the 1960's ethno-cultural historians were insisting that voting behavior often reflected cultural, religious, and ethnic affiliations, which to many individuals were far more important than strictly economic issues.

The first organizationally minded historians tended to come out of the fields of business and economic history. This was not entirely unexpected, since business firms were among the earliest to develop complex and bureaucratically structured organizations in order to raise large amounts of capital and to carry out complex functions that extended over a wide geographical area. Among the first to study business and economic history in organizational terms was Alfred D. Chandler, Jr. Unwilling to accept the value-laden approach characteristic of Progressive historians who had made the corporation a symbol of greed and avarice, Chandler focused on the origins of economic organizations and their complex structures. A number of factors, he noted, provided an environment conducive to the growth of organizations: the westward expansion of population; the construction of a national railroad network; the application of new sources of power (the internal combustion engine and electricity) to industry and transportation; and the application of findings in the natural and physical sciences.

> The coming of the large vertically integrated, centralized, functionally departmentalized industrial organization altered the internal and external situations in which and about which business decisions were made. Information about markets, supplies, and operating performance as well as suggestions for action often had to come up through the several levels of the departmental hierarchies, while decisions and suggestions based on this data had to be transmitted down the same ladder for implementation. Executives on each level became increasingly specialists in one function—in sales, production,

purchasing, or finance—and most remained in one department and so handled one function only for the major part of their business careers. Only he who climbed to the very top of the departmental ladder had a chance to see his own company as a single operating unit. Where a company's markets, sources of raw materials, and manufacturing processes remained relatively stable... the nature of the business executive's work became increasingly routine and administrative.

Although his work was confined to business organizations, Chandler's use of organizational and bureaucratic concepts were capable of being applied in modified form to other kinds of organizations as well.[7]

While Chandler was analyzing the characteristics of the modern corporation, other scholars were beginning to apply organizational insights to the study of American society generally. Especially notable in this regard was the work of Samuel P. Hays, who emerged during the 1960's and 1970's as one of the leading spokesmen for the use of social and behavioral science concepts in historical research. In 1957 Hays published *The Response to Industrialism 1885–1914,* in which he described the all-pervading influence of industrialism and organizational change. Neither businessmen, farmers, nor workers individually could escape from an increasingly impersonal market. They soon discovered, however, that by uniting in groups they could wield considerable power. Producers joined together to control the conditions under which they sold their commodities; distributors organized to influence marketing and transportation; workers joined unions in order to have a say in the determination of wages, hours, and working conditions. The organizational revolution, Hays pointed out, "revealed the degree to which industrialism had shifted the context of economic decisions from personal relationships among individuals to a struggle for power among well-organized groups."[8]

In 1965 Hays spelled out his specific criticisms of the older Progressive synthesis that had posited a simple dualism between the "people" and special interests. The Progressive approach, he noted, "prevented historians from giving full attention to the political role of working people, the influence of ethno-cultural factors in politics, the changing characteristics of elites, the role of the business community in reform, the treatment of urban life as a system of social organization, the source of anti-reform impulses, the conflict between local and cosmopolitan cultures, the growth of bureaucracy and administration, the growth of education as a process of cultural transmission and social mobility, the development of ideology and its relationship to practice, and the exam-

---

[7]Alfred D. Chandler, Jr., "The Beginnings of 'Big Business' in American Industry," *Business History Review,* XXXIII (Spring, 1959), pp. 1–31. See also his book *Strategy and Structure: Chapters in the History of Industrial Enterprise* (Cambridge, 1962).

[8]Samuel P. Hays, *The Response to Industrialism 1885–1914* (Chicago, 1957), p. 48.

ination of inter-regional economic relationships." Most important, Hays concluded, the Progressive approach obscured the changes in decision-making in a "highly systematized society."[9]

In the first selection in this chapter, Hays delineates the changing political and organizational structures of modern American industrial cities. Eschewing the Progressive interpretation that identified "reformers" as those individuals concerned with solving urban problems, Hays argues that urban development can best be understood in terms of a constant tension between those forces making for decentralization and those making for centralization in human relationships and institutions, between social differentiation and social integration, between those who wanted to establish smaller contexts of life in home, church, and school, and those who wanted to discipline and to link the activities of people into more highly organized systems. Although a community of human relationships continued to exist in most cities, Hays finds that the forces working for centralization triumphed, thus completely altering the character of urban life, its productive organizations, and its political structures.

By the 1960's a number of historians were employing organizational themes in their work. Especially notable was Robert H. Wiebe's *The Search for Order 1877–1920*, which gained immediate recognition from his fellow historians. For much of the nineteenth century, according to Wiebe, America was a "society of island communities" weakly linked and largely autonomous in character. The heart of this social system was "local autonomy." Few Americans could even conceive of managerial government; almost "all of a community's affairs were still arranged informally." By the 1880's and 1890's, however, Americans confronted a crisis of the first magnitude. The "island communities" broke down because of rapid economic, technological, and demographic change. Americans, according to Wiebe, then adopted a bureaucratic solution to fill the threatening void. The rise of a "new middle class" of professionals holding bureaucratic and organizational values provided the American people with a new kind of social order. By the First World War the complex of institutional arrangements had become so entrenched that few people contemplated any other alternatives.[10]

While Hays and Wiebe were describing organizational changes in the late-nineteenth and twentieth centuries, other scholars were beginning to study how and why bureaucratic values were disseminated throughout American society. In a quantitative study employing content analysis, Louis Galambos studied the growing acceptance of organizational and bureaucratic values among Americans generally. Taking certain key occupational groups and their attitudes toward big business

---

[9]Hays, "The Social Analysis of American Political History," pp. 392–393.

[10]Robert H. Wiebe, *The Search for Order 1877–1920* (New York, 1967), p. xiii.

from 1880 to 1940 (which centered on antitrust), Galambos noted that the middle classes first manifested anger toward large corporate enterprise. The process of accommodation and toleration, however, began as early as the 1890's and was all but completed by the Second World War. "The people," he concluded, "seem content with organizational values and giant bureaucracies. For most Americans, antitrust exists only as a chapter in history, an episode they study while preparing themselves for a bureaucratic career in a society steeped in the values of the corporate future."[11]

Concern with bureaucratization also stimulated interest in the phenomenon of professionalization. Before the Civil War only law, medicine, and religion were regarded as legitimate professions. Indeed, a profession traditionally was defined by the "character" of its members rather than by their knowledge or training. After 1880, on the other hand, the concept of a profession underwent fundamental changes. In a modernized society a profession was defined by the possession of a series of specific attributes: the existence of a presumably systematic body of special knowledge; authority derived from the possession of formal knowledge not understood by laypeople; community sanction, often in the form of a legal grant of powers and privileges (licensing); an implicit or explicit code of ethics; and a unity and corporateness in the membership.

In one of the early studies of the process of professionalization Roy Lubove applied the insights of organizational history to the development of social work as a profession. "Specialization and the idealization of expertise, the growth of an occupational subculture, and bureaucratization were instrumental in shaping the character of twentieth-century social work," Lubove concluded. "These typical features of an urban-industrial society have affected not only the professions but most spheres of life, and their controlling influence will undoubtedly remain potent." Modern social work, then, reflected the bureaucratic goals of efficiency and detached rationality. Nor was social work atypical. In a similar vein Raymond E. Callahan insisted that the ideals of efficiency and administrative rationality were borrowed from business by educational innovators who wanted to emulate the successes of the modern corporation.[12]

Organizational historians also attempted to demonstrate the widespread pervasiveness of the values of efficiency and detached rationality in American society. In an influential study Samuel P. Hays insisted that the conservation movement between 1890 and 1920 was motivated by a

[11]Galambos, *The Public Image of Big Business in America*, p. 268.

[12]Roy Lubove, *The Professional Altruist: The Emergence of Social Work as a Career 1880–1930* (Cambridge, 1965), p. 220; Raymond E. Callahan, *Education and the Cult of Efficiency* (Chicago, 1962). See also Samuel Haber, *Efficiency and Uplift: Scientific Management in the Progressive Era, 1890–1920* (Chicago, 1964).

concern with the rational, scientific, and efficient use of natural resources. The conservation movement, he noted, was not antibusiness,
as Progressive historians had inferred, nor were businessmen necessarily opposed to conservation. Indeed, many large corporations were in
the vanguard of the movement to exploit resources in a rational and
scientific manner. Hays found that small farmers and individual entrepreneurs tended to oppose conservation; they desired a free hand to do as
they pleased in the hope of gaining instant wealth. [13]

Organizationally minded historians, however, were by no means the
only group that challenged the validity of the Progressive and neo-
conservative syntheses. During the 1960's a small group of "new social
historians"—most of whom had absorbed the insights of the organizational school—had begun to alter the scope of historical inquiry. Less
interested in individuals or small elites, they were concerned, to quote
Hays, "with human interaction, no matter what its manifest topical
content, whether economic, political, religious or intellectual.... [S]o-
cial history assumes that when large numbers of people exist in relationship to each other... patterns of common and distinct characteristics
emerge. The task of social history is to describe and analyze these patterns."[14]

The roots of the "new" social history were, of course, varied. Part of
the impetus to create new ways of looking at the past came from French
scholarship, which since the 1930's had sought to end traditional disciplinary barriers in order to understand the totality of human activities
within a given society. Equally significant were the contributions of
English scholars like Edward Thompson and Eric Hobsbawn, which
recreated the lives of English workers. Thompson and Hobsbawn were
less concerned with labor organizations than with the culture and experiences of workers and the ways in which they resisted or accommo-
dated themselves to new patterns of life and work. At the same time
many American scholars in the social and behavioral sciences were beginning to appreciate the persistence of group loyalties. The result was a
partial repudiation of the "melting pot" approach and a renewed concern with ethnic and racial groups.

Still another influence on the "new" social history came from individuals associated in part with the "New Left." Rejecting an emphasis
on the role of elites, these scholars charged that their colleagues had
failed to take into account the life experiences of the inarticulate masses
of Americans. Instead of focusing on those groups who achieved recognition and success, historians had an obligation to interpret American
history from the point of view of those who spent their lives in obscurity

---

[13]Samuel P. Hays, *Conservation and the Gospel of Efficiency: The Progressive Conservation
Movement, 1890–1920* (Cambridge, 1959).

[14]Samuel P. Hays, "A Systematic Social History," in *American History: Retrospect and
Prospect,* ed. by George A. Billias and Gerald N. Grob (New York, 1971), pp. 317–318.

and who never shared the fruits of affluence. The American past, "New Left" historians insisted, included such elements as racism, poverty, exploitation, discrimination, and violence, and the profession had an obligation to study such phenomena. Indeed, the historical profession generally and not only the "New Left" was clearly influenced by the persistence of social problems, civil strife, and dissensions caused by the Vietnam War during and after the 1960's. Consequently, there was widespread interest in the study of hitherto neglected groups and the kinds of social problems that had been an enduring source of tension and conflict in American society.

Finally, by the 1960's a number of American historians were explicitly testing hypotheses and concepts first developed in the social and behavioral sciences, a development that clearly strengthened the "new" social history. Moreover, the rapid development of quantification and increased use of computer technology aided historians as they turned to hitherto neglected sources such as manuscript census schedules in their efforts to recreate the American social order and to illuminate the lives of millions of inarticulate persons who left little in the way of a written record.

Indicative of the growing interest in social history was the publication in 1964 of Stephan Thernstrom's *Poverty and Progress*. A student of Oscar Handlin—whose own studies of immigration and acculturation had laid the foundation for future work in this specialty—Thernstrom attempted to integrate a large body of data from original sources with concepts and methodologies taken from the social and behavioral sciences. Taking a small New England community in the late-nineteenth century (Newburyport, Massachusetts), he examined the manuscript census schedules between 1850 and 1880 to study a large number of ordinary men and women, most of whom began life without the advantages of family ties or property, during a time of rapid social and economic change. Thernstrom was particularly interested in testing the allegation that the United States was a land of opportunity for all people, irrespective of their origins. His findings were somewhat ambiguous. Few children of working-class families rose very far on the social scale; class antagonisms persisted in various forms; there was considerable out-migration by those who succeeded the least; and the lives of workers were by no means without their perils or rigors. Nevertheless, many ordinary working people did view America as a land of opportunity. The gains registered by them were modest—a step up the occupational scale and the acquisition of a small amount of property. "Yet *in their eyes*," Thernstrom concluded with some surprise, "these accomplishments must have loomed large."[15]

---

[15]Stephan Thernstrom, *Poverty and Progress: Social Mobility in a Nineteenth Century City* (Cambridge, 1964), pp. 164–165. See also Thernstrom's *The Other Bostonians: Poverty and Progress in the American Metropolis, 1880–1970* (Cambridge, 1973).

In subsequent work Thernstrom sought to explain why radical ideologies never found a fertile recruiting ground among American workers, a group that was adversely affected by the "brutality and rapacity" of the process of industrialization. By way of explanation, he noted that the working class was drawn into the new industrial society by a process "that encouraged accommodation and rendered disciplined protest difficult." Many workers and their children were provided with modest opportunities for advancement; those who failed to find such opportunities were tossed hopelessly about, "alienated but invisible and impotent."[16]

Thernstrom's pioneering work was symptomatic of the growing interest in studying the lives of working people (as compared with the Progressive and neo-conservative emphasis on prominent individuals or elite groups). The 1960's and 1970's saw the publication of a number of books and articles dealing with the experiences of blacks, Italians, Jews, Slavs, and Irish, to mention only a few. Nor were groups defined solely in ethnic or racial terms; an increasing number of scholars undertook research on woman and changing sex roles. Moreover, urban historians began to study the ways in which groups perceived of and related to each other. The result was the appearance of a number of community studies that dealt in part with the experiences of working-class persons.

The emphasis on the social, cultural, and ethnic environments of American workers soon created within the "new" social history a new subspecialty concerned with the history of the American working class. Before 1960 historians concerned with American labor generally dealt with the development of unions and strikes. Intellectual descendents of John R. Commons (an institutional economist who fathered a particular approach to the history of American workers), labor historians assumed that the hopes and aspirations of laborers could best be understood through an examination of unions and their leaders. These scholars were concerned with the evolution of the trade union as an institution and its role in the market place. "New social historians," on the other hand, were prone to point out that the majority of workers were not union members, and that an emphasis on unions as economic organizations tended to isolate the history of workers from their social and cultural environments. Like Thernstrom, most of these newer historians were concerned with the varied ways in which workers reacted to the changing industrial and technological scene.

Symptomatic of the new interest in the history of the working class was the work of Herbert G. Gutman. In his major attempt to synthesize his findings, Gutman divided American social and working-class history into three distinct periods: 1815–1843, 1843–1893, and 1893–1919. In the

---

[16]Stephan Thernstrom, "Urbanization, Migration, and Social Mobility in Late Nineteenth-Century America," in *Towards a New Past: Dissenting Essays in American History,* ed. by Barton J. Bernstein (New York, 1968), pp. 172–173.

first period the United States remained a preindustrial nation and drew its labor force from people who lived in a preindustrial culture. After 1843, however, industrial developments transformed the nation's social structure, thereby creating a profound tension "between the older American preindustrial social structure and the modernizing institutions that accompanied the development of industrial capitalism." After 1893 the United States reached industrial maturity. In each of these three periods, Gutman observed, there was a recurrent tension between native and immigrant workers fresh to factories whose success rested upon the inculcation of regular work habits and an industrially oriented discipline. In his closing statement Gutman called upon fellow historians to study "the transition of native and foreign-born American men and women to industrial society, and how that transition affected such persons and the society into which they entered."[17]

In earlier articles Gutman attempted to demonstrate that many of the older generalizations about workers were not completely warranted. His study of Paterson, New Jersey, during the 1870's, for example, rejected the view that industrialists reigned supreme in the late-nineteenth century. On the contrary, argued Gutman, the industrialist and not the worker was often perceived as a disruptive outsider challenging the small workshops and personal relationships characteristic of smaller cities as they entered a period of social and technological change. Consequently, when industrialists made certain demands on the citizenry—including the use of police during labor strife or the suppression of a newspaper—the action often provoked opposition among all elements of the population. In Paterson and other medium-size industrial cities, public opinion frequently favored the worker over the capitalist. Even in the absence of strong unions, workers were by no means powerless; they were able to mobilize significant support among non-working-class groups in their struggles with rising industrialists. Gutman's study of Paterson is included as the second selection in this chapter.

Paralleling the "new" social history was the rise of two closely related specialties, the "new" political history and the "new" urban history. Indeed, in many ways there was little to distinguish among the three fields. All were concerned with groups and group interaction; all were explicitly committed to the systematic testing of hypotheses borrowed from the social and behavioral sciences; all were influenced by contemporary social tensions in defining the questions they sought to answer; and all welcomed the application of quantitative techniques and computer technology to historical problems.

During the 1960's and 1970's "new political historians" posed sharp

---

[17]Herbert G. Gutman, "Work, Culture and Society in Industrializing America, 1815–1919," *American Historical Review*, LXXVIII (June, 1973), pp. 531–587. See also the recent collection of Gutman's articles, *Work, Culture, and Society in Industrializing America: Essays in American Working-Class and Social History* (New York, 1976).

challenges to both the Progressive school thesis that conflict arose out of socioeconomic differences and the neo-conservative allegation that Americans agreed as to certain basic philosophical postulates. "New political historians," by way of contrast, argued that ethno-cultural factors were key elements in political history. Americans, they insisted, did not vote along class lines. The most important elements in determining voter behavior rather were national origins and religious affiliation, both of which involved a particular world view and consequently gave rise to differences over such moral and cultural issues as prohibition, nativism, female suffrage, and Sunday observance laws. Political parties in turn adopted different positions on such issues, thereby appealing to different ethno-cultural groups.

Paul Kleppner, for example, in his social analysis of Midwestern politics from 1850 to 1900, wrote that ethno-cultural issues far exceeded in importance strictly economic concerns in the mind of the electorate. Studying voting behavior in terms of a series of variables that included occupation, ethnicity, religion, rural–urban differences, and wealth, Kleppner found that Republican strength was greatest among more evangelically inclined people, while the Democratic party tended to attract more ritualistic individuals. Similarly, Samuel P. Hays, using precinct returns from gubernatorial elections in Iowa from 1887 to 1914, found that the differences between the two parties were overwhelmingly ethnic and cultural; prohibition and woman's suffrage far exceeded in importance the so-called trust issue. When the Republicans (traditionally "dry") in 1916 nominated a "wet" candidate and the Democrats a "dry" one, many traditionally Democratic precincts went Republican, and some Republican precincts went Democratic. Hays concluded that historians had to "examine what people feel and think and experience, and see their political action as a product of these inner events" rather than imposing their own ideological views on the study of political history.[18]

Similarly, the questions posed by urban historians reflected the concerns of the organizational school and the "new" social and political history. In his study of New York City during the 1860's and 1870's, Seymour Mandelbaum insisted that machine politics was largely a means of bringing order to an urban area increasingly fragmented by social and economic change. "In a society of independent, individual decision-makers," Mandelbaum observed, "the mechanisms of the market place, which gave every commodity and every man a price, dominated society." Given weak lines of communication, the absence of

[18]Paul Kleppner, The Cross of Culture: A Social Analysis of Midwestern Politics 1850–1900 (New York, 1970); Samuel P. Hays, "History as Human Behavior," Iowa Journal of History, LVIII (July, 1960), pp. 196–197. For an extended treatment of ethno-cultural historians see Richard L. McCormick, "Ethno-Cultural Interpretations of Nineteenth-Century American Voting Behavior," Political Science Quarterly, LXXXIX (June, 1974), pp. 351–377.

patterns of deference and a legitimate leadership, only "a universal payment of benefits—a giant 'pay-off'—could pull the city together in a common effort." Ironically, the ultimate destruction of Boss Tweed and his machine in the name of "reform" in the early 1870's left New York City "without direction." The implications of Mandelbaum's work were clear. Urban machine politics was less a struggle between honesty and corruption and more an effort to deal with complex problems arising out of social and economic change in a society lacking appropriate institutions and certain kinds of leadership patterns. Implicit in his book was the conviction that organizational elaboration and group interaction were crucial to an understanding of urban politics in the late-nineteenth century.[19] Other urban historians studied the experiences of various ethnic and racial groups, the development of municipal services, social welfare, religious and philanthropic institutions, patterns of violence, physical growth, geographical and social mobility, the structure of economic opportunity, and the relationship between the electorate and government.[20]

By the 1970's scholars associated with the organizational school or the "new" social, political, and urban history had produced a significant body of work. One important result was a breakdown in the unity that had marked the Progressive and neo-conservative schools of American historiography. While a commitment to progress, consensus, and continuity was by no means absent, the bulk of American scholars were less inclined to erect the type of broad conceptual framework that characterized the work of their predecessors. Indeed, many contemporary American historians thinking about the problem would probably agree with a foreign scholar who denied that the very concept of progress was applicable to the study of history. "There is no universal content corresponding to the universal time-framework of history," he noted. "In the dimension of concrete historical reality there is only a multiplicity of particular contents, as partial and piecemeal as the particular portions of time to which particular men direct themselves with a view to realizing particular ends."[21]

Despite the increasing fragmentation of American history, certain questions will continue to be of interest to scholars and students alike, if only because any answer will have a bearing upon present concerns. At a time when Americans continue to debate policy issues involving social

---

[19]Seymour Mandelbaum, *Boss Tweed's New York* (New York, 1965), pp. 5, 58, 181.

[20]For a discussion of recent contributions to urban history see Stephan Thernstrom, "Reflections on the New Urban History," *Daedalus*, C (Spring, 1971), pp. 359–375, and Raymond A. Mohl, "The History of the American City," in *The Reinterpretation of American History and Culture*, ed. by William H. Cartwright and Richard L. Watson, Jr. (Washington, D.C., 1973), pp. 165–205.

[21]Nathan Rotensreich, "The Idea of Historical Progress and Its Assumptions," *History and Theory*, X (No. 2, 1971), p. 220.

justice, urban problems, war, economic opportunity, and discrimination of various kinds, there will probably remain an abiding concern with their historical roots and relationships to the structure of American society. What were the origins of organizational change? Was the impact of such change a mixed or unmixed blessing? How did Americans react to fundamental social and economic change, and to what degree did they welcome or struggle against bureaucratic and organizational values? Can the study of inarticulate groups explain with any degree of clarity the authoritative decisions that shape a nation's history? Is an emphasis on group pluralism a better conceptual tool than the older dualism that posited a conflict between the mass of people and special interests? So long as Americans debate their future, these and similar questions will be of concern to historians.

Samuel P. Hays

SAMUEL P. HAYS (1921–   ) is Professor of History at the University of
Pittsburgh. His books include *Conservation and the Gospel of Efficiency: The
Progressive Conservation Movement, 1890–1920* (1959), and *The Response to In-
dustrialism, 1885–1914* (1957).

The rapid development of urban history in the past few years has witnessed far greater progress in the expansion of subject matter than of
conceptual framework. Most urban history has been written as a narrative with a minimum of deliberately fashioned concept. As a result, the
"reform" framework, inherent in the contemporary self-image of the
city from year to year in the twentieth century, has become unconsciously transferred into the historical imagination to establish the prevailing pattern of writing about the city. Its sequence is simple: cities
grew, they gave rise to problems, and reform forces arose to cope with
those problems. The classic political contest in urban history is the
struggle between those who would solve the difficulties of the city and
their opponents.

The persistence of the "reform" context is surprising in view of the
vast fund of information and ideas readily available for other approaches, which gives rise to concepts about patterns of human relationships in the city on a broader and less overtly normative basis. From one
point of view, these concepts enable us to place the contemporary conceptions of the city's problems in context—namely, as the particular
definition of problems from the particular vantage point or "image" of
the city of particular groups of people. We can examine the special roots
and perspectives of "reform" movements. From another point of view,
they enable us to examine the entire range of human life within the city,
the variety of people, the patterns they generate, and the relationships
they establish among themselves, irrespective of our own normative
concerns about the city. The conceptual possibilities for reconstructing
the historical dimension of the city are readily available.

The "reform" context is even more unsatisfactory because it constitutes a rejection of the city, constant unwillingness to consider the city in
its own right and a constant search, through history, for something

Samuel P. Hays, "The Changing Political Structure of the City in Industrial America,"
Journal of Urban History, Vol. 1, No. 1 (November, 1974), pp. 6–34, reprinted by permission
of the Publisher, Sage Publications, Inc.

which to each writer the city instead should be. We must develop an approach which accepts the city as it is—its heterogeneity of ethnicity, religion, and race; its inequalities and the process by which vertical mobility constantly transforms one pattern of inequality into another; its tension between parochial and cosmopolitan life; its administrative and technical systems which order people as between those who manage and those who are managed. This enormous variety of human life on the part of thousands and millions of people we must appreciate and comprehend in its own right—for what it was, not for what it failed to be—and order into patterns so as to enhance that appreciation and comprehension.

The following essay constitutes a conceptual framework which I have found useful in comprehending the evolution of the city since the mid-nineteenth century. It has been influenced heavily by works in geography and sociology. Yet by the practitioners of those arts it would be considered primitive and elementary. Here I attempt to translate simple concepts from the relatively static framework of the social sciences into a historical context so as to stress change over time. In its broadest outline, urban development is considered a constant tension between forces making for decentralization and forces making for centralization in human relationships and institutions, between centrifugal and centripetal tendencies, between social differentiation and social integration. The city holds in balance in one historical context those attempts to separate out from the wider world to establish smaller contexts of life in home, church, education, and recreation, and those attempts to discipline and link the productive and occupational activities of man into more highly organized systems. The city is an excellent context in which to examine the evolution of these tensions in modern industrial society.

I

During the last half of the nineteenth century, the physical limits of cities expanded constantly. In some cases, people moved outward from the center to the periphery to establish new residential communities. In others, new migrants settled in areas adjacent to but distinct from the city's older districts. These brought about a greater dispersion of urban population, a more varied and decentralized life, and the development of subcommunities. These were not similar; each had distinct ethnic, cultural, occupation, and class characteristics. The physical growth of cities, then, involved social differentiation; new subcommunities created more varied cultures and cities became more heterogeneous. This had a profound impact on the patterns of human relationships in the city so that by the end of the century it was far more decentralized than it had been seventy years before.

Prior to industrialization, cities had been relatively small, compact and integrated. They were "pedestrian communities" in that the location of activities was determined by the time it took to walk between them, between residence and occupation, church and school, store and recreation facilities. The community tended to be a face-to-face community, in which human relationships were established by personal contact over limited areas. These relationships were close. Individuals could not live free from the view of others, from their approval or disapproval. In such a social situation, those who became dominant in economic, social, and religious life established and maintained acceptable patterns for the entire community. Differences in values which might lead to differences in public demands were not readily revealed in political affairs.

Two characteristics of these relatively integrated communities stood out. One was the physical intermixture of different social groups. Although the earlier cities were relatively homogeneous ethnically and religiously, they were heterogeneous in class terms, exhibiting distinct gradations from lower to upper. Different classes had long existed in the American city. But their geographical separation was not as sharp as it became in the late nineteenth century. Factory owners often built their residences next to their factories and within sight of workingmen's homes. Laborers often lived in the back alleys in blocks where the more well-to-do lived on the main street. Clear-cut expression of the particular values of a social group requires geographical separateness and distinctiveness. Since in the pedestrian community distinct social classes did not live in distinct geographical areas but were intermixed, the clarity of their political impulses was limited.

Urban political leadership reflected the integrated community. City councils were usually elected in a town meeting to represent the city as a whole. Invariably, they were composed of men dominant in the community's social and economic life—bankers, commission merchants, lawyers. Rarely were those in the lower three-quarters of the vertical social order selected. In later years, when councilmen were chosen by wards, working-class wards frequently elected workingmen. Election at large gave an opportunity for those dominant in its formal political life as well. This, it should be emphasized again, was not due to the lack of social differentiation. There is ample evidence to demonstrate inequalities in wealth, and there is no reason to believe that these inequalities did not lead to differences in political outlook. But the lack of geographical distinctiveness of social differentiation reduced the capacity of the middle and lower classes to develop and express effectively their political views.

This pedestrian community of the early nineteenth century changed radically by 1900. The drive toward social differentiation had proceeded apace; it found expression in a variety of urban subcommunities, each with a distinct geographical identity, residential life, cultural pattern, and representation in city government. Many of these subcommunities grew out of migration from abroad. Irish and German migration brought into almost every city newcomers who divided along both national and religious lines. German Catholics, Lutherans, and Jews settled in different areas of the city and established separate churches, schools, and social organizations. Later southern and eastern Europeans added to the variety. By seeking to live in close proximity to those of similar nativity and religion, they created distinctive ethno-religious subcultures.

Subcommunities also arose from upward social mobility which became transformed into geographical movement from the city's center to its periphery. As the economy grew, opportunities at all occupational levels expanded. People moved upward in occupation and income; the drive toward social differentiation became intense. The upwardly mobile desired to establish new ways of life, to separate out from their older environments and to live in a different community, where cultural patterns were similar to their new aspirations. They sought more space for play in the form of larger yards, wished their daughters to meet more acceptable future husbands, or wanted to associate in their nonwork hours with people of their own patterns of living. Outward urban migration arose from the desire to establish new residential subcommunities with church, school, and recreational facilities in areas distinct from older subcommunities. The desire for social differentiation could be realized only through geographical differentiation.

Cheap urban transportation, the trolley and the automobile, made this process possible. Horse-drawn vehicles on rails were in operation as early as the 1850s. In the 1880s cable-cars powered by central steam plants were experimented with but soon gave way to the electric trolley. At first trolley lines radiated out from the central city to only a few areas, but by the end of the century the electric trolley had opened up almost all the surrounding territory save that which defied penetration because of natural barriers. These innovations were as profound an element of the transportation revolution as were the steamboats and the steam railroads. They generated an extensive movement of population and restructured the urban social order.

The simplest expression of this change lay in the increasing distance between place of residence and place of work. Whereas formerly one had to live within walking distance of work, now he or she could live much farther away. Professionals and businesspeople who worked in the central city established residential communities elsewhere. Factory owners no longer lived beside their factories. Lawyers whose work required that they be near the centralized public records and legal institutions of the city and county courts lived out in newer and economically more substantial communities. Doctors, if they were specialists such as surgeons, lived in one place and carried on their practice in another.

This distance between work and residence created more distinct geographical specialization of activities in the city. Residential communities served the family; they included home, church, school, and recreation facilities, including residential play areas—yard space—as well as country clubs and golf courses. Communities became distinctive in terms of nationality, religions, and class patterns of residential life. While residential institutions could be decentralized, work institutions could not. The individual could readily move where he lived but not where he worked. His place of work, in fact, depended upon centralizing rather than decentralizing forces, those bound up with the organization of economic life into larger systems of production, merchandising, and banking. While the desire for social differentiation enticed people into a centrifugal movement of residential dispersion, their occupations involved them in centripetal and integrative forces. During the last half of the nineteenth century, decentralizing tendencies were the dominant of the two.

The heightened geographical mobility created by the trolley greatly complicated the process of conserving residential communities. Each desired to maintain its distinctive patterns of residential life. This was extremely difficult to do, because mobility and stability were incompatible. One could not easily prevent other people of different classes, nationalities, races, or religions from moving into his community. Freedom to buy and sell property might quickly undermine established patterns. To protect themselves, communities experimented with a variety of techniques. That these were rarely successful testifies to the high degree of motion in the modern city. Upper-class communities experienced especially observable difficulties in self-maintenance. During the latter half of the nineteenth century, new upper-class residential areas arose in which the wealthy, old and new, sought to disassociate themselves from the institutions and people of the older city. But, unable to control land transactions, these communities rarely lasted more than one or two generations. Real estate promoters converted their estates into smaller lots for middle- and lower-income families.

Decentralization of residential life created decentralization of related economic institutions. Community growth rapidly dispersed property ownership as larger holdings, usually in the form of estates owned by the well-to-do, were divided into smaller lots. One property owner frequently was replaced by several hundred, each one of which now had a tangible stake in community life and demanded a voice in community affairs. Since the apportionment of city council seats to various wards frequently depended upon the number of property taxpayers in the ward, expansion of property ownership directly affected municipal government. Diffusion of property ownership diffused political impulses.

New subcommunities gave rise to new consumer-oriented stores, designed to fill immediate personal and family needs. Grocery, drug, confectioner, milk, eating, and liquor stores each served a market within walking distance. Many were family-owned stores; almost all had a vital interest in the area's property conditions and its general growth and development. Ethnic communities gave rise to stores which provided the particular food, dress, and other goods distinctive to the nationality of the residents. Consumer-oriented small businesses expanded especially rapidly in urban immigrant settlements. The immigrant storekeeper became the backbone of the urban small-business community.

The physical development of the community generated economic enterprises which facilitated that growth in banking, real estate, contracting, and transportation. These firms were often confined in their activities to a particular region of the city, were identified with it and had a stake in its physical growth. They catered to a wider community than did the small retailer, to a larger subsection of the city than the neighborhood best called the urban region. Real estate firms arose to change large estates owned by single individuals into innumerable small lots owned by many; banks grew up to finance these real estate transactions and the building and development that followed; contractors built the new structures, streets, and sidewalks. These men identified closely with their regions; they became recognized as leaders by the people of the region.

Urban physical expansion provided opportunities for new entrepreneurs; regional developers were very different from those who had been concerned with growth in the older section of the city. Many were immigrant leaders who, while profiting from development, provided essential services for community growth and became influential community spokesmen. New real estate development provided opportunities for new entrepreneurs in the new banks, trolley lines, real estate agencies, and construction firms. The boards of directors of community banks, for example, contained far more men of recent immigrant origin and Catholics and Jews than did the older, central-city banks. The more successful immigrant businessmen often combined real estate development and rental property with banking service. They worked closely with ethnic political leaders in their projects; both rested ultimately for their influence and their leadership upon the development of urban subcommunities.

Differentiation and decentralization in social and economic life gave rise to a decentralized political system. Increasingly the ward became the focus of politics. Each community demanded separate representation so that its particular needs would be dealt with. Even prior to 1850, a ward system had begun to replace citywide representation; elected by wards, councilmen now represented their communities in the council's deliberations. School government often developed in a similar manner. Each ward had its own elementary school, often a focal point for community social affairs, administered by a ward-elected school board. Ward-oriented political life took precedence over a citywide political life. Through it, the varied urban sub-communities could express their distinctive viewpoints on public affairs.

Ward representation changed the kinds of men chosen as councilmen. Whereas earlier the great majority were from upper occupational and socioeconomic classes, by the end of the century they were from the middle and lower levels. Outward migration and geographical differentiation greatly reduced the number of upper-class and increased the number of middle- and lower-class wards. Each ward tended to select as representatives people who were like the majority of its inhabitants; the character of representation changed, as did that of the communities represented. At the same time, economic leaders of the new, decentralized communities began to play a larger role as councilmen. Identified with the real estate and business concerns of the community, they established personal ties with large numbers of residents in their business affairs. Economic and social leadership became translated into political leadership. By 1900, the typical ward-elected city councilman was a small businessman—retailer, director of a funeral home, real estate promoter and contractor, director of a community bank—a clerk, a skilled artisan, or an unskilled laborer. Professional and large business classes were greatly outnumbered.

The major concern of urban government lay with the city's physical development. The overwhelming number of demands made upon city council and of city ordinances pertained to the approval of subdivisions, of streets and drainage systems, of lighting and transportation. City taxes came from property owners and city expenditures went for services to development; major council controversies came over taxation and expenditure. Considerable disagreement arose, also, over the question of private or public enterprise. Should private services be permitted without restriction, or should they be licensed and regulated? Should property owners pay for the development of adjacent streets, or should they be paid for through a general system of taxation and municipal expenditure? Whatever the answers to these questions, city government in the last half of the nineteenth century came to be a major instrument of physical growth and community development.

Because the city council consisted of representatives of different geographical areas, controversies over taxing and expenditure for urban development became controversies between different areas of the city. This process developed in the same way as it did in the state with conflicts between different counties, or in the nation between sections. Each urban community wished assistance for development; each wanted a gas light on this or that corner. Decisions were often made by "log-rolling," in which one councilman voted for the proposals of others in exchange for their vote for his own. These controversies frequently sorted themselves out into disagreements between the city's older and newer sections. The older feared the newer. They often argued that the geographical expansion of the city was neither necessary nor desirable. Their taxes would be used to finance development in expanding areas in which they had no direct interest. They stood aghast at the willingness of the city council to incur indebtedness to finance new development. The older city usually was in the minority, for urban expansion and ward representation brought into government a large number of councilmen who reflected the views of the newly developing communities and who outvoted their opponents.

The use of city funds in community development, and the award of franchises to provide services such as transportation created opportunities for corruption. But this should not obscure the more important phenomenon of decentralized urban growth. Many controversies over physical development were, in fact, phrased in terms of the issue of corruption. The most sensational case involved the New York City "Tweed ring." That controversy was fundamentally one between old and new New York City, a belief on the part of lower Manhattan that New York did not need to expand physically, and a demand on the part of those preoccupied with development further up the island that it did. The city government threw in its lot with expansion and development and increased municipal indebtedness to help carry it out. Tweed's downfall was triggered by revelations of corruption in this venture, but the underlying opposition came from disagreement with the substance of his policies.

II

While decentralization characterized urban development in the nineteenth century, by 1900 integration, although in evidence even earlier, was emerging as a dominant force. Decentralization continued, but it became overlaid with new patterns of social organization which drew people together into more closely-knit groups. As the density of population increased, the intensity of claim and counter-claim in decision-making also increased. A new political order arose to limit the variety of such claims, to channel them into fewer centers of decision-making, and to integrate more activities into a relatively small number of systems of human relationships. While the older city witnessed a process of dispersion, the new involved centralization.

Integrative tendencies in urbanization grew out of the transition from locality patterns of human relationships, which emphasized interaction among people living in the same geographical area, to functional and administrative forms of organization, which emphasized interaction among people of particular functions, no matter where they lived, and among people playing different roles in the vertical hierarchy of organized administrative systems. While the locality group was inclusive, encompassing all those living in a given geographical area, functional and administrative groups were exclusive, involving only those who had a common functional interest or were within a given administrative system. Whereas in former decades the locality contest had been crucial in the effective expression of political impulses, new forms of social and political organization were more divorced from location in particular segments of the city. These new forms of organization rested on patterns of human relationships which cut across community and constituted a superstructure of contacts above and beyond it.

Behind these new patterns of human relationships lay the growth of organizational technologies. Whereas production technologies, those which substituted machines for manual labor, dominated in the last half of the nineteenth century, organizational technologies came to the fore after 1875, which dramatically increased the speed and flexibility of human contacts. The telephone replaced the messenger boy, permitting contact and control—integration—in ways which had not been possible before. Organizational technologies gave rise to more precise coordination of human interaction so as to dovetail efforts efficiently. They made possible the new, more systematized, more coordinated patterns of human interaction.

The most visible expression of urban integration was the newly reorganized central city. Formerly a mixture of residences, professional offices, factories, and public buildings, the central city declined as a residential and factory area on the advent of rapid transit which stimulated movement out of the city's core to the periphery. In their place came new activities which emphasized the central city as the location of organization which reached out to gather in the entire urban area. The large office building was the most dramatic physical expression of this change. Within a few decades, these buildings replaced homes, churches, schools, the whole range of residentially related activities, in the city's center. Although innovation in structural steel and the elevator made this possible, the growth of rapid interpersonal communication reflects more precisely the state of organizational integration which lay behind it. The telephone first became a popular means of communication in the center city.

These changes can be charted also in the shifting location of private corporate management activities. In the nineteenth century, when management and coordination were relatively small compared with production, the former were carried out in the same building as the factory. As management functions grew, their physical location became more of a problem. At times, the mansions of factory owners, located near the factories, became a convenient location as the owners moved to upper-class communities. It came to be more convenient to locate near related institutions such as banks and advertising agencies, whose expertise was frequently called upon. The central office building located in the center of the city was the answer. Many of these were built either by industries for their management or by the estates of deceased entrepreneurs and then rented to the firm. In any case, the growing importance of coordination, internal and external, gave rise to a series of moves which led to the concentration of activities in the central city.

Here there grew rapidly a host of other centralizing institutions: large-scale retail establishments drawing customers from the entire city; specialized professionals, such as doctors, architects and engineers who had a citywide clientele; lawyers whose work required that they be near legal records and the courts; banks whose financial networks fanned out to link transactions throughout the city and the region; public administrative agencies in recreation, planning, health, and welfare. The larger organizational life of the city focused on the center because here a host of interrelated activities associated with coordinating human relationships took place. The reorganization of the central city was not merely a matter of physical change, but of more intense human interaction at a level high on the vertical scale of social organization.

These integrative activities found organizational, as well as locational expressions, the most important of which were the Chambers of Commerce representing the city's most powerful businessmen. There were several types of such bodies, distinguishable in terms of the geographical extent of their activities and clientele, on the one hand, and their role in the scale of human contacts on the other. The neighborhood boards of trade represented small, consumer-oriented businesses in the relatively small communities; the regional chambers of commerce drew in banks, real estate firms, merchants, and professionals whose activities were larger than the neighborhood but smaller than the entire city; citywide Chambers of Commerce, composed of manufacturers, downtown merchants, central-city bankers, and managers of central-city property, represented the largest integrative tendencies of the city. These citywide Chambers of Commerce, rather than the smaller bodies, came to play an increasingly important role in municipal affairs. They constituted a crucial political force in the years from 1897 to 1929.

The rapid rise of the empirical professions such as public health and education greatly accelerated urban integration. The public health doctor was one of the most politically active professionals. The germ theory of disease not only enhanced understanding of the causes of diseases but also made abundantly clear what needed to be controlled in order to prevent them. Moreover, public health innovations could be brought about more effectively through one citywide context than many community ones. The dynamics of school politics was similar. Professional educators urged a host of innovations, such as longer school terms, more training for teachers, better facilities and equipment, teacher pensions, and new methods of capturing the interest of the pupil. But how to bring about change? Many school boards were conservative. The answer was to shift the context of school decisions from the many, local ward school boards to a central body where a more citywide perspective could be fostered and to which professionals would have direct access.

Two other professional groups, civil engineers and architects, were more concerned with urban physical organization. Civil engineers became the technical experts behind large public works such as water reservoirs, sanitary sewage systems, bridges, and paved streets. Since such matters affected the city at large, plans to facilitate them required a perspective far more extensive than that of the urban small community. And the same for that segment of architects who became interested in city planning. Often concerned with central-city office buildings, they became enamored of the possibilities of large-scale changes in the city and especially the center. This included the rearrangement of streets and buildings, the development of open spaces and parks, the extension of landscaping and beautification at the city center and elsewhere. Like the engineers, their citywide perspective prompted them to seek large- rather than small-scale physical changes.

These professional concerns were universal rather than particularist. The problems they dealt with cut across parochial community lines. The public health expert faced tuberculosis and typhoid fever not simply in Ward 6, but in the entire city; the school professional wished to educate more rather than fewer children and for longer periods of time. The civil engineer and the architect sought to rearrange diverse and far-flung sections of the city according to more universal standards of efficiency and design. Professionals were not content merely to learn more; they wished to use their knowledge to change society. The new empirical professions were not inert, but highly political. They became infused with a missionary spirit to reduce disease, to lengthen human life, to enhance the quantity and quality of education, and to redesign the physical city.

Only a few, however, shared the professional expert's values, his vision, and the urgency of his concern. He constantly had to educate others, to search for political allies, and, to overcome resistance from opponents. Since he sought to influence a wide range of people and affairs, he chose mechanisms of decision-making and action which were equally broad in scope. At the municipal level, he constructed public health departments, relatively independent of community political impulses and of the city councils which reflected those impulses, so that he could operate freely from his own professional guidelines. He supported increased executive authority in the mayor in order to protect himself from popular forces. The new empirical professions played a major role in the integration of the twentieth-century city.

The urban upper class constituted still a third force in urban integration. In its residential institutions, the urban upper class was separatist; it sought to establish homes, churches, schools, and clubs apart from other classes, and increasingly beyond the city's boundaries. In this, the upper class was no different in its localistic impulses than were other classes, thereby contributing to the decentralization and fragmentation of the city. But economic concerns required that it move in the opposite direction as well and stimulate integration. The occupations of the upper class were often in the central city, the corporate systems in which it worked were headquartered there, and the property it owned often was either there physically or represented by investments in corporations based there. The urban upper class faced two ways at once; decentralist in residential institution, it was integrative in its economic and occupational life. While it sought to separate itself from the city in one way, in another it was propelled back into the center of urban affairs.

The recent history of the upper class added a special integrative factor in the early twentieth century. Many of the upper class had grown up in the center city. Faced with an infusion of new people, a rise in property values and taxes and the deterioration of their residential environment, they only recently had moved out. But many retained a strong nostalgia for the old area and could not avoid an interest in what happened there. The relocation of churches revealed this ambivalence. Congregations invariably sold downtown churches for a healthy profit because of the rapid rise in land values. With the proceeds, they could build a new church in the suburbs and have funds left over. Many members, and usually those from long residence in the former location, wished these resources to be used for social welfare programs in the community where the church had been. Adding to this nostalgia was the fact that the location of the places of residence and of work of the upper class required that they pass through lower-class areas on their way between home and work, making the conditions there particularly visible to them. Such experiences as these added to the concern for welfare among the working class to limit its "disruptive" and "disintegrative" tendencies. Upward mobility reduced interclass communication drastically, but the peculiar experiences of the upper class in the early twentieth-century city gave rise to a desire on the part of some to reestablish some semblance of contact.

The urban upper class became involved in a host of social welfare programs: prohibition, control of prostitution, language instruction for immigrants, religious evangelism, public baths, playgrounds, better housing, restriction of child labor, and improvement of the working conditions of women. The most visible and dramatic example of upper-class welfare was the settlement house. Located in the midst of lower-class neighborhoods, the settlement house provided educational and social services for lower-income groups. Boards of directors and financing came from the upper class, who lived in outlying residential areas. They also provided the volunteer workers for settlement house activities. In this fashion, the settlement house constituted an instrument of interclass communication. The "gatekeeper" between the two classes was the settlement house director who lived and communicated within two different worlds, the world of the lower-class immigrant and the world of the affluent.

In these relationships between social classes in different sections of the city, women played an important role. Active in social welfare reforms, the members of women's organizations were drawn heavily from the upper classes who had the leisure time to give to civic affairs. "Society" clubs served as headquarters for many civic reform groups; "society" newspapers provided one of the most extensive sources of information about welfare reform; "society" women often propelled their husbands into reform activities. While men became involved in urban integration through the economic system and professional life, women did so through intuitive sympathy for other women and children, their common religion and ethnicity, and their nostalgia for their childhood communities. Much of the interclass communication which lay behind this aspect of urban integration came through special lines of interaction generated by upper-class women.

Forces making for integration in economic, professional, and social life came together in a drive for integration and centralization in decision-making. Reformers arose to modify the formal structure of municipal and school government and decision-making in welfare and charitable activities. They were most disturbed about the ward system of city and school affairs which gave considerable influence to the decentralizing tendencies of urban communities. This, they felt, hindered a focus on a more comprehensive view of the city—the "public interest" they called it—in order to deal with its problems. As each urban group sought to implement integrative objectives, it became dissatisfied with ward government and supported more highly centralized methods of decision-making.

One innovation was to increase the power of the mayor—for example, that he propose a budget which the council then might modify rather than vice versa. Another was the commission form of government. A third was the city manager system in which an "expert" was hired to administer the city's affairs. Almost all such plans proposed a centralization of representation, a modification or abolition of ward representation in favor of citywide representation. The most successful attempt to centralize decision-making came in school government. By the 1920s, almost every city in the nation had eliminated the ward in favor of the citywide school board. At times these were elected at large, but often they were appointed—for example, by judges of the municipal courts. Control in the school system shifted from the community to the city at large.

These drives for centralization of decision-making came primarily from the upper levels of the social order. The "good government" organizations were composed of people from upper occupational groups; the candidates they preferred for public office were from the same levels. Entirely missing from the reform movement were the typical ward leaders of the previous era—the small storekeeper, the white-collar clerk, the skilled artisan. Instead, it was dominated by the central-city businessman, the advanced professional, and the upper social classes. Chambers of Commerce often took the lead in reform activities; allied with them were a variety of voters leagues and civic organizations which brought in professionals and upper-class women. Their success in centralizing decision-making shifted sharply up the occupational social levels from which decision makers were drawn. Now the vast majority of council and school board members were from the upper-middle and upper classes. The greatest change came in school boards. By 1924, such boards across the country were dominated by business and professional leaders. A virtual revolution had taken place, reflecting the triumph of centralizing over decentralizing forces in municipal and school affairs.

These changes in urban government marked the re-entrance into political life of members of the upper class after several decades of relative absence. Dominating urban politics in the early pedestrian community, these groups had retired from municipal government as the city expanded, as ward government generated lower- and middle-class leadership and as they were unable to exercise control in a city of varied and decentralized communities. Their old methods of influence, via day-to-day contacts in the pedestrian community, no longer sufficed. By the early twentieth century, however, they had learned new methods of integrative control from their experience with corporate systems. They became increasingly adept at communications technologies and the role of the professional expert in fashioning a stable and manipulable social order. Wishing to apply these techniques to public affairs and the model of the corporation to city government, they re-entered public life through reform organizations. They were not expressing just personal values; they were reshaping the political order according to the inner dynamic of the changing economic and social order. They constituted the counter-thrust toward integration within the decentralizing society of the late nineteenth century.

Tendencies toward urban integration took place at a level far above the local community. They created networks of extra-community relationships. In the face of this new social order, the local community lost much of its autonomy and its salience. Whereas in the nineteenth century it was the dominant focus of urban life, in the twentieth century it became far less viable as more of the articulate sector of the city became involved in the development of functional groups and corporate systems. Although the urban community remained as a focal point of primary group relationships for many people, its significance and importance for the wider community declined as it became transformed from a creative urban force into an object of action generated elsewhere. Political institutions at the ward level declined; political involvement diminished; ward institutions became local representatives of wider systems. As innovation developed apace at the upper levels of the social order, community institutions at the lower levels atrophied and declined.

III

By 1929, these integrative tendencies had run their first course of development. During the next four decades, a new phase appeared in which both decentralizing and centralizing tendencies appeared with new vigor and a forceful interplay. The automobile and the telephone gave rise to greater mobility and flexibility in human contacts, generating a new phase of outward movement. Systematization also moved on apace, creating ever larger units of administrative action which restrained the growth of autonomous units and integrated them into more universal perspectives and more centrally directed strategies. Interaction between centripetal and centrifugal forces remained the major context of urban history.

The twentieth-century city served as a giant social escalator, involving a constant flow of individuals upward through levels of occupation, income, and standards of living and outward to newer residential areas. Children and grandchildren of post-1880 southern and eastern European immigrants moved upward rapidly after the Great Depression. Whites and blacks from the rural United States moved onto and up the same escalator. As occupations and income rose, so did the distance of residence from the center city; one study of the 1960 census detailed this process for blacks for whom the dynamics of upward mobility were similar to those for whites. Upward mobility accelerated rapidly after the early 1950s as the mid-twentieth-century income revolution proceeded. National median family income in current dollars rose from less than $1,500 in 1939 to $3,390 in 1950 to $5,620 in 1960 and $8,632 in 1968.

Technological innovations in transportation and communication—the automobile and the telephone—made possible this outward movement. By its speed and flexibility, the automobile increased the range of short-term movement between home and work or between home and shopping areas. Now one could live five, ten, or fifteen miles from work and commute. Until the early twentieth century the telephone had linked business firms almost exclusively. It soon spread to households, permitting those living in widely scattered areas to establish intensive patterns of interaction and facilitating outward movement.

These innovations generated an outward thrust of business as well, the development of manufacturing, research centers, and storage and warehouse facilities on the periphery rather than in the center of the city. The gasoline motor truck and paved streets permitted close physical contact between such businesses and their markets, their suppliers, and their administrative headquarters. The telephone permitted a constant flow of communication and enabled the firm's headquarters to exercise supervision and control over elements physically decentralized. Decentralization in the location of industry should not be taken to involve autonomy of decision-making, for such firms were integral parts of a larger system. Technology facilitated both physical decentralization and administrative control; the first depended upon the second.

This phase of suburbanization had several characteristics different from that of the nineteenth century. First, the outward spread of industry gave rise to an occupationally more varied set of suburbs; those who worked in suburban industries—blue-collar, white-collar, and professional—chose to live relatively close to them. Suburban areas did not contain middle- and upper-class groups alone, but a wide variety of classes. Second, the mere size of the suburban scene provided a far larger number of communities and of choices of residence. Since these choices were made in terms of the class level of the community with which one wished to associate, the range of suburban communities reflected a more varied and precisely defined spectrum of classes than in previous years. Third, the vast size of the suburban spectrum gave rise to lateral movement within it, increasingly becoming more important relative to the center-periphery patterns which previously dominated. A structure arose within the periphery distinguishing those who lived and worked in the same suburb, those who lived in one suburb and worked in another, and those who lived in the suburb and worked in the central city.

These outward movements took place across rather than within city legal boundaries. Because the outlying areas wished to be included in the city's services, nineteenth-century urban boundary expansion met little opposition. Much outward population flow took place within the city's legal limits. By 1930, many cities were ringed with independent towns, boroughs, and townships, each with autonomous legal power derived from the authority not of the city but of the state. Many suburbanites had moved beyond the city's borders precisely to be in a community which had such political independence. In the city, residential communities had little power to maintain their stability; they were always threatened by forces which sought to change the patterns of land use and thereby to undermine its physical base. Outside the city, in a separate corporate town or township, such control could be exercised. Here it was possible to require that house lots be of a minimum size and houses of a minimum value.

Suburban political units reflected a desire to separate out one's com-

munity from the larger urban world. Nineteenth-century decentralization, within the city, did not lead to permanent political subunits. In
fact, the urban community had little staying power in the face of integrative forces. Twentieth-century decentralization took place across the
city's borders and enjoyed political jurisdictions separate from the city
and capable of maintaining autonomous political and legal, as well as
social existence. Twentieth-century decentralization had far greater staying power than did that of the nineteenth.

The process of urban integration also continued. As the city grew, so
did the range of people, activities, and land use which large urban
systems sought to influence. One form of this impulse was the drive for
metropolitan government, to extend the city's boundaries outward to
encompass growing suburban areas, often to make the city's boundaries
synonymous with the county's. The drive for metropolitan government
extended the former drive for centralization of city government; once the
latter movement had succeeded, it began to advocate a larger metropolitan system. Such a movement developed in almost every city, some as
early as the late 1920s, but succeeded only rarely.

More successful was the growth of specialized public functions
which extended beyond the city's boundaries. Suburbanites demanded
effective transportation to their work in the city; they supported metropolitan transit authorities to develop systems of public transit which
went far beyond the city's borders. Because of their wider jurisdiction,
county governments usually created such authorities. Similar agencies
developed for countywide trash disposal and garbage collection, sanitary sewers, water systems, and health departments. These innovations
gave rise to governmental institutions as wide in scope as the metropolitan area itself, and an almost imperceptible shift in decision-making
power from suburban units to the larger authority.

Metropolitan authorities were corporations established for specific
purposes with general powers to achieve them. Like similar state and
federal corporations, they were free from traditional restraints by council
and mayor. Still further removed from the city's active political impulses
than were the mayor or council elected-at-large, they could carry out
their task in terms of technical standards of professional expertise at the
upper levels of the political order rather than have to respond to the
constant suggestions and objections of open political debate. Innovations in government in the years between 1897 and 1929 narrowed the
actors in the decision-making process and the range of alternatives and
debate; the authorities continued this process. Once given a grant of
power, it became difficult to render the authority accountable to any
other governmental body.

The urban redevelopment authority—the prime example—was not
only divorced from other governmental bodies but also had the power of
eminent domain. It arose to change urban patterns of land use, most

frequently in the central city. What land uses should prevail? Invariably redevelopment involved a shift from buildings of lower value and tax return to those of higher. This meant the substitution of large-scale for small-scale enterprise, a perspective consistent with integrative objectives and congenial to those involved in large-scale private enterprise rather than those at the middle and lower levels of the social order. With the power of eminent domain, the authority could force property owners to sell. In this way, the expansion of the property-stake in urban affairs, which came with the decentralization of ownership in the nineteenth century, was reversed. Land used by many small property holders was transferred to a relatively few large ones through the process of urban renewal.

Professional and technical experts continued to extend their manipulative ventures as the drive toward more universal contexts of action grew. So also did the gap between these and impulses of smaller scale. Public health leaders pushed such measures as fluoridation and air pollution control. Mental health programs expanded rapidly. The drive for education continued unabated, with emphasis on better facilities, more intensive instruction, influence over preschool and home environment, and junior colleges. In such programs as these, the practice of control from the top by experts grew apace. School boards, already under such a system of decision-making, concentrated on utilizing it more extensively. Public health experts were less fortunate. The fluoridation issue became especially critical. Left to community popular vote, fluoridation was rejected more often than accepted. By the 1960s, therefore, public health leaders sought to bypass the urban general suffrage, argued that public health matters were not fit subjects for democratic control, and sought legislation to impose fluoridation on the entire state.

Preference for top-level decision-making on the part of professional experts was reflected in several political tactics. One was the creation of neighborhood groups, such as parent-teacher associations and neighborhood welfare councils, which served both to convey information about potential sources of discontent to central agencies and to implement general citywide policies. Their power, however, was confined to suggestion rather than decision. Another was the heightened interest in a systematic understanding of opposition to administrative proposals, not as a means to modify objectives, but so as to implement them more effectively. They began to study the sociology of public health, of education, of mental health. They were, of course, far more interested in the sociology of those whom they confronted than of their own values and professional social systems. They simply wished a more complete understanding of their political opposition so that they could better implement their goals.

Reaction against integrative tendencies in the city took several new forms and led to new types of balance between centrifugal and centripetal forces. As centralization rose in the pre-1929 years, the community declined as a viable political force. In the depression years of the 1930s, however, a reverse trend set in momentarily. Some smaller cities abolished the city manager system; Cleveland, unique among the larger cities in adopting the plan, rejected it in the late 1920s. Other cities returned to the ward system of representation in the 1930s, and a noticeable increase took place in representation from working-class areas. In many instances, even with citywide elections, city councils contained more representatives of workingmen, but invariably these were prominent union officials who represented not geographical communities but functional organizations.

Not until the political activation of urban blacks, when community became expressed through race, did community resistance against integrative tendencies revive significantly. The process was sharpened by urban redevelopment which physically destroyed urban communities, most frequently black residential areas, in sections with the lowest property values. "Urban renewal" is "Negro removal" was the cry. This threat to the black community came at a time of rising black income, education, and awareness. Moreover, concentration of blacks in limited areas of the city gave a clear spatial and community form to the expression of black political aims. In the midst of a city and school government dominated by whites, blacks frequently demanded that a ward plan of representation and government supersede citywide forms which provided minority groups little chance to express effectively their demands.

Those involved in smaller-scale economic, social, and political affairs and at the middle and lower segments of the political order found themselves cast in a defensive rather than a creative role. Initiative as to the formulation of goals for urban policy had shifted to institutions far above them. Because it focused on community change, urban redevelopment helped to reactivate these community impulses and met increasing opposition from them. A variety of spokesmen arose to voice objections: homeowners, storekeepers, real estate firms, often the same types of people who once had represented the wards in city councils and school boards. Often they succeeded in changing a project, sometimes by postponing but at other times by preventing its development. To the authorities, these were major irritants; following modern views of "conflict management," they sought to overcome resistance but not always with success.

Confrontation between officials who represented dominant political institutions and those who reflected community impulses revealed the institutional strength of the former and the weakness of the latter. Officials had a myriad of institutions into which they could retreat for strength. They could parry opposition by seeking more information, by reconsidering, by shifting to a different administrative channel. The institutional routines through which they could counter-thrust, hide, escape, or protect themselves, stall and wear down opponents, seemed almost endless. Community representatives were far more exposed. Their constituencies were institutionally weak, with few information resources to provide support and backing, and few agencies to constitute a legitimate source of waiting, parrying, and regrouping. The weakness of community impulses was reflected in the weakness of institutions into which community leaders could retreat and return with new political strength.

Forces from outside the community arose to aid the reconstruction of its institutions. Social workers and federal anti-poverty program employees urged residents of poor communities to organize and exercise political power, to make demands upon city government for help in improving their neighborhoods. These efforts to re-energize people at the lower levels of the political order were only sporadically successful. The apathy of residents, often highly mobile, uninvolved in their neighborhood, let alone the city, was difficult to overcome. Most frequently these efforts at community-building aroused only a small segment—one or two percent—of the inhabitants, and served to speed them up the escalator and out into the wider urban society. Their major impact was to demonstrate that the disengagement of the bottom third from the larger political order was a permanent fact of life in modern American society.

The community's weakness within the city stood in stark contrast to its strength outside the city. The independent legal status of the suburban community gave it an enormous capacity for strength and persistence in the face of integrative urban impulses. It enabled them to ward off intrusions of influence from the city, such as lower income or black migrants. They could frustrate efforts at metropolitan government, either by organizing suburban units into an opposition bloc or by influencing state legislatures to stipulate electoral provisions which loaded the vote on metropolitan government in their favor. The power of the state could also be used to reduce suburban autonomy, as in school district reorganization, carried out through state legislative and administrative agencies. Against such integrative pressures from either city or state, however, the suburban communities could throw a considerable and continual counter-force. Their capacity for resistance was far greater than was that of the urban community.

Within the city, the upper third of the social order, often similar in socioeconomic composition to the most influential suburbs, exercised far more influence than did the lower or middle third. But the form of their political involvement shifted from geographical or area organization to functional organization. Increasingly, the active elements of the city came to be organized not by locality or community, but by specialized interests or functions, some in terms of occupation, trade associations, trade unions, or professional organizations; some in terms of specialized institutions such as libraries, art galleries, colleges, and schools; still others in terms of religion or ethnicity. Active elements in each of these functional groups were not the urban masses, but those in the upper occupational and organizational levels. The setting of urban politics came to be the interplay among functional groups in the upper levels of the political order, producing a pluralist political system, but distinctively within the top segment of vertical organization.

Membership in city councils and school boards reflected functional politics. Officials elected citywide were nominated by parties or, if in a nonpartisan election, by a nonpartisan group. In each case, the nominating body usually sought to "represent" all segments of the city; these "segments" in turn were thought of in functional terms. Positions were "reserved" for labor, for each of the major religious or nationality groups, for blacks, for merchants, bankers, or manufacturers. These functional representatives came from the top levels of vertical organization. The upward shift in the scale of representation and functional representation seemed to go hand in hand. Spokesmen for working-class people were no longer skilled or unskilled workmen, as in the earlier city, but top union officials who came from managerial levels of society. Ethnic and religious groups came to be represented by the very highest vertical levels of the different ethnic and religious class systems. Black members of city councils and school boards were professionals and businessmen from the upper levels of the black community.

Functional group politics created a new context of active urban political life limited to the upper levels of the political order, and a new balance of urban forces in which centrifugal tendencies came to be the functional groups at that level. No longer did the centralization-decentralization balance encompass the entire social order as it had in the late nineteenth and twentieth centuries. Now it was confined, for the most part, to the active, articulate segments of the upper levels. Those seeking to integrate urban affairs more fully sought support, placated the opposition, and developed a firm political base largely within this context. Save for an occasional instance of an election, the active urban political order was limited to the upper levels of the vertical scale of society and the middle and lower levels either remained apathetic and aloof or were cast in a negative or veto role.

As American cities moved into the last half of the twentieth century, their patterns of human relationships were far different than in the mid-nineteenth century. A structure of human contacts, growing out of the greater speed and scale of communications, and the expanded range of human thought, awareness, and action had developed, far broader in scope than that of a century before. The community of primary human relationships remained, but its influence in the entire political order had declined sharply. Above and beyond it, a network of functional and corporate institutions had developed which now constituted the context of active political life. Innovation in the political order came from this level, the "public consciousness" generated by media of mass communications was largely confined to it, and the interplay of day-to-day political differences took place within it. Over a century or more of development, the entire urban political order had expanded greatly, rearranged itself, and had undergone a sharp change in the location of political interaction and decision-making. From a previous balance which had tipped the scales of the city's active political impulses toward decentralization, they had shifted strongly toward centralization and upward in the vertical social and political order.

Herbert G. Gutman

HERBERT G. GUTMAN (1928–   ) is Professor of History at the City College of the City University of New York. He is the author of a number of works on American social history, including *The Black Family in Slavery and Freedom, 1750–1925* (1976) and *Work, Culture, and Society in Industrializing America: Essays in American Working-class and Social History* (1976).

Much is known about the early history of New England textile towns, but too much is inferred from this single source about the nineteenth-century American industrial city. Although little is known about the development of the industrial city, urban historians as well as labor and business historians have generalized much about it. Unwarranted assumptions about the social and economic structure of the early industrial city, however, have distorted significant patterns in its early development. Paterson, New Jersey, an industrial city that attracted the attention of men as diverse as Alexander Hamilton, William Haywood, and William Carlos Williams and that had as its official motto *Spe et Labore* (With Hope and Labor), serves as a case study to test some of the generalizations and assumptions.

I

Little is known of the inner history of the nineteenth-century American industrial city. Historians have detoured around Paterson and other nineteenth-century industrial cities for many reasons. Perhaps the landscape seemed unattractive. Perhaps the roadways into and out of the city seemed simple and one-dimensional. Whatever the cause, specialists have built roadblocks that deny access to a rich and hitherto untapped social history. The urban historian apparently finds the large, complex metropolis a greater challenge and a more accessible source for information than the simpler, intensely specialized, and grim factory town. The labor historian learns quickly that industrial cities lacked permanent labor organizations, and since he is by tradition little more than the chronicler of trade union history he just ignores the factory town. And the business historian, anxious to trace the detailed internal development of a particular firm or industry, all too often takes for granted its external relationships to the larger community. These attitudes, among others, have focused attention away from the industrial city as a legitimate subject for detailed and careful inquiry.

Only two elements in Paterson's history, for example, have attracted detailed attention: Alexander Hamilton's ill-fated effort to start "the Society for establishing useful Manufactures" in the 1790s and William Haywood's equally troubled effort to organize the immigrant silk workers into the Industrial Workers of the World, in 1913. No less than 120 years separates these two incidents—a period of time that sheds light on the transition from Hamilton to Haywood. But historians have not filled in the void between these two men in ways that make the transition meaningful. Instead, they have too often relied on crude and utterly misleading generalizations about the industrial city, its social order, and its power structure. Here one of these misleading generalizations, perhaps the most important, is subjected to close and critical examination: the widely held view that from the start, industrialists had the social and political power and prestige to match their economic force, and that they controlled the towns. This generalization has several corollaries: industrialists faced ineffective opposition; town politics reflected their interests; other property owners—particularly small businessmen and professionals—identified with industrialists and applauded their innovations and pecuniary successes. Factory-workers enter this version of history only as passive, ineffective, and alienated victims, practically helpless before their all-powerful employers. Stated in another fashion, it is the proposition that from the beginning, there existed a close relationship between economic class, social status, and power and that control over "things"—especially industrial property and machinery—was quickly and easily transformed into authority and legitimized so that industrialists could do little wrong and, better still, quoting Max Weber, "realize their own will in communal action even against the resistance of others who are participating in the action." In place of this common view, another is argued. Through its early years, for at least a generation, the factory and its disciplines, the large impersonal corporation, and the propertyless wage-earners remained unusual and even alien elements in the industrial town. They disrupted tradition, competed against an established social structure and status hierarchy, and challenged traditional modes of thought. In these years, therefore, the factory-owner symbolized innovation and a radical departure from an older way of life. His power was not yet legitimized and "taken for granted." Surely powerful because of his control over "things," the factory-owner nevertheless found it difficult to enforce noneconomic decisions essential to his economic welfare. He met with unexpected opposition from nonindustrial property-owners, did not dominate the local political structure, and learned that the middle and professional classes did not automatically accept his leadership and idolize his achievements. Moreover, the new working class, not entirely detached from the larger community, had significant ties to that community which strengthened its power at critical moments and allowed it, despite the absence of strong permanent labor organizations, often to influence events at the expense of the factory-owner.

Men hold authority in particular setting, Robert M. MacIver has observed, when they possess "the established right to determine policies, to pronounce judgments on relevant issues, or, more broadly, to act as the leaders or guide to other men." The industrial town was too new at the start for the industrialist to command this kind of prestige and to hold this kind of authority. Class position and social status were closely related. But as a new class, the industrialists had not yet achieved high social status. In fact, the absence of the kind of authority described by MacIver shaped much of dramatic early history of the industrial city. The owners of disruptive and radical innovations—power-driven machinery, the factory, and the large corporation—sought to legitimize their economic power in these years. And Paterson is a good illustration of the frustrating search by the industrialist for status and unchallenged authority.

II

By the early 1870s, Paterson ranked as a major American industrial city. Located fourteen miles from New York City, its factories manufactured mainly locomotives, machinery, iron goods of all kinds, and silks and other textiles. Its three locomotive firms contained 25 per cent of the nation's locomotive capacity, and the products of its large ironworks helped construct the Philadelphia Centennial Exposition buildings; many eastern bridges; and New York's Metropolitan Museum of Art, its Lenox Library, and its first elevated railroad. Paterson also stood as America's preeminent silk manufacturing center, and its separate jute, flax, and mosquito net mills were each the largest of their kind in the nation. With a few exceptions, most of the mills came to Paterson after 1850 so that their owners ranked as relative newcomers to the city twenty years later. Older Patersonians saw their small city change radically between 1850 and 1870.

Before 1850 Paterson had grown fitfully. Early in the nineteenth century, small cotton factories started there to take advantage of available water power and the New York market and port nearby. Although the city had twenty cotton mills in 1832, inability to compete with more efficient New England firms caused them to stagnate in the 1840s and

1850s. According to its official industrial historian, as late as 1838 most New Yorkers regarded Paterson as "an upcountry hamlet, chiefly noted for its fine waterfall and valuable waterpower."

But the cotton mills attracted machinists to repair and build textile machinery, and the start of the railroad era in the 1830s led one of them, aided by New York capital, to begin locomotive manufacturing in 1836. His pioneer factory grew slowly before 1850, as did a number of smaller machine and iron shops. The great increase in the demand for railroad equipment, iron, and machinery after 1850 stimulated the rapid growth of these industries. Two more locomotive factories opened, and between 1850 and 1873 the three together produced 4,437 locomotives and sold them over the entire nation. In 1873, 3,000 men worked in the locomotive shops. Other iron works grew as quickly. Two Lancashire millwrights, for example, started a machine works in 1845 with ten hands and employed 1,100 in 1873.

The silk industry grew even more quickly and spectacularly than the iron and locomotive industries. The pattern was quite simple. A declining cotton industry made available water power, cheap mills, and a resident labor force. These first attracted English silk manufacturer John Ryle to Paterson in 1839, after a successful start as a New York silk importer. Small spinning and weaving shops began in the 1840s and 1850s. But the great stimulus came from outside the city in the 1860s, when New York and Boston silk and textile manufacturers and importers moved their mills to Paterson or built new ones there. A few examples suffice. A Coventry Englishman brought his silk mill from New York in 1860. In the next two years, the nation's leading importer of tailor trimmings left Boston for Patterson, as did another Bostonian, a pioneer American silk manufacturer. In 1868, one of New York's great silk importers became a Paterson manufacturer. From the start, these men of wealth constructed large mills and introduced power machinery, and other innovations. One imported a whole English factory. These men transformed the industry. In 1860 four silk mills employed 590 workers. In 1876, eight silk ribbon and six broad silk factories gave work to 8,000 persons, two thirds of them women. One of every four silk workers was under sixteen years of age. Outside capital also financed other large textile mills in these years. A mosquito net factory came from New York, and Scottish money built the nation's largest jute mill. Eighty-one years after its founding in Northern Ireland, in 1865, Barbour Brothers opened a linen factory that quickly became one of Paterson's great mills. Smaller workshops' continued, but by the 1870s the large mills dominated the local economy.

Older Paterson residents in 1873 lived in a different city than they had known in 1850. The coming of the large mills, particularly from outside the city, transformed Paterson in many ways. The mill-owners, a new industrial leadership mostly alien to the older city, represented a power unknown in earlier years. More than this, their factories drew in increasing numbers of immigrant and native workers and the city boomed. In 1846 Paterson had only 11,000 inhabitants. In the next twenty-four years, its population increased to 33,000. Immigrants made up more than a third of its residents. French and German skilled silk workers, but especially English skilled hands and an increasing number of unskilled Irish laborers, found work in the rapidly expanding factories. Built on two major industries, iron and textiles, the Paterson economy offered employment to whole families: the iron factories hired only men and textile mills relied mainly on female and child labor. Rapid growth in the 1850s and 1860s illustrated in Paterson all the severe social dislocations incident to quick industrialization and urbanization everywhere, but it also opened new opportunities for small retail businesses. Between 1859 and 1870, for example, the number of grocers rose from 105 to 230 and the number of saloonkeepers from 46 to 270. Paterson's industrial leaders in the early 1870s, mostly new to the city, had innovated boldly and caused a city to change radically in less than twenty years from one characterized by small workshops to one typified by large factories. Between 1873 and 1878 a severe depression halted temporarily this process.

III

It is sufficient to report briefly that this first of modern industrial crises, 1873–1878, crippled the Paterson economy and strained the city's total resources and all its citizens. "Among all classes," it was noted as early as October 31, 1873, "there is a feeling of gloom and intense anxiety in regard to the future." Nearly three years later, a silk worker reported with good reason that "Paterson is in a deplorable condition." The unemployed regularly overtaxed limited public and private charities and occasionally paraded the streets demanding public works. The locomotive workers especially felt the diminished demand for labor. From 1871 to 1873 the three locomotive factories produced 1,185 engines; in 1875, 1876 and 1877 the figure totalled only 195. The 1873 wage bill for 3,172 locomotive workers came to $1,850,000; four years later (1877) the same firms paid 325 workers only $165,000. The silk and other textile workers apparently suffered less unemployment, but recurrent wage cuts between 1873 and 1877 ranged from 10 to 30 per cent and meant exceedingly hard times for nearly 10,000 textile workers. Sporadic silk strikes, particularly in 1876, illustrated the workers' reactions to these deplorable conditions. Despair permeated the city. Its population fell almost 10 per cent between 1875 and 1878. With good reason, a New York Sun reporter in September 1876 called Paterson an industrial ghost town comparable to a southern city after Lee's surrender.

In analyzing the consequences of the 1873–1878 depression, historians have argued that the hardship resulting from extensive unemployment and lowered wages shattered labor organizations and immeasurably strengthened employers. But this exclusively economic interpretation ignores the fact that the same cyclical crisis, coming after two decades of radical economic and social change, also tested the status and power of Paterson's new industrialists and workers within the community. The depression created grave economic difficulties for the entire population, and, in trying to solve certain of their problems, the Paterson industrialists sought support and sanction at critical moments from the local community and its leaders. Their successes, but more importantly their failures, revealed much about their status and power in the city, measured the stability and legitimacy of the new industrial order, and gauged the attitudes of shopkeepers and merchants, professionals, politicians, and other prestigious persons in the precorporate city toward the new order and its leaders.

Four incidents between 1877 and 1880 involving Paterson's "public"—two textile strikes and two libel suits against a socialist newspaper editor—will be examined briefly in order to explore the early relationship between economic class, social status, and power.

IV

The first incident illustrated the inability of the new large manufacturers to commit the city government to their interests. It occurred between June and August, 1877 and was an unprecedented general strike of ribbon-weavers, mostly English, French, and German immigrants, against the biggest silk manufacturers. They protested a 20 per cent wage cut and an irksome labor contract and demanded a 10 per cent wage increase and a board of arbitration modeled on English and French precedent. At its peak, the strike—the greatest in Paterson to that time—idled 2,000 workers and closed the mills. After ten weeks, a compromise including restoration of the wage cut took place. What allowed the workers to effect this compromise in the absence of permanent labor organization and after forty-four months of depression? Why did the silk manufacturers fail? In part, the staying power of the weavers frustrated the manufacturers, but even more serious obstacles denied them success.

Important and powerful groups in the community refused to sanction and support the mill-owners. Nonstrikers and elected city officials either supported the strikers or, more significantly, rejected pressure and commands from the mill owners. Small shopkeepers extended credit and subscribed relief funds to the strikers. A weekly, German-language newspaper also supported them. Although critical of the strikers, the two daily newspapers did not cheer the manufacturers and they even lectured the mill owners to "put conscience as well as capital" into their enterprises. The local courts displayed their independence of the manufacturers and on several occasions weavers charged with disorderly conduct went free or suffered, at best, nominal fines. After manufacturer William Strange successfully prosecuted two weavers for violating written contracts, pressure from city officials, including the mayor, convinced a local judge to postpone indefinitely forty additional trials.

The Republican mayor, Benjamin Buckley, and the Democratic-controlled Board of Aldermen gave the manufacturers their greatest trouble. The aldermen were mostly self-made men: skilled workmen of independent means and retail shopkeepers. Their number included neither factory workers nor manufacturers. Mayor Buckley personified the precorporate American dream. Born in England in 1808, he had come to Paterson as a young man, worked first in a cotton factory, and then achieved wealth and high status. By 1877, he owned a small spindle factory, headed a local bank, and looked back on a successful career in Republican politics including several terms in the state legislature and the presidency of the state senate. He started the first of his several terms as Paterson's Republican mayor in 1875. Because he viewed his role as maintaining the public peace and little more, Buckley infuriated the silk manufacturers. During the dispute, he used his powers, especially the small police force, with great skill and tact to suppress overt disorders only. This angered the mill-owners. They insisted that inadequate civic authority allowed a few agitators to intimidate hundreds of loyal workers. In the strike's seventh week, therefore, the Paterson Board of Trade, dominated by the largest silk and iron manufacturers, called a special meeting to pressure the city authorities to enlarge the police force and also to declare a state of emergency limiting the strikers' use of the streets and their freedom of action. The Board publicly charged that "the laws of the land are treated with contempt and trampled upon by a despotic mob" led by immigrant radicals and "communists." A silk manufacturer warned that unless the authorities put down these troublemakers Paterson soon would be "a city without manufactories ... with nothing ... but the insignificant industries of an unimportant town." Other manufacturers expressed even graver anxieties: one urged that strike leaders be "taken out and shot" and another offered to finance a private militia. Iron manufacturer Watts Cooke admitted their deepest fear—the absence of sufficient status and respect in the city. "All the classes of the community," Cooke lamented, "are coming to lean towards and sympathize with the men rather than the employers." He and the others demanded the protection of the city authorities. But Mayor Buckley and the Board of Aldermen turned a deaf ear toward the complaints and demands of the large manufacturers. Buckley did not issue a proclamation, defended his use of civic authority, and advised the aldermen that the Board of Trade did "great injury to the credit of the city." He especially commended "the good sense of the working people." The Democratic Board of Aldermen upheld the Republican mayor. It unanimously passed three resolutions: the first tabled without discussion the request for a larger police force; the second applauded Buckley's "wise and judicious course"; and the third, as if to reiterate the independence of the city government from the manufacturers, urged immediate prosecution of mill owners who violated local fire-escape ordinances. The manufacturers were unable to alter public policies during the strike. City officials—all property-owners—maintained an independence of judgment and explicitly rejected iron manufacturer Watts Cooke's insistence that the Board of Trade was "best able to judge what the city needed to protect it."

After the strike, although the *Paterson Guardian* advised the Board of Trade to get into local politics and "pay the proper attention to the men . . . elected to the city council," the large manufacturers turned away from politics and to the private militia. The Board listened approvingly to a member who found "more virtue in one well drilled soldier than in ten policemen or in one bullet than in ten clubs in putting down a riot." Silk manufacturer Strange led the group that subscribed the first $4,500 for arms and equipment. And of the 120 militiamen signed up by January, 1880, at least 50 per cent were manufacturers, merchants, clerks, salespeople, and professionals. It proved easier to subscribe funds for a militia than to "reform" the city government. The manufacturers had more than enough wealth to finance a private militia but inadequate prestige and power to dominate the city government. In 1877, Paterson had one police officer for every 1,666 residents; ten years later, it had a militia company but the ratio of police to population remained the same. The manufacturers' use of private power indicated weakness, not strength *vis a vis* the body politic and the city government.

V

A year after the ribbon-weavers' strike, a second dispute involving textile workers again illustrated the limited power of the Paterson manufacturers. A third wage cut in less than a year convinced 550 unorganized workers, mostly women and children, to quit the textile mills owned by two brothers, Robert and Henry Adams. One of the East's great textile mills, R & H Adams and Company symbolized the rapid rise of the new industrialism in Paterson. It had moved a small factory there from New York City in 1857 and had thrived in the next twenty years, adding several large and efficient mills to its original plant. By far the largest of its kind in the country and perhaps in the world, the firm exported huge quantities of mosquito netting overseas, especially to Africa and Asia. Two more unequal adversaries than the unorganized Adams strikers and their employer hardly could be found. Yet, after a strike lasting nine months, the company conceded defeat in March 1879, and its senior partner, Robert Adams, who vigorously and publicly combatted the strikers, quit the firm and left Paterson.

Once again, community attitudes toward the dispute shaped its outcome, and Robert Adams, not the striking women, had no allies in this battle. The Board of Trade kept silent. No one publicly protested Adams' recurrent threat to move the mills. The press remained neutral. With one exception noted below, Adams got no overt encouragement from other manufacturers, retail businessmen, or politicians. He even had trouble with his foremen and had to fire a few who defended the strikers. Unlike Adams, the strikers found strength in the community. Many took jobs in other local textile mills. Strike funds gathered mainly from local workers, shopkeepers, and merchants fed the others. Concerts and picnics buoyed their spirits and added to their funds. At least one of every eight Patersonians signed a petition attacking Adams. Frequent street demonstrations indicated additional support. Soon after the trouble began, an outspoken Irish socialist, Joseph P. McDonnell, came to Paterson from nearby New York to encourage the strikers. He organized them into the International Labor Union, an industrial union for unskilled factory workers led by immigrant socialists and Yankee eight-hour reformers. McDonnell stayed on and soon started a socialist weekly newspaper, the Paterson *Labor Standard*. Although its masthead quoted Karl Marx and its columns heaped abuse on local mill-owners and called Adams "Lucifer" and his mills "a penitentiary," its back pages contained numerous local business advertisements. Forty-five retail enterprises, mostly saloons, groceries, and clothing, drygoods, and boot and shoe shops sustained the paper as it railed against manufacturer Adams.

Adams' power against the workers was limited to his firm's income. He sent special agents to Fall River and other New England towns to recruit new workers. Adams hired many new hands but retained few because the strikers made full use of the streets. The strikers and their sympathizers, at one time as many as 2,000 persons, met the new workers at the rail depot or in the streets, urged them to quit Adams, and even financed their way home. This tactic worked: the first time jeers, taunts, and ordinary discourse convinced twenty-two of twenty-five Fall River workers to leave immediately. Although the city authorities arrested a few workers when tempers flared, they quickly released them and made no effort to restrain strikers using the streets peacefully. By carefully separating "peaceful coercion" from "violence," the authorities effectively if unintentionally strengthened the strikers and Adams' wealth gained him no advantage. The freedom to use the streets to persuade outsiders from taking their jobs together with support from shopkeepers allowed the otherwise weak strikers to check Adams' power, thereby revealing his impotence and finally forcing him to surrender and to leave the city.

VI

The third and fourth events centered on Joseph McDonnell and his socialist newspaper, the *Labor Standard*. Dublin-born McDonnell had crowded much radical experience into his thirty-two years before coming to Paterson in 1878 to aid the Adams strikers. He had edited several Dublin and London Irish nationalist journals, engaged in Fenian "conspiracies," represented Ireland at the 1872 Hague Congress of the First International and sided with the Marxists, organized several huge London labor free-speech demonstrations, and served four prison terms before coming to the United States in January, 1873. Soon after his arrival, McDonnell exposed steerage conditions in indignant letters, edited a New York socialist weekly, and traveled all over the East condemning capitalism, advocating socialism, and organizing weak socialist trade unions. According to traditional historical stereotypes, McDonnell should have been a pariah to all but a few Patersonians and therefore easy game for his opponents. But even though the Irish socialist had serious legal troubles and went to prison, he and his newspaper soon won acceptance as legitimate and useful critics of the new industrial order.

McDonnell's difficulties began in October 1878, before the ink had dried on the *Labor Standard*'s first issue, and continued unabated for eighteen months. The formal complaint of a few loyal Adams workers whom the *Labor Standard* attacked as "scabs" convinced the County Grand Jury to indict McDonnell for libel. A petit jury found him guilty and a judge fined him $500 and court costs. A few months later, McDonnell apparently averted a second libel indictment. But in the fall of 1879, a second Grand Jury indictment did come, for McDonnell had printed a bitter letter by a young worker, Michael Menton, exposing inadequate working and living conditions in a Passaic River brickyard, where Menton had labored and become severely ill. In February, 1880 a jury found McDonnell and Menton guilty of libel and a judge sent them to the Passaic County Jail for three months. Viewed only in these narrow terms, McDonnell's difficulties prove to traditional labor historians only the repressive power of "capital" and the pliancy of the judiciary. Actually, McDonnell's difficulties strengthened him. If these legal troubles were intended to drive him from Paterson, the opposite resulted. Support from workers, mostly nonsocialists, and from other persons prominent in the community assured his survival.

Although new to Paterson, McDonnell was not a complete outcast during his first trial. His lawyer, an old Patersonian, had grown wealthy as a real-estate speculator, fathered the state's first ten-hour law and important banking reforms, organized the city's waterworks, and been a prominent Republican for twenty years before becoming Greenback candidate for New Jersey governor. Despite the county prosecutor's plea to convict McDonnell as a "woman libeler," a "threat" to established order and a "foreign emissary" sent by English manufacturers to "breed discontent" in America, the jury, composed mostly of storekeepers and skilled workmen, remained deadlocked for three days and three nights. Only unusual pressure by the presiding judge finally brought conviction. The $500 fine, substantially less than the maximum $2,000 fine and two-year prison term, told much. A second judge, in the case, himself originally a Lancashire worker and then the owner of a small bobbin pin factory, convinced the presiding judge to go easy on McDonnell. After the conviction, storekeepers and merchants contributed handsomely to McDonnell's "defense fund."

McDonnell's lower-class supporters made known their displeasure with the trial and used the threat of their potential political power. They crowded the courtroom to cheer McDonnell and after the conviction, raised the fine and court costs quickly and carried their hero through the streets. More important, the trial occurred during the bitter 1878 congressional election, and they humiliated the county prosecutor, a Democratic politician. Workers joined by sympathetic storekeepers crowded the annual Democratic election meeting and in a raucous demonstration refused to let it start until the prosecutor left the hall. The meeting ended quickly. McDonnell's supporters then jammed a second meeting and hundreds silently walked out when the prosecutor rose to speak. Politicians competing for labor votes got the point. A Republican argued that only free speech and a free press could preserve American liberty. Fearing the loss of labor votes, the Democrats publicly defended the right to strike and one Democrat declaimed: "Away with the government of the aristocracy! Away with legislators only from the wealthy classes! We have had enough of them!" A nearby newspaper sympathetic to McDonnell concluded: "In Paterson, he [McDonnell] is stronger than his accusers. Today he has the sympathy of the people, and his paper from this time forth is deeply rooted in Paterson."

The second trial and subsequent imprisonment of McDonnell attracted national attention but only its local significance concerns us. The support McDonnell received this time revealed his growing local prestige and power. Except for the litigants, no one publicly attacked him. His competitor, the Democratic *Paterson Guardian*, found the verdict "to say the least, a great surprise to those who heard or read the testimony." The judge justified sending McDonnell to prison only because he feared that others again would pay a fine. This time, McDonnell's lawyers were the son of a former Democratic mayor and Socrates Tuttle, Paterson's most respected attorney, who had been Republican mayor some years before. Ably defending his client, Tuttle warned that a conviction would endanger the free press and mean that the working classes would "henceforth never be allowed to complain." Three northern New Jersey nonlabor weeklies emphasized the same point. McDonnell's sympathizers were led by two former silk factory foremen, one German and the other English, and both now successful entrepreneurs. Two clergymen, one a Baptist and the other a Methodist (both active in Republican politics and Paterson's most popular clergymen) condemned McDonnell's treatment and counseled the socialist. Several aldermen, former aldermen, and county freeholders visited him in prison. Garrett A. Hobart, a Paterson corporation lawyer, President of the State Senate and that year elected chairman of the Republican State Committee, sent McDonnell ten dollars for his defense, offered "to do his best" and sought to amend the state libel law. Even the son of Henry Adams and nephew of Robert Adams, McDonnell's 1878 adversary, gave the socialist twenty dollars and visited him in jail.

McDonnell's jail experience, surely one of the most unusual in American penal history, depended upon John Buckley, the former mayor's son. He had been a locomotive worker as a young man, a prominent Republican, and warden of the county prison. Apparently distressed over the conviction, Warden Buckley did his best to assure McDonnell's comfort and his freedom while in prison. McDonnell kept a prison diary, and its entries record many surprising amenities. The warden let him edit his newspaper and organize a national and local protest campaign against his imprisonment. McDonnell's supporters visited him daily and often brought their children along. Buckley allowed them to meet in his office. One day as many as twenty-one persons called on McDonnell. Every day his meals arrived from outside, and saloon- and boardinghouse-keepers kept him overstocked with cigars, wines, and liquors. Others brought fresh fruits, cakes, and puddings. On St. Patrick's Day shamrocks came, and on his birthday, two fancy dinners. The day of his release, Warden Buckley publicly commended the good behavior of prisoner Joseph P. McDonnell.

Let out ten days early, McDonnell benefited from a demonstration of popular support unprecedented in Paterson's history. Organized by a committee of seventy-five that was dominated by workers but included twelve saloon- and inn-keepers and five grocers, the demonstration counted between fifteen and twenty thousand persons. After that, few Patersonians doubted the labor agitator's place and power in their city. McDonnell's *Labor Standard* survived until his death in 1908. He founded the New Jersey Federation of Trades and Labor Unions and pioneered in pushing protective labor legislation. Several clues indicate his rapid acceptance as a radical critic. Soon after his imprisonment, the Democratic prosecutor who had called him a "woman libeler" and a "foreign emissary" sent by British manufacturers began advertising his legal services in the *Labor Standard*. The city government regularly bought space to print legal public notices. In 1884, less than six years after he had come to Paterson and four years after his release from jail, socialist McDonnell was appointed New Jersey's first deputy inspector of factories and workshops.

McDonnell never lost feeling for those who helped in the early days. In 1896, although the *Labor Standard* still carried Karl Marx's words on its masthead, McDonnell printed kind words about Garrett Hobart, then running with William McKinley against William Jennings Bryan. He called Hobart "a rare specimen of manhood in the class in which he moves" and, remembering Hobart's aid in 1880, concluded that "to know him is to like him whether you agree with his opinions or not."

VII

What general meaning can be inferred from these Paterson events? If they are unique to that city, then only the local historian profits from them. In fact, they typified obstacles encountered by industrialists in other post-Civil War industrial towns and cities during crises similar to the 1877 and 1878 Paterson textile disputes. Time and again, the industrialist found his freedom of action confined by particular local "circumstances." Several examples illustrate his difficulties. A western Pennsylvania jury convicted a mine operator when violence resulted after he brought Italians there. The merchant mayor of an Illinois mining town disarmed Chicago Pinkerton police sent to guard an operator's properties. A sheriff raised a posse to chase special New York police sent to protect railroad repair shops in eastern Pennsylvania. Ohio Valley newspapers condemned iron manufacturers for arming strikebreakers. Northern Pennsylvania merchants housed striking evicted coal miners. A pronounced pattern emerges from these and similar events. Unorganized or poorly organized workers displayed surprising strength and staying power and found sympathy from other groups in the community. Local political officials often rejected or modified the pressures of industrialists. Nonindustrial capitalists—persons with power and prestige locally and persons committed to competitive private enterprise and the acquisitive spirit in their own dealings—responded equivocally or critically to the practices of the new industrialists. Such behavior is quite different from that usually characterized as typical of early industrial America. And yet it occurred frequently in the first decades of the industrial city. How can this pattern of behavior be explained?

Unless two misleading and erroneous conceptions are disregarded, this pattern of response seems anomalous and even meaningless. The first is the idea that the industrialist achieved status and legitimized his power quickly and easily in his local community. The second is the belief that urban property owners as a group shared a common ideology in responding to the severe dislocations resulting from rapid industrialization and in reacting to the frequent disputes between workers and factory-owners. Because Congress gave huge land grants to railroads, and state governors frequently supplied militia to "settle" industrial disputes, it does not follow that the industrialists in Paterson and other cities so dominated the local political and social structure that their freedom of action remained unchecked. Because a grocer owned his business and a mayor presided over a bank, it does not mean they sympathized with the social policies of a large factory-owner. Because Andrew Carnegie applauded Herbert Spencer, it does not mean that jungle ethics reigned supreme in the industrial city. If we are free of these distorting generalizations, it is possible to look afresh at social behavior and conflict in Gilded Age America. Take the example of the use of state troops in industrial disputes. Such action may have resulted from the low status and power the industrialist had in his local community. Unable to gain support from locally elected officials and law-enforcement groups and unable to exercise coercive power in the community, he reached upward to the state level, where direct local pressures were felt less strongly. If, as E. D. Baltzell writes, "power which is not legitimized tends to be either coercive or manipulative," much is explained by the low status of the new industrialists. Careful examination of particular local industrial conflicts that involved the use of state as opposed to local police might help explain the widespread violence and corruption so often condemned by Gilded Age historians and yet so little understood.

In nineteenth-century America, power and status had meaning on several levels of society. Here the focus is a particular community. If the industrialist is viewed as an innovator in a local context, the Paterson events take on broader meaning. The new industrialist—especially if he came from elsewhere—was a disruptive outsider. He did not create an entirely new social structure, but he confronted an existing one. He found a more-or-less static city, which thrived on small and personal workshops and an intimate and personal way of life. It was hardly ideal, but it was settled and familiar. Making goods and employing people differently, the industrialist abruptly disrupted this "traditional" way of work and life and, as a person, symbolized severe local dislocations. The older residents and the newer workers responded to these changes in many ways. But if the industrialist, in cutting costs and rationalizing production, violated traditional community norms or made unusually new demands upon the citizenry—such as the special use of a police force or the suppression of a newspaper—his decision often provoked opposition.

The size of the industrial city and the particular composition of its population made the industrialist's innovations more visible and his power more vulnerable there than in the larger complex metropolis. Residents of the early factory town had a more direct relationship with one another and with the innovations. Even persons indirectly affected by industrialism could hardly avoid close contact with the larger factory, the corporation, and the propertyless wage-earners. The closeness of the middle class and the old resident population to the new industrialism gave such persons the opportunity to judge the industrial city's social dislocations and social conflicts by personal experience, and not simply through the opaque filter of ideologies such as laissez-faire liberalism and Darwinism. In addition, the worker had more power as a consumer and as a voter and could express particular needs more effectively in the factory town than in the metropolis. Street demonstrations had a greater impact in Paterson than in New York or Chicago. In the industrial city, the retail merchant depended heavily on a narrow class of consumers (mostly workers) and the politicians appealed to more homogeneous voting groups. All of these considerations contributed to the industrialist's difficulties. So, too, did the rapid growth of the mill-town itself weaken their chances for civic and police control. A number of studies of the mobility patterns of Paterson men (three thousand fathers and sons between 1870 and 1890) show that the more ambitious and able workers found expanding opportunities outside the factories in small retail business, politics, and city employment (including the police force)—the very areas in which the industrialists demanded cooperation or control. Conservative in many ways, these men had a stake in the new society. Some identified entirely with their new class and repressed their origins. But others—a large number in the early years—still had memories, roots, and relatives among the workers. Some had even suffered from the same employers they were now called on to protect. In crisis situations such as those that occurred in the 1870s, their social origins and older community ties may have created a conflict between their fellow-feeling and even family sentiment and their material achievements. The evidence does not make explicit such conflict, but it makes clear that during strikes and other crises the industrialists could not expect and did not get unswerving loyalty or approval from them.

VIII

Historians have not emphasized sufficiently the subtle and complex patterns of response to social change in nineteenth-century America—particularly to the coming of industrial capitalism. Much has been omitted in these pages: No judgement is passed on working conditions or standards of comfort in the industrial city; nothing is said of the important but little studied working class sub culture that thrived in the industrial city, and no attempt is made to precisely measure the strength of the opposing forces of workers and industrialists. The conclusions stated here are that economic power was not easily translated into social and political power, and that the changes resulting from rapid industrialization stimulated sufficient opposition to the industrialist to deprive him of the status and the authority he sought and needed. The theme of this chapter illustrates Dorothy George's (*England in Transition*, 1953) view that "social history is local history" but local history in a larger context that permits the careful examination of grand and sweeping hypotheses. It is finally suggested, indirectly, that knowledge of the early history of American industrialization and urban growth tells much about modern society and the contemporary city: its social structure, its power relationships, and its decision-making process. The nineteenth-century city differed from its twentieth-century counterpart; so much of what "makes" a city has changed in the past seventy years. In *Victorian Cities* (1963), Asa Briggs wisely argued for historical specificity and interdisciplinary approaches to the study of nineteenth-century cities. Free of the nostalgia of those historians who compare the "city" only to the "country" but sensitive to the acute social disorganization that accompanied rapid industrialization and urban development, Briggs showed that different British cities each had a distinct history (shaped by particular inner social patterns) and also that their histories should not be confused with the later city so powerfully affected by radical innovations such as the automobile, the national corporation, and the revolution in communications. All too often, however, social scientists and even historians view the contemporary city in exceedingly ahistorical terms or only study its past by projecting present "trends" backward. For them, as Barrington Moore notes, the past becomes "merely a storehouse of samples," and "facts" are "drawn upon as if they were colored balls from an urn." Stephan Thernstrom's pioneering study of nineteenth-century Newburyport, Massachusetts, *Poverty and Progress* (1964), splendidly illustrates the grave pitfalls of an ahistorical view of urban social mobility. It further shows that however carefully the present is studied and however refined the techniques of analysis, the present is not fully comprehended if the past is ignored or distorted.

Class and status altered as the industrial city matured. The industrialist's power became legitimized. The factories and their owners dug deeper into the lives of the mill towns and became more accepted and powerful. The old middle class, and those who revered the old, precorporate town, lost influence and disappeared. They were replaced by others who identified more fully with the corporate community. The city government became more bureaucratic and less responsive to popular pressures. Why and how these changes occurred remain important subjects for study. But in order to grasp the magnitude of these changes it is necessary to discard the notion that the nineteenth-century factory-owners moved into control of the industrial town overnight. This myth masks reality and prevents us from focusing on the differences between the nineteenth-century city and the contemporary city. If these differences are located and analyzed, "trends" no longer seem timeless, and the "modern condition"—so often tied to the "urban condition"—assumes a meaningful historical dimension because it is rooted in an understandable past.

5

The Transformation of American Foreign Policy 1890–1917

Altruism or Imperialism?

During the last quarter of the nineteenth century the United States emerged as a recognized world power. Its industrial and agricultural productivity, large size, growing population, and modern navy gave it a prominence that could not be ignored. The acquisition of an overseas empire added to America's stature. In 1898 and 1899 the United States suddenly acquired the Hawaiian Islands and gained control over Puerto Rico, the Philippines, and part of the Samoan archipelago. Within a year and a half America had become a dominant power in both the Caribbean and the Pacific. America's entry into the First World War merely confirmed the nation's new-found status as a world power.

Curiously enough, many Americans were ambivalent about their country's new role. Some feared that America's democratic institutions were incompatible with an overseas empire and the large military establishment that would be required to sustain it. Others rejected the concept of empire because they opposed bringing under the American flag groups they regarded as racial or social inferiors. Some Americans, on the other hand, favored the entry of the United States into world affairs, either because of a crusading zeal to spread American institutions or an economic desire to find new markets. There was a comparable division in public opinion between 1914 and 1917 over whether America's rights and interests were threatened by the actions of the Allies or Central Powers. Most Americans believed their nation should remain at peace, but disagreements persisted over the exact policies to be used to reach that goal. Although the United States entered the twentieth century as a recognized world power, its people remained quite divided over the desirability of pursuing their new destiny.

These divisions among the public over foreign policy had their counterpart among diplomatic historians. Just as Americans debated the wisdom of particular policies, so historians disagreed about interpretations of past events. The historical debate, in reality, was not confined to an analysis of the past; implicit in many diplomatic interpretations was a view of America's present and future. To argue that the United States traditionally had been a champion of freedom and democracy was to take a position on certain contemporary policies toward the nondemocratic world. Similarly, the argument that America had been an imperialistic nation bent on imposing its economic and military power on the rest of the world had implications for contemporary foreign policy questions.

The historical literature dealing with the Spanish-American War is a case in point. Charles and Mary Beard, whose *Rise of American Civilization* symbolized the Progressive school of American historiography, implied that economic issues led President William McKinley to ask for a declaration of war. The Spanish government, after all, had practically acceded to his demands. McKinley, Beard insisted, revised Cleveland's policy of neutrality, presumably because of the threat to American investments in and trade with Cuba. In the final analysis war grew out of a desire to protect America's economic interests in that region. The ensuing acquisition of overseas territory provided further proof of Beard's charge that the nation's business community played an important role in determining the country's foreign policy. Although Beard's thesis was presented in somewhat qualified form, it clearly implied the primacy of economic forces.[1]

A decade later Julius W. Pratt rejected the Beardian emphasis on economic determinism. The forces responsible for the new expansionism, according to Pratt, were intellectual and emotional in nature. The emergence of Social Darwinism, with its emphasis on competition and the survival of the fittest, provided some people with an intellectual justification for expanding America's sphere of influence. They argued that nations, like individuals, were engaged in a remorseless test of their fitness to survive. The criterion of success was dominion over others; failure to expand, on the other hand, meant stagnation and decline. Other expansionist-minded persons were affected by religious and humanitarian concerns; they wished to bring American civilization and morality to less advanced peoples. Still others accepted the doctrines developed by Captain Alfred Thayer Mahan, who saw growing American sea power as the key to the nation's greatness. Sea power, however, required overseas naval bases. Pratt, interestingly enough, noted that the business community, which was still recovering from the depression

---

[1]Charles A. Beard and Mary R. Beard, *The Rise of American Civilization* (2 vols.: New York, 1927), II, pp. 369–382.

that began in 1893, opposed intervention in Cuba for fear that it might block the road to economic recovery. With Admiral Dewey's dramatic victory in the Philippines, American businessmen became converted to the expansionist cause by the prospect of dominating the potentially large market in China. Those same businessmen now found it easy to apply the same rationale in the Caribbean and supported expansion in that area. The reasons why the United States went to war, therefore, were quite different from the reasons that led its government to acquire an overseas empire. Indeed, Pratt concluded that American imperialism consisted of a blend of religious, humanitarian, and economic components.[2]

Pratt and Beard agreed, at least in part, that foreign policy was determined by domestic influences. There were significant differences, nevertheless, between their approaches. To Beard the business community, with its emphasis on profits, pushed the nation to go to war. In Pratt's eyes, on the other hand, a variety of influences—domestic and foreign—came into play, though no one in particular exercised the decisive role. These two approaches were to dominate the writing of American diplomatic history to a considerable degree. Those in the tradition of Beard would see America's foreign policy primarily in terms of domestic concerns. The others would emphasize in addition the importance of actions taken by foreign governments. While the two approaches would on occasion come together in the work of an individual scholar, more often than not they would remain distinct and separate.

After the publication of Pratt's work in 1936, scholarly interest in the Spanish-American War tended to flag. Between the 1930's and 1960 diplomatic historians were primarily concerned in dealing with the causes of the First and Second World Wars. But in 1959 William Appleman Williams published his influential book, *The Tragedy of American Diplomacy*, which had a profound impact on the writing of all of diplomatic history. His book, indeed, became the starting point for the work of many revisionist and "New Left" historians, who believed that America's foreign policies were dominated by economic interests.

The Williams thesis, briefly stated, rested on the premise that foreign policy was a function of the structure and organization of American society. Business groups during the depression of the 1880's and 1890's had concluded that foreign markets were indispensable for America's economic well-being. These markets would help to avoid any internal problems that might arise from economic stagnation resulting from America's tendency to produce surplus goods. The result was a fundamental change in America's foreign policy. Policy makers adopted what became known as the Open Door Policy—an open door "through which

---

[2]Julius W. Pratt, *Expansionists of 1898* (Baltimore, 1936), and *America's Colonial Experiment: How the United States Gained, Governed, and in Part Gave Away a Colonial Empire* (New York, 1950).

America's preponderant economic strength would enter and dominate all underdeveloped areas of the world. . . . [T]he Open Door Policy was in fact a brilliant strategic stroke which led to the gradual extension of American economic and political power throughout the world."[3] Much of America's diplomacy in the twentieth century, Williams wrote, was directed toward the goal of assuring the nation's economic supremacy on a global scale.

The origins of modern American foreign policy, Williams insisted, could be traced back to the economic crisis of the 1890's. During that decade, a new national consensus had been reached. Americans no longer debated whether or not an expansionist policy should be pursued, but rather what form expansionism should take. This expansionist policy was based on the conviction that American diplomacy and prosperity went hand in hand and required access to world markets. Any restrictions on the flow of American goods and capital would lead to a depression and social unrest. Support for economic expansion, therefore, played a crucial role in precipitating the Spanish-American War and in the subsequent debate over the desirability of acquiring overseas possessions. The first selection in this chapter is an excerpt from *The Tragedy of American Diplomacy.*

In 1963 Walter LaFeber published a prize-winning volume on American expansionism from 1860 to 1898 that gave strong support to the Williams thesis. The Civil War, LaFeber noted, marked an important dividing line in America's expansionist policies. Before 1860 expansionism was confined to the American continent; it reflected the desire of an agrarian society to find new and fertile lands. Post–Civil War expansionism, on the other hand, was motivated by the belief that foreign markets were vital to America's well-being. To a society dominated by businessmen, it appeared that additional foreign markets "would solve the economic, social, and political problems created by the industrial revolution." Given Europe's imperialist penetration in many regions of the world, Americans concluded that their country needed strategic bases if they were to compete successfully. The diplomacy of the 1890's and the Spanish-American War grew out of these concerns. "By 1899," concluded LaFeber, "the United States had forged a new empire. American policy makers and businessmen had created it amid much debate and with conscious purpose."[4]

The Williams-LaFeber interpretation of the origins of modern America's foreign policy had a powerful appeal during the 1960's and 1970's, particularly as disillusionment with American society grew during the

---

[3]William Appleman Williams, *The Tragedy of American Diplomacy* (2d. rev. and enl. ed.: New York, 1972), pp. 45–46.

[4]Walter LaFeber, *The New Empire: An Interpretation of American Expansionism 1860–1898* (Ithaca, 1963), pp. 416–417. See also Thomas McCormick, *China Market: America's Quest for Informal Empire 1893–1901* (Chicago, 1967).

Vietnam War. The argument that the country's diplomacy was based less on altruism and idealism and more on a desire to safeguard an international order that made possible America's economic supremacy, of course, had important implications for contemporary concerns. The Cold War, for example, rather than resting on a moral foundation that pitted freedom against Communism, was seen as a product of America's continued insistence on structuring a world order along lines that preserved its capitalist hegemony. Thus American foreign policy—which grew out of domestic institutions and developments—was allegedly responsible in large measure for initiating and perpetuating the Cold War and causing the Vietnam conflict.[5] Williams's work spawned a whole school of historians who proceeded to write revisionist accounts of the history of American foreign policy.

The Williams thesis, however, did not gain universal acceptance in historical circles. Not all scholars, for example, agreed with his portrait of American society. Others were critical of a viewpoint that emphasized the importance of domestic factors in the determination of foreign policy and belittled the role of other nations. In their eyes diplomatic policies were also influenced by the external actions and reactions of foreign governments. A more balanced approach, they argued, called for an understanding of the behavior of other governments, which, in turn, implied a multinational approach to diplomacy and multiarchival research. Rejecting the idea of American omnipotence in world affairs, they stressed other than economic factors and attempted to demonstrate that the purposefulness attributed to American policy makers was not justified by a critical examination of the sources.

Typical of this approach was Ernest R. May's *Imperial Democracy: The Emergence of America as a Great Power*, published in 1961. May argued that in the 1890's the United States had not sought to play a new role in world affairs. On the contrary, diplomatic problems concerning Hawaii, China, Venezuela, and Cuba had almost intruded upon the domestic issues in which most statesmen and political leaders were primarily interested. "Some nations," May observed, "achieve greatness; the United States had greatness thrust upon it."

President McKinley, for example, rather than being the harbinger of imperialism, was portrayed as a leader who was trying to keep his country out of war and at the same time resolve the Cuban dilemma that had inflamed public opinion. His initiatives were ultimately doomed to failure, for Spain would neither grant Cuba autonomy nor suppress the rebellion. McKinley then gave Spain an ultimatum, which included

[5]See the following: LaFeber, *America, Russia, and the Cold War 1945–1966* (New York, 1967); Lloyd C. Gardner, "American Foreign Policy 1900–1921: A Second Look at the Realist Critique of American Diplomacy," in *Towards a New Past: Dissenting Essays in American History*, ed. by Barton J. Bernstein (New York, 1968), pp. 202–231; David Healy, *U.S. Expansionism: The Imperialist Urge in the 1890s* (Madison, 1970).

American mediation in the event Spain and the Cubans could not reach some arrangement (a mediation that in all likelihood would have meant Cuban independence). To the Spanish government such an ultimatum was unacceptable. McKinley then faced a crucial choice. He could embark upon a war that he did not want or could defy public opinion and accept some compromise. The latter course might have led to the unseating of the Republican party if not the overthrow of constitutional government. "When public emotion reached the point of hysteria, he succumbed," said May.

Did McKinley accept the decision for war because of a need for foreign markets and strategic bases, as Williams argued? Most assuredly not, insisted May:

> Neither the President nor the public had any aim beyond war itself. The nation was in a state of upset. Until recently its people had been largely Protestant and English; its economy predominantly rural and agricultural.... Now, however, the country was industrialized and urbanized. Catholics were numerous and increasing. People of older stock found themselves no longer economically or even socially superior to members of immigrant groups or to others.... The panic of 1893 made this new condition even more visible by depressing agricultural prices, rents, investment income, professional fees, and white-collar salaries.... In some irrational way, all these influences and anxieties translated themselves into concern for suffering Cuba. For the people as for the government, war with monarchical, Catholic, Latin Spain had no purpose except to relieve emotion.[6]

Six years later, May published an extended essay in which he used concepts drawn from the social sciences in order to present a fuller portrait of the diplomacy of those years. In that work May examined the structure and role of public opinion in order to illuminate how the United States briefly became imperialistic in outlook and then even more quickly turned away from overseas expansion. After analyzing public opinion in terms of various categories involving elites with different interests and concerns, May argued that the anticolonialist consensus was briefly broken in 1898–1899, which resulted in the transfer of leader-

---

[6]Ernest R. May, *Imperial Democracy: The Emergence of America as a Great Power* (New York, 1961), pp. 268–270. In a certain sense May's thesis was anticipated a decade earlier by Richard Hofstadter. In 1952 Hofstadter published an article that rejected an economic explanation of American diplomacy in the 1890's and suggested instead that the hysteria and jingoism of this decade grew out of the anxieties occasioned by social and economic change. (Shortly thereafter Hofstadter proposed a comparable explanation of the roots of "McCarthyism.") Although sympathetic to liberalism, Hofstadter's work in the 1940's and 1950's contributed to the emerging rejection of the basic tenets of the Progressive school of American historiography. In his eyes modern American liberalism reflected less a concern for the welfare of the masses of Americans and more the inner feelings of select middle-class persons alienated from their society because of technological and economic change. Foreign policy, Hofstadter implied, mirrored these nonrational and noneconomic influences. See his "Manifest Destiny and the Philippines," in *America in Crisis: Fourteen Crucial Episodes in American History*, ed. by Daniel Aaron (New York, 1952), pp. 173–200.

ship to a wider circle. The outcome was a new consensus that accepted the desirability of acquiring foreign possessions and owed much of its inspiration to European and especially British opinion. Shortly thereafter the more traditional anticolonial view prevailed, especially after the difficulties faced by the British during the Boer War in South Africa and the growth of an antiimperialist movement in Britain. May concluded by insisting that the imperialist–antiimperialist debate could not be understood solely in terms of what Americans said or did, for they were members of a much broader Atlantic civilization.[7]

Paul A. Varg, in a similar vein, noted that a careful examination of the specific actions by the United States in world affairs precluded any simple or facile generalizations about imperialism or America's world power status. China was *not* of major importance to American policy officials. Even the dominant role of the United States in the Caribbean was never pursued solely for economic considerations; strong opposition to any American intervention in that area arose during each crisis. In Varg's view, few American leaders pursued foreign policy concerns out of a conviction that the nation's welfare was dependent upon developments in other parts of the world. Although the United States did become a world power, it was not because of any master plan designed to control the destiny of other nations. The second selection in this chapter is from an article by Varg.[8]

Although the implications of the work of scholars like May and Varg were not immediately evident, their approach involved an explicit rejection of the Williams critique of American foreign policy. Diplomacy, they insisted, could not be separated from the ideas and actions of other nations, for the United States functioned within a system of nation-states in which more than economic considerations counted. May and Varg were, at least by implication, much less critical of American leaders, and they certainly did not share the view that diplomacy was the function of America's rigid class structure.

Just as America's involvement in the Spanish-American War proved controversial among historians, so too did its involvement in the First World War. The circumstances leading to America's entry generated conflict over the proper role of the United States in world affairs and the desirability of participation in foreign conflicts. More than anything else, the divisions among historians who dealt with American diplomacy from 1914 to 1917 reflected differing views as to what America's policy should have been.

---

[7]Ernest R. May, "American Imperialism: A Reinterpretation," *Perspectives in American History*, I (1967), 123-283, also published as *American Imperialism: A Speculative Essay* (New York, 1968).

[8]For other examples of work in this tradition see Howard K. Beale, *Theodore Roosevelt and the Rise of America to World Power* (Baltimore, 1956); Raymond A. Esthus, *Theodore Roosevelt and the International Rivalries* (Waltham, 1970); and Paul A. Varg, *The Making of a Myth: The United States and China, 1897–1912* (East Lansing, 1968).

Generally speaking, most of the contemporary or near-contemporary accounts—none of which were based upon wide research in the sources simply because relevant manuscript materials were as yet unavailable—took a favorable view of America's diplomatic moves between 1914 and 1917. The two most widely read works in this regard in the 1920's were semi-autobiographical accounts that dealt with the careers of Walter Hines Page, the American ambassador to England, and Colonel Edward House, Wilson's close friend and adviser. Both men had advocated intervention; both had shown concern lest America's policy obstruct the Allies; and both were of the opinion that German militarism would have represented a real threat to American democracy if the Central Powers had emerged victorious. When the United States entered the war, they argued, it did so for reasons of morality and self-interest, both of which coincided in 1917.[9]

The controversy over the Versailles peace treaty and the growing disillusionment with Wilsonian idealism, however, set the stage for a reexamination of the problem of America's entry into the war. During the 1920's a new school of historians known as the revisionists emerged to offer different explanations for America's involvement. John K. Turner, a veteran socialist writer who published a book entitled *Shall It Be Again?* in 1922, was among the first of the revisionists. Rejecting the interpretation that the United States intervened to protect commerce and lives and to uphold national honor and international law, Turner argued that Wilson, a pseudo-liberal, went to war because of the greed of Wall Street bankers. His book, however, had little influence at the time of its publication, one reason being its polemical tone.[10]

A few years later a more significant statement of the revisionist point of view was presented by Professor Harry Elmer Barnes, who became interested in the general problem of war guilt. In 1926 Barnes published his *Genesis of the World War* in which he repudiated the idea that Germany had been responsible for the outbreak of war in 1914. He contended that America's participation in the war had been a mistake brought about by Wilson's acquiescence in Britain's illegal maritime restrictions and his misguided desire to save the Allies from defeat. By throwing American power into the conflict on the side of the Allies, Wilson set the stage for the disastrous and one-sided Versailles peace settlement that followed.[11] Barnes continued for more than forty years to reiterate his belief that the United States should have stayed out of the First World War. Implicit in his point of view was the assumption that

---

[9]Burton J. Hendrick, *The Life and Letters of Walter Hines Page* (3 vols.: Garden City, N.Y., 1922–1925); Charles Seymour, ed., *The Intimate Papers of Colonel House* (4 vols.: Boston, 1926–1928).

[10]John K. Turner, *Shall It Be Again?* (New York, 1922).

[11]Harry E. Barnes, *The Genesis of the World War: An Introduction to the Problem of War Guilt* (New York, 1926).

America had no stake in the European conflict. A much fairer peace treaty between the warring powers could have been negotiated had American power not thrown the balance in favor of England and the Allies.

During the 1920's and 1930's the revisionists continued to build up their thesis that America entered the war because of Wilson's unneutral diplomacy. C. Hartley Grattan, one of Barnes's former students, published a long and detailed revisionist work in 1929. Working on the assumption that neither the world nor the United States had gained anything from the war, Grattan in his book *Why We Fought* examined the circumstances that led to American involvement. He pointed to Wilson's shift in policy from true neutrality to a pro-Allied position—a shift brought about by Anglophilism; the influence of capitalists, financiers, and munition makers who had an economic stake in an allied victory; and the skill of British propagandists. In view of America's pro-English policy, Grattan concluded, Germany by late 1916 had no choice but to counter with unrestricted submarine warfare.[12]

The revisionists found a very receptive climate of opinion for their views in the 1930's because of the deterioration in the world situation. By this time it was evident that the international structure erected at Versailles and at various conferences in the 1920's was failing to keep the peace. In Italy Mussolini and the fascists exercised dictatorial control; in Germany Hitler was well on the road to rebuilding Germany's war potential; and in the Far East Japan was already beginning its policy of expansion on the mainland of Asia.

To many Americans these developments were particularly distressing. The United States presumably had gone to war in 1917 not only to protect its own interests, but also, as Wilson had so eloquently put it, "to make the world safe for democracy." More than ever before, the rise of dictatorships abroad seemed to be making a mockery of the high idealism with which America had entered the First World War.

The disillusionment of the American people in the 1930's was reflected in their growing distrust and suspicion of foreign nations. As a result, the United States entered a period of semi-isolationism. In its foreign policy moves, America seemed to be intent upon cutting itself off from membership in the community of nations as much as possible. At the same time, steps were taken to prevent a repetition of the mistakes many felt had been made in the period prior to America's entry into the First World War. In the mid-1930's a series of neutrality acts were passed in an obvious effort to prevent history from repeating itself. The Johnson Act of 1934, for example, forbade American citizens to lend any money to a nation which was in default of its war debts to America. The intent of this act, in part, was to prevent the establishment of an American

---

[12]C. Hartley Grattan, *Why We Fought* (New York, 1929).

financial interest in the survival of any foreign country. The three neutrality acts written between 1935 and 1937 had other provisions to prohibit aid to belligerent nations in time of war.

The isolationist mood of the 1930's was further strengthened as a result of the Senate investigation of the American munitions industry. A Senate committee headed by Senator Gerald P. Nye of North Dakota was given the task in 1934 of investigating the influence of munitions makers on American foreign policy. Although the evidence gathered by the committee came closer to refuting rather than supporting the thesis that the munitions industry played a Machiavellian role in influencing foreign policy, the findings of the committee were used indirectly by some revisionist historians to buttress their case against Wilsonian diplomacy.

Coupled with the rise of isolationism was that of pacifism. The pacifist movement in this era was a potent force in shaping the minds of many Americans and creating an intense desire throughout the nation for peace. Many American citizens became convinced that war was to be avoided at all costs because of its immoral nature, its threat to civilization, and its failure as a means of achieving any worthwhile objectives.

The desire to avoid involvement in any future European war had the effect of reawakening interest in the reasons why America had entered World War I. How had America become involved in the war and who was responsible? In asking a question of this nature, many historians started with the assumption that America's entry into the war had been a gross error that could have been avoided. By revealing the process whereby the United States had undertaken a mistaken commitment, the revisionists hoped to provide contemporary statesmen and diplomats of the 1930's with the knowledge and wisdom to avoid similar pitfalls in the future.

Some of the revisionists deplored America's participation on different grounds. These historians felt that war and liberal reform were incompatible. War, they argued, always sounded the death knell of domestic reform and often inaugurated periods of conservatism or reaction. The First World War, for example, had weakened if not destroyed the commitment to liberal values that had been characteristic of the Progressive era.

Such was the thesis presented by Charles A. Beard during the 1930's. Although Beard did not write specifically on Wilsonian diplomacy, he was one of the most articulate of the anti-war critics. In his book *The Open Door at Home,* which was published in 1934, as well as in testimony before Congressional committees, he argued that America's strength and character had derived from its relative isolation from European power politics and chicanery. Committed to a program of liberal reform, Beard staunchly opposed America's involvement in any future European war. His position seemed to support by implication the revisionist critique of American foreign policy between 1914 and 1917, though for different reasons. [13]

The most mature and complete revisionist account came when Charles C. Tansill published his massive work *America Goes to War* in 1938. In writing this book, Tansill explored a huge mass of manuscript and printed material. Tansill believed that there were multiple causes for America's entry into the war: he stressed the great growth of the munitions trade with the Allies; the unneutral biases of Lansing, House, and Page; and the inability of Wilson to cope with the pressures put on him. But above all, Tansill's argument rested mainly on one premise—that the United States had no valid reason for helping the Allies and opposing Germany and that a German victory would have been a lesser evil than American participation. Reflecting the disillusionment of the 1930's and the intense desire of the nation to avoid any future conflict, Tansill's work seemed to offer conclusive evidence for support of the revisionist thesis.

There were a number of historians in the 1930's, however, who took issue with the revisionist point of view. The outstanding opponent of the revisionists was Professor Charles Seymour of Yale University who edited *The Intimate Papers of Colonel House* (4 vols., 1926–1928), published *American Diplomacy During the World War* in 1934, and *American Neutrality, 1914–1917* in 1935. Unlike the revisionists, Seymour never discussed the issue of whether or not the United States *should* have gone to war; he approached the question of America's entry into the war as a historical problem rather than a moral issue. Nor were Seymour's writings in a didactic vein; he was not concerned with the problem of how America might stay out of a future conflict. Seymour succeeded, therefore, in ridding his work of the present-mindedness that had characterized the writings of many other historians on this issue.

As a result of his approach, Seymour came to certain conclusions regarding Wilson's diplomacy that differed sharply from those of the revisionists. Seymour admitted that Wilson and his advisers were pro-English in their sympathies, but he felt that the President made a determined effort to follow the principles of international law. Indeed, Seymour pointed out, there were periods when America's relations with the Allies were far more vexatious and troublesome than those with Germany. At certain times in the course of the war, Wilson seriously considered the possibility of imposing economic sanctions against the Allies.

Seymour's major thesis, however, was that the United States went to war primarily because of Germany's decision to wage unrestricted submarine warfare. If Germany was permitted to have her own way, the

---

[13]Charles A. Beard, *The Open Door at Home* (New York, 1934) and *The Devil Theory of War* (New York, 1936).

economic well-being of neutral nations and the lives of their citizens would have been seriously threatened. Since Wilson was unwilling to surrender to German demands, Seymour concluded, he had no alternative—given Germany's intransigence on the submarine issue—but to ask Congress for a declaration of war.

The wide range of opinion that existed among historians during the 1930's regarding America's involvement in the First World War was lucidly demonstrated in the work of Walter Millis. A graduate of Yale and an editorial writer for the New York *Herald Tribune,* Millis became interested in American diplomacy between 1914 and 1917. In 1935 he published *Road to War: America, 1914–1917,* a book that caused a stir because the author refused to pinpoint with precision the reasons why America had entered the war. That same year Millis also published an article which was more explicit. After examining the events from 1914 to 1917, Millis concluded that a conspiratorial thesis about Wilson and his advisers simply could not be proved and that the problem of causation was far more complex than anyone had imagined. In discussing the work of other historians on this problem, Millis observed that their interpretations often depended in large measure upon their starting assumptions regarding the nature of the state and upon their philosophy of international relations. "The facts of the period from 1914 to 1917," he noted, "are complex enough to support almost any theory of historical causation that one may apply to them, at the same time that they are obstinate enough to resist almost any theory of how the ultimate entanglement could have been prevented. An examination of the facts must remain as an essential foundation of any policy designed to control a similar situation in the future. Yet it is to be suspected that before the facts can be of much use there will have first to be agreement upon many profound issues as to the ends which the control should serve, the proper philosophy of international relations, the real character and objects of the state in the international and domestic complex—issues the very existence of which seems to be scarcely realized as yet by most of those participating in the current debate. They have so far confined themselves to the problem of how the nation is to avoid entanglement in another foreign war. The far more important question of whether the nation (whatever they may conceive that to mean) will want to avoid entanglement has hardly even been raised."[14]

The outbreak of World War II tended to quiet for a time the debate over the reasons for America's participation in World War I. But one work—Walter Lippmann's *U.S. Foreign Policy: Shield of the Republic,* published in 1943—touched upon the problem and cast the issue in a different light. Lippmann argued that America had gone to war in 1917

---

[14]Walter Millis, "How We Entered the Last One," *The New Republic,* LXXXIII (July 31, 1935), pp. 323–327.

because a German victory ultimately would have threatened the nation's security. When Germany embarked on its campaign of unrestricted submarine warfare, Lippmann claimed, the United States responded by declaring war because it was unwilling to risk an Allied defeat which would have jeopardized America's safety. Lippmann admitted that Wilson had never educated the American people to the dangers involved in an Allied defeat nor clearly defined America's national interests. But the events of the Second World War were demonstrating that America could not afford to stand idly by while the rest of the Atlantic community was overrun by aggressors. With the United States fighting a two-front war against Germany and Japan at the time his book was published, it is not too difficult to understand why Lippmann wrote as he did.[15]

Lippmann's work foreshadowed the position many historians were to take in the period after 1945 as well as to suggest some of the assumptions they would make. As a result of the epochal events in world affairs between 1933 and 1945, historians and political scientists began placing more emphasis upon power politics and the national interest as significant factors in the shaping of international relations. This tendency was reinforced by the increasingly important role that the United States was playing as leader of the free world after World War II. Many argued that America's foreign policy had to be based upon realistic rather than moral considerations and a keen appreciation of the national interest. Viewing America's diplomatic moves in the period prior to 1917 in these terms, some scholars were very critical of Wilson's foreign policy. Now Wilson began to be criticized not because America had entered the war in 1917, but because he had never clearly defined the reasons why the country had gone to war. His excessive moralism, some scholars claimed, prevented Wilson from defining America's national interest and placed him at a serious disadvantage when it came to writing a treaty of peace in the postwar period.

Such was the argument advanced by two writers, George Kennan and Hans Morgenthau, in 1951. According to both of these scholars, America's national interest required the preservation of a balance of power in Europe. If one accepted this premise, the United States indeed had had a vital interest in the outcome of World War I. America's national interest made it mandatory, as Kennan put it, that the war "be brought to an end as soon as possible on a basis involving a minimum maladjustment and as much stability as possible for the future."[16] Wilson's policy, on the other hand, had been founded on precisely the opposite assumption—that one of the aims of the war was to end once and for all the balance of power concept.

What was the result of the implementation of Wilson's policy? Ac-

---

[15]Walter Lippmann, *U.S. Foreign Policy: Shield of the Republic* (Boston, 1943).
[16]George Kennan, *American Diplomacy 1900–1950* (Chicago, 1951), p. 66.

cording to Kennan and Morgenthau, it resulted in diplomatic disaster for America. Wilson's policies fatally weakened the European balance of power and thereby prepared the way for the ultimate emergence of Fascism and Nazism. Germany, bitter and resentful over its treatment at Versailles, found that the breakup of its traditional institutions brought about a decade of profound social unrest; Austria-Hungary was dismembered and carved up into a series of unstable nation-states; Russia was no longer a potential ally of France to help contain German power; and England and France lay weakened by the vicissitudes of war and unable to do much to maintain world peace. Wilson's insistence upon the total destruction of German power, plus his reliance upon abstract moral principles, had isolated him from reality and caused him to embark on a mistaken policy. "If Woodrow Wilson erred," one political scientist concluded, "it was not because he led the United States into war but because he failed to do everything in his power to prepare the people to see their entrance into a foreign war as an act consistent with imperative principles of national self-interest, as well as with national ideals and sentiments. . . . Armed intervention might well have been the wisest alternative from the long-run standpoint of American ideals and interests, but the great majority of the people did not choose war upon mature deliberation; they simply drifted into war, guided largely by impulses—some noble, some mean—with but a tenuous relation to broad and enduring national policy. Consequently, it is little wonder that the motives which led to war seemed inadequate in the perspective of peace, and that America's vaunted moral leadership revealed itself once more as the irresponsible outburst of a nation physically mature but emotionally and intellectually adolescent—a quick-tempered, good-hearted giant of a nation, moved by impulses it would later regret, undertaking commitments it would not fulfill, and never quite comprehending either the circumstances or the consequences of its erratic behavior."[17]

Realists like Morgenthau and Kennan, of course, judged Wilson in the light of their own philosophy of international relations. In one sense, their works were primarily intended to serve as a message to Americans after the Second World War. They were less interested in understanding Wilson and the dilemmas that he faced than they were in showing that America's foreign policy during the First World War had been based too much on moral grounds. Unlike the revisionists, the school of realists represented by Kennan and Morgenthau was not critical of Wilson because he had taken the United States into war; they criticized him instead because he had taken the nation into war *for the wrong reasons.*

While the realists were evaluating Wilson in terms of what he should

[17]Robert E. Osgood, *Ideals and Self-Interest in America's Foreign Relations: The Great Transformation of the Twentieth Century* (Chicago, 1953), pp. 262–263.

have done, other recent historians, following the approach of Charles Seymour, were examining in great detail the situation that Wilson actually faced. Taking a more detached rather than a didactic approach, they were not interested in criticizing the diplomacy of 1914–1917; their primary objective was to understand and define the issues that the Wilson Administration faced, the pressures imposed upon America's leaders, and how these leaders responded to such pressures. These historians did not have to deal specifically with the issue of whether the United States should have stayed out of war in 1917 or whether it should attempt to avoid any future conflicts because the problem of American intervention did not exist in the same form as it had at the time of the First World War. The profound change in America's international role and position after 1945 made any discussion of such an issue a meaningless one. Research by these recent historians was facilitated also by two other developments. The private papers of many public officials who played an active and important part in the Wilson administration became available with the passage of time, and materials in foreign archives were placed at their disposal. As a result, these historians were able to view the problem of America's entry into the First World War in a somewhat different light than earlier writers.

This picture drawn by these historians of the 1950's and 1960's—and since they did not establish a distinct school these scholars cannot be given a specific designation—was far more complex than that of their predecessors. Rejecting a moralistic or conspiratorial approach, they viewed Wilson as a leader confronted with a variety of pressures—pressures that limited his choices of alternative policies. They sought to understand how Wilson responded to the foreign and domestic problems that arose in rapid succession after the outbreak of war in Europe in 1914. In so doing they sketched a portrait of a wartime leader that was both tragic and sympathetic, but by no means uncritical

Unlike the revisionists of the 1930's or the realists of the 1950's—who wrote under the assumption that Wilson had considerable leeway in determining the nation's foreign policies—these more recent historians have emphasized the complexity of events between 1914 and 1917. Arthur S. Link, the foremost Wilson scholar, drew a complex portrait of Wilsonian diplomacy in *Wilson the Diplomatist*, published in 1957. Link pointed to the many factors with which the President had to contend: the desire of most Americans to remain neutral; the pressure for continued trade, particularly with the Allies; the existence of pacifist, interventionist, and preparedness groups; the growing restrictiveness of the British maritime system; and challenges posed by the German submarine policy. Added to these problems was the fact that Wilson ardently desired to act as a mediator between the warring European powers in order to bring about a just peace. To Link, Wilson was not as simple a figure as he had been presented by the revisionists or realists.

On the contrary, Wilson was a complex individual who combined both idealistic and realistic traits. Given the circumstances that he faced and the numerous pressures that were piled upon him, Link implied that Wilson had far less freedom than had been supposed in determining the course of events. Many of the major decisions were beyond his control and were made by the English and German leaders. The result was that by the spring of 1917, according to Link, Wilson reached the tragic conclusion that the United States had no alternative but to intervene once the Germans had decided to sink all vessels bound for Allied ports.

Several other historians have also argued that the range of choices open to Wilson was limited from the very beginning and that as time went on the available alternatives grew fewer and fewer. Considering that neither the Allies nor the Central Powers were willing to accept a peace without victory in 1917 and that the Germans believed that unrestricted submarine warfare could defeat the Allies before American aid became effective, Wilson had to accept either the sinking of American ships and the loss of American lives or else defend his nation's rights. Reviewing the history of this period, Ernest R. May wrote in the late 1950's: "one has a sense that it could not have ended otherwise. . . . There was no way out. Triumph for the immoderates was only a matter of time. . . . Despite its tragic ending, the struggle [for peace] was heroic."[18]

While Link and May were explaining American involvement in the First World War as a tragic choice for Wilson and the nation, others— influenced by the Williams school—attempted to reinterpret Wilsonian diplomacy in more or less economic terms. In his analysis of Woodrow Wilson and world politics, N. Gordon Levin, Jr., argued that "Wilsonians laid the foundations of a modern American foreign policy whose main thrust, from 1917 on, may be characterized as an effort to construct a stable world order of liberal-capitalist internationalism, at the Center of the global ideological spectrum, safe from both the threat of imperialism on the Right and the danger of Revolution on the Left."[19] Although Levin did not argue that the United States went to war in 1917 primarily for economic reasons, he did imply that Wilsonian ideology, with its interest in a world order conducive to America's economic interests, helped set the stage for the country's participation in the First World War.

In surveying the literature covering the rise of America as a world power between 1890 and 1917 and its involvement in two wars, one is struck by the fact that the attitude taken by different generations toward

---

[18]Ernest R. May, *The World War and American Isolation 1914–1917* (Cambridge, 1959), p. 437.

[19]N. Gordon Levin, Jr., *Woodrow Wilson and World Politics: America's Response to War and Revolution* (New York, 1968), p. 1.

the nature of American society, war, and war causation have all played a significant role in determining particular interpretations. To scholars like Williams America's involvement in the Spanish-American War and the First World War grew out of the desire of the United States to dominate the world economy; humanitarian, moral, and religious factors played a minor role at best. The implication of the Williams hypothesis was that only a radical reorientation of American society could have altered its imperialistic and aggressive foreign policies. Other scholars were influenced by moral considerations in making historical judgments on Wilson's presidency. The revisionists of the 1930's were convinced that the United States had little to gain by foreign entanglements; thus they tended to project their beliefs back to the period from 1914 to 1917. War was the great enemy of progress, and in their eyes Wilson was either duped or part of an evil conspiracy. The realists of the 1950's, on the other hand, felt that war and the use of force were an integral part of the prevailing international system. Their criticism of Wilson, therefore, was not that he took the nation to war, but that he did not make clear to the people why America's national interests required such action. Even historians like Arthur S. Link and Ernest R. May—neither of whom was within the realist tradition—looked upon war as part of the tragic human condition; they emphasized the limitations of political leaders in dealing with international problems. Finally, recent revisionists and "New Left" scholars of the 1960's tended to see war as an outgrowth of America's concern with economic supremacy; either directly or indirectly their historical contributions allocated a large share of the blame for the tragic events of the twentieth century to American foreign policy.

As long as Americans continue to debate the proper role of their nation in world affairs, the events of 1898–1899 and 1914–1917 will continue to hold interest for historians. In studying those two wars, scholars will in all probability continue to raise many of the same questions asked by their predecessors for nearly half a century. Did the United States go to war in order to resolve basic contradictions within its economic and social system? Was the acquisition of overseas territories a cause or a consequence of war? To what degree did moral, religious, and humanitarian sentiments play a role in the diplomacy of the 1890's? Did the United States in fact abandon its interests in empire after 1900, or did it create a new form of colonialism through its economic power? Similarly, why did America go to war in 1917? Were its vital national interests threatened by Germany? Did American involvement arise out of its unneutral policies, its misguided sentimentalism and utopianism, and its desire to maintain the integrity of the Atlantic Community, or was its true interest to preserve the balance of power in Europe? Was America's singular concern with a world order that was conducive to its economic interests responsible for the breakdown of neutrality between 1914 and 1917? Above all, did the United States become a world power because its leaders consciously recognized the importance of other regions to the nation's well-being, or did it simply stumble into its new status without a clear grasp of the underlying issues? Americans will struggle with these and other questions as long as they continue to debate foreign policy issues.

William Appleman
Williams

WILLIAM APPLEMAN WILLIAMS (1921–   ) is Professor of History at Oregon State
University. He has written a number of major interpretive works on the
history of American foreign policy as well as a general interpretation of
American history entitled *The Contours of American History* (1961).

Because of its dramatic and extensive nature, the Crisis of the 1890s
raised in many sections of American society the specter of chaos and
revolution. Conservatives and reformers came to share the same conviction that something drastic had to be done, not only to solve the immediate problem, but to prevent the recurrence of such crises. That an
expansionist foreign policy would provide such relief and prevention
rapidly became an integral and vital part of all but an infinitesimal segment of the response to the general crisis. The issue that in a few years
developed into what in the 1950s would have been called a Great Debate
concerned *not* whether expansion should be pursued, but rather what
kind of expansion should be undertaken.

This broad support for expansion, and particularly overseas economic expansion, rested upon agreement among conservatives and liberals (even many radicals joined in for a few years), and Democrats and
Republicans, from all sections and groups of the country. A strong
majority agreed that foreign policy could and should play an
important—if not crucial—part in recovering from the depression of the
1890s and in forestalling future difficulties. . . .

The second idea about expansion was much broader and took account of the particular outlook of all special interests. It explained
America's democracy and prosperity in the past as the result of expansion across the continent and, to a lesser degree, overseas into the markets of the world. Either implicitly or explicitly, depending on the form
in which it was presented, the idea pointed to the practical conclusion
that expansion was the way to stifle unrest, preserve democracy, and
restore prosperity. . . .

Such general and active support for economic expansion is often neglected when considering the coming of the Spanish-American War. It is customary to explain the war as a crusade to save the Cubans or to interpret it in psychological terms as a release for national frustrations arising from the depression. But while it may be granted that economic leaders preferred not to go to war as long as they could attain their objectives without it, and although it may be useful to talk about Americans developing a national compulsion to punish Spain for mistreating Cuba, it is equally apparent that such interpretations do not take account of several key aspects of the coming of the war. For one thing, it is clear that various groups saw war with Spain over Cuba as a means to solve other problems. They reached that conclusion, moreover, at the end of a conscious exercise in considering alternatives—not in a blind and irrational outburst of patriotic or ideological fervor. Many agrarians viewed it as a way to monetize silver at home and thus pave the way for a general expansion of their exports to the sterling areas of the world. Some labor groups thought it would ease or resolve immediate economic difficulties. And many important businessmen, as contrasted with the editors of some business publications, came to support war for specific commercial purposes as well as for general economic reasons.

If there is any one key to understanding the coming of the war with Spain, it very probably lies in the growing conviction among top economic and political leaders that American military intervention was necessary in order to clean up the Cuban mess so that domestic *and other foreign policy* issues could be dealt with efficiently and effectively. It should be made clear, however, that in suggesting this explanation of the war there is no direct or implicit argument that other considerations were nonexistent or unimportant. Nor is it being hinted that the whole affair was the product of some conspiracy in high places. Consciousness of purpose is not conspiracy, even if those who are addicted to explaining everything in terms of irrational psychology often seem unable to distinguish between the two. There was consciousness of purpose in high places—as there should be, whatever one's individual judgment on either the goals or the means—but there was no conspiracy.

It likewise seems wise to emphasize the obvious, but nevertheless often overlooked, distinction between explicit economic motives and a more general economic estimate of the situation. Men have on occasion acted in certain ways because their pocketbook nerve prompted them to do so. They still do. Even historians have been known to change jobs (or their points of view) for more money, as well as for their egos, or for better research facilities. And the actions of some influential figures during the period leading up to the war with Spain can only be understood in that light. They wanted intervention to save and extend their property holdings. In a similar way, other men can and do act on the basis of an equally narrow political calculation. Some Americans wanted intervention on the grounds that it would save their personal and party political fortunes.

Yet it is also quite possible, and not at all unusual, for men to act on the basis of a broader, more inclusive organization and integration of information and desires. Sometimes such a conception of the world—or *Weltanschauung*, as it is more formally called—orders data in such a way that political, religious or cultural values are held to be the crucial factors. Thus some Americans undoubtedly supported war against Spain because according to their view of the world it was impossible to have peace or prosperity or good government in Cuba as long as it was ruled by Catholics.

To an extensive degree, however, American leaders of the 1890s entertained a *Weltanschauung* that organized data around economic criteria. They explained difficulties, and likewise advanced solutions and alternatives, by reference to economic phenomena. This did not make them economically motivated in the pocketbook sense, but it did lead them to believe that their objectives in the political and social realms could only be attained through economic means. To somewhat over-simplify the point to gain clarity, it can be summarized in this way.

Men like McKinley and other national leaders thought about America's problems and welfare in an inclusive, systematized way that em-phasized economics. Wanting democracy and social peace, they argued that economic depression threatened those objectives, and concluded that overseas economic expansion provided a primary means of ending that danger. They did not want war per se, let alone war in order to increase their own personal fortunes. But their own conception of the world ultimately led them into war in order to solve the problems in the way that they considered necessary and best. These general remarks bearing on historical analysis and interpretation should be kept in mind. . . .

There are three central considerations to be evaluated and connected when explaining and interpreting the war against Spain. The first is that the basic policy of presidents Cleveland and McKinley was to secure the defeat of the revolution in Cuba and what they repeatedly and explicitly called "the pacification of the island" under Spanish rule. Both presidents wanted to get on with other domestic and foreign programs and policies; in particular, both were intensely concerned with vigorous overseas economic expansion into Latin America and Asia.

The outbreak of the Sino-Japanese War in 1894 upset Cleveland con-siderably, for example, and he formally warned the Congress and the country that the conflict "deserves our gravest consideration by reason of its disturbance of our growing commercial interests." Cleveland not only repeated the same general theme in his message of December 2, 1895, but explicitly tied that problem to the outbreak of revolution in Cuba that was "deranging the commercial exchanges of the island, of which our country takes the predominant share." Shortly thereafter, in March and April 1896, Secretary of State Olney told the Spanish that the United States wanted to help "pacify the island."

Speaking with "candor," Olney explained Cleveland's "anxiety," and bluntly repeated the President's "earnest desire for the prompt and permanent pacification of that island." The United States wanted to avoid "a war of races" within the island, and sought "the non-interruption of extensive trade relations [and] . . . the prevention of that wholesale destruction of property on the island which . . . is utterly destroying American investments that should be of immense value, and is utterly impoverishing great numbers of American citizens."

After waiting eight months, Cleveland, on December 7, 1896, personally and publicly reiterated his desire for "the pacification of the island." America's concern, he bluntly pointed out, was "by no means of a wholly sentimental or philanthropic character."—"Our actual pecuniary interest in it is second only to that of the people and government of Spain." In the original draft of his message, Cleveland proposed to conclude with a warning strikingly reminiscent of the *Harper's* magazine remark of 1893 that "if we have fighting to do, it will be fighting to keep the peace." Cleveland originally put it this way: either Spain must end the rebellion promptly or "this government will be compelled to protect its own interests and those of its citizens, which are coincident with those of humanity and civilization generally, by resorting to such measures as will promptly restore to the Island the blessings of peace." He even added, again in the original draft, a deadline specified as "the coming of the New Year."

The increasing vigor and militance (and even self-righteousness) of Cleveland's approach to Cuban affairs cannot be explained or understood in isolation. The ever more threatening agitation of the agricultural businessmen was a major factor. So was the rising American concern about developments in the Far East. Japan's attack on China had thrown open the lid of Pandora's Box of Imperialistic Rivalries, and American interests such as the American China Development Company (and other firms and banks) were caught and whipsawed in the resulting free-for-all between Japan, Russia, France, England, and Germany.

In the fall of 1896, however, China turned to the United States in an effort to protect its own position by aligning itself with a major power that had not indicated any significant interest in territorial concessions. At the same time they offered a railroad concession to Americans, a delegation of Chinese officials visited the United States. Received and entertained by public and private leaders, the Chinese clearly accomplished their initial objective of intensifying American interest in and concern over economic gains in Asia.

Cleveland's remarks on Cuba in the first draft of his December 1896 message would clearly seem to follow from that anticipated involvement in Asia—particularly since the President had called for the "gravest consideration" of that issue as early as 1894. But Cleveland had just been defeated by McKinley in the election of November 1896, and his position was obviously difficult. As a responsible politician, Cleveland no doubt realized that it would be unfair (and against tradition) to issue an ultimatum that would entrap his successor. He may even have been explicitly advised that McKinley had told Lodge that he "very naturally does not want to be obliged to go to war as soon as he comes in." Nor is it very likely that Cleveland judged it wise on second thought to go out of office as the man who gave the country a war as his farewell gift. In the message as delivered, therefore, he contented himself with the clear warning that "it can not be reasonably assumed that the hitherto expectant attitude of the United States will be indefinitely maintained."

Upon entering the White House, McKinley reiterated Cleveland's demand for prompt "pacification of the island." But in acting on that policy he began very quickly to squeeze Spain (and himself and the United States) into an ever more difficult position. To some extent, this pressure on Spain was prompted by the activity of various groups within the United States which insisted on more vigorous and dramatic action. This has led some historians to conclude that the pro-rebel newspaper campaign against Spain was primarily responsible for the war. Others have reduced the problem to a political issue, arguing that McKinley ultimately accepted war to sustain or save the influence and power of the Republican Party (and his position within it).

These interpretations which stress domestic pressure on the administration do define and raise the second principal consideration in any evaluation of the war. But the wild and irresponsible press campaign initiated and directed by William Randolph Hearst and Joseph Pulitzer never succeeded in whipping up any sustained hysteria for war until early in 1898—*if even then*. The evidence is overwhelming that the psychological Rubicon was not crossed until a few weeks after the sinking of the battleship *Maine* on February 15, 1898. As for the argument that politics was the key to the war, that begs the real point about what provoked the political pressure. The agitation that scared metropolitan (and other) Republicans came from militant agriculturalists who wanted markets—and a symbolic and a real assault on autocratic European power throughout the world.

Several other factors appear far more significant in explaining McKinley's increasing pressure on Spain. One of them is intimately connected with his continuation of Cleveland's policy of demanding prompt pacification. For along with other Americans, McKinley reacted against the very ruthlessness that the thinly veiled warnings from the United States encouraged Spain to employ. In insisting upon certain ends while prohibiting the use of forceful measures, McKinley was more the victim of his own irresponsibility than a puppet jerked about by the yellow press of Pulitzer and Hearst.

Furthermore, McKinley was being increasingly pressured by metropolitan expansionists. Some of those men were economic entrepreneurs acting on narrow interest-conscious motives. They wanted their property protected and their opportunities secured. That outlook was typified by Chauncey M. Depew of the New York Central Railroad, Alonzo B. Hepburn of the National City Bank, Edward F. Cragin of the Union League Club who had ties with the Nicaraguan Canal Company and Standard Oil, Collis P. Huntington of the Southern Pacific Railroad, financier August Belmont, and John S. McCook of New York who was a railroad lawyer also active in organizing overseas economic ventures. Still another group was made up of broad-gauged expansionists like Roosevelt and Lodge, who saw a war with Spain as a way to bring empire to America by Caesarean section. "I have been hoping and working ardently," Roosevelt candidly admitted, "to bring about our interference in Cuba."

Finally, McKinley himself made it precisely clear in July 1897, that he was determined to finish up the Cuban crisis in order to proceed with other matters. This became apparent in the long instructions given his new minister to Spain (who was also a close friend). The document should also serve to correct once and for all the mistaken impression that McKinley drifted this way and that in response to whatever political winds were blowing. He knew quite well what he desired to accomplish. "The chronic disturbance in the social and political condition of our own peoples. . . . A continuous irritation within our own borders injuriously affects the normal functions of business, and tends to delay the condition of prosperity to which this country is entitled."

Though it was not unique in the archives of diplomatic history, this assignment of responsibility for domestic welfare to a foreign power was a very striking and unequivocal example of that approach. It revealed beyond any possibility of misunderstanding the inner logic of all expansionist thought *whereby both opportunity and difficulty, good and evil, are externalized.* As Frederick Jackson Turner once acknowledged in a moment of deep insight, the frontier itself was "a gate of escape" from existing responsibilities; and when men began to act on the frontier thesis they merely sustained that pattern of defining issues in such a way that the solutions became progressively dependent upon external factors. Stated as directly as possible, the point is that none of the foreign powers involved—either in Cuba or in Asia—actually threatened the United States, nor did they have any inherent primary responsibility for what McKinley called "the prosperity to which this country is entitled." It was only the definition of American well-being primarily in terms of overseas economic expansion, a definition formulated by

Americans, that led to the conclusion that the foreign nations had such obligations.

The related consideration concerning the way that McKinley and other influential Americans envisaged the relationship linking prosperity, social peace, and foreign policy became increasingly clarified during the late summer and early fall of 1897. By August, for example, businessmen were generally convinced that recovery from the depression was being generated and sustained by overseas economic expansion. As a result, many of them began to change their earlier fears that intervention in Cuba would delay prosperity. Instead, they began to feel that it would be wise to remove that distraction so that the new frontier of exports could be given full attention.

In addition, many of those who had sympathized with or actively supported the rebels began to fear that a successful revolution would cause grave difficulties by bringing the lower class to power. McKinley was advised of this very explicitly by a correspondent who reported the growing anxiety that "the troublesome, adventurous, and non-responsible class" would control the island "causing chaos, injury, and loss beyond redemption."

Probably even more important in strengthening the inclination to intervene to pacify Cuba was the renewed outbreak of trouble in the Far East. Germany's seizure of Kiaochow on November 14, 1897, intensified existing fears that Japan and the European powers were going to divide China among themselves. Whether they defined the issue in narrow interest-conscious economic terms, or in a broader analysis that stressed the need of the American economic *system* to expand overseas, American leaders became very disturbed. Most of them looked to Asia, and to China in particular, as the great market which would absorb the surplus. It is beside the point that this did not happen; at issue is the nature of American thought and action at that time.

The influence of these events in the late summer and fall of 1897 was revealed in many striking episodes. In September, for example, Roosevelt discussed personally with McKinley a memorandum in which he advocated war in November, *and specifically recommended that "we take and retain the Philippines."* [Emphasis added.] In November, Senator Orville H. Platt and a member of the House of Representatives saw McKinley and added their advice that Manila was the key to the entire Asian crisis. In January 1898, a petition from over 35 leading New York businessmen (many of whom had raised their voices—and pens—as early as May 1897) asked McKinley to intervene with "prompt and efficient measures" in Cuba to put an end to their "tremendous losses" and restore "a most valuable commercial field." And in February other entrepreneurs of the New York State Chamber of Commerce asked for similar action in Asia. Deeply concerned about the crisis in China and its effect upon "the privileges enjoyed under existing treaty rights by

Americans," they "respectfully and earnestly" requested "prompt and energetic defense" of such rights and "the preservation and protection of their important commercial interest in that Empire."

These activities clarify the third central aspect of the coming of the war: the McKinley Administration knew that an important and growing segment of the business community wanted prompt and effective action in Cuba and Asia. Until some time in the latter part of March (or perhaps even the first week in April), McKinley undoubtedly wanted to end the Cuban affair without war. This seems quite clear despite his series of ultimatums to Spain that included a demand for independence (under American guidance) if the United States thought it necessary. But by the last 10 days in March (by which time Germany had secured a 99-year lease to Kiaochow with extensive economic concessions throughout the province of Shantung), the business community was ready to accept war.

A special emissary sent by McKinley to sound out the New York area reported that such key figures as John Jacob Astor, Thomas Fortune Ryan, William Rockefeller, Stuyvesant Fish, and spokesmen for the House of Morgan were "feeling militant." Then Lodge advised McKinley on March 21, 1898, that Boston economic leaders had concluded that "one shock and then an end was better than a succession of spasms such as we must have if this war in Cuba went on." And four days later, the President received by telegram the following intelligence from a New York correspondent. "Big corporations here now believe we will have war. Believe all would welcome it as relief to suspense. . . . Don't think it necessary now mince matters."

Now the purpose of all this analysis is not to argue or suggest that McKinley went to war because important economic leaders told him to do so. Neither is it to imply that the public clamor that arose after the sinking of the *Maine* was insignificant. The point is quite different. It is that American leaders went to war with Spain as part of, and as the consequence of, a general outlook which externalized the opportunity and the responsibility for America's domestic welfare; broadly in terms of vigorous overseas economic expansion into Latin America and Asia; and specifically in terms of Spain's inability to pacify Cuba by means (and within time limits) acceptable to the United States, and the separate but nevertheless related necessity of acting in Asia to prevent the exclusion of American interests from China. . . .

Discounted in recent years as a futile and naive gesture in a world of harsh reality, the Open Door Policy was in fact a brilliant strategic stroke which led to the gradual extension of American economic and political power throughout the world. If it ultimately failed, it was not because it was foolish or weak, but because it was so successful. The empire that was built according to the strategy and tactics of the Open Door Notes engendered the antagonisms created by all empires, and it is that opposition which posed so many difficulties for American diplomacy after World War II.

At the outset, it is true, the debate between imperialists and anti-imperialists revolved around an actual issue—colonialism. Touched off by the specific question of what to do with Cuba and the Phillipines, the battle raged over whether they should be kept as traditional colonies or established as quasi-independent nations under the benevolent supervision of the United States. Though the differences were significant at the beginning of the argument, it is nevertheless clear that they were never absolute. The Open Door Notes took the fury out of the fight. And within five years the issue was almost nonexistent. The anti-imperialists who missed that changing nature of the discussion were ultimately shocked and disillusioned when Bryan became Secretary of State and began to practice what they thought he condemned.

Such critics were mistaken in attacking Bryan as a backslider or hypocrite. Bryan's foreign policy was not classical colonialism, but neither was it anti-imperial. He had never shirked his share of the white man's burden, though perhaps he did shoulder a bit more of the ideological baggage than the economic luggage. He was as eager for overseas markets as any but the most extreme agrarian and industrial expansionists. As with most other farmers, labor leaders, and businessmen, economic logic accounts for much of Bryan's anticolonialism. Looking anxiously for markets abroad as a way of improving conditions at home, all such men feared and opposed the competition of native labor. It was that consideration, as much as racism and Christian fundamentalism, that prompted Bryan to assert that "the Filipinos cannot be citizens without endangering our civilization."

Bryan's program for the Philippines symbolizes the kind of imperial anticolonialism that he advocated. Once the Philippine insurrection was crushed, he proposed that the United States should establish "a stable form of government" in the islands and then "protect the Philippines from outside interference while they work out their destiny, just as we have protected the republics of Central and South America, and are, by the Monroe Doctrine, pledged to protect Cuba." Opposition spokesmen gleefully pointed out that this was the substance of their own program. . . .

Though many of them felt that they had suffered a terrible defeat in the decision to retain the Philippines, the antiimperialists actually won their domestic war over fundamental policy with the issuance of the Open Door Notes. Hay's dispatches of 1899 and 1900 distilled the conglomeration of motives, pressures, and theories into a classic strategy of noncolonial imperial expansion. Based on the assumption of what Brooks Adams called "America's economic supremacy," the policy of the open door was designed to clear the way and establish the conditions under which America's preponderant economic power would extend the American system throughout the world without the embarrassment and inefficiency of traditional colonialism. As Hay indicated with obvious anticipation and confidence in September 1899, the expectation was that "we shall bring the sweat to their brows."

Hay's first note of September 6, 1899, asserted the proposition that American entrepreneurs "shall enjoy perfect equality of treatment for their commerce and navigation" within all of China—*including the spheres of interest held by foreign powers.* That principle was soon extended to other underdeveloped areas. His second note of July 3, 1900, was designed to prevent other nations from extending the formal colonial system to China. That axiom was also applied to other regions in later years. Hay also circulated a third dispatch among the powers. Though rarely linked with the first two in discussions of the Open Door Notes, it was nevertheless an integral part of the general policy statement. In that document, Hay made it plain that the United States considered loans to be an inherent part of commerce. The connection was always implicit, if not rather obvious. "It is impossible to separate these two forms of business activity," as one businessman remarked at the time, "since it is axiomatic that trade follows the loan." The relationship was also and without any question in the minds of American policy-makers when the first notes were written, since such loans were being sought and discussed as early as 1897. Hay's purpose was to close every formal loophole through which America's competitors might seek to counter the strategy of the open door.

The Open Door Notes took the substance out of the debate between the imperialists and the anti-imperialists. The argument trailed on with the inertia characteristic of all such disagreements, but the nation recognized and accepted Hay's policy as a resolution of the original issue. Former Secretary of State John W. Foster summarized this point quite accurately in the *Independent* at the end of 1900. "Whatever difference of opinion may exist among American citizens respecting the policy of territorial expansion, all seem to be agreed upon the desirability of commercial expansion. In fact it has come to be a necessity to find new and enlarged markets for our agricultural and manufactured products. We cannot maintain our present industrial prosperity without them."

It took some years (and agitation) to liquidate the colonial status of the territory seized during the war against Spain. It also required time to work out and institutionalize a division of authority and labor between economic and political leaders so that the strategy could be put into operation on a routine basis. And it was necessary to open the door into existing colonial empires as well as unclaimed territories. But the strategy that had been set was followed through the Potsdam Conference at the end of World War II, when President Harry S. Truman sought with considerable insistence to re-establish the open door for

American economic and political influence in Eastern Europe and on the Asian mainland. . . .

The most dramatic confluence of these currents of ideological and economic expansion did not occur until the eve of American entry into World War I. For this reason, among others, it is often asserted that the United States did not take advantage of the Open Door Policy until after 1917, and some observers argue that the policy never led to the rise of an American empire. In evaluating the extent to which Americans carried through on the strategy of the Open Door Notes, there are two broad questions at issue with regard to statistics of overseas economic expansion, and they cannot be mixed up without confusing the analysis and the interpretation. One concerns the over-all importance of such expansion to the national economy. The answer to that depends less upon gross percentages than upon the role in the American economy of the industries which do depend in significant ways (including raw materials as well as markets) on foreign operations. Measured against total national product, for example, the export of American cars and trucks seems a minor matter. But it is not possible at one and the same time to call the automobile business the key industry in the economy and then dismiss the fact that approximately 15 per cent of its total sales in the 1920s were made in foreign markets. . . .

In summation, the true nature and full significance of the Open Door Policy can only be grasped when its four essential features are fully addressed.

First: it was neither a military strategy nor a traditional balance-of-power policy. *It was conceived and designed to win the victories without the wars.* In a truly perceptive and even noble sense, the makers of the Open Door Policy understood that the war represented the failure of policy. Hence it is irrelevant to criticize the Open Door Policy for not emphasizing, or not producing, extensive military readiness.

Second: it was derived from the proposition that America's overwhelming economic power could cast the economy and the politics of the poorer, weaker, underdeveloped countries in a pro-American mold. American leaders assumed the opposition of one or many industrialized rivals. Over a period of two generations the policy failed because some of those competitors, among them Japan and Germany, chose to resort to force when they concluded (on solid grounds) that the Open Door Policy was working only too well; and because various groups inside the weaker countries such as China and Cuba decided that America's extensive influence in and upon their societies was harmful to their specific and general welfare.

Third (and clearly related to the second point): the policy was neither legalistic nor moralistic in the sense that those criticisms are usually offered. It was extremely hard-headed and practical. In some respects, at any rate, it was the most impressive intellectual achievement in the area of public policy since the generation of the Founding Fathers.

Fourth: unless and until it, and its underlying *Weltanschauung*, were modified to deal with its own consequences, the policy was certain to produce foreign policy crises that would become increasingly severe. The ultimate failures of the Open Door Policy, in short, are the failures generated by its success in guiding Americans in the creation of an empire.

Once these factors are understood, it becomes useful to explore the way that ideological and moralistic elements became integrated with the fundamentally secular and economic nature of the Open Door Policy. The addition of those ingredients served to create a kind of expansionism that aimed at the marketplace of the mind and the polls as well as of the pocketbook.

Paul A. Varg

PAUL A. VARG (1912–   ) is Professor of History at Michigan State University. He has written a number of books on American diplomatic history, including *Foreign Policies of the Founding Fathers* (1964), *The Making of a Myth: The United States and China, 1879–1912* (1968), and *The Closing of the Door: Sino-American Relations, 1936–1946* (1973).

In 1899 John Bassett Moore, then serving as assistant secretary of state, wrote that the United States, during the preceding ten years, had moved "from a position of comparative freedom from entanglements into the position of what is commonly called a world-power." "Where formerly we had only commercial interests," he explained, "we now have territorial and political interests as well." The annexation of the Philippines, Hawaii, and Puerto Rico and the temporary occupation of Cuba appeared to have thrust the United States into the vortex of international politics.

However, no one explanation of the United States' reaction to its new power position is possible. A study of the course pursued in relations with China shows that the administrations in Washington moved with a restraint approaching that of a mere observer. In Cuba the same administrations acted with energy. These two case studies, constituting the body of this essay, argue against any simple explanation of American policy in the years after the Spanish-American War.

The differences in response do not alter the fact that measured in economic terms, the United States had achieved great power status. By 1900 there were 193,000 miles of railroad track spanning the continent linking even remote hamlets to great metropolitan centers. The prime result was a national economy based upon the availability of great natural resources and a market of continental dimensions. The value of manufacturers by 1899 stood at $13,000,000,000 and surpassed in value the products of agriculture. In 1900 the value of iron and steel products reached $803,968,000. The production of iron and steel almost equaled that of Germany and Great Britain combined. The conditions for mass production had already been achieved. At the turn of the century, it was

"The United States a World Power, 1900–1917: Myth or Reality?", by Paul A. Varg, was published originally in *Twentieth-Century American Foreign Policy*, edited by John Braeman, Robert H. Bremner, and David Brody (*Modern America*, no. 3), and is copyright © 1971 by the Ohio State University Press. All rights reserved. It appears here in an abridged version by permission of the author, the editors, and the publisher.

estimated that the per capita consumption of manufactures in the United States was 50 percent higher than in Great Britain and twice as great as that in Germany and France.

Unprecedented material success inspired confidence among many Americans that the world at large would inevitably follow in America's wake. The more sober-minded among them pondered the question of the relations of this new economic colossus to the outside world. Some, like the historian John Fiske and the sociologist Franklin Henry Giddings, envisioned an extension of Anglo-Saxon political and economic institutions to more remote parts of the world. Others, like Brooks Adams and Alfred T. Mahan, impressed by contemporary struggles for security, prestige, and markets, concluded that the United States must for reasons of survival build a strong navy, protect the sea lanes of the world's commerce and extend its own trade for purposes of counteracting the influence of other powers.

At the same time there emerged the view among many congressmen, journalists, and some business representatives that the capacity to produce goods was outrunning the economic demand of the home market. All were agreed that foreign markets were of increasing importance because of the danger of an industrial surplus. Some set forth a reciprocal trade program as the best answer to this problem. Others adhered to the traditional protective tariff policies and thought the solution to the surplus lay in a policy of opening up foreign markets by aggressive pursuit of colonies, or by strong pressure on governments to open the door to American goods.

The new look outward captured the churches and expressed itself in a rapid growth of interest in the expansion of Christianity. The organization of the Student Volunteers for Foreign Missions at Dwight L. Moody's Northfield in the summer of 1887 marked the beginning of a church crusade calling for "the evangelization of the world in this generation." China soon gained the highest priority and became by 1900, as Sherwood Eddy said, the lodestar of young college students ready to Christianize the world. The crusade never lost its religious orientation, but many of the vigorous young men became passionate crusaders for sheering away anachronisms of superstition, ignorance, and social injustice. In turn they aroused an interest in China among a part of the churchgoing public and encouraged the belief that in the whole realm of foreign relations, China occupied a position of prime importance.

Those charged with the conduct of foreign relations shared the view that the United States was entering upon a new era. Among these were Theodore Roosevelt, his two secretaries of state John Hay and Elihu Root, his friend Henry Cabot Lodge, a leader in the Senate, and other senators including Cushman Davis of Minnesota. Roosevelt's predecessor in the presidency, William McKinley, although a man with a reputation for moving cautiously, shared the vision of a new role for the United States.

McKinley, for all his later protestations of anguish in making up his mind on the question of annexing the Philippines, had acted decisively on that issue in the summer of 1898, when he dictated the basis for negotiations with Spain. On no point was he more firm than on the stipulation that negotiations could only be entered into if Spain agreed that the islands were negotiable. Neither, according to the testimony of John Bassett Moore, was McKinley averse to demanding a sphere of influence in China when the outbreak of the Boxers in June, 1900, opened up the prospect of a partition of China. In spite of his earlier caution in moving toward war with Spain, McKinley was on the side of those who advocated an energetic foreign policy.

The transition to a new age of bold engagement in world affairs, greeted with eagerness by many, evoked the concern of others. Entangling alliances continued to be anathema, and not even the most ardent proponents of the "large policy" advocated a departure from the tradition against them. Usually, moves toward involvement had to be clothed in terms of duty and national obligation or described as necessary to protect the helpless against the imperialism of others. Those opposed to the new developments tended to phrase the argument in terms of anti-imperialism versus imperialism; those in favor more often saw the issue as narrow, self-centered nationalism versus internationalism.

The propensity toward moralistic argument obfuscated the more vital concerns of those who preferred to eschew moralistic arguments or purely intellectual speculation on cosmic tendencies. The public debate set up categories that were often irrelevant to the more immediate questions of what were the vital interests of the nation and how they could be defended or advanced. Those charged with direct responsibility for foreign relations concerned themselves with the more immediate. Although they sometimes contributed to the confusion by resorting to generalizations loaded with value judgments, they reached decisions on the basis of pragmatic and mundane considerations.

What appeared to be a defense of the sovereignty and independence of less-favored nations evoked popular support as long as the defense was limited to moral support. In advising Secretary of State John Hay, John Bassett Moore pointed to the popularity of the Monroe Doctrine. Its popularity, said Moore, was due to the generally held notion that the policy had saved Latin America from European imperialism. No one knew better than Moore the falsity of this popular idea, but he urged Hay to issue the circular note of July 3, 1900, calling for support of China's territorial and administrative integrity and independence, for reasons of national interest, and assured him that the public would interpret the notes in altruistic terms and therefore approve of them.

At the turn of the century, Europeans expressed concern over the future United States role in world affairs. Their concern had its source in the obvious capacity of American industry to flood the markets of Europe and the world with manufactured goods and also in the fears aroused by United States acquisition of an empire as a result of her victory over Spain. A writer for a British magazine, the *Spectator*, worried over the towering strength of the United States, but he was even more puzzled and disturbed by the failure of American policy to conform to familiar standards of big-power behavior. He dreaded an American monopoly of world trade and efforts to control the wealth of the world, but he feared equally the American unwillingness to see any but the native powers in control of the richest countries of Asia and America's refusal to take South America or let anyone else take it.

The catapulting of the United States onto the stage of world politics understandably caused concern in the capitals of Europe. Americans appeared to decry alliances, colonization, and imperialism. Among Europe's statesmen, these were not evils but devices for ordering the world's affairs so as to protect the interests of individual nations while at the same time preserving the peace. The behavior of the United States appeared unpredictable to European leaders while at the same time they acknowledged her power.

Americans who welcomed the new role of the United States boldly justified the uniqueness of their policy. The editor of the *Journal of Commerce* replied to the writer in the *Spectator* that Americans did not aim to control all the wealth in the world, but neither were they prepared to deny themselves the gains within their reach. Like all nations not infected with Oriental fatalism, he wrote, Americans were "doing the best we can for ourselves, and our energy and wealth are such that we are quite likely to end by dominating some important industries, and though we shall not own all the wealth of the world, we may be creditors of all nations."

The editor of the *Journal of Commerce* also gave his own explanation of the policy of the United States in Asia and South America. The Chinese and the South Americans were entitled to independent governments. Americans, he wrote, wished exclusive control nowhere, but they likewise were determined not to be excluded. As to South America, Americans had no reason to take it, but neither would they permit their own security to be threatened by permitting European states to establish themselves there. "The South Americans have their own governments," he wrote, and he found them no worse than some European governments. "What they need," he concluded, "is less of Europe; not more of it."

However flamboyant American rhetoric, the American government usually behaved with restraint. When examined closely, specific actions of the United States in world affairs argue against easy generalizations about imperialism or world power status. The variety of approaches reflected the different assessments placed upon the importance of national interests in the many areas of the world. A comparative study of the developments in each major theater, the Far East, Latin America, and Europe, reveals a common tendency toward greater involvement but likewise marked differences.

A series of half-truths have become part of the popular lore concerning relations with China in the years between 1890 and American entry into World War I. It has been too readily assumed that China was considered to be of major importance by the policy-makers, that altruistic considerations advocated by both missionary leaders and church organizations weighed heavily in the councils of statesmen charged with foreign affairs, that the China market was viewed as so important to the American economy that an alliance of business groups and the Department of State assumed a major role in Chinese affairs, and that the Open Door policy provided at least a minor shield for the protection of China against European and Japanese imperialism.

The acquisition of the Philippines was both a result of an awakening interest in China and, later, a reason for being concerned about developments on the mainland of Asia. Yet, possession of the islands did not give to the United States the leverage in Chinese affairs that was anticipated. Other powers—Russia, Japan, Great Britain, and, to a somewhat lesser degree, France—were much more effective in making their influence felt in Peking. The weak government of the Manchu dynasty could only effectively resist demands made upon it by any one of these if it could enlist the support of one or more of the others. China did, on occasion, turn to the United States for support; but Washington had little influence because everyone, including the Chinese, recognized that the American government was not ready to resist a determined foe. Other governments, especially Russia and Japan, having much more at stake, were more adamant in demanding or in opposing the demands of others. Their own security, and likewise their important trade and investments, assured firmness in their negotiations.

The United States, on the other hand, had strictly limited interests. Its major concern was the security of the Philippines, and the islands were far removed from the path of the storm brewing in Manchuria at the close of the Boxer Revolt. To be sure, American trade centered in the northern provinces, and the inroads of Russia and Japan raised the specter of Americans being excluded, but this trade was not of sufficient importance to call for a strong policy. Although protests in the defense of equality of commercial opportunity flowed from Washington with regularity, these were conveyed in a spirit of pious hope rather than from a posture of unswerving determination. Moreover, the promise of a future market increasingly faded, especially after 1905, when exports to China failed to increase. Even at the peak of the optimism concerning the China market, the American business community made little effort to expand sales in that part of the world. American investments in China were even less important.

Consequently, the government in Washington treaded water whenever it found itself headed toward a dangerous confrontation. Only when American lives were in danger was there a willingness to proceed boldly. The Boxer Revolt provided such an occasion, and there was no hesitancy in sending a military expedition. On lesser occasions the navy went to the rescue or displayed sufficient force to calm the waters.

The caution of the Department of State before deciding on the Circular Note of 1900 illustrates the point. Pressed to pledge support of China's integrity by Consul-General John Goodnow, who spoke for the leading viceroys in the Yangtze Valley, Hay weighed this proposal and at the same time pondered upon the support of President McKinley and his attorney general for seizing a leasehold and laying claim to a sphere of influence. Hay strongly opposed the latter. In issuing the Circular Note calling for support of China's independence and territorial and administrative integrity, he sought no more than to provide a catalyst whereby the nations would, for a brief time, be enabled to extricate themselves from a race for partition and find security for their interests in a common program of restraint. China could not herself resist their demands, and they could not themselves find security unless there was a mutual commitment to restraint. John Bassett Moore remarked to Hay "that the idea might, by many, be thought to be fanciful, but that after all it might not be found to be impracticable."

Hay had no need to worry that he was making a hazardous commitment. He did no more than commit his own government not to violate the principle enunciated; other parties were invited to join in the policy of self-denial, but they were not served notice that the United States would come to China's aid if her independence and administrative and territorial integrity were threatened. Hay did not show concern that Russia would probably reject the pledge she was to be invited to make and that France would blindly follow in the steps of the czar's government, but if this should happen, Hay would suffer no more than minor embarrassment.

Moore, in advising Hay, made no reference to the importance of the China market. He advanced only two arguments in favor of the United States' taking a stand. The United States, he said, had an immediate interest "in the fate of China in consequence of holding the Philippines. If Russia, or Russia and powers in alliance with her, held China," Moore argued, "we should be at their mercy in the Philippines." Second, he pointed out "that the idea of supporting the independence and integrity of China would accord with the sentiments of our people; that it was the principle of helping other nations to maintain their independence and integrity that had made the Monroe Doctrine so popular amongst them...."

Moore not only eschewed the argument of the importance of the China market but dismissed as foolish the other consideration that held the attention of missionary-minded interests. According to Moore's memorandum of his conversation with Hay, Moore remarked

> that some of our people, mostly students and men unfamiliar with practical affairs, had conceived that it would be a good thing if the Powers would take China under their tutelage, and reorganize her and transform her; that this seemed to leave out of consideration the 300,000,000 or 400,000,000 people in China, with an ancient and persistent civilization, and was, in my opinion, on the whole a fantastic conception, based on erroneous principles.

Placing the Circular Note of 1900 in the context out of which it emerged reduces it from a ringing declaration in behalf of China to a cautious pronouncement by a government that did not view China as of vital importance to its own interests.

The estimate of the Department of State of China's importance to American interests did not change, although there were occasions when the vigor of diplomatic notes suggested the contrary. In spite of apparent determination to affect the course of developments, the United States moved with a restraint that accorded with the relatively low estimate the nation at large placed upon its interests in Asia.

There were, however, those in the United States who held those interests to be vital and, therefore, called for a policy of unyielding opposition to the aggressiveness of Russia or Japan. Before the Russo-Japanese War the most ardent advocates of a strong posture were the small group of commercial interests within the business community who spoke through the American Asiatic Association and the *Journal of Commerce and Commercial Bulletin*. The editorials of the New York weekly newspaper affirmed that the nation's economic future hung on access to the China market and that the United States as a Pacific power could not sit idly by while Russia unilaterally absorbed Manchuria and put itself in a position to dominate Peking. "Opinions may be divided as to the source from which the most serious obstacles to an agreement have come." wrote the editor in March, 1901, "but unless western civilization is to confess itself baffled by the Chinese problem, there must be an end to the pursuit of individual ambitions at the expense of the common cause." He closed by proclaiming: "The United States is in a position to lend a powerful impulse to greater unity of action, and it is to be hoped that no weak fear of foreign entanglements will allow the opportunity to slip."

Russia's attempts to strengthen its hold over Manchuria after the Boxer Revolt did cause the Department of State to make some moderately vigorous protests. For a brief period the policy seemed to harmonize with the position of the *Journal of Commerce*. Given the lead taken by Japan and Great Britain, the United States could show firmness without facing the danger inherent in being in the forefront of the resistance. The alignment with Tokyo and London reached its peak when Washington turned its negotiations of a new commercial treaty with China into a campaign for opening cities in Manchuria to foreign trade and residence. Russia saw a threat in the requests of the United States to its own program and therefore used its influence in Peking to have the Chinese decline the American request. Throughout the spring and early summer of 1903, Secretary of State John Hay and W. W. Rockhill, his adviser on Far Eastern affairs, doggedly pushed forward. An almost pathological distrust and dislike of Russia increased their firmness.

In July, 1903, they changed course. It was during that month that Japan and Russia entered upon negotiations that clearly portended a showdown. Too close alignment with Japan and Great Britain posed the danger of involvement in possible war. Neither American interests nor public opinion provided support for a dangerous course. By the end of July the United States quietly withdrew from insisting that three cities in Manchuria be opened by a specific date and that they be open for foreign residence. The removal of these two points by the United States enabled Russia to withdraw her opposition to the commercial treaty. Russia's opposition had rested largely on the fear that her own sphere in Manchuria would be inundated by Japanese settlers if the cities were open to foreign settlement.

Manchuria was clearly not worth military involvement. However, after Japan's victory over Russia in 1905, American attention was once again focused on the sprawling plains north of China proper. Americans had looked upon Japan as fighting their war and believed that a victory over Russia was a victory for the principles of the Open Door. War did not solve the problem. Russia and Japan, within their newly defined spheres, sought to improve their positions. . . .

Looking back on the relations between the United States and China in the years 1900 to 1917, it is clear that the United States, although involved in the China question, did not wield the same degree of influence in the Asian area as that exerted by the other world powers. Her restraint was dictated by an awareness that neither her security interests nor her economic interests at the time justified a bold course. China's importance, as American statesmen saw it, lay in the future. Whatever the importance of the China market might become, it was not important at that time. Other nations had heavy investments in railways, mining, and other enterprises. As late as 1914, the United States portion of these investments was only 3 percent. To the degree that there was a public interest in China, it was in large part an intangible, nonmaterial interest associated with dreams of providing tutelage of China in the transition from an ancient to a modern society. Missionaries and their allies in the church leadership at home shared this vision, but their point of view struck almost no response among men of practical affairs, whose concern was bound by considerations of security and the state of the economy.

By almost any standard, the United States record in the Caribbean area differed sharply from the minor role it played in Asia. By World War I, five Caribbean states had been subordinated to protectorate status, and no nation would have openly challenged the dominance of the United States. The differences lay in felt concerns as to security and the presence of economic interests. In contrast to the restraint that characterized the response to developments in Asia, the United States overreacted to both dangers and opportunities in the Caribbean. In part, the difference can be explained by the proximity of the small island republics and by the absence of any power capable of seriously testing American capability.

In fact, the most serious deterrent to Yankee imperialism in the Caribbean came from within the American body politic and not from without. Imperialism had a free rein from the public when American action could be defended as negating Europe's imperialism. It met strong opposition when American behavior came into conflict with democratic values antithetic to domination of another people. Sometimes the opposition was based on no more than the defense of special economic interests. At other times, the opposition came from politicians seeking political gains by putting the ruling party's policies in the worst possible light. Regardless of motives, those who were opposed, by appealing to traditional values, paid tribute to their survival.

Historians have parted ways over the question as to whether strategic considerations or economic interests shaped the policy of intervention. It is probably futile to weigh the comparative importance of these two factors and more profitable to recognize that the new industrial society that had come into being fostered ambitions to achieve those attributes by which greatness among nations was measured. Among these badges of greatness were the capacity to wield an influence abroad and to dominate some one region.

In the aftermath of the Spanish American War, the problem of future relations between the island of Cuba and the republic that had intervened to make it independent of Spain served as a test as to whether the old or the new ideals were to dominate. Whatever private motives existed aiming at the advancement of personal or corporate interests, Congress and the country at large saw the goal as emancipation of the Cubans from Spanish rule. The Teller Amendment promised that Cuba was to be independent, not only of Spain, but likewise of the United States. Some privately questioned the wisdom of the self-denying amendment but did not dare do so publicly.

Senator Teller of Colorado gave expression to the sentiment of the great majority when he introduced his resolution. To be sure, there were those who had never favored independence for Cuba. They probably voted for the amendment simply for the political reason that they did not wish to stand apart from an obviously popular move. Their votes do not explain the general support of the amendment.

The granting of independence to Cuba was something assumed by a majority of Congress in the debates that preceded the war. Senator Teller later explained that he introduced his measure for another reason than that of curbing annexationist moves on the part of the United States. Independence for Cuba was so generally accepted, said Teller, that a resolution was not necessary. The reason for the Teller Amendment, according to its author, was to diminish the danger of European intervention. President McKinley, according to one senator, greatly feared that Europe would intervene in one way or another. He warned two senators who called upon him: "Remember, Senators, if this war breaks out, it may be a world's war." Europe was cynical about the aims of the United States and did not believe that she would go to war against Spain and then set Cuba free. Senator Spooner explained that it had been necessary to dispel this cynicism because it could have led some European governments to intervene. That a nation should take over a colony of the other would set a most dangerous precedent. It was thought that the Teller Amendment, put before the Senate by the Committee on Foreign Relations and approved by the Senate, would deprive the European powers of a reason for intervening.

Once the fighting started, the pious resolutions lost their sanctity. Raw motives of self-interest and irrational fears cradled in a sense of Anglo-Saxon superiority came to the surface as Americans came face to face with Cuba's insurgents. The army showed its attitude when it restricted its commands to the rebels, our Cuban allies, to orders to carry out the menial tasks of transporting supplies and digging ditches. After the battle of San Juan Hill, General Lawton complained that the Cuban troops sat on a high hill to the rear of the scene of battle and failed to join in the attack. When Santiago was under siege, General Shafter protested that the Cuban troops failed to prevent the entry of Spanish reinforcements.

This was only the beginning of complications. The Cubans, led by General García, were bitter over the Americans ignoring them. And the Americans reciprocated. Upon the close of hostilities, Stephen Crane, correspondent for the *New York World,* reported that the Americans had come to despise the Cubans. The contempt for the Cubans carried over to the political realm, raising questions about their capacity to govern themselves. General Shafter, after his return to the United States in December, 1898, was asked: "How about self-government for the Cubans?" "Self-government!" he replied. "Why, these people are no more fit for self-government than gun-powder is for hell."

The opinions of soldiers and correspondents found their way into the newspapers. The Cubans, so recently the heroic resistors of Spanish tyranny, were soon dismissed as rabble and as wholly unprepared to govern themselves. The revised view was expressed by the Cleveland *Leader:* "While our Government disavowed a purpose of conquest, it may be absolutely necessary for us to keep Cuba and make it a part of the United States."

The distrust that attended the fighting increased in the months ahead. President McKinley reassured the Cubans that they would establish their own government once tranquility had been achieved, but the Cubans also heard Americans who seemed to favor annexation. In June, 1899, General Leonard Wood, in an interview with the *New York Times,* said that the propertied classes and Spaniards in Cuba favored annexation by the United States. These groups, he reported, wanted a stable government. Wood observed that "the establishment of another Haitian Republic in the West Indies would be a serious mistake."

The Teller Amendment became an object of regret. General James Harrison Wilson, who was in command of one part of Cuba, did not propose to alienate the Cubans by breaking the pledge, but he envisioned arrangements that would tie Cuba to the United States economically and in foreign affairs. Senator Joseph B. Foraker of Ohio supported General Wilson. When Elihu Root became secretary of war on August 1, 1899, he took over responsibility for governing Cuba. Root, fearful that Cuban resentment would trap the United States into the same bitter kind of warfare in which it was already involved in the Philippines, moved cautiously and tried to reassure the Cubans that there was no plan for annexation. Root proposed the establishment of local governments before moving to the problem of drafting a Cuban constitution. Like many others, Root feared the control of Cuba falling into the hands of the illiterate and propertyless classes. Consequently, he prescribed a suffrage based on literacy, property, or service in the army.

On July 25, 1900, the military government of Cuba called for the election of a constitutional convention. The convention began its sessions the following November. The Cubans enjoyed complete freedom in framing their own government, but soon found that the United States notions on the subject of the relations of the two countries did not conform to their own. Root wrote to Hay early in January, 1901, outlining his ideas on this subject. He wished to have incorporated in the Cuban constitution four provisions. The United States should have the right to intervene "for the preservation of Cuban independence and the maintenance of a stable government." The Cuban government should not be free to enter into agreements with foreign powers "which may tend to impair or interfere with the independence of Cuba, or to confer upon such foreign power any special right or privilege without the consent of the United States." The United States should have the right to acquire naval stations. Finally, actions taken during the American occupation and all rights acquired during the course of the occupation should be maintained and protected. . . .

The more interesting question to be answered is why Congress and the McKinley Administration found the degree of control retained by the United States necessary. The explanation seems to lie in its distrust of Cuban society even more than in its concern for American economic investments or any concern for the security of the proposed isthmian canal. As concerns the latter, there was almost no mention of the canal. Security considerations did enter the discussion, but it was the security of the coastline from the mouth of the Mississippi to Florida. . . .

The idealism that led to intervention in 1898 was employed in 1902 to justify the Platt Amendment. The reasoning was logical even if it ignored a number of realities. If concern for human rights was a legitimate concern, the legitimacy would not, in the eyes of its ardent exponents, become illegitimate when it transcended national boundaries. The imperialists condemned such a view as parochial. However, the logical next question would have been the legitimacy of the use of force. Few questioned the rightness of employing force to free the Cubans from Spain. Why should they have questioned provisions for the use of force in Cuba itself as long as the end was to them legitimate? . . .

Concern for economic interests and security contributed to the support of the Platt Amendment, but liberal ideology facilitated intervention in the Caribbean.

Some found it necessary to justify every move by idealistic argument. It was wholly irrelevant to the consideration of others. A year after Congress debated the Platt Amendment, the Committee on Ways and Means of the House of Representatives held hearings on commercial reciprocity with Cuba. No more mundane discussion could have taken place. Cuban representatives, spokesmen for New York merchants, agents of the cane growers of Louisiana, and sugar beet interests in California, Colorado, and Michigan argued with the vehemence of bargainers at an Oriental bazaar. Two questions dominated the discussions. Did the price of sugar production in Cuba, given current market prices, make the harvesting of the current crop unprofitable, and would, therefore, the Cuban economy spin into bankruptcy and lead to widespread unemployment and violence? Second, if this were true, did the United States have an obligation to rescue the sugar economy by opening the American market to sugar, or should the obligation be met, as the sugar beet representatives argued, by the American people as a whole and not by the small segment who happened to be domestic producers of sugar?

The backdrop for this sugar extravaganza was the situation of the world market. World sugar production had gradually increased from

1,481,000 tons in 1853–54 to 10,710,000 tons in 1901–2. Germany was by far the greatest producer of sugar. Austria, France, and Russia were next in order. The world price was determined by Hamburg. To promote exports, Germany and France subsidized exports of sugar so that the price of German beet sugar in London averaged 25 percent of the price in Germany. In 1898 an international cartel had been established whereby both production and prices could be controlled. In brief, the problem facing the sugar planters in Cuba had its source in capitals far removed from both Havana and Washington. Yet, if the United States lowered the duty on sugar imports from Cuba alone by a reciprocal agreement, the Cubans would gain at least temporary relief.

Cuba's distress was also the United States' opportunity. Members of the Ways and Means Committee showed at least as great an interest in capturing the Cuban market for American goods as the Cubans showed in gaining access to the American market. The best informed witness on this phase, Colonel T. H. Bliss, collector of customs at Havana, testified that the United States had a monopoly of the markets in fresh beef, pork, eggs, flour, coal, coal oil, machinery, and railroad iron. This, however, was more than counterbalanced by the imports of a list of ninety articles chiefly from other countries. Others controlled the Cuban markets in cattle, rice, wines, olive oil, salt, preserved fruits, dried beef, cottons, linens, woolens, silk, shoes, hats, and many other commodities.

These articles, said Bliss, could be secured from the United States, and would be if a tariff was arranged that gave the price advantage to the American products. "Thus," he said, "a tariff arrangement that would give the United States the control of the trade tabulated . . . would enable her to control at least 86 percent of the entire inward trade of Cuba." "This," he estimated, "on the basis of last year's figures, would have made their export trade to Cuba amount to $56,904,000 or just double what it actually was."

The casual estimate interested the committee members, but only in the long run would the proposed reciprocal trade program have these results. Bliss informed them of many of the difficulties. Almost all importers in Cuba were Spaniards with long associations with European business houses. New ties would not be established at once. There were other problems, too. Bliss cited the willingness of European cotton manufacturers to meet highly exact weight requirements and to guarantee the exact number of threads in a piece of goods. These determined in part the rate of import duty, and this in turn made the difference between profit and loss. Bliss likewise stressed how the practice of limiting credit to thirty days handicapped American sales.

Cubans pleaded for reciprocity because of the desperate situation of the sugar industry, and they recognized that it would be necessary to offer concessions in return. However, they were not unaware of the danger of Cuba becoming an economic colony of the United States. Their fears were nourished by the British minister, Sir Lionel Carden, who advised them that the principal benefits would go to the Americans and that the Cuban government would suffer sharp losses in revenue. In his report to the Foreign Office, Sir Lionel stated that the very existence of British trade with Cuba was threatened. "These arguments," he wrote "I have not failed to urge on several of the leading Cuban delegates, who are already opposed on political grounds to too intimate a connection with the United States, and it is to be hoped that their efforts may have the effect of neutralizing the action of the planters and their sympathizers."

President McKinley, Secretary of War Root, and General Leonard Wood put the argument for a reciprocal trade treaty in terms of the plight of the Cuban sugar economy and the moral obligation of the United States, inherent in its intervention in Cuba, to enable the Cubans to achieve economic recovery. Economic disaster at the close of the United States military occupation would reflect unfavorably upon the nation and upon the administration. This was the overriding consideration. Theodore Roosevelt, calling on Congress to approve a reciprocal trade treaty, stressed the obligation of the United States to assist the Cubans. At the same time these leaders expressed sympathy for the Cubans, they were mindful of other dimensions of the question than the immediate crisis. When the final bill was before the House of Representatives, Roosevelt urged its approval "not only because it is eminently for our own interests to control the Cuban market and by every means to foster our supremacy in the lands and waters south of us, but also because we, of the giant republic of the north, should make all our sister nations of the American Continent feel that whenever they will permit it, we desire to show ourselves disinterestedly and effectively their friend."

Winning the confidence of the peoples of the Caribbean by recognizing their problems and responding to their pleas for assistance guided Roosevelt and Root. The administration saw as its goal constructive leadership and friendly relations based upon mutual interests. The hope of a future market was almost incidental. However, the frankness of Roosevelt in stating that the United States aimed at control of the Cuban market and supremacy "in the lands and waters south of us" supports the Cuban critics who later charged that the aim was to reduce the island to an economic colony.

The negotiation of a reciprocal trade treaty went forward, but there was strong opposition from the domestic beet-sugar interests, and Elihu Root for a time had little hope of getting the approval of Congress. In December, 1902, the treaty was completed, and it was approved by Congress the following March. The beet sugar interests won a major concession when a provision was introduced making the 20 percent reduction in duty on Cuban sugar dependent upon the continuation of the high Dingley tariff duties on sugar from all other countries.

Some historians charge that the aim of the United States in negotiating the treaty was economic domination of Cuba. Eventually, Cuba did become an economic colony, but this was not a result of the trade treaty. Shortly after Congress approved of the treaty, Parker Willis, an economist who had long favored reciprocal trade, criticized the treaty as falling far short of the ideals of reciprocity. He maintained that the Cuban reduction of duties on American manufacturers was not sufficient to promise any real increase of exports to Cuba.

The reciprocal trade agreement did not lead to immediate American domination of the Cuban economy. It was Cuba that derived the greater gain. Imports from Cuba rose from $31,371,704 in 1900 to $122,528,037 in 1910. Sugar accounted for $93,543,897 of these imports. The 20 percent reduction of the regular duties on sugar originating in Cuba explained in part the increasing importance of the commercial tie. Almost the entire amount of sugar produced in Cuba was exported to the United States. Imports of tobacco were valued at $17,915,616 in 1910 and likewise benefitted by the 20 percent reduction.

The exports of the United States to Cuba in 1910 fell far short of the optimistic predictions that had been made during the discussion in 1902 of the benefits to be gained by a reciprocal agreement. Exports did increase from $26,513,400 in 1900 to $52,858,758 in 1910, but Cuba continued to buy from Europe in large part rather than from the United States. British cotton goods far outsold American cottons.

American investments in Cuba spiraled upward much more rapidly than exports of goods. In 1898, prior to the war with Spain, they approximated $50 million. By 1911 they had risen to more than $200 million.

The question of whether the United States had attained the status of a world power depends obviously on how the term is defined. By the turn of the century, the United States had by any economic measure moved to the front rank. It was likewise a major power in the Pacific Ocean area, where it possessed a series of important island bases and the Philippines plus a strong navy. Any nation seeking to bring about change in this region would have confronted a determined United States. However, while it exerted a modest influence in Eastern Asia and had established its right to a voice in international affairs in that area, the United States had only minor interests in China, and it did not affect significantly the course of events in the Manchu empire. Only in the Caribbean did the United States take on heavy commitments and dominate political developments. In Europe it was aloof. Except for its lasting impact on Spain in depriving her of the last of her empire and participation in the Algeciras Conference of 1906, the United States played no part in European affairs, although she was important to Europe as an economic competitor and as a supplier of both agricultural and manufactured goods.

The most significant development in American foreign relations was not an increasing impact on the course of world diplomacy but the emergence of foreign relations as a major problem. Varied responses to the question came to the fore ranging from a clamor for markets, speeches, and editorials on America's mission in the world, to thoughtful probing of the question of national interests. Much of the debate centered on duty and on opportunity and almost none of it on the complexities.

The heritage of a generation determines in large part the conduct of its diplomacy. At the turn of the century the heritage included neither a sense that the nation's welfare was in any way dependent upon developments abroad nor any significant public awareness that the existing world order, so benign in terms of American interests, rested on the complex arrangements of treaties, dominance of underdeveloped areas by the European powers, and control of the seas by Great Britain. Apart from a few leaders, such as Theodore Roosevelt and, to a lesser degree, Woodrow Wilson, there was no recognition of the advantages to the United States of the existing order in Europe. The heritage continued to nourish parochialism and counterbalanced the thrust of new forces. However, the dawn of a new era was at hand. New concerns made themselves felt and new ambitions came to the fore.

6

The Progressive Movement

Liberal or Conservative?

The rise of American industry in the decades following the Civil War was a development whose impact can hardly be exaggerated. It involved more than a shift from a commercial and agrarian economy to an urban and industrial one; indeed, it effected fundamental changes in the nature and quality of American society. The far-reaching technological and industrial innovations forced Americans to reexamine their traditional values and beliefs many of which seemed obsolete, if not irrelevant, to the problems of a new age.

Traditionally, Americans were accustomed to think in terms of individualistic values. The rise of industry itself was often rationalized in the ideology of the self-made man who claimed he attained success by virtue of his own talents, drive, and ambition. By the end of the nineteenth century, however, it was becoming more difficult to conceive of industrial progress solely in terms of the achievements of a few creative individuals. The growth of a national transportation and communications system, which led to the rise of a national market, had stimulated the formation of large industrial units. This organizational revolution, to use Kenneth Boulding's convenient phrase,[1] was to have profound implications. Americans at the turn of the twentieth century found that their nation was being increasingly dominated by large corporations whose establishment resulted in the partial curtailment, if not abolition, of competition—a development that collided sharply with the ideology of individualism and freedom.

The position of the individual within the nation's increasingly industrialized society became a major source of concern for many Americans. If America's greatness was related to individual achievement, what would happen as freedom and social mobility were more and more

[1]Kenneth E. Boulding, *The Organizational Revolution: A Study in the Ethics of Economic Organization* (New York, 1953).

circumscribed by giant corporations with their impersonal and machinelike qualities? Did not the emphasis of corporations on efficient production and material objectives distort the human qualities that had been responsible for America's rise to greatness? Was not the growing disparity between rich corporations and poor workingmen creating a situation akin to that existing in many European countries where there was open class strife? These and similar questions led many Americans to advocate reforms that would restore dignity to the individual and give meaning to his life.

The forces of reform gradually gathered momentum in the last quarter of the nineteenth century. Although critics of American society could not agree upon a specific diagnosis, let alone remedial measures, they were united in a common conviction that some changes would have to be made if the United States was to survive with its historic values intact. The solutions presented were often diffuse. Many were all-embracing panaceas that called for the preservation of a competitive and individualistic society, but, at the same time, did not sacrifice the affluence associated with technological progress. Henry George, for example, gained international fame by presenting his single tax scheme in 1879 in his book *Progress and Poverty*, while Edward Bellamy, in his utopian novel *Looking Backward* (1886), argued that only the nationalization of all the means of production and distribution would solve most of America's major problems. In a similar vein, many Protestant clergymen who were disturbed by the cleavages in American society offered their own answers in what came to be known as the Social Gospel. These religious critics argued that an immoral society was incompatible with the ideals of moral men. Society, therefore, would have to be remade in the form of a Christian socialist commonwealth, thereby offering individuals an opportunity to lead moral lives. Others, including the Populists, socialists, advocates of civil service reform, and academic critics also contributed to the swelling chorus of reform.

Between 1900 and 1917, these uncoordinated efforts at reform were institutionalized in what came to be known as the Progressive movement. Pluralistic rather than unitary, the Progressive movement was actually a series of movements operating at the local, state, and national levels of government and society. The movement consisted of a loose coalition of reformers who sought a variety of goals: political reforms such as the initiative, referendum, recall, and the destruction of urban political machines and corruption; economic reforms such as the regulation of public utilities and the curtailment of corporate power; and social reforms such as the Americanization of the immigrant, the amelioration of the lot of the urban poor, and regulation of child and woman labor as well as many others. Among the symbolic leaders of the movement were two presidents, Theodore Roosevelt and Woodrow Wilson. These two men not only revived the moral authority and leadership-potential inherent in the presidency, but they supported the enactment of a series of laws embodying major social reforms.

Until the period after the Second World War, there was relatively little controversy among historians about the nature and character of the Progressive movement. Most American historians were writing within the tradition of the Progressive school. Consequently, they interpreted these reform movements and reformers within a liberal framework. In their eyes, the reformers in the movement had been challenging the dominant position of the business and privileged classes. The reformers' goals had been clear and simple: to restore government to the people; to abolish special privilege and ensure equal opportunity for all; and to enact a series of laws embodying principles of social justice. These reformers, Progressive historians emphasized, were not anticapitalist; they had not advocated the abolition of private property nor sought the establishment of a socialist society. On the contrary, they had taken seriously the American dream; their fundamental goal had been a democratic and humane society based on egalitarian ideals and social compassion. The real enemies of society were the businessmen, dishonest politicians, and "special interests," all of whom posed a serious threat to the realization of American democracy.

Such an approach put Progressivism squarely within the American liberal tradition and on the side of the "people" as opposed to the forces of wealth, self-interest, and special privilege. Vernon L. Parrington, one of the best known Progressive historians, saw Progressivism as a "democratic renaissance"—a movement of the masses against a "plutocracy" that had been corrupting the very fabric of American society since the Civil War. Thus, the movement concerned itself not only with political democracy, but with economic democracy as well. To Parrington Progressivism was a broad-based movement that included members of the middle class, journalists, and scholars—men, in other words, whose consciences had been aroused by the "cesspools that were poisoning the national household," and who had set for themselves the task of reawakening the American people.[2]

Implicit in this point of view was the conviction that the course of American history had been characterized by a continuous struggle between liberalism and conservatism, democracy and aristocracy, and equal opportunity and special privilege. Most historians writing in the Progressive tradition believed that reformers, regardless of their specific goals or the eras in which they appeared, were cast in the same mold because they invariably supported the "people" against their enemies. Such was the position of John D. Hicks, an outstanding American historian whose textbooks in American history were used by tens of

---

[2]Vernon L. Parrington, *Main Currents in American Thought* (3 vols: New York, 1927–1930), III, p. 406.

thousands of high school and college students between the 1930's and
1960's. Hicks in 1931 published *The Populist Revolt*, the first major account of Populism based on wide research in the original resources. To
Hicks the Populists carried the banner of reform in the 1890's and represented the first organized protest of the masses against the encroachments of a monopolistic plutocracy. Although the Populist movement
ultimately failed, it was victorious in the long run, Hicks held, because
much of its program was taken over by later reformers and enacted into
law during the first two decades of the twentieth century. To a large
extent his thesis rested on the assumption that American reform efforts
drew much of their inspiration from the Jeffersonian agrarian tradition
which had survived intact among the nation's farmers and rural population.[3]

Not all historians were as friendly and well-disposed toward
Populism and Progressivism as was Hicks. Those historians writing
within a socialist and Marxian tradition, for example, were highly critical
of Progressivism because of its superficial nature and its refusal to adopt
more radical solutions to meet the basic needs of American society. To
John Chamberlain, a young Marxist who in 1932 published a devastating
critique of American reform, the Progressive movement was an abysmal
failure. Its adherents, claimed Chamberlain, were motivated by an es-
capist desire to return to a golden past where honesty and virtue had
dominated over egoism and evil.[4]

Oddly enough, many of the detractors of the achievements of the
reform movement from 1890 to 1917 were, like Chamberlain, within the
Progressive school of history in that they accepted the idea that class
conflict had been the major determinant of progress and social change in
America. Many of them, particularly during the depression of the
1930's, condemned the Progressive reforms as being piecemeal and superficial in nature. The failure of the Progressive generation, these critics
emphasized, had led to the reaction of the 1920's, which in turn had
resulted in the disastrous depression of the 1930's. Disillusionment with
the Progressive movement, however, did not necessarily imply disillusion with the efficacy of reform or with the aspirations and ideals of the
liberal tradition in America. Even those intellectuals who flirted with
Marxism during the depression did so out of their conviction that
America could still be redeemed from the hands of its enemies.

Beginning in the 1940's, and continuing in the 1950's and 1960's, the
mood of American historians began to change. The increasing
homogeneity of American society began to dissolve the sectional, class,
and ethnic groupings that had been employed by the Progressive school

---

[3]John D. Hicks, *The Populist Revolt: A History of the Farmers' Alliance and the People's Party*
(Minneapolis, 1931).

[4]John Chamberlain, *Farewell to Reform* (New York, 1932).

of history. No longer did historians have to vindicate the claims of the West against the East, the South against the rest of the nation, or to establish conclusively the contributions of the Puritans, the immigrant, the working class, or the businessman. Such narrow loyalties appeared parochial in a milieu where national similarities seemed to be more significant than group differences.

The change in mood, however, was due to far more fundamental factors than a mere shift in the class and ethnic backgrounds of historians. Much more basic was the change in attitude and outlook that accompanied the revolutionary changes in the world since the 1940's. To scholars writing after 1940, the Progressive ideology appeared much too facile and simplified. Like many philosophers and theologians, they began to criticize Progressive historians for underestimating man's propensities for evil and for overestimating his capacity for good. In brief, these critics argued that the interpretation of the Progressive school of history rested on an unrealistic evaluation of human nature. The result, they concluded, was that Americans had been unprepared for the dilemmas and challenges that they faced in the great depression of the 1930's and the world-wide conflict of the 1940's because of their tendency to view history in terms of a simple morality play where good always triumphed over evil.

The challenge to democracy by communism since World War II has given rise to a new group of scholars—the neo-conservative historians—who have been critical of the Progressive school and who embarked upon their own reevaluation of the American past. Writing from a conservative point of view, these historians stressed the basic goodness of American society and the consensus that has characterized the American people throughout most of their past. Thus these scholars insisted that American history could not be written in terms of a struggle between democracy and aristocracy or the people against the special interests. On the contrary, they tended to stress the unity and homogeneity of the American past, the stability of basic institutions, and the existence of a monistic national character. While they did not deny that there have been conflicts and struggles between sections, classes, and special interest groups in the past, the neo-conservative historians insisted that such struggles were always fought within a liberal framework and that the protagonists were never really in disagreement over fundamentals. Moreover, these scholars were also much less certain about the value or desirability of social change. Having witnessed the effects of revolutionary movements in other parts of the world, the neo-conservatives questioned whether conflict and change would necessarily lead to a better society.

The result of this changed outlook was a sharp shift in the way that historians interpreted the Progressive movement. The Progressive school of history had looked upon the Progressive era as but one phase in the continuing struggle against special privilege and business. The newer neo-conservative school, in rejecting the older view, now began to ask new and different questions. If Progressivism was not in the Jeffersonian liberal tradition, in what tradition could it be placed? If Progressives were not necessarily moral individuals fighting on behalf of the masses, who were they and what did they stand for? If they did not democratize and reform America by their efforts, just what did they accomplish? Such were the questions raised by historians who rejected the older Progressive view.

The attack on the Progressive school interpretation of the Progressive movement was led by Richard Hofstadter, the distinguished Columbia University historian. Oddly enough, Hofstadter was writing within the Progressive tradition and as a liberal partisan. Yet he could not find very many constructive achievements to attribute to the American liberal tradition. Indeed, he found the liberal ideology to be narrow and deficient in many respects. In a number of brilliant books, Hofstadter attempted to expose, by historical analysis, the shortcomings, the inadequacies, and the failure of American liberalism.

In 1948 Hofstadter published *The American Political Tradition and the Men Who Made It*. In this book he attempted to delineate the basic characteristics of the American political tradition by studying the careers of nearly a dozen presidents and political leaders, including Andrew Jackson, John C. Calhoun, Abraham Lincoln, Theodore Roosevelt, Woodrow Wilson, and Franklin Delano Roosevelt. Hofstadter's thesis was that the liberal tradition had failed because it was based upon the idea of a return to an ideology that emphasized acquisitive and individualistic values. Thus, the Populists and Progressives had similar deficiencies; neither had faced up to the fundamental problems of an industrialized and corporate America. Even Franklin Delano Roosevelt, who did not share the nostalgia common to the Progressive tradition, was a pragmatist whose attraction lay in the force of his personality rather than in any consistent ideology or philosophy.

Seven years later, Hofstadter spelled out his case in even greater detail in *The Age of Reform: From Bryan to F.D.R.* The Populists, he argued, were unsophisticated and simplistic reformers. Rather than approaching the farm problem within a broad national and international context, they placed the blame for their difficulties upon elements of American society which were alien to them—Easterners, Wall Street bankers, Jews, and foreigners. Associated with Populism, therefore, was a combination of attitudes made up of a curious blend of racism, nativism, and provincialism—attitudes that helped to explain the fears of agricultural and rural America that later manifested themselves in national paranoic scares. "The Populists," Hofstadter emphasized, "looked backward with longing to the lost agrarian Eden, to the republican America of the early years of the nineteenth century in which there were few millionaires and, as they saw it, no beggars, when the laborer had excellent prospects and the farmer had abundance, when statesmen still responded to the mood of the people and there was no such thing as the money power. What they meant—though they did not express themselves in such terms—was that they would like to restore the conditions prevailing before the development of industrialism and the commercialization of agriculture."[5]

Nor were the Progressives, according to Hofstadter, very much more sophisticated. Traditionally, Progressivism had been viewed by historians as a liberal reform movement aimed at readjusting American institutions to the imperatives of a new industrial age. To Hofstadter, on the other hand, Progressivism was something quite different. Borrowing heavily from the work of behavioral scientists, he argued that Progressivism was related to other influences, notably status anxiety. Playing down the role of economic factors in individual and group motivation, Hofstadter maintained that to a large extent American political conflicts reflected the drive of different ethnic and religious groups for a secure status in society. By the latter third of the nineteenth century, a number of groups—clergymen, lawyers, professors, older Anglo-Saxon Protestant families—were finding themselves displaced from the seats of power and their traditional positions of leadership by a dangerous plutocracy and new political machines under the control of alien elements. The response of this displaced elite was a moral crusade to restore older Protestant and individualistic values—the Progressive movement. This crusade was based on the simple idea that only men of character—the "right sort of people"—should rule. Few Progressive leaders, including Theodore Roosevelt and Woodrow Wilson, were realistic in their appraisals of and solutions to America's problems. "In the attempts of the Populists and Progressives to hold on to some of the values of agrarian life, to save personal entrepreneurship and individual opportunity and the character type they engendered, and to maintain a homogeneous Yankee civilization," Hofstadter wrote, "I have found much that was retrograde and delusive, a little that was vicious, and a good deal that was comic."[6] Blinded by their moral absolutism and their righteous convictions, the Progressives were unable to foresee that much of their ideology was narrow and undemocratic and would prepare the groundwork for a later reaction that would threaten the very fabric of American liberty.

The implications of Hofstadter's interpretation were indeed striking. In brief, his line of thought led to the conclusion that American liberalism was not a liberal movement, but a movement by fairly well-to-do middle class groups alienated from their society because of

---

[5]Richard Hofstadter, *The Age of Reform: From Bryan to F.D.R.* (New York, 1955), p. 62.
[6]*Ibid.*, p. 11.

technological and industrial changes. There is no doubt that Hofstadter himself was writing from the left of the political spectrum, but it is clear also that he felt strongly that the United States never had had a viable and constructive liberal tradition. Implicit in his views, therefore, was the assumption that American history occurred within an illiberal or conservative mold, that a genuine struggle between classes—as portrayed by the Progressive historians—had never taken place.

Hofstadter's general interpretation of Progressivism rested to a large degree upon the research of others, particularly the work of George E. Mowry. Author of a number of important books on Theodore Roosevelt and the Progressive movement, Mowry was one of the first historians to see Progressivism as a movement by a particular class aimed at reasserting its declining position of leadership. Motivated by an intense faith in individualistic values, these groups opposed the rapid concentration of power in the hands of large corporate entities and the consequent emergence of an impersonal society. The Progressives, Mowry concluded, sought to recapture and reaffirm the older individualistic values, but they attempted to do so without undertaking any fundamental economic reforms or altering to any great extent the structure of American society.[7]

While the specific formulations of the Mowry-Hofstadter thesis have not been universally accepted,[8] most recent historians seem to agree that the older interpretation of Progressivism as a struggle between the people and special interests is oversimplified, if not erroneous. Thus Louis Hartz in his fascinating book *The Liberal Tradition in America: An Interpretation of American Political Thought Since the Revolution* (1955) argued that because America never had a feudal tradition, it did not experience the struggles between conservatives, reactionaries, liberals, and Marxians that characterized the history of most European countries. On the contrary, the United States had a three-century-long tradition of consensus, wherein all Americans subscribed to the Lockean tenets of individualism, private property, natural rights, and popular sovereignty. The differences between Americans, Hartz maintained, have been over means rather than ends. Thus, Americans never had a conservative tradition in the European and Burkean sense of the term, because American liberalism, by virtue of its continuity, was a conservative

---

[7]George E. Mowry, "The California Progressive and His Rationale: A Study in Middle Class Politics," *Mississippi Valley Historical Review*, XXXVI (September, 1949), pp. 239–250.

[8]A number of historians have pointed to what they regard as a methodological flaw in the Mowry-Hofstadter analysis. To argue—as Mowry and Hofstadter have done—that the Progressives were a cohesive group requires that they show that the anti-Progressives represented a quite different social and economic group. One recent historian who did a study of the anti-Progressives in one state found that their social and economic and ideological characteristics were almost identical with those of the Progressives. See Richard B. Sherman, "The Status Revolution and Massachusetts Progressive Leadership," *Political Science Quarterly*, LXXVIII (March, 1963), pp. 59–65.

tradition. To view American history in terms of class struggle, said Hartz, was to misunderstand the basic agreements that united all Americans.

As a result of the rise of the neo-conservative school of historians, the Progressive movement has begun to be interpreted in a new and different light. Some of these scholars, for example, neatly reversed the Progressive school approach. Instead of seeing early twentieth-century Progressivism as a liberal movement, they argued that it was essentially conservative in nature—a characteristic that was a source of strength rather than of weakness. Thus the historical stature of Theodore Roosevelt rose as historians such as John M. Blum saw him as a conservative though responsible president who was flexible enough to deal with the major issues of the day in a constructive yet practical manner. Conversely, the reputation of Woodrow Wilson among some historians tended to decline because of his righteous moralism. Wilson's New Freedom, they wrote, was unrealistic because of its worship of a bygone age where all individuals had equal opportunity in the economic sphere. His foreign policies also turned out to be dismal failures because they rested on an exclusively moral foundation that omitted any appreciation of the national interest or the realities of international affairs.[9]

Conversely, the reputation of many American reformers suffered as a result of the writings of neo-conservative historians. Rather than writing about their contributions and achievements, historians have shown the shortcomings and failures of various reform leaders. They have exposed the personal and selfish factors that supposedly motivated the behavior of reformers and implicitly determined their unrealistic approach to contemporary problems. Above all, such historians scored the reformers for accepting an optimistic moralism based on their faith in progress. According to neo-conservative scholars, Progressive reformers tragically misunderstood man's propensity for evil and thereby failed to prepare Americans for the inevitable reaction that followed their failure to establish a democratic utopia at home and a peaceful international community of nations abroad in the first two decades of the twentieth century.

At the same time that neo-conservative scholars were attempting to undermine the Progressive school emphasis on reform and class conflict, other historians were in the process of developing an entirely new synthesis to explain American history since the late-nineteenth century. Influenced by work in the social and behavioral sciences, they began to apply organizational theory to historical study. Building on the impressive contributions of Max Weber and others, organizational historians saw American society as being increasingly dominated by hierarchical

---

[9]John M. Blum, *The Republican Roosevelt* (Cambridge, 1954). For a critical, but by no means unsympathetic, interpretation of Wilson see Arthur S. Link, *Woodrow Wilson and the Progressive Era 1910–1917* (New York, 1954).

and bureaucratic structures, which were accompanied by a sharp acceleration in the process of professionalization. Associated with these developments was a corresponding shift in the nation's value system. Through the mid-nineteenth century individualistic values remained dominant; after that time they were replaced by an orientation that stressed ideals of efficiency, order, rationality, and systematic control.[10]

The organizational model—as we have already seen—had been employed by business historians such as Alfred D. Chandler, Jr., to explain the emergence of large corporations. But such a model was also capable of being applied in a far more inclusive manner. A number of historians, for example, advanced the thesis that Progressivism represented largely an attempt to govern society in accordance with the new ideals of scientific management and efficiency. The conservation movement, to take one concrete illustration, was not—as historians of the Progressive school had maintained—a struggle by the American people and their champions against special interests and large corporate enterprises bent on depriving the nation of its natural resources and despoiling the landscape. On the contrary, the conservation movement, according to Samuel P. Hays, was a movement of scientists and planners interested in "rational planning to promote efficient development and use of all natural resources." Frequently, large corporations—which were profoundly influenced by the ideals of scientific management—were ardent supporters of conservationist policies because of their interest in long-range resource planning. Conversely, small farmers, small cattlemen, homesteaders, and other groups that Progressive historians equated with the democratic masses, often opposed conservation because it conflicted with their hopes of becoming rich quickly. "The broader significance of the conservation movement," Hays concluded, "stemmed from the role it played in the transformation of a decentralized, nontechnical, loosely organized society, where waste and inefficiency ran rampant, into a highly organized, technical, and centrally planned and directed social organization which could meet a complex world with efficiency and purpose."[11] Implicit in this approach was the assumption that conservation had little or nothing to do with the liberal-conservative categories of the Progressive school of historiography.

In stressing the role of the "expert" and the ideals of scientific management as basic to an understanding of the Progressive era, organizational historians also reinterpreted other aspects of early twentieth century American history. Many of the Progressive reforms, they stressed, were directed not at making the government more democratic and re-

---

[10]For a penetrating discussion of this problem see Louis Galambos, "The Emerging Organizational Synthesis in Modern American History," *Business History Review,* XLIV (Autumn, 1970), pp. 279–290.

[11]Samuel P. Hays, *Conservation and the Gospel of Efficiency: The Progressive Conservation Movement, 1890–1920* (Cambridge, 1959), pp. 2, 265.

sponsive to the wishes of the American people, but to making it and the economy more efficient. The movement for federal regulation of business was not, as the Progressive school of historians had argued, motivated by fear or hatred of large corporate enterprise. Its goal, according to these newer historians, was the elimination of senseless and destructive competition in the economic system by making business and government partners in the effort to eliminate the ups and downs of the business cycle. Progressivism, therefore, reflected the desire of various professional groups to substitute planning for competition, to raise the "expert" to a position of paramount importance, and to end the inherent defects of democratic government by making government conform to the ideals of efficiency and rational planning.

The decline of the older view of the Progressive era was also evidenced in the changing historical interpretation of business and businessmen. For a good part of the twentieth century, the liberal assumptions of most historians led them to portray the business community not only as monolithic in character, but as being made up of men who were grasping, selfish, and narrow in their outlook. In recent scholarship, on the other hand, the businessman has been studied within a quite different framework. Business historians found in the careers of great entrepreneurs a creative and constructive leadership that brought into being America's phenomenal industrial capacity. Similarly, a number of recent scholars have denied that the business community was necessarily reactionary or that all businessmen shared a common ideology. Instead, they attempted to demonstrate that businessmen divided into various groups with conflicting ideas and that many of the Progressive reforms of the early-twentieth century were actually introduced, supported, and endorsed by businessmen. In a study of the relationship between businessmen and the Progressive movement, for example, Robert H. Wiebe found a complex situation. Businessmen, he noted, rarely tried to improve the lot of low-income groups; they fought against unions and social insurance legislation; and while desiring to purify democracy, they opposed its extension. Economic regulation, on the other hand aroused a quite different response, for "at least one segment of the business community supported each major program for federal control. In this area businessmen exercised their greatest influence on reform and laid their claim as progressives."[12]

In *Businessmen and Reform* (1962) Wiebe had referred to the Progressive era as an "age of organization." Businessmen, he averred, turned to organization as a means of survival in an impersonal and changing world. Five years later in a major work Wiebe carried his analysis much further and provided one of the first attempts to synthesize American

---

[12]Robert H. Wiebe, *Businessmen and Reform: A Study of the Progressive Movement* (Cambridge, 1962), p. 212.

history around an organizational core. For much of the nineteenth century American society was composed of autonomous and semi-
autonomous "island communities." The United States was a nation
more in name than in fact, for most individuals resided in relatively
small, personal centers which managed its affairs independently of
other communities. By the 1880's, however, these communities no
longer functioned in their traditional manner, for technological and economic forces had undermined their cohesiveness and caused "dislocation and bewilderment." The result, according to Wiebe, was a "search
for order." Some attempted to restore the local community to a position
of significance; others turned to agrarian reform; still others joined moral
crusades in the belief that a return to traditional values would solve
many problems. Ultimately most Progressives turned to organization to
bring a new order and equilibrium to American society. In such diverse
fields as law, medicine, economics, administration, social work, archi-
tecture, business, labor, and agriculture—to cite only a few examples—a
new middle class appeared, tied together by their conviction that their
expertise and occupational cohesiveness provided the means of ordering
a fragmented society. "The heart of progressivism," wrote Wiebe, "was
the ambition of the new middle class to fulfill its destiny through
bureaucratic means."[13] Slowly but surely America was brought "to the
edge of something as yet indefinable. In a general sense, the nation had
found its direction early in the twentieth century. The society that so
many in the nineties had thought would either disintegrate or polarize
had emerged tough and plural; and by 1920 the realignments, the
reorientations of the Progressive era had been translated into a complex
of arrangements nothing short of a revolution could destroy."[14]

Curiously enough, neo-conservative, consensus, and organizational
interpretations of the Progressive movement that grew in influence in
the 1950's and 1960's were also echoed by "New Left" historians. Disillusioned by the continued existence of war, poverty, and racism, "New
Left" scholars tended to write about the shortcomings and failures of
American reform, a point of view that grew out of their own belief that
only radical changes in the framework and structure of American society
would solve these problems. Consequently, the "New Left" interpretation of early-twentieth-century Progressivism was written within a partial consensus framework (although those individuals writing within
this radical tradition clearly rejected the consensus on which this movement was based) and an awareness of the importance of organizations in
twentieth-century America.

To "New Left" historians the Progressive movement was anything
but a reform movement. In one of the most significant studies of early-

[13]Robert H. Wiebe, *The Search for Order 1877-1920* (New York, 1967), p. 166.
[14]*Ibid.*, pp. 301-302.

twentieth-century American history, Gabriel Kolko argued that both major political parties shared a common ideology and set of values. This ideology—what Kolko called political capitalism—sought the elimination of a growing competition in the economy. Political capitalism, he noted, "redirected the radical potential of mass grievances and aspirations"; rather than federal regulation *of* business the norm became federal regulation *for* business. Between 1900 and 1916 a unique synthesis of economics and politics occurred. Progressivism, argued Kolko,

> was initially a movement for the political rationalization of business and industrial conditions, a movement that operated on the assumption that the general welfare of the community could be best served by satisfying the concrete needs of business. But the regulation itself was invariably controlled by leaders of the regulated industry, and directed toward ends they deemed acceptable or desirable. In part this came about because the regulatory movements were usually initiated by the dominant businesses to be regulated, but it also resulted from the nearly universal belief among political leaders in the basic justice of private property relations as they essentially existed, a belief that set the ultimate limits on the leaders' possible actions.

Since neither Populism nor the Socialist party developed a specific diagnosis of existing social dynamics and relationships, Americans had no viable alternatives, for the two major political parties became the means through which business domination was institutionalized. "The Progressive Era," concluded Kolko, "was characterized by a paucity of alternatives to the status quo, a vacuum that permitted political capitalism to direct the growth of industrialism in America, to shape its politics, to determine the ground rules for American civilization in the twentieth century, and to set the stage for what was to follow."[15]

The reaction against the liberal interpretation of the Progressive movement, however, has not been shared by all historians. While admitting that older historians may have been wrong in their emphasis on a class conflict of the people versus the special interests, some scholars continue to see Progressivism as an attempt to deal effectively with many social and economic problems that grew out of industrialism and the resulting concentration of power in the hands of a few individuals and groups. J. Joseph Hutchmacher, for example, explicitly rejected the Mowry-Hofstadter idea that Progressivism was a middle-class movement dominated by a system of values espoused by rural-Yankee-Protestant groups. On the contrary, Hutchmacher maintained that Progressivism was much more broadly based, and that lower-class groups played an important role in the movement. Implicitly rejecting the neoconservative thesis, Hutchmacher argued that Progressivism was an attempt to cope with the complex dilemmas of an urban-industrial society.

---

[15]Gabriel Kolko, *The Triumph of Conservatism: A Reinterpretation of American History, 1900–1916* (New York, 1963), pp. 2–3, 285, 305.

Although he clearly rejected the Jeffersonian agrarian interpretation of Progressivism, his point of view was essentially a modification and elaboration of the Progressive school that saw the reform movement of 1900–1920 as a continuing phase in the perennial struggle of liberalism versus conservatism. [16]

In a similar vein, David P. Thelen examined closely the Mowry-Hofstadter thesis that status tensions and insecurity were central to the origins of Progressivism. Using Wisconsin as a case study, Thelen could find no correlation between an individual's social characteristics and his political affiliation and ideology. Rejecting the sociological and psychological interpretation that Progressivism was rooted in social tensions, he argued instead that its roots went back into the nineteenth century. The depression of the 1890's was of particular importance, for it dramatized the failures of industrialism and gave rise to a search for alternatives. Out of this search came a broad consensus on a series of reform programs that cut across class lines. All groups could unite on the urgent necessity for tax reform and the need to control "corporate arrogance." "When the progressive characteristically spoke of reform as a fight of 'the people' or the 'public interest' against the 'selfish interests,' he was speaking quite literally of his political coalition because the important fact about progressivism, at least in Wisconsin, was the degree of cooperation between previously discrete social groups now united under the banner of the 'public interest.' . . . Both conceptually and empirically it would seem safer and more productive to view reformers first as reformers and only secondarily as men who were trying to relieve class and status anxieties." Thelen's article is included as the first selection in this chapter.

Most interpretations of Progressivism rested on studies of Midwestern or Eastern states. In a significant analysis of Alabama during the Progressive era, on the other hand, Sheldon Hackney found that many of the standard generalizations were open to question. He noted, for example, that there was little continuity between Populism and Progressivism in Alabama; following the demise of their party, Populists either voted Republican or else withdrew from politics. Holding a social philosophy that viewed society in static terms, they clearly preferred a minimal rather than an activist government; they were "primitive rebels." Nor were Progressives motivated by status anxiety or committed to producer values; they saw society in dynamic terms and insisted that economic opportunity could come about only through greater economic growth stimulated in part by positive governmental action. Unlike their forebears, Progressives were earnestly interested in changing Southern

---

[16]J. Joseph Hutchmacher, "Urban Liberalism and the Age of Reform," *Mississippi Valley Historical Review*, XLIX (September, 1962), pp. 231-241.

society and bringing it into the modern industrial era. Indeed, Hackney found that Alabama Progressivism resembled more the Eastern, urban Roosevelt brand than the Western, rural Bryan variety.

But Progressivism, as Hackney observed, also had sharp implications for the status of black Americans in Alabama. During the years from 1890 to 1910, the pattern of race relations in that state was highly fluid; inconsistency was its primary characteristic. One manifestation of this uncertainty was the high frequency of lynchings. Stability came to Alabama only when the Constitutional Convention of 1901 in effect eliminated black citizens from political participation. Curiously enough, the movement for disfranchisement was led by opponents of reform. Their success helped Progressives to create a new coalition from the purged electorate that owed little to Populist antecedents. Progressivism in Alabama, therefore, rested on the institutionalization of legal and political inequality. Hackney's book raised significant questions about the nature of Progressivism and gave little support to either liberal, conservative, or radical schools of historical interpretation. The second selection in this chapter is an excerpt from Hackney's book.

Oddly enough, virtually all historians, whether they are in the older Progressive or the newer neo-conservative, organizational, or "New Left" traditions, seem to be in agreement on at least one major point; namely, that Progressivism was an urban rather than a rural-centered movement. Once again, historians seem to have been reflecting their milieu. In the past many of the major historians had come out of an environment dominated by rural and agrarian values; their attitude toward cities was partly conditioned by the prevailing view that American democracy was the creation of a rural agrarian society. Within the past two or three decades, however, the majority of historians have tended to come from a society and regions of the country much more concerned with the problems of urban life. They do not share the anti-urban attitudes held by many of their predecessors. As a result, these historians have written about the contributions of cities and growing urban areas to American history. In this respect, they have shared the mounting concerns of most present-day Americans with the problems of an urban society.

As the historiography of the Progressive movement shows, it is difficult to evaluate the specific contributions of the movement without dealing with certain moral values that inevitably influence the historical judgments of scholars studying the subject. To the Progressive school of historical scholarship, Progressivism was one of the first efforts to adjust American values to an industrialized society wherein the concentration of economic power was thwarting the workings of American democratic institutions as well as corrupting the moral fibre of its citizens. Since they agreed with the goals of reformers who were attempting to ameliorate this situation, the writings of the Progressive school of historians on the movement tended to be a favorable one. More recent scholars, on the other hand, operated within quite a different value structure. Business and other neo-conservative historians, precisely because they emphasized the constructive achievements of American business, did not see much good in a movement which they believed was based on superficial knowledge, amateurism, and demagoguery. Because these historians were more complacent, even proud, of the accomplishments of American society, they saw less need for radical reforms in America's past history. Hence, they either emphasized the conservative nature of Progressivism or else pointed to its lack of realism or its optimistic illusions in order to show why the movement failed. Similarly, "New Left" scholars were equally hostile in their analysis of Progressivism; they saw the movement as one dedicated to the control of government by business, giving it a reactionary rather than a reform character. Some historians who identified themselves with the liberal tradition also argued that American liberalism fell far short of enacting truly meaningful reforms during the Progressive era. Thus it was possible for neo-conservative, liberal, and radical scholars to be critical of the Progressive movement from their respective viewpoints. And even organizational historians evidenced considerable ambivalence; they were not at all certain that a society based on bureaucratic values and structures was necessarily good.

The problem of evaluating the nature of the Progressive movement, therefore, is by no means easy or simple. Despite considerable research on this important era of American history, the divisions among historians are not necessarily disappearing. On the contrary, these divisions are in some respects growing sharper because of differences among historians pertaining to the nature and meaning of the American liberal tradition. In the final analysis, when historians are assessing Progressivism, they are assessing also the ability of Americans to adapt themselves to new problems in any given era.

Aside from the ideological and philosophical conflicts among historians, there are several major questions and problems that must be dealt with in evaluating the Progressive movement. Was there a relationship between the Progressive movement and earlier as well as later reform movements, including Populism and the New Deal? Who were the Progressives and what did they represent? Similarly, what groups opposed Progressivism and why did they do so? Were the reforms that were enacted between 1900 and 1917 constructive? What impact, if any, did they have upon American life? What significance did Progressivism have for black Americans and other minority groups? Why did the Progressive movement come to an end as an organized movement, or did it, indeed, come to an end at all?

These are only a few of the questions that historians have dealt with in an effort to understand the development of American society during the first two decades of the twentieth century. It is difficult, if not impossible, to avoid addressing oneself to these issues because of the bearing they have upon the larger question of understanding the nature of the American experience.

David P. Thelen

DAVID P. THELEN (1939-   ) is Professor of History at the University of Missouri. He has written *The New Citizenship: Origins of Progressivism in Wisconsin, 1885–1900* (1972).

Recent historians have explained the origins of the Progressive movement in several ways. They have represented progressivism, in turn, as a continuation of the western and southern farmers' revolt, as a desperate attempt by the urban gentry to regain status from the new robber barons, as a thrust from the depths of slum life, and as a campaign by businessmen to prevent workers from securing political power. Behind such seemingly conflicting theories, however, rests a single assumption about the origins of progressivism: the class and status conflicts of the late-nineteenth century formed the driving forces that made men become reformers. Whether viewed by the historian as a farmer, worker, urban elitist, or businessman, the progressive was motivated primarily by his social position; and each scholar has painted a compelling picture of the insecurities and tensions felt by the group that he placed in the vanguard of progressivism. Pressures and threats from other social groups drove men to espouse reform. In these class and status conflicts can be found the roots of progressivism.

How adequately does this focus on social tensions and insecurities explain the origins of progressivism? Since some of these scholars have invoked concepts from social science to support their rejection of earlier approaches, the validity and application of some of the sociological and psychological assumptions which make up the conceptual framework for the idea that social tensions impelled the progressive require analysis. Is the focus on social classes relevant to the rise of political movements like progressivism? Is it useful to rely upon a narrow, untestable and unproved conception of motivation when other approaches are available? How much of a concrete situation does an abstract model explain?

First, theories borrowed from one discipline are not designed to encompass the data of another. In questioning the application of models from physiology and physics to psychology, the noted personality

David P. Thelen, "Social Tensions and the Origins of Progressivism," *Journal of American History*, LVI (September, 1969), pp. 323–341. Reprinted by permission of the Organization of American Historians.

theorist George A. Kelly explained: "We are skeptical about the value of copying ready-made theories which were designed for other foci of convenience"; and he urged his fellow psychologists to resist the temptation of "poking about in the neighbors' back yards for methodological windfalls." Just as physiology and physics encompass only part of the psychologist's realm, so psychology, sociology, and political science are concerned with only part of the historian's realm.

Those historians who have borrowed the idea that social stratification explains the rise of political movements like progressivism illustrate the dangers inherent in borrowing theories from other fields. Most sociologists and political scientists now doubt the relevance of social stratification to the emergence of political movements. Reinard Bendix, for example, maintained that "the study of social stratification, whether or not it is adumbrated by psychological analysis, is not the proper approach to an understanding of the role of cumulative political experience." In their pleas for more pluralistic approaches to political power, such political scientists as Nelson W. Polsby and Robert A. Dahl have found that social stratification is largely irrelevant to the exercise of political power. So severe were these criticisms of the assumption that social class determined political power that one sociologist, reviewing the literature of the field in 1964, concluded that "the problem has simply been dropped."

But an even greater problem with placing emphasis on social tensions is that it is ahistorical. Even sociologists like Seymour M. Lipset and Bendix have complained about the "increasingly ahistorical" drift of the focus of this field. After analyzing the major models of social change, another sociologist concluded that the fundamental error of these models was their failure to incorporate the dimension of time. Few scholars would deny that social tensions exist at all times and in all societies. For at least twenty years before 1900, various business groups had tried to take political power away from workers and bosses. But to focus on the social class motivation of businessmen is to obscure the basic historical problem of why progressivism emerged when it did. Conflicts between businessmen and workers were hardly unique to the years around 1900. The emphasis on social tensions obscures chronology. When sociologists are disturbed about this problem, historians should be wary indeed.

The assumption that progressivism derived from social tensions is at least as vulnerable to attack by psychologists. If the kinds of questions historians generally ask about the origins of political and social movements are reduced to the psychological level, then the theories of class and status motivation would seem to be premised on very debatable assumptions about individual motivation. Most historians would want to know the conditions that existed before a change occurred, why the change happened, and what were the results of that change.

The first problem—the conditions before a change occurred— reduces in psychological terms to the way an individual perceives himself, his self-image. Psychologists have approached this question in many ways, but a theory of change which assumes that social tensions were the basic cause implicitly accepts only one of these approaches. It assumes that an individual defines himself primarily in terms of his particular social role, that his behavior is motivated mainly by his class and status role perceptions. Only about one out of every three psychologists, however, would accept this premise to any real extent. Even some sociologists and anthropologists who have traditionally seen individual behavior as primarily determined by culture, have retreated from that position and now see a more symmetrical interaction in which personality also influences culture. An overwhelming majority of psychologists have rejected role theory as an adequate explanation for the way an individual who enlists in a reform movement forms his self-image.

The second problem—why the change happened—reduces in psychological terms to the mechanism by which an individual feels impelled to join a political movement like progressivism. Here again those scholars who emphasize social tensions have implicitly chosen only one of several alternatives offered by psychologists. They assume that the threat from some other social group frustrated the would-be progressive who, in turn, reacted aggressively against that threat. Very few psychologists, however, would claim that social tensions are the main source of frustration. Furthermore, individuals are generally capable of reacting to new roles without experiencing any major frustrations. The different ways in which Theodore Roosevelt and Calvin Coolidge, for example, remade the role of the presidency to fit their own personalities suggest how flexible roles can be without deeply frustrating an individual. Furthermore, different members of the same social class will perceive social challenges in different ways; many will experience no frustration at all.

Even if historians concede that social stresses can frustrate an individual, does it follow that he will react aggressively toward the source of that frustration? The frustration-produces-aggression model is one of the most debated propositions in psychology. Extreme critics have called it "nonsensical." Others have shown that frustration more often produces anxiety, submission, dependence, or avoidance than aggression. Even presumably simpleminded creatures like rats and pigeons do not necessarily react aggressively when they are frustrated. If some psychologists have shown that aggression is only one possible result of frustration, others have shown that frustration is only one possible source of aggression. Indeed, prior to 1939 most psychologists accepted Sigmund Freud's *Beyond the Pleasure Principle*, which contended that aggression derived from the Death Wish. Others have found the source of aggression in neither frustration nor the Death Wish. The assumption that social tensions will frustrate an individual and drive him to react aggressively has been riddled by the artillery of a great many psychologists. For historians to continue to assume that men react primarily to social threats is to ignore an impressive body of psychological literature.

The third problem—what were the results of that change—reduces in psychological terms to the way an individual outwardly expresses the internal change. If an individual felt angry following threats from another social group, how would he express that anger? The idea that he will sublimate his aggressive propensities into cries for political reform is one which is endorsed by many Freudians who follow *Civilization and Its Discontents.* But even some psychoanalysts claim that Freud never adequately explained sublimation. Other personality theorists have asserted that "everyone recognizes . . . that at present we have no theory which really explains the dynamics" of sublimation. Many psychologists have seen sublimation as only one possible way of expressing aggressive proclivities. Political reform is only one of hundreds of directions an individual can channel hostile impulses. But most personality theorists are so unimpressed by the concept of sublimation that they simply ignore it in their own theories.

By assuming that social tensions produced progressivism, historians have approached the basic questions about social and political movements from a very narrow psychological viewpoint. Even more important, the psychological underpinnings of this assumption are either disproved, disputed, ignored, or "untestable" by modern psychologists.

Moreover, the whole psychological framework which includes these theories has recently come under attack. Both behaviorists and psychoanalysts had previously assumed that individuals were motivated by "a state of tenseness that leads us to seek equilibrium, rest, adjustment, satisfaction, or homeostasis. From this point of view, personality is nothing more than our habitual modes of reducing tension." Men became reformers to relieve tensions, perhaps impelled by class and status anxieties. Now, however, many psychologists contend that personality theorists too long overemphasized the irrational components in motivation. As early as 1953 Gordon Allport reported that the trend in motivational theory was away from the tension reduction approach and toward an emphasis on the rational and healthy side of individuals. By stressing the rationality of free choice, these psychologists have argued that a commitment to reform, for example, may in fact be the ultimate expression of a mature personality and reflect a man who is capable of getting outside of his self-preoccupation. Indeed, Erich Fromm has said that the revolutionary leader might well be the only "sane person in an insane world." The decision to embrace progressivism may simply represent a conscious choice between alternative programs, not an attempt to reduce tensions which grew out of a man's efforts to maintain his social position.

There is another problem in borrowing models: the more inclusive the model, the farther it is removed from the reality it is attempting to explain. The data must be squeezed and distorted to make them conform to the model. Many social scientists themselves have revolted against the topheavy and abstract models which have prevailed in their fields. One student of social stratification, for example, concluded from a review of 333 studies that his field suffered from "the disease of overconceptualization." Similarly, many psychologists have rejected the abstract personality constructs used to explain motivation because they are too far removed from the reality of individual people. Arguing for a focus on the "life style" of each person, Allport has attacked theories which emphasize "the abstract motivation of an impersonal and therefore non-existent mind-in-general," preferring "the concrete, viable motives of each and every mind-in-particular." In a like vein, Kelly has argued that most psychological constructs ignore an individual's "private domain, within which his behavior aligns itself within its own lawful system." These abstract constructs can only account for the individual as "an inert object wafted about in a public domain by external forces, or as a solitary datum sitting on its own continuum." Allport even charged that psychologists who build universal models to explain human motivation are seeking a "scientific will of the wisp"; the " 'irreducible unlearned motives' of men" they are seeking cannot be found because they do not exist.

This is not a critique of any particular psychological theory or approach to behavior. Rather it is a plea to be aware of the dangers in building a conceptual approach to such a problem as progressivism upon so many rickety psychological foundations. Historians should recognize that psychologists are not that different; they are at least as divided in their interpretations as we are. For historians to accept the assumptions that underlie the idea that social tensions produced progressivism would be similar to a psychologist borrowing Frederick Jackson Turner's frontier hypothesis for his research. Many of us would complain that there are other explanations for the development of American history; and a great many psychologists, in effect, are shuddering at the weak psychological underpinnings of the assumption that their social backgrounds made men become reformers.

The real test for the soundness of any approach is not theoretical, of course, but empirical. In this case the inadequacy of the sociological and psychological ideas which inform the assumption that social tensions produced progressivism becomes obvious after an examination of the types of men who became progressives and conservatives. If social tensions were relevant to the rise of progressivism, then clearly the class and status experiences of progressives should have differed in some fundamental way from those of the conservatives.

How different, in fact, were the social origins of progressives and conservatives? Following George E. Mowry's publication in 1951 of *The California Progressives*, several scholars examined the external social class attributes of progressive leaders and concluded that the reformers were drawn from the young urban gentry. But because they neglected to sample a comparable group of conservatives, these studies failed to prove their contention that class and status experiences impelled the progressives. Subsequent profiles of both progressive and conservative leaders in the election of 1912 and the legislative sessions of 1911 in Washington and 1905 in Missouri showed that both groups came from nearly the same social background. Objective measures of their social origins failed to predict the programs and ideologies of political leaders.

Scholars may not accept this finding because they question whether the 1914 campaign reflected political ideologies so much as the personalities of leaders and the desire for office. The studies of legislatures in Washington and Missouri might be questioned because in a single session such extraneous pressures as the personality of a powerful governor or the use of bribes might have interfered with a legislator's expression of his natural preferences. Furthermore, neither Washington nor Missouri was ever noted as a banner progressive state. Perhaps the issues in these states were not as hotly contested—and hence did not reveal as sharp social tensions—as in the more radical states.

The following profile of Wisconsin legislators was designed to avoid some of the possible objections to the other studies. Since contemporaries and historians alike have agreed on the pivotal position of Wisconsin, it is an ideal state to test whether social tensions were important in the development of progressivism. This sample begins with the 1897 session because it was then, for the first time, that the Progressive Republicans identified in their speeches, platforms, and votes the issues which divided them from the stalwarts, and concludes with the 1903 session, when many of their programs were enacted. The index for "progressivism" was based on votes growing out of the campaigns for a more equitable distribution of the tax burden, for regulation of quasi-public corporations, and for purification of the electoral and legislative processes. These were the issues which gave the thrust and tone to Wisconsin progressivism and served as the dividing lines between the old guard and the insurgents.

During these four sessions there were 286 roll calls on these issues. A "progressive" legislator was defined as one who voted for more than 75 percent of the progressive measures; a "moderate" favored between 50 and 75 percent of the progressive measures; and a "conservative" opposed more than half of the progressive measures. Of the 360 Republican legislators included in this profile, 40 percent were progressives, 38 percent were moderates, and 22 percent were conservatives.

TABLE I

	FARMER	MER-CHANT	PROFES-SIONAL	MANU-FAC-TURER	FINAN-CIER	WORKER
	Percent	*Percent*	*Percent*	*Percent*	*Percent*	*Percent*
Progressives	20	27	26	13	9	5
Moderates	22	24	29	6	13	6
Conservatives	12	27	32	16	10	3

If social conflicts were important to the emergence of progressivism, the variable which would be most likely to reveal that fact would be the occupations of legislators. Convincing generalizations from the following chart would need to be based upon large statistical differences, since the relatively small sample is divided so many ways. Occupation clearly made little difference in a legislator's vote on progressive measures.

The extent of a man's education helps to locate his social position. In Wisconsin neither progressives (22 percent), moderates (24 percent), nor conservatives (27 percent) were dominated by college graduates. At a time and place where college degrees were rare, perhaps a better measure of educational aspirations would be the proportion of men who sought any kind of formal schooling—high school, business college, night school—beyond the level of the common school. Here again, however, the differences in achievement between progressives (58 percent), moderates (60 percent), and conservatives (66 percent) are insignificant.

The place of a man's birth also indicates his social background. But the nativity of Wisconsin's legislators failed to differentiate progressives from conservatives (see Table II).

If the Wisconsin sample corresponds roughly to those of other states in the occupations, education, and nativity of political leaders, it differs from them in two other respects. Students of the 1912 election found the progressives to be considerably younger than the conservatives in both age and political experience, a fact which led them to see progressivism as a revolt of the young, would-be politicians. In Wisconsin, however,

TABLE II

	MIDWEST	EAST AND NEW ENGLAND	CANADA	EUROPE
	Percent	*Percent*	*Percent*	*Percent*
Progressives	47	29	6	18
Moderates	61	24	2	13
Conservatives	49	30	5	16

TABLE III

	NONE	ONE	TWO OR MORE
	Percent	*Percent*	*Percent*
Progressives	52	28	20
Moderates	62	27	11
Conservatives	35	37	28

progressives and conservatives both had an average age of forty-eight, and the moderates averaged forty-six. The median ages of progressives (49), moderates (45), and conservatives (47) likewise fail to suggest the existence of any generational conflict between progressives and conservatives.

Nor were Wisconsin's progressives the most politically immature of the rival factions. While service in the legislature is only one measure of political experience, it does reveal the effectiveness of politicians in winning renomination from their local organizations. Although Wisconsin's conservatives had the longest tenure in the legislature, they contrasted not so much with the progressives as with the moderates. Table III indicates the number of previous sessions attended by legislators.

The social origins of Wisconsin legislators between 1897 and 1903 clearly suggest that no particular manner of man became a progressive. Such variables as occupation, education, nativity, age, and previous legislative experience fail to differentiate the average progressive from the average conservative. The theories that progressivism was motivated by status or class tensions felt by the urban gentry, the businessmen, the workers, the farmers, or the incipient politicians are challenged in Wisconsin by the fact that members of these groups were as likely to become conservatives as progressives. And the Wisconsin profile parallels other studies. To the extent that social class allegiance can be measured by such attributes as occupation, nativity, education, and age, social tensions were apparently irrelevant to the formation of progressivism since the "typical" progressive and conservative came from the same social background.

Collective statistical profiles can, however, obscure more than they reveal. The five more prominent early Wisconsin progressive leaders, the men who forged the issues which Robert M. La Follette subsequently adopted, were most noteworthy for their different social origins. The man contemporaries hailed as the "father of Wisconsin progressivism" was Albert R. Hall, a small dairy farmer in the western part of the state. Nephew of national Grange head Oliver Kelley, Hall was basically an agrarian radical who developed the reputation of a fearless enemy of the railroads and other large corporations. No less important was John A. Butler, the lengthened shadow of the powerful Milwaukee

Municipal League. A sharper contrast to Hall could scarcely be found than this independently wealthy and highly educated Brahmin who seemed to spend more time in his villa than he did in his Milwaukee law office. Milwaukee also contributed Julius E. Roehr, organized labor's leading champion in the legislature. Born in New York City—the son of German immigrants—this hardworking lawyer and dissident Republican politician would have been extremely uncomfortable with the smells of either Hall's farm or Butler's villa. James H. Stout, the most respected of the early progressives in the legislature, was born and raised in Iowa and educated at the University of Chicago. A fabulously wealthy lumber baron, Stout used his company town of Menomonie to pioneer in vocational education and in welfare benefits for his workers. The orator of these early legislative progressives was James J. McGillivray, a self-made Canadian-born architect and manufacturer who lived in Black River Falls and authored the state's antitrust acts. It would seem almost pointless to hunt for a common social "type" in these early progressives. A Brahmin man of leisure and self-made manufacturer, an agrarian radical who knew no workers and a lawyer who never lived outside a large city and was the workers' champion, young men and old men, Yankees and immigrants, these were the leaders who made common cause in Wisconsin and developed the progressive program.

The widely scattered backgrounds of the most prominent early leaders and the remarkable collective similarity between the average progressive and conservative confirm the weaknesses in the sociological and psychological framework for the assumption that progressivism was rooted in social tensions. The widespread emphasis on social tensions is unsound sociologically because it draws upon only a narrow spectrum of personality theory, and those models upon which it does draw are either unproved or unprovable. The statistical profiles from Wisconsin and elsewhere reveal empirically that the origins of progressivism cannot be found by studying the social backgrounds and tensions of progressive leaders. Remembering Kelly's injunction to avoid "poking about in the neighbors' back yards for methodological windfalls," historians must develop alternative approaches which encompass not only the realm of sociology and psychology but also that of history.

Such an alternative approach should at least restore chronology, a major casualty in the repeated emphasis on men's class and status feelings, to a more prominent position. At this point it is possible to offer a tentative explanation for the origins of progressivism when that movement is placed in the context of the chronological evolution of both industrialism and reform.

When the Progressive era is put against the backdrop of the growth of industrialism in America, the remarkable fact about that period is its relative freedom from social tensions. If conflicts between city and farm, worker and boss, younger and older generations, native-born and immigrant are more or less natural results of industrialization, then the years between the late 1890s and the early 1910s stand as a period of social peace when contrasted with either the Gilded Age or the 1920s, when those conflicts were raw and ragged. Not competition but cooperation between different social groups—ministers, businessmen, workers, farmers, social workers, doctors, and politicians—was what distinguished progressivism from such earlier reform movements as Mugwumpery, Populism, the labor movement, and civil service reform. To the extent that men and groups were motivated by tensions deriving from their class and status perceptions, they would have been unable to cooperate with men from different backgrounds. In focusing on the broadly based progressive thrust, the real question is not what drove groups apart, but what drove them together? To answer this question, progressivism must be located in the development of reform in the late-nineteenth century.

The roots of progressivism reach far back into the Gilded Age. Dozens of groups and individuals in the 1880s envisioned some change that would improve society. Reformers came forward to demand civil service reform, the eight hour day, scientific agriculture, woman suffrage, enforcement of vice laws, factory inspection, nonpartisan local elections, trust-busting, wild-life conservation, tax reform, abolition of child labor, businesslike local government, regulation of railway rates, less patronizing local charity, and hundreds of other causes which would subsequently be identified with progressivism. Younger social scientists, particularly economists were not only beginning to lambast the formalism and conservatism in their fields and to advocate the ideas which would undergird progressivism but they were also seeking to force governments to accept their ideas. Richard T. Ely's work on the Maryland Tax Commission in the mid-1880's, for example, pioneered in the application of the new economics to government and generated many of the programs which future reformers and politicians would soon adopt.

But this fertility of reform in the Gilded Age did not conceal the basic fact that individuals and groups remained fragmented. There was no common program which could rally all groups, and the general prosperity tended to reassure people that industrialism might cure its own ills. As late as 1892 one editor, reflecting this optimistic frame of mind, could state that "the rich are growing richer, some of them, and the poor are growing richer, all of them." Men and groups seeking major changes, whether elitists or Populists, were generally stereotyped as cranks who were blind to the vast blessings and bright future of industrialism. Circumscribed by such problems and attitudes reformers were understandably fragmented in the Gilded Age.

The catastrophic depression of 1893–1897 radically altered this pattern of reform. It vividly dramatized the failures of industrialism. The widening chasm between the rich and the poor, which a few observers had earlier called a natural result of industrialism, could no longer be ignored. As several tattered bands of men known as Coxey's Army tramped from town to town in 1894, they drew attention to the plight of the millions of unemployed and vividly portrayed the striking contrasts between the way of life of the poor and the "conspicuous consumption" of the rich. Furthermore, as Thorstein Veblen observed, they showed that large numbers of Americans no longer cherished the old gospel of self-help, the very basis for mobility in a democratic society. As desperation mounted, businessmen and politicians tried the traditional ways of reversing the business cycle, but by 1895 they realized that the time-honored formulas of the tariff and the currency simply could not dispel the dark pall that hung over the land. Worse still, President Grover Cleveland seemed utterly incapable of comprehending, let alone relieving, the national crisis.

The collapse of prosperity and the failure of national partisan politicians to alleviate the crisis by the traditional methods generated an atmosphere of restless and profound questioning which few could escape. "On every corner stands a man whose fortune in these dull times has made him an ugly critic of everything and everybody," wrote one editor. A state university president warned his graduates in 1894 that "you will see everywhere in the country symptoms of social and political discontent. You will observe that these disquietudes do not result from the questions that arise in the ordinary course of political discussion . . . but that they spring out of questions that are connected with the very foundations of society and have to do with some of the most elemental principles of human liberty and modern civilization." Was the American dream of economic democracy and mobility impossible in an industrial society? Would the poor overthrow an unresponsive political and economic system? Such questions urgently demanded answers, and it was no longer either wise or safe to summarily dismiss as a crank anyone who had an answer. "The time is at hand," cried one editor, "when some of the great problems which the Nineteenth century civilization has encountered are crying for a solution. . . . Never before in the history of the world were people so willing to accept true teaching on any of these subjects and give to them a just and practical trial." A man's social origins were now less important than his proposals, and many men began to cooperate with people from different backgrounds to devise and implement solutions.

This depression-inspired search for answers sprouted hundreds of discussion groups at which men met, regardless of background, to propose remedies. These groups gave men the habit of ignoring previously firm class lines in the face of the national crisis. When Victor Berger urged the Milwaukee Liberal Club to adopt socialism as the answer, for example, his audience included wealthy bankers, merchants, and lawyers. In the same city, at the Church and Labor Social Union, banker

John Johnson urged a "new society" where "class privileges will be abolished because all will belong to the human family," and the discussion was joined by Populists and Socialists as well as clergymen and conservative editors. In this context, too, all types of people sought the wisdom of the men who had made a career of studying the social and economic breakdown. No one was surprised when unions, Granges, women's clubs, and other groups wanted University of Wisconsin economists like Ely to address them. Maybe they had an answer. The social unrest accompanying the depression weakened class and status allegiances.

The direct political effects of the depression also broke down the previous rigidity and fragmentation of reform. The depression created a clear sense of priorities among the many causes which Gilded Age reformers had advocated. It generated broadly based new issues which all classes could unite behind. One such program was the urgent necessity for tax reform. When the depression struck, individuals and corporations were forced to devise ways of economizing as property values, sales, and revenues declined precipitously. Caught between higher taxes to cover the rising costs of local government and their own diminishing revenues, many wealthy individuals and corporations began to hide their personal assets from the assessors, to lobby tax relief through local governments, and even to refuse to pay any taxes. The progressive program was forged and received widespread popular support as a response to these economies. Citizens who lacked the economic or political resources to dodge their taxes mounted such a crusade against these tax dodgers that former President Benjamin Harrison warned the wealthiest leaders that unless they stopped concealing their true wealth from the tax assessors they could expect a revolution led by enraged taxpayers. The programs for tax reform—including inheritance, income, and ad valorem corporation taxes—varied from place to place, but the important fact was that most citizens had developed specific programs for tax reform and had now agreed that certain individuals and corporations had evaded a primary responsibility of citizenship.

A second major area which proved capable of uniting men of different backgrounds was "corporate arrogance." Facing declining revenues, many corporations adopted economics which ranged from raising fares and rates to lobbying all manner of relief measures through city and state governments. Even more important, perhaps, they could not afford necessary improvements which elementary considerations of safety and health had led local governments to demand that they adopt. Corporate arrogance was no longer a doctrinaire cry of reformers. Now it was an unprotected railway crossing where children were killed as they came home from school or the refusal of an impoverished water company to make improvements needed to provide the healthful water which could stop the epidemics of typhoid fever. Such incidents made the corporation look like a killer. These specific threats united all classes: anyone's child might be careless at a railroad crossing, and typhoid fever was no respecter of social origins.

From such new, direct, and immediate threats progressivism developed its thrust. The more corporations used their political influence to resist making the small improvements, the more communities developed increasingly radical economic programs like municipal ownership or consumer-owned utilities and fought to overthrow the machines that gave immunity to the corporations. Political reforms like the initiative, direct primary, and home rule became increasingly important in the early stages of progressivism because, as William Allen White said, men had first to get the gun before they could hit anything with it. But it was the failure of the political system to respond to the new and immediate threats of the depression that convinced people that more desperate programs were needed.

Perhaps there are, after all, times and places where issues cut across class lines. These are the times and places where men identify less with their occupational roles as producers and more with their roles as consumers—of death-dealing water, unsafe railway crossings, polluted air, high streetcar rates, corrupt politicians—which serve to unite them across social barriers. There are also universal emotions—anger and fear—which possess all men regardless of their backgrounds. The importance of the depression of the 1890s was that it aroused those universal emotions, posed dramatic and desperate enough threats to lead men of all types to agree that tax dodging and corporate arrogance had to be ended and thereby served to unite many previously fragmented reformers and to enlist the support of the majority that had earlier been either silent or enthusiastic only about partisan issues like the tariff on symbols like Abraham Lincoln. The conversion of the National Municipal League showed how issues were becoming more important than backgrounds. Originally composed of elitists who favored such Mugwumpish concerns as civil service reform, the League by 1898 had become so desperate with the domination over political machines by utility companies that it devoted its energies to municipal ownership and to political devices which promised "more trust in the people, more democracy" than its earlier elitism had permitted. The attitude of moral indignation, such an obvious feature of the early stages of progressivism, was not rooted in social tensions but in the universal emotion of anger.

Whether this emphasis on the results of the depression—unrest, new threats and new issues, and cooperation among social groups—has widespread relevance or validity remains to be seen, but it does help to explain the roots of progressivism in Wisconsin. The most important factor in producing the intensity of Wisconsin progressivism was the cooperation between previously discrete and fragmented social groups both in forging popular issues and getting reforms adopted. And the most important factor in defining the popular issues was the arrogance of certain corporations. In Milwaukee the traction and electricity monopoly between 1894 and 1896 alone, for reasons ranging from extreme overcapitalization to confidence in its political powers raised both its lighting and streetcar fares, refused to arbitrate with its striking employees, enjoined the city from enforcing ordinances lowering its fares, and used its political power—the company's chief manager was the state's leading Republican boss—to cut its tax bill in half, kill an ordinance which would have prevented it from polluting the air, and thwart generally popular attempts at regulation. Each time the monopoly refused to obey an order, lobbied special favors from the city or state, or prostituted the Republican party to the company, the progressive coalition grew. By the end of the depression, the coalition drew together both ends of the economic spectrum—the Merchants and Manufacturers Association and the Chamber of Commerce as well as several labor unions and the Federated Trades Council. Politically it included the county Republican Club, the Democratic Jefferson Club, and the Socialists and Populists. The Mugwumpish and upper-class Municipal League was joined by German social clubs like the Turnvereine. So defiant was the company—so desperate were the people—that the traction managers became the state's most hated men by 1899; and humorist-politician George Peck observed that Wisconsin's parents "frighten children when they are bad, by telling them that if they don't look out," the traction magnates "will get them." Four hundred miles away, in Superior, the story was remarkably similar. Angered by the repeated refusals of that city's water company to provide the city with healthful enough water to prevent the typhoid fever epidemics that killed dozens of people each year, and blaming the company's political power within both parties for the failure of regulation, labor unions and Populists cooperated with business and professional men and with dissident politicians to try to secure pure water and to overthrow the politicians owned by the company. In Superior, political debate had indeed narrowed, as an editor observed, to a fight of "the people against corporate insolence." The water company, like the traction monopoly at Milwaukee, stood isolated and alone, the enemy of men from all backgrounds. In Wisconsin, at least, the community's groups continued to perform their special functions; and, by the end of the depression, they were all agreed that corporate arrogance had to be abolished. Their desperation made them willing to speak, lobby, and work together.

If, as the Wisconsin experience suggests, cooperation was the underpinning of progressivism, historians should focus on reformers not as victims of social tensions, but as reformers. At any given time and place, hundreds of men and groups are seeking supporters for their plans to change society and government. The basic problem for the reformer is to win mass support for his program. In Wisconsin a reformer's effectiveness depended on how well he manipulated acts of corporate and individual arrogance that infuriated everyone in order to demonstrate the plausibility of his program. Desperate events had made tax dodging, corporate defiance and control of politics the main political issues and had allowed this program to swallow the older reformers at the same time that they created a much broader constituency for reform. The question then becomes: Why did some succeed while others failed? North Dakota never developed a full-blown progressive movement because that state's progressives never demonstrated the plausibility of their programs. Wisconsin's early progressives did succeed in drawing together such diverse groups as unions, businessmen, Populists, and dissident politicians because they adapted their program and rhetoric to the menacing events which angered everyone. Reformers operate in their hometowns and not in some contrived social background which could as easily apply to New York or Keokuk, and it is in their hometowns that they should be studied. Historians should determine why they succeeded or failed to rally the support of their communities to their programs, for the most significant criterion for any reformer is, in the end, his effectiveness.

When the progressive characteristically spoke of reform as a fight of "the people" or the "public interest" against the "selfish interests," he was speaking quite literally of his political coalition because the important fact about progressivism, at least in Wisconsin, was the degree of cooperation between previously discrete social groups now united under the banner of the "public interest." When the progressive politician denounced the arrogance of quasi-public corporations and tax-dodgers, he knew that experiences and events had made his attacks popular with voters from all backgrounds. Both conceptually and empirically it would seem safer and more productive to view reformers first as reformers and only secondarily as men who were trying to relieve class and status anxieties. The basic riddle in progressivism is not what drove groups apart, but what made them seek common cause.

Sheldon Hackney

SHELDON HACKNEY (1933–   ), formerly Professor of History at Princeton University, is now president of Tulane University. His book, *Populism to Progressivism in Alabama* (1969), received the Albert J. Beveridge prize of the American Historical Association.

Emancipation Day was celebrated on January 1, 1901 in Negro communities throughout Alabama just as it had been for many years. Numerous Negro speakers enumerated and detailed the progress of Negroes since the Civil War: progress made in literacy, land ownership, business, the professions, and the aggregate of personal achievements that reflected material progress. Measured against the lowly status of Negroes 35 years before, these advances seemed spectacular. But measured against the promise of American life, they were not great enough to dissuade whites from their belief in the doctrine of Negro inferiority. Some people felt Negroes had failed their test as Americans and deserved to be proscribed. Others, such as those for whom Tom Heflin spoke, feared that Negroes were succeeding too well. For whatever reason, most white men in Alabama agreed on the necessity of disfranchisement. It was the biggest and most important downward readjustment in the long and bitter process of redefining the Negro's place in Southern life.

The trend in race relations had been evident in the South ever since Florida enacted the first Jim Crow law in 1887. The tendency was to replace informal, fluctuating, and nonuniform patterns with legal, static, and uniform methods of treating Negroes. For example, Negroes could vote and participate in politics in various ways in some places during the 1890s. In other places countless stratagems of dubious morality were employed to neutralize or utilize their votes. The Constitutional Convention, said James Weatherly, was called to replace "this revolutionary method by legal machinery...."

The revolutionary methods had grown out of the vague feeling among many whites that there was something impermanent and not right about existing relations between the races. As a friend wrote to John W. DuBóse, probably in 1902, "The Civil War ... did not settle the problem. It is still unsettled and must remain so until settled right." But with no model of "right," there was no agreement on the spheres of life from which even the deferential Negro should be excluded.

Consequently the pattern of race relations was highly fluid in Alabama in the period 1890 to 1910. Inconsistency was the primary characteristic. The law in its various guises brought increasing order to the situation, and in doing so abolished both the freedom and the insecurity that went with inconsistency. The workings of the law could be seen in various fields. The city council of Montgomery passed an ordinance segregating the seating on streetcars in 1900. A Negro boycott that year failed to reverse the decision. Jim Crow did not come to the railroad stations until January 6, 1902, when the Alabama Railroad Commission issued an order to the railroads operating in the state to maintain comfortable waiting rooms for their passengers. The order also required railroads to furnish separate waiting rooms for the two races. The last company of Negro state militia, the Capitol City Guards, was not disbanded until 1905. Meanwhile Eirmingham's mayor announced that the new Birmingham jail, famed in folk song and pamphlets of protest, would be segregated at last.

While recognizing the law's creative role in the structure of segregation, the growing separation of the races did exist independent of the law. This separation was even extended to the domain of death. A Negro newspaper noticed in 1900 that the Mississippi legislature had ordered the removal of remains of the Honorable James Lynch from the white cemetery where they had rested since his death. Two years later a Birmingham paper reported that "Will Mathis has requested Judge Lowry to have his hanging at a different hour from the time that the negro, Orlando Lester, will be hanged, and also that he be hanged from a different set of gallows."

Labor was a particularly sensitive area of race relations. The vice president of the Alabama Federation of Labor in 1902 was J. H. Beanes, a Negro, who was host for the organization's annual convention in Selma in that year. Community pressure was strong for the meeting to be segregated, but there was resistance. A delegate from Typographical Union Local 104 in Birmingham stated that "rather than see one accredited delegate, black or white, thrown out of this convention I would go to the woods and hold this meeting." Union locals were thoroughly segregated, but conventions and governing bodies admitted Negroes in order to protect unionism from an increasingly hostile Negro labor force.

Perhaps nothing better captures the flux of patterns of segregation in the South at the turn of the century than the case of a Southerner with an impeccable pedigree, Mary Custis Lee, the daughter of Robert E. Lee. In 1902 she was arrested on the Washington, Alexandria & Mt. Vernon Railroad for refusing to move from the Negro section of the car where she had taken her seat. She was not a freedom rider; she simply was not aware that there was a law segregating the races on that railroad, and evidently she was not used to such a practice being dictated by custom.

Pathological evidence of the disturbed state of race relations was available in the statistics on lynching. The 10-year period 1889 to 1899 witnessed the most dramatic rise and decline of lynch law. The peak years were 1891 and 1892; in each year 24 people were dispatched by mobs in Alabama. The low point of a mere four lynchings was reached in 1900. But in 1901, a year of prosperity and rising cotton prices, contrary to the notion that the frequency of lynchings fluctuated in response to deviations from the long-term trend in cotton prices, there were 16 mob murders. It was no accident that disfranchisement was the single most important public issue that year. This raises the question of the cause of the ebb and flow in this form of physical aggression. It is certainly true that "respectable" groups in society carried on campaigns to discourage people from resorting to rope and faggot. Thomas G. Jones went so far as to argue that the Thirteenth and Fourteenth Amendments gave federal courts jurisdiction in lynching cases against mob members who deprived Negro victims of equal protection and due process of law. Governor William Dorsey Jelks (1901–1906) was sincerely devoted to the prevention of lynching, for which he suffered some criticism. He was deeply disturbed by the fact that "human life is about as cheap in Alabama as it is anywhere...." Yet he was unable to get lynchers convicted even when the evidence appeared overwhelming. In view of the continued immunity of lynchers it would seem that some factor other than social disapproval was responsible for the decline of lynching.

It is likely that the high rate of extralegal sanctions against Negroes in the 1890's was related to the fluidity and uncertainty in patterns of race relations. The potential for conflict was greater as long as patterns of permissible conduct were poorly defined and changing. At the end of the decade and after, as legal devices were used increasingly to define and make uniform the prescribed boundaries of the permissible in race relations, anxious whites felt less need to assert their superiority. The Negro leader and president of Alabama A. and M. College at Normal, W. H. Councill, sensed this when he told an Emancipation Day audience in 1901 "that the salvation of the negro in this country depends upon drawing the social lines tighter, tighter all the while, North and South. The moment they become slack the white man becomes brutal— the negro goes down forever."

Councill's statement also reflected the deepening disillusionment of Negroes in the face of their increasing proscription. This despair was expressed in the half-dozen extant Negro newspapers in Alabama. As the 1890s wore on, Negroes postponed their quest for full citizenship through political self-assertion and turned to the more traditional paths favored by Booker T. Washington and W. H. Councill. Accommodation, material self-improvement, and dependence on upper class whites seemed to be the only choice short of emigration for Negroes. H. C. Binford, schoolteacher, city alderman, and newspaper editor, in 1899 told his readers: "there is nothing in politics for us, it makes no difference which side wins none of them want the Negro." A year later he glumly admitted that "we have gotten use to being slighted and have ceased to kick. What's the use?" Negro newspapers of all shades of opinion put increased emphasis on the need to acquire education and property.

Prospects were so gloomy that Washington thought that "before we [Negroes] can make such progress we must decide whether or not the Negro is to be a permanent part of the South." Not only was there a Negro emigration movement of unknown strength, and white propagandists of colonization like John Temple Graves, Thomas Pearce Bailey, and John Tyler Morgan, but newspapers were full of plans to replace the Negro labor force and population of the South with white immigrants. The atmosphere was so tense that W. H. Councill surrendered to pessimism. In a controversial article in *The Forum* in 1899 he arrived at the conclusion that everything the Negro had was at the sufferance of the whites and that there was no future for the Negro in America.

Councill's despair led to two patterns of thought. On the one hand there was the policy of accommodation—and Councill was an expert accommodator. In 1901, as always, he needed funds from the state government, and applied to Governor Samford hat-in-hand. His letter argued that the state was getting a good deal because "all of this vast property is deeded to the State of Alabama. The State has donated money only for a normal school which is putting into rural districts as well as the towns teachers who are not only competent to teach, but who are in harmony with the institutions and customs of the South." To complete this example of the policy of accommodation, Councill's request was endorsed by General William C. Oates who played the role of upper-class paternalist. Oates wrote that he thought "Councill a good man and fine manager of this school and politically all right."

The other fork of Councill's two-pronged pessimism was the assertion of a perennial American Negro myth, "repatriation." The redemption of Africa from barbarism by American Negroes was a satisfying dream for Negroes who were alienated from American life and suffering from a poor self-image.

The progressive alienation of Negroes sprang from several sources. One prime cause was the dwindling sphere of economic opportunity. Negro newspapers in Alabama were aware, as was Councill, of the Negro's weakening position in the job market. But while the Negro is anxious to work," commented the *Southern Watchman*, "there are those who are using every effort to deprive him of the wherewithal to earn his daily bread."

But it was the total impact of adverse change that Negroes experienced. One Negro newspaper reacted with bitterness, indignation, despair, bewilderment, and resignation:

> The 'Jim Crow' car law, which forces the respectable and the disrespectable Negro to travel in the same car is infamous enough, an insult is being added to injury continually. Have those in power forgotten that there is a God, and do they not know that every seed of unjust discrimination sown will in some due time come up. . . . The Negro is as docile as he can be . . . and day after day he is reminded through the daily papers . . . that some additional project is on foot, or is about to be promulgated to stand as a menace to his development, or a curb to his ambitious manhood . . . and we wonder what the harvest will be.

Leaders of the white community were as aware as Negroes were of the deterioration in race relations, for the future of the Negro was a popular topic of public discussion. One evidence of this concern and interest was The Southern Society for the Promotion of the Study of Race Conditions and Problems in the South. Edgar Gardner Murphy conceived the idea and quickly enlisted Hilary Herbert and a blue-ribboned membership. The result was a widely publicized meeting in May 1900 in Montgomery. The conference aired a broad range of opinion, from John Temple Graves' call for colonization of Negroes in Africa to William A. MacCorkle's insistence that Negroes be treated as citizens. A Negro observer reported that there was no support for Graves' proposal nor for the argument of a North Carolina man that Southern states ought not to educate Negroes. Other speakers evidently met significant opposition when they expressed their belief in the inherent inferiority of Negroes, when they maintained that Negro criminality was getting worse, and when they thought that Negro religious life should be guided and controlled by whites. Everyone was opposed to lynch law. According to Murphy, even Northerners agreed that enfranchising Negroes was a mistake.

This is an important indication of the state of informed opinion at the time of the Alabama Constitutional Convention. Booker T. Washington himself was yielding before it. In November 1899 he had tried unsuccessfully to rally Negro opposition to a disfranchising measure pending before the Georgia Assembly. At the same time, however, he was talking of backing an educational qualification for suffrage as a means of insuring that Negroes would be judged on the same basis as whites. G. W. Atkinson of West Virginia questioned the wisdom of such a deal with white leaders. Atkinson advised Washington that he thought the Democratic leaders of the South were using Washington and that any voting law would be administered so as to discriminate against Negroes.

As later events proved, it was naïve of Washington to think registrars would apply suffrage tests fairly to both races. Atkinson grasped the essential evil of the Southern system when he understood this. But Washington understood that he had very little choice; he was simply trying to use his contacts among white leaders to make the best deal possible under the circumstances.

The problem was, those bent on disfranchisement were no longer restrained by the federal government or by opposition from within the state. The small force of 14 Populists and Republicans in the 155-member convention could do little, though they stood fast against limiting suffrage. The sizable opposition to disfranchisement registered in the referendum, more interested in white votes than black, was not nearly sufficient to block the powerful coalition whose divergent interests happened to focus on disfranchisement. There was so little resistance of any kind that there was little need to camouflage the purpose and intent of the convention.

"And what is it that we want to do?" asked John B. Knox in his presidential address to the Constitutional Convention of Alabama as it opened its deliberations on May 22, 1901. "Why it is within the limits imposed by the Federal Constitution, to establish white supremacy in this State." The subordinate position of the Negro race was about to be written into the fundamental law. "Our purpose is plain," delegate Thomas Watts asserted some days later. "It is not denied by any man upon the floor of this Convention or in this State."

There was such a consensus on disfranchising Negroes that the main question facing the convention was not whether to do it but how to do it without violating the federal constitution on the one hand and the pledge not to disfranchise any white men on the other hand. . . .

Article VIII, as finally passed, contained two distinct "plans." The permanent plan contained the disfranchising provisions, the qualifications that were to be a permanent part of the organic law. The temporary plan consisted of the devices designed to permit those of the favored race (or party) who would not be able to qualify under the permanent rules to register under special provisions. The temporary plan expired on January 1, 1903.

The permanent plan set up a most elaborate maze through which one had to grope to claim the privilege of becoming an elector. The basic conditions for registration were that a person must be a male citizen, or alien who had declared his intention of becoming a citizen, 21 years of age who had resided in the state for two years, the county for one year, and the precinct for three months. The second requirement was the ability to read and write any article of the United States Constitution, unless physical disability caused the deficiency. Except for the physically disabled, the prospective elector also must have been engaged in some lawful employment for the greater part of the preceding 12 months. If this requirement could not be met there was the alternative property qualification of 40 acres of land on which the prospective elector lived, or the ownership of real or personal property assessed for taxes at a value of $300 and on which the taxes had been paid. There was, in addition, a long list of disqualifying crimes, including vagrancy. Having become an elector, the last cul-de-sac in the labyrinth was the cumulative poll tax of $1.50 per year that had to be paid on or before the first day of February preceding the election in which the elector offered to vote.

Those who could meet all but the literacy and property qualifications were provided with loopholes that were to be open for only a few months. For this purpose Louisiana's famous "Grandfather Clause" was adapted by Alabama, indeed the only novelty of the suffrage article, so that it became the "Fighting Grandfather Clause." This device allowed those to register who had served honorably in the land or naval forces of the United States or Confederate States in any war from 1812 on, or who were descendants of such veterans. If this were not enough, there was the further provision to register "all persons who are of good character and who understand the duties and obligations of citizenship under a republican form of government." . . .

The continuing argument about the nature of political conflict in the United States might be put into better perspective by the realization that between 1890 and 1910 Alabama experienced the two major varieties in turn. Populism was an attempt to create a mass political party. It was led by men with little claim to elite status and was supported by a following normally unorganized and in some cases socially disorganized. Faced with such a disruption in the natural order of society, those who identified their own welfare with the continuation of the existing status structure refused to join. The various elites within the state, the advocates of change as well as the defenders of the status quo, cooperated sufficiently to defeat Populism. But they did not cease their own pluralistic squabbles, and, with the demise of Populism and the disfranchisement of the Negro, the community was free to reorient its politics around the seething contentions of elite-led interest groups. The Progressive movement, then, was a loose federation of the leadership and membership of different associations and informal groups interested in short-term reform. Contrary to Robert Wiebe's stimulating thesis in his book, *The Search for Order, 1877–1920*, Populism was a protest of the alienated against the established community, and the Progressives were the true spokesmen for the local community against the forces linking Alabama to the outside world: the low-down thieving Yankees and their tyrannical railroads.

The alienated on whom Populism drew for support came mainly from the section of the social spectrum that included tenant and yeoman farmers of both races, urban labor, and thwarted merchants and professional men from small towns. The Progressives got less enthusiastic and less constant help from organized labor in the cities than did the Populists, but they received much more substantial support from merchants and professional men of more secure status. The Bosses naturally drew support from the industrial managers and those, of whatever class, who linked their identities to the fate of the economic elites. But the greatest reservoir of power was the Black Belt.

The support of the Black Belt was the key to victory in Alabama. Without it, the Populists could come close but could never win. With it, the Bosses controlled the state except for the four-year-period after 1896 when the emergent Progressive movement, benefiting from Joseph Johnston's personal connections in the Black Belt, gained enough Black Belt backing in the Democratic primaries to secure possession of the party. This was but an interim; the Big Mule-Black Belt alliance was back in power in 1900 when Johnston's attempt to maintain power by attracting political immigrants from the moribund Populist party failed repeatedly. As the Populist party declined, its leaders dispersed along many political and ideological paths ranging from socialism to fascism. Similarly the membership scattered. The politically homeless Populist masses did not inflate Democratic ranks; most withdrew from politics or voted Republican. In order for the Progressive faction of the Democratic party to achieve real ascendancy it had to find support among the politically active Democrats, and this meant Black Belt Planters.

An analysis of the voting in the Constitutional Convention of 1901 shows there was a potential pool of support in the Black Belt for some Progressive measures, particularly railroad regulation. The Progressive urge there was inhibited by anti-Negro fixations among the Planters and by the fact that Negro suffrage was used by the machine to maintain itself in power. Disfranchisement, therefore, was a prerequisite of Progressivism in Alabama. The melange of motives that made disfranchisement a reality in Alabama, against the wishes of Populists and poor whites, included both the desire to make reform possible and the wish to make it impossible. Progressives, and Populists too for that matter, were no less racist or prejudiced than their fellow Alabamians, but among the proponents of Negro disfranchisement the majority and the moving spirit were composed of the opponents of reform. The disfranchisers thought they could cleanse their consciences, retain their power, and prevent a further recurrence of Populism all at the same time. They were wrong. Once the political aspect of the Negro problem had been solved by abolishing the Negro's political rights, and the rights of plenty of poor whites in the bargain, the way was open for the Progressives to assemble from the purged electorate a winning coalition, a coalition that owed little to Populist antecedents.

The Populists were neither backward-looking nor revolutionary; they were merely provincial. Though they were anxious to modernize their own farms to increase their leverage in the marketplace, they were not interested in the modernization of their region. Though they saw clearly what was happening to the yeoman farmer in America, they did not know what to do about it. They distrusted middle class reformers, so they could not cooperate with the budding Progressive movement. They had not rejected the outmoded tenets of Jeffersonianism, so they repeatedly voted against measures to equalize taxes, curb corporations, and provide the services needed by an industrial society. In fact, the Populists resembled primitive rebels. Unlike the issue-oriented Progressives, the Populist program was symbolic of a more basic urge for power that in turn grew from feelings of distrust, betrayal, frustration, and impotence. Unable to create a new, more appropriate system of values for their situation, and hampered by the lack of leaders drawn from traditional sources, the Populists were also unable to stimulate the sort of commitment in the electorate that could withstand adversity. They failed because they were neither revolutionaries nor reformers.

Revolutions are made possible by the perceptions of gaps between expectations and reality, gaps caused by the structure of society. The Populist experience suggests that when the gap between aspiration and achievement is caused by the deterioration of real conditions, the insurgents may reject traditional rulers but will find it difficult to substitute new values for the old, to focus discontent on common goals, or to sustain motivation among the following. However, reformers such as the Progressives are motivated by the dissonance between conflicting cultural commandments. For them the problem was to institutionalize the older ethical mandates while at the same time providing for stability and progress. The contradictory values of Christian brotherhood and American competitive success were thus rationalized, and the result was a powerful force that was restricted in its operation by the Progressives' sense of class loyalty and notions of a conflict-free society. In contrast to Populism, Progressivism's narrow commitment excluded any but the most traditional humanitarian concern for the working classes.

On one thing the two movements could agree: equality of opportunity was a good thing. The problem was, their views of the nature of reality differed sharply. In action, if not in words, the Populists clung to their traditional idea that the way to insure equality of opportunity was to keep taxes low and government small. For most of them the barrier to opportunity came from too much of the wrong kind of government interference and the barrier could be removed simply by returning government to the hands of the people and by abolishing privilege. The Populists had a static conception of social reality, an outlook they shared with their enemy, the Bosses.

The Progressives viewed reality in dynamic terms. For them, abolishing privilege was not enough. Greater equality of opportunity could only come through greater economic growth to multiply the chances of success, and such a goal could only be realized through increased governmental services to stimulate growth and enable individuals to take advantage of the greater opportunity. With such a commitment it was obvious that, even though they honored the myths of the Southern past, the Progressives were earnestly interested in changing Southern society.

There is a great deal more than irony in the fact that the myth of the Old South was created and sponsored by the groups in the post-Reconstruction South that were doing the most to alter the nature of Southern life. The new facts of defeat and poverty successfully challenged the assumptions that had supported the plantation-centered culture of the antebellum South, and the new men who "redeemed" the ex-Confederate states from the regimes of Reconstruction neither sprang from the old ruling class nor adhered to its ideology. Instead they championed industrialization or at least allied themselves with the capitalists of the North who wished to exploit the South's great natural and human resources. At the same time, however, the Redeemers and their heirs, the Bosses, masked their break with the past by defending the existing institutional structure of society and celebrating the virtues of the Old South and the Lost Cause. Though it is not unusual for revolutionaries to stress their agreement with traditional values, the truth is that the Redeemers were not the modernizing elite that students of modernization see as a prerequisite of substantial change in the social structure. They did not propose the creation of new institutions and they advocated no change of function for any existing institution. Retrenchment in governmental services and opposition to an expansion of the regulatory functions of government lay at the heart of their program. In fact, the Redeemers were so intent on exploitation that they were more analogous to colonialists than to a nationalistic leadership eager to adjust society to the needs of development. The Progressives, however, did resemble an innovating elite dedicated to rational growth.

Southern Progressivism, of course, was not all of a piece, but Alabama's divergence from the norm, if there was one, exceeded even the most generous limits previously recognized. In its program and accomplishments, Alabama Progressivism resembled more the Eastern, urban, Roosevelt brand than the Western, rural, Bryan variety. Perhaps the reason for this is that the movement early came under the influence of B. B. Comer, an urban businessman who differed markedly from the stereotype of the Western or the Southern Progressive leader who had to rely on emotionalism to motivate the electorate, as Robert Wiebe has pointed out in *The Search for Order*. Alabama's early Progressivism is also at variance with Wiebe's observation that Southern and Western Progressivism lagged behind the national movement.

If the profile of national Progressivism created by George Mowry in his book, *The Era of Theodore Roosevelt*, is accurate, then Alabama was not completely harmonious with national trends, and one suspects that the phenomenon in Alabama was more truly national than the ideal type

sketched by Mowry. In some characteristics there was agreement between Alabama and the Mowry model. According to both conceptions,
the reformers were young, well educated, with a fundamental faith in
the soundness of the American system, and with a distrust of organized
labor. It is not surprising that Alabama Progressives held a restricted
definition of "the people," a belief in a leadership elite, an insistent
belief in the compatibility and mutual dependence of all classes within
society, and a faith in individualism. As Robert Wiebe points out in his
book, *Businessmen and Reform,* these were tenets shared by comfortable
Americans everywhere.

Strikingly like the reform-minded businessmen in Wiebe's study and
in contrast to Mowry's Progressives, Alabama's Progressives were not
optimistic about human nature. They were confident of the future and
believed in manmade progress, but they also thought a crucial function
of law was to restrain the human propensity for evil. Far from wishing to
extend democracy, Progressives in Alabama wanted to purify it and
actually assisted in restricting it. Though Alabama Progressives in cases
may have boasted of family backgrounds superior to those of their
enemies, the biographical data of the Constitutional Convention show
that it was not status anxiety, or a rejection of materialism, but rather
their new role as upwardly-mobile businessmen that led Comer and his
cohorts to Progressivism. Comer's campaign rhetoric was overwhelmingly economic and political rather than moral. It is true that the character of the movement was deeply influenced by reformers whose projects
did not stem directly from economic self-interest, but those men and
women might more logically be seen as responding to the urgent commands of traditional anti-machine politics and humanitarianism than to
a status squeeze. Nostalgia for old rural virtues and distrust of the city
were absent from Alabama Progressivism. Unlike the version of Progressivism portrayed by Mowry, the Alabama variety was realistically
concerned with the problems of an urbanizing and industrializing society.

Alabama Progressivism was not dominated by producer values such
as Mowry attributes to the national Progressives. Along with the
Populists, Alabama Progressives shared in a value system derived from
the Puritan ethic and the American success myth, but while the
Populists emphasized the work ethic in hopes that laborers and farmers
who did their own manual work could get a larger share of America's
unequally distributed wealth, the Progressives stressed the code of ethical business practices that was a part of the success myth. They wanted
the state to enforce these ethical commandments primarily by promoting
growth with stability. The chaos and corrupting competition could then
be abolished through state regulation and state-sanctioned self-
regulation by business. In this way men of character would properly get
a larger share of the community's wealth while other classes would

benefit from the resulting economic growth as the enlarged fund of wealth radiated through society from the middle class.

The final way in which Alabama Progressives differed from the Mowry portrait of Progressivism is that the Alabama Progressives were not opposed to reform in the 1890s and their views underwent little change after the turn of the century. It was merely opportunity that was altered. That Populism was too radical for them does not negate the fact that while the Populists were calling for the people to take control of government, Progressive leaders were advocating free silver and moderate reform. As the old silver faction slowly came to power in Alabama after 1902, Populism withered. But it did not disappear, because the evils that called it forth did not disappear. Just as the Progressives unsuccessfully offered a moderate alternative in the 1890s, such organizations as the Farmers Union and political leaders of various accents from time to time in this century have offered the dispossessed and powerless a semblance of the radical alternative Populism might have been. That Progressivism was the path chosen is a significant fact in the recent history of the United States.

7

The 1920's

Decade of Decline or Destiny?

The decade of the 1920's occupies an ambiguous position in American history. Sandwiched between two exciting eras—the Progressive era and World War I on the one side and the New Deal on the other—the 1920's appear almost out of place. Certainly the presidents—Harding, Coolidge, Hoover—were not of the stature of men like the two Roosevelts and Woodrow Wilson. Few legislative landmarks or creative social experiments emerged from the decade of the postwar era. Indeed, one important attempt at reform—prohibition—came close to being a fiasco. For these reasons, popular writers, movies, and television in recent years have depicted the decade in terms of a decline in morality, an orgy of financial speculation, a reaction against authority, an increase in organized crime, and a withdrawal from world affairs; in short, a time when established institutions and standards were in the process of disintegration. The popular designation of these years—the Roaring Twenties—sums up the traditional view.

Upon closer examination, however, the 1920's become far more complex than the picture presented in the popular stereotype. While Americans in later years looked back at the postwar era with distaste—even hostility—partly because it ended in the worst depression in American history—contemporaries viewed the period in a quite different light. One group in American society, the businessmen, felt that they were living in a new era. To them the twenties were marked not by conservatism but by change and innovation. The application of scientific procedures and new measures of efficiency in industry, businessmen believed, would bring about a level of prosperity that would eliminate poverty from the country completely. Under an enlightened and informed business leadership and a government sympathetic to business ideals, they predicted a new golden age for America.[1]

The optimistic outlook on the part of businessmen was expressed in a variety of ways. Spokesmen of industry never tired of proclaiming that the nation's greatness resulted from the labors of individual entre-

---

[1]See James W. Prothro, *The Dollar Decade: Business Ideas in the 1920's* (Baton Rouge, 1954).

preneurs who had raised America to a level of prosperity hitherto un-matched in history. Perhaps the most spectacular glorification of business values and ideals was exemplified in a biography of Jesus by Bruce Barton in 1925. Barton's book was ostensibly an effort to write about the career of Jesus in a popular vein. But Barton's conclusion was cast in business terms that were simple to understand: Jesus was the greatest organizer and promoter in history because he had succeeded in "selling" Christianity to millions of persons over the centuries. As Barton put it in his preface of the book:

> A physical weakling! Where did they get that idea? Jesus pushed a plane and swung an adze; he was a successful carpenter. He slept outdoors and spent his days walking around his favorite lake. His muscles were so strong that when he drove the moneychangers out, nobody dared to oppose him!
>
> A kill-joy! He was the most popular dinner guest in Jerusalem! The criticism which proper people made was that he spent too much time with publicans and sinners (very good fellows, on the whole, the man thought) and enjoyed society too much. They called him a "wine bibber and a gluttonous man."
>
> A failure! He picked up twelve men from the bottom ranks of business and forged them into an organization that conquered the world. . . . [For the story of Jesus is] the story of the founder of modern business.[2]

Confidence in the 1920's was by no means confined to businessmen. Even American historians, who were traditionally hostile to business because of their liberal sympathies, saw much to praise. Charles and Mary Beard, for example, were not particularly impressed with either the Harding or Coolidge administrations when they published *The Rise of American Civilization* in 1927. Yet they did not view the twenties as a decade of reaction. Although the Beards admitted that Harding and Coolidge were dealing with complex problems in much the same manner as William McKinley and Marcus A. Hanna of bygone days, they noted that a large group of rebels in Congress fought the Republican presidents and occasionally won an issue. But the outstanding development of the 1920's to the Beards was not the political battles; it was rather the rapid growth of industry and mechanization in this era which left its imprint on virtually every phase of American life. "The most common note of assurance," they concluded in their work, "was belief in unlimited progress. . . . Concretely it meant an invulnerable faith in democracy, in the ability of the undistinguished masses, as contrasted with heroes and classes, to meet by reasonably competent methods the issues raised in the flow of time—a faith in the efficacy of that new and mysterious instrument of the modern mind, 'the invention of inven-

---

[2]Bruce Barton, *The Man Nobody Knows: A Discovery of the Real Jesus* (Indianapolis, 1925), Preface.

tion,' moving from one technological triumph to another, overcoming the exhaustion of crude natural resources and energies, effecting an even wider distribution of the blessings of civilization—health, security, material goods, knowledge, leisure, and aesthetic appreciation, and through the cumulative forces of intellectual and aesthetic reactions, conjuring from the vasty deeps of the nameless and unknown creative imagination of the noblest order, subduing physical things to the empire of the spirit—doubting not the capacity of the Power that had summoned into being all patterns of the past and present, living and dead, to fulfill its endless destiny."[3]

The sociologists, like the historians, also found much to be optimistic about during the decade. Although they were critical of many aspects of American life, most sociologists were confident that existing defects could be remedied. In the past, they argued, few statesmen or political leaders had possessed an adequate understanding of how American society functioned and judgments were often made on the basis of inadequate or misleading information. Only rarely had scientific methods been applied to social problems. What was required now, claimed the sociologists, was the gathering of quantitative and objective data that would enable leaders to define factors that governed society. Armed with the knowledge provided by sociologists, future statesmen would be able to make decisions in a truly enlightened manner.

As a general rule, sociologists during the 1920's were fond of emphasizing what they called a "cultural lag," that is, the condition wherein the institutions of a given society lagged behind the advances in technological and scientific knowledge. Such a lag was responsible for the internal tensions and difficulties in America, they maintained. The solution was obvious: existing institutions had to be brought up to date to conform to the findings of science. Once these institutions were modernized, the American millennium would begin. If American society would only accept the findings and recommendations of the social scientists, the sociologists claimed, a new utopia lay just ahead.

Sociologists, therefore, asserted with confidence that the 1920's represented the beginnings of a new era in American history. Even Thorstein Veblen, one of the most devastating commentators on the irrationality of the capitalistic profit system, seemed to think that most of society's pressing problems could be solved. All that was required, he concluded in *The Engineers and the Price System*, was a transference of power and authority from the businessman—who viewed industry in terms of profits rather than efficiency and social utility—to the engineer—an individual to whom productivity and efficiency were ends in themselves.

---

[3]Charles A. and Mary R. Beard, *The Rise of American Civilization* (2 vols.: New York, 1927), II, p. 800.

Although Veblen had little confidence that America's leaders would seize upon opportunities presented to them, he did imply that possible solutions to America's major problems lay close at hand.[4]

One serious note of dissent in this chorus of optimism and self-congratulation was struck by the literary intellectuals of the 1920's. Many of them saw a decade of decline and degradation in America rather than one of destiny. They pictured Americans as being caught up in an irresistible surge of materialism—a people who had failed to grasp the meaning and significance of life. American society as a result lacked depth and was noted for the superficiality of its cultural, artistic, and intellectual achievements.

Among the earliest indictments by intellectuals was the symposium edited by Harold E. Stearns. Published in 1922 under the title *Civilization in the United States,* the book was a biting commentary on the superficial quality of American life. Stearns pointed out in his preface that each of the thirty contributors was a native American who had written his piece independently of the others, but that all had reached virtually the same conclusions. First, that hypocrisy was a major characteristic of American life; to most Americans the cardinal sin was not the immoral or dishonest act itself, but rather being found out or caught. Second, that America lacked a genuine sense of nationalistic self-consciousness—a fact that prevented the country from living up to its promise. Third—and most important—that America's social life was one of "emotional and aesthetic starvation," one in which "the mania for petty regulation, the driving, regimentating, and drilling, the secret society and its grotesque regalia, the firm grasp on the unessentials of material organization of our pleasures and gaieties are all eloquent stigmata." Could America be changed, asked Stearns? The answer was "yes." "There must be an entirely new deal of the cards in one sense; we must change our hearts. For only so, unless through the humbling of calamity or scourge, can true art and true religion and true personality . . . grow up in America to exorcise these painted devils we have created to frighten us away from the acknowledgement of our spiritual poverty."[5]

Most of Stearns' contributors agreed with his general indictment. To Lewis Mumford the American city was both an index of the nation's material success and a symbol of its spiritual failure. To H. L. Mencken the American politician was a cowardly and frightened individual whose primary concern was holding fast to his office. To Harold E. Stearns America's intellectuals were confined in a spiritual prison by a regimented and standardized society. To John May the press was controlled by advertising and the public was gullible and uncritical in accepting at

---

[4]Thorstein Veblen, *The Engineers and the Price System* (New York, 1921).

[5]Harold E. Stearns, *Civilization in the United States: An Inquiry by Thirty Americans* (New York, 1922), pp. vi–vii.

face value whatever appeared in their newspapers. The other chapters in *Civilization in the United States* included discussions of art, law, education, radicalism, business, advertising, and other aspects of American life, and all were equally critical in their approach. Most of the writers left the impression that America was a cultural wasteland and an intellectual desert with few redeeming features. So widespread was deception and hypocrisy, they concluded, that democracy itself seemed threatened.

Although many of the literary intellectuals were critical of American society in the twenties, few could agree upon a specific remedy, let alone a general diagnosis of its malaise. Some writers migrated to Paris in order to find an environment conducive to their art. Other artists congregated in Greenwich Village, in New York City, where they could remain aloof from the sordid materialism that seemed to permeate every nook and corner of American life. Still others related the decline in American civilization to the breakdown of Western civilization as a whole. Led by Irving Babbitt and Paul Elmer More, these "New Humanists," as they were called, insisted upon the necessity of man's "inner check" to control his desires and impulses. They emphasized the need for a "natural aristocracy" and scoffed at the idea of progress that was generally accepted by most Americans. Yet many of these alienated intellectuals—a group that included such outstanding figures as F. Scott Fitzgerald, Sinclair Lewis, Ernest Hemingway, John Dos Passos, and William Faulkner—were capable of creating a rich and enduring literature in the twenties and providing a cultural renaissance in America that perhaps had had no equal since the transcendentalist era of nearly a century before.

The great depression of the 1930's that began with the stock market crash in 1929, however, provided a new perspective from which to judge the previous decade. Now the optimistic outlook of the twenties seemed erroneous if for no other reason than the fact that America's prosperity had culminated in the worst economic disaster that the nation had ever known. With the seemingly imminent collapse of the capitalist system, business values and ideals were cast into disrepute. Businessmen who had been the heroes of the 1920's became the villains of the 1930's in the popular mind.

The view of the 1920's by the social scientists was less affected by the depression than was that of the businessmen. Having emphasized the application of intelligence and science to social problems in a period of prosperity, sociologists were even more adamant about taking such an approach during the depression. However, there was a growing realization among the social scientists that certain difficulties would impede the realization of their technocratic and scientific utopia. The famous report by the President's Committee on Social Trends in 1933, a project commissioned in 1929, came to the conclusion that the task of social understanding and control was far more complex than had been previously imagined. There were elements in American life to which concepts and projects involving mechanization, efficiency, and change simply could not be applied. What was required was not an outright rejection of older approaches to social problems, but a careful analysis of modern society that struck a correct balance between tradition and change.[6]

The interpretation of the twenties by historians was much more influenced by the depression than was that of the sociologists. However, this change in outlook was hardly surprising. Those historians who had written about the 1920's earlier had done so in a rather casual and superficial manner. For one thing, many of the sources required for an understanding of the so-called era of "normalcy" were only just becoming available by the end of the decade. But a much more basic reason for the shift in emphasis lay in the intellectual orientation of the profession itself. Having been reared in the liberal ideology of Progressivism, many historians of the Progressive school tended to interpret American history within the framework of a continuous class conflict that resulted in alternating periods of reform and reaction. Each era of liberal reform, they believed, was succeeded by a period of conservative consolidation or reaction. Caught up in the maelstrom of New Deal reform, these historians looked back at the 1920's as a time of reaction—a decade dominated by ultra-conservative presidents who reflected the selfish and narrow desires of the business community. In many respects such historians accepted at face value the claim by Franklin Delano Roosevelt that the New Deal was simply a continuation of America's traditional liberal values that had been momentarily subverted by the First World War and the ensuing era of disillusionment in the postwar period.

The typical interpretation of the twenties by such Progressive historians ran along the following lines. By 1920 the American people had tired of the moralistic fervor that had been characteristic of the Progressive era and of Wilsonian idealism. Having lived through two crusades lasting for over two decades—one for domestic reform and the other to make the world safe for democracy—the American people were ripe for a return to "normalcy," to use the word coined by Warren G. Harding during the presidential campaign of 1920. But "normalcy" turned out to be anything but normal. In contrast to both the Progressive and New Deal periods, which were exciting ones—if only because the American people and their leaders recognized and attempted to cope with the problems facing them and set out in a resolute and imaginative manner to come to grips with them—the twenties had a decidedly negative atmosphere. Under the conservative, and at times reactionary, Republican leadership, the American people abdicated their responsibilities.

---

[6]President's Research Committee on Social Trends, *Recent Social Trends* (2 vols.: New York, 1933).

They withdrew from the efforts on the part of other nations to ensure lasting peace; they rejected Progressive attempts to grapple with the problems of an increasingly complex industrial society and retreated instead into an outdated idea of individualism; and they turned the affairs of state over to the business community which was interested only in the pursuit of the almighty dollar.

Given this negative interpretation, it is not difficult to understand the events and developments that Progressive historians chose to document their case. Generally speaking, they were prone to write about the suppression of dissent, the near prostration of the labor movement, and the relative decline in the economic position of the farmer and worker in American society. In their eyes the twenties was a period of bigotry marked by the rise of the Ku Klux Klan, the abandonment of the ideal of America as a haven for the oppressed peoples of the world, and the resurgence of anti-Catholicism and anti-Semitism. It was a time of corruption, symbolized by the scandals of the Harding administration; even the restoration of "honesty" under Coolidge simply meant a policy whereby the federal government turned many of its functions over to business. But worst of all, it was a time when idealism seemed sadly out of date—when the youth of America were alienated from their society and the homogeneity of the nation seemed threatened by competing group loyalties. If any one theme stood out in the writings of Progressive historians, it was their assumption that the 1920's had been an irresponsible decade.

The picture of the "Roaring Twenties" or the "Jazz Age," to use designations that later became popular, was evident in the work of many historians. Vernon L. Parrington, writing within the Progressive tradition, sharply criticized the literary figures of the 1920's for throwing away their democratic-liberal heritage to emulate Europe's radical writers. To those historians writing within a Marxian framework—such as Lewis Corey or John Chamberlain—the decade was an exercise in futility—a period marked by the triumph of monopolistic capitalism which inevitably concluded with the worst depression in American history. Perhaps the most savage indictment of the decade appeared in John Dos Passos's brilliant trilogy, U.S.A. In this literary masterpiece, Dos Passos drew an unforgettable picture of the era. Using a variety of literary techniques to create an impressionistic view of a period, he emphasized the corrupting nature of materialism upon potentially "good" individuals.[7]

The critical approach to the 1920's continued to hold the allegiance of some leading contemporary historians writing within the Progressive

---

[7]Vernon L. Parrington, *Main Currents in American Thought* (3 vols.: New York, 1927–1930), III; Lewis Corey, *The Decline of American Capitalism* (New York, 1934), and *The Crisis of the Middle Class* (New York, 1935); John Chamberlain, *Farewell to Reform, Being a History of the Rise, Life and Decay of the Progressive Mind in America* (New York, 1932).

tradition down to the 1950's and 1960's. Arthur M. Schlesinger, Jr., in *The Crisis of the Old Order 1919–1933* spelled out in great detail the failure of that period. Unlike other historians who had dealt with the 1920's before him, Schlesinger was in a position to write in an authoritative manner because of the greater mass of source materials that were available. Although Schlesinger took note of the intellectual and technological advances in the twenties, his picture of the period remained a relatively hostile one. In his view the 1920's were but a prelude to the New Deal.[8]

Similarly, John D. Hicks, in *Republican Ascendancy 1921–1933* (1960), a volume in the New American Nation series, took much the same approach as Schlesinger. "It is not unfair," wrote Hicks in another essay, "to characterize the period . . . as an age of disillusionment. The high hopes with which the United States had entered World War I had been shattered; neither the League of Nations, nor the World Court, nor the disarmament program, nor the outlawry of war provided adequate guarantees of peace. . . . Politically speaking, the swing to conservatism had brought little comfort. The Harding scandals had left an ugly smell that even the puritanical Coolidge had found it difficult to eradicate; but for the ills of the times the Progressives under LaFollette could suggest only shopworn remedies of little relevance to the new age. American society was on the loose. . . . Then, despite business control of every aspect of American economic and political life, including a successful businessman in the White House, business had gone broke. Small wonder that the very bottom had fallen out of American confidence."[9]

The first selection in this chapter, by John Kenneth Galbraith, a Harvard economist and an individual active in a variety of liberal and reform movements, discusses the state of the American economy in the twenties. In presenting his argument, Galbraith makes a distinction between the stock market crash in October, 1929, and the ensuing depression because the first did not automatically cause the second. The depression of the 1930's, he writes, followed the stock market crash because the American economy had been unsound. Being in a vulnerable position, the economy was unable to withstand the blow it received from Wall Street. Although Galbraith is by no means completely hostile toward the 1920's, his interpretation falls largely within the Progressive tradition of American historiography because of the picture it presents of a maldistribution of income and unsound corporate and banking structure, and a generally weakened economy in the world at large during the decade. Given these conditions, Galbraith concludes, the depression was a logi-

---

[8]Arthur M. Schlesinger, Jr., *The Crisis of the Old Order 1919–1933* (Boston, 1957).

[9]John D. Hicks, *Normalcy and Reaction 1921–1933: An Age of Disillusionment* (Washington, D.C., 1960), p. 21.

cal outgrowth of the economic developments that took place in the twenties.

The popular stereotype of the 1920's, however, had already begun to undergo a reevaluation in the late 1930's, and this changing view gained momentum in the 1940's. During the drab days of the depression, many persons and especially the youth of America looked back upon the gaiety and irresponsibility of the twenties with a strange fascination and even a longing as they contemplated the bleak present and uncertain future. But the major shift in interpretation came during the Second World War. Concerned with maintaining the nation's morale during the war, certain critics began to denigrate the literature of the 1920's for its negative outlook and its blanket condemnation of American society. In 1944 Bernard De Voto, the famous historian and literary critic, argued that American civilization had not been bankrupt in the twenties; the bankruptcy lay in the negative literary interpretation of that decade. Indeed, De Voto found much that was appealing as well as constructive during the 1920's.[10]

While De Voto was condemning the literary rebels of the twenties for their negative and irresponsible outlook, other literary historians were beginning to approach the decade with a more appreciative eye. In 1955 Frederick J. Hoffman published his work *The Twenties: American Writing in the Postwar Decade*. After a thorough examination of the subject, Hoffman concluded that the writers of the 1920's had lived in a world that appeared to be cut loose from the past and therefore had sought to discover new ways of expressing the human condition. These literary artists, he continued, "had to invent new combinations of spirit and matter and new forms of expressing the human drama. They were not aided by any secure ordering of social or religious systems. . . . Their restless desire for the new was always motivated by their distrust of the old. . . . the 1920's were an opportunity and a challenge offered to a group of persons who were freshly and naively talented, anxious to learn *how* to restate and redramatize the human condition, morally preoccupied with the basic problem of communicating their insights into their present world."[11]

Although De Voto and Hoffman came to sharply divergent judgments about the literature of the 1920's, they were not very far apart in their general view of the period as a whole; both found much that was constructive and exciting during those years. Their break with the prevailing critical approach was soon echoed by other scholars. Indeed, shortly after the end of World War II, the pendulum began to swing

---

[10]Bernard De Voto, *The Literary Fallacy* (Boston, 1944).

[11]Frederick J. Hoffman, *The Twenties: American Writing in the Postwar Decade* (2nd edition: New York, 1962), pp. 434–436.

away from the Progressive interpretation of the twenties. Rejecting the older and more critical view of the period, historians as well as other social scientists took a fresh look at the twenties, and in doing so offered a new perspective for understanding the events that transpired between 1921 to 1933.

The new view of the twenties was actually the joint product of scholars in a number of disciplines. George Soule, for example, an economic historian, concluded in his study of the 1920's that the economic picture traditionally drawn of the period was an erroneous one. It was true that the rich became richer in the 1920's, Soule wrote, but at the same time the poor were also getting richer—albeit at a slower rate. In his view the depression that began in 1929 had much more deeply-rooted causes than those previously advanced. To Soule the depression grew out of a fundamental maladjustment of productivity and purchasing power—a maladjustment that was not indigenous to the 1920's but whose origins stretched back into American history for a good many decades.[12]

Other historians in the post-World War II era joined in the growing chorus of praise that celebrated the achievements of American capitalism rather than emphasizing its defects. They argued that it was America's productive capacity, after all, that had made possible the Allied victory during World War II and provided the free world with the means to resist the Soviet challenge after 1945. At the same time, American capitalism had given to the American people an affluent society hitherto unattainable and did so without resorting to a government-owned or managed economy. This new perspective was particularly evident in David M. Potter's challenging book, *People of Plenty: Economic Abundance and the American Character,* published in 1954. In this work Potter maintained that economic abundance had been the most important determinant in the shaping of the American character. Although Potter was not writing in terms of specific time periods, his interpretation placed the 1920's squarely within the mainstream of American history. In this context, the depression of the 1930's became the exception to the general rule of American prosperity. To put it another way, there was nothing unique or different about the twenties from an economic point of view.

The changing picture of the 1920's was reflected too in the way that historians began to look at the politics of the period. Arthur S. Link in a key article written in 1959 questioned whether the portrayal of the twenties as a reactionary decade actually fit the known facts. He argued that historians for too long had accepted uncritically the hypothesis that Progressivism had disintegrated at the end of World War I. Progressive

[12]George Soule, *Prosperity Decade* (New York, 1947).

ideals and Progressive leadership supposedly had been submerged by the rising tide of reaction and bigotry during the postwar era. This was not the case, said Link. Progressivism, after all, had never been a single national movement; it had been composed of a number of diverse reform movements operating at different levels of society. The war had shattered the coalition of Progressive reformers, but many of the individual reform efforts continued into the postwar period—albeit with less vigor. There were still many Progressive leaders in Congress in the twenties, Link maintained. This development was often obscured by the reactionary and conservative figures who were either elected to the presidency or dominated the excutive branch of government. The apparent conservatism of the period concealed from public view the continued existence of Progressive ideals that asserted themselves later in the New Deal era. Link implicitly rejected the Progressive historiography of the twenties which saw the decade as a reactionary one. Link's picture was far less negative because of his desire to redress the balance by stressing the achievements as well as the failures of the twenties. [13]

Other historians in the 1950's echoed the same view by stressing the continuity of social and cultural trends from the pre-war years into the 1920's. Rather than representing a deviation in the normal course of American history, the decade was seen as a natural outgrowth of the country's past. Henry F. May in an article suggested that the break-up of America's traditional culture began closer to 1910 than to 1920. He argued that after the first decade of the twentieth century the upper middle-class Protestant aristocracy that had largely dictated American mores gradually lost influence to other groups which gained power—the rising new middle class, working class, and ethnic minorities. The cultural disintegration of the 1920's—a movement synonymous with the decline of the old Protestant literary and moral tradition—was a complex development. To divine the true nature of the decade, May concluded, would require an examination not only of politics, economics, literature, and science of the period, but also of the relationship between them all. Much of the work since the 1950's has reflected May's call for new methods, as well as his argument along with that of Link, for continuity rather than reaction as the major theme of the 1920's. [14]

During the 1960's and 1970's, scholarly interest in the 1920's steadily mounted. Link in his article had called the decade "the exciting new frontier of American historical research." Burl Noggle, the leading his-

---

[13] Arthur S. Link, "What Happened to the Progressive Movement in the 1920's?" *American Historical Review* LXIV, (July, 1959), pp. 833–851. For a continuation of welfare reforms into the 1920's as evidence of the enduring force of Progressivism, see Clarke Chambers, *Seedtime of Reform* (Minneapolis, 1963).

[14] Henry F. May, "Shifting Perspectives on the 1920's," *Mississippi Valley Historical Review*, XLIII (December, 1956), pp. 405–427.

toriographer on the twenties, writing in the mid-1960's agreed that more historians had been drawn to the decade.[15] The reasons for the growing interest were many. Papers of major public figures had become available, memoirs had been written, and scholars were able to view events with a sharper focus as a result of this new evidence. The question of whether the 1920's served as a bridge or a chasm to the 1930's continued to intrigue historians. Most important of all, historians began to employ new research strategies and to follow May's call for a cross-disciplinary approach to the period.

The "new social historians," for example, sought to find links between religion, prohibitionism, and nativism. These scholars were less inclined to view American society of the 1920's in simplistic, dichotomous terms of the Progressives. They doubted that social conflict could be understood best in terms of polarized social groups or classes such as urban versus rural, working class versus middle class, Catholic versus Protestant, fundamentalist versus modernist, immigrant versus nativist, and "wet" versus "dry." These groups in their view were much more complicated; they did not conform neatly to the definitions assigned them by earlier scholars. The "new social historians" sought to illuminate America's complex social structure and to study the social and political changes that took place not as isolated events but as closely related phenomena which had some continuity with social changes in earlier and later eras.

The concerns of the "new social historians" in these matters was evident in a series of essays that appeared in a volume entitled *Change and Continuity in Twentieth Century America: The 1920's*, published in 1968. Several scholars stressed the theme of anxiety as one that was common to some social movements in the twenties, and used an interdisciplinary approach to study them. Paul A. Carter traced the fears and reactions of the Fundamentalists to the growing encroachment of secularism and science. Joseph R. Gusfield, a sociologist, applied the insights of his discipline to study prohibition. But the significance of anxiety as a motivating force and the methods used to study its nature could best be seen in Robert Miller's essay on the Ku Klux Klan.[16]

To Miller the Klan reflected a reaction to the tensions of what Klansmen considered to be an age of social revolution. The K.K.K. was a counterrevolutionary movement by citizens in all parts of the country—

---

[15]Link, "What Happened to the Progressive Movement in the 1920's?" p. 834, and Burl Noggle, "The Twenties: A New Historiographical Frontier," *Journal of American History*, LIII (September, 1966), pp. 299–314.

[16]Paul A. Carter, The Fundamentalist Defense of Faith," pp. 179–214; Joseph R. Gusfield, "Prohibition: The Impact of Political Utopianism," pp. 257–308; and Robert M. Miller, "The Ku Klux Klan," pp. 215–256 in John Braeman, *et. al.* eds., *Change and Continuity in Twentieth-Century America: The 1920's* (Columbus, Ohio, 1968). See also Gusfield's book, *Symbolic Crusade: Status Politics and the American Temperance Movement* (Urbana, 1963).

not only the South—to push back the changes in modern America and to restore its older and more pure past. Its membership was heterogeneous and made up of many splinter groups. Although its values were those of small-town rural America, it was based in urban as well as rural areas. Each Klansman identified change with a particular enemy. To some the enemy was the black who threatened a white man's country. To others it was the Catholics who endangered a Protestant America. The immigrant was seen by many Klansmen as polluting the purity of America's Anglo-Saxon blood. Foreign radicals, like Bolsheviks, could undermine American ways. What held the fragmented and amorphous Klan together, concluded Miller, was a "fellowship of belief" that the country faced a myriad of such enemies, as well as a shared anxiety about America's future and a longing to return to the past.[17]

One fragment group of the "new social historians"—the urban historians—were able to arrive at new insights by applying the term "urban" with greater precision as they studied more meticulously the changing distribution of population. The 1920 census marked a significant change in the urban-rural ratio, showing for the first time that the majority of Americans lived in what were defined as "urban" areas— incorporated communities of 2500 persons or more. But urban historians were no longer content to use the city as a static unit of analysis. They employed imaginative techniques to study residential patterns—the growth of suburbs, zoning laws, and urban planning. By viewing the role of the city in a more dynamic way, they revised some old ideas. Charles Glaab discovered, for example, that many solutions applied in urban plans and programs in the 1930's had been actually worked out by the urban theorists in the 1920's. George E. Mowry in his book, *The Urban Nation, 1920–1960*, pointed out the profound impact urbanization had on shaping American society during the decade. He stressed the marked acceleration of this trend in succeeding decades, thereby tying the 1920's more closely to the period that followed.[18]

The work of the "new political historians"—another fragment group of the "new social historians"—was characterized by a greater sophistication in the use of quantitative techniques which also shed new light on the 1920's. Samuel Lubell, the pollster, had advanced a thesis regarding the election of 1928 in a book written in the early 1950's in which he argued that Al Smith had brought about a critical realignment of voters in the Northeast. The "Al Smith revolution" attracted to the

---

[17]Miller, "The Ku Klux Klan," p. 217.

[18]Charles Glaab, "Metropolis and Suburb: The Changing American City," in Braeman, et al., eds., *Change and Continuity in Twentieth-Century America: The 1920's*, pp. 399–437; George E. Mowry, *The Urban Nation, 1920–1960*, (New York, 1965); and Burl Noggle, "Configurations of the Twenties," in William H. Cartwright and Richard L. Watson, Jr., eds., *The Reinterpretation of American History and Culture* (Washington, D.C., 1973), pp. 470–471.

Democratic party the urban dwellers, second-generation immigrants, Catholics, and labor voters, all of whom identified with the candidate, and thereby setting into motion the train of events that led to the Democratic coalition resulting in Roosevelt's election in 1932. Lubell's thesis was strengthened by Richard Hofstadter's analysis of the same election written a few years later. But two scholars—Jerome Clubb and Howard Allen—who developed highly sophisticated quantitative techniques for studying election returns, came up with evidence contrary to the Lubell-Hofstadter hypothesis in the late 1960's after studying closely twenty major metropolitan areas over a long time span. Smith's appeal appeared to have little carry-over effect, and Roosevelt's election seemed to be rooted more in the depression of the 1930's than in the 1920's.[19]

Another fruitful area of research into the 1920's for the "new social historians" was sparked by the renewed interest in minority groups resulting from the tensions experienced in the 1960's and 1970's. The social protest movements in these decades—civil rights and women's liberation in particular—aroused a desire among some scholars to search deeper for the part that blacks and women had played in America's past. Books on black history dealing with the 1920's cast new light on some significant developments and personalities: the growth of the Harlem ghetto; the "Harlem Renaissance;" black leaders like Marcus Garvey; and the role of black intellectuals. The study of women's history in the same period, however, proved less extensive and less rewarding, perhaps because of the rapid disintegration of certain organizations after the achievement of women's suffrage in 1920. Scholars, nevertheless, studied the continuing though unsuccessful efforts of women to gain other rights and privileges in the feminist movement during the decade.[20]

Biographers recently have rehabilitated also the reputation of two presidents—Harding and Hoover—and in doing so have by implication dealt a blow to the idea of the 1920's as a decade of reaction and inertia. Robert K. Murray's biography of Warren G. Harding portrays him as a politically adept president and one who was quite competent in managing the nation's domestic and foreign affairs. More significant was the

---

[19]Samuel Lubell, *Future of American Politics* (New York, 1952); Richard Hofstadter, "Could a Protestant Have Beaten Hoover in 1928?," *The Reporter* (March 17, 1960), pp. 31–33; Jerome Clubb and Howard Allen, "The Cities and the Election of 1928: Partisan Realignment?," *American Historical Review* LXXIV (April, 1969), pp. 1205–1220.

[20]For studies in black history see: Gilbert Osofsky, *Harlem: The Making of a Ghetto* (New York, 1966); Theodore G. Vincent, *Black Power and the Garvey Movement* (Berkeley, 1971); and Harold Cruse, *The Crisis of the Negro Intellectual* (New York, 1967). For women's history, see William L. O'Neill, *Everyone was Brave: The Rise and Fall of Feminism in America* (Chicago, 1969); and J. Stanley Lemons, *The Woman Citizen: Social Feminism in the 1920's* (Urbana, 1973). For a work that studies blacks, women, and the peace movement in the twenties, see Paul A. Carter, *Another Part of the Twenties* (New York, 1977).

reevaluation of Herbert Hoover which reversed the image of his presumably inept presidency and gave him credit for starting policies supposedly inaugurated by the New Deal. Joan H. Wilson's study labeled Hoover a Progressive, and showed that he personified Progressive ideals while serving in the government during the early and mid-1920's. If these two presidents were, indeed, less conservative and more energetic than portrayed in the past, then the line of continuity between the 1920's and 1930's was more direct and less marked by abrupt change than previously supposed.[21]

The historians of the "New Left," who figured more prominently in revising other periods of American history during the 1960's, all but ignored the 1920's. When they discussed the decade at all, their point of view—a reflection of their hostility toward and alienation from American society in the 1960's—was in many ways similar to that of the Progressive scholars. Barton J. Bernstein in his essay on the New Deal described the 1920's as a period "more properly interpreted by focusing on the continuation of progressive impulses, demands often frustrated by the rivalry of interest groups, sometimes blocked by the resistance of Harding and Coolidge, and occasionally by Hoover. Through these years while agriculture and labor struggled to secure advantages from the federal government, big business flourished."[22]

Paradoxically, the more radical New Left historians were responsible for rehabilitating, in part, the reputation of the presumably conservative Herbert Hoover. William Appleman Williams (who helped to found the "New Left" school, but who was not always in agreement with its viewpoint), refurbished Hoover's reputation in foreign affairs because both men were critics of America's foreign policy as it developed along more imperialistic lines after 1890. Both men favored a more limited American intervention in global affairs, though for quite different reasons and from widely divergent perspectives.[23]

Other scholars besides the "New Left" have continued in the tradition of the Progressive school of historians in evaluating the 1920's as a decade of reaction. The application of social science concepts and techniques by recent historians sometimes tended to confirm the critical portrait of the decade etched by the Progressives. Paul L. Murphy, in his

---

[21]Robert K. Murray, *The Harding Era* (Minneapolis, 1969); Carl Degler, "The Ordeal of Herbert Hoover," *Yale Review* LII (Summer, 1963), pp. 564–583; and Joan H. Wilson, *Herbert Hoover: Forgotten Progressive* (Boston, 1975).

[22]Barton J. Bernstein, "The New Deal: The Conservative Achievements of Liberal Reform," in *Towards a New Past: Dissenting Essays in American History*, Barton J. Bernstein, ed. (New York, 1968), p. 265. In this same book, see the only essay by a New Left historian on the 1920's—Robert F. Smith, "American Foreign Relations 1920–1942," pp. 232–262.

[23]William A. Williams, *The Tragedy of American Diplomacy* (Cleveland, 1959); Wilson, *Herbert Hoover: Forgotten Progressive*, p. 276; and Selig Adler, "Herbert Hoover's Foreign Policy and the New Left," in Martin L. Fausold and George T. Mazuzan, eds., *The Hoover Presidency* (Albany, 1974), pp. 153–163.

article written in the 1960's on the nature and sources of intolerance during the twenties, emphasized the impact of World War I in inaugurating measures of repression. After the war ended, repression continued because many Americans believed that a large number of domestic problems arose from the activities of groups and individuals who rejected the established order. Murphy argued also that the Americans who were most receptive to a movement directed at seemingly dangerous groups shared certain characteristics: they were rural or rural-oriented, homogeneous in their religious structure and values, adhered to traditional status arrangements, and exhibited a low social mobility. American society between 1919 and 1930, he concluded, was characterized by "intolerance and its shrewd manipulation." Murphy's article provides the second selection for this chapter.

It should be noted, in conclusion, that some historians like Murphy have stressed the decade of the 1920's as one having unique characteristics that set it apart because of the extraordinary reaction against Progressive ideals and reforms. Other scholars have argued that there was a greater continuity between the politics and culture of the twenties and the Progressive era that preceded, and the New Deal that followed it. In trying to decide whether the decade was one of continuity or reaction, the student should keep in mind the following questions. Is it accurate to speak about the economic developments in the twenties in terms of presidential administrations? Indeed, can important economic changes be properly understood within such a restricted time span as a single decade? Would it not be more accurate for historians—as some have done—to study the emergence of a complex industrial economy in the twentieth century as a whole? Were the Progressives correct in understanding the nature of social conflict in terms of class and geographical differences? Or were the "new social historians" more accurate because of their stress upon sociological and psychological influences? Is it possible—or even desirable—to view the twenties as a decade apart? Or is it more plausible to emphasize the continuity between the twenties and the periods that went before and after it? These are only a few questions one must answer if the true nature of the 1920's is to be correctly assessed.

John Kenneth Galbraith

JOHN KENNETH GALBRAITH (1908–   ) was Professor of Economics at Harvard University until his retirement in 1975 and also served as Ambassador to India under President John F. Kennedy. He has written a number of widely read and controversial works, including *American Capitalism* (1952), *The Affluent Society* (1958), and *The New Industrial State* (1967), *Economics and the Public Purpose* (1973), and *Money, Whence It Came, Where It Went* (1975).

After the Great Crash came the Great Depression which lasted, with varying severity, for ten years. In 1933, Gross National Product (total production of the economy) was nearly a third less than in 1929. Not until 1937 did the physical volume of production recover to the levels of 1929, and then it promptly slipped back again. Until 1941 the dollar value of production remained below 1929. Between 1930 and 1940 only once, in 1937, did the average number unemployed during the year drop below eight million. In 1933 nearly thirteen million were out of work, or about one in every four in the labor force. In 1937 one person in five was still out of work.

It was during this dreary time that 1929 became a year of myth. People hoped that the country might get back to twenty-nine; in some industries or towns when business was phenomenally good it was almost as good as in twenty-nine; men of outstanding vision, on occasions of exceptional solemnity, were heard to say that 1929 "was no better than Americans deserve."

On the whole, the great stock market crash can be much more readily explained than the depression that followed it. And among the problems involved in assessing the causes of depression none is more intractable than the responsibility to be assigned to the stock market crash. Economics still does not allow final answers on these matters. But, as usual, something can be said.

I

As already so often emphasized, the collapse in the stock market in the autumn of 1929 was implicit in the speculation that went before. The only question concerning that speculation was how long it would last. Sometime, sooner or later, confidence in the short-run reality of increasing common stock values would weaken. When this happened, some people would sell, and this would destroy the reality of increasing values. Holding for an increase would now become meaningless; the new reality would be falling prices. There would be a rush, pellmell, to unload. This was the way past speculative orgies had ended. It was the way the end came in 1929. It is the way speculation will end in the future.

We do not know why a great speculative orgy occurred in 1928 and 1929. The long accepted explanation that credit was easy and so people were impelled to borrow money to buy common stocks on margin is obviously nonsense. On numerous occasions before and since credit has been easy, and there has been no speculation whatever. Furthermore, much of the 1928 and 1929 speculation occurred on money borrowed at interest rates which for years before, and in any period since, would have been considered exceptionally astringent. Money, by the ordinary tests, was tight in the late twenties.

Far more important than rate of interest and the supply of credit is the mood. Speculation on a large scale requires a pervasive sense of confidence and optimism and conviction that ordinary people were meant to be rich. People must also have faith in the good intentions and even in the benevolence of others, for it is by the agency of others that they will get rich. In 1929 Professor Dice observed: "The common folks believe in their leaders. We no longer look upon the captains of industry as magnified crooks. Have we not heard their voices over the radio? Are we not familiar with their thoughts, ambitions, and ideals as they have expressed them to us almost as a man talks to his friend?" Such a feeling of trust is essential for a boom. When people are cautious, questioning, misanthropic, suspicious, or mean, they are immune to speculative enthusiasms.

Savings must also be plentiful. Speculation, however it may rely on borrowed funds, must be nourished in part by those who participate. If savings are growing rapidly, people will place a lower marginal value on their accumulation; they will be willing to risk some of it against the prospect of a greatly enhanced return. Speculation, accordingly, is most likely to break out after a substantial period of prosperity, rather than in the early phases of recovery from a depression. Macaulay noted that between the Restoration and the Glorious Revolution Englishmen were at a loss to know what to do with their savings and that the "natural effect of this state of things was that a crowd of projectors, ingenious and absurd, honest and knavish, employed themselves in devising new schemes for the employment of redundant capital." Bagehot and others have attributed the South Sea Bubble to roughly the same causes. In 1720 England had enjoyed a long period of prosperity, enhanced in part by war expenditures, and during this time private savings are believed to have grown at an unprecedented rate. Investment outlets were also few and returns low. Accordingly, Englishmen were anxious to place their savings at the disposal of the new enterprises and were quick to believe that the prospects were not fantastic. So it was in 1928 and 1929.

Finally, a speculative outbreak has a greater or less immunizing effect. The ensuing collapse automatically destroys the very mood speculation requires. It follows that an outbreak of speculation provides a reasonable assurance that another outbreak will not immediately occur. With time and the dimming of memory, the immunity wears off. A recurrence becomes possible. Nothing would have induced Americans to launch a speculative adventure in the stock market in 1935. By 1955 the chances are very much better.

II

As noted, it is easier to account for the boom and crash in the market than to explain their bearing on the depression which followed. The causes of the Great Depression are still far from certain. A lack of certainty, it may also be observed, is not evident in the contemporary writing on the subject. Much of it tells what went wrong and why with marked firmness. However, this paradoxically can itself be an indication of uncertainty. When people are least sure they are often most dogmatic. We do not know what the Russians intend, so we state with great assurance what they will do. We compensate for our inability to foretell the consequences of, say, rearming Germany by asserting positively just what the consequences will be. So it is in economics. Yet, in explaining what happened in 1929 and after, one can distinguish between explanations that might be right and those that are clearly wrong.

A great many people have always felt that a depression was inevitable in the thirties. There had been (at least) seven good years; now by an occult or biblical law of compensation there would have to be seven bad ones. Perhaps, consciously or unconsciously, an argument that was valid for the stock market was brought to bear on the economy in general. Because the market took leave of reality in 1928 and 1929, it had at some time to make a return to reality. The disenchantment was bound to be as painful as the illusions were beguiling. Similarly, the New Era prosperity would some day evaporate; in its wake would come the compensating hardship.

There is also the slightly more subtle conviction that economic life is governed by an inevitable rhythm. After a certain time prosperity destroys itself and depression corrects itself. In 1929 prosperity, in accordance with the dictates of the business cycle, had run its course. This was the faith confessed by the members of the Harvard Economic Society in the spring of 1929 when they concluded that a recession was somehow overdue.

Neither of these beliefs can be seriously supported. The twenties by being comparatively prosperous established no imperative that the thirties be depressed. In the past, good times have given way to less good times and less good or bad to good. But change is normal in a capitalist economy. The degree of regularity in such movements is not great, though often thought to be. No inevitable rhythm required the collapse and stagnation of 1930–40.

Nor was the economy of the United States in 1929 subject to such physical pressure or strain as the result of its past level of performance that a depression was bound to come. The notion that the economy requires occasional rest and resuscitation has a measure of plausibility and also a marked viability. During the summer of 1954 a professional economist on President Eisenhower's personal staff explained the then current recession by saying that the economy was enjoying a brief (and presumably well-merited) rest after the exceptional exertions of preceding years. In 1929 the labor force was not tired; it could have continued to produce indefinitely at the best 1929 rate. The capital plant of the country was not depleted. In the preceding years of prosperity, plant had been renewed and improved. In fact, depletion of the capital plant occurred during the ensuing years of idleness when new investment was sharply curtailed. Raw materials in 1929 were ample for the current rate of production. Entrepreneurs were never more eupeptic. Obviously if men, materials, plant, and management were all capable of continued and even enlarged exertions a refreshing pause was not necessary.

Finally, the high production of the twenties did not, as some have suggested, outrun the wants of the people. During these years people were indeed being supplied with an increasing volume of goods. But there is no evidence that their desire for automobiles, clothing, travel, recreation, or even food was sated. On the contrary, all subsequent evidence showed (given the income to spend) a capacity for a large further increase in consumption. A depression was not needed so that people's wants could catch up with their capacity to produce.

III

What, then, are the plausible causes of the depression? The task of answering can be simplified somewhat by dividing the problem into two parts. First there is the question of why economic activity turned down in 1929. Second there is the vastly more important question of why, having started down, on this unhappy occasion it went down and down and down and remained low for a full decade.

As noted, the Federal Reserve indexes of industrial activity and of factory production, the most comprehensive monthly measures of economic activity then available, reached a peak in June. They then turned down and continued to decline throughout the rest of the year. The turning point in other indicators—factory payrolls, freight-car loadings, and department store sales—came later, and it was October or after before the trend in all of them was clearly down. Still, as economists have generally insisted, and the matter has the high authority of the National Bureau of Economic Research, the economy had weakened in the early summer well before the crash.

This weakening can be variously explained. Production of industrial products, for the moment, had outrun consumer and investment demand for them. The most likely reason is that business concerns, in the characteristic enthusiasm of good times, misjudged the prospective increase in demand and acquired larger inventories than they later found they needed. As a result they curtailed their buying, and this led to a cutback in production. In short, the summer of 1929 marked the beginning of the familiar inventory recession. The proof is not conclusive from the (by present standards) limited figures available. Department store inventories, for which figures are available, seem not to have been out of line early in the year. But a mild slump in department store sales in April could have been a signal for curtailment.

Also there is a chance—one that students of the period have generally favored—that more deep-seated factors were at work and made themselves seriously evident for the first time during that summer. Throughout the twenties production and productivity per worker grew steadily: between 1919 and 1929, output per worker in manufacturing industries increased by about 43 percent. Wages, salaries, and prices all remained comparatively stable, or in any case underwent no comparable increase. Accordingly, costs fell and with prices the same, profits increased. These profits sustained the spending of the well-to-do, and they also nourished at least some of the expectations behind the stock market boom. Most of all they encouraged a very high level of capital investment. During the twenties, the production of capital goods increased at an average annual rate of 6.4 percent a year; non-durable consumers' goods, a category which includes such objects of mass consumption as food and clothing, increased at a rate of only 2.8 percent. (The rate of increase for durable consumers' goods such as cars, dwellings, home furnishings, and the like, much of it representing expenditures of the well-off to well-to-do, was 5.9 percent.) A large and increasing investment in capital goods was, in other words, a principal device by which the profits were being spent. It follows that anything that interrupted the investment outlays—anything, indeed, which kept them from showing the necessary rate of increase—could cause trouble.

When this occurred, compensation through an increase in consumer spending could not automatically be expected. The effect, therefore, of insufficient investment—investment that failed to keep pace with the steady increase in profits—could be falling total demand reflected in turn in falling orders and output. Again there is no final proof of this point, for unfortunately we do not know how rapidly investment had to grow to keep abreast of the current increase in profits. However, the explanation is broadly consistent with the facts.

There are other possible explanations of the downturn. Back of the insufficient advance in investment may have been the high interest rates. Perhaps, although less probably, trouble was transmitted to the economy as a whole from some weak sector like agriculture. Further explanations could be offered. But one thing about this experience is clear. Until well along in the autumn of 1929 the downturn was limited. The recession in business activity was modest and underemployment relatively slight. Up to November it was possible to argue that not much of anything had happened. On other occasions, as noted—in 1924 and 1927 and of late in 1949—the economy has undergone similar recession. But, unlike these other occasions, in 1929 the recession continued and continued and got violently worse. This is the unique feature of the 1929 experience. This is what we need really to understand.

IV

There seems little question that in 1929, modifying a famous cliché, the economy was fundamentally unsound. This is a circumstance of first-rate importance. Many things were wrong, but five weaknesses seem to have had an especially intimate bearing on the ensuing disaster. They are:

THE BAD DISTRIBUTION OF INCOME

In 1929 the rich were indubitably rich. The figures are not entirely satisfactory, but it seems certain that the 5 percent of the population with the highest incomes in that year received approximately one third of all personal income. The proportion of personal income received in the form of interest, dividends, and rent—the income, broadly speaking, of the well-to-do—was about twice as great as in the years following the Second World War.

This highly unequal income distribution meant that the economy was dependent on a high level of investment or a high level of luxury consumer spending or both. The rich cannot buy great quantities of bread. If they are to dispose of what they receive it must be on luxuries or by way of investment in new plants and new projects. Both investment and luxury spending are subject, inevitably, to more erratic influences and to wider fluctuations than the bread and rent outlays of the $25-a-week workman. This high-bracket spending and investment was especially susceptible, one may assume, to the crushing news from the stock market in October of 1929.

THE BAD CORPORATE STRUCTURE

In November 1929, a few weeks after the crash, the Harvard Economic Society gave as a principal reason why a depression need not be feared its reasoned judgment that "business in most lines has been conducted with prudence and conservatism." The fact was that American enterprise in the twenties had opened its hospitable arms to an exceptional number of promoters, grafters, swindlers, impostors, and frauds. This, in the long history of such activities, was a kind of flood tide of corporate larceny.

The most important corporate weakness was inherent in the vast new structure of holding companies and investment trusts. The holding companies controlled large segments of the utility, railroad, and entertainment business. Here, as with the investment trusts, was the constant danger of devastation by reverse leverage. In particular, dividends from the operating companies paid the interest on the bonds of upstream holding companies. The interruption of the dividends meant default on the bonds, bankruptcy, and the collapse of the structure. Under these circumstances, the temptation to curtail investment in operating plant in order to continue dividends was obviously strong. This added to deflationary pressures. The latter, in turn, curtailed earnings and helped bring down the corporate pyramids. When this happened, even more retrenchment was inevitable. Income was earmarked for debt repayment. Borrowing for new investment became impossible. It would be hard to imagine a corporate system better designed to continue and accentuate a deflationary spiral.

THE BAD BANKING STRUCTURE

Since the early thirties, a generation of Americans has been told, sometimes with amusement, sometimes with indignation, often with outrage, of the banking practices of the late twenties. In fact, many of these practices were made ludicrous only by the depression. Loans which would have been perfectly good were made perfectly foolish by the collapse of the borrower's prices or the markets for his goods or the value of the collateral he had posted. The most responsible bankers—those who saw that their debtors were victims of circumstances far beyond their control and sought to help—were often made to look the worst. The bankers yielded, as did others, to the blithe, optimistic, and immoral mood of the times but probably not more so. A depression such as that of 1929–32, were it to begin as this is written, would also be damaging to many currently impeccable banking reputations.

However, although the bankers were not unusually foolish in 1929, the banking structure was inherently weak. The weakness was implicit in the large numbers of independent units. When one bank failed, the assets of others were frozen while depositors elsewhere had a pregnant warning to go and ask for their money. Thus one failure led to other failures, and these spread with a domino effect. Even in the best of times local misfortune or isolated mismanagement could start such a chain reaction. (In the first six months of 1929, 346 banks failed in various parts of the country with aggregate deposits of nearly $115 million.) When income, employment, and values fell as the result of a depression bank failures could quickly become epidemic. This happened after 1929. Again it would be hard to imagine a better arrangement for magnifying the effects of fear. The weak destroyed not only the other weak, but weakened the strong. People everywhere, rich and poor, were made aware of the disaster by the persuasive intelligence that their savings had been destroyed.

Needless to say, such a banking system, once in the convulsions of failure, had a uniquely repressive effect on the spending of its depositors and the investment of its clients.

THE DUBIOUS STATE OF THE FOREIGN BALANCE

This is a familiar story. During the First World War, the United States became a creditor on international account. In the decade following, the surplus of exports over imports which once had paid the interest and principal on loans from Europe continued. The high tariffs, which restricted imports and helped to create this surplus of exports remained. However, history and traditional trading habits also accounted for the persistence of the favorable balance, so called.

Before, payments on interest and principal had in effect been deducted from the trade balance. Now that the United States was a creditor, they were added to this balance. The latter, it should be said, was not huge. In only one year (1928) did the excess of exports over imports come to as much as a billion dollars; in 1923 and 1926 it was only about $375,000,000. However, large or small, this difference had to be covered. Other countries which were buying more than they sold, and had debt payments to make in addition, had somehow to find the means for making up the deficit in their transactions with the United States.

During most of the twenties the difference was covered by cash—i.e., gold payments to the United States—and by new private loans by the United States to other countries. Most of the loans were to governments—national, state, or municipal bodies—and a large proportion were to Germany and Central and South America. The underwriters' margins in handling these loans were generous; the public took them up with enthusiasm; competition for the business was keen. If unfortunately corruption and bribery were required as competitive instruments, these were used. In late 1927 Juan Leguia, the son of the President of Peru, was paid $450,000 by J. and W. Seligman and Company and the National City Company (the security affiliate of the National City Bank) for his services in connection with a $50,000,000 loan which these houses marketed for Peru. Juan's services, according to later testimony, were of a rather negative sort. He was paid for not blocking the deal. The Chase extended President Machado of Cuba, a dictator with a marked predisposition toward murder, a generous personal line of credit which at one time reached $200,000. Machado's son-in-law was employed by the Chase. The bank did a large business in Cuban bonds. In contemplating these loans, there was a tendency to pass quickly over anything that might appear to the disadvantage of the creditor. Mr. Victor Schoepperle, a vice-president of the National City Company with the responsibility for Latin American loans, made the following appraisal of Peru as a credit prospect:

> Peru: Bad debt record, adverse moral and political risk, bad internal debt situation, trade situation about as satisfactory as that of Chile in the past three years. Natural resources more varied. On economic showing Peru should go ahead rapidly in the next 10 years.

On such showing the National City Company floated a $15,000,000 loan for Peru, followed a few months later by a $50,000,000 loan, and some ten months thereafter by a $25,000,000 issue. (Peru did prove a highly adverse political risk. President Leguia, who negotiated the loans, was thrown violently out of office, and the loans went into default.)

In all respects these operations were as much a part of the New Era as Shenandoah and Blue Ridge. They were also just as fragile, and once the illusions of the New Era were dissipated they came as abruptly to an end. This, in turn, forced a fundamental revision in the foreign economic position of the United States. Countries could not cover their adverse trade balance with the United States with increased payments of gold, at least not for long. This meant that they had either to increase their exports to the United States or reduce their imports or default on their past loans. President Hoover and the Congress moved promptly to eliminate the first possibility—that the accounts would be balanced by larger imports—by sharply increasing the tariff. Accordingly, debts, including war debts, went into default and there was a precipitate fall in American exports. The reduction was not vast in relation to total output of the American economy, but it contributed to the general distress and was especially hard on farmers.

THE POOR STATE OF ECONOMIC INTELLIGENCE

To regard the people of any time as particularly obtuse seems vaguely improper, and it also establishes a precedent which members of this generation might regret. Yet it seems certain that the economists and those who offered economic counsel in the late twenties and early thirties were almost uniquely perverse. In the months and years following the stock market crash, the burden of reputable economic advice was invariably on the side of measures that would make things worse. In November of 1929, Mr. Hoover announced a cut in taxes; in the great no-business conferences that followed he asked business firms to keep up their capital investment and to maintain wages. Both of these measures were on the side of increasing spendable income, though unfortunately they were largely without effect. The tax reductions were negligible except in the higher income brackets; businessmen who promised to maintain investment and wages, in accordance with a well-understood convention, considered the promise binding only for the period within which it was not financially disadvantageous to do so. As a result investment outlays and wages were not reduced until circumstances would in any case have brought their reduction.

Still, the effort was in the right direction. Thereafter policy was almost entirely on the side of making things worse. Asked how the government could best advance recovery, the sound and responsible adviser urged that the budget be balanced. Both parties agreed on this. For Republicans the balanced budget was, as ever, high doctrine. But the Democratic Party platform of 1932, with an explicitness which politicians rarely advise, also called for a "federal budget annually balanced on the basis of accurate executive estimates within revenues . . ."

A commitment to a balanced budget is always comprehensive. It then meant there could be no increase in government outlays to expand purchasing power and relieve distress. It meant there could be no further tax reduction. But taken literally it meant much more. From 1930 on the budget was far out of balance, and balance, therefore, meant an increase in taxes, a reduction in spending, or both. The Democratic platform in 1932 called for an "immediate and drastic reduction of governmental expenditures" to accomplish at least a 25 percent decrease in the cost of government.

The balanced budget was not a subject of thought. Nor was it, as often asserted, precisely a matter of faith. Rather it was a formula. For centuries avoidance of borrowing had protected people from slovenly or reckless public housekeeping. Slovenly or reckless keepers of the public purse had often composed complicated arguments to show why balance of income and outlay was not a mark of virtue. Experience had shown that however convenient this belief might seem in the short run, discomfort or disaster followed in the long run. Those simple precepts of a simple world did not hold amid the growing complexities of the early thirties. Mass unemployment in particular had altered the rules. Events had played a very bad trick on people, but almost no one tried to think out the problem anew.

The balanced budget was not the only strait jacket on policy. There was also the bogey of "going off" the gold standard and, most surprisingly, of risking inflation. Until 1932 the United States added formidably to its gold reserves, and instead of inflation the country was experiencing the most violent deflation in the nation's history. Yet every sober adviser saw dangers here, including the danger of runaway price increases. Americans, though in years now well in the past, had shown a penchant for tinkering with the money supply and enjoying the brief but heady joys of a boom in prices. In 1931 or 1932, the danger or even the feasibility of such a boom was nil. The advisers and counselors were not, however, analyzing the danger or even the possibility. They were serving only as the custodians of bad memories.

The fear of inflation reinforced the demand for the balanced budget. It also limited efforts to make interest rates low, credit plentiful (or at least redundant) and borrowing as easy as possible under the circumstances. Devaluation of the dollar was, of course, flatly ruled out. This directly violated the gold standard rules. At best, in such depression times, monetary policy is a feeble reed on which to lean. The current economic clichés did not allow even the use of that frail weapon. And again, these attitudes were above party. Though himself singularly open-minded, Roosevelt was careful not to offend or disturb his followers. In a speech in Brooklyn toward the close of the 1932 campaign, he said:

> The Democratic platform specifically declares, "We advocate a sound currency to be preserved at all hazards." That is plain English. In discussing this platform on July 30, I said, "Sound money is an international necessity, not a domestic consideration for one nation alone." Far up in the Northwest, at Butte, I repeated the pledge... In Seattle I reaffirmed my attitude...

The following February, Mr. Hoover set forth his view, as often before, in a famous letter to the President-elect:

> It would steady the country greatly if there could be prompt assurance that there will be no tampering or inflation of the currency; that the budget will be unquestionably balanced even if further taxation is necessary; that the Government credit will be maintained by refusal to exhaust it in the issue of securities.

The rejection of both fiscal (tax and expenditure) and monetary policy amounted precisely to a rejection of all affirmative government economic policy. The economic advisers of the day had both the unanimity and the authority to force the leaders of both parties to disavow all the available steps to check deflation and depression. In its own way this was a marked achievement—a triumph of dogma over thought. The consequences were profound.

V

It is in light of the above weaknesses of the economy that the role of the stock market crash in the great tragedy of the thirties must be seen. The years of self-depreciation by Wall Street to the contrary, the role is one of respectable importance. The collapse in securities values affected in the first instance the wealthy and well-to-do. But we see that in the world of 1929 this was a vital group. The members disposed of a large proportion of the consumer income; they were the source of a lion's share of personal saving and investment. Anything that struck at the spending or investment by this group would of necessity have broad effects on expenditure and income in the economy at large. Precisely such a blow was struck by the stock market crash. In addition, the crash promptly removed from the economy the support that it had been deriving from the spending of stock market gains.

The stock market crash was also an exceptionally effective way of exploiting the weaknesses of the corporate structure. Operating companies at the end of the holding-company chain were forced by the crash to retrench. The subsequent collapse of these systems and also of the investment trusts effectively destroyed both the ability to borrow and the willingness to lend for investment. What have long looked like purely fiduciary effects were, in fact, quickly translated into declining orders and increasing unemployment.

The crash was also effective in bringing to an end the foreign lending by which the international accounts had been balanced. Now the accounts had, in the main, to be balanced by reduced exports. This put prompt and heavy pressure on export markets for wheat, cotton, and tobacco. Perhaps the foreign loans had only delayed an adjustment in the balance which had one day to come. The stock market crash served nonetheless to precipitate the adjustment with great suddenness at a most unpropitious time. The instinct of farmers who traced their troubles to the stock market was not totally misguided.

Finally, when the misfortune had struck, the attitudes of the time kept anything from being done about it. This, perhaps, was the most disconcerting feature of all. Some people were hungry in 1930 and 1931 and 1932. Others were tortured by the fear that they might go hungry. Yet others suffered the agony of the descent from the honor and respectability that goes with income into poverty. And still others feared that they would be next. Meanwhile everyone suffered from a sense of utter hopelessness. Nothing, it seemed, could be done. And given the ideas which controlled policy, nothing could be done.

Had the economy been fundamentally sound in 1929 the effect of the great stock market crash might have been small. Alternatively, the shock to confidence and the loss of spending by those who were caught in the market might soon have worn off. But business in 1929 was not sound; on the contrary it was exceedingly fragile. It was vulnerable to the kind of blow it received from Wall Street. Those who have emphasized this vulnerability are obviously on strong ground. Yet when a greenhouse succumbs to a hailstorm something more than a purely passive role is normally attributed to the storm. One must accord similar significance to the typhoon which blew out of lower Manhattan in October 1929.

Paul L. Murphy

PAUL L. MURPHY (1923–   ) is Professor of History and American Studies at the University of Minnesota. He has written a number of studies of American constitutional history, including *The Constitution in Crisis Times, 1918–1969* (1972) and *The Meaning of Freedom of Speech: First Amendment Freedoms from Wilson to FDR* (1972).

In approaching that seamy side of the national character which periodically displays broad-scale intolerance, prejudice, nativism, and xenophobia, many American historians have sought in recent years to draw upon the findings of scholars in related disciplines in their attempts at meaningful analysis. Especially suggestive in this area has been recent work in sociology, social psychology, cultural anthropology, and American studies. Differences exist, however, as to how such findings can actually aid the historian and the degree of reliance he can confidently place upon them. Given the fact that the average historian must work in a past context in which precise empirical research is impossible, particularly as it applies to a broad spectrum of public attitudes, and given the fact that modern social science studies draw the great body of their evidence from current materials, a question of relevance is raised. How safe is it for the historian to project such modern findings backwards in an attempt better to understand and grasp the tensions and pressures of a prior era? Are modern social science techniques reliable in the analysis of imprecise historical materials?

Some members of the historical guild feel that such borrowing of either materials or techniques is too dangerous to be acceptable. Others at times have relied too heavily upon such interdisciplinary aids in order to validate general presumptions otherwise difficult of documentation. Still others have used such materials cautiously and carefully, so cautiously and so carefully that they have come to differ among themselves concerning their applicability. In the study of past intolerance, for example, there have been those who drew heavily upon a sociologically oriented emphasis on status rivalries and who have emphasized ongoing tensions ever present in the slow process of ethnic integration in our dynamic society. Yet such persons have subsequently been challenged

Paul L. Murphy, "Sources and Nature of Intolerance in the 1920s," *Journal of American History*, LI (June, 1964), pp. 60–76. Reprinted by permission of the Organization of American Historians.

to explain the plausibility of the cyclical nature of waves of intolerance and its frequently differing character as unique situations have produced unique expressions geared to immediate needs. Others who have made careful use of stereotyping or who have placed reliance upon ideological factors have been questioned. So too have those who have focused upon the concrete facts of the immediate situation, especially upon the influence of men of passion with ability to create or nurture moods of alarm by exploiting irrational myths. This has forced such persons to deemphasize the constant factor of human irrationality in normal times even though it is always basic in assessing causation in all historical events.

In many ways the study of intolerance in the 1920s raises in exaggerated form both a question of the applicability of related materials and of proper permissible use of such materials. That decade, despite its surface prosperity and supposed gaiety and exuberance, was characterized by waves of public intolerance seldom felt in the American experience. Much of this intolerance was merely an outbreak of familiar subsurface prejudices with antecedents in earlier expressed antipathies toward radicals, Catholics, Jews, Negroes, Orientals, and other minority groups. Yet such intolerance was not traditional. Fostered frequently, although seldom led directly by men seeking gratuities as brokers for that community or as brokers for men of property, it quickly gained its sanctions from that national consensus so clumsily branded "normalcy" and involved many Americans previously immune to its toxicity. As such it was an integral part of the 1920s, participated in consciously or unconsciously by the great majority of Americans. That it took on a changing character as the decade advanced is apt testimony to its virulence. That it either disappeared or took on different forms with the depression seems to reveal that it was specially suited to the peculiar culture and society of the jazz age.

The historian would be delighted if by merely adding the materials and utilizing the techniques of the social scientists he could say precise and scientific things both about the roots, nature, and manifestations of intolerance at this time. Yet, despite the siren's call of being able through empirical social research to reach quantitative answers, he is tempted to concentrate on the imprecise approaches of history, relying upon interdisciplinary tools as analytical devices only when they seem to have an obvious relation to known and documentable reality.

Clearly the sources of the intolerance of the 1920s can be traced to at least the late Progressive period, with obvious roots in the immediately preceding years. Clearly such intolerance had a relation to growing Progressive apprehensions over alarming developments which did not seem to be responding to normal controls. The IWW, the first effectively organized movement of militant workingmen to challenge the whole American economic system, sent chills through the hearts and outrage through the souls of upper and middle class Americans. Here in the early years of the century was a group with the effrontery to make demands no decent citizen could honor and employ techniques no moral American could tolerate. But worse than this, these people and their Socialist "cousins" rejected the premises upon which the American system rested, namely that rights and privileges were open in a free society to anyone who was willing to work up patiently within the system. Or if the individual was incapable of utilizing this technique he would eventually be taken care of in a spirit of paternalism by the affluent class, as long as he stood with his hat in his hand and patiently waited. The alarming fact was that the IWW's and Socialists were no longer willing to wait. They were unwilling to accept the fact that only after one had gained a stake in society was he warranted in becoming a critic or a reformer. As one Progressive editor wrote during the Lawrence textile strike of 1912 (at the point which Paul Brissenden called "the high tide of the IWW activity"):

> On all sides people are asking, Is this a new thing in the industrial world? . . . Are we to see another serious, perhaps successful, attempt to organize labor by whole industrial groups instead of by trades? Are we to expect that instead of playing the game respectably, or else frankly breaking out into lawless riot which we know well enough how to deal with, the laborers are to listen to a subtle anarchistic philosophy which challenges the fundamental ideas of law and order, inculcating such strange doctrines as those of "direct action," "sabotage," "syndicalism," "the general strike," and "violence"? . . . We think that our whole current morality as to the sacredness of property and even of life is involved in it.

Also involved in it was the IWW practice of utilizing the rhetoric of American democracy as a device for obtaining their ends. The "free-speech fight" which assumed national proportions after 1910 was distressingly successful at times and was painfully difficult to counteract. For while many Americans could argue that utilizing free speech to gain personal economic ends was an abuse of American ideals, the alternative of arbitrary suppression hardly preserved them.

For those in this dilemma World War I afforded a satisfying rationalization for suppression. Woodrow Wilson's prediction, "once lead this people into war and they'll forget there ever was such a thing as tolerance," was clairvoyant, as the government quickly set out to turn the President's words into official policy that succeeded frighteningly well. Every element of American public opinion was mobilized behind "my country, right or wrong," dissent was virtually forbidden, democracy at home was drastically curtailed so that it could be made safe abroad, while impressionable children were either "educated" in Hun atrocities, or their time was employed in liberty loan, Red Cross, war saving stamp, or YMCA campaigns. It was not difficult then to channel an aroused nation's wrath against earlier boatrockers—a development made easier by the fact that many IWWs and Socialists stood out boldly against war from the start. The Espionage Act of 1917, while ostensibly a measure to strike at illegal interference with the war effort, was so worded that is could be, and was, used to stamp out radical criticism of the war. Its subsequent 1918 amendment, the Sedition Act, was a less subtle device. Passed by the pressure of western senators, and modeled after a Montana IWW statute, its purpose was to undercut both the performance and advocacy of undesirable activity. There was a clear implication that people who utilized speech as a means of gaining improper ends had to be restricted. And with the subsequent federal prosecution of 184 members of the IWW in 1918 and 1919, to say nothing of a crackdown on Socialists, German-Americans, conscientious objectors, and Non-Partisan Leaguers, the intent of the federal legislative and administrative program became crystal clear.

With peace and the end of conservative labor's wartime honeymoon, there was renewed fear on the part of the reinvigorated business community that an unholy union of dissident malcontents and elements of more orthodox labor, now feeling callously betrayed, was not only possible but probable. The strikes of the immediate postwar period could only be rationalized by business in these terms. And to create further alarm, not only was Bolshevism a reality in Russia, but American workers and even some influential leaders were studying its economic and political implications with interest if not with admiration. Catholics, when under fire in the past, had consistently denied their allegiance to the Vatican, but some of these Bolshevik admirers even proclaimed proudly and openly their allegiance to a new order from the Kremlin.

Fear led to irrationality and business found it impossible to analyze the meaning and implications of these developments or to understand what Gutzon Borglum called in 1919 the "real labor problem," which was labor's dependent condition. In response to a speech by Nicholas Murray Butler, rebuking labor for its lack of "reasonableness," Borglum wrote:

> Labor's recent political activity is due to a deep consciousness of the necessity of self-reliance to secure any and all improvement in its condition. And further, the political color that has recently appeared in its methods, is forced because of the utter faithlessness and failure of partisan government to give it relief.

But to conservative leaders, protection was more important than understanding. With the wartime legislation now generally inapplicable, they sought to get onto the statute books peacetime sedition and criminal syndicalism laws to take its place. To accomplish this, business was frequently able to transfer its own fears of Bolshevism both to a broader public and to state legislators who served that public. The result was that such propagandizing, plus added apprehensions triggered by frequently specious bomb scares, produced wide demand for restriction. Thus, although much of the new legislation was enacted in a sincere desire to control agitators and dangerous seditionists, other more responsive legislators took care to be sure that resultant laws were carefully worded and did not appear to be class legislation. By 1920 thirty-five states had enacted some form of restrictive, precautionary legislation enabling the rapid crackdown on speech that might by its expression produce unlawful actions geared toward stimulating improper political or economic change. Such legislation was couched in terms which in Connecticut permitted punishment of "disloyal, scurrilous, or abusive language about the form of government of the United States," and in Colorado, "advocacy by word or in print of forcible resistance to constituted government either as a general principle, or in particular instances as a means of affecting governmental, industrial, social or economic conditions."

That there was no legal need or justification for such legislation (the criminal codes of the states adequately covered conspiracy and libel) further underlined the fact that its purpose was devious. It constituted intimidating legislation by which business subtly sought to institutionalize forms of prior curtailment and thereby free itself from the necessity of having personally to restrict those it considered a threat to the existing order. Henceforth such restriction and subtle regimentation could be left to the discretion of administrative officials who could develop standards to fit immediate and local needs, and who, as the decade progressed, were to add the injunction as a further precautionary weapon.

Although this legislation was quickly implemented in 1919 in a number of states, it did not quiet all malcontents. Prompted by a multiplication of strikes and labor discontent, the more hysterical began to fear that local sanctions were not enough and proceeded to advocate a form of federal "direct action." Powerful federal activity such as the Palmer raids, the army-conducted deportation of 249 "dangerous Reds" aboard the "Soviet Ark" *Buford*, the contemporaneous effort of representatives and senators to rush through a federal peacetime sedition act, while a product of and response to excessive public hysteria should also be understood as the partial culmination of an increasingly more pressing apprehensiveness which had obsessed conservatives for well over a decade. And the fact that many Americans were at the time able to rationalize and condone the most disgraceful, wholesale departure from fundamental guarantees of basic liberty and due process of law in American history further underscores the extent of their fears.

Yet the Red scare of the 1920s introduced a new permanent dimension of intolerance. This was the aspiring, self-seeking individual or special interest group which sought to exploit the hysteria and intolerance of the moment for personal advantage. Such individuals and groups were not new in American history. But the breadth of their operations was more sweeping in the 1920s, and the ambitiousness of their calculations was greater, as was the number of Americans they sought to affect. For aggressive politicians like A. Mitchell Palmer, Leonard Wood, or Albert S. Burleson, the ability to project themselves into the role of master defender of the endangered order could mean nomination to high office, hopefully the presidency. To an Anthony Caminetti, the first person of Italian extraction to be elected to Congress and by then Commissioner of Immigration, this was an opportunity to demonstrate that he, as well as others of his national origin, were fully 100 percent American. To an aggressive bureaucrat like William J. Flynn, head of the Bureau of Investigation, or J. Edgar Hoover, head of the Bureau's newly created General Intelligence (antiradical) Division, here was a chance to enhance the power of the Bureau, and his own power and domain simultaneously. To Flynn's successor, William J. Burns, the ability to guide public fears and even create fears where only apprehensions had existed was also an opportunity to stimulate a brisk business for the Burns International Detective Agency until an increasingly more hostile public forced a curtailment and a housecleaning in the Department of Justice.

At the group level motivations were equally divergent. The American Legion epitomized the service-oriented organizations, obligated to deliver a variety of specific benefits to its wide membership. To do this entails sufficient flattering and assisting of those in power to convince them that the organization deserved favors. But to write the Legion off as "apple-polishing, flag-wavers of patriotism" is to miss the fact that most legionnaires received great satisfaction from ousting "Reds" and Americanizing everyone completely. Such patrioteering afforded an opportunity for members to demonstrate and articulate their faith and allegiance to basic ideals and institutions and thereby to gain acceptance and status with those who felt a similar need. Thus in this and similar organizations there was a natural tie between aiding the "establishment" and crusading to save America. The professional patriots, on the other hand, had simpler and even less commendable motives. Primarily propaganda organizations, and the mouthpieces of single leaders or small cabals, their purpose was to ingratiate themselves with large private or corporate donors and thereby insure their continuation. This meant showing results, not only in broad distribution of literature but in providing speakers to help in mobilizing large elements of the general public against all manner of enemies of "the American way." Thus Harry A. Jung of the powerful National Clay Products Industries Association and later the American Vigilant Intelligence Federation could write to a potential subscriber:

> We cooperate with over 30 distinctly civic and patriotic organizations. . . . It would take me too long to relate how I "put over" this part of our activities,

namely, "trailing the Reds." Should you ever be in Chicago, drop in and see me and I will explain. That it has been a paying proposition for our organization goes without saying. . . .

And again, Fred R. Marvin, head of the Keymen of America, could for six dollars per annum supply potential private radical hunters with his *Daily Data Sheets* which conveyed the doings of the Bolsheviks and parlor pinks to nervous and apprehensive individuals. It was Marvin's aim to inspire the leadership of such a group as the DAR to draw up and enforce a national "blacklist" of undesirable speakers that included such public disturbers of the peace as Jane Addams, Sherwood Eddy, James Harvey Robinson, and William Allen White. In all, over thirty such ultrapatriotic organizations came and went in the 1920s, all to a greater or lesser degree dependent upon the success with which they could mobilize and direct public intolerance and intemperance.

In this context the Ku Klux Klan played a unique role. Although it was geared to financial gain, especially as the decade progressed and its leadership fell more and more into the hands of those who sought to utilize it solely for personal profit, it was content to draw its money and support largely from private citizens in small towns and rural communities, a fact which set it apart from most other intolerance purveyors in the 1920s. This also meant, however, that it operated upon poorly underpinned grounds, a fact graphically illustrated by its rapid collapse well before the onset of the economic crisis of the depression years.

The success which all these individuals and groups achieved would still not have been possible if great segments of the American public had not been highly susceptible to the various types of appeal which they made. The source of this susceptibility was neither simple, nor always rational. It stemmed from the turbulence of the decade as value patterns underwent modification from the impact both of external pressures and internal conflict. When the German sociologist Ferdinand Tönnies delineated in his 1926 volume between what he called Gemeinschaft-Gesellschaft social structure, he inadvertently suggested the root of one of the sources of the chronic distress of the American middle class mind. Tönnies' Gemeinschaft structure well described that segment of American society which was basically rural or rural oriented, homogeneous in its ethnic and religious structure and values, a society which functioned through traditional status arrangements and which was characterized by low mobility. The members of such a society had always in America fought off what they considered the deleterious effect of foreign values endemic in a Gesellschaft structure with its urban orientation, secular focus, heterogeneous ethnic makeup, its preference for ordering social and economic relations through contract, and its tradition of high mobility which too often seemed to operate on questionable standards. In fact, the decade had opened on the crest of a successful counterattack

of superimposed Gemeinschaft values in the "noble experiment," prohibition. But such a victory was a nervous one as open defiance and
hostility grew and as erosion seemed to be occurring elsewhere with the
nation succumbing to the excitement and immediacy of a new, generally
urban dispersed popular culture. Formerly insulated value orientations
now were subjected to the lure of new behavioral patterns suggested by
the radio, the movies, romance magazines, and national service clubs.
Moreover, the automobile, and in time the airplane, were affording the
physical mobility which inevitably speeded up actual social contact with
those whose values may earlier have only been slightly known. This
does not suggest that either form of social organization was bound to
prevail. What it does suggest is that with the pressures to standardize,
elements of formerly isolated groups were being subjected to a new
challenge to modify the intensity with which they held to their own
unique ways as the only acceptable ones.

Those who were thus disturbed accepted dominant American values. However, they found that their interpretation of these values or the
techniques that they found acceptable in attaining them frequently had
to undergo more modification than they found comfortable. Yet "normalcy," incorporating as it did a multitude of simple virtues along with
carefully contrived selfish ends, proved an acceptable home for most
rural Victorians and Babbitts alike. Their concern, and often it was held
with equal intensity by each, was not the system, but the deviator, who
for one reason or another was unwilling to accept the system with its
fairly rigid formulae as to how to succeed and who might succeed. Here
two types of troublemakers invariably stood out. The one was made up
of those who sought unjustifiably to reach the pinnacle of full attainment
of the success symbols which the system held out. The other consisted
of those whose hierarchy of values and, of necessity, methods for attaining them were totally at odds with the standards of the day. In the
former group one inevitably found the targets of Klan antipathy, for
example: the ambitious immigrant, non-Anglo-Saxon, non-Protestant,
whose frequent tendency to "overachieve" led to actions to "keep him
in his place." But the quiet "consensus" of the 1920s backed up the
Klan's overt censuring with a type of silent coercion which was often far
more effective, especially if a Jew wanted admission to the local country
club, or a Catholic wanted the presidency of the nation. Although
Americans may never be fully ready for "the functionally strategic con-
vergence of the standards by which conduct is evaluated," to use Robin
Williams' phrase, they were not ready in the 1920s even to consider such
a possibility as a desirable national objective. The deviators, although
small in number, were even more of a threat. Radicals, militant labor
leaders, other loud and unreasonable critics of the system, and the honest and misguided average citizens whom they seemed to be perverting,
had to be clamped into place even more quickly and thoroughly and by

virtually any means possible. In this many welcomed an aid of any and all self-proclaimed champions of 100 percent Americanism.

This position constituted an interesting modification of an earlier confidence in progress through broad public participation and discussion, a process long boasted as inherent in American institutions. In 1931 Roger Baldwin attributed this to the manifestly declining postwar faith in democracy. Others attributed it to the general insecurity of all Americans and especially the chronic dissatisfaction with what many had been led to believe would be the glorious life of a postwar world. Regardless of the cause, the effect was to undercut one of the potentially important sources which might have brought significant relief. Having convinced themselves that deviators from the status quo were potential Bolsheviks, many Americans found it a simple step to renounce the mildest type of reformer or reform program, a view in which they had the most thorough encouragement from the self-seeking patriots of the decade. An organization like the American Civil Liberties Union, the Federal Council of Churches, various social justice elements within specific religious groups, explicit social reform organizations like the American Birth Control League, the Consumer's League, the National Child Labor Committee, although in reality seeking to strengthen the system by eliminating its many defects, found basic communication difficult with a public conditioned to look askance at any but practitioners of normalcy.

Despite the general similarity through the decade of the sources of broad scale intolerance, its public manifestations took a variety of changing forms. The early fears of Bolshevism could not be exploited indefinitely especially when the sins committed in the name of its suppression were revealed and its purveyors were shown to be using it as a device for unscrupulous personal gain. Public indignation toward the excesses of the Palmer raids, for example, came quickly following the issuance by the National Popular Government League of the devastating report on the *Illegal Practices of the United States Department of Justice* in late May 1920. Such indignation was sufficient to drive those who might have sought to extend similar techniques to adopt far more subtle and clandestine modes of approach, and also to turn hysteria-making over to the private professional patriot organizations. Thus, William J. Burns, for example, after carefully instituting the Bridgeman raids of August 1922 turned to Ralph Easley of the National Civic Federation, Richard M. Whitney of the American Defense Society, and Joseph T. Cashman of the National Security League to arouse the public to a fever pitch over their implications.

Yet even Burns's string ran out in 1923–1924 as the misrule of the Department of Justice could no longer be ignored and as antiradicalism (labor by this time having been quite thoroughly tamed) was becoming a tiresome broken record. This is not to say, as Sidney Howard wrote bitterly at the time, that certain business interests might not find it useful to tar their critics by turning to the "services of radicalism in almost any one of their patriotic clashes with social liberalism or rambunctious unions, or, even, child labor reformers." But for the moment different targets were needed.

For those distressed with the growing disruption of their Gemeinschaft society, the Ku Klux Klan offered avenues for assaulting those most surely responsible. And while all Americans might not have agreed with C. Lewis Fowler, editor of the *American Standard,* that a heinous conspiracy to destroy America was afoot between Roman Catholicism and anti-Christian Jewry, the irrational myths and stereotyping surrounding these groups were sufficient to convince many they needed surveillance, if not repression. The Klan also impressed many with its pious objectives of uplifting the nation's morality through attacking its immoral desecrators. Atypical of the conservative, service-and-fellowship oriented organizations, or the professional patriot groups, stemming primarily from outside the urban business community, the Klan, nonetheless, for three or four years in the mid-1920s successfully attacked and insidiously exploited the shattering of old moral standards. Thereby the Klan could resort to direct action against progenitors of public immorality, as it did in the case of Judge Ben "Companionate Marriage" Lindsey in Denver. Indirectly, it could also inspire others to heed the clarion call to expose the evil forces which had to be behind the callous disregard of traditional ways, a call answered by Calvin Coolidge, for example, in his public exposé of "Reds" in our women's colleges, or by Texas representative Thomas L. Blanton's public assault on the ACLU which he branded the "UnAmerican Criminal License Union."

For those patriots seeking essentially to play a broker's role for powerful interests, intriguing new opportunities were opening up in antipacifism and the baiting of antimilitarists. The official demise of Burns left the tradition of his office to the War Department. By that time the Department was growing more apprehensive over the potential threat to its authority from antiwar sentiments that were increasingly prevalent as disillusion with the war experience intensified. As early as 1923, General Amos Fries, head of the Chemical Warfare Service, had publicly committed the government to support Preparedness Day, and by inference the continuation of an expanded military establishment. Fries had also encouraged Mrs. Lucia R. Maxwell, librarian of the Service, to prepare and circulate the famed "Spider Web Chart," which purported to study women's peace organizations in the United States and show, by ramification and association, that they were all Bolshevik inspired or at least deep pink. Although the War Department eventually ordered retraction, and directed Fries to inform persons to whom the chart had been circulated that its information was erroneous, the retraction fell on few careful ears. The chart was still being used by the Legion and the DAR in the early 1930s as an authentic exposé of the enemies of America. Such sentiments were also purveyed by such a professional militarist as General John J. Pershing, who in a series of lectures for the American Defense Society warned that "our situation is seriously complicated by the teachings of numerous pacifist organizations. . . ."

The concern with pacifism does not imply, however, that earlier hostility toward radicals, social reformers, and other public disrupters had ended. On the contrary, the development of pacifism as a term of opprobrium was merely adding another liability to the large series of undesirable personality traits that these enemies of America were supposed to possess, one which could be stressed more strongly when public apprehensions of radicalism were relatively deflated. Certainly as explosive public episodes developed—the Passaic Textile Strike, the furor over New York City's Stuyvesant High School, and by implication the use of any public building as a public forum even for liberals, the Colorado Mine War of late 1927, and above all the execution of Sacco and Vanzetti—the "Reds" and their dupes were held largely to blame, both for the episodes and for any number of people taking a remotely liberal view on the questions they raised. However, the dangers of such people could be brought home to a far more diversified audience if one talked of the "whole Pacifist-Radical-Communist movement in America [which] is foreign in its conception, if not actually under foreign influence, direction and control," or referred to such a leader as Roger Baldwin as a "slacker, radical, draft evader, and Leavenworth ex-convict."

And the most effective agents of intolerance came more and more to have this focus. By 1925, the heyday of the Klan was over. The enactment of the National Origins Act in 1924, internal strife (endemic in the order from its beginnings), and burgeoning prosperity, all undercut prior strength. In its annual report for 1927, the American Civil Liberties Union announced that the principal purveyors of intolerance in the country were the War Department, the American Legion, and professional patriot societies. It declared that the American Legion had by then "replaced the Klan as the most active agency of intolerance and repression in the country." The report was editorially criticized by Joseph Pulitzer's liberal New York *World* for such a value judgment, stating: "With scores of different organizations seeking to curtail liberty in scores of different ways, it is a wise man who can say that one is more active than any of the others." To which Forrest Bailey, Director of the ACLU, responded by merely pointing out that this was the consensus of all the state units reporting to national headquarters for the year.

It is not the purpose of this paper to attempt to explain the effect of the depression upon what had become fairly standard patterns of intolerance and intolerance-making. Nonetheless, certain clear developments can be recognized. On one hand, the professional patriots quickly found their traditional sources of income drying up. The National Civic Federation, for example, previously one of the bellwethers of such groups, was reduced to such belt-tightening by 1930 and the years following that its activities had to be cut to virtual ineffectiveness. Other comparable groups collapsed completely. Faced with similar problems the American Legion and the DAR found it expedient to do some of their cutting back in the area of antiradical activity. Pacifist-baiting no longer seemed a highly meaningful or relevant response to public problems.

On the other hand, vast evidence suggests that many businesses stepped up their antiradical activity. Deserting the intolerance purveyors who had formerly performed the function of subtly undermining and discrediting their critics, they now preferred to spend their money for direct action in the form of company guards, labor spies, strike breakers, and arms. Thus the American Civil Liberties Union could report a vast increase in the number of cases it received in the early depression years and generally the greatest suppression of individual liberties in the country since the days of the Red scare. Similarly, the number of instances of police brutality and flagrant abuse of local governmental power were well known.

If one is to talk in terms of meaningful and internally consistent cycles of public intolerance, an era ends in 1929–1930. By this time, to defend the status quo as unassailable was to make oneself ludicrous, since a casual glance revealed the magnitude of its defects. Significantly, when Representative Hamilton Fish auspiciously launched a series of congressional investigations in 1930 in an attempt to throw the blame for the depression on domestic "Reds," the results of his crusade were to produce either large-scale public apathy or large-scale public antipathy.

The imperfect public record of the 1920s then would seem to reveal that many interwoven factors produced a concatenation of syndromes which made the country a peculiarly fertile seedbed both for intolerance and its shrewd manipulation. These undoubtedly included the tensions of economic dynamism, grossly unequal distribution of wealth, enhanced urbanization with the dislocation it produced both in the urban area and in its rural recruitment grounds, virulent disillusionment with democracy, and the confusing and contradictory assumptions concerning the increasingly unpopular war experience.

A moot question still exists as to whether more precise results could not have been reached by placing heavier reliance on social science. Undoubtedly if public opinion poll information were available or if scientific attempts had been made at the time to quantify a variety of public attitudes, the record would be more approachable. Certainly steeping ourselves in a more sophisticated analysis of present and future events enhances the understanding of social and human processes in general and affords a more precise appreciation of human behavior in a past context. Certainly the types of questions which the empirical social researcher is currently asking can be asked of that decade and the historian is derelict if he fails to ask them. Yet the basic problem is still how to gain essential information now lacking and difficult or impossible to obtain. The social science researcher is not much help here. In fact, he operates on the assumption that unless sufficient information is available to permit arrival at quantitative answers, little of value can be produced and one's energies are wasted in the effort.

The historian, proceeding on the assumption that almost all important questions are important precisely because of their subtle implications and overtones, their complexities, ambiguities, and ambivalences—because in other words, they are not susceptible to quantitative answers—then must plod on his dogged and imperfect way. He must approach incomplete materials not only semi-analytically, but impressionistically and eclectically, even at times attempting to devise his own ways to evaluate a great divergency of data which the social scientist scarcely feels worth considering due to its impreciseness and unsuitability to quantitative analysis. But the historian likes to feel that only if serious attempt is made to assess all the data, regardless of its nature or its incompleteness, can anything resembling past reality possibly be attained. And as a humanist viewing essentially human phenomena, even if in so imprecise a fashion, the historian also likes to feel that he may, as Arthur M. Schlesinger, Jr., has suggested, "yield truths about both individual and social experience which quantitative social research by itself could never reach."

8

The New Deal

Revolutionary or Conservative?

Franklin Delano Roosevelt was perhaps the most controversial president ever to occupy the White House. For over twelve years he led the American people, first through the worst depression in their history and then through a war that encompassed virtually the entire globe. To his admirers he was an individual of heroic stature, a leader who firmly believed that it was possible to preserve free and democratic institutions by internal reforms without adopting authoritarian or totalitarian methods and overturning the basic structure of American society. To his enemies he was a misguided, even immoral, individual who mistakenly believed that he could save American democracy by taking the people down the road to the welfare state—a road that would eventually end in socialism and therefore the negation of individual freedom. Unlike some other presidents, Roosevelt had the uncanny ability to arouse strong passions. He was a person who was either loved or hated; few remained neutral toward him or reacted blandly to his personality or accomplishments.

Why did Roosevelt arouse such strong passions? The answer to this ostensibly simple question is anything but simple. Certainly there was little in his background or his accomplishments prior to 1933 that would explain the controversial nature of his presidential tenure. Even those friends and associates who worked closely with Roosevelt during his dozen years in the White House were not always able to grasp his many-sided personality or understand why he acted as he did. Frances Perkins, his long-time Secretary of Labor, described him as "the most complicated human being I ever knew," a comment that was echoed by others such as Henry Morgenthau and Robert E. Sherwood.

The controversy that surrounded Roosevelt's years in the White House has almost been matched by the quantity and quality of books written about him by friends, associates, and enemies. Unlike other presidents whose careers were not chronicled until decades after their death, Roosevelt has already been the subject of literally hundreds of books and articles. Part of the reason for this situation undoubtedly lies in the fact that much of the source material left by Roosevelt[1] and his associates was opened up to scholars within a surprisingly short time after his death in 1945. But part of the reason surely lies in the fascination with the New Deal and the changes that American society underwent during the years from 1933 to 1945. However the Roosevelt years were interpreted, it is difficult to avoid the conclusion that the United States was a very different nation in 1945 as compared with 1933.

It was the sheer magnitude of the New Deal innovations early in his presidential career that caused Roosevelt to become such a highly controversial figure. Although his victory in 1932 was relatively broad-based, he soon alienated many businessmen as well as other powerful interest groups. As a result, he came under increasingly harsh attacks as the 1930's progressed. Some accused him of subverting traditional American ideals of individualism and liberty by moving toward a welfare state that could end only in socialism and an omnipotent state. Such a staunch Democrat as Al Smith, for example, hotly argued during the presidential campaign of 1936 that Roosevelt was indeed taking the American people down the road to socialism. "It is all right with me if they [the Roosevelt Administration] want to disguise themselves as Norman Thomas or Karl Marx, or Lenin, or any of the rest of that bunch," Smith shouted, "but what I won't stand for is allowing them to march under the banner of Jefferson, Jackson and Cleveland."[2]

The attack on Roosevelt's New Deal from the right was echoed also by the critics of the left. There were many who felt that the traditional American attachment to individualistic values had been rendered obsolete by the nation's industrial and technological advances. Rexford G. Tugwell, a professor of economics and one of the early New Deal "brain trusters" was one such critic. He was convinced that America's competitive economy had never worked well; to attempt to reform it with minor changes would prove hopelessly inadequate. What was required, Tugwell concluded, was thorough and effective governmental planning for all aspects of the economic system; only in this way could the economy be stabilized and future depressions avoided. Much to his disappointment, the New Deal seemed too pragmatic. Roosevelt, he finally concluded, was either unwilling or unable to plan in a rational and systematic manner. To the left of men like Tugwell stood the Socialist and Communist groups in America. Their criticism was that the New Deal was too conservative; the only proper approach to the depression was a complete overhaul of America's social and economic system and the establishment of a socialist state.

---

[1] It has been estimated that Roosevelt's personal papers occupy more than 9,000 cubic feet at the Hyde Park Library; this figure does not include the papers of other important New Deal officials.

[2] Quoted in William E. Leuchtenburg, *Franklin D. Roosevelt and the New Deal 1932–1940* (New York, 1963), p. 178.

Thus, during the depression years the New Deal was attacked from many points of view. To some it was too radical; to others it was too conservative or reactionary. Still others viewed Roosevelt's policies as a series of pragmatic and expedient moves in response to specific events and deplored the fact that the President never seemed to give much thought to the overall dimensions of the crisis facing the American people. To be sure, many of these critics were reflecting to a large extent the passions and emotions of the age in which they were living. Faced with the problem of coming to grips with the greatest depression the country had ever known, they did not have the perspective nor the dispassionate attitude required to view the issues at stake in a detached or objective manner. Their criticisms, nevertheless, helped to establish the framework of reference with which later writers were to approach the New Deal. In brief, the question usually raised by contemporary commentators and later historians revolved around the role of the New Deal in American life. Was the New Deal simply an extension of the Progressive tradition, or did it involve a radical departure from the mainstream of American history?

For historians reared in the tradition of the Progressive school there was little doubt about the basic nature of the New Deal. Viewing America's past in terms of a conflict between liberalism and conservatism and the people versus the vested interests, they saw the New Deal as simply another phase in the struggle against monopoly, privilege, and special interests. To them the New Deal was related to earlier reform movements, including Jeffersonian and Jacksonian Democracy, Populism, and Progressivism, all of which had represented the people in their continuing struggle to achieve a greater measure of political, economic, and social equality. While they often referred to the revolutionary character of the New Deal, their use of the term "revolutionary" did not necessarily imply a sharp break with the past. Louis Hacker, although not squarely in the Progressive tradition, referred to the New Deal as the "Third American Revolution" in the mid-1940's. His description of the New Deal, however, was anything but revolutionary. Some of its policies, he wrote, were improvisations; some were descended from Populism and Progressivism; but always "there existed the thought that the responsibility of public authority for the welfare of the people was clear and that the intervention of the state was justifiable."[3] Hacker's last point, while by no means acceptable to all Americans, was hardly novel; reformers and intellectuals had been urging government-sponsored reforms since the mid-nineteenth century.

To Henry Steele Commager, one of America's most distinguished historians, the relationship between the New Deal and earlier reform movements was obvious. Writing at the time of Roosevelt's death,

---

[3]Louis M. Hacker, *The Shaping of the American Tradition* (New York, 1947), pp. 1125–1126.

Commager explicitly denied the revolutionary character of the New Deal. What was simply a new deal of old cards appeared radical for two reasons: the rapidity with which the New Deal program was enacted into law; and the fact that the movement contrasted so sharply with the do-nothing attitude of the Harding-Coolidge-Hoover administrations. If the New Deal was compared with the Progressive era rather than the 1920's, Commager maintained, "the contrast would have been less striking than the similarities. . . . [For] precedent for the major part of New Deal legislation was to be found in these earlier periods." The achievements of Roosevelt—the restoration of self-confidence, the reassertion of faith in democracy, and the rehabilitation of the nation's human and natural resources—all demonstrated the affinity of the New Deal to the earlier reform movements in American history.[4]

Perhaps the fullest and most eloquent argument favoring the idea that the New Deal was a continuation and extension of America's liberal past was advanced by the outstanding historian writing in the Progressive tradition, Arthur M. Schlesinger, Jr. A former professor at Harvard University, Schlesinger has been the most persuasive and brilliant historian writing within and in defense of America's liberal tradition. He was, of course, much more than a historian. A leading intellectual, important member of the Kennedy administration, and shrewd commentator on current affairs, Schlesinger has been an activist as well as a scholar. As a historian, Schlesinger since the close of World War II has championed a modified brand of American liberalism whose roots, he believed, go far back into the nation's history. Thus, his Pulitzer-prize winning study, *The Age of Jackson* (1945), argued that Jacksonian Democracy was a liberal political movement based on a coalition of urban workers and other democratic groups in American society. Schlesinger attempted also to rebuild the intellectual foundations of the liberal ideology in his writings. His book, *The Vital Center* (1948), incorporated Niebuhrian theology into the corpus of American liberalism so as to give the latter a more realistic and viable character. Taking cognizance of the reaction against liberal ideas since the 1940's, Schlesinger borrowed Reinhold Niebuhr's emphasis on original sin and reinterpreted the liberal ideology in order to purge that ideology of the charge that its utopian optimism had been unrealistic and its adherents had been incapable of meeting the challenge of totalitarianism since the 1930's.

All of American history, according to Schlesinger, was characterized by a cyclical movement which saw periods of liberal reform followed by alternate periods of conservative consolidation. In his eyes Jacksonian Democracy followed the decline of Jeffersonian Democracy, the Progressive era followed the age of the Robber Barons, and the New Deal

[4]Henry Steele Commager, "Twelve Years of Roosevelt," *American Mercury*, LX (April, 1945), pp. 391–401.

came after the sterile conservatism of the 1920's. Indeed, Schlesinger argued, the New Frontier of John F. Kennedy and the Great Society of Lyndon B. Johnson were themselves reactions to the inaction of the Eisenhower years. The generative force behind this cycle was social conflict—conflict which arose from a constant accumulation of dis- quietude and discontent within American society. Schlesinger spelled out his thesis in a series of books and articles, one of which was *The Age of Roosevelt,* a multi-volumed study of the New Deal.[5]

In the first selection Schlesinger discusses the origins of the New Deal. To him the New Deal represented much more than a mere re- sponse to the depression. On the contrary, the New Deal was an integral part of the history of American liberalism; it was another phase of the liberal-conservative cycle in American history. By the 1920's, Schlesinger claimed, the nation had tired of the Progressive crusade. National disinterest in politics meant that power gravitated inevitably toward powerful economic interests, and government increasingly came under the control and influence of the business community. As a result of this shift in power, there was a progressive alienation of various groups from American society, including the farmers, workers, minority ethnic groups, and disenchanted intellectuals. Even without a depres- sion, Schlesinger suggested, the New Deal was bound to have hap- pened in one form or another. What the depression did was to give the New Deal its particular character—a political movement responding to the immediate problem of an impending economic collapse. The New Deal, he concluded, rejected the dogmatic absolutes and the simplistic dichotomies posed in contemporary ideologies such as Communism and fascism. To Schlesinger the New Deal was a practical, energetic, and pragmatic movement based on the assumption that a "managed and modified capitalist order achieved by piecemeal experiment could com- bine personal freedom and economic growth."

Schlesinger's approach to the New Deal was echoed by other histo- rians. Frank Freidel, author of what appears to be the most definitive multi-volumed biography of Roosevelt, wrote in much the same his- toriographical tradition as that of Schlesinger. Freidel, however, posed the discussion in quite different terms. To him the New Deal was basi- cally the work of a number of persons who had grown to maturity during the Progressive era and who still shared the moral fervor of that period. Like Roosevelt, they were conservative men whose primary goal was to save rather than to destroy the free enterprise system. These humanitarian reformers were willing to use the machinery and authority of government to improve the lot of the common man. Taken as a

---

[5]Schlesinger has to date published three volumes of this study: *The Crisis of the Old Order, 1919–1933* (Boston, 1957), *The Coming of the New Deal* (Boston, 1958), and *The Politics of Upheaval* (Boston, 1960).

whole, the New Deal was based on "American objectives and experience in the Progressive Era and during the first World War."[6] To put it another way, Roosevelt's program was squarely within the American tradition; his goals were essentially to conserve the existing economic and social system by eliminating obvious defects rather than changing it by radical programs.

Historians such as Commager, Schlesinger, and Freidel were all favorably disposed to the New Deal because they identified themselves with the American liberal or Progressive tradition. This is not to imply that they were uncritical toward Roosevelt and the New Deal; in many instances they found much that was inadequate, wrong, or misleading about the goals, program, and administration of many New Deal experiments. Generally speaking, however, they wrote with approval of Roosevelt's pragmatism, his faith in American democracy, and his obvious distaste for totalitarian methods. The alternative to the New Deal, they hinted, might very well have been a dictatorship of the right or left if the nation had continued to drift along as it had under Hoover.

While such historians who identified themselves in the Progressive tradition were interpreting the New Deal in a favorable light, others, particularly those adhering to a conservative ideology, were writing in quite a different vein. Conceiving of individual freedom and competition in almost absolutist terms, they saw the New Deal as a violent departure from traditional American values. To them the New Deal was anything but a continuation of America's political tradition; it represented rather an outright rejection of everything that was good and desirable within that tradition. During the decade of the thirties, many critics, especially spokesmen of conservative social groups and businessmen, took this position on the New Deal. Former President Hoover, for example, sounded a note of warning in 1934 when he condemned the expansion of the federal government's role and the subsequent regimentation of American life. "It is a vast shift," he wrote, "from the American concept of human rights which even the government may not infringe to those social philosophies where men are wholly subjective to the state. It is a vast casualty to Liberty if it shall be continued."[7]

Hoover's hostility was matched by other writers like John T. Flynn, a former liberal who had become progressively disillusioned by America's liberal tradition. Author of several books on Roosevelt, Flynn's antagonism against the New Deal reached a peak in his work *The Roosevelt Myth*. Specifically denying the achievements that liberal historians had credited to the New Deal, he argued that Roosevelt had substituted for

---

[6]Frank Freidel, *The New Deal in Historical Perspective* (2nd ed.: Washington, D.C., 1965), p. 6. To date Freidel has published four volumes of his study of Roosevelt: *Franklin D. Roosevelt: The Apprenticeship* (Boston, 1952), *The Ordeal* (Boston, 1954), *The Triumph* (Boston, 1956), and *Launching the New Deal* (Boston, 1973).

[7]Herbert Hoover, *The Challenge to Liberty* (New York, 1934), p. 103.

the free enterprise system one that operated upon "permanent crises and an armament economy." In the process of implementing New Deal programs, the vigor of state governments had been sapped, the authority of Congress had been eroded, and unprecedented power had been concentrated in the hands of the president. One result of Roosevelt's New Deal policies was the appearance of a staggering federal debt; "a debt that can never be paid and which can be taken off our shoulders only by a great and devastating inflation."[8]

The charge by conservative writers that the New Deal represented a break with the past, interestingly enough, was echoed by some Progressive historians. One of these was Richard Hofstadter who, although writing within a liberal framework, was among the severest critics of America's liberal tradition. American liberalism, Hofstadter argued, had failed because of its moralizing tendencies and its inability to come to grips with the fundamental issues of the day. In *The Age of Reform: From Bryan to F.D.R.*, he insisted that the New Deal could not under any circumstances be interpreted as a continuation of the liberal-Progressive tradition. The section in his book devoted to the New Deal was appropriately entitled "The New Departure."

To Hofstadter the New Deal was markedly different from any other indigenous American political movement. Past reform movements, Hofstadter noted, had generally operated under the assumption that their purpose was to clear the way for new enterprises and new men—to smash established privilege and monopoly and to provide all Americans with an equal opportunity in life. Within this context, the national government was considered to be either negative in its nature or an obstacle in the way of success. Earlier reform movements had taken it for granted that American society was essentially a healthy society but one that needed further democratization to reach its full potential.

The New Deal, according to Hofstadter, was based on entirely different premises. Instead of viewing American society as healthy, New Deal reformers saw it as a sick society in need of changes that could only be instituted through federal action. Thus the New Deal accepted the idea of federal responsibility for the relief of the unemployed, supported legislation for social security, unemployment insurance, wages and hours, and public housing, and did not fear massive expenditures that resulted in deficit spending. Many of the traditional aims of past reform movements—to restore government to the people and to destroy big business and monopolies—were simply bypassed or ignored by Roosevelt. Considering the nature and magnitude of New Deal programs, Hofstadter concluded, the movement had to be considered a new departure in American life. "The New Deal, and the thinking it engendered," wrote Hofstadter, "represented the triumph of economic

---

[8]John T. Flynn, *The Roosevelt Myth* (rev. ed.: New York, 1956), pp. 414, 445.

emergency and human needs over inherited notions and inhibitions. . . .
At the core of the New Deal, then, was not a philosophy (F.D.R. could
identify himself philosophically only as a Christian and democrat), but
an attitude, suitable for practical politicians, administrators, and technicians, but uncongenial to the moralism that the Progressives had for the
most part shared with their opponents."[9]

The New Deal, Hofstadter pointed out with an ironic touch, represented a reversal of the usual ideological roles of American conservatives
and reformers. The conservatives had traditionally prided themselves
on their sense of realism, their distrust of abstract plans for remaking
society, and their belief in the necessity for institutional continuity. Reformers, on the other hand, had invariably appealed to moral sentiments, denounced existing injustices, and aroused the indignation of
the community. By the 1930's, however, the traditional roles of the two
had become reversed. Reformers appealed not to moral abstractions, but
to concrete grievances of specific groups—farmers without markets, unemployed men without bread, laborers seeking to organize in unions of
their own choosing, and to those groups concerned with the soundness
of banks, investment markets, and manufacturing enterprises. Conservatives were now in the position of moral critics—they denounced the
New Deal precisely because of its violation of traditional rules, its abandonment of the nation's moral heritage, its departure from sound principles, and its imposition of a federal tyranny upon the American
people.

Oddly enough, Hofstadter was unhappy with the efforts of both
conservatives and reformers. The reformers from the New Deal on,
according to him, had refused to think in terms of rational planning and
remained content to respond in a pragmatic way to individual pressures
and situations as they arose. The criticisms of the conservatives, on the
other hand, were "hollow and cliche-ridden," the complaints of a class
increasingly cut off from the world of reality. But all that Hofstadter
could do—at least in his role as historian and contemporary critic—was
to hope that a better understanding of America's past political tradition
might help future politicians to formulate a more realistic philosophy.

A similar criticism was voiced by Rexford G. Tugwell, a Columbia
University professor who had joined Roosevelt's administration in the
early 1930's as a strong advocate of governmental economic planning.
The old faith in a self-regulating market, he maintained, had never been
justified; it was part of the American mythology of a free enterprise
system. Distrustful of business and businessmen, Tugwell felt that only
the federal government was in a position to control the economy in such
a way as to make it run smoothly and efficiently.

---

[9]Richard Hofstadter, *The Age of Reform: From Bryan to F.D.R.* (New York, 1955), pp. 314,
323.

After leaving government service to return to the academic world, Tugwell set out to write a biography of Roosevelt, which was finally published in 1957, although parts had appeared in a series of long articles somewhat earlier. The picture Tugwell drew of Roosevelt and the New Deal was a friendly one, but one also marked with a sense of disappointment. According to Tugwell, the productive capacity of the American economy by the late 1920's had far outrun purchasing power, thus giving rise to a fundamental maladjustment which resulted in the depression. The Republicans under Hoover initially denied that the economic situation was serious. Later they adopted half-way measures and encouraged private rather than public relief. When Roosevelt came to power, he was faced with a grave emergency but one which gave him an unprecedented opportunity such as no other president had had. Although he was a master improviser and politician, Roosevelt never conceived of New Deal measures in terms of rational planning. Many of the New Deal innovations, indeed, resulted from careful balancing between the claims of various competing pressure groups. Roosevelt, Tugwell concluded, was a political pragmatist with a progressive bent. Despite his essential greatness, he was unable or unwilling to seize the opportunity and institute far-reaching reform measures. Whether future historians would continue to look upon the New Deal in this manner, Tugwell admitted, was an open question. [10]

Both Hofstadter and Tugwell were critical of Roosevelt because of his political opportunism and his pragmatic approach to serious problems. Implicit in their writings was the belief that the New Deal could not be interpreted as a part of America's liberal tradition. Oddly enough, they were in agreement with recent neo-conservative historians who had also rejected the thesis that American history could be understood in terms of class and ideological conflict. In the eyes of these more recent historians, American history had been marked not by conflict and divisions, but by stability and unity. Domestic struggles in the United States, they maintained, were over means, never over ends. To look upon the politics of the 1930's as an expression of fundamental divisions among the American people, they concluded, was a mistake.

But if the New Deal did not reflect fundamental class and ideological divisions, what did it reflect? To Heinz Eulau, a political scientist at Stanford University writing in essentially a neo-conservative vein, the New Deal defied ideological classification. It is true, he admitted, that many individuals associated with Roosevelt had their own particular blueprints for the reconstruction of American society. Taken as a whole, however, the New Deal had many sides, and for this reason was not the

---

[10]Rexford G. Tugwell, "The New Deal in Retrospect," *Western Political Quarterly*, I (December, 1948), pp. 373–385. See also Tugwell's full length study of Roosevelt, *The Democratic Roosevelt* (New York, 1957).

product of a cohesive and rational ideology. Nor did the New Deal articulate a faith in a better tomorrow; it did not call upon people to join a crusade to remake their society or to experiment with new and untried schemes. But if the New Deal was not an ideology, a faith, a crusade, an experiment, a revolt, or a charisma, what was it? To Eulau the answer to this question was clear. The New Deal, he suggested, was "both a symbol and evidence of the nation's political maturity"; it represented an effort to solve problems "through politics rather than through ideology or violence." In Eulau's eyes a mature politics involves adjustment, compromise, and integration. By this standard the New Deal symbolized a mature politics because it was seeking solutions to problems rather than imposing preconceived solutions on problems.[11]

By implication Eulau was agreeing with those neo-conservative historians who rejected class and ideological interpretations of American history in favor of an approach that emphasized the stability of American institutions and the pragmatism of American culture. The distinguishing characteristic of American history, therefore, was a rejection of the unrealistic intellectual and ideological characteristics of European thought and the substitution in their place of common sense. To writers like Eulau the New Deal must be understood as part of the basic common-sense approach of most Americans and their rejection of the world of ideology. In this sense the New Deal was not comparable to earlier liberal movements; the New Deal was simply an attempt to cope with unique problems in a simple and sensible manner.

During the 1960's the stature of Franklin D. Roosevelt and the New Deal again began to change as younger scholars asked some searching questions. If the New Deal had modified and humanized American society, why did poverty and racism continue to exist? If the New Deal had truly reformed an unbridled capitalism and made it more responsive to the needs of people, why were so many different groups—blacks, Puerto Ricans, Mexican Americans, and middle-class youths—alienated from their society? If the New Deal had led to a change for the better in terms of America's role in world affairs, how had the nation become involved first in the Korean War and then in the Vietnam conflict? Given the tensions and crises of the 1960's, it was perhaps inevitable that the historical image of the New Deal would once again change.

Perhaps the sharpest critique—though by no means the only one— came from the pens of historians identified with the "New Left." Many of these scholars were committed to radical changes in the structure of American society and they saw history as a discipline that would illuminate the present by a searching examination of the past. We have "sought explicitly," wrote the editor of a book of essays representing in

---

[11]Heinz Eulau, "Neither Ideology Nor Utopia: The New Deal in Retrospect," *Antioch Review*, XIX (Winter, 1959–1960), pp. 523–537.

part "New Left" scholarship, "to make the past speak to the present, to ask questions that have a deep-rooted moral and political relevance. In moving occasionally beyond description and causal analysis to judge significance, we have, by necessity, moved beyond objective history in the realm of values."[12]

Given their own values and commitment to social change, it was natural that radical historians would see the New Deal in an unfavorable light. In an essay discussing the place of the New Deal in American history, for example, Barton J. Bernstein argued that the liberal reforms of the 1930's had not transformed the American system; rather they conserved and protected corporate capitalism. Nor had the New Deal significantly redistributed power in any way, or granted any meaningful recognition to unorganized peoples. Even its bolder programs had not extended the beneficence of government beyond affluent groups or used the wealth of the few for the needs of the many. The New Deal followed essentially conservative goals, for it was intended to maintain the American system intact. "The New Deal," Bernstein concluded, "failed to solve the problem of depression, it failed to raise the impoverished, it failed to redistribute income, it failed to extend equality and generally countenanced racial discrimination and segregation. It failed generally to make business more responsible to the social welfare or to threaten business's pre-eminent political power.... In acting to protect the institution of private property and in advancing the interests of corporate capitalism, the New Deal assisted the middle and upper sectors of society. It protected them, sometimes, even at the cost of injuring the lower sectors. Seldom did it bestow much of substance upon the lower classes."[13]

From the vantage point of the political left, therefore, the New Deal was a failure. Committed to capitalism, it could not offer the lower classes anything but rhetoric and psychological comfort. So wrote even Paul K. Conkin in a penetrating analysis of Roosevelt and the New Deal. Judging the New Deal more from the perspective of a social democrat rather than a partisan of the "New Left," he expressed considerable admiration for Roosevelt's political astuteness and charismatic qualities. Yet Conkin denied that Roosevelt was even a pragmatist, for his thought was too shallow and superficial and concerned largely with immediate issues. "For the historian," noted Conkin in his critical but compassionate summation, "every judgment, every evaluation of the past has to be tinged with a pinch of compassion, a sense of the beauty and nobility present when honest hopes and humane ideals are frustrated. He sees

---

[12]Barton J. Bernstein, ed., *Towards a New Past: Dissenting Essays in American History* (New York, 1968), p. xiii.

[13]Barton J. Bernstein, "The New Deal: The Conservative Achievements of Liberal Reform," in *ibid.*, pp. 264, 281–282.

that the thirties could have brought so much more, but also so much worse, than the New Deal. The limiting context has to be understood— the safeguards and impediments of our political system, Roosevelt's intellectual limitations, and most of all the appalling economic ignorance and philosophic immaturity of the American electorate. . . . The New Deal solved a few problems, ameliorated a few more, obscured many, and created new ones. This is about all our political system can generate, even in crisis."[14]

Much of the historiography of the New Deal, therefore, reflected to some degree personal ideological commitments. To Progressive scholars Roosevelt was a hero; to conservatives he was too radical; and to radicals he was too conservative, if not reactionary. Each group, of course, judged Roosevelt in terms of the direction they felt America *should* have taken.

In a major study of New Deal economic policy, however, Ellis W. Hawley approached the problem quite differently. Americans, he noted, shared a commitment to two value systems that were not wholly compatible. On the one hand, they cherished liberty and freedom, which implied a competitive economic and social order. On the other hand, they valued order, rationality, and collective organization and associated large business units and economic organizations generally with abundance, progress, and a rising standard of living. Yet the latter value posed a potential threat to the former; monopoly negated, at least in theory, freedom and competition. Much of twentieth-century American history, Hawley observed, revolved around the search for a solution "that would preserve the industrial order, necessarily based upon a high degree of collective organization, and yet would preserve America's democratic heritage at the same time." New Deal economic policy mirrored this basic ambivalence; it vacillated between rational planning and antimonopoly, neither of which was completely compatible. Hawley's conclusion offered little support to any of the competing ideologies that underlay many of the historical interpretations of Roosevelt and the New Deal. "If the experiences of the nineteen thirties have any relevance at all," he wrote, "it is in illustrating the limitations of logical analysis, the pitfalls inherent in broad theoretical approaches, the difficulty of agreeing on policy goals, and the necessity of making due allowances for the intellectual heritage, current trends of opinion, and the realities of pressure-group politics." The second selection in this chapter is an excerpt from Hawley's influential study.

Considering, then, the many ways historians have written about the New Deal, is it possible to come to any sort of definitive conclusions about its essential nature? Can Roosevelt and the New Deal be positioned precisely in terms of their place within the American political

---

[14]Paul K. Conkin, *The New Deal* (New York, 1967).

tradition? In dealing with this question, it should be emphasized that many of the apparent differences between students writing about the New Deal are partly semantical in nature. When describing the operation of specific New Deal programs, for example, the differences of opinion between historians tend to narrow sharply. Thus, what the W.P.A., N.R.A., and other federal agencies *did* is often not a subject of dispute. The issue that invariably leads to conflict is the *intent* of the participants involved. The controversy involves not the relief activities of the 1930's, to cite one instance, but whether or not the concept of federal relief undermined the cherished American ideals of individualism and liberty.

The semantic difficulty may be seen in the various ways historians have used the word "pragmatic." When Roosevelt was described as a "pragmatic leader," what did this mean? Actually the term was used in at least three different ways. Edgar E. Robinson, for example, has described Roosevelt's personal leadership as "pragmatic—an individual playing by ear." What Robinson meant by his characterization was that Roosevelt, in order to gain an immediate political advantage, never considered the long-range effects of his policies. "Roosevelt's failure," Robinson concluded, "lay in his unsuccessful attempt to justify the means or establish the ends he had in view." Underlying Robinson's thesis was the criticism that the New Deal resulted in an almost fatal concentration of power in the hands of the executive—a "power that could destroy the world or build it in the image of an entirely new scientific perspective."[15]

A second use of the term "pragmatic," as we have already seen in Tugwell's case, involved the criticism that Roosevelt never even understood the need for long-range economic planning. Roosevelt limited himself to immediate problems and tended to neglect more fundamental issues. Consequently, he never took advantage of the unparalleled opportunity for reform that arose out of the greatest single economic crisis that the American people had ever faced. While New Deal measures were important in giving status and material benefits to groups in American society that had been hitherto neglected, relatively speaking, these reforms fell short of their real potential. This view of Roosevelt, which has been echoed by many writers, is based on the underlying assumption that New Deal pragmatism and rational governmental planning were incompatible.

The term "pragmatic" has been used in a third way to describe a mental attitude and frame of mind that rejected the dogmatic thinking of the 1930's and remained open and receptive to new ideas. William E. Leuchtenberg, a Columbia University historian, has argued that the

---

[15]Edgar Eugene Robinson, *The Roosevelt Leadership 1933–1945* (Philadelphia, 1955), pp. 383, 397, 408.

"pragmatism" of the New Deal seemed striking only because the period as a whole was characterized by rigid ideological thinking. The New Deal was pragmatic, Leuchtenberg maintained, "only in contrast to the rigidity of Hoover and of the Left." Moreover, the movement was pragmatic in the sense that reformers themselves remained skeptical about final utopias and ultimate solutions and were always open to experimentation. To Leuchtenberg the New Deal was more than a movement to experiment or to improvise; it was a movement led by men who were committed to the proposition that it was possible to make human life more tolerable, that depressions were by no means inevitable events, and that human affairs were not necessarily guided by inexorable deterministic laws.[16]

The problem of understanding and assessing the achievements of the New Deal and its place in American history, therefore, is one whose answer will largely be determined by a series of prior assumptions about the nature of the American past and the nation's ideals in both the present and the future. To those historians whose view is that America is founded upon an atomistic philosophy—that the nation's greatness arose from the achievements of talented and ambitious individuals and was not related to the activities of the government—the New Deal will always appear as a movement alien and hostile to traditional values. In this context the New Deal represents a new departure in American history that will end perhaps in a collectivistic and authoritarian government. On the other hand, to those scholars who adhere to a corporate philosophy—that society is more than a mere aggregate of private individuals and that a modern complex industrial economy requires a certain amount of public regulation as well as government-sponsored reform—the New Deal becomes a political movement inspired by proper ideals. Instead of being an aberration in terms of the American political tradition, the New Deal was a movement consonant with previous struggles for justice and equality. Finally, to those historians who maintain that only a radical restructuring of American society could eliminate poverty, racism, war, and inequality, the New Deal appears as a palliative or sham designed to gloss over fundamental defects.

The problem of judging the nature and accomplishments of the New Deal is, then, a difficult one, for it involves the entire fabric of the American past. Indeed, to avoid any broad judgments is in effect to render a judgment, albeit on an unconscious level. In the final analysis, therefore, historians will continue to grapple with the place of the New Deal in American life. Was the New Deal a continuation of America's liberal tradition or was it a repudiation of that tradition? Did the New Deal reflect an attempt by corporate capitalism to maintain its power

---

[16]William E. Leuchtenberg, *Franklin D. Roosevelt and the New Deal 1932–1940* (New York, 1963), pp. 344–345.

intact by forging a partnership with the federal government with the latter in a subordinate position? Or did the New Deal give a significant voice to minority groups that in the past had been powerless? Can the New Deal even be understood in ideological terms or should it be viewed as a political movement characterized by an underlying pragmatism? Or were the alleged inconsistencies of the New Deal a reflection of the underlying commitment of Americans to the values of order and freedom, which in turn gave rise to ambivalent policies? These are only some of the broad questions that must be answered in order to assess the nature and significance of the New Deal.[17]

[17]For a penetrating analysis of the historical literature on the New Deal see Alfred B. Rollins, Jr., "Was There Really a Man Named Roosevelt?," in *American History: Retrospect and Prospect,* edited by George A. Billias and Gerald N. Grob (New York, 1971), pp. 232–270.

Arthur M. Schlesinger, Jr.

ARTHUR M. SCHLESINGER, JR. (1917–   ) is Albert Schweitzer Professor of the Humanities at the City University of New York. He was also a Special Assistant to President John F. Kennedy. Among his many published works are *The Age of Jackson* (1945), *The Age of Roosevelt* (1956–   ), and *A Thousand Days: John F. Kennedy in the White House* (1965).

In the background of any historical episode lies all previous history. The strands which a historian may select as vital to an understanding of the particular episode will vary widely according to his interest, his temperament, his faith and his time. Each man must unravel the seamless web in his own way. I do not propose here any definitive assessment of the sources of the New Deal. I doubt whether a final assessment is possible. I want rather to call attention to certain possible sources which may not have figured extensively in the conventional accounts, including my own—to the relation of the New Deal to the ebb and flow of American national politics and then its relation to the international dilemma of free society in this century.

Such relationships are speculative; nonetheless, an attempt to see them may perhaps cast light on some of the less discussed impulses behind the New Deal itself. To begin—and in order to make a sharp issue—let me ask this question: would there have been a New Deal if there had been no depression? Without a depression, would we have had nothing but a placid continuation, so long as prosperity itself continued, of the New Era of the Twenties?

I would answer that there would very likely have been some sort of New Deal in the Thirties even without the Depression. I think perhaps our contemporary thinking has come too unreflectively to assume depression as the necessary preliminary for any era of reform. Students of American history know better. The fight against depression was, to be sure, the heart of the New Deal, but it has not been the central issue of traditional American reform: it was not the heart of Jeffersonian democracy nor of Jacksonian democracy nor of the anti-slavery movement nor of the Progressive movement.

What preceded these other epochs of reform was an accumulation of

Arthur M. Schlesinger, Jr., "Sources of the New Deal: Reflections on the Temper of a Time," *Columbia University Forum*, II (Fall, 1959), pp. 4–12. Copyright © 1959 by Columbia University. Reprinted from *The Columbia University Forum* by permission.

disquietudes and discontents in American society, often non-economic in character, and producing a general susceptibility to appeals for change—this and the existence within society of able men or groups who felt themselves cramped by the status quo and who were capable of exploiting mounting dissatisfaction to advance policies and purposes of their own. This combination of outsiders striving for status and power and a people wearying of the existing leadership and the existing ideals has been the real archetype of American reform.

The official order in the Twenties presented perhaps the nearest we ever came in our history to the identification of the national interest with the interests, values and goals of a specific class—in this case, of course, the American business community. During the generation before Harding, the political leaders who had commanded the loyalties and the energies of the American people—Theodore Roosevelt and Woodrow Wilson—expressed strains in American life distinct from and often opposed to the dominant values of business. They represented a fusion of patrician and intellectual attitudes which saw in public policy an outlet for creative energy—in Lippmann's phrase, they stood for mastery as against drift. In the service of this conception, they led the people into great national efforts of various sorts, culminating in the convulsive and terrible experience of war. Two decades of this—two decades under the glittering eyes of such leaders as Roosevelt and Wilson, Bryan and La Follette—left the nation in a state of exhaustion.

By 1920 the nation was tired of public crisis. It was tired of discipline and sacrifice. It was tired of abstract and intangible objectives. It could gird itself no longer for heroic moral or intellectual effort. Its instinct for idealism was spent. "It is only once in a generation," Wilson himself had said, "that a people can be lifted above material things. That is why conservative government is in the saddle two-thirds of the time." And the junior official to whom he made this remark, the young Assistant Secretary of the Navy, also noted soon after his unsuccessful try for the Vice-Presidency in 1920, "Every war brings after it a period of materialism and conservatism; people tire quickly of ideals and we are now repeating history." John W. Davis, the Democratic candidate in 1924, said a few years later: "The people usually know what they want at a particular time . . . In 1924 when I was a candidate what they wanted was repose."

A nation fatigued with ideals and longing for repose was ready for "normalcy." As popular attention receded from public policy, as values and aspirations became private again, people stopped caring about politics, which meant that political power inevitably gravitated to society's powerful economic interests—the government of the exhausted nation quite naturally fell to the businessmen. And for nearly a decade the business government reigned over a prosperous and expanding country.

Yet, for all the material contentment of the Twenties, the decade was also marked by mounting spiritual and psychological discontent. One could detect abundant and multiplying symptoms of what Josiah Royce, after Hegel, used to call a self-estranged social order. The official creed began to encounter growing skepticism, and even opposition and ridicule, in the community at large. Able and ambitious groups, denied what they considered fitting recognition or opportunity, began to turn against the Establishment.

If the economic crash of 1929 astonished the experts, a spiritual crash was diagnosed well in advance. "By 1927," reported Scott Fitzgerald, "a widespread neurosis began to be evident, faintly signalled, like a nervous beating of the feet, by the popularity of crossword puzzles." In the same year Walter Lippmann pointed more soberly to the growing discrepancy between the nominal political issues of the day and the actual emotions of the people. If politics took up these real issues, Lippmann said, it would revolutionize the existing party system. "It is not surprising, then, that our political leaders are greatly occupied in dampening down interest, in obscuring issues, and in attempting to distract attention from the realities of American life."

What was wrong with the New Era was not (as yet) evidence of incompetence or stupidity in public policy. Rather, there was a profound discontent with the monopoly of power and prestige by a single class and the resulting indifference of the national government to deeper tensions. Those excluded from the magic circle suffered boredom, resentment, irritation and eventually indignation over what seemed the intolerable pretensions and irrelevances of their masters. Now it is the gravest error to underrate the power of boredom as a factor in social change. Our political scientists have pointed out convincingly how the human tendency toward inertia sets limits on liberalism; I wish they would spend equal time showing how the human capacity for boredom sets limits on conservatism. The dominant official society—the Establishment—of the Twenties was an exceedingly boring one, neither bright nor witty nor picturesque nor even handsome, and this prodded the human impulse to redress the balance by kicking up heels in back streets.

All this encouraged the defection of specific groups from a social order which ignored their needs and snubbed their ambitions. Within the business community itself there were dissident individuals, especially in the underdeveloped areas of the country, who considered that opportunities for local growth were unduly restrained by Wall Street's control of the money market. The farmers felt themselves shut out from the prevailing prosperity. Elements in the labor movement resented their evident second-class citizenship. Members of foreign nationality groups, especially the newer immigration and its children, chafed under the prevalent assumption that the real America was Anglo-Saxon, Protestant, middle-class and white. In time some of the younger people of the nation began to grow restless before the ideals held out to them; while others, in accepting these ideals, acquired a smug mediocrity which even depressed some of their elders.

Gravest among the symptoms was the defection of the intellectuals: writers, educators, newspapermen, editors—those who manned the machinery of opinion and who transmitted ideas. The fact of their particular estrangement and discontent guaranteed the articulation, and thus, to a degree, the coordination of the larger unrest. The intellectuals put the ruling class in its place by substituting for its own admiring picture of itself a set of disrespectful images, which an increasing number of people found delightful and persuasive; the insiders, who had before been seen in the reverent terms of Bruce Barton and the *American Magazine,* were now to be seen less reverently through the eyes of H. L. Mencken and Sinclair Lewis. Satire liberated people from the illusion of business infallibility and opened their minds to other visions of American possibility. The next function of the intellectuals was precisely to explore and substantiate those other visions. They did so with zest and ingenuity; and the result was that, beneath the official crust, the Twenties billowed with agitation, criticism and hope. Dewey affirmed man's capability for social invention and management; Beard argued that intelligent national planning was the irresistible next phase in history; Parrington insisted that Jeffersonian idealism had a sound basis in the American past, and indeed, expressed a truer Americanism than did materialism. Together the satirists and the prophets drew a new portrait of America—both of the American present and of the American promise—and the increasingly visible discrepancy between what was and what might be in America armed the spreading discontent.

The well of idealism was rising again; energies were being replenished, batteries recharged. Outsiders were preparing to hammer on the gates of the citadel. The 1928 election, in which an Irish Catholic challenged Yankee Protestant supremacy, illustrated the gathering revolt against the Establishment. And, though Hoover won the election, Samuel Lubell has pointed out that "Smith split not only the Solid South, but the Republican North as well." Smith carried counties which had long been traditionally Republican; he smashed the Republican hold on the cities; he mobilized the new immigrants. In losing, he polled nearly as many votes as Calvin Coolidge had polled in winning four years before. He stood for the vital new tendencies of politics; and it is likely that the prolongation of these tendencies would have assured a national Democratic victory, without a depression, in 1932 or certainly by 1936. And such a Democratic victory would surely have meant the discharge into public life of able and ambitious people denied preference under a business administration—much the same sort of people, indeed, who eventually came to power with the New Deal; and it would have meant new opportunities for groups that had seen the door slammed in their faces in the Twenties—labor, the farmers, the ethnic minorities, the intellectuals.

The suspicion that a political overturn was due even without a depression is fortified, I think, by the calculations of my father in his essay of some years back "The Tides of National Politics." In this essay he proposed that liberal and conservative periods in our national life succeeded themselves at intervals of about fifteen or sixteen years; this alternation takes place, he wrote, without any apparent correlation with economic circumstances or, indeed, with anything else, except the ebb and flow of national political psychology. By this argument, a liberal epoch was due in America around 1934 or 1935, depression or no.

In short, the New Deal was, among other things, an expression of what would seem—to use a currently unfashionable concept—an inherent cyclical rhythm in American politics. The Depression did not cause the cycle: what the Depression did was to increase its intensity and deepen its impact by superimposing on the normal cycle the peculiar and unprecedented urgencies arising from economic despair. One might even argue—though I do not think I would—that the Depression coming at another stage in the cycle would not necessarily have produced a New Deal. It is certainly true, as I said, that depressions did not induce epochs of reform in 1873 or in 1893. I think myself, however, that the magnitude of the shock made a political recoil almost certain after 1929. Still, the fact that this recoil took a liberal rather than a reactionary turn may well be due to the accident that the economic shock coincided with a liberal turn in the political cycle.

In any event, the fact remains that the historical New Deal, whether or not something like it might have come along anyway, was after all brought into being by the Depression. It assumed its particular character as it sought to respond to the challenge of economic collapse. And, in confronting this challenge, it was confronting a good deal more than merely an American problem. Mass unemployment touched the very roots of free institutions everywhere. "This problem of unemployment," as Winston Churchill said in England in 1930, "is the most torturing that can be presented to civilized society." The problem was more than torturing; it was something civilized society had to solve if it were to survive. And the issue presented with particular urgency was whether representative democracy could ever deal effectively with it.

Churchill, in the same Romanes lecture at Oxford in 1930, questioned whether it could: democratic governments, he said, drifted along the lines of least resistance, took short views, smoothed their path with platitudes, and paid their way with sops and doles. Parliaments, he suggested, could deal with political problems, but not with economic. "One may even be pardoned," Churchill said, "for doubting whether institutions based on adult suffrage could possibly arrive at the right decisions upon the intricate propositions of modern business and finance." These were delicate problems requiring specialist treatment. "You cannot cure cancer by a majority. What is wanted is a remedy."

The drift of discussion in the United States as well as in Britain in the early Thirties revealed an increasingly dour sense of existing alternatives; on the one hand, it seemed, was parliamentary democracy with economic chaos; on the other, economic authoritarianism with political tyranny. Even more dour was the sense that history had already made the choice—that the democratic impulse was drained of vitality, that liberalism was spent as a means of organizing human action. Consider a selection of statements from American writers at the time, and their mortuary resonance:

> The rejection of democracy is nowadays regarded as evidence of superior wisdom. (Ralph Barton Perry)
> The moral and intellectual bankruptcy of liberalism in our time needs no demonstration. It is as obvious as rain and as taken for granted. (Nathaniel Peffer)
> To attempt a defense of democracy these days is a little like defending paganism in 313 or the divine right of kings in 1793. It is taken for granted that democracy is bad and that it is dying. (George Boas)
> 'Liberalism is dead.' So many people who seem to agree upon nothing else have agreed to accept these three sweeping words. (Joseph Wood Krutch)
> Modern Western civilization is a failure. That theory is now generally accepted. (Louise Maunsell Fields)
> Why is it that democracy has fallen so rapidly from the high prestige which it had at the Armistice? . . . Why is it that in America itself—in the very temple and citadel of democracy—self-government has been held up to every ridicule, and many observers count it already dead? (Will Durant)

Only the most venerable among us can remember the creeping fear of a quarter of a century ago that the free system itself had run out of energy, that we had reached, in a phrase Reinhold Niebuhr used as a part of the title of a book in 1934, the "end of an era." What this pessimism implied for the realm of public policy was that democracy had exhausted its intellectual and moral resources, its bag of tricks was played out, and salvation now lay in moving over to a system of total control.

In affirming that there was no alternative between laissez-faire and tyranny, the pessimists were endorsing a passionate conviction held both by the proponents of individualism and the proponents of collectivism. Ogden Mills spoke with precision for American conservatives: "We can have a free country or a socialistic one. We cannot have both. Our economic system cannot be half free and half socialistic . . . There is no middle ground between governing and being governed, between absolute sovereignty and liberty, between tyranny and freedom." Herbert Hoover was equally vehement: "Even partial regimentation cannot be made to work and still maintain live democratic institutions." In such sentiments, Hoover and Mills would have commanded the enthusiastic assent of Stalin and Mussolini. The critical question was whether a middle way was possible—a mixed system which might give the state more power than conservatives would like, enough power, indeed, to assure economic and social security, but still not too much as to create dictatorship. To this question the Hoovers, no less than the Stalins and Mussolinis, had long since returned categorical answers. They all agreed on this, if on nothing else: no.

As I have said, economic planning was not just an American problem. Great Britain, for example, was confronting mass unemployment and economic stagnation; moreover, she had had since 1929 a Labor government. In a sense, it would have been hard to select a better place to test the possibilities of a tranquil advance from laissez-faire capitalism to a managed society. Here was a Labor leadership, sustained by a faith in the "inevitability of gradualness," ruling a nation committed by tradition and instinct to the acceptance of empirical change. How did the British Labor government visualize its problem and opportunity?

The central figures in the Labor government of 1929 were Ramsay MacDonald, now Prime Minister for the second time, and Philip Snowden, his sharp and dominating Chancellor of the Exchequer. Both were classic Socialists who saw in the nationalization of basic industry the answer to all economic riddles. Yet in the existing political situation, with a slim Labor majority, nationalization was out of the question. With socialism excluded, MacDonald and Snowden—indeed, nearly all the Labor party leaders—could see no alternative to all-out socialism but nearly all-out laissez-faire. A capitalist order had to be operated on capitalist principles. The economic policy of the Labor government was thus consecrated as faithfully as that of Herbert Hoover's Republican administration in the United States to the balanced budget and the gold standard—and, far more faithfully than American Republicanism, to free trade.

Socialism across the Channel was hardly more resourceful. As the German Social Democrat Fritz Naphtali put it in 1930, "I don't believe that we can do very much, nor anything very decisive, from the point of view of economic policy, to overcome the crisis until it has run its course." In this spirit of impotence, the democratic Socialists of Europe (until Léon Blum came to power some years later) denied the possibility of a middle way and concluded that, short of full socialization, they had no alternative but to accept the logic of laissez-faire.

The assumption that there were two absolutely distinct economic orders, socialism and capitalism, expressed, of course, an unconscious Platonism—a conviction that the true reality lay in the theoretical essences of which any working economy, with its compromises and confusions, could only be an imperfect copy. If in the realm of essences socialism and capitalism were separate phenomena based on separate principles, then they must be kept rigorously apart on earth. Nor was this use of Platonism—this curious belief that the abstraction was somehow more real than the reality, which Whitehead so well called the "fallacy of misplaced concreteness"—confined to doctrinaire capitalists and doctrinaire socialists. The eminent Liberal economist Sir William Beveridge, director of the London School of Economics, braintruster for the Lloyd George welfare reforms before the First World War, spoke for enlightened economic opinion when he identified the "inescapable fatal danger" confronting public policy in the Depression as "the danger of mixing freedom and control. We have to decide either to let production be guided by the free play of prices or to plan it socialistically from beginning to end . . . Control and freedom do not mix." Beveridge, encountering Donald Richberg in Washington in the glowing days of 1933, asked a bit patronizingly whether Richberg really believed that there was "a half-way between Wall Street and Moscow." As for Britain, "there is not much that anyone can do now to help us," Beveridge said. "We must plan to avoid another crisis later. We shall not by conscious effort escape this one."

So dogma denied the possibility of a managed capitalism. But could dogma hold out in Britain against the urgencies of depression? Some Englishmen dissented from the either/or philosophy. In the general election of 1929, for example, John Maynard Keynes and Hubert Henderson had provided the Liberal party with the rudiments of an expansionist policy, based on national spending and public works. As unemployment increased in 1930, so too did the pressure for positive government action. That year Sir Oswald Mosley, a member of the Labor government, proposed to a cabinet committee on unemployment an active program of government spending, accompanied by controls over banking, industry and foreign trade. But he could make no impression on the capitalist orthodoxy of the Socialist leaders; Snowden rejected the Mosley memorandum. Another minister suggested leaving the gold standard; Snowden covered him with scorn. To the party conference of 1930, MacDonald said, "I appeal to you to go back to your Socialist faith. Do not mix that up with pettifogging patching, either of a Poor Law kind or Relief Work kind." In other words, socialism meant all or—in this case—nothing!

As economic pressure increased, more and more had to be sacrificed to the balancing of the budget; and the implacable retrenchment meant more governmental economy, reduction in salaries, reduction in normal public works, until, in time, the frenzy for economy threatened the social services and especially the system of unemployment payments on which many British workers relied to keep alive. The summer crisis of 1931, after the failure of *Kreditanstalt*, weakened the pound; and to

Snowden and the Labor government nothing now seemed more essential than staying on the gold standard. To keep Britain on gold required American loans; American loans would not be forthcoming unless satisfactory evidence existed of a determination to balance the budget; and the evidence most likely to satisfy J. P. Morgan and Company, which was arranging the American credit, was a cut in unemployment benefits.

In August 1931, MacDonald and Snowden confronted the cabinet with this dismal logic. Arthur Henderson made it clear that the whole cabinet absolutely accepted Snowden's economic theory: "We ought to do everything in our power to balance the Budget." But MacDonald's proposal for a cut in the dole seemed downright wrong; the Labor government fell. MacDonald soon returned to office as head of a National government. The new government, slightly more adventurous than its predecessors, took Britain off gold in a few weeks. Sidney Webb, Labor's senior intellectual, provided the Labor government its obituary: "No one ever told *us* we could do that!"

The Labor government having immobilized itself by its intellectual conviction that there was no room for maneuver, no middle way, now succeeded through its collapse in documenting its major premise. Then the experience of 1931 displayed the Right as too hardboiled ever to acquiesce in even the most gradual democratic change. "The attempt to give a social bias to capitalism, while leaving it master of the house," wrote R. H. Tawney, "appears to have failed."

If piecemeal reforms were beyond the power of the Labor government, as they were beyond the desire of a Tory government, then the only hope lay in the rapid achievement of full socialism; the only way socialism could be achieved seemed to be through ruthlessness on the Left as great as that on the Right. Such reasoning was responsible for the lust for catastrophic change that suffused the British Left and infected a part of the American Left in the early Thirties. No one drew more facile and sweeping conclusions than Harold Laski. The fate of the MacDonald government, Laski wrote, was "tantamount to an insistence that if socialists wish to secure a state built upon the principles of their faith, they can only do so by revolutionary means."

From this perspective Laski and those like him quite naturally looked with derision on the advocate of the middle way. In December 1934, for the perhaps somewhat baffled readers of *Redbook* magazine, Laski debated with Maynard Keynes whether America could spend its way to recovery. Public spending, Laski said with horror, would lead to inflation or heavy taxation or waste; it would mean, he solemnly wrote, "an unbalanced budget with the disturbance of confidence (an essential condition of recovery) which this implies": it would bequeath a "bill of staggering dimensions" to future generations. "Government spending as anything more than a temporary and limited expedient," he concluded, "will necessarily do harm in a capitalist society." This was, of course, not only the argument of Ramsay MacDonald but of Herbert Hoover; Laski's novelty was to use it to defend, not a balanced budget and the gold standard, but—socialist revolution.

One way or another, the British Left began to vote against liberal democracy. Sir Oswald Mosley, who had championed the most constructive economic program considered within the MacDonald government, indicated the new direction when, with John Strachey and others, he founded the authoritarian-minded New Party in 1931. Mosley's excesses soon led him toward fascism and discredit; but plenty of others were reaching similar conclusions about the impossibility of reform under capitalism. Sidney and Beatrice Webb abandoned Fabianism for the mirage of a new civilization in the Soviet Union. All peaceful roads to progress seemed blocked. After a visit with Roosevelt in Washington, Cripps wrote, "My whole impression is of an honest anxious man faced by an impossible task—humanizing capitalism and making it work." "The one thing that is not inevitable now," said Cripps, "is gradualness."

Both Right and Left—Hoover and Stalin, John W. Davis and Mussolini, Ogden Mills and Stafford Cripps—thus rejected the notion of a socially directed and managed capitalism, of a mixed economy, of something in between classical free enterprise and classical socialism. And the either/or demonstration commanded considerable respect in the United States—self-evidently on the American Right; and to some degree on the American Left. So Laski had made clear in *Democracy in Crisis* that the American ruling class would be as tough and hopeless as any other:

> What evidence is there, among the class which controls the destiny of America, of a will to make the necessary concessions? Is not the execution of Sacco and Vanzetti, the long indefensible imprisonment of Mooney, the grim history of American strikes, the root of the answer to that question?

In 1932 both Right and Left thus stood with fierce intransigence on the solid ground of dogma. In so doing, they were challenging an essential part of the American liberal tradition. When Professor Rexford G. Tugwell of the Columbia University economics department, on leave in Washington, revisited his campus in 1933, he rashly bragged of the New Deal's freedom from "blind doctrine," and the *Columbia Spectator*, then edited by a brilliant young undergraduate named James Wechsler, seized on this boast as the fatal weakness of Tugwell's argument and of the whole New Deal. "This is the crux of the problem," the *Spectator* said; "the blind stumbling in the most chaotic fashion—experimenting from day to day—without any anchor except a few idealistic phrases—is worthless. It is merely political pragmatism."

Merely political pragmatism—to ideologists, whether of Right or of Left, this seemed conclusive evidence of intellectual bankruptcy. As the conservatives had said that any attempt to modify the capitalist system must mean socialism, so the radicals now said that any attempt to maintain the capitalist system must mean fascism. "Roosevelt's policies can be welded into a consistent whole," wrote I. F. Stone, "only on the basis of one hypothesis . . . that Mr. Roosevelt intends to move toward fascism." "The essential logic of the New Deal," wrote Max Lerner, "is increasingly the naked fist of the capitalist state."

Convinced of the fragility of the system, the radicals saw themselves as the forerunners of apocalypse. "American commercial agriculture is doomed," wrote Louis Hacker; capitalism was doomed, too, and the party system, and the traditional American way of life. In 1934 Sidney Hook, James Burnham, Louis Budenz, V. F. Calverton, James Rorty and others addressed "An Open Letter to American Intellectuals." "We cannot by some clever Rooseveltian trick," the letter warned,

> evade the unfolding of basic economic and political developments under capitalism . . . Let us not deceive ourselves that we shall not have to face here also the choice between reaction, on the one hand, and a truly scientific economy under a genuine workers' democracy on the other.

In 1935 *The New Republic* stated with magisterial simplicity the argument of the radicals against the New Dealers, of New York against Washington, of the Marxists against the pragmatists.

> Either the nation must put up with the confusions and miseries of an essentially unregulated capitalism, or it must prepare to supersede capitalism with socialism. *There is no longer a feasible middle course.*

Both radicalism and conservatism thus ended in the domain of either/or. The contradictions of actuality which so stimulated the pragmatists of Washington, only violated the properties and offended the illusions of the ideologists. While they all saw themselves as hardheaded realists, in fact they were Platonists, preferring essence to existence and considering abstractions the only reality.

The great central source of the New Deal, in my judgment, lay precisely in the instinctive response of practical, energetic, and compassionate people to those dogmatic absolutes. This passion to sacrifice reality to doctrine presented a profound challenge to the pragmatic nerve. Many Americans, refusing to be intimidated by abstractions or to be overawed by ideology, responded by doing things. The whole point of the New Deal lay in its belief in activism, its faith in gradualness, its rejection of catastrophism, its indifference to ideology, its conviction that a managed and modified capitalist order achieved by piecemeal experiment could combine personal freedom and economic growth. "In a world in which revolutions just now are coming easily," said Adolf Berle, "the New Deal chose the more difficult course of moderation and rebuilding." "The course that the new Administration did take," said Harold Ickes, "was the hardest course. It conformed to no theory, but it did fit into the American system—a system of taking action step by step, a system of regulation only to meet concrete needs, a system of courageous recognition of change." Tugwell, rejecting laissez-faire and communism, spoke of the "third course."

Roosevelt himself, of course, was the liberal pragmatist *par excellence*. His aim was to steer between the extremes of chaos and tyranny by moving always, in his phrase, "slightly to the left of center." "Unrestrained individualism" he wrote, had proved a failure; yet "any paternalistic system which tries to provide for security for everyone from above only calls for an impossible task and a regimentation utterly uncongenial to the spirit of our people." He constantly repeated Macaulay's injunction to reform if you wished to preserve.

Roosevelt had no illusions about revolution. Mussolini and Stalin seemed to him, in his phrase, "not mere distant relatives" but "blood brothers." When Emil Ludwig asked him about his "political motive," he replied, "My desire is to obviate revolution... I work in a contrary sense to Rome and Moscow." He said during the 1932 campaign:

> Say that civilization is a tree which, as it grows, continually produces rot and dead wood. The radical says: 'Cut it down.' The conservative says: 'Don't touch it.' The liberal compromises: 'Let's prune, so that we lose neither the old trunk nor the new branches.' This campaign is waged to teach the country to march upon its appointed course, the way of change, in an orderly march, avoiding alike the revolution of radicalism and the revolution of conservatism.

I think it would be a mistake to underestimate the extent to which this pragmatic attitude was itself a major source of New Deal vitality. The exaltation of the middle way seems banal and obvious enough today. Yet the tyranny of dogma was such in the early years of the Great Depression that infatuation with ideology blocked and smothered the instinctive efforts of free men to work their own salvation. In a world intoxicated with abstractions, Roosevelt and the New Dealers stood almost alone in a stubborn faith in rational experiment, in trial and error. No one understood this more keenly than the great English critic of absolutes; Keynes, in an open letter to Roosevelt at the end of 1933, stated the hopes generated by the New Deal with precision and eloquence. "You have made yourself," Keynes told Roosevelt,

> the trustee for those in every country who seek to mend the evils of our condition by reasoned experiment within the framework of the existing social system. If you fail, rational choice will be gravely prejudiced throughout the world, leaving orthodoxy and revolution to fight it out. But, if you succeed, new and bolder methods will be tried everywhere, and we may date the first chapter of a new economic era from your accession to office.

The question remains: why did the New Deal itself have the pragmatic commitment? Why, under the impact of depression, was it not overborne by dogma as were most other governments and leaders in the world? The answer to this lies, I suspect, in the point I proposed earlier—in the suggestion that the New Deal represented, not just a response to depression, but also a response to pent-up frustration and needs in American society—frustrations and needs which would have operated had there been no depression at all. The periodic demand for forward motion in American politics, the periodic break-through of new leadership—these were already in the works before the Depression. Depression, therefore, instead of catching a nation wholly unprepared, merely accelerated tendencies toward change already visible in the national community. The response to depression, in short, was controlled and tempered by the values of traditional American experimentalism, rather than those of rigid ideology. The New Deal was thus able to approach the agony of mass unemployment and depression in the pragmatic spirit, in the spirit which guaranteed the survival rather than the extinction of freedom, in the spirit which in time rekindled hope across the world that free men could manage their own economic destiny.

Ellis W. Hawley

ELLIS W. HAWLEY (1929–   ) is Professor of History at the University of Iowa. He
is the author of *The New Deal and the Problem of Monopoly: A Study in Economic
Ambivalence* (1966).

The Great Depression, however, with its mass unemployment and declining incomes, brought a new and acute awareness of the monopoly
problem, a new consciousness of the gap between ideal and reality.
Along with the concern over centralization, injustice, and loss of individual freedom, came a new concern, a growing belief that the misuse of
business power was responsible for the economic breakdown and the
persistence of depression conditions. Reorganization and reform of the
business system, so many Americans felt, had now become an imperative necessity; as one might expect, the approaches to the problem
tended to follow the patterns established earlier. Once again, opinion
divided along lines that were roughly similar to those which had divided
the New Freedom, the New Nationalism, and the "new competition."

Like the advocates of the New Freedom, for example, the antitrusts
or neo-Brandeisians favored a policy of decentralizing the business
structure and enforcing competitive behavior. They did so both with the
idea of implementing democratic and individualistic ideals and with a
growing conviction that enforced competition was the best way to
achieve sustained prosperity. The depression, as they saw it, was a
product of monopolistic rigidities. The businessmen, because of their
market power, had been able to maintain prices even though their costs
of production were falling. This had resulted in excessive profits, over-
savings, and a failure of consumer purchasing power. And the only real
solution, they felt, if such crises were to be averted in the future, was a
program that would restore flexible prices and allow competitive forces
to keep the economy in balance. They believed, moreover, that these
goals were attainable. They could be attained by rigorous antitrust prosecution, by limits on size, by a tax on bigness, by controls over business
financing and competitive practices, and by other measures that would
encourage more reliance on free markets.

The economic planners, on the other hand, like the New Nationalists
of an earlier period, felt that antitrust action was a hopeless anach-

ronism. In a modern economy, they maintained, concentrations of economic power were inevitable. They were necessary for efficient mass production, technical progress, and reasonable security; and while the abuse of this power was largely responsible for the depression, the idea that it could be dispersed was both impractical and dangerous. The only real answer lay in systematic organization and planning, in conscious and rational administrative control of economic processes so as to restore economic balance and prevent future breakdowns.

Again, however, there was strong disagreement as to who should do the planning and the degree and type that would be necessary. On the political left were national economic planners who would deprive businessmen of their power and transfer much of it to the state or to organized non-business groups. In the center were those who felt that some scheme of business-government cooperation could be effective. On the right were industrialists and pro-business planners, men who drew their ideas from the war experience or the Associational Activities of the nineteen twenties, and who felt that an enlightened business leadership, operating through self-governing trade associations, should make most of the decisions. The depression, so some of these business planners argued, was due mostly to irresponsible "chiseling" and "cutthroat competition"; and the government, if it wanted to bring about recovery, should help "responsible and enlightened businessmen" to force the "chiselers" into line.

Under depression conditions, this clash of values and policies became particularly acute. On the one hand, the depression produced insistent demands for planning, rationalization, and the erection of market controls that could stem the forces of deflation and prevent economic ruin. On the other, it intensified antimonopoly sentiment, destroyed confidence in business leadership, and produced equally insistent demands that big business be punished and competitive ideals be made good. The dilemma of the New Deal reform movement lay in the political necessity of meeting both sets of these demands, in the necessity of creating organizations and controls that could check deflationary forces and provide a measure of order and security while at the same time preserving democratic values, providing the necessary incentives, and making the proper concessions to competitive symbols. From a political standpoint, the Roosevelt Administration could ignore neither of these conflicting currents of pressure and opinion; and under the circumstances, it could hardly be expected to come up with an intellectually coherent and logically consistent set of business policies. . . .

From the viewpoint of a logical economist, about the only term that could adequately describe these conflicting policies and gyrations would be "economic confusion." The New Deal began with government sponsorship of cartels and business planning; it ended with the antitrust campaign and the attack on rigid prices; and along the way, it engaged in minor excursions into socialism, public utility regulation, and the establishment of "government yardsticks." Certainly, there was little in the way of economic consistency. Nor was there much success in terms of restoring prosperity and full employment. Neither the planning approach nor antitrust action nor any of the compromises in between ever contributed much to economic recovery, although they did lead to increased governmental activities of each sort. Recovery, when it came, was largely a product of large-scale government spending, and not of any major reorganization of the business system.

From a political standpoint, however, there was a certain amount of consistency and logic to the New Deal programs. In dealing with business, Roosevelt faced a political dilemma. On the one hand he was confronted with strong pressures for punitive action against big business and with the necessity of making proper obeisance to the antitrust tradition. On the other was the growing pressure for some sort of planning, control, and rationalization. As a practical matter, his Administration did a fairly respectable job of satisfying both sets of demands. The denunciations of "monopoly" and the attack on unpopular groups like Wall Street, the Power Trust, and the Sixty Families kept the antitrusters happy, while at the same time organized industrial pressure groups were being allowed to write their programs of market control into law, particularly in areas where they could come up with the necessary lobbies and symbols. . . .

The problem of reconciling liberty and order, individualism and collective organization, was admittedly an ancient one, but the creation of a highly integrated industrial system in a land that had long cherished its liberal, democratic, and individualistic traditions presented the problem in a peculiarly acute form. Both the American people and their political leaders tended to view modern industrialism with mingled feelings of pride and regret. On one hand, they tended to associate large business units and economic organization with abundance, progress, and a rising standard of living. On the other, they associated them with a wide variety of economic abuses, which, because of past ideals and past standards, they felt to be injurious to society. Also, deep in their hearts, they retained a soft spot for the "little fellow." In moments of introspection, they looked upon the immense concentrations of economic power that they had created and accused them of destroying the good life, of destroying the independent businessman and the satisfactions that came from owning one's own business and working for oneself, of reducing Americans to a race of clerks and machine tenders, of creating an impersonal, mechanized world that destroyed man as an individual.

The search in twentieth-century America, then, was for some solution that would reconcile the practical necessity with the individualistic ideal, some arrangement that would preserve the industrial order, necessarily based upon a high degree of collective organization, and yet would preserve America's democratic heritage at the same time. Americans wanted a stable, efficient industrial system, one that turned out a large quantity of material goods, insured full employment, and provided a relatively high degree of economic security. Yet at the same time they wanted a system as free as possible from centralized direction, one in which economic power was dispersed and economic opportunity was really open, one that preserved the dignity of the individual and adjusted itself automatically to market forces. And they were unwilling to renounce the hope of achieving both. In spite of periodic hurricanes of anti-big-business sentiment, they refused to follow the prophets that would destroy their industrial system and return to former simplicities. Nor did they pay much attention to those that would sacrifice democratic ideals and liberal traditions in order to create a more orderly and more rational system, one that promised greater security, greater stability, and possibly even greater material benefits.

There were times, of course, when this dilemma was virtually forgotten. During periods of economic prosperity, when Americans were imbued with a psychological sense of well-being and satiated with a steady outflow of material benefits, it was hard to convince them that their industrial organization was seriously out of step with their ideals. During such periods, the majority rallied to the support of the business system; so long as it continued to operate at a high level, they saw no need for any major reforms. So long as the competitive ideal was embodied in statutes and industrial and political leaders paid lip service to it, there was a general willingness to leave it at that. If there were troubled consciences left, these could be soothed by clothing collective organizations in the attributes of rugged individuals and by the assurances of economic experts that anything short of pure monopoly was "competition" and therefore assured the benefits that were supposed to flow from competition.

In a time of economic adversity, however, Americans became painfully aware of the gap between ideal and reality. Paradoxically, this awareness produced two conflicting and contradictory reactions. Some pointed to the gap, to the failure of business organizations to live by the competitive creed, and concluded that it was the cause of the economic debacle, that the breakdown of the industrial machine was the inevitable consequence of its failure to conform to competitive standards. Others pointed to the same gap and concluded that the ideal itself was at fault, that it had prevented the organization and conscious direction of a rational system that would provide stability and security. On one hand, the presence of depression conditions seemed to intensify anti-big-business sentiment and generate new demands for antitrust crusades. On the other, it inspired demands for planning, rationalization, and the creation of economic organizations that could weather deflationary forces. The first general effect grew directly out of the loss of confidence in business leadership, the conviction that industrial leaders had sinned against the economic creed, and the determination that they should be allowed to sin no more. The second grew out of the black fear of economic death, the urgent desire to stem the deflationary tide, and the mounting conviction that a policy of laissez-faire or real implementation of the competitive ideal would result in economic disaster.

During such a period, moreover, it would seem practically inevitable that the policy-making apparatus of a democracy should register both streams of sentiment. Regardless of their logical inconsistency, the two streams were so intermixed in the ideology of the average man that any administration, if it wished to retain political power, had to make concessions to both. It must move to check the deflationary spiral, to provide some sort of central direction, and to salvage economic groups through the erection of cartels and economic controls. Yet while it was doing this, it must make a proper show of maintaining competitive ideals. Its actions must be justified by an appeal to competitive traditions, by showing that they were designed to save the underdog, if this was impossible, by an appeal to other arguments and other traditions that for the moment justified making an exception. Nor could antitrust action ever be much more than a matter of performing the proper rituals and manipulating the proper symbols. It might attack unusually privileged and widely hated groups, break up a few loose combinations, and set forth a general program that was presumably designed to make the competitive ideal a reality. But the limit of the program would, of necessity, be that point at which changes in business practice or business structures would cause serious economic dislocation. It could not risk the disruption of going concerns or a further shrinkage in employment and production, and it would not subject men to the logical working out of deflationary trends. To do so would amount to political suicide.

To condemn these policies for their inconsistency was to miss the point. From an economic standpoint, condemnation might very well be to the point. They were inconsistent. One line of action tended to cancel the other, with the result that little was accomplished. Yet from the political standpoint, this very inconsistency, so long as the dilemma persisted, was the safest method of retaining political power. President Roosevelt, it seems, never suffered politically from his reluctance to choose between planning and antitrust action. His mixed emotions so closely reflected the popular mind that they were a political asset rather than a liability.

That New Deal policy was inconsistent, then, should occasion little surprise. Such inconsistency, in fact, was readily apparent in the National Industrial Recovery Act, the first major effort to deal with the problems of industrial organization. When Roosevelt took office in 1933, the depression had reached its most acute stage. Almost every economic group was crying for salvation through political means, for some sort of rationalization and planning, although they might differ as to just who was to do the planning and the type and amount of it that would be required. Pro-business planners, drawing upon the trade association ideology of the nineteen twenties and the precedent of the War Industries Board, envisioned a semicartelized business commonwealth in which industrial leaders would plan and the state would enforce the decisions. Other men, convinced that there was already too much planning by businessmen, hoped to create an order in which other economic groups would participate in the policy-making process. Even under these circumstances, however, the resulting legislation had to be clothed in competitive symbols. Proponents of the NRA advanced the theory that it would help small businessmen and industrial laborers by protecting them from predatory practices and monopolistic abuses. The devices used to erect monopolistic controls became "codes of fair competition." And each such device contained the proper incantation against monopoly.

Consequently, the NRA was not a single program with a single objective, but rather a series of programs with a series of objectives, some of which were in direct conflict with each other. In effect, the National Industrial Recovery Act provided a phraseology that could be used to urge almost any approach to the problem of economic organization and an administrative machine that each of the conflicting economic and ideological groups might possibly use for their own ends. Under the circumstances, a bitter clash over basic policies was probably inevitable.

For a short period these inconsistencies were glossed over by the summer boomlet of 1933 and by a massive propaganda campaign appealing to wartime precedents and attempting to create a new set of cooperative symbols. As the propaganda wore off, however, and the economic indices turned downward again, the inconsistencies inherent in the program moved to the forefront of the picture. In the code-writing process, organized business had emerged as the dominant economic group, and once this became apparent, criticism of the NRA began to mount. Agrarians, convinced that rising industrial prices were canceling out any gains from the farm program, demanded that businessmen live up to the competitive faith. Labor spokesmen, bitterly disillusioned when the program failed to guarantee union recognition and collective bargaining, charged that the Administration had sold out to management. Small businessmen, certain that the new code authorities were only devices to increase the power of their larger rivals, raised the ancient cry of monopolistic exploitation. Antitrusters, convinced that the talk about strengthening competition was sheer hypocrisy, demanded that this disastrous trust-building program come to a halt. Economic planners, alienated by a process in which the businessmen did the planning, charged that the government was only sanctioning private monopolistic arrangements. And the American public, disillusioned with rising prices and the failure of the program to bring economic recovery, listened to the criticisms and demanded that its competitive ideals be made good.

The rising tide of public resentment greatly strengthened the hand of those that viewed the NRA primarily as a device for raising the plane of competition and securing social justice for labor. Picking up support from discontented groups, from other governmental agencies, and from such investigations as that conducted by Clarence Darrow's National Recovery Review Board, this group within the NRA had soon launched a campaign to bring about a reorientation in policy. By June 1934 it had obtained a formal written policy embodying its views, one that committed the NRA to the competitive ideal, renounced the use of price and production controls, and promised to subject the code authorities to strict public supervision. By this time, however, most of the major codes had been written, and the market restorers were never able to apply their policy to codes already approved. The chief effect of their efforts to do so was to antagonize businessmen and to complicate the difficulties of enforcing code provisions that were out of line with announced policy.

The result was a deadlock that persisted for the remainder of the agency's life. Putting the announced policy into effect would have meant, in all probability, the complete alienation of business support and the collapse of the whole structure. Yet accepting and enforcing the codes for what they were would have resulted, again in all probability, in an outraged public and congressional opinion that would have swept away the whole edifice. Thus the NRA tended to reflect the whole dilemma confronting the New Deal. Admittedly, the NRA was accomplishing little. Yet from a political standpoint, if the agency were to continue at all, a deadlock of this sort seemed to be the only solution. If the Supreme Court had not taken a hand in the matter, the probable outcome would have been either the abolition of the agency or a continuation of the deadlock.

The practical effect of the NRA, then, was to allow the erection, extension, and fortification of private monopolistic arrangements, particularly for groups that already possessed a fairly high degree of integration and monopoly power. Once these arrangements had been approved and vested interests had developed, the Administration found it difficult to deal with them. It could not move against them without alienating powerful interest groups, producing new economic dislocations, and running the risk of setting off the whole process of deflation again. Yet, because of the competitive ideal, it could not lend much support to the arrangements or provide much in the way of public supervision. Only in areas where other arguments, other ideals, and political pressure justified making an exception, in such areas as agriculture, natural resources, transportation, and to a certain extent labor, could the government lend its open support and direction.

Moreover, the policy dilemma, coupled with the sheer complexity of the undertaking, made it impossible to provide much central direction. There was little planning of a broad, general nature, either by businessmen or by the state; there was merely the half-hearted acceptance of a series of legalized, but generally uncoordinated, monopolistic combinations. The result was not over-all direction, but a type of partial, piecemeal, pressure-group planning, a type of planning designed by specific economic groups to balance production with consumption regardless of the dislocations produced elsewhere in the economy.

There were, certainly, proposals for other types of planning. But under the circumstances, they were and remained politically unfeasible, both during the NRA period and after. The idea of a government-supported business commonwealth still persisted, and a few men still felt that if the NRA had really applied it, the depression would have been over. Yet in the political context of the time, the idea was thoroughly unrealistic. For one thing, there was the growing gap between businessmen and New Dealers, the conviction of one side that cooperation would lead to bureaucratic socialism, of the other that it would lead to fascism or economic oppression. Even if this quarrel had not existed, the Administration could not have secured a program that ran directly counter to the anti-big-business sentiment of the time. The monopolistic implications in such a program were too obvious, and there was little that could be done to disguise them. Most industrial leaders recognized the situation, and the majority of them came to the conclusion that a political program of this sort was no longer necessary. With the crisis past and the deflationary process checked, private controls and such governmental aids as tariffs, subsidies, and loans would be sufficient.

The idea of national economic planning also persisted. A number of New Dealers continued to advocate the transfer of monopoly power from businessmen to the state or to other organized economic groups. Each major economic group, they argued, should be organized and allowed to participate in the formulation of a central plan, one that would result in expanded production, increased employment, a more equitable distribution, and a better balance of prices. Yet this idea, too, was thoroughly impractical when judged in terms of existing political realities. It ran counter to competitive and individualistic traditions. It threatened important vested interests. It largely ignored the complexities of the planning process or the tendency of regulated interests to dominate their regulators. And it was regarded by the majority of Americans as being overly radical, socialistic, and un-American.

Consequently, the planning of the New Deal was essentially single-industry planning, partial, piecemeal, and opportunistic, planning that could circumvent the competitive ideal or could be based on other ideals that justified making an exception. After the NRA experience, organized business groups found it increasingly difficult to devise these justifications. Some business leaders, to be sure, continued to talk about a public agency with power to waive the antitrust laws and sanction private controls. Yet few of them were willing to accept government participation in the planning process, and few were willing to come before the public with proposals that were immediately vulnerable to charges of monopoly. It was preferable, they felt, to let the whole issue lie quiet, to rely upon unauthorized private controls, and to hope that these would be little disturbed by antitrust action. Only a few peculiarly depressed groups, like the cotton textile industry, continued to agitate for government-supported cartels, and most of these groups lacked the cohesion, power, and alternative symbols that would have been necessary to put their programs through.

In some areas, however, especially in areas where alternative symbols were present and where private controls had broken down or proven impractical, it was possible to secure a type of partial planning. Agriculture was able to avoid most of the agitation against monopoly, and while retaining to a large extent its individualistic operations, to find ways of using the state to fix prices, plan production, and regularize markets. Its ability to do so was attributable in part to the political power of the farmers, but it was also due to manipulation of certain symbols that effectively masked the monopolistic implications in the program. The ideal of the yeoman farmer—honest, independent, and morally upright—still had a strong appeal in America, and to many Americans it justified the salvation of farming as a "way of life," even at the cost of subsidies and the violation of competitive standards. Agriculture, moreover, was supposed to be the basic industry, the activity that supported all others. The country, so it was said, could not be prosperous unless its farmers were prosperous. Finally, there was the conservation argument, the great concern over conservation of the soil, which served to justify some degree of public planning and some type of production control.

Similar justifications were sometimes possible for other areas of the economy. Monopolistic arrangements in certain food-processing industries could be camouflaged as an essential part of the farm program. Departures from competitive standards in such natural resource industries as bituminous coal and crude oil production could be justified on the grounds of conservation. Public controls and economic cartelization in the fields of transportation and communication could be justified on the ground that these were "natural monopolies" in which the public had a vital interest. And in the distributive trades, it was possible to turn anti-big-business sentiment against the mass distributors, to brand them as "monopolies," and to obtain a series of essentially anti-competitive measures on the theory that they were designed to preserve competition by preserving small competitors. The small merchant, however, was never able to dodge the agitation against monopoly to the same extent that the farmer did. The supports granted him were weak to begin with, and to obtain them he had to make concessions to the competitive ideal, concessions that robbed his measures of much of their intended effectiveness.

In some ways, too, the Roosevelt Administration helped to create monopoly power for labor. Under the New Deal program, the government proceeded to absorb surplus labor and prescribe minimum labor standards; more important, it encouraged labor organization to the extent that it maintained a friendly attitude, required employer recognition of unions, and restrained certain practices that had been used to break unions in the past. For a time, the appeals to social justice, humanitarianism, and anti-big-business sentiment overrode the appeal of business spokesmen and classical economists to the competitive ideal and individualistic traditions. The doctrine that labor was not a commodity, that men who had worked and produced and kept their obligations to society were entitled to be taken care of, was widely accepted. Along with it went a growing belief that labor unions were necessary to maintain purchasing power and counterbalance big business. Consequently, even the New Dealers of an antitrust persuasion generally made a place in their program for social legislation and labor organization.

The general effect of this whole line of New Deal policy might be summed up in the word counterorganization, that is, the creation of monopoly power in areas previously unorganized. One can only conclude, however, that this did not happen according to any preconceived plan. Nor did it necessarily promote economic expansion or raise consumer purchasing power. Public support of monopolistic arrangements occurred in a piecemeal, haphazard fashion, in response to pressure from specific economic groups and as opportunities presented themselves. Since consumer organizations were weak and efforts to aid consumers made little progress, the benefits went primarily to producer groups interested in restricting production and raising prices. In the distributive trades, the efforts to help small merchants tended, insofar as they were successful, to impede consumer purchasing power. In the natural resource and transportation industries, most of the new legislation was designed to restrict production, reduce competition, and protect invested capital. And in the labor and agricultural fields, the strengthening of market controls was often at the expense of consumers and in conjunction with business groups. The whole tendency of interest-group planning, in fact, was toward the promotion of economic scarcity. Each group, it seemed, was trying to secure a larger piece from a pie that was steadily dwindling in size.

From an economic standpoint, then, the partial planning of the post-NRA type made little sense, and most economists, be they antitrusters, planners, or devotees of laissez-faire, felt that such an approach was doing more harm than good. It was understandable only in a political context, and as a political solution, it did possess obvious elements of strength. It retained the antitrust laws and avoided any direct attack upon the competitive ideal or competitive mythology. Yet by appealing to other goals and alternative ideals and by using these to justify special and presumably exceptional departures from competitive standards, it could make the necessary concessions to pressure groups interested in reducing competition and erecting government-sponsored cartels. Such a program might be logically inconsistent and economically harmful. Perhaps, as one critic suggested at the time, it combined the worst features of both worlds, "an impairment of the efficiency of the competitive system without the compensating benefits of rationalized collective action." But politically it was a going concern, and efforts to achieve theoretical consistency met with little success.

Perhaps the greatest defect in these limited planning measures was their tendency toward restriction, their failure to provide any incentive for expansion when an expanding economy was the crying need of the time. The easiest way to counteract this tendency, it seemed, was through government expenditures and deficit financing; in practice, this was essentially the path that the New Deal took. By 1938 Roosevelt seemed willing to accept the Keynesian arguments for a permanent spending program, and eventually, when war demands necessitated pump-priming on a gigantic scale, the spending solution worked. It overcame the restrictive tendencies in the economy, restored full employment, and brought rapid economic expansion. Drastic institutional reform, it seemed, was unnecessary. Limited, piecemeal, pressure-group planning could continue, and the spending weapon could be relied upon to stimulate expansion and maintain economic balance.

One major stream of New Deal policy, then, ran toward partial planning. Yet this stream was shaped and altered, at least in a negative sense, by its encounters with the antitrust tradition and the competitive ideal. In a time when Americans distrusted business leadership and blamed big business for the prevailing economic misery, it was only natural that an antitrust approach should have wide political appeal. Concessions had to be made to it, and these concessions meant that planning had to be limited, piecemeal, and disguised. There could be no over-all program of centralized controls. There could be no government-sponsored business commonwealth. And there could be only a minimum of government participation in the planning process.

In and of itself, however, the antitrust approach did not offer a politically workable alternative. The antitrusters might set forth their own vision of the good society. They might blame the depression upon the departure from competitive standards and suggest measures to make industrial organization correspond more closely to the competitive model. But they could never ignore or explain away the deflationary and disruptive implications of their program. Nor could they enlist much support from the important political and economic pressure groups. Consequently, the antitrust approach, like that of planning, had to be applied on a limited basis. Action could be taken only in special or exceptional areas, against unusually privileged groups that were actively hated and particularly vulnerable, in fields where one business group was fighting another, in cases where no one would get hurt, or against practices that violated common standards of decency and fairness.

This was particularly true during the period prior to 1938. The power trust, for example, was a special demon in the progressive faith, one that was actively hated by large numbers of people and one that had not only violated competitive standards but had also outraged accepted canons of honesty and tampered with democratic political ideals. For such an institution, nothing was too bad, not even a little competition; and the resulting battle, limited though its gains might be, did provide a suitable outlet for popular antitrust feeling. Much the same was also true of the other antitrust activities. Financial reform provided another outlet for antitrust sentiment, although its practical results were little more than regulation for the promotion of honesty and facilitation of the governmental spending program. The attacks upon such practices as collusive bidding, basing-point pricing, and block-booking benefited from a long history of past agitation. And the suits in the petroleum and auto-finance industries had the support of discontented business groups. The result of such activities, however, could hardly be more than marginal. When the antitrusters reached for real weapons, when they tried, for example, to use the taxing power or make drastic changes in corporate law, they found that any thorough-going program was simply not within the realm of political possibilities.

Under the circumstances, it appeared, neither planning nor antitrust action could be applied in a thorough-going fashion. Neither approach could completely eclipse the other. Yet the political climate and situation did change; and, as a result of these changes, policy vacillated between the two extremes. One period might see more emphasis on planning, the next on antitrust action, and considerable changes might also take place in the nature, content, and scope of each program.

Superficially, the crisis of 1937 was much like that of 1933. Again there were new demands for antitrust action, and again these demands were blended with new proposals for planning, rationalization, and monopolistic controls. In some respects, too, the results were similar. There was more partial planning in unorganized areas, and eventually, this was accompanied by a resumption of large-scale federal spending. The big difference was in the greater emphasis on an antitrust approach, which could be attributed primarily to the difference in political circumstances. The alienation of the business community, memories of NRA experiences, and the growing influence of antimonopolists in the Roosevelt Administration made it difficult to work out any new scheme of business-government cooperation. These same factors, coupled with the direct appeal of New Dealers to the competitive ideal, made it difficult for business groups to secure public sanction for monopolistic arrangements. The political repercussions of the recession, the fact that the new setback had occurred while the New Deal was in power, made it necessary to appeal directly to anti-big-business sentiment and to use the administered price thesis to explain why the recession had occurred and why the New Deal had failed to achieve sustained recovery. Under the circumstances, the initiative passed to the antitrusters, and larger concessions had to be made to their point of view.

One such concession was the creation of the Temporary National Economic Committee. Yet this was not so much a victory for the antitrusters as it was a way of avoiding the issue, a means of minimizing the policy conflict within the Administration and postponing any final decision. Essentially, the TNEC was a harmless device that could be used by each group to urge a specific line of action or no action at all. Antimonopolists hoped that it would generate the political sentiment necessary for a major breakthrough against concentrated economic power, but these hopes were never realized. In practice, the investigation became largely an ineffective duplicate of the frustrating debate that produced it, and by the time its report was filed, the circumstances had changed. Most of the steam had gone out of the monopoly issue, and antitrust sentiment was being replaced by war-induced patriotism.

The second major concession to antimonopoly sentiment was Thurman Arnold's revival of antitrust prosecutions, a program that presumably was designed to restore a competitive system, one in which prices were flexible and competition would provide the incentive for expansion. Actually, the underlying assumptions behind such a program were of doubtful validity. Price flexibility, even if attainable, might do more harm than good. The Arnold approach had definite limitations, even assuming that the underlying theories were sound. It could and did break up a number of loose combinations; it could and did disrupt monopolistic arrangements that were no necessary part of modern industrialism. It could and, in some cases, did succeed in convincing businessmen that they should adopt practices that corresponded a bit more closely to the competitive model. But it made no real effort to rearrange the underlying industrial structure itself, no real attempt to dislodge vested interests, disrupt controls that were actual checks against deflation, or break up going concerns. And since the practices and policies complained of would appear in many cases to be the outgrowth of this underlying structure, the Arnold program had little success in achieving its avowed goals.

Even within these limits, moreover, Arnold's antitrust campaign ran into all sorts of difficulties. Often the combinations that he sought to break up were the very ones that the earlier New Deal had fostered. Often, even though the arrangements involved bore little relation to actual production, their sponsors claimed that they did, that their disruption would set the process of deflation in motion again and impair industrial efficiency. Arnold claimed that his activities enjoyed great popular support, and as a symbol and generality they probably did. But when they moved against specific arrangements, it was a different story. There they succeeded in alienating one political pressure group after another. Then, with the coming of war, opposition became stronger than ever. As antitrust sentiment was replaced by wartime patriotism, it seemed indeed that the disruption of private controls would reduce efficiency and impair the war effort. Consequently, the Arnold program gradually faded from the scene.

It is doubtful, then, that the innovations of 1938 should be regarded as a basic reversal in economic policy. What actually happened was not the substitution of one set of policies for another, but rather a shift in emphasis between two sets of policies that had existed side by side throughout the entire period. Policies that attacked monopoly and those that fostered it, policies that reflected the underlying dilemma of industrial America, had long been inextricably intertwined in American history, and this basic inconsistency persisted in an acute form during the nineteen thirties. Policy might and did vacillate between the two extremes; but because of the limitations of the American political structure and of American economic ideology, it was virtually impossible for one set of policies to displace the other. The New Deal reform movement was forced to adjust to this basic fact. The practical outcome was an economy characterized by private controls, partial planning, compensatory governmental spending, and occasional gestures toward the competitive ideal.

In conclusion one might ask whether the experiences of the New Dealers have any relevance for the problems of today, and for various reasons he might doubt that they do. After all, the setting has changed. The concern with business power, mass employment, and rigid prices has given way to concern over inflation, labor power, and the price-wage spiral. In the increasingly affluent society of the organization man, there is less criticism of big business, less agitation for government-supported cartels, and less awareness of the gap between economic reality and the competitive ideal. Some economists, in fact, argue that the gap has largely disappeared. They claim that the process of economic concentration has been reversed, that technological innovation has stimulated a "revival of competition," and that any realistic definition of workable competition should include a variety of behavior patterns that economists in the nineteen thirties would have regarded as monopolistic. Others disagree about the prevalence of competition, but maintain that the concentrations of economic power involved in big business, big labor, big agriculture, and big government are not so bad after all. For example, they argue that the power is being used wisely, that one power concentrate tends to offset the other, or that excessive power can be checked by public opinion. Democracy, they seem to think, is still possible in an organizational system, and concentrated power can be used to liberate as well as oppress.

The concern with monopoly as a major cause of economic depression has also faded from the scene. The majority of economists seem to doubt that there is much connection between concentration and rigid prices or that price flexibility, even if it could be attained, would insure full employment and sustained prosperity. In any event, they seem convinced that tampering with the price-wage structure is one of the most difficult and least desirable ways of controlling the business cycle. Consequently, most current discussions of countercyclical programs tend to revolve about the use of fiscal and monetary policies rather than central planning or antitrust action. The return of prosperity, however, has had less effect on the older indictment of monopoly. The fear of centralized economic power has not completely vanished. The older charges that monopoly is unfair, wasteful, uneconomic, and injurious to consumer welfare are still repeated. A number of economists, politicians, and scholars are still concerned about the gap between ideal and reality, about the continued growth of collectivization, planning, and administrative controls in a land that professes to believe in free markets and economic individualism.

Those concerned with the problem, moreover, are still puzzled by the ambivalence of the attitudes involved and the inconsistency and irrationality of policies relating to competition and monopoly. The deep respect for efficiency, they point out, is counterbalanced by sympathy for the "little fellow" and concern about the political and economic power that giant successful enterprises can wield. The belief in free competition is offset by substantial support for tariff barriers, private controls, and limitations on the entry of new entrepreneurs in a number of industries and trades. The desire for competitive incentives is tempered by a strong drive for economic security, for protection against such hazards as unemployment, declining incomes, shrinking markets, and price wars. And the general tradition in favor of a free market economy is combined with an amazing array of exceptions, with a wide range of activities designed to insulate economic groups from the rigors of market rivalry. Current policy, it seems, like that of the New Deal era, is still a maze of conflicting cross-currents, and so long as the intellectual heritage remains and conflicting goals persist, it seems doubtful that any set of simple, consistent policies can be drawn up and implemented.

In some respects, then, the problems with which current policy-makers must deal are comparable to those facing the New Dealers. If the experiences of the nineteen thirties have any relevance at all, it is in illustrating the limitations of logical analysis, the pitfalls inherent in broad theoretical approaches, the difficulty of agreeing upon policy goals, and the necessity of making due allowances for the intellectual heritage, current trends of opinion, and the realities of pressure-group politics. The margin within which innovations could be made was considerably broader during the nineteen thirties than at present; yet the New Dealers were never able to agree upon a clear-cut program or to impose any rational and consistent pattern. The planners discovered that centralized, over-all planning was not really feasible, that because of political, practical, legal, and ideological considerations, any attempt to apply such an approach quickly degenerated into a type of single-industry, pressure-group planning that brought few of the benefits presumably associated with rationalized collective action. The antitrusters, too, discovered that their approach had to be economized, that it could be applied only on a limited basis or in special areas and special cases. The attempts to combine the two approaches, to work out pragmatic tests and choose between regulation and antitrust action on a case-by-case, industry-by-industry basis, ended typically in the same clash of values that lay behind the original battle of principles.

It seems doubtful, moreover, that research, investigation, and logical analysis can ever resolve this clash of values. In any event, decades of debate, coupled with massive investigations like that conducted by the TNEC, have failed to produce any general consensus about the causes of business concentration and combination, their results and effects, and the proper methods of dealing with them. Barring a revolution or drastic changes in techniques, attitudes, values, and institutions, it seems likely that policy in this area will remain confused and contradictory, that programs designed to combat monopoly will still be intermingled with those designed to promote it.

This is not to say, of course, that research and analysis are useless. Within limits they can be of great aid to the policy-maker. They can help to define the issues, identify points of pressure, and clarify national objectives. They can evaluate existing programs in terms of these goals and provide evidence as to the nature, feasibility, and relative effectiveness of the various methods whereby they might be attained. And they can acquaint the policy-maker with the range of alternatives at his disposal, and the probable consequences of choosing any one of them. This study, it is hoped, will contribute something in all of these areas, and further inquiries into particular periods, problems, or developments can contribute a good deal more. Yet such studies are unlikely to resolve the underlying policy dilemma. They are unlikely to come up with any line of policy that will be acceptable to all and that will really reconcile the conflicting goals, attitudes, and values that Americans have inherited from the past.

Consequently, the conflict in American ideology and American economic policy seems likely to continue. The gap between ideal and reality, particularly if the economy should falter, will continue to generate demands for economic reorganization and reform. Yet the possibilities for planning and rationalization will still be limited by the popular belief in free markets, and those for antitrust action by the pressure-group politics. The relative strength of the conflicting forces and ideologies may change, and new debates concerning the location, use, and control of power may develop; but so long as the competitive ideal and democratic heritage continue to mean anything, the dilemma itself seems likely to persist. And the problem of monopoly, in its broadest aspects, will remain unsolved.

9

The Coming of World War II

Avoidable or Inevitable?

During the great depression of the 1930's the American people and their leaders remained preoccupied for much of the period with a myriad of domestic concerns. Concentrating on solving the problems of unemployment, underproduction, agricultural distress, and an economy that seemed to be on the verge of collapse, most individuals gave relatively little thought to events on the international scene. With a few notable exceptions, the aim of Americans was to solve their internal problems; foreign relations were important only to the extent that they threatened to involve the nation in another world holocaust similar to the one that began in 1914 and ended tragically four years later. Indeed, the desire to remain isolated from developments on the international scene was so pervasive that between 1934 and 1937 the Congress enacted and the President signed a series of acts designed precisely to prevent a repetition of the events from 1914 to 1917 that eventually ended in America's participation in World War I.

The outbreak of World War II in Europe in 1939 proved to be an important turning point in the development of American foreign policy. Domestic concerns such as the great depression and mass unemployment receded into the background as the fear of war swept over the country. Unlike Woodrow Wilson, Roosevelt refused to ask his countrymen to remain neutral in thought as well as action. "This nation," he told the American people in a fireside chat in September, 1939, "will remain a neutral nation, but I cannot ask that every American remain neutral in thought as well." From the very beginning of hostilities, Roosevelt's hope was to offer as much military aid to the Allies as he could without going to war. Upon presidential urging, Congress repealed the arms embargo that was then in effect because the two year cash-and-carry clause of the neutrality act of 1937 had expired. The fall of France in the spring of 1940 intensified Roosevelt's desire to rebuild

America's military forces and to give England all aid short of war. In 1941 the program of military aid to the Allied cause was expanded considerably by the Lend-Lease Act that was passed in March. By the summer of that year, the United States was involved in an undeclared naval war with Germany as American naval forces assumed the responsibility of protecting shipping in the western half of the North Atlantic. The most dramatic gesture of American sympathy for the British cause came in August of 1941, when Roosevelt and Churchill met off the coast of Newfoundland and agreed to a joint statement on mutual war aims. Known as the Atlantic Charter, the document not only spelled out the hopes of the two leaders for a better world, but referred specifically to "the final destruction of the Nazi tyranny" as a war aim.

The situation in Asia was equally explosive. Beginning in 1937 Japan renewed her attack upon the Nationalist regime of Chiang Kai-shek. The United States, having long been committed to the preservation of the territorial integrity and independence of China, found itself facing a diplomatic crisis. Nazi victories in Europe had the effect of stimulating Japanese ambitions even further; after the fall of France, Japan occupied northern Indo-China and signified its desire to establish a "co-prosperity sphere" throughout eastern Asia—a euphemism for Japanese hegemony.

Roosevelt responded slowly to these developments in Asia. First, the American government adopted various forms of economic pressure. After Japan occupied southern Indo-China in July of 1941, Roosevelt took the decisive step of imposing all-inclusive economic sanctions. At this point Japan faced the choice of curtailing its ambitions, particularly in China, or breaking the restrictions by resorting to armed conflict. During the remainder of the year, Japan and the United States remained on a collision course that finally culminated in the fateful attack on Pearl Harbor on December 7, 1941.

Throughout the course of World War II, few Americans expressed any doubts over the issue of war guilt or their own involvement. Faced by totalitarian regimes in Germany, Italy, and Japan—regimes committed to the goal of regional or world domination—the United States, most felt, had no choice but to defend itself and become the champion of the free world. Roosevelt tried his best to avoid war and the use of American troops overseas, but the march of events seemed to destroy his hopes. The Japanese attack on Pearl Harbor settled the issue of going to war in a conclusive manner. From that point on, America committed its industrial and military might against the forces of aggression. Such was the position taken by most contemporary scholars and writers who dealt with American diplomacy from 1937 to 1941.

The first criticisms concerning America's foreign policies in the years prior to 1941 came toward the end of World War II. Not until after the war was over, however, did the revisionists—as those critical of Roosevelt came to be known—spell out their case in great detail. The reaction against Roosevelt's policies after 1945 was not a totally unexpected or surprising development. After each of America's past wars, a debate had taken place over the question of whether the nation ought to have become involved in overt hostilities. More important in explaining the criticisms of Roosevelt's diplomacy, however, was the widespread disillusionment in the United States with the results of World War II. America had gone to war in 1941 to destroy the forces of totalitarianism and then found itself faced with an even greater menace—the Soviet Union. Germany was divided, half of Europe lay under Russian domination, and the United States and the Soviet Union entered upon a period of tense diplomatic relations in the postwar era that quickly became known as the "Cold War." When the Soviet Union developed an atomic bomb of its own in 1949, America felt its physical security threatened for the first time since 1783. America's wartime allies, Britain and France, could no longer be considered first-rate powers, and the British Commonwealth was facing a severe crisis as a result of the rise of Asian and African nationalism. In the Far East the situation looked equally bleak: the destruction of Japanese power left a vacuum that was quickly filled by the Chinese Communist regime; India, gaining its independence, was weak; and Korea was left divided. At home the coming of the Cold War posed problems of internal security as some persons feared that the nation was being threatened by subversives and Communists. The result was a period of repression in the early 1950's that seriously impaired the civil rights that American citizens had traditionally enjoyed under the Constitution. All of these developments raised some doubts over the wisdom of America's participation in World War II.

Many of the major critics of Roosevelt's foreign policies, interestingly enough, had taken an isolationist position as regards America's foreign policy in the 1930's and some even had been associated with the school of revisionist writers who opposed America's entry into World War I. Harry Elmer Barnes, the father of World War I revisionism, consistently opposed Roosevelt's diplomatic policies and addressed meetings of the America First Committee—an isolationist organization of the 1930's and early 1940's. Charles A. Beard spoke out against any American entanglements in the 1930's and testified before the Senate Foreign Relations Committee in opposition to the idea of a lend-lease program. And Charles C. Tansill, who published the leading study in the 1930's critical of Wilson's foreign policies between 1914 and 1917, also played a key role in attacking New Deal diplomacy.

One of the first scholarly attempts to discredit Roosevelt's diplomacy came in 1946 and 1948, when Charles A. Beard published *American For-*

eign Policy, 1932–1940, and *President Roosevelt and the Coming of the War, 1941,* respectively. Beard's works, receiving a good deal of attention because of the eminent reputation of their author, were quickly followed by a series of other books. Although the positions they took varied markedly, all the revisionists were in basic agreement on certain fundamental points. Moreover, most of them had nothing but contempt for historians who refused to accept their anti-Roosevelt thesis. Harry Elmer Barnes, for example, characterized those who disagreed with him as "court historians," thereby implying that they had sacrificed their scholarly integrity to gain favor in government circles.

The revisionist hypothesis was based on a number of assumptions. First, the revisionists denied that the Axis powers had threatened America's vital interests. Germany had no plans to attack the Western Hemisphere, they claimed, and the Japanese were concerned only about Asia. Roosevelt's charge that the American people were being directly threatened from abroad, therefore, had little or no substance. Secondly, Roosevelt's foreign policy was one that he knew would inevitably lead to war in Europe and Asia. Indeed, some revisionists went so far as to suggest that Roosevelt deliberately misled the American people by telling them that he was working for peace while, in reality, he was laying the foundation for war. His famous speech in Boston during the presidential campaign of 1940 in which he promised that American boys would not fight on foreign soil was simply one example of his cupidity. Finally, the revisionists emphasized that the long-term results of America's involvement in World War II were largely negative—if not disastrous; the United States, by upsetting the European balance of power and creating a power vacuum, made possible the emergence of the Soviet Union—a nation that presented a far more serious threat to American security than did Nazi Germany.

Many, though not all, of the revisionists looked upon Roosevelt as a leader who deliberately misled and lied to the American people. In his critical study of New Deal diplomacy, Charles A. Beard made this point quite explicit. Roosevelt, Beard wrote, kept reassuring the American people that he was doing everything he could to avoid war and maintain a neutral position. Yet every action that he took belied his statements. He gave military aid and assistance to Britain, first through the destroyer-base exchange, then through the Lend-Lease program, and finally by ordering American naval vessels to escort convoys. All of these steps were undertaken consciously; they were not forced upon a reluctant or unwilling president by events beyond his control. Roosevelt, claimed Beard, acted on the assumption that he was wiser than the American people and consequently did not feel that he had to tell them the truth. The American people, Beard concluded, were faced with the fact "that the President of the United States possesses limitless authority publicly to misrepresent and secretly to control foreign policy, foreign affairs, and the war power."[1] Beard's thesis was echoed by other revisionists. As William Henry Chamberlain put it in 1953: "One is left, therefore, with the inescapable conclusion that the promises to 'keep America out of foreign wars' were a deliberate hoax on the American people, perpetrated for the purpose of insuring Roosevelt's re-election and thereby enabling him to proceed with his plan of gradually edging the United States into war."[2]

Although the revisionists were critical of Roosevelt's European diplomacy, they usually reserved their heaviest ammunition for his Far Eastern policy. Indeed, most of the criticism of Roosevelt centered around his dealings with Japan in the period from 1937 to 1941. Reduced to its simplest form, the revisionist indictment boiled down to the fact that Roosevelt deliberately provoked the Japanese into attacking Pearl Harbor. At that point the President was able to take the American people into a war that he secretly wanted, but had not desired to ask for publicly.

Such a thesis, of course, rested on the assumption that the Japanese leaders wanted peace—but that Roosevelt's maneuverings had forced them into an untenable position that could be resolved only by war. Although not all revisionists argued along precisely the same lines, their general arguments were remarkably similar. They maintained that Japan's desire for peace was sincere and that she wished to end her four-year old war in China. Facing a crucial shortage of oil and other resources, the Japanese hoped to end the conflict on the Asiatic mainland in order to assure themselves continued access to those materials that were indispensable to the economic well-being of the nation. To achieve these objectives, the Japanese leaders did everything within their power to arrive at a satisfactory *modus vivendi* with the United States.

President Roosevelt, according to the revisionists, was not interested in peace; he wanted war. Instead of dealing with Japan on the basis of justice and equity, he pursued a policy that he knew would ultimately provoke Japanese retaliation. During 1941 the United States increased its economic pressures upon Japan by curtailing the shipments of oil and other raw materials. At the same time, America refused to agree to any concessions to Japan regarding China. By mid-1941 all Japanese assets in the United States had been frozen and in August Roosevelt sent a strong warning to Japan to abandon her expansionist policies. All of these moves, the revisionists claimed, were deliberately designed to provoke Japan into some form of retaliation.

The final step, said the revisionist writers, was taken in late November, 1941, when Secretary of State Cordell Hull submitted a ten-

---

[1]Charles A. Beard, *President Roosevelt and the Coming of the War, 1941: A Study in Appearances and Realities* (New Haven, 1948), p. 598.

[2]William Henry Chamberlain, "The Bankruptcy of a Policy," in *Perpetual War for Perpetual Peace*, edited by Harry Elmer Barnes (Caldwell, 1953), p. 491.

point proposal to Japan. This document demanded that Japan pull out of China and Indo-China. To the revisionists the document represented an American "ultimatum" and not one that could serve as the basis for diplomatic discussions. The perfidy of American leaders became even clearer in the days preceding the attack on Pearl Harbor. Some time earlier, the United States had broken Japan's secret code. Roosevelt and his advisers, therefore, knew that Japan really desired peace, but that she was ready to take military action if the American government persisted in its unyielding course. High American officials, including the President, even knew that a Japanese attack on the military and naval installations at Pearl Harbor was imminent. According to the revisionists, the desire of the Roosevelt Administration for war was so strong that government officials did not inform the military commanders in Hawaii of the possibility of an attack. In the end, then, Roosevelt's harsh policies provoked the Japanese into an attack on the unprepared military at Pearl Harbor, and gave him the declaration of war that he had so ardently desired. To achieve his goal, some revisionists maintained, Roosevelt knowingly sacrificed American lives as well as a large part of the American fleet at Pearl Harbor. As Harry Elmer Barnes wrote in *Perpetual War for Perpetual Peace*—a volume in which a number of leading revisionists spelled out their case—"The net result of revisionist scholarship applied to Pearl Harbor boils down essentially to this: In order to promote Roosevelt's political ambitions and his mendacious foreign policy some three thousand American boys were quite needlessly butchered. Of course, they were only a drop in the bucket compared to those who were ultimately slain in the war that resulted, which was as needless, in terms of vital American interests, as the surprise attack on Pearl Harbor."[3]

For the most part, American historians have rejected this revisionist hypothesis. They have done so largely on the grounds that it rests upon a simplistic conspiracy theory of history. Human beings, they claim, are complex creatures who are affected by complex motives. To argue that Franklin Delano Roosevelt knew the precise results of his policies would be to credit him with an omniscience that no human could possibly possess. As a leading nonrevisionist historian pointed out, it is one thing to charge that the Roosevelt Administration misunderstood Japan's intentions and underestimated her military strength; it is quite another matter to conclude that the tragic disaster of December 7, 1941, was a matter of calculated diplomatic planning by a scheming American president.[4]

---

[3]*Ibid.*, p. 651. By far the most detailed revisionist interpretation of the events leading up to Pearl Harbor is Charles C. Tansill, *Back Door to War: Roosevelt Foreign Policy, 1933–1941* (Chicago, 1952).

[4]Robert H. Ferrell, "Pearl Harbor and the Revisionists," *The Historian*, XVII (Spring, 1955), p. 233.

The revisionist argument—at least in a modified version—nevertheless offers a historical thesis that cannot be easily dismissed. In the first selection in this chapter, Paul W. Schroeder discusses America's policy toward Japan in the crucial months preceding Pearl Harbor. Schroeder raises a number of issues which cast some doubt upon the wisdom of America's diplomatic moves. The major point at stake was whether the United States had been well-advised in taking a "hard" line toward Japan. The issue raised two interesting questions: should the United States have made the liberation of China a central aim of its policy, thereby requiring the immediate evacuation of Japanese troops; and should Roosevelt have declined the invitation of the Japanese premier to a personal meeting between the two leaders to discuss their differences? To Schroeder the answer to both these questions is an emphatic "no." Until mid-1941 American planners had consistently sought two reasonable and rather limited objectives; that of splitting the three Axis powers and stopping Japan's advance with Asia. With these goals within its reach, the United States then added a third; the liberation of China. The last objective, however, was not a limited one, nor could it be attained short of war. Because of its misguided sympathy toward China, the American government drove Japan back into the arms of the Axis powers and made inevitable an armed confrontation between the two nations. American policy makers, Schroeder concluded, were not evil men determined to bring about war; they were instead men who were blinded by a sense of their own moral righteousness and had abandoned that pragmatism required of all human beings if differences between nations are not always to end in war.

Schroeder's thesis, in many respects, had already been anticipated by other writers on this subject. George F. Kennan, the former ambassador to Russia, State Department official, and historian, for example, had argued in 1951 that the United States erred grievously in the twentieth century when it committed itself to the Open Door and the preservation of the territorial and administrative integrity of China. Although a nation-state, Kennan wrote, China had many attributes which failed to coincide with the European national state that had evolved in the eighteenth and nineteenth centuries. Consequently, the Open Door policy was difficult to implement because it rested on the fallacious assumption that China was no different from other states. More important, Kennan insisted, the United States continuously "hacked away, year after year, decade after decade, at the positions of the other powers on the mainland of Asia, and above all the Japanese, in the unshakeable belief that, if our principles were commendable, their consequences could not be other than happy and acceptable. But rarely could we be lured into a discussion of the real quantities involved: of such problems as Japan's expanding population, or the weaknesses of government in China, or the ways in which the ambitions of other powers could be practicably countered. Remember that this struck a particularly sensitive nerve in the case of countries whose interests on the Asiatic mainland were far more important to them than our interests there were to us. . . . There was always a feeling, both among the Japanese and among the British, that we were inclined to be spendthrift with their diplomatic assets in China for the very reason that our own stake in China meant so much less to us than theirs did to them."[5] The result, he concluded, was that the United States never exploited the possibility of arriving at a mutually satisfactory compromise with Japan. Like Schroeder, however, Kennan vehemently denied that the failure to reach a meaningful compromise was a deliberate choice of evil and scheming leaders.

The majority of writers dealing with America's diplomacy in the years prior to Pearl Harbor, however, took an exactly opposite point of view from the revisionists. The internationalist or interventionist school—to differentiate it from the revisionist school—based its arguments upon an entirely different set of assumptions. Writers of the internationalist school began with the proposition that the Axis powers had, in fact, posed a very serious threat to America's security and national interests. By the summer of 1940, the Nazis had conquered most of Western and Central Europe and Britain seemed to be on the verge of surrender. When Hitler invaded the Soviet Union in June, 1941, a German victory appeared to be a certainty. The danger, according to the internationalist school, was that America might have to face the victorious Axis powers alone. German and Italian campaigns in North Africa created a fear that control of that continent might provide a springboard for an attack upon the Western hemisphere. Axis successes in Europe, meanwhile, had stimulated the Japanese to increase their aggressive moves in Asia on the theory that the Allies were too preoccupied in the West to divert any forces to the Far East.

Roosevelt, according to the internationalist school, believed that Germany represented the greatest threat to America's security. It was in the national interest, therefore, to follow a policy designed to bring about a German defeat. Thus, Roosevelt embarked upon a program of extending to England all aid short of war in the belief that such a policy might prevent a Nazi victory and contribute to the eventual downfall of Germany. Although renouncing impartial neutrality, Roosevelt hoped that aid to England would permit his nation to protect its security without committing American troops to a foreign conflict. The undeclared naval war in the North Atlantic against Germany represented the limit of America's involvement.

Roosevelt's primary interest lay in Europe, the internationalist interpretation continued, and his Far Eastern policy was designed to avert any showdown with Japan. The steps that he took in 1940 and 1941 were

---

[5]George F. Kennan, *American Diplomacy 1900–1950* (Chicago, 1951), p. 48.

intended to check Japan by all means short of war. The embargo on oil and other resources, the freezing of Japanese assets in the United States, the aid to China, and the massing of the American fleet in the Pacific were aimed at deterring, not provoking, the Japanese. America's objective was to seek a peaceful settlement with Japan, but a settlement that would uphold American security and principles, protect China, and honor the British, French, and Dutch interests in the Far East. Japan's expansionist ambitions, however, proved to be too great and Roosevelt came to realize that an armed conflict between the two nations was inevitable. According to the internationalist school of writers, his policy at this point became one of stalling for time in order to permit an American military build-up.

Although the internationalist school by no means approved of all of Roosevelt's diplomatic policies, they believed that the fundamental causes for America's involvement in the war lay outside the United States and in the trend of world events over which this country had little, if any, control. Most of them were convinced that Roosevelt had sought the goal of peace with great sincerity. In fact, many argued that his desire for peace led him to overestimate the opposition to his internationalist policies, which he could have pursued even more vigorously than he did.

Almost all of the historians in the internationalist school violently rejected the revisionist point of view—particularly the insinuation that Roosevelt had plotted to provoke the Japanese assault on Pearl Harbor. While many admitted that there might have been some blundering in both Washington and Hawaii, there was general agreement that the attack came as a genuine surprise. In Washington neither civilian nor military authorities had interpreted the decoded Japanese messages correctly; virtually everyone assumed that the Japanese were moving to attack British and Dutch installations in the Southwest Pacific. Although it was true that the army and navy commanders in Hawaii were not given all of the information gained from breaking the Japanese code, most internationalist historians believed that the military officials on the spot would have interpreted the messages in the same light as their superiors in Washington. Even if they had been able to divine Japanese intentions correctly, there is some doubt as to whether a military disaster could have been avoided; the American fleet was extremely vulnerable to air attack and there were insufficient land-based planes to ward off a Japanese raid. In retrospect, then, the internationalist historians looked upon Pearl Harbor as a tragic disaster that grew out of faulty military and diplomatic planning rather than part of a presidential conspiracy.[6]

The second selection in this chapter is by Dexter Perkins, one of the deans of American diplomatic history, and represents the views of in-

---

[6]See especially Roberta Wohlstetter, *Pearl Harbor: Warning and Decision* (Stanford, 1962).

ternationalist scholars while vigorously attacking the revisionist school. To Perkins historical revisionism at the close of a military conflict seems to be a common occurrence among Americans. In part, this response stems from the letdown or disillusionment that results from a failure to secure all of the goals for which the war was fought; it is related also to the inevitable reaction against the strong executive leadership that characterizes most wartime administrations. Whatever the reasons for its rise, Perkins defines such revisionism as "history by hypothesis"; it suggests that the world would have been a better place had the United States remained aloof from any involvement in World War II. Perkins goes on to argue that a victorious Germany would have been a very serious menace to America. Nor did Roosevelt deceive the American people, according to Perkins. The President was basically in accord with public opinion for even the Republican party nominated Wendell Willkie in 1940 and took an internationalist position on foreign affairs. Although Roosevelt may have been devious in his public statements from time to time, he accurately reflected the mood and thinking of his fellow countrymen. In the final analysis, Perkins ends up with a favorable, though by no means uncritical, appraisal of Roosevelt's foreign policy prior to the war.

Other internationalist scholars have also argued strongly against the revisionist thesis that Roosevelt deliberately exposed the American fleet at Pearl Harbor in order to provoke a Japanese attack. Herbert Feis, for example, insisted that Japan was bent on dominating Asia, thus threatening America's interests in that part of the world. Had the United States not placed an embargo on trade with Japan, it would have been in the strange position of having undertaken preparations for war while at the same time strengthening the opponent it might meet in battle. Feis denied that there was conclusive evidence that Prince Konoye's offer to meet with Roosevelt in the autumn of 1941 might have averted a conflict. He rejected also the thesis that Secretary of State Cordell Hull's note of November 26, 1941, was in any sense an ultimatum. The basic cause of the war, concluded Feis, was Japan's insistence on becoming the dominant power in the Far East. Short of a complete surrender on America's part, the chances of avoiding war by means of diplomatic negotiations had always been remote.[7]

It should be emphasized that there are many points of disagreement among individual historians of the internationalist school even though all of them rejected the revisionist hypothesis. The differences between internationalist historians frequently reflected the same divisions that existed among Roosevelt's advisers prior to December 7, 1941. For example, Secretary of State Cordell Hull was generally cautious in his

---

[7]Herbert Feis, "War Came at Pearl Harbor: Suspicions Considered," *Yale Review*, XLV (Spring, 1956), pp. 378–390.

approach; he favored limiting overt action to steps short of war. Secretary of War Henry L. Stimson, on the other hand, believed that the policy of all aid short of war would not result in the defeat of the Axis powers, and that America would have to intervene sooner or later. Indeed, Stimson believed that American people would have supported Roosevelt in a declaration of war even before Pearl Harbor. Similarly, some internationalist historians, including Herbert Feis and Basil Rauch, were sympathetic to Hull and Roosevelt, while others, notably William L. Langer and S. Everett Gleason, argued that Roosevelt overestimated isolationist opposition to his policies and that the President actually lagged behind public opinion on the desirability of taking strong measures against the Axis powers.[8]

Beginning in the late 1950's, however, the internationalist school began to come under sharp attack from scholars who saw a close relationship between foreign and domestic policy, with the former growing out of the latter. These scholars took a quite different approach to the problem of war causation; rather than focusing on the immediate events that led to Pearl Harbor, they studied the long-range trends in American foreign policy and provided an alternative framework for understanding our entry into the Second World War. Perhaps the most influential scholar in this regard was William Appleman Williams, who offered in a series of important books a view of American diplomacy that was sharply at variance with his internationalist contemporaries.

The Williams thesis, in its simplest form, was that American foreign policy since the late-nineteenth century reflected a particular ideology known as "Open Door" imperialism. A reflection of American capitalism, this policy was based on the premise that foreign markets were indispensable for domestic prosperity and tranquility. By the 1890's, therefore, the United States had moved to acquire overseas possessions, strategically situated so as to facilitate trade and provide naval bases but involving few of the usual responsibilities associated with an extensive overseas empire. The Open Door policy, argued Williams, was designed to win victories without wars; "it was derived from the proposition that America's overwhelming economic power would cast the economy and the politics of the poorer, weaker, underdeveloped countries in a pro-American mold."[9] Ultimately the ideology of the Open Door would lead the United States into a more and more militant opposition to any economic system—socialist, communist, totalitarian—that might diminish its overseas trade.

---

[8]Herbert Feis, *The Road to Pearl Harbor: The Coming of War Between the United States and Japan* (Princeton, 1950); Basil Rauch, *Roosevelt: From Munich to Pearl Harbor* (New York, 1950); William L. Langer and S. Everett Gleason, *The Challenge to Isolation, 1937–1940* (New York, 1952) and *The Undeclared War, 1940–1941* (New York, 1953).

[9]William Appleman Williams, *The Tragedy of American Diplomacy* (rev. ed.: New York, 1962), p. 49. See also Williams' *The Roots of the Modern American Empire* (New York, 1969).

Williams' thesis led directly to a new interpretation of the diplomacy of the 1930's and the coming of the Second World War. The New Deal, according to Williams, was intended to define and institutionalize the roles, functions, and responsibilities of three important segments of industrial society—capital, labor, government—and to do so in harmony with the principles of capitalism. In foreign policy the New Deal continued to seek the overseas markets on which American prosperity supposedly rested; even Secretary of State Cordell Hull's reciprocal trade program was intended to control foreign sources of raw materials while simultaneously providing for the selling of American surpluses abroad. The result was a strengthening of free trade imperialism, which in turn led to a rising distrust of the United States by nations increasingly fearful of domination by American capitalism. When Japan began to move south into China in 1937 and Germany became more active in Latin America, Roosevelt and his advisers moved toward an activistic and interventionist foreign policy because of the threat to our economic interests throughout the world. During the Second World War America's economic leaders also became enthusiastic converts to the mission to reform the world. This crusading zeal, in conjunction with Open Door imperialism, was in large measure responsible for the advent of the Cold War and the disastrous course that involved the nation in two wars in the 1950's and 1960's. [10]

The Williams thesis about the nature of foreign policy proved extraordinarily attractive to individuals and groups committed to fundamental changes in American society in the 1960's. Indeed, Williams himself concluded that the United States had to adopt a new foreign policy that rejected the assumptions that an informal empire was necessary for our welfare, that trade was a weapon against those nations with whom we had disagreements or was necessary in order to pay for the costs of military security abroad. Moreover, the United States had to stop seeing Communism in terms of an absolute evil. "Once freed from its myopic concentration on the cold war, the United States could come to grips with the central problem of reordering its own society so that it functions through such a balanced relationship with the rest of the world, and so that the labor and leisure of its own citizens are invested with creative meaning and purpose." [11] While Williams himself was more within a social democratic tradition, other historians—particularly those associated with the "New Left"—picked up where Williams had left off. In the eyes of these scholars war, racism, and poverty were all

---

[10] A detailed study of New Deal diplomacy in the Williams tradition is Lloyd C. Gardner's *Economic Aspects of New Deal Diplomacy* (Madison, 1964).

[11] Williams, *Tragedy of American Diplomacy*, p. 306. Walter LaFeber's *America, Russia, and the Cold War 1945–1966* (New York, 1967), and Lloyd C. Gardner's *Architects of Illusion: Men and Ideas in American Foreign Policy 1941–1949* (Chicago, 1970), are both in the Williams tradition.

outgrowths of the evil nature of American capitalism, a system that rested on the exploitation of the many by the few. Only radical changes that involved a sharp redistribution of economic and political power would make it possible for the American people to confront their problems and develop appropriate solutions.[12]

Curiously enough, relatively few "New Left" historians have written about the events that immediately preceded American entry into the Second World War. While emphasizing American culpability for the advent of the Cold War, they tended to shy away from dealing with the Second World War, perhaps because of the difficulty of ignoring the nature of Nazi Germany. With the exception of Williams's general interpretation of American diplomacy and Lloyd C. Gardner's study of the economic aspects of New Deal diplomacy, relatively little has been written on the origins of the Second World War by those with an affinity for the "New Left."

To evaluate in a fair and objective manner the events leading up to Pearl Harbor, then, is not a simple task for scholars. The complexity of this historical problem arises from many reasons: the tangled web of interrelated events in the period before December, 1941, which makes it difficult, if not impossible, to separate causes and to point to any particular one as "definitive"; the fact that some of the goals for which America went to war were not achieved by the end of the conflict; and the problem of ascertaining the precise motives of the national leaders and various interest groups of the period. Historical judgment, furthermore, rests to a large degree upon the starting assumptions held by various scholars; different historians approach the problem with a different set of starting assumptions and hence reach conflicting conclusions.

In contrasting the revisionist with the international school of historians, several differences are clearly discernible. First, both deal in a very different way with the issue of whether or not the Axis powers represented an immediate threat to American security. The revisionists maintained that there was no evidence showing that Hitler hoped to move into the Western Hemisphere. Even if he had, the revisionists held that the best policy would have been for America to have waited until Germany and Russia had destroyed each other; such a policy would have avoided the power vacuum that developed in Europe in the postwar period that enabled the Soviet Union to expand without checks. In the Far East, America also made a mistake by pushing Japan into war by an inflexible policy and a refusal to offer any reasonable compromises. The internationalists, on the other hand, believed that a victorious Germany posed a serious threat to American security, especially if one considers the military prowess and scientific potential of the Third Reich. Given

---

[12]See Gabriel Kolko, *The Politics of War: The World and United States Foreign Policy 1943–1945* (New York, 1968) and *The Roots of American Foreign Policy* (Boston, 1969).

Hitler's past behavior, there was no reason to assume that his ambitions would have been satisfied after conquering England and the Soviet Union. Insofar as the Far East was concerned, the internationalists took the view that Japan's unwillingness to abandon its imperialist policy was the prime cause of the war. Scholars within the Williams tradition tended to see the diplomacy of the 1930's as an outgrowth of American economic expansionism; they paid relatively little attention to the Axis powers and to the question whether or not American security was, in fact, threatened by developments in Europe and the Far East.[13]

A second issue that scholars dealt with was the motivation behind Roosevelt's foreign policy. Did Roosevelt deceive the American people by telling them that his policy would lead to peace when in reality he wanted war? To this question the revisionists answered in the affirmative and the internationalists in the negative. The Williams school as well as those scholars writing within the tradition of the "New Left," on the other hand, tended to occupy a middle position, if only because this question was not central to their analysis. All schools had a serious problem on this score, however, because the issue revolved about the motivation and intentions of one man. How can the historian gauge the motives of any individual, particularly when so few human beings ever record their innermost convictions or are completely honest with themselves?

In many respects the most important difference separating the various schools was their judgment concerning the results of the war. To the revisionists the outcome of the war was dramatic evidence of the blundering and evil policy followed by Roosevelt and his advisers. The United States, after all, had gone to war to destroy the menace of totalitarianism. Instead, it was confronted after 1945 with the Soviet Union, a far greater menace than Nazi Germany. On the continent Russia controlled all of Eastern and a good part of Central Europe; in the Far East the destruction of Japanese power created a situation that ultimately led to a Communist takeover in China. The internationalist school, by way of comparison, readily admitted that the results of the war were anything but desirable, but its adherents also argued that these results did not necessarily make Hitler the lesser of two evils. Moreover, history suggests a tragic view of human destiny; for each problem solved more arise in its place. To expect a final solution to all problems is to be unrealistic. While Roosevelt may have miscalculated in some of his policies, he did not do so knowingly or deliberately; his mistakes were due to the limitations that characterize all human beings. The Williams school and "New Left" historians saw in the Second

---

[13]Cf. Alton Frye, *Nazi Germany and the American Hemisphere, 1933–1941* (New Haven, 1967); James V. Compton, *The Swastika and the Eagle: Hitler, the United States, and the Origins of World War II* (Boston, 1967); and Bruce M. Russett, *No Clear and Present Danger: A Skeptical View of the United States Entry into World War II* (New York, 1972).

World War the origins and beginnings of the Cold War, for during that time America's economic imperialism was fused with a messianic sense; the result was a crusade against any system not modeled after the example of the United States.

In general, then, the differing interpretations of America's entry into the Second World War reflect the personal faith of the historians in the particular policy they are advocating. The internationalist school believed that the United States, as a world power, could not neglect its responsibilities nor ignore events in other parts of the world. The world is far too small a place for the provincial isolationism that characterized American diplomacy in the early years of the republic. Consequently, they believed that Roosevelt was on the right track even though some of his specific moves may not have been correct ones. The revisionists, on the other hand, argued that America's national interest could have been best served by remaining aloof from conflicts that did not immediately threaten the United States. Roosevelt, therefore, made a grievous error when he committed his nation—against the will of its people—to a world conflict. The American people, the revisionists concluded, are still paying the price of that mistake. Those in the tradition of Williams or the "New Left," argue by way of contrast that only a basic transformation in America's foreign policy (and hence domestic policies) can bring peace and an atmosphere conducive to meaningful social change. Consequently—with some exceptions—they see American diplomacy in the 1930's as a grievous error.

Which of these schools of thought is correct? Were the revisionists justified in their claim that the United States should have stayed out of World War II? Were they right in attributing evil and invidious motives to Roosevelt and his advisers? Or were the internationalist historians right in arguing that World War II involved vital American interests and that Roosevelt was simply trying to safeguard these interests even though it meant that the nation might eventually enter the war? Or were Williams and "New Left" historians correct in attributing war to Open Door imperialism? These are some of the basic issues confronting the student who is attempting to understand the background and events that led up to Pearl Harbor.

Paul W. Schroeder

PAUL W. SCHROEDER (1927–   ) is Professor of History at the University of
Illinois. He is the author of several books on diplomatic history; the book
from which the present selection is taken was the recipient of the Beveridge
Prize of the American Historical Association.

In judging American policy toward Japan in 1941, it might be well to
separate what is still controversial from what is not. There is no longer
any real doubt that the war came about over China. Even an administration stalwart like Henry L. Stimson and a sympathetic critic like Herbert
Feis concur in this. Nor is it necessary to speculate any longer as to what
could have induced Japan to launch such an incredible attack upon the
United States and Great Britain as occurred at Pearl Harbor and in the
south Pacific. One need not, as Winston Churchill did in wartime,
characterize it as "an irrational act" incompatible "with prudence or
even with sanity." The Japanese were realistic about their position
throughout; they did not suddenly go insane. The attack was an act of
desperation, not madness. Japan fought only when she had her back to
the wall as a result of America's diplomatic and economic offensive.

The main point still at issue is whether the United States was wise in
maintaining a "hard" program of diplomatic and economic pressure on
Japan from July 1941 on. Along with this issue go two subsidiary questions: the first, whether it was wise to make the liberation of China the
central aim of American policy and the immediate evacuation of
Japanese troops a requirement for agreement; the second, whether it
was wise to decline Premier Konoye's invitation to a meeting of leaders
in the Pacific. On all these points, the policy which the United States
carried out still has distinguished defenders. The paramount issue between Japan and the United States, they contend, always was the China
problem. In her China policy, Japan showed that she was determined to
secure domination over a large area of East Asia by force. Apart from the
legitimate American commercial interests which would be ruined or
excluded by this Japanese action, the United States, for reasons of her
own security and of world peace, had sufficient stake in Far Eastern
questions to oppose such aggression. Finally, after ten years of Japanese

From *The Axis Alliance and Japanese-American Relations, 1941,* by Paul W. Schroeder, pp.
200–216. Copyright © 1958 by the American Historical Association. Used by permission of
Cornell University Press.

expansion, it was only sensible and prudent for the United States to demand that it come to an end and that Japan retreat. In order to meet the Japanese threat, the United States had a perfect right to use the economic power she possessed in order to compel the Japanese to evacuate their conquered territory. If Japan chose to make this a cause for war, the United States could not be held responsible.

A similar defense is offered on the decision to turn down Konoye's Leaders' Conference. Historians may concede, as do Langer and Gleason, that Konoye was probably sincere in wanting peace and that he "envisaged making additional concessions to Washington, including concessions on the crucial issue of the withdrawal of Japanese troops from China." But, they point out, Konoye could never have carried the Army with him on any such concession. If the United States was right in requiring Japan to abandon the Co-Prosperity Sphere, then her leaders were equally right in declining to meet with a Japanese Premier who, however conciliatory he might have been personally, was bound by his own promises and the exigencies of Japanese politics to maintain this national aim. In addition, there was the serious possibility that much could be lost from such a meeting—the confidence of China, the cohesiveness of the coalition with Great Britain and Russia. In short, there was not enough prospect of gain to merit taking the chance.

This is a point of view which must be taken seriously. Any judgment on the wisdom or folly of the American policy, in fact, must be made with caution—there are no grounds for dogmatic certainty. The opinion here to be developed, nonetheless, is that the American policy from the end of July to December was a grave mistake. It should not be necessary to add that this does not make it treason. There is a "back door to war" theory, espoused in various forms by Charles A. Beard, George Morgenstern, Charles C. Tansill, and, most recently, Rear Admiral Robert A. Theobald, which holds that the President chose the Far East as a rear entrance to the war in Europe and to that end deliberately goaded the Japanese into an attack. This theory is quite different and quite incredible. It is as impossible to accept as the idea that Japan attacked the United States in a spirit of overconfidence or that Hitler pushed the Japanese into war. Roosevelt's fault, if any, was not that of deliberately provoking the Japanese to attack, but of allowing Hull and others to talk him out of impulses and ideas which, had he pursued them, might have averted the conflict. Moreover, the mistake (assuming that it was a mistake) of a too hard and rigid policy with Japan was, as has been pointed out, a mistake shared by the whole nation, with causes that were deeply organic. Behind it was not sinister design or warlike intent, but a sincere and uncompromising adherence to moral principles and liberal doctrines.

This is going ahead too fast, however; one needs first of all to define the mistake with which American policy is charged. Briefly, it was this.

In the attempt to gain everything at once, the United States lost her opportunity to secure immediately her essential requirements in the Far East and to continue to work toward her long-range goals. She succeeded instead only in making inevitable an unnecessary and avoidable war—an outcome which constitutes the ultimate failure of diplomacy. Until July 1941, as already demonstrated, the United States consistently sought to attain two limited objectives in the Far East, those of splitting the Axis and of stopping Japan's advance southward. Both aims were in accordance with America's broad strategic interests; both were reasonable, attainable goals. Through a combination of favorable circumstance and forceful American action, the United States reached the position where the achievement of these two goals was within sight. At this very moment, on the verge of a major diplomatic victory, the United States abandoned her original goals and concentrated on a third, the liberation of China. This last aim was not in accord with American strategic interests, was not a limited objective, and, most important, was completely incapable of being achieved by peaceful means and doubtful of attainment even by war. Through her single-minded pursuit of this unattainable goal, the United States forfeited the diplomatic victory which she had already virtually won. The unrelenting application of extreme economic pressure on Japan, instead of compelling the evacuation of China, rendered war inevitable, drove Japan back into the arms of Germany for better or for worse, and precipitated the wholesale plunge by Japan into the South Seas. As it ultimately turned out, the United States succeeded in liberating China only at great cost and when it was too late to do the cause of the Nationalist Chinese much real good.

This is not, of course, a new viewpoint. It is in the main simply that of Ambassador Grew, who has held and defended it since 1941. The arguments he advances seem cogent and sensible in the light of present knowledge. Briefly summarized, they are the following: First is his insistence on the necessity of distinguishing between long-range and immediate goals in foreign policy and on the folly of demanding the immediate realization of both. Second is his contention that governments are brought to abandon aggressive policies not by sudden conversion through moral lectures, but by the gradual recognition that the policy of aggression will not succeed. According to Grew, enough awareness of failure existed in the government of Japan in late 1941 to enable it to make a beginning in the process of reversal of policy—but not nearly enough to force Japan to a wholesale surrender of her conquests and aims. Third was his conviction that what was needed on both sides was time—time in which the United States could grow stronger and in which the tide of war in Europe could be turned definitely against Germany, time in which the sense of failure could grow in Japan and in which moderates could gain better control of the situation. A victory in Europe, Grew observed, would either automatically solve the problem of Japan or make that problem, if necessary, much easier to solve by force. Fourth was his belief that Japan would fight if backed to the wall (a view vindicated by events) and that a war at this time with Japan could not possibly serve the interests of the United States. Even if one considered war as the only final answer to Japanese militarism, still, Grew would answer, the United States stood to gain nothing by seeking a decision in 1941. The time factor was entirely in America's favor. Japan could not hope to gain as much from a limited relaxation of the embargo as the United States could from time gained for mobilization; Roosevelt and the military strategists were in fact anxious to gain time by a *modus vivendi*.

There is one real weakness in Grew's argument upon which his critics have always seized. This is his contention that Konoye, faced after July 26 with the two clear alternatives of war or a genuine peace move, which would of necessity include a settlement with China, had chosen the latter course and could have carried through a policy of peace had he been given the time. "We believed," he writes, "that Prince Konoye was in a position to carry the country with him in a program of peace" and to make commitments to the United States which would "eventually, if not immediately" meet the conditions of Hull's Four Points. The answer of critics is that, even if one credits Konoye's sincerity and takes his assurances at face value, there is still no reason to believe that he could have carried even his own cabinet, much less the whole nation, with him on any program approximating that of Hull. In particular, as events show, he could not have persuaded the Army to evacuate China.

The objection is well taken; Grew was undoubtedly over-optimistic about Konoye's capacity to carry through a peaceful policy. This one objection, however, does not ruin Grew's case. He countered it later with the argument that a settlement with Japan which allowed Japanese garrisons to remain in China on a temporary basis would not have been a bad idea. Although far from an ideal solution, it would have been better, for China as well, than the policy the United States actually followed. It would have brought China what was all-important—a cessation of fighting—without involving the United States, as many contended, in either a sacrifice of principle or a betrayal of China. The United States, Grew points out, had never committed herself to guaranteeing China's integrity. Further, it would not have been necessary to agree to anything other than temporary garrisons in North China which, in more favorable times, the United States could work to have removed. The great mistake was to allow American policy to be guided by a sentimental attitude toward China which in the long run could do neither the United States nor China any good. As Grew puts it:

> Japan's advance to the south, including her occupation of portions of China, constituted for us a real danger, and it was definitely in our national interest that it be stopped, by peaceful means if possible, by force of arms if neces-

sary. American aid to China should have been regarded, as we believe it was regarded by our Government, as an indirect means to this end, and not from a sentimental viewpoint. The President's letter of January 21, 1941, shows that he then sensed the important issues in the Far East, and that he did not include China, purely for China's sake, among them. . . . The failure of the Washington Administration to seize the opportunity presented in August and September, 1941, to halt the southward advance by peaceful means, together with the paramount importance attached to the China question during the conversations in Washington, gives rise to the belief that not our Government but millions of quite understandably sympathetic but almost totally uninformed American citizens had assumed control of our Far Eastern policy.

There remains the obvious objection that Grew's solution, however plausible as it may now seem, was politically impracticable in 1941. No American government could then have treated China as expendable, just as no Japanese government could have written off the China Affair as a dead loss. This is in good measure true and goes a long way to explain, if not to justify, the hard American policy. Yet it is not entirely certain that no solution could have been found which would both have averted war and have been accepted by the American people, had a determined effort been made to find one. As F. C. Jones points out, the United States and Japan were not faced in July 1941 with an absolute dilemma of peace or war, of complete settlement or open conflict. Hull believed that they were, of course; but his all-or-nothing attitude constituted one of his major shortcomings as a diplomat. Between the two extremes existed the possibility of a *modus vivendi*, an agreement settling some issues and leaving others in abeyance. Had Roosevelt and Konoye met, Jones argues, they might have been able to agree on a relaxation of the embargo in exchange for satisfactory assurances on the Tripartite Pact and southward expansion, with the China issue laid aside. The United States would not have had to cease aid, nor Japan to remove her troops. The final settlement of the Far Eastern question, Jones concludes,

> would then have depended upon the issues of the struggle in Europe. If Germany prevailed, then the United States would be in no position to oppose Japanese ambitions in Asia; if Germany were defeated, Japan would be in no position to persist in those ambitions in the face of the United States, the USSR, and the British Commonwealth.

Such an agreement, limited and temporary in nature, would have involved no sacrifice of principle for either nation, yet would have removed the immediate danger of war. As a temporary expedient and as an alternative to otherwise inevitable and useless conflict, it could have been sold by determined effort to the public on both sides. Nor would it have been impossible, in the writer's opinion, to have accompanied or followed such an agreement with a simple truce or standstill in the China conflict through American mediation.

This appraisal, to be sure, is one based on realism. Grew's criticism of Hull's policy and the alternative he offers to it are both characterized by fundamental attention to what is practical and expedient at a given time and to limited objectives within the scope of the national interest. In general, the writer agrees with this point of view, believing that, as William A. Orton points out, it is foolish and disastrous to treat nations as morally responsible persons, "because their nature falls far short of personality," and that, as George F. Kennan contends, the right role for moral considerations in foreign affairs is not to determine policy, but rather to soften and ameliorate actions necessarily based on the realities of world politics.

From this realistic standpoint, the policy of the State Department would seem to be open to other criticisms besides those of Grew. The criticisms, which may be briefly mentioned here, are those of inconsistency, blindness to reality, and futility. A notable example of the first would be the inconsistency of a strong no-compromise stand against Japan with the policy of broad accommodation to America's allies, especially Russia, both before and after the American entrance into the war. The inconsistency may perhaps best be seen by comparing the American stand in 1941 on such questions as free trade, the Open Door in China, the territorial and administrative integrity of China, the maintenance of the prewar *status quo* in the Far East, and the sanctity of international agreements with the position taken on the same questions at the Yalta Conference in 1945.

The blindness to reality may be seen in the apparent inability of American policy makers to take seriously into account the gravity of Japan's economic plight or the real exigencies of her military and strategic position, particularly as these factors would affect the United States over the long run. Equally unrealistic and more fateful was the lack of appreciation on the part of many influential people and of wide sections of the public of the almost certain consequences to be expected from the pressure exerted on Japan—namely, American involvement in a war her military strategists considered highly undesirable. The attitude has been well termed by Robert Osgood, "this blind indifference toward the military and political consequences of a morally-inspired position."

The charge of futility, finally, could be laid to the practice of insisting on a literal subscription to principles which, however noble, had no chance of general acceptance or practical application. The best example is the persistent demand that the Japanese pledge themselves to carrying out nineteenth-century principles of free trade and equal access to raw materials in a twentieth-century world where economic nationalism and autarchy, trade barriers and restrictions were everywhere the order of the day, and not the least in the United States under the New Deal. Not one of America's major allies would have subscribed wholeheartedly to Hull's free-trade formula; what good it could have done to pin the Japanese down to it is hard to determine.

But these are all criticisms based on a realistic point of view, and to judge the American policy solely from this point of view is to judge it unfairly and by a standard inappropriate to it. The policy of the United States was avowedly not one of realism, but of principle. If then it is to be understood on its own grounds and judged by its own standards the main question will be whether the policy was morally right—that is, in accord with principles of peace and international justice. Here, according to its defenders, the American policy stands vindicated. For any other policy, any settlement with Japan at the expense of China, would have meant a betrayal not only of China, but also of vital principles and of America's moral task in the world.

This, as we know, was the position of Hull and his co-workers. It has been stated more recently by Basil Rauch, who writes:

> No one but an absolute pacifist would argue that the danger of war is a greater evil than violation of principle.... The isolationist believes that appeasement of Japan without China's consent violated no principle worth a risk of war. The internationalist must believe that the principle did justify a risk of war.

This is not an argument to be dismissed lightly. The contention that the United States had a duty to fulfill in 1941, and that this duty consisted in holding to justice and morality in a world given to international lawlessness and barbarism and in standing on principle against an unprincipled and ruthless aggressor, commands respect. It is not answered by dismissing it as unrealistic or by proscribing all moral considerations in foreign policy. An answer may be found, however, in a closer definition of America's moral duty in 1941. According to Hull, and apparently also Rauch, the task was primarily one of upholding principle. This is not the only possible definition. It may well be contended that the moral duty was rather one of doing the most practical good possible in a chaotic world situation and, further, that this was the main task President Roosevelt and the administration had in mind at least till the end of July 1941.

If the moral task of the United States in the Far East was to uphold a principle of absolute moral value, the principle of nonappeasement of aggressors, then the American policy was entirely successful in fulfilling it. The American diplomats proved that the United States was capable of holding to its position in disregard and even in defiance of national interests narrowly conceived. If, however, the task was one of doing concrete good and giving practical help where needed, especially to China, then the American policy falls fatally short. For it can easily be seen not only that the policy followed did not in practice help China, but also that it could not have been expected to. Although it was a pro-China and even a China-first policy in principle, it was not a practical fact designed to give China the kind of help needed.

What China required above all by late 1941 was clearly an end to the fighting, a chance to recoup her strength. Her chaotic financial condition, a disastrous inflation, civil strife with the Communists, severe hunger and privation, and falling morale all enfeebled and endangered her further resistance. Chiang Kai-shek, who knew this, could hope only for an end to the war through the massive intervention of American forces and the consequent liberation of China. It was in this hope that he pleaded so strongly for a hard American policy toward Japan. Chiang's hopes, however, were wholly unrealistic. For though the United States was willing to risk war for China's sake, and finally did incur it over the China issue, the Washington government never intended in case of war to throw America's full weight against Japan in order to liberate China. The American strategy always was to concentrate on Europe first, fighting a defensive naval war in the Far East and aiding China, as before, in order to keep the Japanese bogged down. The possibility was faced and accepted that the Chinese might have to go on fighting for some years before eventual liberation through the defeat of Japan. The vehement Chinese protests over this policy were unavailing, and the bitter disillusionment suffered by the Chinese only helped to bring on in 1942 the virtual collapse of the Chinese war effort during the later years of the war.

As a realistic appraisal of America's military capabilities and of her world-wide strategic interests, the Europe-first policy has a great deal to recommend it. But the combination of this realistic strategy with a moralistic diplomacy led to the noteworthy paradox of a war incurred for the sake of China, which could not then be fought for the sake of China and whose practical value for China at the time was, to say the least, dubious. The plain fact is that the United States in 1941 was not capable of forcing Japan out of China by means short of war and was neither willing nor, under existing circumstances, able to throw the Japanese out by war. The American government could conceivably have told the Chinese this and tried to work out the best possible program of help for China under these limitations. Instead, it yielded to Chinese importunities and followed a policy almost sure to eventuate in war, knowing that if the Japanese did attack, China and her deliverance would have to take a back seat. It is difficult to conceive of such a policy as a program of practical aid to China.

The main, though not the only, reason why this policy was followed is clearly the overwhelming importance of principle in American diplomacy, particularly the principle of nonappeasement of aggressors. Once most leaders in the administration and wide sections of the public became convinced that it was America's prime moral duty to stand hard and fast against aggressors, whatever the consequences, and once this conviction became decisive in the formulation of policy, the end result was almost inevitable: a policy designed to uphold principle and to punish the aggressor, but not to save the victim.

It is this conviction as to America's moral duty, however sincere and understandable, which the writer believes constitutes a fundamental misreading of America's moral task. The policy it gave rise to was bad not simply because it was moralistic but because it was obsessed with the wrong kind of morality—with that abstract "Let justice be done though the heavens fall" kind which so often, when relentlessly pursued, does more harm than good. It would be interesting to investigate the role which this conception of America's moral task played in the formulation of the American war aims in the Far East, with their twin goals of unconditional surrender and the destruction of Japan as a major power, especially after the desire to vindicate American principles and to punish the aggressor was intensified a hundredfold by the attack on Pearl Harbor. To pursue the later implications of this kind of morality in foreign policy, with its attendant legalistic and vindictive overtones, would, however, be a task for another volume.

In contrast, the different kind of policy which Grew advocated and toward which Roosevelt so long inclined need not really be considered immoral or unprincipled, however much it undoubtedly would have been denounced as such. A limited *modus vivendi* agreement would not have required the United States in any way to sanction Japanese aggression or to abandon her stand on Chinese integrity and independence. It would have constituted only a recognition that the American government was not then in a position to enforce its principles, reserving for America full freedom of action at some later, more favorable time. Nor would it have meant the abandonment and betrayal of China. Rather it would have involved the frank recognition that the kind of help the Chinese wanted was impossible for the United States to give at that time. It would in no way have precluded giving China the best kind of help then possible—in the author's opinion, the offer of American mediation for a truce in the war and the grant of fuller economic aid to try to help the Chinese recover—and promising China greater assistance once the crucial European situation was settled. Only that kind of morality which sees every sort of dealing with an aggressor, every instance of accommodation or conciliation, as appeasement and therefore criminal would find the policy immoral.

What the practical results of such a policy, if attempted, would have been is of course a matter for conjecture. It would be rash to claim that it would have saved China, either from her wartime collapse or from the final victory of communism. It may well be that already in 1941 the situation in China was out of control. Nor can one assert with confidence that, had this policy enabled her to keep out of war with Japan, the United States would have been able to bring greater forces to bear in Europe much earlier, thus shortening the war and saving more of Europe from communism. Since the major part of the American armed forces were always concentrated in Europe and since in any case a certain proportion would have had to stand guard in the Pacific, it is possible that the avoidance of war with Japan, however desirable in itself, would not have made a decisive difference in the duration of the European conflict. The writer does, however, permit himself the modest conclusions that the kind of policy advocated by Grew presented real possibilities of success entirely closed to the policy actually followed and that it was by no means so immoral and unprincipled that it could not have been pursued by the United States with decency and honor.

Dexter Perkins

DEXTER PERKINS (1889–   ) is Emeritus Professor of History at the University of Rochester. He is the author of many books on various phases of American diplomatic history, including three volumes on the Monroe Doctrine.

Revisionism may be defined as an after-the-event interpretation of American participation in war, with the accent on the errors and blunders that provoked the struggle and on the folly of the whole enterprise. If we accept this definition, we shall certainly agree that there has been plenty of revisionism in the course of our history. The war of 1812 has sometimes been judged to have been futile and sometimes described as a war of intended conquest. The Mexican War has come in for harsh treatment as a war of unnecessary aggression. James G. Randall, one of the foremost students of the Civil War period, suggests that a less passionate view of the sectional problem might have made the conflict avoidable. Again and again it has been stated by reputable historians that William McKinley might have prevented the war of 1898 had he stressed in his message to Congress the very large concessions that had been made by Spain. The First World War was brilliantly represented by Walter Millis as the product of a blundering diplomacy and of economic pressures not entirely creditable. And since 1945 we have had a crop of historians, headed by so eminent a member of his historical generation as Charles A. Beard, attempting to show that the maddest folly of all was our entry into the conflict that ended less than a decade ago. Clearly, revisionism is an American habit; though, in saying this, I do not mean to imply that it is unknown in other lands.

The roots of the revisionist tendency are worth speculating about. Such a point of view, I take it, is particularly apt to find expression in a country where peace is highly treasured and where the glorification of war is relatively uncommon. Just as many Americans easily put away the hates and resentment of war at the end of the struggle and display a tendency towards reconciliation with the vanquished, so they tend to forget the passions that animated them and drove them into the conflict, and to view what at the time seemed reasonable and natural as something that with a little more forbearance or wisdom could have been

"Was Roosevelt Wrong?," *Virginia Quarterly Review*, XXX (Summer, 1954), pp. 355–372. Reprinted with permission of the *Virginia Quarterly Review* and Dexter Perkins.

avoided. And there are other factors that reinforce this point of view. Wars are apt to end in disillusionment. After the glorious hopes of the years 1917 and 1918 came the clash of national selfishnesses at Versailles, and a distraught and threatened world. In 1945 the defeat of Hitler and Japan was soon seen to have left grave problems ahead. In the East, the American defense of China and the hopes of a strong democratic nation in the Orient ended in the victory of the Chinese Reds. And in Europe, though the peril from the ambitions of Hitler was exorcized, the United States found itself face to face with a new totalitarianism, far-ranging in its ambitions like the old. In such a situation it was natural to forget the menace that had been defeated, and to ask whether there might not have been a better solution to the problems that ended with the capitulation ceremonies at Rheims and on the deck of the *Missouri*.

After every large-scale war, moreover, there is a reaction against that strong executive leadership which is almost inevitably associated with periods of crisis in the life of the nation. This was true in 1920; and it was true after 1945. During the conflict the personality of Mr. Roosevelt loomed large, and almost immune from attack. But under the surface there was hostility, and this was to take the form of criticism of his war policies. Sometimes this criticism came, as in the case of Frederic R. Sanborn in his "Design for War," from one who had a strong animus against the New Deal, and who approached the record of the administration in the field of foreign policy with this animus. Sometimes, on the other hand, as in the case of Charles A. Beard, it came from one who regarded the Roosevelt diplomacy as jeopardizing and perhaps wrecking far-reaching programs of internal reform. In these two cases, and in virtually every other, strong emotions entered into the account. It has been a satisfaction to the revisionists to tear down the President; and there has always been—and it was inevitable that there should be—a reading public to fall in with this point of view, either from personal dislike of Roosevelt or from partisan feeling.

Revisionism, then, has roots in the very nature of the case. But, if we analyze it coolly, what shall we think of it? This is the question I propose to examine in this essay.

It seems to me fair to say at the outset that it is impossible to avoid the conclusion that revisionism is essentially history by hypothesis. It suggests—indeed in some instances it almost claims—that the world would have been a better place, or that at any rate the present position of the United States would have been happier, if this country had not intervened in the Second World War. Such a proposition can be put forward, but it cannot be established like a theorem in geometry. We cannot go back to 1939 or 1941 and reenact the events of those stirring and tumultuous years. In a sense, we are bound by the past.

None the less, it seems worth while, even though we are in the realm of speculation rather than scientific history, to state the revisionist point of view. First, with regard to Germany the point of view is advanced that the United States was in no essential danger from Adolf Hitler, that he demonstrated no very great interest in the American continents, that he desired until almost the day of Pearl Harbor to keep out of trouble with the United States, that there is no reliable evidence that he meditated an assault upon the New World. It is possible for the revisionist to go further. The ambitions of Hitler, it would be maintained, would have been checked and contained within limits by the presence of the great totalitarian state to the East. The two colossi would act each as a restraint on the other. It needed not the intervention of the American government to preserve the safety of the New World. As to Asia, the argument runs somewhat differently. Less emphasis is placed on the question of national security and more on a certain interpretation of national interest. The United States, we are told, had only a meager interest in China; its trade and investments there were insignificant, and were likely to remain so. They were distinctly inferior to our trade and investments in Japan. The shift in the balance of the Far East that might come about through a Japanese victory over Great Britain was no real concern of the United States. As to the Philippines, they might have been left alone had we stayed out of the war, or conversely, they were not worth the sacrifice involved in maintaining our connection with them. Such are the assumptions, implied, if not always expressed, in the revisionist view of the problem of the Orient.

Now some of the assertions in this rationale are unchallengeable. It is true that Hitler desired to avoid a clash with the United States until just before Pearl Harbor. It is true that the economic interests of the United States in China were inferior to our interests in Japan. These are facts, and must be accepted as facts. But there still remain a good many questions about the revisionist assumptions. For example, was there in 1940 and 1941 no danger of the destruction of British naval power, and would that destruction have had no unhappy consequences for the United States? Granted that the documents show great reluctance on the part of the Fuehrer to challenge the United States, would this reluctance have outlasted the fall of Great Britain? Granted that the Kremlin might have exercised a restraining influence on the Germans, is it certain that the two powers might not have come to an understanding as they did in 1939, and had at other periods in the past? Just how comfortable a world would it have been if the psychopathic leader of Germany had emerged from the Second World War astride a large part of the Continent, with the resources of German science at his command? There are questions, too, that can be asked about the Orient. Did the United States have no responsibility for the Philippines, and would the islands have been safe for long if the Japanese had dominated the Far East? Could the United States divest itself of all concern for China, abandoning a policy of nearly forty years duration and a deep-seated American tradition? Was the destruction of British power in this part of the world a matter of no concern to this country? Could the defeat of Britain in the East be separated from the fate of Britain in the world at large? These are extremely large questions, and it is a bold man who will brush them aside as inconsequential or trivial, or who will reply to them with complete dogmatism. Indeed, it is because they raise so many problems cutting to the root of our feelings, as well as our opinions, that they arouse so much controversy. Nor is there any likelihood that we can ever arrive at a complete consensus with regard to them.

We must, I think, seek a somewhat narrower frame of reference if we are to answer the revisionists with facts, and not with speculations. One of the ways to answer them, and one particularly worth pursuing with regard to the war in Europe, is to analyze the policy of the Roosevelt administration in its relation to public sentiment.

Foreign policy, in the last analysis, depends, not upon some logical formula, but upon the opinion of the nation. No account of American diplomacy in 1940 and 1941 can pretend to authority which does not take into account the tides of sentiment which must always influence, and perhaps control, the course of government. It is not to be maintained that a President has no freedom of action whatsoever; he can, I think, accelerate or retard a popular trend. But he does not act independently of it; the whole history of American diplomacy attests the close relationship between the point of view of the masses and executive action. A peacefully-minded President like McKinley was driven to war with Spain; a President who set great store by increasing the physical power of the nation, like Theodore Roosevelt, was limited and confined in his action; and Franklin Roosevelt himself, when, in the quarantine speech of October, 1937, he sought to rouse the American people against aggression, was compelled to admit failure, and to trim his sails to the popular breeze. These things are of the essence; to fail to observe them is to fail to interpret the past in the true historical spirit.

Let us apply these conceptions to the period 1939 to 1941. It will hardly be denied that from the very beginning of the war public sentiment was definitely against Germany. Indeed, even before the invasion of Poland, the public opinion polls show a strong partiality for the democratic nations. As early as January, 1939, when asked the question [of] whether we should do everything possible to help England and France in case of war, 69 percent of the persons polled answered in the affirmative, and the same question in October produced a percentage of 62 percent on the same side. No doubt this sentiment did not extend to the point of actual participation in the war, but it furnished a firm foundation for the action of the President in calling Congress in special session, and in asking of it the repeal of the arms embargo on shipments of war in the interest of the Allies. The measure to this effect was introduced in the Congress towards the end of September; and it was thoroughly debated. There are several things to be said in connection with its passage. The first is that after its introduction there was a consistent majority of around 60 percent in the polls in favor of passage. The second is that, though there was a strong partisan flavor to the debate, the defections when they came were more numerous on the Republican than on the Democratic side. It is true that, without the leadership of the President, the repeal could not have been enacted. But also it did not fly in the face of public sentiment (so far as that can be measured), but on the contrary reflected it.

With the fall of France there took place a deep and significant development in public opinion. This change the revisionists usually do not mention. They prefer to treat of American policy as if it were formed in a vacuum without regard to the moving forces that have so much to do with the final decisions. Yet the evidences are ample that in June of 1940 the American people were deeply moved. Take, for example, the action of the Republican nominating convention. There were several outstanding professional politicians in the running in 1940, Senator Taft, Senator Vandenberg, Thomas E. Dewey. Each one of these men represented a policy of caution so far as Europe was concerned. Yet what did the convention do? It turned to a relatively unknown figure, to a novice in politics who had, however, more than once declared himself as advocating extensive assistance to the democracies. The choice of Wendell Willkie as the Republican candidate for the Presidency is a fact the importance of which cannot be denied. It is worth while calling attention to other like phenomena. One of these is the overwhelming majorities by which the Congress appropriated largely increased sums for the armed forces, not only for the navy but for the army and the air force as well. Perhaps the American people, or the representatives of the American people, ought not to have been perturbed at what was happening in Europe. But the fact is that they were perturbed. They were perturbed in a big way. And the votes in the legislative halls demonstrate that fact.

Or take another example. The movement for a conscription law in time of peace developed rapidly after June of 1940. It developed with very little assistance from the White House. It cut across party lines. And it resulted in a legislative enactment which reflected the excitement of the public mind. How can we interpret the measure otherwise? Was there not a substantial body of opinion in the United States that feared a German victory?

Another important factor to be noted is the formation in June of 1940 of the Committee to Defend America by Aiding the Allies. It is highly significant that this movement arose at all. It is doubly significant that it found a leader in a Kansan Republican such as William Allen White. It is trebly significant that, once initiated, it spread like wild-fire, and that by September there were more than 650 chapters in the United States. And it is also to be noted that in New York there soon came into being a more advanced group, the so-called Century Group, which advocated war if necessary to check the aggressions of Germany.

And it is further to be observed that out of the Committee to Defend America came an agitation for what was eventually to be the bases-destroyer deal of September 2, 1940. This deal, by the way, was approved by 62 percent of the persons polled on August 17, 1940, two weeks before it was actually consummated.

Let us go further. The next important step forward in American policy was the lend-lease enactment of the winter of 1941. This measure, it would appear from the polls, was based on a very distinct evolution of public sentiment. In July of 1940 59 percent of the persons polled preferred to keep out rather than to help England at the risk of war, and 36 percent took the contrary view. In October the percentages were exactly reversed: they were 36 to 59. By January of 1941 68 percent of those interviewed thought it more important to assist Great Britain than to keep out of war. And the lend-lease enactment, when presented to the Congress, passed the Lower House by the impressive vote of 317 to 71 and the Senate by 60 to 31. As in the legislation of 1939, though the vote again had a partisan flavor, there were more defections from the Republicans in favor of the measure than of Democrats against it. And there is something more to be added to the account in this instance. By the winter of 1941 the America Firsters had appeared upon the scene. A counter-propaganda was now being organized against the administration. Yet this new group, despite its vigorous efforts, failed signally to rally majority opinion. And Senator Taft, who represented the most thoughtful opposition to the administration, himself proposed a measure of assistance to Great Britain.

I shall treat a little later of the various measures requiring no legislative sanction which the President took in the course of the year 1941. But it is important to observe that throughout the period there was a strong public sentiment that believed that it was more important to defeat Germany than to keep out of war. This view was held, according to the polls, by 62 percent of those interrogated in May of 1941 and by 68 percent in December of 1941. As early as April, 1941, 68 percent of the pollees believed it important to enter the war if British defeat was certain.

We should next examine the legislation of the fall of 1941. By this time the Congress was ready to authorize the arming of American merchant ships, and this by a heavy vote. The measure was passed by 259 to 138 in the House and the Senate amended it and passed it by 50 to 37. Congress was ready, more reluctantly, to repeal those provisions of the neutrality acts which excluded American vessels from the so-called war zones. It was moving in the direction of fuller and fuller engagement against Hitler. We shall never know, of course, what the next step would have been had not that step been taken by Germany. It was the dictator of the Reich who declared war on the United States, not the American national legislature that declared war on the Fuehrer and his minions. But in the period between 1939 and 1941 it seems safe to say that the foreign policy of the Roosevelt administration was in accord with the majority opinion accepted, and pursuing a course of action which majority opinion approved.

This circumstance is naturally either ignored or obscured in the revisionist literature. And what makes it easier to forget is the undeniable fact that Franklin Roosevelt was unhappily sometimes given to equivocation and shifty conversation. Very early, it is true, as early as the quarantine speech of October, 1937, he sounded the alarm against the totalitarians. Very often he stated his conviction that their continued progress presented a threat to the United States. On occasion he took his courage in his hands as, when at Charlottesville in June of 1940, in an election year, he came out frankly in favor of aid to the democracies, or in the declaration of unlimited emergency in the address of May 27, 1941. There is little doubt that he deemed the defeat of Hitler more important than the avoidance of war (as did many other Americans, as we have seen). Yet he was often less than frank in his approach, and the emphasis he laid on his devotion to peace was often excessive. He shocked even his ardent admirer, Robert Sherwood, in the election of 1940. His presentation of the case for lend-lease does not at all times suggest candor; indeed, the very phrase seems a bit of cajolery. With regard to the question of convoy, in the spring of 1941, he was clever and, though verbally correct, hardly wholly open in his approach to the problem. In the famous episode of the *Greer* (an attack by a German submarine on a vessel which was reporting its position to a British destroyer), he misrepresented the facts, or spoke without full knowledge of them. All this it is only right to admit. Yet we must not exaggerate the importance of these considerations. The country knew where it was going with regard to Germany. It accepted lend-lease as desirable. Of the patrolling of the ocean lanes which followed, the President spoke candidly in the speech of May 27, 1941. There was nothing clandestine about the occupation of Greenland or Iceland. The pattern in the fall of 1941 would most probably not have been much altered if Roosevelt had been more scrupulous with regard to the *Greer*. In the last analysis we come back to the essential fact that Roosevelt represented and expressed in action the mood of the country with regard to Germany.

The question is, I believe, more difficult when we come to examine American policy towards Japan. We can say with some assurance that the denunciation of the treaty of commerce of 1911, undertaken by the administration in July of 1939 as an indication of American displeasure with Japanese policy, was distinctly well received. Indeed, if the State Department had not acted, the legislature might have. We can also say that in August of 1939 there was an overwhelming feeling against sending war materials to Nippon. When in September of 1940, an embargo on the export of scrap iron was imposed, 59 percent of the persons polled on this issue approved the step that had been taken. And in 1941 the number of persons who believed that some check should be put on Japan even at the risk of war rose from 51 percent to 70 percent between July and September, and stood at 69 percent at the time of Pearl Harbor.

But we have fewer indications of the direction of public sentiment in the action of Congress, and no actual votes on which to base our estimate of how the representatives of the American people felt with regard to the important problem of our course of action in the Orient. We must, I think, speak less confidently on this question of public opinion than in the case of Germany. We must turn rather to an analysis of the policy of the administration, and to revisionist criticism of that policy.

First of all, let us look at some of the uncontroverted facts. We know that there were militarist elements in Japan. We know that as early as 1934 Japan proclaimed its doctrine of a Greater East Asia in the famous Amau statement. We know that in the same year it upset the naval arrangements made at Washington and London. We know that it set up a special régime in North China in 1935. We know that it became involved in a war with China in 1937. This, of course, was only prelude. The outbreak of the European conflict in Europe, and the collapse of France, offered to the sponsors of further aggressive action a great opportunity. The occupation of northern Indo-China followed. In the summer of 1940, the impetuous and aggressive Matsuoka came to the Foreign Office. On September 27, 1940, there was signed a tripartite pact with Japan, which bound Nippon to come to the assistance of the Axis powers if they were attacked by a power then at peace with them. In other words, the Tokyo government sought to confine and limit American policy. In April of 1941 came a neutrality pact with Russia which freed the hands of the Japanese militarists for a policy of advance towards the South. In July came the occupation of the rest of Indo-China. The occupation of *northern* Indo-China made some sense from the point of view of blocking the supply route to the Chinese Nationalists. The occupation of *southern* Indo-China made no sense, except as the prelude to further acts of aggression. And in due course the aggression came.

Admittedly, this is only one side of the story. The question to be examined is, did these acts take place partly as a result of American provocation? Was it possible for a wiser and more prudent diplomacy to have avoided the rift that occurred in December, 1941? Revisionist criticism of our Oriental policy has been expressed in a variety of ways. In its most extreme form, it suggests that the President and his advisers actually plotted war with Japan. In its less extreme form, it directs its shafts at a variety of actions, of which I shall examine the most important. They are the conversations with the British as to the defense of the Far East, the commitments made to China, the severance of commercial relations, the failure to accept the proposals of Prince Konoye for direct conversations with the President, and the breakdown of the *modus vivendi* proposal of November, 1941. I shall examine each of these briefly, but let us first turn to the accusation that American policy was directed towards producing and not avoiding an armed conflict in the Orient.

It seems quite impossible to accept this view on the basis of the documentation. During the greater part of 1940 and 1941, it was certainly not the objective of the Roosevelt administration to bring about a clash in the Far East. On the contrary such a clash was regarded as likely to produce the greatest embarrassment in connection with the program of aid to Britain. The military and naval advisers of the President were opposed to it, and said so again and again. Even on the eve of Pearl Harbor this was the case. In addition, Secretary Hull was opposed to it. Ever the apostle of caution, he made his point of view quite clear almost up to the end. And as for the President, it is worth pointing out that on the occasion of the Japanese occupation of southern Indo-China he came forward with a proposal for the neutralization of that territory in the interests of peace, and that in August he frankly stated it to be his purpose to "baby the Japanese along." That he feared Japanese aggression is likely, almost certain; that he desired it is something that cannot be proved.

But let us look at the various specific actions which have awakened criticism on the part of the revisionists. In the first place I cannot see that staff conversations with the British were open to any objections whatsoever. If the object of the Roosevelt administration was to limit Japanese aggression in the Far East, then it seems wholly rational to take precautions against such aggression, and surely it could reasonably be expected that such precautions would serve as a deterrent rather than as an incitement to action. It is, in my judgment, rather distorted thinking that regards such action as provocation. This is precisely the point of view of the Kremlin today with regard to the North Atlantic treaty and the European defense pact, or, to take another example, very like the contention of the Germans when they invaded Belgium in 1914. Because the British had engaged in military conversations with the Belgians looking to the possible violation of the neutrality treaty of 1939, it was claimed by apologists for Germany that the violation of neutrality was defensible. Where is the possible justification for such reasoning?

There is more to be said with regard to the breaking off, by the United States, of commercial and financial relations with Japan on the heels of the Japanese occupation of southern Indo-China in the summer of 1941. Undoubtedly this created an extraordinarily difficult situation for the government in Tokyo. Undoubtedly the cutting off of the oil supply from the United States gave great additional force to the arguments of the militarists. Undoubtedly, in the absence of a far-reaching diplomatic arrangement, it presented a strong reason for "bursting out" of the circle, and going to war. If the administration put faith in this measure of economic coercion as a substitute for physical resistance, its faith was to turn out to be groundless. For myself, I have for a long time believed that economic coercion against a strong and determined power is more likely to produce war than to prevent it. But there are circumstances that ought to be mentioned in favor of the action of the administration. It is to be emphasized that the severance of commercial and financial relations resulted not in a breach of the negotiations with Japan but in a resumption of those negotiations. It is to be remembered that Prince Konoye's proposal for a personal conference with the President came after and not before the President's action. American policy by no means put an end to the efforts of those substantial elements in Japan who feared a clash with this country and who were laboring to prevent it. It must be pointed out, also, that the alternative was by no means a pleasant one. At a time when we were deeply engaged in the Atlantic, when we were being more and more deeply committed with regard to the war in Europe, when our domestic supply of oil might have to be substantially curtailed, the continuation of our exports to the Far East to assist Japan in possible projects of aggression was a very difficult policy to follow. It may even be that it would have proven to be totally impracticable from a political point of view.

We come in the third place to the efforts of Premier Konoye to establish direct contact with President Roosevelt. It is well known that Ambassador Grew believed at that time, and that he has more than once stated since, that a good deal was to be hoped from such a meeting. And it is by no means clear why, if the objective were the postponement of a crisis, the experiment should not have been tried. Secretary Hull brought to this problem, as it seems to me, a rigidity of mind which may properly be criticized. In insisting on a previous definition of the issues before the meeting was held, he was instrumental in preventing it. While we cannot know what the result of such a meeting would have been, we are entitled, I think, to wish that it had been held. All the more is this true since it would appear likely that Prince Konoye was sincere in the effort which he made to avoid war.

But there is another side to the matter. We cannot be absolutely sure of Konoye's good faith. We can be still less sure of the willingness of the Tokyo militarists to support him in the far-reaching concessions that would have been necessary. And in the final analysis we cannot be sure of the ability of the American government to make concessions on its own part.

And here we come, as it seems to me, to the crux of the matter. It was the American policy in China that created an impassable barrier in our negotiations with Japan. It is necessary to examine that policy. From one angle of vision the patience of the American government in dealing with the China incident seems quite remarkable. There was a good deal to complain of from 1935 onward, certainly from 1937 onward, if one were to think in terms of sympathy for an aggressed people and in terms of the traditional policy of the United States with regard to this populous nation. The Roosevelt administration moved very slowly in its opposition to Japan. It made its first loan to Chiang Kai-shek in the fall of 1938. It denounced the commercial treaty of 1911 with Nippon only in the summer of 1939. And it embarked upon a policy of really substantial aid to China only contemporaneously with the signing of the tripartite pact in the fall of 1940. Its increasing assistance to Chiang is intelligible on the ground that to keep the Japanese bogged down in China was one means of checking or preventing their aggressive action elsewhere.

The fact remains, however, that it was the Chinese question which was the great and central stumbling block in the long negotiations that took place in 1941. Though the Japanese had entered into an alliance with the Axis powers, it seems not unlikely that, in 1941, as the issue of peace or war defined itself more clearly, they would have been willing to construe away their obligations under that alliance had they been able to come to terms with the United States on the Chinese problem. But by 1941 the American government was so far committed to the cause of Chiang that it really had very little freedom of maneuver. The various Japanese proposals for a settlement of the China incident would have involved a betrayal of the Chinese Nationalist leader. The proposal for a coalition government, a government of the Nationalists and the puppet régime of Wang Ching-wei, could hardly have been accepted. The proposal that America put pressure on Chiang to negotiate, and cut off aid to him if he refused, was by this time equally impracticable. And the question of the withdrawal of the Japanese troops in China presented insuperable difficulties. True it is that in October of 1941 the idea of a total withdrawal seems to have been presented to Mr. Welles by Mr. Wakasugi, Admiral Nomura's associate in the negotiations. But the idea was emphatically rejected by the militarists in Tokyo, and perhaps there was never a time when they would have agreed to any proposal that at the same time would have been acceptable to Chungking. The American government had been brought, by its policy of association with the Chinese Nationalists, to the point where understanding with Japan was practically impossible.

This fact is dramatically illustrated by the negotiations over the *modus vivendi* in November, 1941. At this time, as is well known, proposals were brought forward for the maintenance of the *status quo*, and a gradual restoration of more normal relations through the lifting of the commercial restrictions, and through the withdrawal of the Japanese from southern Indo-China. At first it seemed as if there were a possibility of working out some such proposal. But the Chinese objected most violently, and Secretary Hull dropped the idea. In the face of Chinese pressure, and of the possible popular indignation which such a policy of concession might produce, and acting either under the orders or at least with the assent of the President, he backed down. We must not exaggerate the importance of this. There is no certainty that the *modus vivendi* would have been acceptable to Tokyo, and, judging by the Japanese proposals of November 20, there is indeed some reason to think otherwise. But the fact remains that our close association with Chiang was a fundamental factor in making the breach with Japan irreparable. And it seems fair to say in addition that our hopes with regard to Nationalist China were at all times, in 1941 as later, very far removed from political reality.

Let us not, however, jump to absolute conclusions with regard to questions that, in the nature of the case, ought not to be a matter of dogmatic judgment. If there was a party in Japan, and a substantial one, which feared war with the United States and earnestly sought for accommodation, there was also a party which regarded the course of events in Europe as a heaven-sent opportunity for national self-aggrandizement. That this party might in any case have prevailed, whatever the character of American policy, does not seem by any means unlikely. It is significant that in July of 1941 the fall of Matsuoka brought no change in policy in the Far East, and that the so-called moderate, Admiral Toyoda, gave the orders for the crucial and revealing occupation of southern Indo-China in the summer of 1941.

Let us not forget, either, that after all it was the Japanese who struck. The ruthless act of aggression at Pearl Harbor was no necessary consequence of the breakdown of negotiations with the United States. If new oil supplies were needed, they were, of course, to be secured by an attack on the Dutch East Indies, not by an attack on Hawaii. Though there were strategic arguments for including America in any war-like move, there were strong political reasons for not doing so. No greater miscalculation has perhaps ever been made than that made by the militarists at Tokyo in December, 1941. By their own act, they unified American opinion and made their own defeat inevitable. It will always remain doubtful when the decisive involvement would have come for the United States had the bombs not dropped on Pearl Harbor on the 7th of December of 1941.

What, in conclusion, shall we say of revisionist history? There is a sense in which it is stimulating to the historian, and useful to historical science, to have the presuppositions, the conventional presuppositions, of the so-called orthodox interpreters of our foreign policy, subjected to criticism. There is surely some reason to believe that the candid examination of the views of these critics will, in the long run, result in a more accurate and a more objective view of the great events of the prewar years and in a better balanced judgment of President Roosevelt himself.

But there is another side of the question which, of course, must be recognized. It is fair to say that virtually all revisionist history (like some orthodox history) is written with a *parti pris*. It is hardly possible to speak of it as dictated by a pure and disinterested search for truth. It is, on the contrary, shot through with passion and prejudice none the less. It also rests upon hypotheses which, in the nature of the case, cannot be demonstrated, and assumptions that will, it is fair to say, never be generally, or perhaps even widely, accepted. As to its practical effects, there are no signs that the isolationism of the present era has important political effects, so far as foreign policy is concerned. Conceivably, it provides some reinforcement for partisan Republicanism. But even here it seems considerably less effective than the unscrupulous campaign of Senator McCarthy and his colleagues to represent the previous administration as one saturated with Communists. The urgency of present issues may make revisionism less of a force in our time than it was two decades ago. As to this, we shall have to see what the future unfolds.

10

America and the Cold War

Containment or Counterrevolution?

After the Second World War the American people faced a succession of external and internal challenges for which they had few historical precedents. By 1945 the United States had emerged as the strongest nation on earth. Having triumphed over the forces of Nazi and Fascist totalitarianism, American citizens looked forward with confidence and optimism to the promise of a bright future. Such hopes and expectations were soon dashed. Within two years after the fighting ended, the United States found itself confronting the Soviet Union, its former ally. Instead of peace, the American people were plunged headlong into an era of "Cold War"—a series of crises that required economic and military mobilization even in the absence of actual hostilities.

Two developments during the war established the context within which the Cold War would be waged. One was the toppling of five major nations from the ranks of first-rate powers. America's enemies—Germany, Japan, and Italy—were defeated. Her friends—Britain and France—spent so much blood and treasure that they found it impossible to regain their prewar military and economic importance. This situation left only two super-powers—the United States and the Soviet Union. The second development was the technological revolution in warfare. With the exploding of the atomic bomb in 1945, and the capability of destroying mankind, diplomacy entered upon a new age. These two considerations led one historian to liken the relations be-

tween the United States and Russia to a scorpion and tarantula together
in a bottle, each tragically committed to trying to outdo the other.[1]

Most historians, but by no means all, agreed that World War II
created the setting for the Soviet-American confrontation. Although
ideological differences existed between the two great powers prior to
that time, the war produced suspicion, distrust, and a gap in understanding that became increasingly difficult to bridge. The Cold War,
most scholars and laymen concluded, arose from two seemingly incompatible conceptions of the ideal shape of the postwar world order.
The American point of view pictured the Soviet Union as a ruthless
power, driven by its Communist ideology, bent upon global revolution
and domination, and headed by leaders like Stalin who embarked upon
an aggressive policy of expansion with the ultimate aim of destroying
the free world. From Russia's perspective, however, America represented the main threat to peace. The Soviet view was that the United
States emerged from the war militantly committed to the idea of a
capitalist would order. America, as an imperialist power, sought to encir-
cle the Soviet Union with hostile capitalist countries, to isolate Russia
from the rest of the world, and to destroy Communist regimes wherever
they existed. Thus, the free world and Communist camp each viewed
the other side as being dedicated to its destruction.

American scholars disagreed, however, when they came to evaluate
the causes of the Cold War and to pass judgment on the roles of the two
adversaries. Since 1945 American historians, when inquiring into the
origins of the Cold War, divided into three schools: the orthodox, or
traditional school; the revisionists; and the realists. Although the arguments of each school changed somewhat with the passing of time and
appearance of new developments, they established the framework of
the important historiographical debate that took place.

The first to appear was the orthodox school, which came into being
during the immediate postwar years. At that time most of the American
people, and the vast majority of scholars, were inclined to accept the
official explanation of events set forth by the Truman administration in
justifying its foreign policy. According to the orthodox interpretation,
Soviet aggression and expansionist desires were primarily responsible
for the coming of the Cold War.

The orthodox or traditional interpretation reflected closely the official
view of the American and British governments at the time. Winston
Churchill, speaking at Fulton, Missouri, in the spring of 1946, set forth
the basic outline of this interpretation. An "iron curtain," said Churchill,
had been lowered across Eastern Europe by the Soviets. No one knew
for sure what secret plans for expansion were being hatched behind the
iron curtain. The British leader viewed not only the Soviet Union, but

---

[1]Louis Halle, *The Cold War as History* (New York, 1967), p. xiii.

Communist ideology, Communist parties, and "fifth column" activities as a growing peril to what he called "Christian civilization." President Truman in 1947 echoed similar sentiments when announcing his now famous Truman Doctrine. Although the United States had made every effort to bring about a peaceful world, he said, the Soviet Union had used "indirect aggression" in Eastern Europe, "extreme pressure" in the Middle East, and had intervened in the internal affairs of many countries through "Communist parties directed from Moscow." Because of the Truman Doctrine, many scholars of the traditionalist school held that the Cold War had officially commenced in 1947.

The orthodox interpretation was presented in scholarly books and journals in the late 1940's and early 1950's by historians like Herbert Feis and policy-makers such as George F. Kennan. These men, too, held that the Cold War had been brought about mainly because of Soviet actions. Motivated by the traditional desires for greater security, power, and larger spheres of influence, they said, the Soviet Union resorted to an expansionist foreign policy. Coupled with these age-old drives was the new ideological zeal of Communism which made the Soviets ambitious to foment revolution and conquest in behalf of their cause. Scholars sometimes disagreed about the primary motivation of the Soviets; some favored the importance of ideology as an explanation, while others believed the main focus should be placed on Russia's traditional policy of imperialism and pursuit of national interest. But they all tended to agree that no matter what the motivation might be, Soviet objectives were expansionist in scope. The orthodox view also argued that the Soviet Union violated its agreements with the Western powers, including the Yalta accords as they concerned the political future of Eastern Europe and, to a lesser extent, the role of China in the postwar world.

America's foreign policy, according to the orthodox interpretation, was in marked contrast to that of the Soviet Union. The United States, at first, held high hopes for a peaceful postwar world. The actions of its leaders were predicated on the principles of collective security, and they looked to the new-born United Nations for the solution to any future conflicts. Faced with Soviet aggressive moves, however, America was reluctantly forced to change its views and foreign policy. To prevent the Soviet Union from spreading its influence over large parts of the world, the United States finally felt compelled to embark upon a policy of "containment." Without this containment policy, argued many, the Soviet Union would probably have become the master of all Europe—instead of dominating only Eastern Europe.

Many of the arguments of the orthodox position were set forth in an article published by George F. Kennan under the pseudonym, "Mr. X," in 1947. Kennan, an American diplomat, provided many of the insights upon which the foreign policy of the Truman administration was based. In his piece Kennan suggested, among other things, an American containment policy to check Russia's expansionist tendencies. Kennan subsequently claimed, however, that he was not thinking primarily in terms of containment along military lines.[2]

The orthodox version, despite challenges, remains the dominant school of thought on the origins of the Cold War. Many of its proponents, however, differ widely in their interpretations. They all place differing emphases upon such crucial matters as the role of ideology, the inevitability of the conflict, the presumed unintentional provocation of the West, and the like. Although it may seem arbitrary to lump them together, they may be identified as "orthodox" because they generally found that responsibility for the Cold War rested to a major degree with the Soviet Union.[3] Even this categorization remains tenuous, however, because men like Kennan and Feis have changed their minds and shifted their views with the passage of time.

The roots of the revisionist interpretation, like that of the orthodox thesis, also originated in the statements from public figures as well as scholars. From the outset of the Cold War, the official explanation of events had not gone unchallenged. Henry Wallace, former Vice President, had raised a powerful voice which questioned the soundness of President Truman's analysis of the international situation during the immediate postwar years. Running as a presidential candidate of a minority party in 1948, Wallace sought to be more sympathetic towards the Russians. But his relatively poor showing revealed how little public support there was for this position.

Walter Lippmann, one of the nation's leading intellectuals and a scholarly journalist, likewise refused to place the blame for international tensions exclusively on the Soviet Union. It was Lippmann who popularized the term "Cold War" by using it in the title of a book he published in 1947.[4] In his work he argued that America's statesmen expended their energies assaulting Russia's vital interests in Eastern Europe. By doing so, they had furnished the Soviet Union with the reasons for rationalizing an iron rule behind the iron curtain. They also gave the Russians grounds to suspect what the Soviets had been conditioned to believe: that a capitalist coalition was being organized to destroy them. As a result of Lippmann's writings, in part, revisionist-

---

[2][George F. Kennan], "The Sources of Soviet Conduct," *Foreign Affairs*, XXV (July, 1947), pp. 566–582.

[3]For a few examples of the orthodox interpretation see Herbert Feis' three books, *The Road to Pearl Harbor* (Princeton, 1950), *The China Tangle* (Princeton, 1953), and *Roosevelt-Churchill-Stalin* (Princeton, 1957); William H. McNeill, *America, Britain, and Russia: Their Cooperation and Conflict, 1941–1946* (London, 1953); Norman Graebner, *Cold War Diplomacy: American Foreign Policy 1945–1960* (Princeton, 1962); and André Fontaine, *History of the Cold War from the October Revolution to the Korean War, 1917–1950* (2 vols.: New York, 1968).

[4]Walter Lippmann, *The Cold War* (New York, 1947). Lippmann's book was a collection of newspaper articles written to counter Kennan's interpretation of the motivation behind Soviet foreign policy.

minded historians began with one underlying assumption contrary to that of the orthodox interpretation: they were skeptical about accepting the claim that the Soviet Union was primarily or solely responsible for precipitating the Cold War.

Over the years, the revisionist approach to the origins of the Cold War gradually came to represent not merely a challenge but an antithetical position to the orthodox thesis. Many revisionists came to the conclusion that the United States and its policies—rather than Russia and Communism—had brought about the Cold War. The conflict had been precipitated by Western—and especially American—moves which threatened the Soviets and compelled them to react defensively. This the Russians had done by resorting to strict control over those areas that had fallen under their influence during World War II.

It is difficult to generalize about the revisionists because of the diversity of approach among this school of scholars. Each historian stressed different aspects of the Cold War, offered different arguments, and professed to see different motives behind the acts of the principal protagonists. Most revisionists, nevertheless, tended to agree that Russia was weak, not strong, after 1945 because of the ravages of war. Beginning with this premise, they then argued that the Soviet Union was neither willing nor able to pursue an aggressive policy after the war ended. Indeed, some revisionists maintained that while the Russians feared America's technological superiority and military power, they still viewed the United States as the main potential source of assistance to enable them to recover from the disastrous effects of the war. Other revisionists stressed that under Stalin the Soviet Union consistently pursued only cautious, defensive, and limited goals of foreign policy, despite the rhetoric of ideological bravado. Thus, the world-wide policy of aggression which the traditionalists believed they had detected in Russia's behavior seemed to the revisionists to be entirely out of character and beyond the means of the Soviet leaders.

During the 1950's and 1960's, many differing shades of revisionism appeared among American historians. Some scholars approached the problem by attempting to evaluate the degree to which the United States had been responsible for precipitating the Cold War. In tackling this issue, these writers sought to explain and justify Soviet actions since the war. Others analyzed American objectives in such a way as to show that these goals had been the basis for the postwar split. Some radical revisionists, expecially those associated with the "New Left," went even further: they viewed the United States as having been an aggressive power in the world not only during the Second World War, but throughout the entire twentieth century.

When revisionist-minded historians came to the matter of America's motivation, they were likewise in disagreement and offered different explanations. Some claimed that the Western powers in general, and the

Truman administration in particular, tried to deny the Soviet Union its due in the matter of the Yalta agreements: the West, they said, had sought to reinterpret the meaning of these accords, and refused to recognize what Roosevelt and Churchill had been compelled by circumstances to concede at Yalta. Other historians argued that America—imbued with the missionary zeal of a latent "manifest destiny"—had hoped to reshape the world to suit its exaggerated attachment to the democratic principles of representative government. Still other scholars stressed the theme of economic expansion—postulating that America's postwar foreign policy represented a drive to capture world markets and to establish this country's economic and political influence all over the globe. Certain historians concluded that the United States used its early monopoly of nuclear weapons and economic strength to browbeat other nation-states and to force them to submit to Washington's leadership. As proof of this position, they pointed out that the Truman administration had refused major economic assistance to the Soviet Union, and that the Marshall Plan had been designed in such a way as to preclude Soviet participation in it.

Despite the complexities within the revisionist school, it is possible to distinguish two main groups in this category—the moderate revisionists and those associated with the "New Left," who were more extreme. Although the revisionist scholars disagreed about the degree of responsibility they assigned to the United States in bringing on the Cold War, they all held America, in large part, accountable for the conflict because of her aggressive and menacing policy towards Russia.

One example of the moderate revisionist position was Denna F. Fleming's two-volume study, *The Cold War and its Origins, 1917–1960,* published in 1961. Fleming focused upon President Truman as the crucial figure in the coming of the Cold War. Within weeks after Roosevelt died, Fleming wrote, Truman dramatically reversed the course of America's foreign policy. Roosevelt had been dedicated to a Wilsonian "internationalism," and, recognizing that the Soviet Union would be the key to any new league of nations in the postwar period, had done his utmost to maintain good relations with Russia. But Truman adopted a tough policy toward the Russians as soon as he assumed the presidency. In April, 1945, he ordered the Soviets to change their policy in Poland or else America would withdraw certain promised economic aid. Contrary to the orthodox version, which generally dated the beginning of the Cold War in 1947 with the Truman Doctrine, Fleming believed it began in 1945.

Fleming's thesis that America provoked the Cold War was amplified by the picture he presented of the postwar era. The United States was invariably portrayed as taking the initiative in relations between the two powers. Russia, on the other hand, was usually depicted as reacting to events in a defensive way. Fleming's interpretation differed greatly from the orthodox version which had pictured the Soviets as the ruthless aggressor, but his findings were suspect because they were not based on solid documentation.[5]

Writing in the same revisionist tradition was Gar Alperovitz. His book *Atomic Diplomacy: Hiroshima and Potsdam*, published in the mid-1960's, held that President Truman had helped to start the Cold War in 1945 by dropping the atomic bomb. Alperovitz added a new viewpoint to the debate by arguing that Truman resorted to "atomic diplomacy." With the United States possessing a monopoly of atomic weapons at the time, Truman adopted a hard line toward the Soviets—one which was aimed at forcing Soviet Russia's acquiescence in America's postwar plans. In short, Truman fell back upon the modern equivalent of saber-rattling to play power politics and drive Russia out of East Europe by a show of force.

Like most of the moderate revisionists, however, Alperovitz did not heap all the blame for beginning the Cold War on the United States. The Russians by their actions also helped to poison the postwar atmosphere, he said. "The cold war cannot be understood simply as an American response to a Soviet challenge," he wrote, "but rather as an insidious interaction of mutual suspicions, blame for which must be shared by all." Nevertheless, the thrust of Alperovitz's work clearly placed responsibility for the beginnings of the Cold War on American shoulders.[6]

Most "New Left" historians were bitter in their condemnation of the orthodox interpretation. In large part this was so because of their own ideological commitments; they were highly critical about the very nature of American society as a whole, and hence unsympathetic with the aims of the United States abroad. Moreover, where the more moderate revisionists tended to picture Roosevelt or Truman as men of limited vision who fumbled their way to disaster in the postwar period, some "New Left" scholars were inclined to view developments against a much broader background. They wrote within a context that stretched far beyond the immediate postwar years: such "New Left" scholars held that America's foreign policy in the 1940's, 1950's, and 1960's was simply an extension of a trend that had been under way since the Spanish-American War at the turn of the century.

The most significant assault on the orthodox position came from William Appleman Williams in his books, *The Tragedy of American Diplomacy* and *The Contours of American History*, published in the late 1950's and 1960's. Although Williams never regarded himself as a member of the "New Left," his writings were seized upon and extended by other radical historians. What Williams did was to provide a provocative hypothesis to explain America's diplomacy throughout our entire his-

---

[5]Denna F. Fleming, *The Cold War and Its Origins, 1917–1960* (2 vols.: New York, 1961).

[6]Gar Alperovitz, *Atomic Diplomacy: Hiroshima and Potsdam* (New York, 1965).

tory. America's foreign policy was expansionist from our very beginnings, he declared. Writing from a neo-Beardian point of view, Williams
went all the way back to the 1760's. He showed that even before gaining
its independence, America had adopted a course to achieve economic
self-sufficiency within the British empire by applying English mercantilist principles in the New World environment. Once independence had
been won, the United States was committed to the idea of an independent American empire to enable the growing new nation to have markets for its products. Until the 1890's that empire lay mostly to the west
on the American continent, but once the frontier was gone the search for
markets led to overseas expansion. Despite the controversy between
imperialists and anti-imperialists around the turn of the century, both
groups agreed that economic expansion overseas was vital to the nation's prosperity and future. The debate was over means rather than
ends. Imperialists felt that physical acquisition of traditional colonies
was necessary; anti-imperialists, on the other hand, believed that
America's economic expansion throughout the world could be achieved
without the expense of maintaining a colonial empire.

The Open Door policy, according to Williams, resolved the dilemma,
and ultimately became the basis for America's future foreign policy.
America's Open Door policy represented an effort to achieve all the
advantages of economic expansion without the disadvantages of maintaining a colonial empire. It called for an open door for trade with all
foreign countries on a most-favored-nation principle—a principle that
had a long tradition in American diplomacy stretching back to 1776.
Although formulated originally to apply to China, the policy was expanded geographically to cover the entire globe and economically to
include American investments as well as trade.[7]

Williams, operating from this premise, saw the Cold War within a
different context than the orthodox school of historians. To him the
postwar period represented nothing more than the extension of the
Open Door policy as America, seeking markets for its goods and money,
hoped to penetrate into Eastern Europe and other parts of the globe.
Thus America was primarily responsible for the Cold War, for in seeking
to extend its economic influence she took whatever steps were necessary
to maintain or put into power governments that would do business with
the United States. Counterrevolution to make the world safe for American capitalism, not containment, was the major motive behind the
postwar policies of the United States.[8]

---

[7]William A. Williams, *The Tragedy of American Diplomacy* (2nd edn: New York, 1962), and
The Contours of American History (Cleveland, 1961).

[8]Christopher Lasch, "The Cold War, Revisited and Re-Visioned," *The New York Times*,
Jan. 14, 1968.

One of Williams' followers—Walter LaFeber (who in 1963 had published an important study of the origins of American expansionism in the late-nineteenth century)—developed and expanded this view in a monograph that appeared in 1967. LaFeber was critical of both the United States and the Soviet Union for failing to maintain peace. Focusing upon the internal reasons behind the formulation of foreign policy in the two countries, he concluded that domestic developments played a large part in determining those foreign policies that finally emerged. In America, domestic events—presidential campaigns, economic recessions, the era of repression identified with Senator Joseph McCarthy of Wisconsin, and the struggle for power by various factions within the government—contributed as much to the making of America's foreign policy as did external events. Within Russia itself, the same was true: the machinations of Stalin and Khrushchev, problems with the Soviet economy, and power struggles within the Communist party laid the basis for most foreign policy changes. In terms of economic penetration, LaFeber found that the United States and the Soviet Union showed equal interest in exploiting foreign markets wherever possible. Both nations, he concluded, created their postwar policies with an eye to maintaining freedom of action in those areas they considered vital to their economic and strategic interests.

Conflicting aims arising from domestic concerns, LaFeber said, led to a continuing rivalry between the two giant powers as they confronted one another over two decades in many parts of the globe. America's foreign policy was based on the assumption that the nation's political, economic, and psychological needs at home dictated those commitments undertaken abroad. During the first phase of the struggle—1945 to 1953—those commitments were Europe-oriented, and even the Korean War was fought, in part, to preserve America's image as the main bulwark in the West against the Communist monolith. But after the mid-1950's, both America and Russia shifted their focus from Europe to the newly emerging nations all over the world, and the Cold War entered its second phase. The Vietnam War, according to LaFeber, represented a "failure" in America's foreign policy because it sought to answer the political and economic global changes posed by the newly emerging nations with military solutions. There was continuity in America's policy, concluded LaFeber, because the American people had decided to accept the responsibility of answering challenges of such a global nature as far back as 1947 with the Truman Doctrine. In a similar vein Lloyd C. Gardner, a student of Williams at the University of Wisconsin, emphasized the commitment of American leaders to a liberal world order based on the "Open Door" policy. Haunted by fears of depression, these leaders strived to create a world economy conducive to American capitalism and prosperity. "Responsibility for the *way* in which the Cold War developed, at least," Gardner concluded, "belongs more to the United States."[9]

Gardner's work in particular influenced a number of revisionist and "New Left" scholars. Athan Theoharis, for example, accepted Gardner's contention that the United States was largely responsible for the way in which the Cold War developed. Theoharis insisted that a wide variety of options were available to American policy makers in 1945; nothing compelled the adoption of policies that led to the Cold War. During the Second World War, for example, Roosevelt followed a diplomatic policy that was strikingly vacillating and ambivalent. At Yalta, on the other hand, Roosevelt pursued a conciliatory path based upon the acceptance of Soviet postwar influence and the need to arrive at an accommodation that would avert disharmony and conflict. His death, however, altered the diplomatic setting by introducing an element of uncertainty. More importantly, it brought Harry S. Truman to the White House, an individual who was more rigidly anti-Soviet. Truman's accession to the presidency, according to Theoharis, provided the opening wedge for policy advisers whose recommendations were ignored at Yalta. The result was that the opportunities for détente provided at Yalta were effectively subverted under Truman, and the stage was set for years of conflict and confrontation. The first selection in this chapter is an excerpt from an article on the origins of the Cold War by Theoharis.

While neither Williams, LaFeber, nor Gardner necessarily included themselves as members of the "New Left," it was clear that their respective studies could easily serve as a point of departure for radical scholars. In 1968 Gabriel Kolko, whose earlier study of the origins of political capitalism from 1900 to 1917 had heralded the advent of the "New Left" school of historiography, brought out a detailed study of the origins of the Cold War that picked up where Williams and LeFeber had left off. Kolko dealt with America's foreign policy within a much narrower chronological framework; he covered only the years from 1943 to 1945. But Kolko felt that the policies forged in that crucial period were the key to the long-range plans of the United States in the postwar era. His work, *The Politics of War*, represented an attempt to document in detail and to extend the general themes introduced by Williams. Kolko advanced the thesis that the United States had acted not only to win the war in these two years, but to erect the structure for peacetime politics in the postwar world. To Kolko America's objectives were two-fold: to use its military power to defeat the enemy; and to employ its political and economic power to gain leverage for extending America's influence throughout the world. Thus, Kolko, like Williams, viewed the United

---

[9]Walter LaFeber, *America, Russia, and the Cold War, 1945–1966* (New York, 1967), and Lloyd C. Gardner, *Architects of Illusion: Men and Ideas in American Foreign Policy, 1941–1949* (Chicago, 1970).

States as a counterrevolutionary force bent on restoring the old order in Europe and making the world safe for American capitalism. [10]

Kolko's assumptions regarding America's postwar policies were typical of many of the "New Left" scholars. He assumed, first of all, that the United States, not Russia, represented the greatest threat to international stability; that America was mainly responsible for bringing on the Cold War. Second, that the United States was dedicated to world-wide counterrevolution: to a policy of employing her military and economic power to extend her influence throughout the world because American capitalism was dependent upon ever-expanding foreign markets for survival. And third, that the origins of the Cold War lay not solely within World War II but stretched back to World War I and beyond.

Significantly, the revisionist view of Cold War diplomacy—both moderate and extremist—developed mainly in the 1960's. This decade was a period of deepening disillusionment among American intellectuals over the nation's foreign policy. Disenchanted by America's intervention in Cuba and Santo Domingo and the escalating involvement in Vietnam, many intellectuals had begun to question whether the United States had not taken too seriously the responsibilities of world leadership and had involved itself unnecessarily in the internal affairs of other nations where it had no business. Moreover, they feared that this country was so conditioned to fighting totalitarianism that American leaders tended to see enemies where none existed. It is not too much to suggest that this reaction among intellectuals helped to shape the unsympathetic view that the revisionists had taken toward America's foreign policy.

If the orthodox and revisionist interpretations represented antithetical views about the origins of the Cold War, the realist school has become, in many ways, a middle-of-the-road position. The realists, unlike the revisionists who followed them, were less likely to dismiss containment because it represented in their eyes a necessary response to Soviet expansionism. On the other hand, they were critical of the orthodox scholars because of the excessive moralism and legalism in the traditional interpretation. The realists were more prone to view foreign relations in terms of *realpolitik* from which the school derived its name, and to place more emphasis upon power politics and conflicting national interests. Historians of the realist school were less concerned with determining the degree of moral responsibility for the Cold War and focused their attention instead on the pragmatic political problems facing the policy-makers.

Like the other two schools of scholars, the realists could trace their

---

[10]Gabriel Kolko, *The Politics of War: The World and United States Foreign Policy, 1943–1945* (New York, 1968). See also Joyce Kolko and Gabriel Kolko, *The Limits of Power: The World and United States Foreign Policy, 1945–1954* (New York, 1972).

origins back to the late 1940's and early 1950's. Their writings began as a response, in part, to the strong criticisms of Roosevelt's role in the developing East-West impasse. These criticisms held that America's supposed weakness in the postwar period had resulted either from Roosevelt's misunderstanding of Soviet intentions or from his failure to foresee the incompatibility of Soviet and American goals. In the eyes of his critics, Roosevelt was responsible for the subsequent subjugation of Eastern Europe. But the realists argued that Roosevelt, in fact, was faced with a *fait accompli* in Eastern Europe with powerful Russian armies occupying that area, and that the diplomatic options open to him were severely limited as a result.

Generally speaking, the realists held that the blame for the Cold War belonged either to both sides or, more accurately, to neither. Indeed, neither the United States nor the Soviet Union had wanted to precipitate a conflict. Both had hoped that cooperation among the allies would continue—but on their own terms, of course. Each country had sought limited objectives but had expected the other to accept them as such. To be specific, the Soviet Union was motivated by fear and acted in the interests of its security rather than out of any expansionist ambitions. However, whenever one side made a move in pursuit of its limited objectives, the other side perceived the act as a threat to its existence and, in reacting accordingly, triggered a countermeasure which led to increasing escalation. As a result, small and otherwise manageable foreign crises had led inevitably to a widening conflict, which gradually assumed global proportions. In short, the realists found that both sides in pursuing their interests had sought limited goals, but the spiraling effect of such measures had inadvertently precipitated the Cold War.

The realist school tended also to view the Cold War as a traditional power conflict rather than a clash of ideologies. To many of these historians the Cold War was comparable to some of the previous struggles that had taken place to prevent a single power from dominating Europe's east-central regions. Other scholars saw the conflict within the context of the age-old battle over the European balance of power.

When viewing the situation in postwar Europe, members of the realist school took a hard look at political realities rather than indulging in speculations about diplomatic possibilities. While stressing Soviet determination to create in Eastern Europe satellite states that would enhance Russia's security, the realists also emphasized how vulnerable the countries in that part of Europe were to outside pressures because their own social, political, and economic systems had proven incapable of solving the problems of their people. These societies were ripe for revolution, the realists concluded, and an easy prey to the indigenous Communist movements that existed and were Moscow-directed. The countries of Western Europe, they argued, were not susceptible to the same pressures; their social, economic and political institutions, though weakened by the war, were still viable. Hence the realists concluded that the fear expressed in the orthodox interpretation—that Soviet influence might extend across Europe to reach the English Channel—was not only exaggerated but revealed a misunderstanding of the nature of the conflict.

The realists usually disagreed with the moderate revisionists who, like Alperovitz, claimed that the United States had used its monopoly of atomic weapons to force other nation-states into submission. On the other hand, they accepted the thesis that in employing nuclear weapons against Japan the American government was motivated not only by a desire to conclude the Pacific war, but by the hope of doing so before the Soviet Union could enter that theater of war. America, they wrote, feared that Moscow might attempt to do in the Far East what it appeared to be doing in Eastern Europe. Thus, the presence of nuclear weapons in American hands was believed by the realists to have had a psychological effect upon both the atomic "haves" and "have-nots" during the initial phases of the Cold War.

The realists likewise disagreed with those revisionists associated with the "New Left." They challenged the assumptions, ideological considerations, and political misconceptions upon which they felt the "New Left" historians based their arguments. In his review of Kolko's *The Politics of War,* Hans J. Morgenthau (one of the leading realist scholars) charged that Kolko was reflecting the mood of his own generation in attributing blame for the origins of the Cold War. That mood, Morgenthau noted,

> . . . reacts negatively to the simple and simplistic equation, obligatory during the war and postwar periods, of American interests and policies with democratic virtue and wisdom, and those of their enemies with totalitarian folly and vice. As the orthodox historiography of the Second World War and the Cold War expressed and justified that ideological juxtaposition, so the revisionism of Professor Kolko expresses and justifies the new mood of ideological sobriety. However, given the moralism behind American political thinking regardless of its content, revisionism tends to be as moralistic in its critique of American foreign policy as orthodoxy is in defending it. While the moralistic approach remains, the moral labels have been reversed: what once was right is now wrong, and vice versa. Yet as historic truth may emerge from the dialectic of opposite extremes, qualified and tempered by charity and understanding, so sound political judgment requires both the recognition of extreme positions as inevitable and of their possible transcendence through a morality which is as alien to the moralism of our political folklore as Thucydidean justice is to the compensatory justice of opposing historical schools.[11]

---

[11]Hans J. Morgenthau, "Historical Justice and the Cold War," *New York Review of Books,* July 10, 1969.

Morgenthau's own writings represented one of the best examples of the realist point of view. In them he was critical of what he called the legalistic-moralistic tradition which presumably prevented American statesmen from perceiving foreign policy in terms of national power and national interest in the past. His book *In Defense of the National Interest: A Critical Examination of American Foreign Policy,* published in 1951, claimed that America's foreign policies since 1776 had been much too utopian in outlook. Only in the years since World War II, he suggested, had Americans become more realistic and formulated their policy on the basis of power politics and national interest.[12] Nevertheless, American policymakers had misunderstood Soviet foreign policy; they failed to see the essential continuity in the expansionist objectives sought by the czars and later by the Communists and focused instead on the new goals supposedly arising out of a revolutionary ideology. Thus, Morgenthau criticized the orthodox interpretation by suggesting that the United States had contributed to the coming of the Cold War by its long-standing tendency to view its relationship to the rest of the world in rather unrealistic terms.

Another member of the realist school, Louis Halle, took a somewhat different approach. In his book, *The Cold War as History,* published in the mid-1960's, Halle was more interested in stressing the tragic nature of the conflict. He suggested that neither side was really to blame for the Cold War. Misconceptions on both sides had led to the rise of ideological myths—myths which often had little relation to existing social realities. The West, led by the United States, was governed by the myth of a monolithic conspiracy among Communists the world over to drive for global domination, initially under the leadership of the Soviet Union. The Communists, on their part—Lenin and his associates in 1917–1918 and Mao Tse-tung a generation later in 1949–1950—were under the spell of another myth. Their world view pictured a globe divided between capitalist-imperialists, on the one hand, and exploited peasants and proletariat on the other. Each of these two Communist leaders in his own time had believed that the historical moment had come when the oppressed lower classes were about to rise up in revolution, to overthrow their upper-class masters, and to establish a utopian society of the brotherhood of man along lines predicted by Karl Marx. It was the belief in such myths which drove the free world and the Communist camp to embark upon what each side considered to be a struggle for survival.

Historical interpretations, of course, often run in cycles. Just as the revisionists challenged their more orthodox predecessors, so too did

---

[12]Hans J. Morgenthau, *In Defense of the National Interest: A Critical Examination of American Foreign Policy* (New York, 1951). In this same regard, it should be noted that George Kennan has come much closer to the realist school by arguing in his memoirs that the Truman administration pursued the wrong priorities in Europe by concentrating on a policy of *military* containment. George F. Kennan, *Memoirs, 1925–1950* (Boston, 1967).

they come under scrutiny as the disillusionment of the 1960's and early 1970's gave way to new moods. Their implicit acceptance of American hegemony, moreover, seemed less tenable after the Arab-Israeli war of 1973, when an oil embargo and a subsequent quadrupling of oil prices demonstrated the vulnerability of the United States as well as its inability to use power without restraint. Some of the attacks on the revisionist interpretation were frontal in nature. In an analysis of the works of seven leading revisionist historians, Robert J. Maddox accused them of distorting facts to prove their thesis. "Stated briefly," he noted in his introduction, "the most striking characteristic of revisionist historiography has been the extent to which New Left authors have revised the evidence itself. And if the component parts of historical interpretations are demonstrably false, what can be said about the interpretations? They may yet be valid, but in the works examined they are often irrelevant to the data used to support them. Until this fact is recognized, there can be no realistic assessment of which elements of revisionism can justifiably be incorporated into new syntheses and which must be disregarded altogether."[13]

While Maddox was faulting revisionists for their improper use of facts, others were challenging the revisionist conceptualization of American foreign policy. In a broad-ranging discussion, Jerome Slater specifically rejected the allegation that America was an imperialist or imperial nation. Conceding that economic considerations played a role in foreign policy, he insisted that they did not occupy a central or dominant position. Moreover, the United States did not employ the traditional methods of imperialism to attain its economic objectives. Nor were the consequences of American foreign policy sufficiently extensive to justify describing them in imperialistic terms. Even the growth of the American economy was not due to the exploitation of others. Although Slater did not minimize the economic, political, and military power of the United States, he maintained that its ability to control the politics of other nations remained minimal after 1945. His analysis represented a clear rejection of those revisionists who insisted that American diplomacy was at base guided by imperialistic considerations even though colonization and political control were absent. Indeed, Slater argued that much of the criticism of the United States reflected the resentment of the Third World about the prevailing inequality in the distribution of wealth. An excerpt from Slater's article is included as the second selection in this chapter.

In reviewing the three schools of thought—the orthodox, revisionist, and realist—students should decide for themselves the fundamental questions raised regarding America's role in world affairs since the

---

[13]Robert J. Maddox, *The New Left and the Origins of the Cold War* (Princeton, 1973), pp. 10–11.

1940's. Did the Cold War commence with the Second World War, or did it stretch back in time? Did the move of the Soviet Union into Eastern Europe represent the realization of a centuries-old Russian dream of a sphere of influence in that region? Or was it an effort by the Kremlin to extend the influence of Communism in the immediate postwar period? Had the course of American diplomacy since the Spanish-American War been committed to the defense of a global status quo in an attempt to find the ever expanding foreign markets supposedly necessary for the survival of American capitalism? Or could the roots of the Cold War crisis be traced back to the mid-1940's when Russian military forces occupied Eastern Europe? Were America's moves dictated by a containment policy aimed at checking what was believed to be a Soviet plan for spreading Communism throughout the world? Or was the United States bent upon a conservative counterrevolution that would maintain the world economic and political order in a state conducive to the purposes of American capitalism? In answering such questions, students will cope not only with the issue of the Cold War but with the very nature of American society itself.

Athan Theoharis

ATHAN THEOHARIS (1936–   ) is Professor of History at Marquette University. He
has written a number of articles and books on American history since 1945,
including *The Yalta Myths: An Issue in U.S. Politics, 1945–1955* (1970), and *Seeds
of Repression: Harry S. Truman and the Origins of McCarthyism* (1971).

Only recently has the question of the origins of the cold war seriously
divided American historians, the emergence of a "revisionist" school
coinciding with intensive research into primary sources. Yet, revisionists
do disagree over whether there existed a discontinuity between President Roosevelt's and President Truman's policies; they disagree in their
evaluations of the relative influence of economic and political considerations and in their estimates of the role of key advisers in shaping the
decisions and priorities of the two presidents.

This paper will emphasize the tactics and personalities of Roosevelt
and Truman, their specific responses to Soviet policy and influence.
Focusing on Yalta, I shall examine the Truman administration's commitment to the agreements concluded at the conference and Roosevelt's
and the State Department's responsibilities for the development of the
cold war. Conceding that the trend of the Open Door ideology was
inimical to accommodation with the Soviet Union, I, nonetheless, contend that the discretion available to policy makers did not demand the
specific policies adopted after April 1945 that led to the cold war. Put
simply, the thesis of this paper is, to quote Lloyd C. Gardner, that "the
United States was more responsible for the *way* in which the Cold War
developed."

At issue for American diplomats during the 1940s was how to deal
with the progress and consequences of World War II. Given the Soviet
Union's strategic political and geographic position and its inevitable
physical presence in non-Soviet territories after the war, the development of U.S. policy toward Eastern Europe, Germany, and the Far East
would influence the climate of Soviet-American relations. Indeed, the
diplomacy of the Roosevelt and Truman administrations in the 1941–46
period was the product, in part, of their conceptions of the Soviet in-

Athan Theoharis, "Roosevelt and Truman on Yalta: The Origins of the Cold War." Reprinted with permission from the *Political Science Quarterly*, 87 (June, 1972), pp. 210–241.
Footnotes omitted.

volvement in the Far Eastern war and its consequences for postwar China and Japan; and of the status of postwar Germany as determined by decisions concerning the level of German reparations payments.

The dominant role of the post-New Deal presidency in the formulation of foreign policy, the consistency of Truman's policies with those of Roosevelt, and the extent to which either president determined policy or followed recommendations of ostensibly subordinate advisers, furthermore, had crucial significance for U.S.-Soviet relations. During the war, and in the postwar years, U.S. policy was made by the president or his advisers, and not simply at the major summit conferences. At best, the role of the public or of Congress had become that of a potential restraint; policy makers did operate on the premise that Congress or the public might seek to counteract policy decisions. Yet, these were possible deterrents; they did not control policy. As one result of the Executive Reorganization Act of 1939, the president had acquired a bureaucratic apparatus that increased his independence and authority. The post-New Deal president, by resorting to public relations and *fait accompli*, had, as a result, greater freedom to create public opinion and structure the policy debate.

Soviet responses, moreover, were based on an appraisal of the policies of the president, and not on the differing priorities of advisers, the Congress, the public, or the press. While, admittedly, the president, especially Roosevelt, might invoke public, congressional, or press opinion during negotiations with Soviet leaders, this bargaining ploy did not lead Stalin or other leaders in the Kremlin to view U.S. policy as determined by domestic considerations. Concessions might be made in the wording of communiques to make an agreement more palatable to the American public or press, but Soviet policy makers operated on the assumption that they were dealing with the president and that his policy was based upon understood commitments. For this reason, the nature of presidential leadership influenced immediate postwar relations between the United States and the Soviet Union. Most significantly, the Truman administration's attempts to "undo" the Yalta commitments led to the cold war.

What was involved was not only the enigmatic and ambiguous nature of Roosevelt's policies, substantial as these ambiguities were, but the noncommitment of key personnel in the State Department to the "soft" line that Roosevelt had adopted at Yalta.... The rigidity of their position, in contrast to Roosevelt's at Yalta, contained the seeds of possible conflict with the Soviet Union after Truman's accession to the presidency. Truman's limited understanding, of both international affairs and Roosevelt's specific commitments, would enable policy advisers to become policy makers after April 1945 when determining the meaning of the Yalta agreements....

I

During the war years, Roosevelt's policies toward the potential problems concerning the postwar status of Eastern Europe, Germany, and the Far East were strikingly vacillating and ambivalent. The president, like his conservative secretary of state, Cordell Hull, sought to postpone difficult political decisions until after the war. For a time, he refused even to enter serious discussions with the Soviet Union over territorial and other political matters. Roosevelt's stance on German reparations particularly dramatizes this ambiguity of policy and preference for postponement. Thus, although Hull had agreed both to the principle of reparations in kind and not in money at the Moscow foreign ministers conference of October 1943 and to the establishment of an European Advisory Commission to outline Allied policy toward postwar Germany, no efforts were made to determine the level or basis of reparations payments and to develop plans for postwar occupation. In October 1944, indeed, Roosevelt halted any planning for postwar Germany. Significantly, while the debate between Treasury and State was raging over the level of German reparations, Roosevelt wrote to Hull that " 'I do not think that at this present stage any good purpose would be served by having the State Department or any other Department sound out the British and Russian views on the treatment of German industry.' " . . .

Throughout 1943 and 1944, Roosevelt sustained this noncommital course, thus strengthening the resistance of the London Poles to serious negotiations and thereby contributing to the deterioration of Soviet-Polish relations. Following the Soviet incursion into Polish territory in January 1944, Roosevelt offered his good offices to Mikolajczyk, the prime minister of the London Polish government, to mediate but not guarantee a solution of the Polish border difficulty. Roosevelt abandoned this stance of studied ambiguity only on November 17, 1944, and then after Soviet troops had crossed the Curzon line (July 22) and after Moscow Radio had announced the formation of a Polish Committee on National Liberation (July 22) and the subsequent signing of a military and political agreement between this committee and the Soviet Union. At that time and with the American presidential election over, Roosevelt informed Mikolajczyk that whatever agreement the Poles and the Soviet Union concluded would be acceptable to the United States but that the United States could not guarantee Poland's frontiers.

U.S. policy had not been simply the product of domestic politics; key policy advisers had continually counseled a firm stand against the Soviets and the need to sustain the London Poles. Indeed, within State, John Hickerson, deputy director of the office of European affairs, recommended, on January 8, 1945, that the United States secure the establishment of a Provisional Security Council, in which the United States would have a major voice, to supervise political developments in Eastern Europe. And, on January 18, 1945, Secretary of State Stettinius made the same recommendation to Roosevelt. Significantly, Stettinius's proposal provided not only for a rotating chairmanship, thereby implying the equality of the powers, but also for establishing the headquarters in Paris. . . .

Throughout, Roosevelt attempted to secure Soviet military involvement in the war against Japan. He continued to operate on the premise that U.S. policy—to make China a great power—was correct and attainable. A Sino-Soviet accord, he believed, would minimize Soviet intervention in China and force the Chinese Communists to come to terms with Chiang Kai-shek. At the same time, Roosevelt never consistently backed General Stillwell's efforts to reform the Chinese Nationalist regime or to alter its military policy. A sense of wishfulness characterized Roosevelt's estimates of the internal strength of the Nationalist regime, of the prospects for resolving the civil conflict between the Nationalists and Communists without civil war, and of the simply military consequences of Soviet involvement in the war against Japan.

II

Roosevelt's decision to go to Yalta constituted, in essence, a change from wishful thinking and postponement. By early 1945, military developments, and prospective military and political developments, ensured that the Soviets would play a dominant role in Eastern Europe, that Soviet unilateral actions in Germany would complicate Allied occupation policy, and that the Soviet role in the Far East possibly could frustrate the attainment of U.S. objectives. To postpone matters to a postwar peace conference might contribute to the establishment of spheres of influence, to the breakdown of Allied unity and cooperation, and to the radicalization of politics throughout Europe and the Far East.

Roosevelt's diplomacy at Yalta, therefore, reflected not so much overconfidence in his ability to placate Stalin through personal diplomacy, though this was a factor, as his recognition of the weakness of the U.S. diplomatic position and the reality—even legitimacy—of Soviet influence in Eastern Europe, the Far East, and Germany. Although the language is vague, the Yalta agreements did confirm this acceptance of Soviet postwar influence and the importance of acccommodation to avert disharmony and conflict.

The most troublesome issue confronting the conferees was Poland. Roosevelt's phrasing of his requests at Yalta clearly conceded the weakness of the Western bargaining position. He emphasized his need to "save face" when pressing for slight territorial concessions to the Poles from the Curzon Line, emphasized the domestic importance of the

Polish-American vote when urging Stalin to make other concessions over the status of the Polish government, and requested "some gesture" to satisfy the demand of the six million Polish-Americans that the United States be "in some way involved with the question of freedom of elections." By basing his requests on American domestic political considerations, Roosevelt undermined his effect on the decisions of the conference. The final communiqué could simply be worded to gloss over what in fact had been conceded. In many respects, this was the result of the negotiations on Poland: Stalin merely agreed to a formula for the formation of a Polish provisional government and the holding of free and democratic elections under tripartite supervision that would not contradict Soviet objectives yet would enable Roosevelt and Churchill to appease the public opinion that they had so regularly cited during conference proceedings.

Moreover, Roosevelt's February 6 demand that a new Polish government be established, maintaining that the Lublin government "as now composed" could not be accepted (a statement which Churchill immediately endorsed), was not pressed at the conference. The reference to Lublin "as *now* composed" and the further assurance to Stalin that the United States would never support in any way any Polish government "that would be inimical to your interests," significantly reduced the impact of this demand. Stalin replied that Poland did not involve merely honor or domestic public opinion, but the security of the Soviet Union. Second, indirectly recalling the example of the Italian surrender, Stalin also emphasized the importance for the Red Army of secure supply lines in its advance into Germany that only a stable, nonhostile local administration could provide.

The result, incorporated in the Declaration on Liberated Europe and the agreement dealing with Poland, amounted to face-saving formulas for the West. The Lublin government was not to be scrapped for a wholly new government, but rather enlarged to provide the basis for the new government. Stettinius's proposal for reorganizing the Lublin government—"fully representative Government based on all democratic forces in Poland and abroad"—was amended by Molotov to "wider democratic basis with the inclusion of democratic leaders from Poland and abroad." And, the language of the amended Declaration on Liberated Europe, by providing for unanimity even before consultations could begin, acknowledged Soviet authority and her right to veto her allies' objections. Further, the initial State Department proposal for "appropriate machinery for the carrying out of the joint responsibilities set forth in this declaration" was also amended by Molotov to provide instead that the three governments "will immediately take measures for the carrying out of mutual consultations." Nor was observation of the proposed future elections by the three governments guaranteed, since, "in effect," ambassadors alone would observe and report on elections.

The Eastern European agreements, one-sided and a tacit repudiation of earlier U.S. policy, indirectly served to create the potential for subsequent U.S.-Soviet problems. The vagueness of the language, the seeming lack (at least as existing published papers of the proceedings reveal) of intensive discussion over significant changes that amounted to U.S. acceptance of the Soviet position, as well as the exclusion of State from a central negotiating role and the implicit rejection of its policy recommendations at Yalta meant that implementation of the agreements would be determined by the commitment of U.S. policy makers to accept the reality of Soviet influence and the spirit underlying the conference.

A similar situation occurred in the Yalta discussions on Germany. Most important matters involving Germany were postponed, though even then it was implicitly agreed that the Big Three would jointly determine occupation and reparations policy. The level of German reparations payments did divide the Allies at Yalta. The final agreement, though, provided for the creation of a reparations commission to discuss this question; the commission was instructed, with Roosevelt and Stalin concurring and Churchill dissenting, that during its deliberations the figure of $20 billion with one-half going to the Soviet Union should provide "the basis for discussion."

At Yalta, Roosevelt had no clearly formulated German policy. Supporting simply a harsh peace, but no longer committed to dismemberment and sizable reparations, he nonetheless remained unwilling to force a dispute with Stalin and accepted the postponement of these issues. Roosevelt's agreement to a stated sum as the basis for discussion, however, could be construed as a commitment in a principle to a fixed figure if not to that sum. The only merit of Roosevelt's temporizing was in avoiding division and disharmony. By not providing clear guidelines for future discussions, it served to complicate future U.S.-Soviet relations.

The Yalta discussions on the Far East were characterized by the same imprecision of agreement and absence of thorough negotiations. The general terms of Soviet involvement had tacitly been agreed to at Teheran and during discussions between Stalin and Harriman in 1944. Both Roosevelt and Stalin remained interested, nonetheless, in a more specific understanding. At Stalin's insistence, the conditions for Soviet involvement were set forth in writing at Yalta and agreed to by the three powers (though Britain did not participate in the discussions). Specifically, the Soviet Union was to receive South Sakhalin and the Kurile Islands from Japan. In addition, Russia secured "lease" rights to Port Arthur; her "pre-eminent interests" were to be safeguarded in an internationalized port of Dairen and in a "jointly operated" Sino-Soviet commission for the Chinese-Eastern Railroad and the South-Manchurian Railroad; and the status of Outer Mongolia was to be "preserved." Roosevelt admitted not having discussed the matters of Outer Mongolia, the ports, or the railroads with Chiang Kai-shek and conceded that, for the moment, military considerations required continued secrecy. Stalin then informed Roosevelt that Chinese Foreign Minister T.V. Soong was coming to Moscow in April, that it might be appropriate at that time to inform him of this matter. Ultimately, it was decided that Roosevelt would take the initiative to inform the Chinese and would make this move when so directed by Stalin, the determining factor to be military developments in Europe. In return for these concessions, Roosevelt secured two qualified Soviet commitments: to enter the war against Japan two or three months after the termination of the war in Europe and to conclude a pact of "friendship and alliance" with the Nationalist government.

The Far Eastern agreements, however, had not defined the extent of the Soviet role in Manchuria, particularly in the area surrounding the ports and railroads; the reference to the "pre-eminent interests" of the Soviet Union could result in the establishment of a Soviet sphere of influence. Moreover, whether Roosevelt had accepted the German or Italian model as the basis for joint occupation policy in postwar Japan was not clear from the discussions or agreements reached at Yalta. No specific agreement had been made concerning this matter—the outright cession of South Sakhalin and the Kuriles to the Soviet Union did not establish physical occupation of Japanese territory and a right to have an equal voice in occupation policy. Roosevelt's Soviet involvement, however, and the spirit of mutual assistance and cooperation provided justification for Soviet insistence on equal participation in occupation policy.

In sum, at Yalta, Roosevelt adopted a conciliatory policy, accepting the reality of Soviet power and the legitimacy of her post-war involvement in Eastern Europe, Germany, and the Far East. . . .

III

Roosevelt's death significantly changed the diplomatic setting, by introducing, for one thing, an element of uncertainty about future U.S.-Soviet relations. More important, it introduced Harry S. Truman, a man more rigidly anti-Soviet and, given also his noninvolvement in Roosevelt's policymaking, more responsive to the suggestions of policy advisers whose recommendations had been ignored at Yalta. He personal political style would have far-reaching consequences for the Yalta understandings: Truman would not feel compelled to honor the commitments and would seek to exploit the vague language of the agreements to avoid compliance.

In part, the Truman administration in 1945 bore the legacies of

Roosevelt's earlier policy of postponing and avoiding clearly defined commitments and the partial continuing of that policy at Yalta. Despite Yalta, doubt remained over Roosevelt's position on, among other things, German reparations and dismemberment, the character of the postwar governments of Eastern Europe, and the nature of the Soviet postwar role in the Far East. More important, in making concessions to the Soviet Union, Roosevelt had acted unilaterally, without securing the understanding or acquiescence of his subordinates. The imprecision of Roosevelt's administrative leadership thereby provided an opportunity for these subordinates to take advantage of the policy vacuum created by Roosevelt's death and Truman's woeful ignorance of both international politics and the Yalta commitments to secure the eventful adoption of their recommendations.

In April, Harriman had a conversation with Stalin that, because it coincided with Roosevelt's death, permitted him to affirm Truman's intention to continue the policies of his predecessor. Capitalizing on Stalin's statement of willingness to work with Truman as he had with Roosevelt, Harriman extracted from the premier a pledge to have Molotov, on his way to San Francisco, stop off in Washington to consult with Truman. Such a move, Harriman insisted, would promote collaboration. Stalin acceded. Intended as a friendly gesture, Molotov's trip was initiated to provide the opportunity for an exchange of views and a testing of cooperation.

Harriman's move, though not necessarily intentionally, coincided with an intensive policy reexamination in Washington involving Truman and key advisers who had urged Truman not to compromise to reach accommodation.

Truman, in fact, adopted a less conciliatory approach in April 1945. On April 16, he and Churchill sent a joint note to Stalin outlining their proposal for resolving the Polish impasse. Their note placed the Western-oriented Polish political leaders on the same basis with the Lublin Poles. Understanding that even the vague language of the Yalta agreements did not support his position, Truman, nonetheless, remained confident that a strong stand would not precipitate a break with the Soviet Union.

The same attitude also prevailed at his meeting with Molotov on April 23. Truman's language at that meeting was blunt and undiplomatic, specifically rejecting the Yugoslav formula (expanding the existing government by adding a new minister for every four already in the cabinet) as the basis for composing the new Polish provisional government. An agreement had been concluded, Truman self-righteously affirmed, and only required Soviet compliance. In response to Molotov's protests, Truman conceded the vagueness of the language of the agreements (the president had earlier been advised by Leahy, among others, that the Soviet position was consistent with the Yalta agreements). Molotov denied that any agreement had been broken and stressed the need for cooperation, to which Truman reiterated his insistence that the U.S. interpretation was the only one possible.

The result of this meeting, if possibly psychologically satisfying to the frustrated Americans, did not lead to diplomatic resolution. Responding to the April 16 note and the April 23 meeting, Stalin emphasized Poland's importance to Soviet security and protested Western efforts to dictate to the Soviet Union. Truman's refusal to accept Lublin as the core of the new government was inconsistent with the Yalta agreements. Soviet actions in Poland were comparable to those of Britain in Belgium and Greece; the Soviet Union had not sought to interfere in these countries or to ascertain whether British actions made possible representative government. The United States and Great Britain were combining against the Soviet Union and the United States was attempting to secure Soviet renunciation of her security interests.

On May 19, in a seeming about-face, Truman consulted Stalin on Harry Hopkins's proposed mission to Moscow for mutual consultations. Significantly, when the Hopkins mission was first considered in early May, Byrnes and the State Department opposed the idea, recognizing that it meant that Truman had decided to make some concessions to the Soviets.

Truman's objectives for the Hopkins mission remain obscure. The trip did not eliminate the tensions that had surfaced in April, though an agreement worked out on the composition of the Polish provisional government did essentially follow the Yugoslav formula, and on July 5, the Truman administration did recognize the reorganized government.

The Eastern European question, however, had not been amicably resolved. At Potsdam, Truman refused to recognize either the Oder-Neisse line as the western boundary of Poland or Soviet primacy in Bulgaria, Hungary, and Romania. In his public report of August 9 on the results of the conference, Truman declared that Bulgaria and Romania were not to be within the sphere of influence of any one power. And earlier on June 1, 12, and 14, the administration had instructed Harriman to propose to Stalin that the United States and Great Britain be accorded veto power over the actions of Soviet commanders in Hungary, Romania, and Bulgaria.

The Truman administration's decision to accept confrontation rather than seek accommodation also underlay its often shifting and confused, but unbending, German policy. Thus, even though, at the time, these decisions did not necessarily reflect a conscious strategy or policy, on May 10, 1945, Truman unilaterally approved Joint Chiefs of Staff (JCS) directive 1067 and replaced Roosevelt's representative to the Moscow Reparations Commission, Isadore Rubin, with Edwin Pauley. The vagueness of JCS 1067 and the unilateral nature of its promulgation, without consultation with the British, Russians, or French, marked a shift toward a softer policy toward Germany. The directive simply provided general discretion to U.S. military zonal authorities to determine the level of German industrial production and, indirectly thereby, German reparations payments.

During the June discussions in Moscow on reparations, Pauley had adopted an uncompromising line on Soviet requests for specific agreement on German reparations levels, thereby effectively averting progress toward any agreement. The Truman delegation adopted the same stance at Potsdam, indirectly avoiding the issue of joint policy. While paying lip service to the Yalta agreement on reparations, Secretary of State Byrnes refused to respond to Soviet efforts to determine the specific reparations sum that the United States would accept. Dismissing the Yalta figure of $10 billion as "impractical," Byrnes supported a policy whereby, in Molotov's words, "each country would have a free hand in their own zone and could act entirely independently of the others." Despite Assistant Secretary of State Clayton's warning that Byrnes's insistence that reparations come from the zone of the occupying power "would be considered by the Russians as a reversal of the Yalta position," Truman did not alter this position. Potsdam, then, contributed to the division of Germany along zonal lines. In addition, Truman's willingness to reject the Yalta formulas, while publicly proclaiming his commitment to them, added the element of distrust to diplomatic relations. The further complication to joint planning provided later by French obstruction heightened this distrust. A high Soviet official told James Warburg in the summer of 1946 that "after six months of French obstruction, we began to suspect that this was a put-up job—that you did not like the bargain you had made at Potsdam and that you are letting the French get you out of it." . . .

The vague wording of the Far Eastern agreements presented formidable unresolved diplomatic problems for the entering Truman administration. On the surface, the concessions did not seem major. In fact, however, the extent of the postwar Soviet role in either China or Japan had not been clearly defined. Thus, as soon as he became president, Truman was beset by pressure from key advisers in State, the Foreign Service, and his cabinet to reappraise the Far Eastern agreements. At an April 23 cabinet meeting, the president himself raised the issue of reappraisal. Distressed over Soviet actions in Eastern Europe, Truman suggested that the failure of a Yalta signatory to fulfill any of its commitments might free the other signatories from fulfilling theirs. The main opposition to this position came from the military. General George C. Marshall, then chairman of the Joint Chiefs of Staff, argued that the concessions had to stand because the Far Eastern war could not be won without Soviet military assistance.

While no formal decision on the concessions was reached in the cabinet then, the German surrender on May 8 led to further administration reevaluation of Yalta. During a May 11 meeting in Forrestal's office, Harriman, who was about to return to Moscow, contended that "it was time to come to a conclusion about the necessity for the early entrance of Russia into the Japanese war." He reiterated this case at State on May 12, and it was agreed that Harriman's views should be formulated precisely "for discussion with the President." . . .

The United States' seeming ambivalence throughout this preliminary negotiating period was indicative not of indifference but of the desire to forestall Soviet involvement in the Far East. Since the Soviet Union had declared its unwillingness to enter the war against Japan until a treaty had been concluded with China, by stalling negotiations on that treaty, the administration could avert the inevitable extension of Soviet influence in China and Japan without formally repudiating the terms laid down at Yalta.

By June, the administration's options had increased as the result of the defeat of Germany. Thereafter, the administration operated on the premise that Soviet military involvement against Japan was not imperative. This shift was revealed on June 18 in another change of position by the Joint Chiefs of Staff, who now described Soviet aid as desirable but not indispensable and recommended that the United States not bargain for Soviet involvement.

With all this in mind, Truman and Byrnes discussed the Far East with Stalin and Molotov at the Potsdam Conference on July 17. First the Soviet leaders informed Truman and Byrnes of their willingness to accept Chinese control of Manchuria as well as to recognize the Nationalists as the sole leaders of China. In reply, Byrnes affirmed that the United States held to a strict interpretation of the Yalta terms. Then, feigning ignorance of the recently concluded Soong-Stalin talks, Byrnes sounded out Stalin about the areas of Sino-Soviet disagreement. On the basis of Stalin's reply, Byrnes and Truman concluded that the differences between the Soviet and Chinese positions were so fundamental that, at least in the immediate future, a Sino-Soviet treaty was highly unlikely.

The Potsdam discussions between the U.S. and Soviet military staffs provided further assurances for the administration that a Sino-Soviet treaty was still a necessary precondition for Russia's entering the Japanese war. Moreover, at Potsdam, the administration remained in contact with the Chinese Nationalists. On July 20, Chiang Kai-shek informed Truman about Soong's mission, arguing that the Chinese had bargained in good faith and could make no further concessions to secure the treaty. Truman agreed—in fact, he directed Chiang specifically to make no more concessions. Despite this, Truman insisted on the implementation of the Yalta terms and urged Chiang to have Soong return to Moscow to continue negotiations.

While the administration continued formally to support the Yalta commitments, in view of the July 17 meeting with Stalin and Molotov, Truman's instructions to Chiang—if Soong followed them—would effectively stymie the conclusion of a treaty. Moreover, the successful testing of the atomic bomb led Marshall to concede to Stimson and Truman on July 23 that Soviet entry into the war against Japan was no longer necessary, but Marshall again maintained that the Soviet Union could enter anyway and obtain "virtually what they wanted in the surrender terms." Byrnes came away from the discussion hoping only that the Sino-Soviet discussions might be stalled and thereby "delay Soviet entrance and the Japanese might surrender." Finally, instead of consulting the Soviets, the administration unilaterally drafted the formal declaration demanding unconditional Japanese surrender; it also decided unilaterally to accept the Japanese request of August 10 for clarification of the surrender terms.

Moreover, once the second phase of the Sino-Soviet discussions began, the United States adopted a more rigid stance, advising the Chinese to stand firm even if that firmness prevented agreement. On August 5, Byrnes asked Harriman officially to inform Soong that the United States opposed concessions beyond those agreed to at Yalta. He specifically warned the Chinese not to make further concessions over the status of Dairen or Soviet reparations demands. The essence of this new administration position was to support the Chinese at the same time that it opposed concessions needed to conclude the treaty; only if the Soviet Union reversed its attitude and radically changed its demands would a treaty result prior to Japanese surrender.

Truman's policy failed to forestall the Soviet Union's entrance into the Japanese war. Although a formal Sino-Soviet treaty had not been concluded and although the United States finally neither requested nor encouraged Soviet intervention, the Russians nonetheless declared war on Japan on August 8 and moved troops into North China and Manchuria. Simultaneously, Stalin warned Soong on August 10 that, should a formal Sino-Soviet agreement not be concluded, Chinese Communist troops would be permitted to move into Manchuria. Fearful of Soviet support of the Chinese Communists, Chiang Kai-shek acceded to the Soviet demands on the unresolved issues. The formal Sino-Soviet treaty was then quickly concluded, and its terms announced on August 14.

The administration's indirect opposition to the Yalta provisions created the potential for U.S.-Soviet division once the war with Japan ended. The rapidity of the Japanese surrender and the last-minute Soviet entry into the war had complicated surrender proceedings. The administration had had little time to devise formal terms indicating to whom Japanese troops should surrender. Indeed, until Soviet entry, there had been no discussion about Soviet rights to direct or control Japan during the period of occupation. Thus, when unilaterally issuing

General Order #1, the United States directed Japanese troops to surrender to the Nationalists in all areas of China south of Manchuria and to the Russians in Manchuria, Korea north of the thirty-eighth parallel, and Karafutu. These surrender orders were intended to achieve two purposes: to preclude Japanese surrender to Chinese Communist troops and to minimize the Soviet occupation role in China and Japan.

Immediately, on August 16, the Soviet Union protested that these surrender provisions violated the Yalta agreements. Stalin demanded that the Soviet surrender zone include the Kuriles and Hokkaido (the northern sector of Japan). Unwilling to create the opportunity for Soviet military presence in Japan, Truman on August 18 acceded to the Soviet request for the Kuriles but not for Hokkaido. At the same time he pressed for an American air base on the Kuriles. In a sharp rejoinder on August 22, Stalin reiterated his earlier demand for Hokkaido and opposed Truman's request for the air base.

This was no mere territorial conflict; it involved the more basic question of the Truman administration's policy toward the Soviet occupation of Japan. At issue was whether the administration was formally prepared for confrontation. Truman at the time hesitated to reject the prospect of a negotiated settlement and replied to Stalin's sharp note of August 22 that the United States had not sought air base but only landing rights on the Kuriles. Truman further pointed out that the Kuriles were not Soviet territory. Yalta had only permitted Soviet occupation, he said; their final status would have to be determined at a future peace conference. On August 30, Stalin acceded to the request for landing rights. He denied, however, that the status of the Kuriles was unclear, contending that the cession had been permanent and that future peace talks would merely ratify this fact.

Directly or indirectly, the objective of limiting Soviet influence in the Far East underlay administration policy toward the Yalta agreements. Truman and Byrnes cunningly, but shortsightedly, here too sought to have it both ways: to avert the effect of the agreements without formally repudiating or renegotiating them.

IV

This clearly contradictory policy required the administration to continue to refrain from publishing the Yalta agreements on the Far East. Publication would have bound the administration to fulfilling them and would have established earlier U.S. insistence on Soviet involvement, negating the limited Soviet military contribution to defeating Japan. Therefore, the Truman administration neglected to publish the Far Eastern agreements on three ostensibly favorable occasions: when the Soviet

Union declared war on Japan on August 8, when the Sino-Soviet treaty was announced on August 14, or when Soviet troops occupied the Kurile Islands on August 27.

The U.S. troop withdrawal that permitted Soviet occupation of the Kuriles precipitated bitter protests by conservatives in both Congress and the press, who charged that Soviet possession of these "strategic" islands would directly threaten the security of the United States and Japan. In a September 4 press conference, on the eve of his departure for the London Foreign Ministers Conference, Byrnes attempted to allay this protest. The decision leading up to U.S. withdrawal, he informed the press, had resulted from "discussions" (as opposed to "agreements," he implied) conducted at Yalta, not Potsdam. Byrnes, claiming that his attendance at Yalta had provided him with "full" knowledge of these "discussions," attributed the responsibility for them to Roosevelt rather than Truman. He then announced his intention to review them at London; a final agreement on the status of the Kuriles, he concluded, could be made only at a forthcoming peace conference.

Byrnes dissembled in two respects at this press conference: first, in implying that the status of the Kuriles had not yet been defined and, second, in failing to report the existence of the other Far Eastern agreements. His statements were to have serious ramifications for the Truman administration.

Byrnes's secretiveness on the second point stemmed from the administration's desire to prevent the Soviets from assuming a controlling role in China and in the occupation of Japan. This objective necessarily conflicted with Soviet policy and contributed to the atmosphere of distrust that prevailed during the September meetings of the Council of Foreign Ministers in London. Although Molotov then protested the unilateral character of U.S. occupation policy in Japan, demanding the establishment of an Allied control commission, Byrnes equivocated and, in the end, succeeded in postponing any final decision on Japan.

This strategy and the attendant necessity not to publish the Far Eastern agreements—or even, for that matter, admit their existence—would seriously compromise the administration's position. The first public hint of the existence of the agreements occurred in November 1945 during the controversy surrounding the resignation of Hurley as U.S. ambassador to China. In resigning, Hurley charged that U.S. foreign policy had been subverted by "imperialists" and "communists" in both the State Department and the Foreign Service, charges which led to special hearings by the Senate Foreign Relations Committee in December.

The tone of the committee's questioning of Hurley was sharp, at times even hostile. Attempting to defend Hurley, who had repeated his charges of employee disloyalty and insubordination, a sympathetic Senator Styles Bridges asked whether at Yalta—given the absence of

Chinese representatives—any agreement concerning China had been concluded. Although he had not attended the conference, Hurley claimed knowledge about the China discussions. He added that Secretary of State Byrnes was a better authority on that subject.

In his prepared statement the next day, Byrnes dismissed Hurley's charges against the personnel of the State Department and the Foreign Service as wholly unfounded. Senator Bridges, however, was much more concerned with the Truman and Roosevelt administrations' China policy. Repeating his question of the day before, he asked Byrnes whether any agreement concerning China was concluded at Yalta in the absence and without the consent of Chiang Kai-shek. Bridges's confident tone, and the possibility that he had secured access to the Yalta text through Hurley or another source in the State Department, complicated Byrnes's reply. To admit that agreements had been concluded at Yalta without advising or consulting Chiang and had not yet been published would put the administration on the defensive and possibly expose its earlier dissembling. Faced with this dilemma, Byrnes neither affirmed nor denied that an agreement had been made:

> I do not recall the various agreements [of the Yalta Conference]. It is entirely possible that some of the agreements arrived at at Yalta affected China some way or another, and I have told you that I would gladly furnish you the communique and then you could decide whether or not they affected China. If they were made they certainly were made by the heads of government and certainly only the three Governments were represented there.

Bridges then observed that had any agreement on China been concluded, the secretary could not have been unaware of its existence. Thus, when the administration would publish the Far Eastern agreements, it would have to offer a convincing rationale both for its earlier failure to publish them and for Byrnes's seeming ignorance of the matter.

This situation came to pass in February 1946. The event precipitating the publication of the Far Eastern agreements was the administration's announcement in January that it had turned over to an international trusteeship certain Pacific islands the United States captured from Japan during World War II. During a January 22 press conference, Acting Secretary of State Dean Acheson was asked whether the Soviet Union would similarly be required to turn over the Kuriles to an international trusteeship. In answer, Acheson pointed out that the Yalta agreements had provided only for Soviet occupation of the Kuriles; the final disposition would have to be determined at a future peace conference. Acheson conceded, however, that such a conference might simply affirm Soviet control. On January 26, Moscow Radio challenged Acheson's remarks, denying that Soviet control of these territories was temporary or that

Soviet occupation was related only to the prosecution of the war against Japan.

At a press conference on January 29, Byrnes announced that the Kuriles and South Sakhalin had in fact been ceded to the Soviet Union at Yalta. He further disclosed that agreements concerning Port Arthur and Dairen had also been concluded. But these agreements would become binding only after the formal conclusion of a peace treaty with Japan.

The most dramatic aspect of Byrnes's press conference was not the disclosure of the agreements themselves but his attempts to explain the Truman administration's earlier failure to release them or indeed even to admit their existence. What Byrnes did was to tell the press that although he had been a delegate to Yalta, he had left the conference on the afternoon of February 10, before the concluding session the next day. He had not learned about the specifics of the Far Eastern agreements until August 1945, a few days after the Japanese surrender. In response to further questions, Byrnes said he did not know whether former Secretary of State Stettinius knew about the agreements or where, in fact, the text was deposited. It was not, he stated, in the State Department archives, but it might be in the White House files.

Once again, Byrnes had adroitly covered his tracks. He had shifted responsibility for both the Yalta agreements and the failure to publish them to the Roosevelt administration's tactics of secrecy. His statement did, however, raise two important questions: first, had the agreements been privately concluded by Roosevelt without the knowledge of other White House or State Department personnel and, second, where was the text.

During a January 31 press conference, Truman sought to resolve these questions. The text, he claimed, had always been in the White House files, except when under review either by members of the White House staff or other administration personnel. While he had always known the whereabouts of the text, Truman said, he had not reviewed it until he began to prepare for the Potsdam Conference. Asked when the agreements would in fact be published, Truman answered that it would be necessary first to consult the British and the Russians. Most of the agreements, he added, had already been made public; the others would be disclosed at the "proper" time.

The Truman administration's policy toward the Yalta Far Eastern agreements and other administration tactics strained the already uneasy relations between the United States and the Soviet Union. It was in the area of tactics and personality that the rigidity and moralistic tone of postwar U.S.-Soviet relations derived important substance, and not simply from conflicting ideologies and objectives. In this sense, the cold war was an avoidable conflict: the "way" it evolved being a product of shortsighted political leadership. The opportunities for détente provided by Yalta were effectively subverted by the Truman administration, and

U.S.-Soviet relations suffered until a change in presidents brought an administration less rigidly bound to the self-righteous politics of confrontation. Eisenhower's politics remained conservative; but, with the Geneva summit conference of 1955, his presidency marked a new, less militant phase of the cold war.

Jerome Slater

JEROME SLATER (1935–   ) is Professor of Political Science at State University of New York at Buffalo. He is the author of *The OAS and United States Foreign Policy* (1967), and *Intervention and Negotiation: The United States and the Dominican Revolution* (1970).

For most of the postwar period the dominant scholarly consensus on the United States role in international politics closely paralleled the image that policy makers themselves held: the United States was a defensive, status-quo power seeking to contain the revolutionary or simply imperialist expansionism of Soviet-led communism. The dominant critique of United States foreign policy operated well within this framework of assumptions; one common argument was that the United States had a tendency to overreach itself, to undertake commitments that excessively taxed its military and economic capabilities. The focus was on the *limits* of American power; critics never tired of quoting Sir Denis Brogan on "the illusions of American omnipotence."

Radical "Imperialist" Theories

In a remarkably short time, this dominant image of the role the United States has played since World War II has shifted, at first only among radicals, but more recently—and more importantly—among a growing number of mainstream historians and political scientists. Since the early 1960s radical critics have seen the American role as imperialistic rather than defensive: a deliberate, planned, and generally quite successful effort at world domination under the pretext of the "containment" of a largely nonexistent communist military or political threat. The central goal of this domination usually is described in terms of the open-door policy—maintaining access on favorable terms to overseas raw materials, markets, and investment outlets for United States private capital. On behalf of the open-door policy the government, acting as an instrument of American corporate interests, has consistently sought to pre-

Jerome Slater, "Is United States Foreign Policy 'Imperialist' or 'Imperial'?" Reprinted with permission from the *Political Science Quarterly*, 91 (Spring, 1976), pp. 63–87. Footnotes omitted.

serve a capitalist status quo around the world, covertly or overtly employing the vast range of power at its disposal to crush all incipient or
actual threats. Even the policy makers, it is argued, do not "really"
believe the threat to be communism per se—witness the growing nor-
malization of relations with an increasingly status-quo Soviet Union and
even China!—but rather revolution, socialism, or even simply
nationalism, for truly socialist or nationalist regimes would close off
their economies to United States penetration and domination. Radical
critics, then, see economic self-aggrandizement at the heart of American
imperialism, although some point to the Wilsonian crusading idealist
tradition—the mission to bring the blessings of capitalist freedom and
democracy to the rest of the world—as a separate but complementary
historical force that only serves to deepen and legitimize the American
expansionist drive.

Implicitly or explicitly, United States expansionism is seen as analogous in both motivation and consequences to nineteenth-century European colonialism. Outright military invasion and occupation (except as a
last resort) is no longer feasible in the era of modern nationalism, countervailing Soviet power, and potential domestic opposition, the argument runs, so neoimperialism has developed new, more subtle
methods. Through its vast economic power—the billions of dollars invested in the Third World by American-controlled multinational corporations; United States government control of economic assistance to underdeveloped countries, either directly in its bilateral programs or indirectly through its domination of the major international financial institutions; the dependence of Third World countries on American markets
for their exports of raw materials and commodities and imports of manufactured goods and modern technology; the centrality of the dollar in the
world monetary system, etc.—the United States works to keep the rest
of the world conservative, capitalist, and docile. As Harry Magdoff, one
of the most influential theorists of neoimperialism puts it: "Colonialism,
considered as the direct application of military and political force, was
essential to reshape the social and economic institutions of many of the
dependent countries to the needs of the metropolitan centres. Once this
reshaping had been accomplished economic forces—the international
price, marketing, and financial systems—were by themselves sufficient
to perpetuate and indeed intensify the relationship of dominance...."

In any case, economic power is supplemented by close American ties
with conservative local elites, whose own continued status and power is
dependent on United States support—the politicians; the bureaucrats;
and especially the forces of repression, the military and the police, who
are trained, financed, equipped, and frequently led by American "ad-
visors." At a more subtle or insidious level, there is the power of "cultural imperialism," the central role of the United States in the world

communications network and mass media, which provides the means to shape popular images and aspirations in ways consistent with the maintenance of world capitalism and United States domination.

If more forceful action is necessary to prevent undesirable change and shore up cooperative client governments, the argument continues, the CIA is always available to provide information, advice, propaganda, subsidies, bribes, weapons, private armies, and a whole repertoire of "dirty tricks," including coups d'etats and/or the murder of particularly stubborn recalcitrants. And if all else fails, direct military action, facilitated by the worldwide network of United States bases and troop deployments, can shore up the empire at its weakest points, as in Lebanon, the Dominican Republic, and Indochina.

Such is the power of neoimperialism, then, that outright colonial occupation and rule is not merely impractical, but it is unnecessary, for the same ends can be attained equally if not even more effectively, precisely because of the more subtle, insidious, unrecognized nature of the new methods of domination and exploitation: *"only imperfect amateurish imperialism needs weapons; professional imperialism is based on structural rather than direct violence."* Indeed, not only are the methods of neoimperialism more effective, but the scope of its domain is greater than even the most extensive of the territorial empires of the past, for modern imperialism "knows no frontiers," "extends its net over the whole planet"; "the empire is everywhere." So goes the radical, neo-Marxist critique of United States foreign policy.

Nonradical "Imperial" Theories

Somewhat unexpectedly, in the last decade or so important aspects of this radical analysis have been accepted by an increasing number of nonradical, non-Marxist students of United States foreign policy, and even by some conservatives. Though it is not accurate to describe the overall United States world role as *imperialist* or *imperialistic,* they argue, it is accurate to describe it as *imperial.* No analyst thus far has thoroughly and systematically contrasted the concept of an "imperial" role with an "imperialist" one, but it seems clear that at least four important distinctions usually are implied. First, imperial policies are seen to be primarily a function of the structure of the *international* rather than the *domestic* system, in particular, of course, the absence of international institutions capable of maintaining peace and performing other critical governmental functions. Second, an imperial policy or posture is not fundamentally economic in nature: it is neither motivated by economic gain, nor (as already suggested) is it structurally rooted in any particular socioeconomic system, such as "capitalism." Imperial relationships are concerned with power, either for its own sake or as an instrument of some larger, primarily noneconomic objective, such as "world order." For example, Robert W. Tucker argues that although United States postwar policy was initially motivated by a concern for national security defined in limited, defensive, traditional terms—the containment of Soviet expansionism and the maintenance of a balance of power in Europe—it later became generalized and diffused into the much broader objective of maintaining a world environment congenial to American values and institutions, which in turn required an activist, interventionist projection of American power overseas on a scale that could only be termed imperial.

Third, writers describing the United States as an "imperial" power are usually less inclined (although they are often somewhat ambiguous on the matter) to attribute to policy makers a *conscious intent* to dominate, whatever their motivations, than those preferring the "imperialist" label. That is, the United States may play an imperial *role* without having an imperial *policy*. The focus is primarily on consequences, not intentions or motivations. The root cause of the American imperial role, or, alternatively, a conception of security so broad as to require imperial policies de facto, is simply power itself. *Any* great power in the present world system is irresistibly drawn toward imperial policies, argues Raymond Aron; only weak states with no alternatives adopt a conception of the national interest restricted to mere political survival. In effect, goes the argument, interests and commitments of states naturally and inevitably expand as their power expands.

The final significant distinction is that terms "imperialist" or "imperialistic" are invariably condemnatory and indicative of a radical disaffection with United States foreign policy, whereas this is not necessarily the case for "imperial." Indeed, if imperial policies are seen as deriving fundamentally from an anarchic international system, the emphasis is far more likely to be on the "responsibilities" than the "abuses" of power. For example, Aron argues that even if the American role in Europe during the postwar period could be accurately described as imperial, it was both right and desired by the people of Western Europe; and relatively conservative writers like George Liska and John Spanier call for a more open, self-conscious, unapologetic imperial role for the United States as the only alternative to global chaos. Even Tucker, who until very recently has been a most forceful critic of the American imperial conception of its national interest, has now (because of the growing power of the Third World) begun to worry about who will maintain a semblance of world order.

The distinctions between "imperialist" and "imperial" conceptions or models are important ones, but it is also of critical importance to take note of what they have in common: both are—indeed, *must*—be based on the premise, implied or explicit, that in the postwar era the extent of United States power and the nature of its behavior—whatever the causes, motivation, intentions, or effects—warrants comparison with the undoubted empires of the past, in particular the European colonial empires of the late nineteenth and early twentieth centuries. Even the mildest, least condemnatory, and most qualified conception of an American imperial, let alone imperialist role, cannot escape that connotation and still remain meaningful. Imperial implies *great* power, not merely unequal power; it implies the capacity to dominate or control other states, not merely to influence them; it implies an empire, not merely a sphere of influence.

How accurately does this central image of American hegemony or control fit the reality of postwar international politics? The remainder of this article will be devoted to examining the validity of the theories that have thus far been briefly summarized. The focus will be on American relations with the Third World, where surely the argument of American imperialism, if valid, must have its greatest force. The discussion will distinguish between radical, neo-Marxist, and nonradical, non-Marxist analyses of (a) the motivation or causes and (b) the consequences or effects of United States foreign policy.

Motivations for "Imperial" or "Imperialist" Policy

We shall begin with a discussion of radical, neo-Marxist theories of the causes or motivations of American policy. Is the open-door policy—unrestricted access to the economies of the Third World—structurally necessary to the survival of United States capitalism, or, more generally, to the health of the economy? Some contemporary neo-Marxists, most notably Gabriel Kolko, do in fact so argue, following Lenin's earlier arguments about the crucial dependence of late monopoly capitalism on overseas economic imperialism. Consider first direct overseas investment. Although the figures vary, all recent analyses demonstrate that private overseas direct investment is only about 5 percent of total investment (i.e., 95 percent of United States direct investment is domestic), and the vast majority of that overseas investment is not in the Third World but in the advanced industrial societies of Western Europe, Japan, Canada, and Australia. The proportion of overseas investment in the Third World, then, is less than 2 percent of all United States investment, which would hardly seem critical. Looked at from a different perspective, as of 1968 the income from corporate investment in the Third World was only 3–4 percent of the total income of United States corporations, and it was declining relative to income from investments in the industrial world.

The figures for trade reveal the same nonessentiality of the Third World to the United States economy. Total American trade with the rest of the world is only about 7–8 percent of GNP and, once again, by far the largest and most rapidly growing proportion of that trade is not with the Third World but with the advanced countries. Only in the case of strategic raw materials is the Third World *possibly* of critical importance to the American economy, and even here the situation is far from clear. For the moment the United States is increasingly dependent on overseas oil as well as other important raw materials such as copper, tin, and bauxite found in Third World countries. But (1) it is still the case that *most* of these raw materials are produced not in the Third World but in the developed countries; (2) mining the deep seabed is likely to soon further reduce United States dependence on Third World countries; and (3) pending that development most economists still argue that substitutes and alternatives to Third World raw materials, even oil, are now or soon will be available, at costs which are higher, but not so much higher as to make Third World importations more of a necessity than essentially a convenience. In any case, it is only very recently that the United States has become dependent on strategic raw materials imports from the Third World countries to any significant degree, whatever the exact magnitude of that dependence might be now and in the future, and thus the matter is entirely irrelevant to the alleged structural necessity of the open-door policy in the past.

Even if the United States economy *was* structurally dependent on access to Third World markets, raw materials, or sources of investment, would it follow that imperial *control* of the Third World is a necessity? The radical argument depends on that assumption, although it is nearly always left implicit; that is, that the choice is the stark, all-or-nothing one of imperial domination or no access at all. When made explicit, though, the assumption is demonstratively preposterous. Indeed, there seems to be a clear *inverse* relationship between "imperialism" and prosperity in the postwar period. Though of course other factors have also played important roles, it is interesting to note that the least imperial countries have had the highest overall growth rates (Japan, West Germany, Canada, the Netherlands, the Scandinavian countries—all dependent in varying degrees on interstate trade and investment), while the most imperial have done least well (France and Britain in the 1940s and 1950s; Portugal, with the lowest per capita income in Europe for the entire postwar period). Nor should this be unexpected: it is not just that the maintenance of political and military imperial control is extremely costly when there is serious indigenous opposition, but also that states perceived by the nationalist and sensitive Third World countries as imperialist, whether accurately or not, are much more likely to suffer economic retaliation than those seen as quite harmless. In case of renewed Arab-Israeli conflict, for example, the Arabs are probably more likely to cut off oil shipments to the United States than to Japan. The radical assumption is best stood on its head: *only* efforts to gain imperialist economic control, to push against a door that is already open, would be likely to provoke nationalistic resentments intense enough to override economic rationality and close off American access to Third World products.

All this may be true, implicitly or explicitly concede some radical analysts, but policy makers, however inaccurately, *believe* that the health of the United States capitalist system requires an open door to the Third World economies and therefore direct political or economic control over them, and act accordingly, i.e., imperialistically. While this is certainly a logical possibility and a neat theory-saver, the evidence is overwhelming that it is a wholly inaccurate description of how policy makers in fact have perceived American interests in the Third World. There is, after all, an enormous body of available material in the form of memoirs, official documents, and scholarly analyses on how American policy makers have defined the "external challenges" to the United States, in the Third World and elsewhere. It rather conclusively shows that genuine security fears; ideological anticommunism; expansionist idealism; or other political, strategic, or psychological factors have been at the roots of the United States postwar policies, including interventionist or, if you will, "imperial" behavior.

Still another variant of the neo-Marxist argument is that open-door imperialism in the Third World, while neither structurally necessary to the United States economy nor genuinely believed to be so by policy makers, *is* necessary to the largest, most powerful banks and corporations which in turn control foreign policy. Both parts of this argument are quite unpersuasive. A number of scholars have demonstrated that, with the exception of the seven oil majors (to be examined below), the largest United States foreign banks and corporations are among those that are *least* dependent on the Third World, as the overwhelming proportion of their investment, sales, and profits come from the American domestic market, Europe, Japan, and Canada. And, more importantly, while it would be beyond the scope of this article to go into detail, no serious scholarship on the foreign policy-making process in the United States government supports the notion that it is controlled or in most cases even substantially influenced by the desires of "big business." Indeed, even in the case of those American-based multinational corporations which *do* have major investments in the Third World, most recent scholarship establishes that the distance between the corporations and the United States government is increasing, as both the policy makers and the corporations are coming to realize that, faced with growing nationalism, *no* interests—economic or political, private or public—are served by government involvement in corporate disputes with indigenous governments.

The final variation of the neo-Marxist argument is at once the most sophisticated but also the least subject to empirical confirmation or refutation. It is not that corporations control foreign policy or that political leaders consciously seek to promote and protect corporate economic interests, but rather that all United States elites are products of American history, institutions, and class structures, and as such have internalized an overall ideology or *weltanschauung* that equates the maintenance of capitalism at home and its extension overseas—i.e., the open-door policy—with the preservation of the entire "American way of life." The problem with this formulation, "sophisticated" as it may be, is that it is so broad as to be quite immune from normal tests of evidence. It is quite easy to show that American foreign policy makers since World War II have not usually defined their objectives in terms of the open-door policy, the preservation of capitalism, or, indeed, in economic terms of any kind, either in their public rhetoric or in their private correspondence, memoirs, or intragovernmental communications, but then it can be claimed that the policy makers were either concealing their "real" objectives or that their anticommunism and security fears were "ultimately," perhaps even unconsciously, rooted in the desire to preserve capitalism as an economic system. Similarly, instances in which United States policy has been oriented toward the protection or promotion of American economic interests overseas are seized upon as irrefutable proof of the theory, whereas the far more numerous instances of United States passivity when confronted with economic nationalism are treated as signs of the growing subtlety of corporate capitalism, which is willing to let minor infractions on its imperial control go unchallenged in the interest of preserving "the system" as a whole. Or, in another version, even intervention which is overwhelmingly counterproductive in economic terms, such as in Vietnam, is explained in terms of "the empire's" need to preserve the system as a whole by supporting even "the weakest links in the chain." As others have pointed out, both in the context of examining this variant of neo-Marxist theory and in discussing the nature of scientific inquiry in general, a theory so broad that it is capable of "explaining" both A and its opposite B (intervention and nonintervention, intervention that is economically productive and intervention that is economically costly), a theory that rests not on the empirical evidence considered in its entirety but on assertion buttressed only by the selected evidence that fits, is no theory at all, but simply dogma.

It is not the contention of this article that economic considerations, including if you will the maintenance of an open-door for products and investment capital, do not play a significant role in United States foreign policy, but only that such economic considerations have not been the central, dominant ones. Certainly it is obvious that the government has sought to promote trade and investment around the world and has often used its economic and political influence on behalf of such objectives. In so acting, political officials have been motivated by several factors: the belief that an open economic world is genuinely in the best interests of all states; the belief that it is beneficial to the United States economy; and the belief that one of the obligations of the government is to protect and promote the legitimate activities of its citizens abroad, at least as long as those activities do not conflict with larger policy objectives. But what is crucial are the *means* used on behalf of the open-door policy, that is, the *intensity* of the government's commitment to it or the *priority* that policy has relative to other foreign policy objectives. Normally, the government has promoted the interests of private corporations by diplomacy only: verbal representations, exhortation, and bargaining. On some, but increasingly exceptional occasions, the government has gone further, making use of both positive and negative economic sanctions, through its bilateral assistance programs and its influence in international financial institutions, on behalf of private economic interests. On most occasions where the government has resorted to economic pressures, though, larger issues than mere nationalization of American property are perceived to be at stake, as in the case of economic and other actions by the United States against Cuba and the Allende government in Chile. Finally, there is *no* case in which it can persuasively be argued that Washington resorted to serious covert political action or the use of armed force on behalf of private economic interests as such. Apparent exceptions to this assertion, such as the CIA's role in the overthrow of Iran's Mossadegh following his nationalization of oil corporations in 1953, on closer inspection do not undermine the argument, for oil is the *one* foreign economic commodity perceived to be absolutely vital, not to private interests but to the United States economy as a whole. Indeed, what is particularly striking about the case of oil is that even *given* its critical importance, the government nonetheless has consistently subordinated easy and favorable access to it to other, noneconomic objectives: as many observers have pointed out, if economic rather than cold-war ideological/moral, or domestic considerations dominated foreign policy, the United States stance in the Arab-Israeli crisis would have been very different over the last three decades. So even in the single case in which one might *expect* to find economic considerations to be dominant, the reality has been different. That being so, it is hardly credible that the United States interventions in Guatemala in 1954 and the Dominican Republic in 1965 were motivated by, respectively, banana and sugar interests, rather than by ideological, cold-war, and even strategic considerations genuinely believed—whether accurately or not is irrelevant—by policy makers to be at stake in those countries.

To summarize, while it is true that in a general way the United States seeks an open-door policy around the world, it is usually quite restrained—i.e., nonimperialistic—in the methods used to attain this goal. The more clearly it is that purely private rather than national economic interests are involved, the less likely it is that the government will take punitive actions against other states. To go even further, to the extent that *only* economic interests are involved, even where those interests are national rather than private in scope, the less likely it is that the government will resort to serious economic coercion, let alone armed force. Put differently, the more important the issue for the United States as a whole, as seen by policy makers, the more likely it is that economic considerations will be subordinated to noneconomic ones whenever they conflict, as in the past they have in the Middle East.

The argument that United States policy is motivated by noneconomic but still imperial pretensions is a far more serious one than the neo-Marxist theories. It is at once more sophisticated and less of an affront to common sense, and it does not suffer from the shoddy scholarship and ideological dogmatism that so frequently mar much of the radical literature. Quite the contrary; scholars of the deserved stature of Robert Tucker, Stanley Hoffmann, Richard Falk, and others have all described United States foreign policy in terms of its imperial nature. Certainly there can be no doubt that policy makers have often, even typically, described their objectives and policies in *rhetoric* that can fairly be called "imperial": the Truman Doctrine's universalist declaration that it was the policy of the United States "to support free peoples who are resisting attempted subjugation by armed minorities or by outside pressures," Kennedy on the United States as "the watchman on the wall of world freedom," Johnson on history "thrusting" the "responsibility" on the United States "to be guardians at the gate," and so on. Still, it is doubtful that this rhetoric accurately reflected the real, operational purposes of policy makers, for the more plausible interpretation of foreign policies since World War II suggests that the guiding motivation was to meet what was perceived as the quite specific challenge by communist forces in quite specific places. The United States has not in fact sought to preserve world freedom; it has not tried to suppress all revolution, let alone all social change; it has not even tried very hard to create or maintain an environment congenial to American institutions and values; and it has certainly not deliberately set out to dominate other nations; it has simply tried to prevent the spread of communism (whether wisely or not is not relevant here) to areas where communism was not already in power. It cannot be denied that the broadening of the goal of the containment of communism from Western Europe to the entire world, combined with the continuing strain of Wilsonian universalism in American thinking, made the United States (in Stanley Hoffmann's words) at least *"implicitly* imperialistic," but the weight of evidence suggests that the concrete day-to-day policies of the government were considerably more limited. Put differently, we may concede that America's ideological universalism was at least potentially imperial and at some level accurately reflected the genuine long-term hopes and aspirations of the postwar political leadership, but yet deny that such sweeping conceptions of the United States "responsibility," requiring a conscious or unconscious effort at benevolent world domination, were at the root of operational policies.

Yet, one hesitates to make too much of this argument. Even if it is correct that anticommunist security fears rather than broader aspirations lie at the root of United States policies, the globalization of those policies might still produce imperialism. Certainly it is hard to avoid the conclusion that meddling in the internal politics of far-away, relatively unimportant states such as Greece, the Congo, and Chile—not to mention Indochina!—reflects what might justly be labeled as an imperial mentality or conception of American security interests. So the more important argument of this article is that the notion of the United States as an imperial power exaggerates its actual *capacities* to control events around the world.

Consequences of United States Foreign Policy

What, then, of the *consequences* or *effects* of the postwar policies, whatever their causes, motivations, or intentions? Has the impact of United States power on the rest of the world, especially on the Third World where surely the impact must be greatest, been sufficiently extensive to justify describing it as "imperialism," "neoimperialism," "indirect imperialism," or "informal imperialism"? At least implicit in such descriptions and often quite explicit is the argument that the extension of American economic, political, and military power into the Third World has been on such a scale as to reduce those countries to a position not substantially different from the past when they were actually under military occupation and direct political rule. The consequences for the Third World, it is argued, are both economic exploitation and political subordination, just as in the past.

In the last decade or so, particularly in the literature on United States–Latin American relations, the theory (or theories) of "dependence" has become the dominant theme in radical writings. In their more sophisticated versions, dependence theories hold that Third World countries have become inextricably integrated in the world capitalist system, dominated in turn by United States capitalism, as producers of raw materials and consumers of manufactured products. Because they are weak and economically undiversified, however, Third World countries are relegated to the "periphery" of the system, kept underdeveloped or impoverished by the low prices they receive for their exports, the high prices they must pay for their imports, and the onerous conditions which they are forced to accept in order to have access to foreign capital through either loans or investment. Although dependence may be partially a consequence of the deliberate exercise of power, it is more fundamentally a function of the capitalist structure. As long as world capitalism continues in its present form, the Third World cannot escape underdevelopment, for its "surplus production" will continue to be in effect appropriated for the benefit of the advanced capitalist societies. Under capitalism, then, underdevelopment is not a transitional stage to development but a permanent condition: "economic development and underdevelopment are the opposite faces of the same coin."

Why do more Third World countries not rebel against this structural exploitation? Because, according to the dependence theorists, although Third World *people* as a whole suffer, the local political, business, and military *elites* benefit: their power, status, and wealth are directly linked to the preservation of the existing "system," i.e., investment and production by local subsidiaries of the giant multinational corporations; military assistance programs; CIA advice, support, and financing; and so on. Without this alliance between the elites of the center and the periphery, the entire structure of indirect capitalist control over the Third World would be impossible. Put differently, it is this mutually symbiotic alliance that is the functional equivalent of the direct military, political, and bureaucratic control structures of the older, colonialist versions of imperialism.

ECONOMIC EXPLOITATION?

Let us examine this theory or argument, looking first at the question of whether the United States economically exploits the Third World. . . .

We may now sum up. Taken as a whole, have the economic ties between the United States and the Third World been economically exploitative? It is obvious that the United States has enormous economic power; that this power has consequences for other, weaker states; that the consequences are sometimes though hardly invariably detrimental; and that while these detrimental consequences may frequently be the unintended result of sheer United States power, they are sometimes undeniably the result of deliberate, self-seeking policies on the part of the United States government. If by exploitation one means absolute deprivation, though, it is clear that the United States has not economically exploited the Third World, for the underdeveloped world as a whole has grown at a rate of 2 percent per annum *per capita* since 1945, and over 5 percent per annum per capita since 1960, rates which are historically very high, higher for example than the growth rates of the United States or the European countries during any comparable length of time prior to World War I. To a substantial degree, this relatively high growth rate is attributable to the sharp increase of foreign aid, investment, and trade between the developing countries and the advanced industrial ones, primarily (at least until fairly recently) the United States.

Has there nonetheless been exploitation in the sense of *relative* deprivation? For most of the postwar period, it is true, the rich got richer faster than the poor got "richer" and thus the gap between them was growing (although it is likely that this trend has ended in the last few years). The most persuasive evidence, though, is that the growth rates of the rich had little or nothing to do with their "exploitation" of the Third World: the rich got richer because of an increase of both domestic productivity and of trade and investment among themselves, while the poor did not develop at higher rates because of their essentially indigenous problems: one-crop economies, high population rates, political instability, etc. To be sure, there can be absolutely no doubt that the rich countries, particularly the United States, *could* and (according to my values) *should* have done more, much more, to help the Third World countries develop. That is, the United States and other developed countries in their total economic relations with the Third World have been guided primarily by self-interest rather than by the desire to help the poor; had their priorities been different the Third World would be substantially better off today. Take the case of foreign aid as an illustration. Radicals have pointed out the variety of ways in which foreign aid is at least in part structured to promote access for private investment, subsidize American shipowners, promote American export industries, and so on. The total effect of the various restrictions on the uses to which recipients may put bilateral United States assistance clearly lowers the real value of that assistance, but equally clearly it does not reduce that value to zero or even less. Foreign aid thus benefits, not exploits the recipients, although the benefits are not as great as they would be if the amounts were larger and unconstrained by restrictions designed to assist American industries. One may still conclude that the economic relationship between the United States and the Third World is deplorable but the problem is not exploitation, at least if understood in a reasonable sense, but rather neglect, indifference, and moral callousness. What the Third World needs from the United States and the rest of the developed countries is not less but more aid, trade, and private investment, though undoubtedly on better terms than in the past.

POLITICAL CONTROL?

None of this analysis denies, of course, that economic power carries with it political leverage. But is this political leverage sufficient to give it political control over the Third World, as the "neoimperialist" or even simply "imperial" argument implies? The evidence from events in the real world, particularly during but not limited to the past few years, hardly suggests that this is the case.

If economic power carried with it considerable political control, one would expect that *at a minimum* such control would be sufficient for the imperial power to protect its major economic interests, particularly in

areas of the world where its economic power
imperialist (or imperial) model would predict—
United States could exert sufficient political con
the position of its major multinational corporat
And yet over the past decade there has been a wa
United States corporations around the world
Ceylon, Egypt, Indonesia, Algeria, Libya—but
America. The United States government has be
prevent these actions against its corporations ar ⋯⋯y several
partial exceptions, has all but ceased to try. The International Petroleum
Corporation (IPC) case in Peru is particularly instructive and historically
significant. During the mid-1960s the liberal Peruvian government of
Fernando Belaunde Terry began taking steps looking toward the
nationalization of IPC, a subsidiary of Standard Oil of New Jersey. IPC,
backed by the U.S. Embassy in Lima, strongly resisted, and from 1964–
1966 Washington withheld economic assistance from Peru in an effort to
force the Belaunde government to back down. In early 1968 Belaunde
and IPC reached a compromise settlement, involving gradual nationalization, compensation, and a continued role for IPC in managing the oil
fields, but the compromise outraged Peruvian nationalistic opinion, and
shortly afterward a nationalist military coup overthrew Belaunde, and
the new government immediately seized all properties of IPC. IPC, it
will be noted, had annual revenues three times as large as Peru's entire
GNP, and its payroll was 25 percent larger than that of the Peruvian
government, the sort of figures frequently cited to demonstrate the
helplessness of Third World governments before the awesome economic
power of multinational corporations. And yet, the Peruvian government
simply marched several hundred troops into IPC properties and expropriated them without compensation! The Nixon administration subsequently tried to help the IPC gain compensation and apparently for a
while informally slowed down assistance to Peru, although it refused to
apply the Hickenlooper Amendment, which by law clearly applied to the
case and would have required the immediate cessation of all economic
assistance until IPC had been "promptly and effectively" compensated.
In the face of Peruvian adamance, after a while even the half-hearted
efforts of the Nixon government were dropped. The Peruvian government subsequently nationalized the huge and "powerful" Grace and
Cerro de Pasco United States-owned multinational corporations, as well
as a number of smaller ones, and dramatically increased taxation and in
other ways imposed restrictions on many others. Relatively little compensation has been forthcoming, and the United States government has
remained on the sidelines.

The lesson of the Peruvian experience and the helplessness of both
the corporations and the United States government has not been lost on
other nationalistic Latin American regimes. In 1969 a Bolivian military

uptly expropriated the United States-owned Gulf Oil Corpo-
and "forced or frightened almost every sizable U.S. firm out of the
try." In 1971, the Allende regime in Chile expropriated without
compensation the huge, American-owned Anaconda Companies; as in
Peru "The efforts of the U.S. government to influence the process of
providing compensation only strengthened Chilean intransigence," and
once again the Nixon administration stopped short of applying the Hickenlooper Amendment.

In the last few years, the wave of nationalization has rapidly spread.
The Peronist regime in Argentina took a number of steps against United
States corporations; even conservative regimes (such as Brazil) who otherwise welcome foreign investment are responding to popular
nationalism and anti-Americanism by tightening controls over United
States enterprises; and, most significantly of all, the Venezuelan government, which has been gradually gaining control over the oil industry
in the past twenty years, will fully nationalize all foreign (mostly United
States) oil corporations by 1976. Though the economic interests involved
are enormous, and Venezuela is still the largest foreign supplier of imported oil, neither the affected corporations nor the United States government have sought to apply any pressure, but rather are passively
accepting the inevitable.

It is now increasingly recognized that as the host countries gain in
knowledge, confidence, and experience, and as European and Japanese
multinational corporations seek to compete with American business for
access to the Third World, the bargaining relationship between multinational corporations and indigenous governments is rapidly shifting in
favor of the latter, with the United States government relatively powerless and increasingly disinclined to try to resist. The "dependencia"
pattern, under which local elites collaborate with foreign investors
against their own national interests, is rapidly disappearing and was
probably always exaggerated anyway. Without local allies, more direct
action on the part of the "metropolitan" countries would be required;
yet, armed force on behalf of private interests is practically out of the
question in this day and age, and economic pressures can be relatively
easily resisted by proud nationalist regimes and only worsen the situation for the multinational corporations. In the past few years it is clear
that most corporations have come to grips with the new realities, seeking to adapt to rising nationalism as best they can, with no recourse to
threats of economic retaliation or United States governmental assistance.

Even short of outright nationalization, the terms of both trade and
investment between the Third World and the advanced industrial world
are rapidly shifting. The rise of OPEC in the Middle East is the most
dramatic example, of course: in the 1920s host oil-producing countries
received in taxation only about 10–15 percent of oil corporation profits

on production: by the mid-1970s the general figure was over 80 percent and that of a far larger pie. Other raw materials producers are now seeking to form price cartels in emulation of OPEC, and while it is doubtful that any will achieve quite the fantastic success of the oil producers, the fact is that collaborative action to restrict production has led to dramatic price rises for Third World producers of bauxite, tin, copper, and other raw materials. Once again, the government has been powerless to prevent these developments, even though they inflict varying degrees of damage not only on United States-based multinational corporations but on the economy as a whole and there are increasing indications that adaptation rather than coercive resistance will be the general American response.

Aside from the rapidly spreading adverse economic developments that the United States has been powerless to prevent, American political and military influence in the Third World has markedly declined in the last decade, nowhere more so than in Latin America, supposedly the stronghold of United States "neo-imperialism," "hegemony," or "domination." Anti-American nationalism is at a peak, and the Latin American bloc is no longer a reliable ally of the United States in the United Nations or in other international organizations. In general Latin American support for overall United States international policies is at a postwar low. Most important, the United States has proven to be, perhaps if not quite powerless, then at least decreasingly powerful in preventing revolutionary social change in Latin America. The Cuban and Peruvian regimes have successfully resisted all pressures (serious and sustained in the former, half-hearted and transient in the latter), and other states "are advancing frankly towards socialization."

Conclusion: If the United States Is an "Imperial" Power, Where Is Its Empire?

Obviously no one would wish to deny that the United States has enormous economic, political, and military power, and that this power must have a significant impact on other states, both intended and unintended. The question, however, is whether this power is so great as to warrant calling it either "imperialist" or "imperial." Even if these terms, or the notion of a United States "empire," are meant to be understood metaphorically rather than literally, we still must decide whether the metaphors are insightful and enlightening rather than misleading.

It seems reasonable to insist that the term "imperialism" (and all its usual variants) not be used as if it were synonymous with power and wealth as such, or alternatively as a mere name for the observable fact of the global expansion of American influence since World War II. Nor should imperialism be equated with *inequality* of power, per se, as some radical writers implicitly or even explicitly do. To define imperialism in such broad terms, or to treat such concepts as power, control, domination, and influence as if they were synonymous and all equal to imperialism, is simply to obscure highly significant distinctions that would only have to be reinvented if we wish to understand the real world.

Benjamin Cohen's definition of imperialism seems reasonably appropriate: "any relationship of effective domination or control, political or economic, direct or indirect, of one nation over another." Such a definition clearly implies that great power is involved, not merely inequalities of power, and that the relationship is nearly wholly one-sided. However, it is possible to distinguish three different dimensions of power: *control,* defined as the invariable capacity to achieve objectives even in the face of opposition; *domination,* implying great power but falling somewhat short of outright control; and *influence,* meaning the capacity to *affect,* to a greater or lesser degree, the policies and behavior of other states. The term "imperialism" and all its usual variants should be limited to cases in which the power of one state over another is sufficient to establish control or at least a high degree of domination; it has no place where the relationship is simply one of influence, even of asymmetrical influence. Given the invariable connotation of the term "imperialism," the scope and degree of control must approximate the kind of control exercised by nineteenth-century European powers over their colonies. This should not prove objectionable, since most analysts describing the United States role as either "imperialist" or "imperial" in fact do equate, implicitly or explicitly, American power today—i.e., its capacity to control—with that of the nineteenth-century colonial powers.

Where in the world, even in the Third World, does the United States actually enjoy *control?* In Asia? In Africa? In the Middle East? A moment's reflection, without further argument, should suffice to reveal the very suggestion as being without foundation. Perhaps in Latin America, then? In which Latin American countries does the United States exercise control or domination: Argentina, Peru, Venezuela, Bolivia, Ecuador, Mexico? Hardly, for the United States had clearly been opposed to many significant policies and actions of those states and has been unable to affect them. What about Brazil and Chile since Allende, where the general drift of affairs is apparently pleasing to Washington? Even though covert actions did play *some* role in the establishment of military dictatorships in those countries, especially in Chile, the bulk of the evidence as well as plain common sense suggests that indigenous forces in such large and complex societies were surely far more important. What, then, about the Caribbean area? Here, indubitably, the United States has considerable leverage, though not control and only doubtfully even domination, except for some extreme cases, such as Cuba before Castro and the Dominican Republic in the 1960s. Certainly countries like Haiti, the Dominican Republic, Guatemala, Honduras, and Nicaragua *are* economically dependent on the United States and make it a practice to support American foreign policies; on the other hand, even leaving aside the rather dramatic Cuban case, other Caribbean countries (such as Panama, Jamaica, Trinidad and Tobago) have charted a clearly independent economic and political course and throughout the entire area anti-American nationalism is on the rise.

The growing acceptance of the "imperial" model or metaphor to the contrary notwithstanding, we may boldly but confidently conclude that the United States today does not "control" *any* country *anywhere*, and in only a slightly more qualified manner we may also reject the notion of United States "domination." That the United States has varying degrees of *influence* in the Third World is of course undeniable, but it is a declining influence, and limited in scope and effectiveness to only certain matters. As noted earlier, the United States has been all but powerless to stop rising nationalism and radicalism, as well as attacks on its interests and policies around the world. How does the United States today typically react to the nationalization of property, to dramatic increases in the prices of critical raw materials, to demands that it remove its military bases, to anti-American riots, to insults and contempt? On increasingly rare occasions with suspension of economic *assistance* to the offending state, more typically with mere diplomatic protest, and, increasingly, simply with silence—a sullen silence borne of futility, perhaps, but significant precisely for that reason. "Imperialism" should be made of sterner stuff—and certainly it used to be.

Thanks to its growing wealth; the rapidly increasing availability of external aid, trade, and investment from sources other than the United States (Japan, Western Europe, the Soviet Union); and the increased domestic and external constraints on the use of military force, the Third World today is less vulnerable to United States power of any kind than at any time since World War II. The relationship cannot be plausibly described as "imperialist" or "imperial" at all, and only doubtfully and decreasingly as "dependent." It would be more accurate to see the relationship between the United States and the Third World in terms of *mutual* dependence, *mutual* power, and *mutual* vulnerability. To be sure, there are still considerable asymmetries of power—the United States has more *potential* power than the Third World, but it has become increasingly costly for it to actually employ that power. Still, so long as inequalities remain, we may expect the attacks on United States "imperialism" to continue, however inaccurate and misleading they in fact are, both because the shibboleth of "imperialism" provides a convenient myth to deflect attention from the indigenous problems of Third World countries and because inequality per se has become the real focus of Third World resentment of the advanced industrial societies.

11

America in the 1950's and 1960's

Consensus to Crisis?

American history in the quarter of a century after World War II underwent a change in the climate of opinion, which appeared to influence profoundly the way intellectuals saw their society. Generally speaking, intellectuals tended to view the 1950's as a decade of consensus and conformity. There seemed to be widespread agreement within the society on certain shared principles and the distinctive features of American life. The 1960's, on the other hand, was seen as a decade characterized by crisis and individualism. Consensus appeared to be replaced by a polarization of views concerning certain domestic and foreign issues.

This change in the climate of opinion took place despite certain continuities that persisted through both decades. First, the twenty-five years after the end of World War II constituted the longest period of sustained prosperity in the country's history. Second, as the United States assumed a new role as leader of the free world, the Cold War reshaped America's image of itself and of its relationship with the rest of the world. The closer involvement of the United States with the world, along with the long-term prosperity, marked two of the most revolutionary changes in all of American history.

America emerged from World War II as the most prosperous and powerful nation on earth. Although the transition from a wartime to a peacetime economy was not easy, the United States economy did not revert to the hard times of the Great Depression. The American people enjoyed instead an almost uninterrupted period of sustained economic growth. America's gross national product was 212 billion dollars in 1945, double that figure by 1960, and reached one trillion dollars by 1971. America stood at the summit of its power and at the center of the world economy, producing half of the world's manufactures, 43 percent of its electricity, 62 percent of its oil, and 80 percent of its cars. No other people on earth had ever achieved such productivity. Unemployment was reduced to minimal levels—remaining at an average annual rate of 4.6 percent in the 1950's and around 5 percent in the 1960's. The labor force, moreover, expanded enormously as women entered industry in huge numbers. Finally, the United States in the 1950's became a major importer of industrial and consumer goods, making America a consumer of foreign products on a heretofore unprecedented scale. America's affluence had cultural as well as economic consequences, for this new-found abundance affected the values by which the people lived.[1]

Demographic and social changes as well as prosperity affected values. The United States underwent a population explosion in the postwar era as a result of a "baby boom" that extended from 1947 to 1960. Population increased from 140 million in 1945 to 205 million by 1970. The population not only grew but became more mobile in geographic and social terms. One in five Americans changed residence every year, and a large number were concentrated in urban and suburban areas. By 1970 only 26.5 percent of Americans lived in rural areas. Prosperity made it possible also for more Americans to move into the middle class as a result of higher incomes, better jobs, and better educational opportunities. At least three-fourths of American adults in the immediate postwar era characterized themselves as middle-class.

American society as a result of these domestic changes seemed to grow more homogeneous, more stable, and more conservative during the 1950's. The country appeared to be divided less by conflict or by sectional and class differences than ever before. There seemed to be a mood of national confidence, which was reflected in the writings of many of the intellectuals of the 1950's who stressed the twin themes of consensus and conformity.

The main aim of America's foreign policy during the postwar era was to stop the spread of Communism. The United States came to look upon itself as the leader of the free world and the main bastion of Western democracy. Since nuclear weapons prohibited the resort to a major "hot" war, the United States engaged in a "cold" war with the leading Communist powers—the Soviet Union and mainland China. America sought to contain Communism by fighting limited wars, forming alliances, and supporting anticommunist forces throughout the world. In Europe the United States embarked upon a series of diplomatic moves and treaties—the Truman Doctrine, Marshall Plan, Berlin airlift, and North Atlantic Treaty—all of which were aimed against the Soviet Union. In the Far East, America intervened in the Korean War in the 1950's and in Southeast Asia in the 1960's to check the expansion of Communism in that part of the world.

Tensions dividing the United States and the Soviet Union came to a

---

[1]Carl N. Degler, *Affluence and Anxiety: America Since 1945* (Glenview, Illinois, 1975), pp. 165–166.

climax in the Cuban missile crisis of 1962 when the two countries stood on the brink of nuclear war. Fidel Castro, the Cuban leader, allowed the Soviets to establish secret missile bases capable of attacking most of America's largest cities. President Kennedy retaliated by setting up a naval blockade to prevent their completion and threatened nuclear war if the Soviets did not dismantle the bases. The Soviets thereupon backed down and withdrew their missiles. Following the Cuban confrontation, there seemed to be a lessening of Cold War tensions. But tensions arose again in the 1960's as America became deeply involved in the Vietnam War. As that conflict drew to a close in the early 1970's, it appeared that the Cold War was ending—if it was not already over.

The Cold War during the 1950's seemed to accentuate the conservative climate of opinion that pervaded the United States. Most Americans supported the government's foreign policies, and in the name of security were willing to accept more governmental controls and restrictions on civil liberties. In the 1960's, however, mainly because of the Vietnam War, some Americans became increasingly disenchanted with America's Cold War policy. They rejected the idea that the United States should assume the responsibility for defending the rest of the world against the challenge posed by Communism.

In the 1950's these changes in domestic and foreign affairs resulted in what seemed to be a greater emphasis upon conformity. One manifestation of this greater conformity was the rise of McCarthyism. Senator Joseph McCarthy gained prominence by warning about the dangers of internal subversion by Communists and by leading investigations into the presumed disloyalty of government officials. McCarthy's "Red Scare" provoked an attack on civil liberties on a scale almost unprecedented in American history.[2]

During the 1950's, the tendency toward conformity was reflected in the work of a group of historians labeled as the neo-conservatives. These scholars adopted a conservative approach and emphasized consensus and continuity when interpreting American history. They rejected the Progressive view of history which had stressed conflict and discontinuity as the main elements of the American past. The neo-conservatives sensed, perhaps, the supposed menace to America posed

---

[2]There is a historiographical controversy regarding the origins of McCarthyism. Richard Rovere, *Senator Joseph McCarthy* (New York, 1959), attributes McCarthy's rise to his gifts as a demagogue. Earl Latham, *Communist Controversy in Washington from the New Deal to McCarthy* (Cambridge, 1966), claims anticommunism was politically inspired by hatred of the New Deal rather than fear of Russia, and that the danger to national security was never serious. Daniel Bell, ed., *The Radical Right* (New York, 1955), provides a "status anxiety" explanation for the rise of McCarthyism. Richard Hofstadter, *The Paranoid Style in American Politics and Other Essays* (New York, 1965), has similar valuable insights into McCarthyism. Michael Paul Rogin, *The Intellectuals and McCarthy: The Radical Specter* (Cambridge, 1967), refutes the argument that McCarthyism grew out of earlier Populism and attributes the phenomenon to a traditional conservative heritage.

by communism during the Cold War and responded by presenting to the rest of the world an image of an America that had been strong and united throughout most of its past.

One of the most prominent among the neo-conservative scholars was Louis Hartz, who stressed the idea of continuity in American history. Hartz, whose book *The Liberal Tradition in America* appeared in 1955, concluded that the key fact in the nation's history was that America was founded after the age of European feudalism. Hence, America never developed the conservative social institutions that characterized the *ancien régime*. America was "born free," a liberal society at its inception, and had never known anything but a liberal tradition throughout its history.

Daniel J. Boorstin, the outstanding exponent of the neo-conservative position, took a somewhat different tack. He emphasized the shared principles that gave the American way of life its distinctiveness. Boorstin wrote two books in the 1950's which denied that European ideas or influences had any impact upon America. The American way of life, he argued, was essentially pragmatic in character and was formed by the experience of dealing with the environment in settling and developing a huge, rich continent. In the course of time, this nontheoretical approach became a distinctive American life-style—one noted for its practicality, which enabled the American people to unite and to become a homogeneous society made up of undifferentiated men sharing the same values.[3]

But the consensus perspective was not the only view to emerge in the 1950's, nor were historians the only intellectuals to be affected by the national mood. Some social scientists searched for the sources of the conformity that appeared to be manifest among the American people during the decade. Other scholars turned to the study of the American national character in an effort to explain why Americans of the 1950's seemed to be so complacent and willing to conform to the dominant values of their times. There was also a resurgence of conservative social thinkers, giving rise to the movement known as the "new conservatism." Finally, there could be heard the stirrings of certain left wing critics of the consensus and conformity interpretation of the 1950's which seemed to prevail among many intellectuals.

Among those social scientists who looked for explanations of conformity was Erich Fromm, the psychoanalyst. Fromm addressed himself on a broad scale to the social and cultural forces that seemed to bring anxiety and insecurity to Western man in general in the twentieth century. In his book *Escape from Freedom,* written in 1941, Fromm had advanced the hypothesis that much of the vaunted freedom for the indi-

---

[3]Daniel J. Boorstin, *The Genius of American Politics* (Chicago, 1953) and *The Americans: The Colonial Experience* (New York, 1958).

vidual which Western society, including America, supposedly had achieved led to greater insecurity rather than to security and peace. Freedom for the individual frequently led to a terrifying sense of helplessness and inadequacy. Western man, he argued, sought to escape from freedom by fleeing into the arms of a dictator or into the mindless middle-class conformity that characterized much of Western democratic culture. In his book *The Sane Society*, written in the mid-1950's, Fromm continued to argue that modern man became a prisoner of the very institutions he had created to free himself from the past.

The renewed interest in the study of the American national character sought also to explain the apparent trend toward conformism among Americans. Some behavioral scientists developed an interpretation of the American national character that focused primarily upon culture as the main determinant in shaping personality. Other scholars turned to a historical explanation. These scholars tended to emphasize materialistic forces—economic, environmental, or technological—as the crucial factors in the formation of national character and the development of an American value system.

The groundwork for some work done by the behavioral scientists in the 1950's was laid by the distinguished cultural anthropologist Margaret Mead, in one of the most significant books written about the American national character. In *And Keep Your Powder Dry*, published in 1942, Mead argued that any analysis of the American character must take into account the fact that American life is geared to success rather than to status. The average American conceived of class hierarchy as a constantly ascending ladder rather than as something that would provide permanent status. From this situation came a second feature of the American character—the excessive concern for conformity. She suggested that immigrants after they had become Americanized rejected the standards of the culture from which they came and sought to perfect their conformity to American ways and to win the approbation of their American neighbors.

David Riesman, a social psychologist, offered yet another view of the problem in his book *The Lonely Crowd: A Study of the Changing American Character*, published in 1950. In this work Riesman postulated a change in the American national character from the nineteenth-century individualist with an "inner-directed personality" to the twentieth-century conformist with an "other-directed personality." Most nineteenth-century Americans had worked in an agrarian rural society in which success depended upon their own resources in overcoming the physical environment. The development of the "other-directed personality" of the twentieth century was due in large part to technological and economic changes that made for a more interdependent world. Twentieth-century Americans were placed in types of employment where success depended more on gaining favor and interacting with other individuals.

Thus, many modern Americans conducted their lives in such a way as to gain approval from the people around them. In other words, Riesman argued that, since the goals in life had been externalized to a large extent, Americans sought the approval of their neighbors rather than looking to themselves and their own values for direction.

William H. Whyte, a journalist, offered an interpretation that stressed the same theme in his book *The Organization Man,* published in 1956. The "organization man," according to Whyte, was a bureaucratized individual whose conformity resulted from the fact that he lived under an imperative to succeed in corporate management where promotion and even survival depended upon effective interaction with others in a hierarchical structure. The old Protestant ethic of work, said Whyte, had been replaced by a new social ethic which legitimized the pressures society now placed on individuals. The articles of faith of this new social ethic were as follows: "a belief in the group as the source of creativity; a belief in 'belongingness' as the ultimate need of the individual; and a belief in the application of science to achieve the belongingness."[4] An essay that ultimately formed a part of Whyte's book is the first selection in this chapter.

One of the most provocative historical interpretations of the nature of the American character came from David Potter's book, *People of Plenty: Economic Abundance and the American Character,* published in 1954. Although a historian, Potter made heavy use of social science concepts in approaching the problem. To Potter the most important influence in shaping the American character was the country's economic abundance, which molded its values and outlook. The abundance of goods produced from the seemingly unlimited natural resources had increased the rewards of competition in production and resulted in placing an increased premium on efficiency. The emphasis on efficiency in the process of competition favored those who were the most aggressive and eager to reap the promised rewards by taking advantage of the unrestricted latitude given to entrepreneurs. The appetite for rewards, however, outstripped the possibility of attaining them, and the desire to gain individual freedom and mobility clashed with the responsibilities and limitations of real life. The quest for abundance led Americans to abandon the system of status and to trade security for opportunity, thereby resulting in the creation of anxiety in the American character.

Potter employed the concept of abundance to explain many of the peculiar traits of the American character. In the United States, for example, the idea of equality came to mean equality in competition or opportunity for social mobility. But in committing themselves to such a concept of equality, Americans deprived many people of the security inher-

---

[4]William H. Whyte, *The Organization Man* (New York, 1957), p. 7.

ent in the idea of status, thereby giving rise to many psychological insecurities.

Another group of intellectuals called the "new conservatives" sought to understand the great social and economic changes of the 1950's from a different perspective. Peter Viereck, a poet and educator, in his book *The Shame and Glory of the Intellectuals* stressed the theme of conservatism. Viereck argued that genuine freedom could exist only in an orderly setting. The truly free man was one whose life was guided by an ethical inner check and the heritage of classical philosophy and religion rather than being dependent upon the coercive restraints of society.[5]

Viereck's ideas were echoed by a whole host of like-minded men including Russell Kirk, historian-philosopher, and Clinton Rossiter, the American historian. In virtually all of this literature, the "new conservatives" relied on the principles of Edmund Burke, the English critic of the French Revolution, and re-examined them in an effort to demonstrate their applicability to the revolutionary changes of the post-World War II era. Conservatism in the Burkean sense, as Russell Kirk pointed out, was not something new in American intellectual history. It had a tradition stretching back to men like John Adams, John C. Calhoun, and Henry and Brooks Adams. What gave the movement importance in the 1950's was its attempt to judge the events of the postwar decade from a fixed vantage point rooted in Western thought. The "new conservatism," although it was not accepted by the majority of Americans, represented an important element in contemporary thinking during the decade.[6]

The view of America that stressed the themes of consensus and conformity was shared by most but not all scholars and intellectuals. The most outspoken critic of the conservative perspective was C. Wright Mills, a sociologist. Mills in his book *The Power Elite*, published in 1956, argued that American politics could be best understood in terms of a "power elite" within the country. The key decisions in the United States, according to Mills, were made by an irresponsible clique of generals and admirals, members of the defense industry, and national legislators who operated beyond the reach of the people and who made choices in keeping with their Cold War ideology. In brief, Mills argued that America was ruled by a military-industrial complex, which used the Cold War ideology to maintain its position, to manipulate the masses, and tolerated no compromise with communism. Dissent from this doctrine was interpreted by the power elite as disloyalty to America or

[5]Peter Viereck, *The Shame and Glory of the Intellectuals* (Boston, 1953). See also his *Conservatism Revisited* (New York, 1959), and Robert Nisbet, *Quest for Community* (New York, 1953).

[6]Russell Kirk, *The Conservative Mind* (Chicago, 1953); Clinton Rossiter, *Conservative Tradition in America* (New York, 1955).

appeasement. Such a state of affairs, Mills maintained, diminished the effectiveness of the "rules" of democratic government as a protection for civil liberties in America. Mills construed the consensus view of American society as a new conservatism that celebrated the status quo rather than seeking the realization of social justice for the poor and oppressed.

The decade of the 1950's, in summary, was seen as a decade of consensus and conformity by many commentators of the period. Some historians, social scientists, and intellectuals saw more diversity in the decade and declared the designation was too simplistic and too much of a stereotype. This latter argument had considerable merit and truth to it, but the popular image of the 1950's continued to stress consensus and conformity.

The decade of the 1960's, on the other hand, was often depicted as one of crisis and individualism. Dramatic developments in both domestic and foreign affairs led many intellectuals to view the decade as one of crisis. First, the escalation of the struggle for racial justice and equality resulted in what was called the black revolution and spawned widespread hostility and violence. Second, America's growing involvement in world affairs, in particular participation in the Vietnam War, polarized American society. The race riots in major cities, massive antiwar demonstrations, and turmoil on college campuses all heightened the sense of crisis throughout the decade.

At the same time, there occurred a renewed expression of individualism among various elements of American society. This development was manifested best in the rise of the counter-culture among American youth who insisted that individuals be recognized for their human dignity rather than for what society said they were. The women's liberation movement likewise expressed a revived interest in individualism by demanding that women be accepted for their qualities as individuals rather than being treated as sex objects or viewed in stereotyped ways. The individualism of the 1960's was evident also in new life-styles, clothing, and hair styles, which symbolized the indifference of young people to distinctions of race or class. There was an increasing rejection of deference to authority and a growing permissiveness. All of these developments gave rise to a wave of criticism of American life which stood in sharp contrast to the confidence and conformity that had seemed to characterize American society during the 1950's.

One of the most significant movements in domestic affairs contributing to the crisis of the 1960's was the renewed drive for civil rights on the part of blacks. The recent civil rights movement had its origins in 1954 with the Supreme Court decision *Brown et al. vs. Board of Education of Topeka.* In that ruling the court overturned the principle of "separate but equal" established in 1896 which had permitted the segregation of black and white children in public schools. Integration, however, proceeded only very slowly during the Eisenhower years.

But in the 1960's the civil rights movement expanded its scope and increased in intensity. As the movement grew, black leaders became divided over goals and means. In the early part of the decade, the civil rights movement focused mainly on the continuation of the program of nonviolent activism initiated in the 1950's which sought integration and equal rights as its goal. The key spokesman and national leader for this movement was the Reverend Martin Luther King, Jr., who had developed his ethic of nonviolence by reading Gandhi, Tolstoy, Thoreau, and the Bible. His books *Stride Toward Freedom* (1958) and *Why We Can't Wait* (1964) explained his position. King emphasized the need for redemption through Christian love and advocated peaceful tactics like boycotts and sit-ins as means for accomplishing integration. King's philosophy was put into practice by such organizations as the Southern Christian Leadership Conference, the Student Non-Violent Coordinating Committee, and the Congress of Racial Equality, which led the struggle for racial justice in the early years of the decade.

As the 1960's progressed, however, black leaders split over the strategy to be followed in achieving racial justice. Some younger black leaders rejected the goal of integration and nonviolent means, advocating instead "Black Power"—a militant term which came to symbolize the idea of separation of blacks from a white society which had exploited them for hundreds of years. Malcolm X and Stokely Carmichael, two prominent leaders, argued that blacks should take greater pride in their cultural heritage and color, and not seek integration into American society. *The Autobiography of Malcolm X* (1964) and *Black Power* by Stokely Carmichael and Charles V. Hamilton (1967) reflected the new militancy and willingness of some younger blacks to resort to violence. This trend was best exemplified by the formation of the Black Panthers, a group of young people who armed themselves. Eldridge Cleaver's *Soul on Ice* (1967) portrayed what went into the making of a Black Panther. But by the 1970's, the Black Panthers had become concerned more with the care, feeding, and education of black children in urban ghettos than in confronting the police with force.

The civil rights movement in the 1960's met with mounting resistance on the part of white Americans in the South and North. Racial tensions resulted in such hostility that some observers came to fear a possible racial war. In the South whites mounted a "massive resistance" movement against racial integration of public schools and often resorted to violence.[7] As the movement spread to the North, there was increasingly a white "backlash" as blacks sought to desegregate school systems and

---

[7]Bob Smith, *They Closed Their Schools: Prince Edward County, Virginia, 1951–1964* (Chapel Hill, 1965); Numan T. Bartley, *The Rise of Massive Resistance: Race and Politics in the South During the 1950's* (Baton Rouge, 1969); James W. Silver, *Mississippi: The Closed Society* (New York, 1964); and Russell H. Barrett, *Integration in Ole Miss* (Chicago, 1965).

residential areas as well as to gain jobs. The demand for equality by blacks and the resistance to it by whites gave rise to race riots in many parts of the country. Beginning in 1965, many blacks grew impatient with the reluctance of white Americans to grant greater racial equality and turned to violence. Urban riots resulted in many deaths and wide-spread destruction of property. The sense of crisis generated by this violence resulted in some reforms. But increasingly the demand for "law and order" and the end to violence, coupled with the assassination of Martin Luther King, Jr., in 1968, halted the forward motion of the civil rights movement.

The second major development contributing to a sense of crisis in the 1960's was America's deepening involvement in the Vietnam War. America's military intervention was aimed at blocking the spread of Communism in the Far East. In 1961 there were only 3,200 American military advisers in Vietnam, but by 1968 that figure had risen to more than 536,000 men. Because of growing troop commitments, mounting casualties, and the belief that American presidents had taken steps to wage a secret war against North Vietnam, public opinion became deeply divided. There was increasing criticism of America's foreign policy and the rise of a massive antiwar movement.

The adverse reaction to America's participation in Vietnam helped to elaborate an interpretation of American foreign policy that had been developed even prior to the country's entry into the Vietnam conflict. William Appleman Williams in *The Tragedy of American Diplomacy*, pub-lished in 1959, revised the traditional view of American diplomatic his-tory. Williams sought to understand America's foreign relations from the perspective of the country's domestic history. America from its ori-gins had been expansionist in purpose, said Williams. Before the Ameri-can revolution the colonies had adopted a mercantilist course that would have enabled them to gain economic self-sufficiency within the British empire. Once independence had been gained, the United States com-mitted itself to the idea of an independent American empire and pur-sued a policy of expansionism led by agrarian interests against the Indi-ans, Spanish, and Mexicans in North America. With the close of the frontier in the 1890's, the idea of expansion was taken over by business interests who embarked upon a policy of economic imperialism. They aimed primarily at acquiring markets for American goods, outlets for surplus capital, and raw materials for domestic manufacturers. This pol-icy was undertaken to prevent social unrest they feared might appear in America as a result of industrial overproduction or depressions. The outcome was global expansionism based upon an open-door policy by which America sought to dominate foreign markets and resources with-out necessarily acquiring new territory or colonies. To Williams the post-World War II period represented an extension of this open-door policy to all parts of the world. The Cold War, according to Williams, was caused primarily by America's seeking to extend its economic influence in this manner.

Walter LaFeber developed and expanded Williams's thesis in a book dealing with the Cold War published in 1967. He criticized both the United States and the Soviet Union for failing to keep the peace, and focused upon domestic developments within the two countries to explain their foreign policies. Viewing the Cold War as a struggle that began in Europe and then spread to the rest of the world, LaFeber saw it as a clash between the two powers to maintain their freedom of action in those regions they considered vital to their economic and strategic interests. The Vietnam War, LaFeber concluded, was a failure of America's foreign policy because it sought to solve global political and economic problems by military means.[8] During the 1960's many New Left critics of America's Vietnam policy seized upon the writings of Williams and LaFeber to support their positions.

The escalation of America's involvement in the Vietnam war led to a widespread antiwar movement within the United States. At first the protests occurred at the nation's most prestigious universities, where students and professors participated in "teach-ins" which emphasized the irrationality and brutality of the war. As the conflict in Vietnam continued, protesters turned to massive demonstrations. One of the first took place in Washington, D.C., in 1967 and drew more than 200,000 citizens. In 1968 thousands of antiwar protesters went to Chicago for the Democratic National Convention to show their opposition to the war and to the political process. The Chicago police attacked the demonstrators in the parks and in the streets precipitating a bloody "police riot" in which protesters, bystanders, newsmen, and convention delegates were indiscriminately assaulted. By 1969 and 1970 as many as 500,000 persons went to Washington to protest the war. Finally, in the spring of 1970 demonstrations and riots erupted on many campuses following the invasion of Cambodia by American soldiers. At Kent State University in Ohio, the protest against the Cambodian invasion resulted in the deaths of four students. These killings sickened the American people and, along with the ending of the draft, virtually put an end to the massive demonstrations against the war.

The civil rights movement and the antiwar protests of the 1960's generated a high level of violence in the United States. Violent confrontations between whites and blacks during the civil rights demonstrations were followed by riots in the ghettos of nearly 100 cities resulting in the loss of many lives and billions of dollars in property from fire and looting. Frequently antiwar demonstrations turned into confrontations between protesters and police or national guardsmen. Such violence, prac-

---

[8] Walter LaFeber, *America, Russia, and the Cold War* (New York, 1967).

tically unknown during the 1950's, heightened still more the sense of crisis in American society.

Historians in the 1960's who dealt with violence as a subject took issue with the neo-conservative historians of the 1950's who had stressed consensus. Neo-conservatives like Hartz and Boorstin had not denied that America had a violent past. But they had emphasized that America's lack of a feudal past had not given rise to the class hostilities that had caused violent upheavals in Europe, and that most Americans did not take ideology seriously enough to be deeply divided by it. Historians of the 1960's examined collective violence in the United States and came to different conclusions. One of the most notable studies on the subject was the report of the National Commission on the Causes and Prevention of Violence, entitled *Violence in America,* published in 1969. This study not only concluded that collective and individual violence was common in the nation's past, but suggested also that it was a normal aspect of American political life. Violence, it was shown, arose from the unsettled social and cultural arrangements characteristic of America, and from the difficulties of relieving the fears and satisfying the anxieties of many peoples living under fluid social circumstances. This view not only helped to explain contemporary violence, but also directly contradicted the image of a homogeneous past presented by the neo-conservative scholars.[9]

The civil rights movement, especially in Northern cities, drew increasing attention to yet another major social problem—that of poverty. In part the renewed interest in this problem came as a result of the publication of Michael Harrington's *The Other America: Poverty in the United States* in 1962. Harrington argued that America's prosperity and affluence had been exaggerated during the 1950's. He found that about 25 percent of all Americans were living in poverty, with a family income of less than $3,000. Poverty, according to Harrington, was a way of life for millions of Americans. Moreover, although most Americans were somewhat better off than they had been a generation earlier, a great many remained barely above the poverty level. These people were living on family incomes between $3,500 and $4,500 a year and fell short of the government's minimum requirements for a "modestly comfortable level of living." Such persons the economist Leon Keyserling called "deprived Americans" and were estimated in 1964 to number 77 million. This group included many low-paid persons—manual laborers, laundry workers, and clerks—who protested their plight. It was with the goal of improving the lot of many of the poor that President Lyndon Johnson proclaimed his goal of achieving a "Great Society" in 1964.

---

[9]Hugh D. Graham and Ted R. Gurr, eds., *Violence in America* (New York, 1969). See also Richard Hofstadter and Michael Wallace, eds., *American Violence: A Documentary History* (New York, 1970).

The protest movements by the blacks, antiwar demonstrators, and the poor in the 1960's were accompanied by similar movements which stressed the idea of individualism. The youth culture and the women's liberation movement sought to change the mental attitudes and lifestyles of individuals involved in those movements. In some ways the two movements were interrelated. One of the major factors in the formation of the new-found consciousness among young people was their participation in the civil rights and the antiwar movements. Many idealistic white and black students in the 1960's protested racial discrimination and prejudice, and participated in demonstrations and voter registration efforts. Likewise the antiwar protest was initiated and widely supported by the young. The most important result of the youth culture and the women's liberation movement was the rejection of many accepted social norms prevalent in America during the 1950's. Countless Americans in the 1960's rejected the conformism of the 1950's and embraced the ideology of individualism.

The heightened sense of individualism among women could be seen in the rapid rise of the feminist movement, which revolutionized the way in which women thought of themselves and their place in society. Betty Friedan's book *The Feminine Mystique,* published in 1963, marked the beginning of the new feminism. Friedan argued that the "feminine mystique," which most American women accepted, could be attributed to the social conditioning to which they were exposed in their upbringing. The family, school, and mass media all conditioned women to accept the traditional roles of mothers and housewives. Women were indoctrinated to accept domesticity, their role as "sex objects," and consumerism as a way of life. American society was dominated by white males, and the social conventions they espoused prevented women from ever reaching their full potential as human beings. Friedan and other feminists in 1963 formed NOW, the National Organization for Women, to fight against the idea of sexual stereotyping, to lobby for legislation favorable to women, and to raise the consciousness of women in general.[10]

Another significant manifestation of individualism in the 1960's was the new-found self-consciousness among American youth—the counter-culture. This movement represented, in part, a reaction against the conformity that seemed to have characterized much of the 1950's. There were many underlying causes for the appearance of this phenomenon. One was the continuing prosperity which enabled many young people to postpone going to work and to attend college where they developed an identity as members of a distinct social group. A second factor was the overwhelming number of young people of college age,

---

[10]The literature on the women's liberation movement is voluminous, but a good general work is William Chafe, *The American Woman: 1920–1970* (New York, 1972).

the result of the baby boom in the 1940's and 1950's. A third was the expansion of federal funds to support higher education which permitted many more students to attend colleges and universities. Although only a minority of American youth was involved in the counter-culture—and even these young people were not always in college—it was the turmoil on college campuses that attracted the greatest attention.

The youth cult of the sixties challenged many of the accepted ideas and ideals of American society. Many young people objected to what they considered to be the materialism, hypocrisy, and lack of sensitivity of the older generation. They attacked the competitiveness, status-seeking, and conformity that seemed to them to characterize American life. The result was a challenge to many of the confining standards of middle-class American society. The "straight" American of the 1950's—wearing short hair and neatly dressed—gave way to the "hippie" of the 1960's who was often bearded, long-haired, and sometimes dressed in outlandish clothing. Turning to sex, drugs, music, and, at times, political radicalism, this segment of youth rejected an American middle-class culture that seemed alien and artificial to them.[11]

Theodore Roszak, the historian who coined the phrase "counter-culture," wrote a book in 1969 called *The Making of a Counter Culture*, which sought to trace the causes of the crisis among American youth. He described America's young people as profoundly alienated from the parental generation because they questioned the conventional world view which stressed science, logic, and reason. The young placed great emphasis instead on emotion and feeling. They were seeking a new way of life, Roszak concluded, one that rejected the hypocrisy, racism, sexism, and callousness to social problems that seemed to characterize the older generation. They rejected the discipline, hard work, and highly organized institutions of the adult world in favor of a more relaxed life-style. Roszak's reflections captured the essence of the opposition of youth to America's technocratic society.

Another work that caught the spirit of the youth movement was Charles Reich's *The Greening of America*, published in 1970. A law professor at Yale University, Reich sought to place the youth movement within a historical context by showing how a technocratic society sacrificed individualistic and humanistic values. Reich described two earlier ages—Consciousness I and Consciousness II—when the earlier ideals of American enterprise, material success, and the corporation life had been fully accepted. He predicted the coming of a new age—Consciousness III—in which the corporate society would be rejected and individuals

---

[11]The literature on the counter-culture and youth movement is vast, and much of it superficial. One serious attempt to place the phenomenon in a much broader setting is Lewis S. Feuer, *The Conflict of Generations* (New York, 1969).

would live in a genuine communitarian spirit instead. His book created great sympathy for the rebellious younger generation, but it appeared at precisely the time when the youth movement was losing its force.

The view of the 1960's as one of crisis and individualism was best expressed, perhaps, in William O'Neill's informal history of the decade called *Coming Apart*, published in 1971. O'Neill's aim was to describe the process of polarization in American society that occurred between Kennedy's coming to power in 1960 and the beginning of Nixon's presidency in 1969. His book depicted the 1960's as a period of great social tension, stress, and divisiveness. He chronicled the change in the climate of opinion which went from optimism and hope at the start of the decade to pessimism and despair. Domestic problems grew serious—the black struggle, student rebellions, and antiwar protests drove the American people apart in a way that would have been thought unimaginable in the 1950's. O'Neill emphasized the crucial role the Vietnam War played in bringing about the increasing fragmentation of society. The second selection in this chapter is drawn from O'Neill's book, and concerns itself with the evolution of the counter-culture in the 1960's. [12]

The turmoil of the 1960's also gave rise to a new group of radical scholars—the "New Left"—who attacked the neo-conservative interpretation of American history. Left-wing critiques of American society had existed throughout the twentieth century, but such attacks seemed to diminish in the conformity that characterized the decade of the 1950's. But the sense of crisis generated in the 1960's—particularly by the hostility to the Vietnam War—brought a new condemnation of capitalism by New Left scholars. They shared a general belief that what American society needed was a thoroughgoing reformation. Unlike the Old Left, however, the "New Left" varied widely in its assessment of the problems facing the nation and the proper remedies to be employed. The "New Left" included a number of historians who produced revisionist studies in many fields—labor, politics, and urban history. But their most important contributions were in the area of American diplomatic history. Building on the works of the older Progressive historians as well as the volumes written by William Appleman Williams and Walter LaFeber, they produced revisionist works that reinterpreted America's role in world affairs. Most of them started from the general assumption that America's foreign policy had invariably been based on the nation's need for markets for its goods and raw materials for its manufacturers. Joyce and Gabriel Kolko, for example, were especially critical of America's part in bringing on the Cold War. Other "New Left" scholars were equally harsh in condemning America's involvement in the Vietnam

---

[12]For an analysis of more formal ideas and systems of thought in the 1960's, see Ronald Berman, *America in the Sixties* (New York, 1968).

War. The revisionist outlook of the "New Left" touched off a spirited historiographical controversy that affected almost all works written on these subjects.[13]

In conclusion, great differences may have existed between the decades of the 1950's and 1960's—as has been suggested—but there is a danger of carrying the contrast too far. To do so would be to oversimplify what was a complex era. The view of the 1950's as a period of consensus represents something of a stereotype, for some of the changes that took place in the 1960's were already in evidence earlier. The black revolution was well under way in the 1950's; the alienation of youth had been anticipated in Jack Kerouac's beatnik novel *On the Road*, published in 1957; and John Kenneth Galbraith's book *The Affluent Society*, written in 1958, had indicated the existence of large-scale core poverty in a supposedly prosperous America. The growing trend toward greater individualism could be seen in the works of artists and architects in the 1950's, as Carl Degler has shown.[14] The 1950's, then, provided considerable evidence of diversity and divisiveness in the controversies over the Korean War, McCarthyism, and domestic politics.

The characterization of the 1960's as a decade of crisis must likewise be qualified. Attitudes toward sexism, racism, and America's role in world affairs changed rapidly, but political and economic reforms proceeded at a slower pace. Despite the changes America underwent during the upheaval in the 1960's, the fact remains that most of the country's economic and political institutions remained intact. The greatest changes that took place were social and ideological in nature. The social protest movements changed the ways in which people thought and acted toward one another; the women's liberation movement changed the relations between men and women; and the black revolution altered relations of blacks to other Americans. The antiwar movement, on the other hand, affected America's role in world affairs and led to a tendency to support a somewhat more isolationist foreign policy.

Any student who attempts to evaluate the differences between the 1950's and 1960's is at a great disadvantage. There are no reflective histories on either decade, and scholars remain too close to events to have much of a sense of perspective. Certain questions, nevertheless, do suggest themselves. Were the continuities that persisted through both

---

[13]Stephen Ambrose, *The Rise to Globalism: American Foreign Policy Since 1938* (London, 1971) along with LaFeber's *America, Russia, and the Cold War* represent revisionist studies of the Cold War period in general. Joyce Kolko and Gabriel Kolko, *The Limits of Power: The World and the United States Foreign Policy, 1945–1954* (New York, 1972), and Lloyd C. Gardner, *Architects of Illusion: Men and Ideas in American Foreign Policy* (Chicago, 1970), are more specific revisionist studies.

There is a burgeoning literature on the revisionists of the Cold War, and two representative works are Robert J. Maddox, *The New Left and the Origins of the Cold War* (Princeton, 1973), and Robert W. Tucker, *The Radical Left and American Foreign Policy* (Baltimore, 1971).

[14]Carl N. Degler, *Affluence and Anxiety: 1945–Present*, 197–207.

decades—prosperity and anticommunism—more significant than the changes that took place? Why did the climate of opinion change despite these continuities? What were the most important causes behind the sense of social crisis that pervaded the 1960's? To what degree could the changes in the 1960's trace their origins back to developments already under way in the 1950's? What is the relationship between the events of the 1950's and the interpretation of American society which stressed consensus and conformity? Were the commentators of the 1950's correct in their perceptions of American society and the American national character? Or were the 1960's more representative of what has happened in American history in the past? Only by answering such questions can the student evaluate whether the contrast between the 1950's and 1960's was as profound as portrayed in this chapter.

William H. Whyte, Jr.

WILLIAM H. WHYTE, JR. (1917–   ) graduated from Princeton University, worked for *Fortune Magazine* from 1946 to 1959, authored many articles and books, and served on various public bodies. His best known work is *The Organization Man* (1956).

A very curious thing has been taking place in this country—and almost without our knowing it. In a country where "individualism"— independence and self-reliance—was the watchword for three centuries, the view is now coming to be accepted that the individual himself has no meaning—except, that is, as a member of a group. "Group integration," "group equilibrium," "interpersonal relations," "training for group living," "group dynamics," "social interaction," "social physics"; more and more the notes are sounded—each innocuous or legitimate in itself, but together a theme that has become unmistakable.

In a sense, this emphasis is a measure of success. We have *had* to learn how to get along in groups. With the evolution of today's giant organizations—in business, in government, in labor, in education, in big cities—we have created a whole new social structure for ourselves, and one so complex that we're still trying to figure out just what happened. But the American genius for cooperative action has served us well. "Human relations" may not be an American invention, but in no country have people turned so wholeheartedly to the job of mastering the group skills on which our industrial society places such a premium.

But the pendulum has swung too far. Take, for example, the growing popularity of "social engineering" with its emphasis on the planned manipulation of the individual into the group role. Or, even more striking, the extraordinary efforts of some corporations to encompass the executive's wife in the organization—often with the willing acquiescence of the wife in the merger. And these, as we hope to demonstrate, are no isolated phenomena; recent public-opinion polls, slick-magazine fiction, current best-sellers, all document the same trend. Groupthink is becoming a national philosophy.

Groupthink being a coinage—and, admittedly, a loaded one—a working definition is in order. We are not talking about mere instinctive conformity—it is, after all, a perennial failing of mankind. What we are

William H. Whyte, Jr., "Groupthink," *Fortune,* XLV (March, 1952), pp. 114–117, 142, 146. Reprinted by permission of *Fortune.*

talking about is a *rationalized* conformity—an open, articulate philosophy which holds that group values are not only expedient but right and good as well. Three mutually supporting ideas form the underpinning: (1) that moral values and ethics are relative; (2) that what is important is the kind of behavior and attitudes that makes for the harmonious functioning of the group; (3) that the best way to achieve this is through the application of "scientific" techniques.

Once grasped, as the work of the social engineers makes clear, these principles lead us to an entirely new view of man. And what a dismal fellow he is! For the man we are now presented with is Social Man— completely a creature of his environment, guided almost totally by the whims and prejudices of the group, and incapable of any real self-determination of his destiny. Only through social engineering—i.e., applied groupthink—can he be saved. The path to salvation, social engineers explain, lies in a trained elite that will benevolently manipulate us into group harmony. And who's to be the elite? Social engineers modestly clear their throats.

The Vanishing Layman

This vision of a new elite guiding us to the integrated life has inspired some interesting speculations (e.g., Aldous Huxley's *Brave New World*, George Orwell's *Nineteen Eighty-Four*). The real danger, however, is something else again. It is not that the layman will be pushed around by the social engineers: it is that *he will become one himself.* Rather than the pawn of the experts, he will be the willing apprentice—and embrace groupthink as the road to security.

Is this coming to pass? Let's look for a moment at the direction American values are taking among the oncoming generations. There has been a rather disturbing amount of evidence that they are changing rapidly—and in a way that must warm social engineers' hearts. Every study made of the younger generation, every portrayal they make of themselves—from their dating habits to their artistic inclinations— uncovers one clear fact: our youth is the most group-minded we have ever had. Gregariousness, *Time*'s recent study indicated, has become a necessity. "They are parts of groups," one girl shrewdly appraises her contemporaries. "When they are alone they are bored with themselves."

While youngsters are not inclined to philosophize, their attitude toward life adds up to a fairly discernible set of values. It could be described as a "practical" relativism. The old absolute moral values are disappearing. There is still black and white, to be sure, but it is no longer determined by fixed precepts; it is determined rather by what the group thinks is black and white—and if someone does things the way his group does, well, who is to censure him for his loyalty?

The colleges furnish documentation of the drift. If recent surveys are any indication, a startling swing has taken place among students to the twin ideals of group harmony and expertism. "These men," one of their mentors says in praise, "don't question the system. Their main aim is to make it work better—to get in there and lubricate the machinery. They're not rebels; they'll be social technicians for a better society."

The registrar's records bear him out. Along with a concurrent drift from the humanities, there has been a tremendous increase in specialized courses—and of specialization within specialties. Significantly, the courses that enjoyed the most phenomenal popularity among postwar classes were those connected with personnel work. "I like people" became a universal cry, and in droves students aiming for business turned thumbs down on the idea of general, executive apprenticeship in favor of personnel work; here, with stop watch and slip stick in hand, they could measure away, safe from the doubts and intangibles of the world without. The picture was a mirage, of course, but it was only by the most strenuous efforts of placement officers and corporation personnel people that students gave it up.

Does entry into business life transform these values? Apparently not. Talk with members of the younger generation of management—and we speak not of the disaffected but of the successful—and one is struck by a curious strain of resignation that often runs through their discussion. Like the heroes of J. P. Marquand's perceptive novels, they are disturbed by a sense of individual impotence. Dispassionately, they describe themselves primarily as members of their environment—men more acted upon than acting. They are neither angry nor cynical about it; they are caught on a "treadmill" from which they will never escape, perhaps—but the treadmill is pleasant enough, they explain, and in the group role they find the emotional security they want so very badly.

So with their wives. No matter what problem they are discussing—from the possibility of advancement to the style of their living—they instinctively phrase their problems in terms of their relations with the group. The relations, they concede are not simple—there are the girls, the gang on Ferncrest Road, Charlie's people at the office, and a host of lesser constellations to conjure with. Tough as the job may be, however, it is a job to which they have dedicated themselves.

The System Lovers

Turn to the image of the good life in popular cultures and you find the same phenomenon at work. Slick-magazine fiction tells the story. It has never, of course, exactly called for a rebellion against the status quo, but back in the thirties it did present heroes and heroines who engaged in some kind of mild strife with their environment, told the boss off, or did something equally contentious. No longer. A FORTUNE analysis of

1935–36 plots and 1950–51 plots indicates that heroes and heroines have been growing remarkably submissive. Not only is the system they abide by—be it an Army camp, a business office, or a small-town environment—shown as more benevolent; in some cases the system itself becomes the *deus ex machina* that solves the problem.

So in serious fiction. More and more, writers are concerning themselves with the relationship of the individual to the group, and more and more resolving it in favor of the latter. The system—and they don't mean God or the universe—is eventually revealed to the hero as bigger than any of us, and thus it is not only foolish but wrong for him not to reconcile himself to it. From the extreme of the angry, to-hell-with-the-whole-lousy-setup tracts of the 1930's we seem to be going whole hog in the opposite direction.

Let us have a look at the current best-seller, Herman Wouk's *The Caine Mutiny*. Since it is about the Navy, the system shown has some aspects peculiar to service life. The basic question posed, however—the individual's place in the system—has great universality, and in an excitingly told tale Wouk sketches one point of view with such striking overtones that the book could almost go down as a landmark in the shift of American values.

The story tells of the terrible dilemma facing the officers of a mine sweeper; their captain, one Queeg, is a neurotic, cowardly incompetent. A typhoon brings the problem to the breaking point. Through hysteria and cowardice, Queeg is about to sink the ship. In vain, Maryk, the stolid, conventional executive officer, tries to get him to keep the ship headed into the wind. Queeg refuses. In the nick of time, Maryk makes his decision. Under Article 184 of Navy Regulations, he relieves Queeg of his command. The ship is saved.

What is the moral? Maryk, we find, shouldn't have done it. Says the author's protagonist, Lieutenant Willy Keith in a letter to his girl (p. 463): "... I see that we were in the wrong.... The idea is, once you get an incompetent ass of a skipper—and it's a chance of war—there's nothing to do but serve him as though he were the wisest and the best, cover his mistakes, keep the ship going, and bear up. So I have gone all the way around Robin Hood's barn to arrive at the old platitudes, which I guess is the process of growing up."

In other times, perhaps, this definition of maturity might have been regarded as downright parody. Obedience and discipline few could have caviled at. But would they have applauded the counseling of an obedience, so abject, so *unquestioning*, that we are asked, in effect, not only to put up with the evils of a system but to regard them as right—to reach out, as Norbert Weiner's phrase goes, and kiss the whip that lashes us? Would they have joined in censuring an act to which the only logical alternative is the passive sacrifice of several hundred lives? Hardly. The executive officer's action might well have been seen as an act of great moral courage—and one, furthermore, in true allegiance to the service; it did, after all, save the ship. The other byproduct, the withdrawal of Queeg from line command, might also have been interpreted as something less than a disaster to the system.

Not so A.D. 1952. The moral, to judge from what critics and readers have been saying about it, has struck exactly the right chord. The exec, as the dust jacket has it, was merely a well-meaning man "beyond his depth," and more to be pitied than censured. It is not for the individual to question the competence of the Queegs a system may contain. Queeg was a teacher. Queegs are necessary. We needed Queegs to win the war. So goes the assent. "It is about time that more books of this sort were written," says J. P. Marquand. "The lesson the newcomer must learn is in many ways the antithesis of democracy. It is essentially a final acceptance of the doctrine that full and unquestioning obedience must be accorded a superior officer, no matter how personally odious or stupid this individual may be—and that without this individual surrender we can never win a war."

Love that system.

The Permissive Way

What makes this wave of the present particularly unsettling is the surprising fact that it is in rhythm with one of the dominant currents in contemporary American academic thought. It would be a mistake, of course, to treat the connection as cause and effect; groupthink's roots go too deep to be so summarily explained. But it would be just as much of an error to dismiss the academic underpinnings, as the layman is so tempted to do, as mere ivory-tower mumbo jumbo. The ideology of groupthink is often incomprehensible to the uninitiated, but it is of great power nonetheless. Translated by its disciples in hundreds of lecture halls and papers, and by their disciples in turn, it has given a purpose and direction to the groupthink movement that it would otherwise lack.

The movement, in a sense, is an offshoot of the great academic revolt at the turn of the century against formalism. To Young Turks of the day the individualistic tradition of American thought needed redefinition. Too much attention, they felt, had been concentrated on the lone individual; as a consequence, the rigid values built up for his protection were inapplicable to the great social upheavals that were taking place. What was needed was a social view of man—man as a unit of the group— and a willingness to adapt society to his needs.

Most of the credit generally goes to John Dewey, who, with William Kilpatrick, gave "progressive" education its impetus. But there were many others—Veblen in economics, for example, and Roscoe Pound in the law ("The law is social engineering"). Like a fresh breeze, through almost every field of American thought, the new concepts swept, as converts enthusiastically fell to whacking away at the restrictions of the old absolutes. Social Man was coming of age.

When the cultural anthropologists got to work on him, his final link to the old moral absolutes was severed. From their comparisons of primitive cultures, and, later, our own, many anthropologists came to the view that the ethics of a people are relative. By this they do not mean that ethics are unimportant, but rather that they are not to be judged by any abstract conceptions of "right" or "wrong." For if we realize that other cultures and ethics are "equally valid," to use Ruth Benedict's phrase, then we will be jogged into giving up all the more readily our outworn traditions and our illusions of individual autonomy. "It is not any particular set of values," another anthropologist explains, "but a way of looking at them that is important."

A half-century has gone by and the relativistic, social view of man idea is still gaining. The appetite for cultural anthropology, for example, has been growing at such a rate that Ruth Benedict's *Patterns of Culture*, first published in 1931, has reached, after a phenomenal newsstand sale, the No. 1 best-seller spot in the Mentor paper-book series.

In several essentials, however, the nature of the movement against formalism has changed drastically. What started as a healthy revolt against dogmatism has produced an offshoot that has succeeded in becoming the new dogmatism itself. And since, like all dogmatisms, it promises respite from uncertainty, a society still shell-shocked by the upheavals of the twentieth century hasn't bothered yet to question its effects too closely. To be sure, those of the groupthink leaning customarily speak of themselves as rebels fighting an uphill battle against the enemy ("medievalists," "academicians," "absolutists") but the dog they are kicking is practically dead. They won that battle long ago.

Certainly so in one sector of education. Thanks to a strenuous academic controversy, the momentum of the militantly "progressive" brand was slowed down some time back. Groupthink, however, cannot be contained by a label, and to a formidable body of educators the basic ideal of adjustment to group values is so taken for granted that the only remaining job would appear to be working up better ways of bringing it about. "The American educator," writes one of them, Professor Stewart Cole, "[must] treat pupils as persons-in-groups-in-American-culture at every stage of their social learning." To do this the teacher should borrow from such disciplines as anthropology, the social sciences, psychology, and group dynamics. "The social interactions" of teachers and pupils should be "the primary channel of learning the good life for America."[1]

In this free, permissive atmosphere, the idea that the individual

---

[1]Educators of this bent cannot be accused of swimming against the current. As a recent Elmo Roper poll indicates, most Americans now feel the second most important reason for sending children to high school is "to teach them to get along better with other people." (No. 1: to get them ready for a job.)

should be regarded as personally accountable for the way he behaves is, of course, old hat. And in the popular view as well. "If your young son sticks his tongue out at you and calls you a nasty old stinkpot," an article in *American Magazine* good-humoredly, but approvingly, counsels, "just ignore the insult and rejoice secretly that you have such a fine normal child. He is simply channeling his aggressive, aggrieved feelings harmlessly by verbal projection."

Where "social interaction" is the watchword, the attitude conditioning is left, in large part, to the child's peers. Even more than their elders, they are quick to reward deviance with hefty interaction; and thus in the natural distaste of the crowd for the individualist we now have a social tool. And this, the child learns from the books written for him, is as it should be. In these tales of fire engines and trains, as David Riesman has documented in his disturbing study, *The Lonely Crowd*, the neophyte groupthinker is taught that one wins by being directed by others— and that the most important thing in the world is to be a team player.

To further ensure that the child need never be a person-not-in-groups, the necessity for little groupthinkers to think as individuals *all by themselves* may soon be obviated altogether. Individual homework is now to be eliminated. Writes Amy Selwyn in the *Reader's Digest*, "Now authorities generally agree that children learn best if they do their learning in groups and talk out loud about lessons as they work. 'No homework' spokesmen also say if children were not required to spend their leisure studying they would not develop the resentment against study which often kills all incentive to learn anything. . . ."

Lest the layman presume to question the drift, groupthinkers explain that their work is rooted in the Scientific Method, and that now being a holy phrase, it is made plain that the debate is closed to outsiders—if indeed any grounds for debate exist at all.[2] "Because this new 'doctrine' has for its base objective findings in anthropology, social psychology, mental hygiene, and scientific child study," Professor Alain Locke of Howard University says, "there is an authoritative consensus back of these newer educational procedures that few would care to challenge."

On the Brink of Nonsense

He is right. Many educators have seriously questioned the excesses of educational groupthink, but a large proportion of them are curiously loath to do it out loud right now. Criticism of the misapplications of science, they know, will be quickly seized as an attack on science itself. To muddy matters even more, those of the extremist fringe (notably

---

[2]"I should like to see teachers and professors as sure of themselves, as confident in their training and experience, as surgeons are, and as impatient of lay advice"—Margaret B. Pickel, Dean of Women, Columbia University; *New York Times Magazine*, June 3, 1951.

Allen Zoll) have succeeded in putting something of the kiss of death on public discussion by their attacks on "progressive" education. They are really attacking something else, of course; their reasoning is erroneous and their motives suspect. Nevertheless, many people who have a respectable argument to make hesitate for fear they will lose their standing as liberals. The debate, however, cannot long be deferred—certainly so when it can be said, with some justification, that the best friend progressive education has today is Allen Zoll.

There are some signs that the wider implications of the groupthink movement may at last provoke a counterrevolution. Significantly, some of the most astringent critiques of groupthink are coming from the ranks of the sociologists (cf. "The image of Man in the Social Sciences"— Reinhard Bendix in *Commentary*, February, 1951). In its application to the law, Roscoe Pound himself has been led to protest the degree to which the social-utility concept has supplanted firm values. Similarly, in England—which suffers groupthink too—educator Sir Walter Moberly has been stirring the universities to a reexamination of the British variant.

But the best hope may well lie in the ambitions of the groupthinkers themselves. They stand poised, finally, on the threshold of pure nonsense. For a long time they have been growing uncomfortable over their apparent denial of ethical relevance. As the anthropologists themselves point out, man does need a firm sense of right and wrong, and an excessively relative view destroys the old firmness.

This does not mean, however, that the groupthinkers are chastened. Quite the contrary. They now propose to cure this pitfall of scientism with more scientism. Ethics are to be made "a matter of scientific investigation." To some, this merely means an objective study of ethics— certainly a proper enough task. To the groupthinker, however, it means nothing less than a theoretical apparatus for the scientific determination of what is "good" or "bad." And thus "to the innermost citadel of dogmatic thinking, the realm of values," they hopefully turn. "The conquest of the field of values," as one sounds the call, "would be almost the concluding triumph." He couldn't be more correct.

Ethics Without Tears

Why should so despairing an ideology be so popularly contagious? In a society where the old family and community ties that so long cemented it have broken down, the impulse for association is an instinctive and healthy response. But a sense of "belonging," a sense of meaningful association with others, has never required that one sacrifice his individuality as part of the bargain. Why, then, do so many rush to embrace a philosophy that tells them it *is* necessary? Why, like the moth, do we fly to the one thing that will consume us? Why, in a country with the sort of healthy political and economic base that has historically nourished individualism, are we so pathetically eager to join up in flatulent brotherhood?

To explain this impulse is to explain our blind faith in scientism as well. For their appeal is common, and many as the variations may be, they come back, eventually, to one simple, compelling theme.

They offer us freedom from moral choice.

Through the deification of group harmony, buck-passing a moral decision becomes itself a moral act; the system—as *The Caine Mutiny* advocates—attends to these things so much better than the individual, and he might just as well relax and enjoy it.

And there is freedom in another sense as well. Moral dilemmas exist because there is uncertainty. If we can now abstract a few parts from the whole of human nature and by analysis predict objectively what will make for group harmony, the intangibles that make individual decisions so poignant may be obviated altogether. Like a general who is blessed with perfect intelligence of the enemy, we will have only one valid course of action before us. We will have finally latched on to certainty.

Why Participate?

Once this denial of moral relevance is made, folly must be the consequence. For groupthinkers go on to assure themselves that in groupthink itself one finds moral fulfillment. It is not put this crudely, of course; by what has now become a ritualistic explanation, our eyes are directed upward to the goal of harmony, group integration, dynamic equilibrium; upward to a golden mean in which everyone will finally attain the blessed state of—grace? No, the state of "participation."

But participation for what? As a fundamental of the democratic process, as a means of self-expression and development, participation is abundantly desirable. In this sense, FORTUNE has argued strongly for participation; it has reported its application to the problems of management and will continue to. But the word, like its blood brothers "communication" and "adjust," is assuming a sort of end-all quality. So let us put the question: *Why* participate?

In the litany of groupthink the answers describe a complete circle. One participates for the end of "social integration," for "community-centered cohesion," for better "interpersonal relations," for "group harmony," for the reduction of "social tensions," for adjustment to the environment. One participates, in other words, that he may participate. And so the end is really only a means after all. Good means, yes— but as an encompassing philosophy, somewhat less than complete.

Even as a means, participation can be a tricky concept. It is easily confused with getting a number of people to do what one did before.

And in this aspect, unfortunately, it provides the resolutely pedestrian with a way of cutting down to size their up-and-coming brethren. Similarly it offers the faint of heart an alibi for ducking responsibility—if a broth is to be spoiled, it's convenient to have too many cooks participate.

Perhaps the most extraordinary aspect of groupthink is the success with which its double-talk has used the old concepts of individualism to justify their opposite. By letting others decide, one decides. By submitting oneself to the group, one becomes an individual. "It is precisely this gradual change in our mental horizon—new assumptions and hypotheses taken as factual description—that is sinister," says Lincoln Reis, professor of philosophy at Bard College. "So that while we are presented with a logical horror, we find it established and accepted widely as a fact. Nowhere vulnerable to intelligence, it is as impervious as a nightmare."

It is impervious because the ideal of unity it holds out obscures for us some disagreeable facts of life—and the necessity for facing them on moral grounds. "Communication" is a term in point. As used in its cult sense, it implies the facile premise that the conflicts that plague us are due simply to "blocks" in the communication flow, and that if we get the technical hang of it, all will be well. Up to a point this is true. But people do not always argue because they misunderstand one another; they argue because they hold different goals. These will always be a matter of debate, and attempts to evade it through "nonpartisan" communication or "education" programs simply beg the question.

Unity—or Monotony?

"Unity" is a double-edged sword. As our young corporation wife is witness, group harmony is not an unmixed blessing; conversely, neither are frustrations and tensions necessarily bad. They can be fruitful; indeed, progress is often dependent on producing rather than mitigating them. In large part, also, they stem from the scores of conflicting loyalties and allegiances we enjoy in a fluid society. Unless we forswear these in complete fealty to one embracing organization, there is no easy way to escape the moral decision they force upon us. *Nor should there be.* The danger, as Clark Kerr points out, "is not that loyalties are divided today, but that they may become undivided tomorrow."

It is precisely this smothering of the individual that the drift to groupthink seems to be making more and more imminent. Few group thinkers, to be sure, believe themselves against the individual. But in looking so intently at man as a member of the group, they have made man seem important in this role only. There is the frequent explanation, of course, that only by group participation is the individual's potential realized. But this is only a half-truth. Individual excellence must involve something more than a respect for the group and a skill in working with it. "The sphere of individual action," writes Bertrand Russell, "is not to be regarded as ethically inferior to that of social duty. On the contrary, some of the best of human activities are, at least in feeling, rather personal than social. . . Prophets, mystics, poets, scientific discoverers, are men whose lives are dominated by a vision. . . It . . . is such men who put into the world the things that we most value."

Few of us are potential geniuses, but the constant admonition to harmonize and integrate affects us nonetheless. Each day we are faced with a multitude of decisions. Should we trust our own judgment? Or does the group's view have an inherent rightness we cannot match?

The new values would incline us to the easy harmony of the group view, for they would have us suppose that the whole is greater than the sum of the parts; that the system has a wisdom beyond the reach of ordinary mortals. But this is not necessarily so. Man can be greater than the group, and his lone imagination worth a thousand graphs.

He is not often a creator, but even as spectator, as "the common man," he can rise in ways his past performance would not predict. To aim at his common denominators in the name of ultimate democracy is to despise him, to perpetuate his mediocrities, and to conceive him incapable of responding to anything better than the echo of his prejudices. The "equilibrium" that is the compact to be made with this boor is inevitably static, and the trouble is not solved by sticking the adjective dynamic in front of it.

Has the individual reached a low enough estate for us to become concerned? When the nation's best-selling novel advocates his abject submission without raising eyebrows; when some corporations make it policy not to hire honor graduates for fear they might not be good mixers; when it is seriously stated that "natural leaders" can be made obsolete, the time has come at least to think about the matter. For if the drift continues, man may soon cease to fret over such things at all. He will finally have engineered for himself that equilibrious society. Gelded into harmonious integration, he will be free from tensions and frustrations, content in the certainties of his special function, no longer tantalized by the sense of infinity. He will at last have become a complete bore.

The answer is not a return to a "rugged individualism" that never was. Nor is it a slackened interest in social science and "human relations." We need, certainly, to find ways of making this bewildering society of ours run more smoothly and we need all the illumination science can give us to do it. But we need something more. Lest man become an ethical eunuch, his autonomy sacrificed for the harmony of the group, a new respect for the individual must be kindled. A revival of the humanities, perhaps, a conscious, deliberate effort by the corporation not only to accommodate dissent but to encourage it—possible approaches to a problem so fundamental cannot easily be spelled out.

Only individuals can do it.

William L. O'Neill

WILLIAM L. O'NEILL (1935–   ) is Professor of History at Rutgers University. He is
the author of a number of studies of recent American history, including *Divorce in the Progressive Era* (1967), *Everyone Was Brave: The Rise and Fall of Feminism in America* (1969), and *Coming Apart: An Informal History of America in the 1960's* (1971).

Counter-culture as a term appeared rather late in the decade. It largely replaced the term "youth culture," which finally proved too limited. When the sixties began, youth culture meant the way adolescents lived. Its central institutions were the high school and the mass media. Its principal activities were consuming goods and enacting courtship rituals. Critics and students of the youth culture were chiefly interested in the status and value systems associated with it. As time went on, college enrollments increased to the point where colleges were nearly as influential as high schools in shaping the young. The molders of youthful opinion got more ambitious. Where once entertainers were content to amuse for profit, many began seeing themselves as moral philosophers. Music especially became a medium of propaganda, identifying the young as a distinct force in society with unique values and aspirations. This helped produce a kind of ideological struggle between the young and their elders called the "generation gap." It was the first time in American history that social conflict was understood to be a function of age. Yet the young were not all rebellious. Most in fact retained confidence in the "system" and its norms. Many older people joined the rebellion, whose progenitors were as often over thirty (where the generation gap was supposed to begin) as under it. The attack on accepted views and styles broadened so confusingly that "youth culture" no longer described it adequately. Counter-culture was a sufficiently vague and elastic substitute. It meant all things to all men and embraced everything new from clothing to politics. Some viewed the counter-culture as mankind's best, maybe only, hope; others saw it as a portent of civilization's imminent ruin. Few recalled the modest roots from which it sprang.

Even in the 1950's and very early sixties, when people still worried about conformity and the silent generation, there were different drummers to whose beat millions would one day march. The bohemians of that era (called "beatniks" or "beats") were only a handful, but they practiced free love, took drugs, repudiated the straight world, and generally showed which way the wind was blowing. They were highly publicized, so when the bohemian impulse strengthened, dropouts knew what was expected of them. While the beats showed their contempt for social norms mostly in physical ways, others did so intellectually. Norman Mailer, in "The White Negro," held up the sensual, lawless hipster as a model of behavior under oppressive capitalism. He believed, according to "The Time of Her Time," that sexual orgasm was the pinnacle of human experience, perhaps also an approach to ultimate truth. Norman O. Brown's *Life Against Death*, a psychoanalytic interpretation of history, was an underground classic which argued that cognition subverted intuition. Brown called for a return to "polymorphous perversity," man's natural estate. The popularity of Zen Buddhism demonstrated that others wished to slip the bonds of Western rationalism; so, from a different angle, did the vogue for black humor.

The most prophetic black humorist was Joseph Heller, whose novel *Catch-22* came out in 1960. Though set in World War II the book was even more appropriate to the Indochinese war. Later Heller said, "That was the war I had in mind; a war fought without military provocation, a war in which the real enemy is no longer the other side, but someone allegedly on your side. The ridiculous war I felt lurking in the future when I wrote the book." *Catch-22* was actually written during the Cold War, and sold well in the early sixties because it attacked the perceptions on which that war, like the Indochinese war that it fathered, grew. At the time reviewers didn't know what to make of *Catch-22*. World War II had been, as everyone knew, an absolutely straightforward case of good versus evil. Yet to Heller there was little moral difference between combatants. In fact all his characters are insane, or carry normal attributes to insane lengths. They belong to a bomber squadron in the Mediterranean. Terrified of combat, most hope for ground duty and are free to request it, but: "There was only one catch and that was Catch-22, which specified that a concern for one's own safety in the face of dangers that were real and immediate was the process of a rational mind. Orr was crazy and could be grounded. All he had to do was ask; and as soon as he did, he would no longer be crazy and would have to fly more missions. Orr would be crazy to fly more missions and sane if he didn't, but if he was sane he had to fly them. If he flew them he was crazy and didn't have to; but if he didn't want to he was sane and had to."

The squadron's success depends more on having a perfect bomb pattern than hitting the target. Milo Minderbinder is the key man in the Theater, though only a lieutenant, because he embodies the profit motive. He puts the entire war on a paying basis and hires the squadron out impartially to both sides. At the end Yossarian, the novel's hero, resolves his dilemma by setting out for neutral Sweden in a rubber raft. This was what hundreds of real deserters and draft evaders would be doing soon. It was also a perfect symbol for the masses of dropouts who sought utopian alternatives to the straight world. One day there would be hundreds of thousands of Yossarians, paddling away from the crazed society in frail crafts of their own devising. *Catch-22* was not just black comedy, nor even chiefly an anti-war novel, but a metaphor that helped shape the moral vision of an era.[1]

Although children and adolescents watched a great deal of television in the sixties, it seemed at first to have little effect. Surveys were always showing that youngsters spent fifty-four hours a week or whatever in front of the tube, yet what they saw was so bland or predictable as to make little difference. The exceptions were news programs, documentaries, and dramatic specials. Few watched them. What did influence the young was popular music, folk music first and then rock. Large-scale enthusiasm for folk music began in 1958 when the Kingston Trio recorded a song, "Tom Dooley," that sold two million records. This opened the way for less slickly commercial performers. Some, like Pete Seeger, who had been singing since the depression, were veteran performers. Others, like Joan Baez, were newcomers. It was conventional for folk songs to tell a story. Hence the idiom had always lent itself to propaganda. Seeger possessed an enormous repertoire of message songs that had gotten him blacklisted by the mass media years before. Joan Baez cared more for the message than the music, and after a few years devoted herself mainly to peace work. The folk-music vogue was an early stage in the politicalization of youth, a forerunner of the counter-culture. This was hardly apparent at the time. Folk music was not seen as morally reprehensible in the manner of rock and roll. It was a familiar genre.

Folk was gentle music for the most part, and even when sung in protest did not offend many. Malvina Reynold's "What Have They Done to the Rain?" complained of radioactive fallout which all detested. Pete Seeger's anti-war song "Where Have All the Flowers Gone?" was a favorite with both pacifists and the troops in Vietnam.

Bob Dylan was different. Where most folk singers were either clean-cut or homey looking, Dylan had wild long hair. He resembled a poor white dropout of questionable morals. His songs were hard-driving,

---

[1]Lenny Bruce was a more tragic harbinger of change. He was a successful night club comedian who created an obscene form of black comedy that involved more social criticism than humor. Bruce was first arrested [for using filthy language] in 1962. Later he was busted for talking dirty about the Pope and many lesser offenses. He may have been insane. He died early from persecution and drug abuse, and then became an honored martyr in the anti-Establishment pantheon. He was one of the spiritual fathers of the yippies.

powerful, intense. It was hard to be neutral about them. "The Times They Are a-Changing" was perhaps the first song to exploit the generation gap. Dylan's life was as controversial as his ideology. Later he dropped politics and got interested in rock music. At the Newport Jazz Festival in 1965 he was booed when he introduced a fusion of his own called "folk-rock." He went his own way after that, disowned by the politically minded but admired by a great cult following attracted as much, perhaps, by his independent life as by his music. He advanced the counter-culture in both ways and made money too. This also was an inspiration to those who came after him.

Another early expression, which coexisteu with folk music, though quite unlike it, was the twist. Dance crazes were nothing new, but the twist was remarkable because it came to dominate social dancing. It used to be that dance fads were here today and gone tomorrow, while the two-step went on forever. Inexpert, that is to say most, social dancers had been loyal to it for generations. It played a key role in the traditional youth culture. Who could imagine a high school athletic event that did not end with couples clinging to one another on the dimly lit gym floor, while an amateur dance band plodded gamely on? When in 1961 the twist became popular, moralists were alarmed. It called for vigorous, exhibitionistic movements. Prurient men were reminded of the stripper's bumps and grinds. They felt the twist incited lust. Ministers denounced it. Yet in the twist (and its numerous descendants), bodies were not rubbed together as in the two-step, which had embarrassed millions of schoolboys. Millions more had suffered when through awkwardness they bumped or trod on others. The twist, by comparison, was easy and safe. No partner was bothered by the other's maladroitness. It aroused few passions. That was the practical reason for its success. But there was an ideological impulse behind it also. Amidst the noise and tumult each person danced alone, "doing his own thing," as would soon be said. But though alone, the dancer was surrounded by others doing their own thing in much the same manner. The twist celebrated both individuality and communality. This was to become a hallmark of the counter-culture, the right of everyone to be different in much the same way. The twist also foretold the dominance of rock, to which it was so well suited.

No group contributed more to the counter-culture than the Beatles, though, like folk music and the twist, their future significance was not at first apparent. Beatlemania began on October 13, 1963, when the quartet played at the London Palladium. The police, caught unawares, were hardly able to control the maddened throngs. On February 9, 1964, they appeared on U.S. television. The show received fifty thousand ticket requests for a theater that seated eight hundred. They were mobbed at the airport, besieged in their hotel, and adored everywhere. Even their soiled bed linen found a market. Their next recording, "Can't Buy Me

Love," sold three million copies in advance of release, a new world's record. Their first movie, *A Hard Day's Night* (1964), was both a critical and a popular success. Some reviewers compared them with the Marx brothers. They became millionaires overnight. The Queen decorated them for helping ease the balance-of-payments deficit. By 1966 they were so rich that they could afford to give up live performances.

For a time the Beatles seemed just another pop phenomenon, Elvis Presley multiplied by four. Few thought their music very distinguished. The reasons for its wide acceptance were hard to fathom. Most felt their showmanship was the key factor. They wore their hair longer than was fashionable, moved about a lot on the stage, and avoided the class and racial identifications associated with earlier rock stars. Elvis had cultivated a proletarian image. Other rock stars had been black, or exploited the Negro rhythm-and-blues tradition. The Beatles were mostly working class in origin but sang with an American accent (like other English rock stars) and dressed in an elegant style, then popular in Britain, called "mod." The result was a deracinated, classless image of broad appeal.

The Beatles did not fade away as they were supposed to. Beatlemania continued for three years. Then the group went through several transformations that narrowed its audience to a smaller but intensely loyal cult following in the Dylan manner. The group became more self-consciously artistic. Their first long-playing record took one day to make and cost £400. "Sergeant Pepper's Lonely Hearts Club Band" took four months and cost £25,000. They were among the first to take advantage of new recording techniques that enabled multiple sound tracks to be played simultaneously. The Beatles learned new instruments and idioms too. The result was a complex music that attracted serious inquiry. Critics debated their contributions to musicology and argued over whether they were pathfinders or merely gifted entrepreneurs. In either case, they had come a long way aesthetically from their humble beginnings. Their music had a great effect on the young, so did their styles of life. They led the march of fashion away from mod and into the hairy, mustached, bearded, beaded, fringed, and embroidered costumes of the late sixties. For a time they followed the Maharishi, an Indian guru of some note. They married and divorced in progressively more striking ways. Some were arrested for smoking marijuana. In this too they were faithful to their clientele.

John Lennon went the farthest. He married Yoko Ono, best known as an author of happenings, and with her launched a bizarre campaign for world peace and goodness. Lennon returned his decoration to the Queen in protest against the human condition. Lennon and Ono hoped to visit America but were denied entry, which, to the bureaucratic mind, seemed a stroke for public order and morality. They staged a bed-in for peace all the same. They also formed a musical group of their own, the

Plastic Ono Band, and circulated nude photographs and erotic drawings of themselves. This seemed an odd way to stop the war in Indochina, even to other Beatles. The group later broke up. By then they had made their mark, and, while strange, it was not a bad mark. Whatever lasting value their music may have, they set a good example to the young in most ways. Lennon's pacifism was nonviolent, even if wildly unorthodox. At a time when so many pacifists were imitating what they protested against, that was most desirable. They also worked hard at their respective arts and crafts, though others were dropping out and holding up laziness as a socially desirable trait. The Beatles showed that work was not merely an Establishment trick to keep the masses in subjection and the young out of trouble.

Beatlemania coincided with a more ominous development in the emerging counter-culture—the rise of the drug prophet Timothy Leary. He and Richard Alpert were scientific researchers at Harvard University who studied the effects of hallucinogenic drugs, notably a compound called LSD. As early as 1960 it was known that the two were propagandists as well as scientists. In 1961 the University Health Service made them promise not to use undergraduates in their experiments. Their violation of this pledge was the technical ground for firing them. A better one was that they had founded a drug cult. Earlier studies of LSD had failed, they said, because the researchers had not themselves taken the drug. In order to end this "authoritarian" practice, they "turned on" themselves. Their work was conducted in quarters designed to look like a bohemian residence instead of a laboratory. This was defended as a reconstruction of the natural environment in which social "acid-dropping" took place. They and many of their subjects became habitual users, not only of LSD but of marijuana and other drugs. They constructed an ideology of sorts around this practice. After they were fired the *Harvard Review* published an article of theirs praising the drug life: "Remember, man, a natural state is ecstatic wonder, ecstatic intuition, ecstatic accurate movement. Don't settle for less."

With some friends Leary and Alpert created the International Foundation for Internal Freedom (IF-IF) which published the *Psychedelic Review*. To advertise it a flyer was circulated that began, "Mescaline! Experimental Mysticism! Mushrooms! Ecstasy! LSD-25! Expansion of Consciousness! Phantastica! Transcendence! Hashish! Visionary Botany! Ololiuqui! Physiology of Religion! Internal Freedom! Morning Glory! Politics of the Nervous System!" Later the drug culture would generate a vast literature, but this was its essential message. The truth that made Western man free was only obtainable through hallucinogenic drugs. Truth was in the man, not the drug, yet the drug was necessary to uncover it. The natural state of man thus revealed was visionary, mystical, ecstatic. The heightened awareness stimulated by "consciousness-expanding" drugs brought undreamed-of sensual pleasures, according to Leary. Even better, drugs promoted peace, wisdom, and unity with the universe.

Alpert soon dropped from view. Leary went on to found his own sect, partly because once LSD was banned religious usage was the only ground left on which it could be defended, mostly because the drug cult *was* a religion. He wore long white robes and long blond hair. And he traveled about the country giving his liberating message (tune in, turn on, drop out) and having bizarre adventures. His personal following was never large, but drug use became commonplace among the young anyway. At advanced universities social smoking of marijuana was as acceptable as social drinking. More so, in a way, for it was better suited to the new ethic. One did not clutch one's solitary glass but shared one's "joint" with others. "Grass" made one gentle and pacific, not surly and hostile. As forbidden pleasure it was all the more attractive to the thrill-seeking and the rebellious. And it helped further distinguish between the old world of grasping, combative, alcoholic adults and the turned-on, cooperative culture of the young. Leary was a bad prophet. Drug-based mystical religion was not the wave of the future. What the drug cult led to was a lot of dope-smoking and some hard drug-taking. When research suggested that LSD caused genetic damage, its use declined. But the effects of grass were hard to determine, so its consumption increased.

Sometimes "pot" smokers went on to the other drugs—a deadly compound called "speed," and even heroin. These ruined many lives (though it was never clear that the lives were not already ruined to begin with). The popularity of drugs among the young induced panic in the old. States passed harsher and harsher laws that accomplished little. Campaigns against the drug traffic were launched periodically with similar results. When the flow of grass was interrupted, people turned to other drugs. Drug use seemed to go up either way. The generation gap widened. Young people thought marijuana less dangerous than alcohol, perhaps rightly. To proscribe the one and permit the other made no sense to them, except as still another example of adult hypocrisy and the hatred of youth. Leary had not meant all this to happen, but he was to blame for some of it all the same. No one did more to build the ideology that made pot-smoking a morally constructive act. But though a malign influence, no one desired such legal persecution as he experienced before escaping to Algeria from a prison farm.

In Aldous Huxley's prophetic novel *Brave New World,* drug use was promoted by the state as a means of social control. During the sixties it remained a deviant practice and a source of great tension between the generations. Yet drugs did encourage conformity among the young. To "turn on and drop out" did not weaken the state. Quite the contrary, it drained off potentially subversive energies. The need for drugs gave society a lever should it ever decide to manipulate rather than repress users. Pharmacology and nervous strain had already combined to make many adult Americans dependent on drugs like alcohol and tranquilizers. Now the young were doing the same thing, if for different reasons. In a free country this meant only that individual problems increased. But should democracy fail, drug abuse among both the young and old was an instrument for control such as no dictator ever enjoyed. The young drug-takers thought to show contempt for a grasping, unfeeling society. In doing so they opened the door to a worse one. They scorned their elders for drinking and pill-taking, yet to outsiders their habits seemed little different, though ethically more pretentious. In both cases users were vulnerable and ineffective to the extent of their addiction. Of such ironies was the counter-culture built. . . .

At its peak the hippie movement was the subject of much moralizing. Most often hippies were seen as degenerate and representative of all things godless and un-American. A minority accepted them as embodying a higher morality. The media viewed them as harmless, even amusing, freaks—which was probably closest to the truth. But before long it was clear that while the hippie movement was easily slain, the hippie style of life was not. Their habit of dressing up in costumes rather than outfits was widely imitated. So was their slang and their talk of peace, love, and beauty. The great popularity of ex-hippie rock groups was one sign of the cultural diffusion taking place, marijuana another. Weekend tripping spread to the suburbs. While the attempt to build parallel cultures on a large scale in places like the Hashbury failed, the hippies survived in many locales. Isolated farms, especially in New England and the Southwest, were particularly favored. And they thrived also on the fringes of colleges and universities, where the line between avant-garde student and alienated dropout was hard to draw. In tribes, families, and communes the hippies lived on, despite considerable local harassment wherever they went.

Though few in number, hippies had a great effect on middle-class youth. Besides their sartorial influence, hippies made religion socially acceptable. Their interest in the supernatural was contagious. Some of the communes which sprang up in the late sixties were actually religious fellowships practicing a contemporary monasticism. One in western Massachusetts was called the Cathedral of the Spirit. Its forty members were led by a nineteen-year-old mystic who helped them prepare for the Second Coming and the new Aquarian Age when all men would be brothers. The Cathedral had rigid rules against alcohol, "sex without love," and, less typically, drugs. Members helped out neighboring farmers without pay, but the commune was essentially contemplative. Its sacred book was a fifty-seven-page typewritten manuscript composed by a middle-aged bus driver from Northfield, Massachusetts, which was thought to be divinely inspired. Another commune in Boston, called the Fort Hill Community, was more outward looking. Its sixty members hoped to spread their holy word through the mass media.

Some of the communes or brotherhoods sprang from traditional roots. In New York City a band of young Jews formed a Havurah (fellowship) to blend Jewish traditions with contemporary inspirations. They wanted to study subjects like "the prophetic mind; new forms of spirituality in the contemporary world; and readings from the Jewish mystical tradition." At the University of Massachusetts a hundred students celebrated Rosh Hashanah not in a synagogue but in a field where they danced and sang all night. Courses in religion multiplied. At Smith College the number of students taking them grew from 692 in 1954 to nearly 1,400 in 1969, though the student body remained constant at about 2,000. Columbia University had two hundred applicants for a graduate program in religion with only twenty openings.

Students saw traditional religion as a point of departure rather than a place for answers. Comparatively few joined the new fellowships, but large numbers were attracted to the concepts they embodied. Oriental theologies and the like grew more attractive, so did magic. At one Catholic university a coven of warlocks was discovered. They were given psychiatric attention (thereby missing a great chance. If only they had been exorcised instead, the Establishment would have shown its relevance). When a Canadian university gave the studentry a chance to recommend new courses they overwhelmingly asked for subjects like Zen, sorcery, and witchcraft. A work of classic Oriental magic, *I Ching* or the *Book of Changes*, became popular. The best edition, a scholarly product of the Princeton University Press, used to sell a thousand copies a year. In 1968 fifty thousand copies were snapped up. Sometimes magic and mysticism were exploited more in fun than not. The Women's Liberation Movement had guerrilla theater troupes calling themselves WITCH (Women's International Terrorist Conspiracy from Hell). During the SDS sit-in at the University of Chicago they cursed the sociology department and put a hex on its chairman.

But there was a serious element to the vogue for magic. Teachers of philosophy and religion were struck by the anti-positivist, anti-science feelings of many students. Science was discredited as an agent of the military-industrial complex. It had failed to make life more attractive. Whole classes protested the epistemology of science as well as its intellectual dominion. Students believed the Establishment claimed to be rational, but showed that it was not. This supported one of the central truths of all religion, that man is more than a creature who reasons. Nor was it only the young who felt this way. Norman Mailer was something of a mystic, so was Timothy Leary. And the most ambitious academic effort to deal with these things, Theodore Roszak's *The Making of a Counter Culture*, ended with a strong appeal to faith. Like the alienated young, Roszak too rejected science and reason—"the myth of objective consciousness" as he called it. Instead of empiricism or the scientific method he wanted "the beauty of the fully illuminated personality" to be "our standard of truth." He liked magic as "a matter of communion with the forces of nature as if they were mindful, intentional presences." What he admired most in the New Left was its attempt, as he thought, to revive shamanism, to get back to the sanity and participatory democracy of prehistoric society. But he urged the left to give up its notion that violence and confrontation would change the world. What the left must do to influence the silent majority "was not simply to muster power against the misdeeds of society, but to transform the very sense men have of reality."

The anti-war movement was strongly affected by this new supernaturalism. On Moratorium Day in 1969 a University of Massachusetts student gave an emotional speech that brought the audience to its feet shouting, "The war is over." "He went into a dance, waving his arms," a campus minister said. "It was the essence of a revival meeting, where the audience makes a commitment to Christ at the end." The great peace demonstrations in 1969 were full of religious symbolism. In Boston 100,000 people gathered before a gigantic cross on the Common. In New York lighted candles were carried to the steps of St. Patrick's Cathedral. Candles were placed on the White House wall during the November mobilization. At other demonstrations the shofar, the ram's horn sounded by Jews at the beginning of each new year, was blown. Rock, the liturgical music of the young, was often played. So was folk music, which continued as a medium of moral expression after its popular decline.

Theology reflected the new supernaturalism, just as it had the aggressive secularism of a few years earlier. Harvey Cox, most famous of the contemporary theologians, published a study of the extra-institutional spiritual revival called *The Feast of Fools* in 1969. "God is Dead" gave way to the "Theology of Hope," after Jurgen Moltmann's book by that title. A German theologian, Moltmann argued that the trouble with Christian theology was that it ignored the future. "The Church lives on memories, the world on hope," he remarked elsewhere. Though he was a Protestant, Roman Catholic theologians in Germany and America agreed with him. Institutional churches responded to the new by absorbing as much of it as they could. Church happenings, rock masses, light shows, and readings from Eastern mystics were used by Protestants and Catholics alike. The home mass gained popularity among Catholics. It gave to formal worship something of the intimate fellowship that the young found so compelling. Thus while church attendance declined from the high levels of the 1950's, this did not mean a decrease in religious enthusiasm. The most striking aspect of the "religious revival" of the 1950's, after all, had been the absence of devotion.

Going to church then was more a social than a religious act. In the late sixties faith was expressed by not going to church.

There were many ways of responding to this spiritual revival. Orthodox churchgoers were offended by it, and even more by the efforts of their denominations to win the inspirited young. More flexible religious leaders saw it as a great opportunity. Secular radicals and educators were more often depressed by it. Men whose lives were dedicated to the pursuit of truth through reason were not about to become shamans. If it was true that science and scholarship had not yet brought the millennium, this did not seem good cause for abandoning them.

The most surprising man to protest this new turn was Paul Goodman. Goodman's life and work were more nearly of a piece than most people's. He was a secular anarchist, but while hoping to wreck the old order, he believed that the old tools—reason, expertise, science—would still be needed. Hence, though he was one of the chief intellectual mentors of the counter-culture, its growing spiritualism, indeed anti-intellectualism, disturbed him.

Late in 1969 he wrote that this first became clear to him while giving a graduate seminar on "professionalism." He hoped to teach the difference between careerism and fidelity to a professional calling. To his astonishment the class rejected the notion that there was such a thing as a true profession. All decisions were made by the power structure. Professionals were merely peer groups formed to delude the public and make money. "Didn't every society, however just, require experts?" he asked. No, they insisted; it was only important to be human, and all else would follow.

> Suddenly I realized that they did not really believe that there was a nature of things. Somehow all functions could be reduced to interpersonal relations and power. There was no knowledge, but only the sociology of knowledge. They had so well learned that physical and sociological research is subsidized and conducted for the benefit of the ruling class that they did not believe there was such a thing as the simple truth. To be required to learn something was a trap by which the young were put down and co-opted. Then I knew that I could not get through to them. I had imagined that the world-wide student protest had to do with changing political and moral institutions, to which I was sympathetic, but I now saw that we had to do with a religious crisis of the magnitude of the Reformation in the fifteen hundreds, when not only all institutions but all learning had been corrupted by the Whore of Babylon.

This was a strange confession from one who specialized in youth and its discontents, as Goodman fully realized. His most influential book, *Growing Up Absurd* (1960), dealt with generational alienation. But he had thought it a specialized deviance then, and was heartened by the new student radicals "who made human sense and were not absurd at all.

But the alienating circumstances had proved too strong after all; here were absurd graduate students, most of them political activists." "Alienation," he continued, "is a powerful motivation of unrest, fantasy, and reckless action. It leads . . . to religious innovation, new sacraments to give life meaning. But it is a poor basis for politics, including revolutionary politics." Mere confrontation was not the answer to society's ills, especially when done hatefully. Gandhi's great point had been that the confronter aims at future community with the confronted. Yet many New Leftists did not regard their enemies as members of the same species. "How can the young people think of a future community when they themselves have no present world, no profession or other job in it, and no trust in other human beings? Instead, some young radicals seem to entertain the disastrous illusion that other people can be compelled by fear. This can lead only to crushing reaction."

The young knew nothing of society's institutions, how they worked, where they came from, what had made them what they were. For many, history began in 1968. "I am often hectored to my face," Goodman said, "with formulations that I myself put in their mouths, that have become part of the oral tradition two years old, author prehistoric." They didn't trust people over thirty because they didn't understand them and were too conceited to try. "Having grown up in a world too meaningless to learn anything, they know very little and are quick to resent it." The most important thing to the young was being together, en masse if possible. At the rock festivals they found the meaning of life which, as they explained it, consisted of people being nice to each other. A group of them passing a stick of marijuana behaved like "a Quaker meeting waiting for the spirit." And, Goodman concluded, "in the end it is religion that constitutes the strength of this generation, and not, as I used to think, their morality, political will, and common sense." Neither moral courage nor honesty was their salient trait, but rather "metaphysical vitality."

Goodman's argument was an exceptionally brave one. No one who had done less for the young could in good conscience have spoken so bluntly of them. And religion as an organizing principle for making sense of the serious young seemed useful. But it didn't help to distinguish what was durable and what merely fashionable in the counter-culture. The term itself was hard to define as it embraced almost everything new and anti-Establishment, however frivolous. On its deepest level the counter-culture was the radical critique of Herbert Marcuse, Norman O. Brown, and even Paul Goodman. It also meant the New Left, communes and hippie farms, magic, hedonism, eroticism, and public nudity. And it included rock music, long hair, and mini-skirts (or, alternatively, fatigue uniforms, used clothes, and the intentionally ugly or grotesque). Most attacks on the counter-culture were directed at its trivial aspects, pot and dress especially. Pot busts (police raids), often involving famous people or their children, became commonplace. The laws against pot were so punitive in some areas as to be almost unenforceable. Even President Nixon, spokesman for Middle American morality that he was, finally questioned them. Local fights against long hair, beards, and short skirts were beyond number. The American Civil Liberties Union began taking school systems to court for disciplining students on that account. New York City gave up trying to enforce dress codes. It was all the more difficult there as even the teachers were mod. At one school the principal ordered women teachers to wear smocks over their minis. They responded by buying mini-smocks. . . .

Taken together the varieties of life among deviant youths showed the counter-culture to be disintegrating. What was disturbing about it was not so much the surface expression as its tendency to mirror the culture it supposedly rejected. The young condemned adult hypocrisy while matching its contradictions with their own. The old were materialistic, hung up on big cars and ranch houses. The young were equally devoted to motorcycles, stereo sets, and electric guitars. The old sought power and wealth. So did the young as rock musicians, political leaders, and frequently as salesmen of counter-cultural goods and services. What distinguished reactionary capitalists from their avant-garde opposite numbers was often no more than a lack of moral pretense. While condemning the adult world's addiction to violence, the young admired third-world revolutionaries, Black Panthers, and even motorcycle outlaws. The rhetoric of the young got progressively meaner and more hostile. This was not so bad as butchering Vietnamese, but it was not very encouraging either. And where hate led, violence followed. . . .

One aspect of the counter-culture deserves special mention: its assumption that hedonism was inevitably anti-capitalist. As James Hitchcock pointed out, the New Left identified capitalism with puritanism and deferred gratifications. But this was true of capitalism only with respect to work. Where consumption was concerned, it urged people to gratify their slightest wish. It exploited sex shamelessly to that end, limited only by law and custom. When the taboos against nudity were removed, merchants soon took advantage of their new freedom. Naked models, actors, even waitresses were one result, pornographic flicks another. Who doubted that if marijuana became legal the tobacco companies would soon put Mexican gold in every vending machine? It was, after all, part of Aldous Huxley's genius that he saw how sensual gratification could enslave men more effectively than Hitler ever could. Victorian inhibitions, the Protestant Ethic itself were, though weakened, among the few remaining defenses against the market economy that Americans possessed. To destroy them for freedom's sake would only make people more vulnerable to consumerism than they already were. Which was not to say that sexual and other freedoms were not good things in their own right. But there was no assurance that behavioral liberty would not grow at the expense of political freedom. It was one thing to say that sex promoted mental health, another to say it advanced social justice. In confusing the two young deviants laid themselves open to what Herbert Marcuse called "repressive de-sublimation," the means by which the socio-economic order was made more attractive, and hence more durable. Sex was no threat to the Establishment. Panicky moralists found this hard to believe, so they kept trying to suppress it. But the shrewder guardians of established relationships saw hedonism for what it partially was, a valuable means of social control. What made this hard to get across was that left and right agreed that sex was subversive. That was why the Filthy Speech Movement arose, and why the John Birch Society and its front groups divided a host of communities in the late sixties. They insisted that sex education was a communist plot to fray the country's moral fiber. They could hardly have been more wrong. As practiced in most schools, sex education was anything but erotic. In fact, more students were probably turned off sex than on to it by such courses. The Kremlin was hardly less orthodox than the Birch Society on sexual matters, sexual denial being thought a trait of all serious revolutionaries. But the sexual propaganda of the young confirmed John Birchers in their delusions. As elsewhere, the misconceptions of each side reinforced one another.

Still, the counter-culture's decline ought not to be celebrated prematurely. It outlasted the sixties. It had risen in the first place because of the larger culture's defects. War, poverty, social and racial injustice were widespread. The universities were less human than they might have been. The regulation of sexual conduct led to endless persecutions of the innocent or the pathetic to no one's advantage. Young people had much to complain of. Rebellious youth had thought to make things better. It was hardly their fault that things got worse. They were, after all, products of the society they meant to change, and marked by it as everyone was. Vanity and ignorance made them think themselves free of the weaknesses they saw so clearly in others. But adults were vain and ignorant too, and, what's more, they had power as the young did not. When they erred, as in Vietnam, millions suffered. The young hated being powerless, but thanks to it they were spared the awful burden of guilt that adults bore. They would have power soon enough, and no doubt use it just as badly. In the meantime, though, people did well to keep them in perspective.

The dreary propaganda about youth's insurgent idealism continued into the seventies. So did attempts to make them look clean-cut. American society went on being obsessed with the young. But all popular manias are seasonal. Each era has its own preoccupations. The young and their counter-culture were a special feature of the 1960's and would probably not be regarded in the old way for very long afterward. And, demographically speaking, youth itself was on the wane. The median age of Americans had risen steadily in modern times, reaching a peak of thirty years of age in 1952. The baby boom reversed this trend, like so many others. In 1968 the median age was only 27.7 years. But as the birthrate fell the median age began to rise. By 1975 it would be over twenty-eight. By 1990 it should be back up to thirty again, putting half the population beyond the age of trust. Their disproportionate numbers was one reason why youth was so prominent in the sixties. It was reasonable to suppose they would become less so as their numbers declined in relation to older people.

Common sense suggested that work and the pleasure principle would both continue. Once life and work were thought to be guided by the same principles. In the twentieth century they had started to divide, with one set of rules for working and another for living. The complexities of a postindustrial economy would probably maintain that distinction. The discipline of work would prevail on the job. The tendency to "swing" off it would increase, and the dropout community too. The economy was already rich enough to support a substantial leisure class, as the hippies demonstrated. The movement toward guaranteed incomes would make idleness even more feasible. A large dependent population, in economic terms, was entirely practical—perhaps, given automation, even desirable. How utopian to have a society in which the decision to work was voluntary! Yet if economic growth continued and an effective welfare state was established, such a thing was not unimaginable, however repugnant to the Protestant Ethic. Perhaps that was what the unpleasant features of life in the sixties pointed toward. Later historians might think them merely the growing pains of this new order. A Brave New World indeed! . . .

While it was difficult in 1969 to tell where the counter-culture could go, it was easy to see where it came from. Artists and bohemians had been demanding more freedom from social and artistic conventions for a long time. The romantic faith in nature, intuition, and spontaneity was equally old. What was striking about the sixties was that the revolt against discipline, even self-discipline, and authority spread so widely. Resistance to these tendencies largely collapsed in the arts. Soon the universities gave ground also. The rise of hedonism and the decline of work were obviously functions of increased prosperity, and also of effective merchandising. The consumer economy depended on advertising, which in turn leaned heavily on the pleasure principle. This had been true for fifty years at least, but not until television did it really work well. The generation that made the counter-culture was the first to be propagandized from infancy on behalf of the pleasure principle.

But though all of them were exposed to hucksterism, not all were convinced. Working-class youngsters especially soon learned that life was different from television. Limited incomes and uncertain futures put them in touch with reality earlier on. Middle-class children did not learn the facts of life until much later. Cushioned by higher family incomes, indulged in the same way as their peers on the screen, they were shocked to discover that the world was not what they had been taught it was. The pleasure orientation survived this discovery, the ideological packaging it came in often did not. All this had happened before, but in earlier years there was no large, institutionalized subculture for the alienated to turn to. In the sixties hippiedom provided one such, the universities another. The media publicized these alternatives and made famous the ideological leaders who promoted them. So the deviant young knew where to go for the answers they wanted, and how to behave when they got them. The media thus completed the cycle begun when they first turned youngsters to pleasure. That was done to encourage consumption. The message was still effective when young consumers rejected the products TV offered and discovered others more congenial to them.

Though much in the counter-culture was attractive and valuable, it was dangerous in three ways. First, self-indulgence led frequently to self-destruction. Second, the counter-culture increased social hostility. The generation gap was one example, but the class gap another. Working-class youngsters resented the counter-culture. They accepted adult values for the most part. They had to work whether they liked it or not. Beating up the long-haired and voting for George Wallace were only two ways they expressed these feelings. The counter-culture was geographical too. It flourished in cities and on campuses. Elsewhere, in Middle America especially, it was hated and feared. The result was a national division between the counter-culture and those adults who admired or tolerated it—upper-middle-class professionals and intellectuals in the Northeast particularly—and the silent majority of workers and Middle Americans who didn't. The tensions between these groups made solving social and political problems all the more difficult, and were, indeed, part of the problem.

Finally, the counter-culture was hell on standards. A handful of bohemians were no great threat to art and intellect. The problem was that a generation of students, the artists and intellectuals of the future, was infected with romanticism. Truth and beauty were in the eye of the beholder. They were discovered or created by the pure of heart. Formal education and training were not, therefore, merely redundant but dangerous for obstructing channels through which the spirit flowed. It was one thing for hippies to say this, romanticism being the natural religion of bohemia. It was quite another to hear it from graduate students. Those who did anguished over the future of scholarship, like the critics who worried that pop art meant the end of art. These fears were doubtlessly overdrawn, but the pace of cultural change was so fast in the sixties that they were hardly absurd.

Logic seemed everywhere to be giving way to intuition, and self-discipline to impulse. Romanticism had never worked well in the past. It seemed to be doing as badly in the present. The hippies went from flower power to death-tripping in a few years. The New Left took only a little longer to move from participatory democracy to demolition. The counter-culture ethic remained as beguiling as ever in theory. In practice, like most utopian dreams, human nature tended to defeat it. At the decade's end, young believers looked forward to the Age of Aquarius. Sensible men knew there would be no Aquarian age. What they didn't know was the sort of legacy the counter-culture would leave behind. Some feared that the straight world would go on as before, others that it wouldn't.

INDEX